THE KLEIN EDITION

THE TEN COMMANDMENTS

ספר

עשרת הדברות

השלם

THE KLEIN EDITION

ספר
עשרת הדברות
השלם

The Ten Commandments

TARYAG LEGACY FOUNDATION

THE KLEIN EDITION

The Ten

TARYAG LEGACY FOUNDATION

ספר עשרת הדברות השלם

Commandments

A Comprehensive, In-depth Presentation of
The Ten Commandments
Featuring Essential Principles, Laws
and Inspirational Insights

Rabbi Dovid Wax
EDITOR-IN-CHIEF

COMPILED BY AN INTERNATIONAL TEAM OF TORAH SCHOLARS

Published by
TARYAG LEGACY FOUNDATION
1136 Somerset Avenue
Lakewood, NJ 08701
732.942.3420
732.942.3630 fax
email: 613@taryag.org

Distributed by
ISRAEL BOOKSHOP
501 Prospect Street
Lakewood, NJ 08701
732.901.3009
732.901.4012 fax

ISBN 1-933296-00-3

PRINTED IN ISRAEL

THIS VOLUME IS DEDICATED
TO THE BELOVED MEMORY OF

Yidel Klein ז״ל

ר׳ יהודה ב״ר דוד הלוי ז״ל

**A man who cared deeply about Torah education
and devoted his life to its perpetuation.**

After surviving the terrible years of the Holocaust,
Yidel Klein and his family arrived on the shores of
the United States and in 1954 settled in Far Rockaway, NY.
As he breathed the free air, the foremost thought in his mind
was to raise his family in the hallowed ways of the Torah.
He sent his children to a school in Forest Hills, Queens,
enduring a long and difficult drive every day,
because he wanted only the best Torah education for them.
In his great concern for *chinuch*, not only for his own children
but also for the entire community,
he helped found Torah Academy for Girls and served
on its Executive Committee for many years.
As a true Torah visionary, it is entirely fitting
that his name should be forever associated
with one of the most important developments
in Torah education in our times.

נפ׳ כ״ז אדר ב׳ תשס״ג

יהי זכרו ברוך.

Motty & Malka Klein

Patrons of Taryag *

—— שצ ——

Inspired by a vision of the centrality of the Taryag Mitzvoth to
Torah study and Jewish tradition, the following philanthropic
individuals are blazing new frontiers in Jewish education by
dedicating a volume of the Encyclopedia of the Taryag Mitzvoth.
Their generosity will promote a deeper understanding of Jewish
identity, enrich our people and unite hundreds of thousands of
Jews in a common love for our timeless heritage.

MOTTY AND MALKA KLEIN
לע״נ ר׳ יהודה ב״ר דוד הלוי ז״ל

———

MORRIS AND DEVORA SMITH
לרפו״ש דניאל דב הלוי בן רשקא שיחי׳

———

A. JOSEPH AND ROCHELLE STERN

* in formation

Guardians of the
Ten Commandments

— ᘏ —

With a profound understanding of the central role of the Ten Commandments in the system of the Taryag Mitzvos, the following noble individuals have generously sponsored the presentation of these mitzvos and thereby linked their names to them for all eternity.

MR. AND MRS. SOL KEST

MICHAEL AND SURI KEST

SETH AND ZAHAVA FARBMAN

MR. AND MRS. RICHARD PARKOFF

MR. AND MRS. RONNIE HERSH

THE HENDELES FAMILY

ERIC AND GALE ROTHNER

SHLOMI AND MIMI GROSS

לע"נ יוסף בן יהושע בנימין ז"ל

לע"נ לאה בת אברהם חיים ע"ה

Founders of Taryag *

With their dynamic and magnanimous patronage, the following individuals have placed themselves at the forefront of a revolution in Jewish education that will greatly enhance the Torah knowledge of Jewish people all over the world and leave an indelible imprint on all future generations.

MR. AND MRS. YOSSI FRIEDMAN

SHLOME AND HEDDY GROSS

THE HERZOG FAMILY

MR. MOSHE KATLOWITZ

LLOYD AND HARRIET KEILSON

EFFY AND TZIVIE LANDSBERG

MELLY AND ROCHELLE LIFSHITZ

MICHAEL AND NANCY OFFEN

SCOTT AND GRACE OFFEN

CHAIM AND SURI SCHARF

YOSSI AND ELKA SHERESHEVSKY

DANIEL AND RACHEL SOLOMONS

MR. AND MRS. JOSEPH M. TABAK

DR. SHIMON AND KARYN TRYFUS

* in formation

Benefactors of Taryag *

Through their generous support, the following individuals were instrumental in launching this project and setting it on its path to success.

NOCHUM AND DENA ABER

לע״נ יוסף יצחק בן גימילה

MR. AND MRS. ARON BIRNBAUM

EZRA AND GITTY BIRNBAUM

MR. AND MRS. JIMMY FENDELMAN

ELAZAR AND SURI FINGERER

MR. AND MRS. MENDY FISHMAN

YITZCHOK AND MINDY FOLLMAN

MR. AND MRS. DAVID FRIEDMAN

ARYEH AND CHAYA GIBBER AND FAMILY

MR. AND MRS. LEON GOLDENBERG

MR. AND MRS. BINYOMIN GROSS

MR. AND MRS. MOISHE HEIMOWITZ

MR. AND MRS. RALPH HERTZKA

MR. AND MRS. RICHARD JEDWAB

MR. AND MRS. STEVEN LANGERT

DANIEL AND BLIMY LEMBERG

MR. AND MRS. MEIR LEVIN (*Los Angeles*)

MR. AND MRS. TZVI LICHTSHEIN

MR. AND MRS. YOSSIE LIEBER

MR. AND MRS. NAFTALI MANELA

MR. AND MRS. HESHY MUEHLGAY

ARONI AND CHANI PARNES

CHANANIA AND CHANI POMERANTZ

MR. AND MRS. YEHUDA RAHMANAN

MR. AND MRS. SHMUEL ROTHMAN

AVI AND CHERYL SAVITSKY

MR. AND MRS. SIMCHA SHAIN

MR. AND MRS. JONATHAN SPETNER

MR. AND MRS. JAY TAUB

MR. AND MRS. YOAV TAUB

ELY AND RACHELI TENDLER

MORDECHAI AND BRUCHIE TEPLER

JOEL AND JOYCE YARMAK

* *in formation*

Friends of Taryag *

The following individuals have joined a select community of Torah activists who appreciate the importance of Taryag mitzvah education and support it enthusiastically.

MR. AND MRS. ROBERT ABERMAN	MR. AND MRS. DOVID GOTTLEIB	WARREN AND TALI NEWFIELD
MR. AND MRS. YOSSI ADEST	RABBI AND MRS. MORDECHAI GOTTLIEB	HILLEL AND JUDY OLSHIN
YANKY AND PESI BASH	MR. AND MRS. MENDY HANDLER	DRS. HERSHEL AND LISA OZICK
DR. AND MRS. STANLEY BIEL	MR. AND MRS. ROBBY HARTMAN	MR. AND MRS. YAAKOV POLLACK
MAYER AND DEVORA BELLER	MR. AND MRS. STEVE HENDERSON	DR. AND DR.CRAIG REISS
MR. & MRS. ARIE BENJAMIN	THE HIDARY FAMILY	MR. AND MRS. MICHAEL RIEDER
BENJY AND BLIMI BERGER	MR. AND MRS. STEVE HORN	RABBI AND DR. YAAKOV ROSENBAUM
MR. AND MRS. BRUCE BERGER	RABBI AND MRS. YAIR JACOBS	MR. AND MRS. REUBEN ROSENBERG
DR. AND MRS. TUVIA BLECHMAN	MR. AND MRS. NOCHUM JOSEPHS	MR. AND MRS. STUART ROSENBLUM
MR. AND MRS. JONAH BRUCK	MR. AND MRS. YANKI JUDOWITZ	MICHAEL AND ALISON SAGE
MR. AND MRS. JAN BUCKLER	MR. HERMAN KATZ	MR. AND MRS. HESHY SCHLOSSER
MORDECHAI AND DEENEE COHEN	MR. AND MRS. SHUI KOHEN	DR. AND MRS. REUVEN SHANIK
MR. AND MRS. DANNY DIENA	MR. AND MRS. CHAIM KRAUSS	YOSSIE AND PEARL SHAPIRO
MR. AND MRS. EZRA ERANI	לע"נ ר' יואל ב"ר יהושע זצ"ל	MR. AND MRS. HERBIE SOMERSTEIN
MR. AND MRS. AVROHOM FARBER	MR. AND MRS. ROBERT KREITMAN	BORUCH AND NAOMI SPIRA
MR. AND MRS. MOSHE FEUER	MR. AND MRS. MICKY KRULL	RABBI GERSHON AND LEAH SPIEGEL
YOSEF AND CHAVI FINK AND FAMILY	MR. AND MRS. MITCH KUSHNER	HERTZY AND NECHAMA STERN
לכבוד תושבי ארץ ישראל	DOVID AND SHULI LACHMAN	SHMULLY AND SURI STERN
MR. AND MRS. JOSH FRANKEL	MR. AND MRS. JOSHUA LANDES	MICHOEL AND ESTHER STYLLER
MR. AND MRS. HAL FRECHTER	MR. AND MRS. BENJAMIN LAPIN	MR. AND MRS. VICTOR SUTTON
MR. AND MRS. ALTY FREILICH	MR. AND MRS. LOUIS LEEDER	MR. AND MRS. KALMAN TABAK
MR. AND MRS. NACHMAN FRIED	NAFTALI AND SHULI LEVIN	MR. AND MRS. J. UNGER
MR. AND MRS. NUSSI FRIED	GIDEON AND SUSAN LEVY	MR. AND MRS. DAVID UNTERBERG
MR. AND MRS. ELI GELB	RONNIEL AND CAROLINE YAFFA LEVY	MR. AND MRS. MITCHELL VILINSKY
DR. AND MRS. ELIOT GHATAN	MR. AND MRS. JOSEPH LICHTMAN	DR. AND MRS. YOSEF WALDER
MR. AND MRS. YISSOCHOR GREEN	MR. AND MRS. MOSHE MAJESKY	MR. AND MRS. LENNIE WEISS
MR. AND MRS. SHUI GOLDBERG	RABBI AND MRS. HENOCH MESSNER	MENDEL AND CHANI WAX
MR. AND MRS. AVI GOLDSTEIN	YEHUDA AND ADINA MUEHLGAY	HESHY AND SURE GITTY WEINBERG
ITCHE AND MATI GOLDSTEIN	MR. AND MRS. CHESKY NEIMAN	ZVI AND PENINA WIENER
DR. AND MRS. NAFTALI GOLOMBECK	MR. AND MRS. MEILICH NEUMAN	RABBI AND MRS. YANKY YARMISH
RABBI AND MRS. YITZCHOK GOTTDIENER	MR. AND MRS. NOCHMAN NEUMAN	RABBI AND MRS. ELIYOHU ZAKS

* in formation

RABBINIC ENDORSEMENTS OF THE TARYAG MITZVAH PROJECT

The Taryag Mitzvah Project has been universally acclaimed and endorsed by a plethora of Torah leaders the world over: Roshei Yeshiva, Rabbonim and Rebbes as well as educators and community leaders. Those listed below alphabetically, representing many diverse communities, have expressed the importance of this work; many of them have advocated its inclusion in their respective school systems, shuls, and homes.

RABBI DOVID ABUCHATZEIRA
RABBI YEHUDA ADAS
RABBI YAAKOV ARYEH ALTER (GER)
RABBI SHLOMO MOSHE AMAR
RABBI EZRIEL AUERBACH
RABBI SHMUEL AUERBACH
RABBI KENNETH AUMAN
RABBI SHLOMO AVINER
RABBI YISROEL BELSKY
RABBI ELIYAHU BEN-HAIM
RABBI GERSHON BESS
RABBI SHIMON NOSSON NOTA BIDERMAN (LELOV)
RABBI HESHY BILLET
RABBI SHMUEL BIRNBAUM
RABBI CHAIM BRESSLER
RABBI NOCHUM DOV BREUER (BOYAN)
RABBI PINCHUS BREUER
RABBI DOVID COHEN
RABBI ZEV COHEN
RABBI HILLEL DAVID
RABBI YOSEF TZVI DUNNER
RABBI YOSEF TZVI DUSHINSKY (DUSHINSKY)
RABBI MORDECHAI ELIAHU
RABBI YOSEF SHALOM ELYASHIV
RABBI REUVEN FEINSTEIN
RABBI NOSSON TZVI FINKEL
RABBI AVROHOM YAAKOV FRIEDMAN (SADIGER)
RABBI ZACHARIAH GELLEY
RABBI ELIEZER HAGER (SERET-VISHNITZ)
RABBI MOSHE YEHOSHUA HAGER (VISHNITZ)
RABBI MOSHE HALBERSTAM
RABBI TZVI ELIMELECH HALBERSTAM (SANZ)
RABBI YOSEF HARRARI RAFUL
RABBI MOSHE HIER
RABBI YAAKOV HILLEL
RABBI DOVID KAHAN (TOLDOS AHARON)
RABBI SHMUEL YAAKOV KAHAN (TOLDOS AVROHOM YITZCHOK)
RABBI YOSEF KALATSKY
RABBI CHAIM KANIEVSKY
RABBI NISSIM KARELITZ
RABBI MOSHE MORDECHAI KARP
RABBI MEIR KESSLER
RABBI ARYEH MALKIEL KOTLER
RABBI ISRAEL MEIR LAU
RABBI MICHEL YEHUDA LEFKOWITZ
RABBI HENACH LEIBOWITZ
RABBI PESACH LERNER
RABBI AVROHOM CHAIM LEVIN
RABBI AHARON LICHTENSTEIN
RABBI MEIR MAZUZ
RABBI YAAKOV ARYEH MILIKOVSKI (AMSHINOV)

RABBI ELI J. MANSOUR
RABBI MEYER H. MAY
RABBI YONA METZGER
RABBI SHLOMO MILLER
RABBI SHLOMO MORGENSTERN
RABBI ELAZAR MUSKIN
RABBI YAAKOV PERLOW (NOVOMINSK)
RABBI YISROEL AVROHOM PORTUGAL (SKULEN)
RABBI STEVEN PRUZANSKY
RABBI GAMLIEL RABINOVITCH
RABBI YISSOCHER DOV ROKEACH (BELZ)
RABBI YAAKOV YISSOCHER BER ROSENBAUM (NADVORNA)
RABBI YOSEF ROSENBLUM
RABBI MATTISYAHU SALOMON
RABBI HERSHEL SCHACHTER
RABBI AARON SCHECHTER
RABBI YAAKOV MEIR SCHECHTER
RABBI CHAIM PINCHAS SCHEINBERG
RABBI YITZCHOK SCHEINER
RABBI AVRAHAM SCHORR
RABBI AVROHOM SHAPIRA
RABBI MOSHE SHMUEL SHAPIRO
RABBI BORUCH SHOCHET (KARLIN-STOLIN)
RABBI AHARON LEIB SHTEINMAN
RABBI YOCHONON SOFER (ERLAU)
RABBI CHAIM STEIN
RABBI SHMUEL ELIEZER STERN
RABBI MOISHE STERNBUCH
RABBI ELYA SVEI
RABBI SHOLOM TENDLER
RABBI AVROHOM TURIN
RABBI DOVID TWERSKI (RACHMASTRIVKE)
RABBI NOCHUM TWERSKI (CHERNOBYL)
RABBI MOSHE TZADKA
RABBI BEREL WEIN
RABBI MENDEL WEINBACH
RABBI NOACH WEINBERG
RABBI YITZCHOK MENACHEM WEINBERG (TOLNO)
RABBI DOVID WEINBERGER
RABBI MOSHE WEINBERGER
RABBI TZVI HERSH WEINREB
RABBI ASHER WEISS
RABBI AVROHOM WEISS
RABBI YITZCHOK TUVIA WEISS
RABBI MORDECHAI WILLIG
RABBI SHLOMO WOLBE
RABBI MOSHE WOLFSON
RABBI SHMUEL HALEVI WOSNER
RABBI OVADIAH YOSEF
RABBI MECHEL ZILBER

TO RECEIVE COPIES OR TRANSCRIPTS OF THEIR ENDORSEMENTS, PLEASE CONTACT THE TARYAG LEGACY FOUNDATION.

ENDORSEMENTS OF LEADING EDUCATORS AND COMMUNITY LEADERS

RABBI CHARLES ABRAMCHIK — *Sol and Tillie Hasson Sephardic Day School Skokie, IL*

RABBI NOSSON ADLER — *Yeshiva Rabbi Samson Raphael Hirsch, New York NY*

RABBI SHIMON ADLER — *Vaad Hachinuch Hadati, Israel*

RABBI ISRAEL M. AXELROD — *Torah Academy of Greater Philadelphia, Ardmore, PA*

RABBI MENACHEM BAASRI — *Sucath David Talmud Torah, Jerusalem, Israel*

RABBI BARUCH L. BARNETSKY — *Bnos Yisroel School for Girls Brooklyn, NY*

RABBI AHARON BARUCH — *Yeshivas Darchei Torah Southfield, MI*

RABBI NAFTALI HERTZ BASCH — *Yeshiva Ketana of Queens Kew Gardens Hills, NY*

RABBI KALMAN BAUMANN — *Toras Emes Academy of Miami North Miami Beach, FL*

RABBI MAYER BELLER — *Hillel Academy Fairfield, CT*

RABBI YAAKOV BENDER — *Yeshiva Darchei Torah Far Rockaway, NY*

RABBI MORDECHAI BESSER — *Manhattan Day School New York, NY*

MRS. R. BLAU — *Bais Yaakov Academy Brooklyn, NY*

MRS. S.E. BRICKMAN — *Bnos Yisroel School for Girls Brooklyn, NY*

RABBI YOEL BURSZTYN — *Bais Yaakov School for Girls Los Angeles, CA*

RABBI CHAIM CIMENT — *New England Hebrew Academy Lubavitz Yeshiva Brookline, MA*

RABBI HERBERT J. COHEN — *Denver Academy of Torah Denver, Colorado*

RABBI JOEL COHN — *S.A.R.Academy Riverdale, NY*

RABBI HARRIS COOPERMAN — *Phoenix Hebrew Academy Phoenix, AZ*

MRS. ODELIA DANISHEFSKY — *Moriah School of Englewood Englewood, NJ*

RABBI MOSHE DEAR — *Yavneh Hebrew Academy Los Angeles, CA*

RABBI SIMCHA DESSLER — *Hebrew Academy of Cleveland Cleveland, OH*

RABBI DR. YAACOV DVORIN — *Hillel Torah North Skokie, Il*

RABBI O. EHRENREICH — *Beth Jacob of Boro Park Brooklyn, NY*

RABBI JOSEPH ELIAS — *Rika Breuer Teachers Seminary New York, NY*

MRS. MIRIAM FELDMAN — *Temima High School for Girls Atlanta, GA*

RABBI MENDEL FELLER — *Lubavitch Cheder Day School St. Paul, MN*

RABBI CHAIM FEUERMAN — *Noted Educational Consultant*

RABBI PHILIP D. FIELD — *Akiba Hebrew Academy Merion Station, PA*

RABBI AVROHOM FIREMAN — *Torah Academy Brookline, MA*

RABBI AVROHOM FISHMAN — *Yeshiva Beth Yehudah Southfield, MI*

RABBI YEHOSHUA FISHMAN — *Executive Director Torah Umesorah*

RABBI YEHUDA FRANKEL — *Yeshiva of Spring Valley Monsey, NY*

RABBI YAAKOV FREEDMAN — *Shalom Torah Academy East Windsor, NJ*

RABBI YOSEF M. GELMAN — *Masores Bais Yaakov Brooklyn, NY*

RABBI ELI GEWIRTZ — *Partners in Torah*

REBBETZIN SURI GIBBER — *Bais Yaakov H.S. of the Twin Cities*

Minneapolis, MN

RABBI S. BINYOMIN GINSBERG — *Torah Academy St. Louis Park, MN*

RABBI HESHY T. GLASS — *Hebrew Academy of Long Beach Long Beach, NY*

RABBI MARK GOTTLIEB — *Maimonides School Boston, MA*

RABBI NECHEMIA GOTTLIEB — *Yeshiva Bais Hatorah Lakewood, NJ*

REBBETZIN TOVA GREENBLATT — *Bais Yaakov H.S. of St. Louis St. Louis, MO*

REBBETZIN N.D. GRONER — *Bnos Yisroel School for Girls Brooklyn, NY*

RABBI HARVEY HORN — *Yeshiva of North Jersey River Edge, NJ*

RABBI YAKOV HOROWITZ — *Yeshiva Darchei Noam Monsey, NY*

MRS. SARA ITZKOWITZ — *Bnos Yisroel of Baltimore Baltimore, MD*

RABBI SHMUEL JABLON — *Fuchs Mizrachi School University Heights, OH*

RABBI YISROEL M. JANOWSKI — *Yeshiva Elementary School Miami Beach, FL*

REBBETZIN ESTHER JUNGREIS — *Hineni*

RABBI CHAIM DOVID KAGAN — *Beis Chaya Mushka Girls H.S. Oak Park, MI*

RABBI BENJAMIN KAMENETSKY — *Yeshiva of South Shore Hewlett, NY*

RABBI BINYOMIN KAPLAN — *Bais Yaakov of Ramapo Monsey, NY*

RABBI NOCHUM Y. KAPLAN — *Director of Education Chabad Schools*

MRS. BESIE KATZ — *Politz Hebrew Academy Philadelphia, PA*

REBBETZIN SHULAMIS KELLER — *Bais Yaakov H.S. of Chicago Chicago, IL*

RABBI JONATHAN KNAPP — *Yavneh Academy Paramus, NJ*

RABBI SHMUEL KLARBERG — *Yeshiva Ktana of Passaic Passaic, NJ*

RABBI YAKOV KRAUSE — *Torath Emeth Yeshiva Rav Isacsohn*

Los Angeles, CA

RABBI EPHRAIM LEIZERSON	Beth Jacob H.S. of Miami North Miami Beach, FL	RABBI MYER J. SCHWAB	Beth Jacob H.S. of Denver Denver, CO
RABBI MICHAEL LEVI	Bais Yaakov D'Rav Meir Brooklyn, NY	RABBI SHLOMO Y. SCHWARTZ	Ramaz Middle School New York, NY
RABBI MENACHEM LEVIN	Lakewood Cheder School Lakewood, NJ	RABBI AVI SHULMAN	World renowned educator
MRS. NECHAMA LEVITANSKY	Torah Prep School St Louis, MO	RABBI SAUL SCHWARTZ	Buffalo Grove Community Hebrew School Buffalo Grove, IL
RABBI JOSHUA LEVY	Torah Academy Ardmore, PA	MR. ROBERT A. SCOTT	Akiba Academy of Dallas Dallas, TX
RABBI HILLEL MANDEL	Yeshiva Ketana of Manhattan New York, NY	RABBI ELIYAHU SHULMAN	Yeshiva Orchos Chaim Lakewood, NJ
MRS. CRAINDELL MANNES	Bais Yaakov H.S. of Chicago Chicago, IL	RABBI YISRAEL SILVERMAN	Moriah School of Englewood Englewood, NJ
MRS. NAOMI MAY	Greenfield Hebrew Academy Atlanta, GA	RABBI AHARON STEINHAUS	Chinuch Atzmai
RABBI ZEV MEISELS	Joan Dachs Bais Yaakov Chicago, IL	REBBETZIN B. STERN	Bais Yaakov of Passaic Passaic, NJ
MRS. L. R. MILLER	Bais Shaindel High School Lakewood, NJ	RABBI SHOLOM STRAJCHER	Emek Hebrew Academy Teichman Family Torah Center Sherman Oaks, CA
RABBI MEIR MUNK	Toras Emes Bnei Brak, Israel	RABBI MORDECHAI SUCHARD	Founder — Gateways
RABBI MICHAEL A. MYERS	Ida Crown Jewish Academy Chicago, Illinois	RABBI SHLOMO TEICHMAN	Bais Yaakov Academy Brooklyn, NY
RABBI RAPHAEL J. NEMETSKY	Haston Hebrew Academy Indianapolis, IN	RABBI ZVI TEICHMAN	Talmudical Academy Baltimore, MD
RABBI YEHUDA OELBAUM	Machon Bais Yaakov Brooklyn, NY	RABBI SHOLOM TENDLER	YULA Los Angeles, CA
MRS. ROCHEL OPPENHEIM	Masores Bais Yaakov Brooklyn, NY	RABBI PESACH WACHSMAN	Emek Hebrew Academy Teichman Family Torah Center Sherman Oaks, CA
RABBI URIEL OVADIA	Vaad HaChinuch Hadati Israel	RABBI NACHUM WACHTEL	Joseph Kushner Hebrew Academy Livingston, NJ
REBBETZIN M. PARETZKY	Bais Yaakov of Spring Valley Monsey, NY	MRS. AHUVA WAINHAUS	Joan Dachs Bais Yaakov Chicago, IL
RABBI MOSHE B. PERLSTEIN	Cheder Lubavitch Hebrew Day School Skokie, IL	MRS. SHOSHANA H. WASSER	Hanna Sacks B.Y.H.S. of Chicago Chicago, IL
RABBI A. MOSHE POSSICK	Torah Umesorah	RABBI CHAIM A. WEINBERG	Yeshivat Ateret Torah Ellis A. Safdeye Elementary School Brooklyn, NY
RABBI DOVID REFSON	Neve Yerushalayim Jerusalem, Israel		
RABBI SHALOM RICHTER	The Frisch School Paramus, NJ	RABBI YISSACHAR WEINER	Yeshiva Ketana Tiferes Yisroel Brooklyn, NY
RABBI JONATHAN RIETTI	World renowned author and lecturer	RABBI SIMCHA WEISER	Soille San Diego Hebrew Day School San Diego, CA
RABBI MOISHE B. RODMAN	Desert Torah Academy Las Vegas, NV	RABBI MOSHE WEITMAN	Torah Academy for Girls Far Rockaway, NY
MRS. LIORA ROSEN	Bais Yaakov School for Girls Owings Mills, MD	RABBI MOSHE WENDER	Hebrew Theological College, Skokie, IL
RABBI VELVEL ROSEN	Torah Institute Yeshivas Kochav Yitzchok Baltimore, MD	RABBI YEHOSHUA WENDER	The Beren Academy Houston, TX
MRS. ETTIE ROSENBAUM	Maalot Seminary Baltimore , MD	RABBI SHIMON WIGGINS	Yeshiva Atlanta Atlanta, GA
RABBI KALMEN ROSENBAUM	Torah Day School of Atlanta Atlanta, GA	MRS. DEVORA WILHELM	Maimonides Jewish Day School Portland, OR
RABBI YISROEL MEIR RUBINFELD	The Deal Yeshiva Ocean, NJ	RABBI LIPA ZILBERMAN זצ"ל	Talmud Torah Kaminetz Jerusalem, Israel
RABBI PERETZ SCHEINERMAN	Hillel Hebrew Academy Beverly Hills, CA	RABBI YECHEZKEL ZWEIG	Bais Yaakov School for Girls Owings Mills, MD
MRS. ZIPORA SCHORR	Beth Tfiloh Community School Baltimore, MD	RABBI MOSHE ZWICK	Shulamith School Brooklyn, NY

TABLE OF CONTENTS

INTRODUCTION

THE TARYAG MITZVAH PROJECT AND ITS GENESIS

s I sit down to write this Introduction, it occurs to me that I am actually writing an Introduction to an Introduction. This book, The Ten Commandments, is the result of an immense effort by a large group of dedicated and talented people, but its successful completion is not an end by any means. It is the inauguration of the Taryag Mitzvah Project, a vast undertaking that will be completed *b'ezras Hashem* over the next several years. And even the completion of the project will not be the end. It is our hope that it will greatly enhance Jewish education by adding an entirely new dimension to the way Torah is taught and learned in schools, shuls and homes all over the world.

OVER A THOUSAND YEARS OF SCHOLARSHIP

The core of our holy Torah is the Taryag Mitzvos, the six hundred and thirteen commandments that are the foundation of Jewish practice and belief. Throughout the ages, our greatest Sages have encouraged and urged people to learn the Taryag Mitzvos on even an elementary level. The systematic study of the mitzvos, they insisted, would ensure observance, and even those commandments that cannot be performed today would be considered to have been fulfilled through their study.

A solid knowledge of the Taryag Mitzvos provides a grasp of the entire Torah. The study of the suggested reasons for the mitzvos and their deeper meanings imbues their performance with a richness of understanding and feeling that enables the performer to reach new heights of commitment and devotion with each repeated performance. Just about everyone can learn the Taryag Mitzvos with relative ease over a reasonably short time and thereby gain a panoramic view of the Torah as a whole.

According to *Rabbi David Vital* in *Kesser Torah*, David HaMelech was already reviewing the mitzvos in numbered sequence nearly three thousand years ago. Over the last thirteen hundred years, some of our greatest Sages have formulated numbered lists of the mitzvos, thereby facilitating their study and quick review. Many others have written extensively on the specifics, the meanings and the significance of the Taryag Mitzvos.

The Taryag Mitzvah Project is a reflection and distillation of the scholarship of the last thirteen hundred years. The centerpiece of the project will be a projected fifteen-volume Encyclopedia of the Taryag Mitzvoth, a landmark work geared to layperson and scholar alike. The encyclopedia will present each of the 613 mitzvos in their richness and detail. It will be accompanied by Mitzvah Cards and curriculum material for use in schools. The Cards contain an encapsulated version of the mitzvos and their reasons. These have been designed for easy learning and quick review. The standard Mitzvah Cards are geared toward young adults and students in the higher grades. In addition, there will also be a set of colorfully illustrated Junior Mitzvah Cards for younger children. The curriculum materials are state-of-the-art, full-color textbooks, designed for classroom use. Visually stunning graphics and illustrations engage the students and draw them into the subject. Accessible text, highlighted points of interest and thought-provoking questions provide an innovative learning experience. These textbooks are accompanied by a teacher's edition, providing the educators with novel teaching strategies and practical integration activities in a pedagogically sound format.

THE GENESIS OF THE PROJECT

In a way, the Taryag Mitzvah Project was born at our Shabbos table. For a number of years, it has been the practice in our home to learn the Taryag Mitzvos at the Shabbos table with our children and even with guests. This has become a highlight of our week and a joyful experience for both children and adults. The rapid growth in knowledge, perception and sensitivity that we witnessed among all who participated was remarkable. We became intrigued by the possibilities that this approach offered for impacting the broad spectrum of Jewish students.

As a result, we decided to create Mitzvah Cards that would offer a bird's-eye view of each mitzvah. The Cards would enhance the experience of studying the mitzvos and transform it into an exciting learning adventure. We showed a prototype of the Cards to educators, who were enthralled by their potential as innovative learning tools. They urged us to introduce the Cards into the schools.

In our discussions with people from many walks of life, an interesting question kept recurring. Why limit this project to students? Why not provide material for fathers and mothers, laypeople and students — in short, people of all ages and backgrounds — to replicate the experience we had found so informative and satisfying?

That is when we began to think seriously about a formal Taryag Mitzvah Project. We would require not only Cards, but a book to provide a wealth of in-depth, comprehensive information from which people of all levels of education could draw material appropriate to their interests. This book would need to include a solid base of laws, and a broad selection of suggested reasons for the mitzvos, all drawn from classical sources. The book would also include a treasury of Medrashic selections and suggested topics for discussion. And so the "book" evolved into the Encyclopedia of the Taryag Mitzvoth, which is expected to comprise fifteen volumes.

This project has been presented to and evaluated by over one thousand educators across the full spectrum of the Torah educational networks, in numerous cities and locales in the United States and across the world. They have embraced the project with great enthusiasm, and consider it such an important development in Jewish education that they have urged its inclusion into the core curricula of Torah schools. Their input and guidance has molded the structure of this project. Many of the exceptional features of this project are a tribute to their keen insight and many years of experience.

Following the enthusiastic reception of the project by so many educators, this program was presented to the greatest Rabbanim, Roshei Yeshiva, and Rebbes of our generation. Their response has been universally supportive. They too have affirmed, in writing, that a period of time should be set aside each day for the study of the Taryag Mitzvos.

The Taryag Mitzvah Project offers benefits far beyond the school setting. It is easily adaptable to short study sessions, making it perfect for shul instruction in the interval between Minchah and Maariv. It can serve as a wonderful focus for discussion at the Shabbos table by presenting a host of fascinating topics related to the weekly parshah. It is ideally suited for use in outreach, as it makes the broad outlines of Torah accessible to newcomers with little or no background. And it offers any serious student of the Torah a structured format to broaden his understanding of the Torah as a whole — by himself or with a study partner — in an easily assimilable fashion.

So this is where we stand, as the inaugural volume goes to print. Both the Mitzvah Cards and Junior Cards are in production. This is the opening volume of the English edition, and the next volume (which will begin with mitzvah #1 and proceed in order) is currently in production. A Hebrew version is soon to follow. We have editorial, educational and administrative offices in New Jersey and Jerusalem, and a staff of seventy working diligently at making this dream into a reality. An international team of educators is hard at work producing curricular materials, and educators the world over are eagerly awaiting the successful completion of the project. The original germ of an idea has become our life's work, and we are humbly grateful to the Almighty for granting us this priceless opportunity.

THE STRUCTURE OF THE ENCYCLOPEDIA

The Encyclopedia of the Taryag Mitzvoth is aimed at two audiences. It is meant to be a stand-alone compendium of information about the Mitzvos, to be used by anyone interested in studying the mitzvos and their intricacies. It is also meant to be used as a companion resource for educators and parents using the Mitzvah Cards to teach the mitzvos, providing them with a wealth of material from which to draw as they see fit. Consequently, the Encyclopedia's treatment of each mitzvah begins with the basic information of the mitzvah, as it is presented on the Card, and then proceeds to elucidate and expand upon it with a broad, in-depth discussion of the many facets of the mitzvah.

Each entry in the Encyclopedia has been divided into eight sections, each dealing with a different component of the mitzvah. This design enables the reader to quickly and easily find the section and topic of his interest. The sections are:

    ☞ The Basic Mitzvah

    ☞ An Expanded Treatment

    ☞ עיונים — A Broader Look at the Laws

    ☞ שיח הלכה — Situations in Halachah

    ☞ ברכת המצוה — The Blessing for the Mitzvah

    ☞ טוב טעם — Illuminations of the Mitzvah: Suggested Reasons and Insights

    ☞ מאוצרות חז״ל — Through the Eyes of the Sages: Stories, Parables and Reflections

    ☞ מוני המצוות — The Count of the Mitzvah

1. THE BASIC MITZVAH. This section corresponds to the Mitzvah Card. It offers the reader a brief but comprehensive outline of the mitzvah, with a suggested reason for it.

We begin with a clear and simple definition of the mitzvah, identifying the action or inaction required for its fulfillment. The verse in the Torah from which the mitzvah is derived is then presented, along with the number of the mitzvah according to *Sefer HaChinuch.*

This section then presents the main Biblical laws and rules of the mitzvah. Regulations decreed by the Sages are identified as Rabbinic laws.

As a general rule, the laws of the mitzvah are formulated according to the rulings of the *Rambam* and *Shulchan Aruch.* Other opinions are cited in the Expanded Treatment section.

Note: It cannot be emphasized enough that neither this section nor the sections that follow constitute a practical guide to halachic observance. While a very comprehensive outline of the mitzvah and the various opinions concerning its details are presented, their application to the complexities of daily life are too involved to be dealt with in this work, and are beyond the scope of this project.

2. AN EXPANDED TREATMENT. This section expands upon the laws presented in the previous section. It provides the sources for those laws, differing opinions, and many additional details and points of interest. It also elaborates on the relationship between the mitzvah being discussed and other related mitzvos. To make it easy to locate the expanded treatment of each point, a number appears on the Basic Mitzvah to identify the paragraph in the Expanded Treatment section in which the discussion may be found. For this reason, the Basic Mitzvah is repeated on each pair of facing pages.

3. **עיונים — A BROADER LOOK AT THE LAWS.** This section highlights a number of points discussed in the previous section and examines them at greater depth. This format enables us to discuss certain complex aspects of the mitzvah in greater detail, yet in a highly readable manner.

4. **שיח הלכה — SITUATIONS IN HALACHAH.** We have taken the liberty of choosing one or two elements of the mitzvah and analyzing their practical application to daily life. In general, the analysis will make reference to a number of different views. Although it is not meant to provide definitive halachic rulings in any given matter, it will serve to illustrate the broad range of issues, concepts and situations that should be considered.

5. **ברכת המצוה — THE BLESSING FOR THE MITZVAH.** The majority of the 248 positive commandments require a blessing to be recited over their performance. [The 365 negative commandments (prohibitions) do not require blessings, because they call for inaction rather than action.] A special section has been added to these mitzvos to elucidate the choice of language used in the blessing and the proper time for its recitation in relation to the performance of the mitzvah. In cases where no blessing is required, it gives the reasons for the omission.

6. **טוב טעם — ILLUMINATIONS OF THE MITZVAH — *Suggested Reasons and Insights.*** Performance of the mitzvos is not predicated on our understanding their reasons. The finite mind of even the wisest person is in any case far too puny to grasp the infinite wisdom of God. His command alone must elicit our unconditional acceptance and observance of them. Nevertheless, Sages and commentators throughout the generations have suggested reasons for the mitzvos, in the certain knowledge that a sense of these provides further inspiration for their proper performance and an enhanced desire to cleave to the ways of Hashem.

In this section, the reader will find a selection of reasons and rationales for each mitzvah culled from the works of the Rishonim and Acharonim, as well as from the great Masters of Mussar and Chassidus. Although we can never be sure of the precise reason for any mitzvah, we can discern its flavor (the literal meaning of the word "taam"), and catch a glimpse of the complex rationales behind it.

7. **מאוצרות חז"ל — THROUGH THE EYES OF THE SAGES — *Stories, Parables and Reflections.*** This section may prove to be the most captivating part of the Encyclopedia for younger readers and their teachers. It aims to capture the moral and ethical dimensions of the mitzvos as perceived through the sayings, parables and histories of the Sages of the Mishnah, Talmud and Medrash. Poignant and enchanting, exhilarat-

ing and sobering, the mitzvos come to life and ring true to life. In citation after citation, we listen to our greatest Sages describe their observations, insights, sentiments and reflections on the mitzvos.

8. **מוני המצוות — THE COUNT OF THE MITZVAH.** The Talmud states that Moshe was given 613 mitzvos at Sinai (*Makkos* 23b). There are, however, far more mitzvos in the Torah. The *Rambam*, in his *Sefer HaMitzvos*, establishes the criteria for which mitzvos are included in the count of the 613 and which are not. *Rambam* formulates fourteen rules for this, some of which are disputed by other authorities, most notably *Ramban*, whose critiques appear alongside *Rambam* in the standard editions of the *Sefer HaMitzvos*. In the main, mitzvos that are not part of the count are considered to be details of one of the mitzvos that do appear.

Over the centuries, a number of great commentators have compiled their formulations of the 613 mitzvos arranged in a specific order. In the course of the last seven centuries, the arrangement of the *Sefer HaChinuch*, which closely follows that of the Rambam, has become the most popular and widely used formulation and sequence, in part because it follows the sequence of the Torah readings. The Encyclopedia and the Mitzvah Cards follow this formulation and sequence, as they appear in current editions of the *Sefer HaChinuch*.

The purpose of this section is to present the views of other major commentators as to whether a particular Mitzvah is listed in the count of the 613, and if so, its place in the sequence. It analyzes the different approaches and their conceptual systems, and explains why some count a particular mitzvah and others do not.

We have listed below the editions of the various seforim used in compiling the Count of the Mitzvah charts, to aid those who wish to research those sources:

- ☞ *Sefer HaChinuch* — Machon Yerushalayim Edition
- ☞ *Rambam, Sefer HaMitzvos* — Frankel Edition
- ☞ *Baal Halochos Gedolos* — Machon Yerushalayim Edition
- ☞ *R' Saadiah Gaon* — With the commentary of R' Yeruchem Fischel Perla
- ☞ *Rabbeinu Eliyahu HaZakein* — Printed by R' M. Slutzki, Warsaw, and listed according to his commentary *Hiddur Zakein*
- ☞ *R' Yitzchak El-Bargeloni* — With the commentary *Nesiv Mitzvosecha*, and listed according to his commentary and notes
- ☞ *Sefer Mitzvos Gadol* — Schlesinger Edition
- ☞ *Sefer Mitzvos Katan* — 5695 Edition
- ☞ *Sefer Yere'im* — *Sefer Yere'im HaShalem*
- ☞ *Maamar HaSechel* — 5622 Edition
- ☞ *Rashbag* — Feldheim Edition, listed according to the footnote numbers of the *Zohar HaRakia*
- ☞ *Zohar HaRakia* — Feldheim Edition

THE TEN COMMANDMENTS

The inaugural volume of the Encyclopedia of the Taryag Mitzvoth is devoted to the Ten Commandments. There are actually fourteen mitzvos included in the Ten Commandments. According to the commentators, all 613 Mitzvos of the Torah are somehow connected to one or the other of these mitzvos. Therefore, in a certain sense, the mitzvos presented in this volume are a microcosm of the entire mitzvah system of the Torah, and this volume is a microcosm of the entire Encyclopedia.

This volume will be a permanent part of the Encyclopedia where it will take its proper place in sequence. It will be an easily recognized reference work for Shavuoth or any other time that a reader feels inspired to revisit the Ten Commandments as a separate unit.

As the inaugural publication of the Encyclopedia, this volume serves the additional purpose of showcasing the efforts of the Taryag Mitzvah Project and allowing educators, parents and the general public to familiarize themselves with the vast instructional potential of the project.

It is our hope that the Encyclopedia of the Taryag Mitzvoth will become a mainstay of Jewish libraries for generations, and that the Taryag Mitzvah Project will spark a major revolution in Torah study. It will make countless thousands of adults and children conversant with the Taryag Mitzvos, thereby giving them, in a real sense, "knowledge of the entire Torah." This volume represents the first step on the road to that future, and we pray that the Almighty will bless our efforts with success.

A project of this scope and magnitude presents both a daunting challenge and an awesome responsibility. The Taryag Mitzvos are the legacy of *Klal Yisrael,* the rules by which all Jews must live. In attempting to present the Taryag Mitzvos in a format easily accessible to today's students, we were always mindful that our task was one of transmission — to take the words and explanations of the *Gedolim* of previous generations and present them in an organized way. This we have done to the best of our ability, and we pray to the Almighty that we have succeeded in providing both accuracy and accessibility. Any shortfall is ours alone.

ACKNOWLEDGEMENTS

he Taryag Mitzvah Project in general, and this inaugural volume in particular, is the fruit of the vision, efforts, and generosity of many people. It is only fitting that I take this opportunity to pay tribute and express my deeply felt gratitude to them.

First and foremost, I pay tribute to the memory and eternal teachings of my *roshei yeshivah* and mentors, HARAV HAGAON RAV AVROHOM PAM ל״צז and HARAV HAGAON RAV REUVEN FEIN ל״צז. During the years I spent under their tutelage in Yeshiva Torah Vodaath, I witnessed firsthand true greatness in Torah and *midos*. Their examples left an indelible impression on me. I would also like to express my gratitude to, *yibadel lechaim*, my *rebbe*, HARAV HAGAON RAV YISROEL BELSKY א״טילש, whose encouragement, wise counsel, and vast fund of knowledge have always been available to me.

From the inception of this project, we have been privileged to enjoy the support and counsel of HARAV HAGAON RAV YOSEF SHOLOM ELYASHIV א״טילש, who has lent his prestige to this work and given of his precious time to advise us on many of its aspects. Under his guidance, a *Vaad HaChinuch* comprised of leading educators has been established for the purpose of reviewing the materials.

I wish to acknowledge the special contributions of HARAV HAGAON RAV EZRIEL AUERBACH א״טילש, and HARAV HAGAON RAV MECHEL ZILBER א״טילש, who saw the great potential of the project in its earliest stages. They have been pillars of support and *chizuk*. Despite their many commitments, they have been actively involved and consistently helpful. We thank them warmly and look forward to a continued collaboration.

Special thanks to: HARAV HAGAON RAV YAAKOV HILLEL א״טילש, and HARAV HAGAON RAV SHMUEL ELIEZER STERN א״טילש, who have made themselves available whenever called upon; and HARAV HAGAON RAV MOSHE ROSMARIN א״טילש, for reviewing significant parts of this work and offering invaluable insights, criticisms and recommendations.

I extend my deepest thanks to HARAV HAGAON RAV CHAIM WALKIN א״טילש, who embraced this project early on. His enthusiastic endorsement opened many doors for us; the debt we owe to him and his family is boundless. It has also been our special honor to have the guidance of

HARAV HAGAON RAV REUVEN FEINSTEIN שליט״א. His advice regarding the curriculum portion of this project has been immensely helpful.

I do not think I can possibly do justice to the contributions of RABBI ELYAKIM WALKIN, my partner and colleague. He is the engine of Taryag, the support upon which I depend, and, most especially, a warm and trusted friend. He takes this opportunity to express his gratitude to his wife, CHAYA RUCHIE שתחי׳, for her encouragement and for her good cheer when, all too often, work on the project preempted everything else.

A special debt of gratitude goes to my dear friend RABBI DOVID ROSMARIN, who devoted two years of his life — heart and soul — to developing and launching this project. The breadth of its scope and the quality of its organization are a most eloquent tribute to his outstanding talents and utter dedication.

A special note of gratitude to RAV YAAKOV YOSEF REINMAN, a noted *talmid chacham*, writer and editor, whose talents and creativity are manifest in the quality of this work, and to RABBI YEHEZKEL DANZIGER, who has drawn on his many years of experience to offer wise and extremely useful suggestions.

We have also been privileged to receive the encouragement and active assistance of many noted rabbinic leaders: RABBI DOVID WEINBERGER, RABBI HESHY BILLET, RABBI MOSHE WEINBERGER and RABBI YOSEF KALATSKY. Their energetic support of so many worthy causes is legendary. Our gratitude goes as well to RABBI MOSHE HIER and RABBI MEYER MAY, whose steadfast devotion to Jewish education is rooted in their cease-less efforts to preserve the memory of the world that was.

Our work has been enhanced by the valuable suggestions of numerous *menahelim* and educators from all corners of the world of *chinuch*. In particular, we must mention the warm encouragement of RABBI YEHOSHUA FISHMAN; the supportive assistance of RABBI YAAKOV BENDER; the unique educational sensitivities of RABBI AVRAHAM ANISFELD and RABBI MENACHEM LEVIN; and the participation of RABBI MAYER BELLER, who started it all. I also extend my special thanks to RABBI SHOLOM STRAJCHER, who continues to share with me his creative insights and years of experience, and whose "out-of-the-box" thinking has greatly enhanced the project. My very special thanks to RABBI NECHEMIAH GOTTLIEB, a dynamic new force in Torah education, whose invaluable suggestions have enhanced many parts of this work.

A special thank you must also be extended to RABBI YOSAIF ASHER WEISS, whose timely advice and unique insights were instrumental in producing this work.

The Encyclopedia of the Taryag Mitzvoth is a project of enormous scope and ambition, whose success requires a great investment of time, energy and resources. The Taryag Legacy Foundation has been privileged to receive the generous support of numerous people who have recognized the vital importance of the work and joined us in making the vision a reality.

We are deeply grateful to MOTTY KLEIN, whose visionary decision to dedicate the inaugural volume of this monumental endeavor has set in motion a Torah revolution that will, with the help of the Almighty, bring the knowledge and appreciation of the mitzvos to hundreds of thousands of men, women and children. The Taryag Legacy Foundation is proud to be associated with the Klein family in this endeavor, and we pray that it will be a source of merit for the continued health and success of the entire Klein family.

We also wish to thank LLOYD KIELSON, a valued friend, who serves as a shining example of what Jewish communal leadership should be; MORRIS SMITH, legendary supporter of Jewish causes, who with his pene-trating and creative insight was among the first to see the promise of our work, and whose example has moti-vated many others; A. JOSEPH STERN, whose passion for building Torah institutions and bringing mitzvah observance to all Jews is changing the Jewish landscape worldwide; AARON HERSH ELBOGEN, a supporter of many worthy causes who has warmly embraced this project as well.

We are grateful as well to all our many friends who have lent their assistance when it was most needed: RABBI MORDECHAI GOTTLIEB, a dear friend, whose wisdom, encouragement and assistance from day one have been our beacon and our strength; DANNY AND BLIMY LEMBERG, who have graciously offered wise and erudite suggestions and unstinting support; RABBI MORDECHAI ROSENZWEIG, who has been a valued friend and confidant and has played a pivotal role whenever called upon; RABBI YITZCHAK FOLLMAN, whose warmth, concern and faith in the project have helped bring it to fruition; RABBI FISHEL TODD, who from an unassuming office on Private Way, is creatively teaching Torah to the masses — in a most public way; RABBI MICHOEL AND ESTHER STYLLER, whose encouragement and assistance from the project's genesis have meant so much; RABBI BINYOMIN HEINEMANN, whose unstinting support and assistance is most appreciated; RABBI LEIB KLEIN, who has been a valued friend, and constant source of inspiration. A special note of thanks to RABBI SHMUEL GRAMA, a talented and dedicated *mechanech*, whose contributions to the project are invaluable.

We have also enjoyed the friendship, inspiration and assistance of the following friends: HESHY APFELBAUM, SHIMSHON BANDMAN, RABBI ARYEH BELSKY, DOVID BERG, RABBI YISROEL DOVID BERGER, SHIMMY AND LAYALA BERTRAM, RABBI SHMUEL HEIMAN, ELAZAR FINGERER, RABBI REUVEN KANAREK, RABBI YISROEL KELLNER, RONNIEL AND CAROLINE YAFFA LEVY, YEHUDAH AND ADINA MUEHLGAY, CHANANIA POMERANTZ, YEHUDAH RAHMANAN, RABBI JONATHAN RIETTI, YERUCHOM SCHECHTER, RIVIE AND LEBA SCHWEBEL, RABBI EFRAIM SHRAGA SHAIN, RABBI YAAKOV SHULMAN, RABBI GERSHON SPIEGEL, MOSHE TAUB, ZVI AND PENINA WIENER, and MENDY YARMISH.

We offer our sincere thanks to the Foundation for the Jewish Community, a Foundation of Donor Advised Funds, whose donors and staff helped make this work possible. FJC's donors support many worthy causes, not only through their grants, but with their mission-based investing. Financing from FJC's Agency Loan Fund was critical in bringing our efforts to fruition.

Their decision to support this project came at a turning point in our work. Multitudes yet unborn will be indebted to FJC's donors, who had the vision to utilize FJC to manage their charitable funds. (FJC, the premier foundation of donor advised funds for discerning philanthropists, is a public charity that provides total management of charitable giving. To learn more about how you can participate in supporting other worthy projects, call 888-GIVE-FJC or visit www.fjc.org.)

Warm acknowledgement is expressed to LENNY ZEHNWIRTH, whose confidence in our vision has meant so much. We are deeply and eternally grateful to him and his esteemed colleagues for their foresight and leadership.

A project of this magnitude requires an exceptionally dedicated and skillful office staff. The Taryag Legacy Foundation office is superbly managed by our office director, MRS. FAIGE SHOSHANA, and our dedicated staff, MRS. CHAYA ALIZA DECKELBAUM and MRS. ESTHER GINSBURG. They have gone far beyond the call of duty in terms of time and effort expended. We thank MRS. AHUVA WEISS for her pioneering work in editing and refining the curriculum, and MRS. CHANI WILHELM, for her creative work on the Teacher's editions.

A special note of gratitude to RABBI DONIEL MANEVICH, whose meticulous and painstaking editing and proofreading enhance every page of this work.

We warmly acknowledge the contributions of RABBI SHIMON FINKELMAN, an eminent *mechanech*, whose skillful editing has added so much to the curriculum; we also wish to acknowledge the contributions of RABBI MOISHE BAK, RABBI MECHEL ROTTENBERG, RABBI BINYOMIN GINSBERG, RABBI HILLEL MANDEL, RABBI YIDEL STRASSER, and MR. RICHARD ALTABEE.

The Taryag organization in Eretz Yisrael is led by a distinguished and dedicated staff. We are grateful to RABBI NAFTOLI ERLANGER, who serves with great distinction and selfless devotion as Editorial Director, overseeing a large staff of researchers, writers and editors; RABBI YAAKOV YOSEF BATTELMAN, chairman of the Vaad HaChinuch and a towering *chinuch* personality, and his distinguished associates RABBI SHOLOM EINHORN and RABBI YITZCHAK MANDELKORN, who work tirelessly to ensure that the students receive age appropriate and child sensitive curriculum material; RABBI SHMUEL ELYASHIV, Director of Taryag activities in Eretz Yisrael, whose life's passion has become to teach Taryag in a thousand schools, and whose energy, enthusiasm and leadership are an inspiration to all.

Our Sages urge us to present the Torah in a most beautiful setting. Raising the bar of excellence in Torah publishing, the Taryag Legacy Foundation has been blessed with a most talented and creative graphics and design team. Their work is truly a *kiddush Hashem*. We are grateful to:

MRS. DEENEE COHEN, whose DC mark of excellence is evident in the beauty and grace of design on all parts of this project; CHAIM MUSHKIN, a warm and sensitive artist who has become the international address for book cover design; our art director, SHEPSIL SCHEINBERG, a person of immense creativity, who has brought the mitzvos to life on the Junior Mitzvah Cards in a truly remarkable fashion and has contributed to many aspects of this work. We also wish to acknowledge the beautiful graphics and photography of MENASHE SCHWARTZ and ALLEN BEN, and to YANKY GOLDMAN, whose creativity and talents breathe life into every page of the student textbook.

We would like to thank MRS. BASSIE GUTMAN, who heads our typesetting department with great professionalism and infinite patience. She deserves special thanks for her painstaking efforts and selfless devotion in preparing the manuscript for completion. She was ably assisted by MRS. SLAVIE GOLDBERGER and NAFTOLI MILLER, who entered the myriad revisions and corrections.

We are grateful to MRS. ROCHELLE GEMAL, MRS. MIRIAM HIRSCH and MRS. CHAYA HOBERMAN for meticulously proofreading the text.

We are also grateful to MR. GERSHON BIEGELEISEN and MRS. CHAYA FUHRER for their friendship, support and business acumen.

We thank YAAKOV YOSEF STENDIG and RAPHAEL ABEND for the beautiful printing and irregular hours that a project of this sort calls for, and whose patience and confidence in the Taryag Mitzvah Project has been a great *chizuk* to us all; SHEA MARKOWITZ, whose creativity in marketing and design are truly a wonder, and whose friendship I deeply value; YANKY ADLER for his constant patience and good cheer.

On a personal note, I would like to express my gratitude to my honored mother MRS. NECHAMAH MOSKOWITZ and her warm hearted husband, MR. SHLOMO MOSKOWITZ, for all they have done for me, and the love and caring they constantly shower upon our family. They have supported us in this endeavor in so many ways. My thanks also go out to my esteemed parents-in-law, MR. ARNOLD AND RUTH BERKOVITS, who have been a constant source of advice and encouragement from the very beginning.

It is my hope that my efforts in the creation of this work will be a *z'chus* for the *neshamah* of my dear and beloved father and mentor, ר׳ יעקב רפאל בן ר׳ מענדל הלוי ז״ל, whose constant striving for perfection is the model that I seek to emulate.

No acknowledgement would be complete without expressing my boundless gratitude to my children: DASSY, MOSHE, REUVEN, YITZY, AVRUMY, YOSSI, ELI and YAAKOV, who are the inspiration for this project, and who accepted the deep involvement of their parents with words of encouragement and good-natured forbearance; and especially to my wife, JUDY, שתחי׳, whose contribution is far greater than the moral support she gives me. Without her efforts and enthusiasm, and her endurance of my protracted absences from home, this project would be just a dream.

I conclude by expressing my most humble gratitude to the Almighty for allowing me to share in the privilege of bringing the enrichment and enlightenment of the Taryag Mitzvos to the Jewish people. May He guide our efforts and bless them with success.

This book, though self-contained, is but the first of a projected fifteen-volume Encyclopedia. As this volume goes to press, work is already well advanced on the next volume. The excitement and the accomplishment are just beginning. We look forward to the continued collaboration of those who have already participated, and to the future friendship of those who have yet to join us in pioneering this historic work.

Rabbi Dovid Wax
אדר ב תשס״ה / *March 2005*

ספר
עשרת הדברות
השלם

The Ten
Commandments

Prologue to the Ten Commandments

CHAPTER 1:

THE SINAITIC EXPERIENCE — THE BEDROCK UPON WHICH JUDAISM RESTS

ome thirty-three hundred years have passed since humanity experienced an event that was to be the single most significant occurrence in human history. It was the moment when the Jewish nation received the Torah at *Har Sinai*. That moment still lives in our consciousness. Not a single moment passes but that at some level we are aware of it. Nothing else can testify as effectively to Israel's undying belief in the truth of God and His Torah, as our steadfastness throughout the ages in affirming it and living by it.

Nothing at all can undermine our knowledge that at that decisive moment we experienced God Himself, in all His Glory. Fathers passed on to their children what they themselves had learned at their own father's knee. We are the recipients of a long, unbroken chain of tradition. It affirms this: That it was God and none other, God, unmediated, He and only He, Who came to us and communicated with us. This is a living tradition. No one among us will ever harbor the slightest doubt. The *Aseres HaDibros* — the "Ten Commandments" — were communicated to us by God Himself.

The Sinaitic Experience was not limited to a single generation. Every Jewish soul was present. [This, of course, does not mean that we were all there physically. However, the tradition is firmly entrenched that all the *neshamos* of *Am Yisrael* were present during the giving of the Torah (see *Shemos Rabbah* 28:4).] All of us became bound to observe the Torah with a solemn oath that we executed then (see *Yoma* 73b et al.). What is the essence of this oath? It means that the Jewish soul is indelibly imprinted by the profoundly moving impact of what we saw and heard. Our very Jewishness, marked, as it is, by having stood in the presence of God, is testimony that it all happened in precisely the way that our tradition has passed on to us. God was there and we were there; He spoke, and we heard, and nothing was ever again the same. Our absolute knowledge that all this occurred, is our oath (see *Meshech Chochmah, Devarim* 33:4).

Here are the inspiring words of the saintly *Chofetz Chaim* in *Nidchei Yisrael:*

> *God was not secretive when He gave us the Torah. He wanted the entire world to know what was happening. Six hundred thousand adult men were physically present. All of them, everyone, without hesitancy or reservation, joined in full-throated unison to call out,* **"Na'aseh VeNishma** — *We will do whatever You may ever ask of us. We ask only that You tell us where our duty lies." Never, ever, would there be any justification to cast doubt upon the tradition. It happened, and we know it.*
>
> *From that moment onward, all Jews scrupulously kept every law in the Torah. Even during dreadful exiles, no law was forgotten and no law was changed. Even when conscientious observance demanded vast expenditures of time and money, as, for example, when lulavim and esrogim had to be imported across thousands of miles, Klal Yisrael, as a whole, never jettisoned even one iota of the halachah's demands.*

Our loyalty went further. Throughout the ages, people have been studying the laws of the mitzvos in all their details and complexities with uncompromising thoroughness and application. No minutiae were too insignificant, no theoretical constructs too abstruse, but that we, in our millions, devoted love and tireless effort to their elucidation. Neither the rigors of exile nor the countless difficulties we were forced to endure, weakened our enthusiasm and dedication.

None of this could ever have occurred had not the truth of the Torah and its Divine origin been accepted and assumed beyond doubt or quibble. Millions went to cruel and agonizing deaths, millions sacrificed their children to gruesome tortures, all for no other reason than that this Torah should remain alive among us. Our tradition is no small matter for us. We know ourselves to be a link in a chain that reaches back to the very beginnings of our national identity. We have no doubts about who we are and what defines us.

REMEMBER!

Since awareness of the Sinaitic Experience is so basic to our faith, Moshe Rabbeinu admonished us never to forget it. Memory lapses are natural enough, but they are disallowed when they concern the very foundation of our beliefs. Here is what the Torah tells us (*Devarim* 4:9-10):

> *Only watch yourself, be exceedingly careful [since it concerns] your very being, that you not forget any of the events that you witnessed. Make sure that, throughout your life, they never leave your consciousness. Moreover, pass them on to your children and your grandchildren. [Tell them the story of] the day on which you stood before Hashem, your God,*

at Chorev [Har Sinai], [the day] when Hashem said to me: Bring all the people together so that I may let them hear My words. [It is imperative that they absorb this well] so that they may learn to fear Me always, and [furthermore] that they may pass it on to their children.

[Previously (ibid. 4:7) the Torah states: For who [else] is a great nation who has gods close to them like Hashem, our God, whenever we call unto Him. Ran (Derashos HaRan §9) links the subsequent verses with this verse, explaining that the latter verses are meant to caution us: Although we may know that Hashem is close to us (because of the wonders He performs for us) we must nevertheless recall the extraordinary event of the giving of the Torah, as it is the foundation upon which Judaism rests.]

Ramban (in his glosses to Rambam's Sefer HaMitzvos, the second mitzvah omitted by Rambam) maintains that this admonition has a formal place among the Taryag Mitzvos. Here is a paraphrase of what he says:

These verses are to be understood as a command, never to forget the Sinaitic Experience and never, throughout our lives, to allow them to pass from our consciousness. This experience is to remain a constant presence for us …

There is a good reason for such stringency. The underlying theory is that the Sinaitic Experience must be lived by us [i.e. the entire nation], not retold to us [by a single person who experienced it by himself]. If we were to know of it only by hearsay, even if it was retold by a prophet whose reliability has been confirmed by miracles, there would always be a danger that, at some time in the future, another prophet might arise, one whose deeds might be even more wondrous than the earlier ones. If he would then attempt to lure us away from our tradition, our convictions might well be compromised.

This cannot occur, now that we ourselves were witnesses at Sinai. No spurious miracles can ever shake our certainty. We would recognize the charlatan for what he is. That is why the Torah commands us so earnestly never to absolve ourselves from the duty to pass these truths on to our children. They trust us because they would realize that, as parents, we would never pass falsehoods on to our children (see the similar thought expressed in Rambam, Hil. Yesodei HaTorah 8:1).

Ramban takes his ideas further in Parashas Va'eschanan (Devarim 4:9). We are to remember not only the fact of the Sinaitic Experience but also those aspects of the event — the sound of the shofar blasts, the flames that enveloped the mountain — which gave the occasion its unique character. He also maintains that besides the prohibition (Lo Saaseh) to forget what happened, there is also an obligation (Aseh) to pass whatever we saw and heard, to our descendants (see Appendix, note 1).

Although Rambam does not understand these verses to constitute commandments (he does not count them in his Sefer HaMitzvos), he states unequivocally that the principle they express is a cornerstone of the Jewish perspective. He does this in his Iggeres Teiman, a letter he wrote to the Yemenite community to encourage them when they were faced with the threat of forced conversions. Here is a paraphrase of what he wrote:

Keep the memory of the Sinaitic Experience alive, never forget it and pass it on intact to your children. God Himself insisted that we do all this ... You are to describe vividly the glory and the beauty of what happened and you are to do this in public, for all to hear. Only thus can you lay a solid foundation for our faith, and only thus will you lead your community to the truth.

Impress the unequalled greatness of that day upon your children's mind. The Torah itself (Devarim 4:32) takes pains to underline its uniqueness.

You, my brothers, must understand that the covenant forged at Sinai between God and ourselves was unique, never repeated. God Himself, the most unimpeachable witness, describes it as such. Never before had God revealed Himself to an entire people, permitting His Glory to be perceived "eye to eye," and never again will this occur.

I will tell you why God did this: To anchor our faith to such mighty pillars of support that no circumstance, be it even the present dreadful situation in which you are being challenged to stand firm in the face of unbearable pressures to convert, would ever be able to move us one whit from the impregnable fortress of our faith.

The Torah (Shemos 20:20) tells us that the purpose of this unique experience was to help us to withstand the harsh tests with which we would inevitably meet up in the course of our history. Do not waver! Do not sin!

Clearly, *Rambam* agrees with *Ramban* that we are obligated to remember the Sinaitic Experience and that we are to pass our memories along to our children, and they to theirs.

[There is a technical reason why *Rambam* does not include these mitzvos among the *Taryag*. In his fourth rule of which mitzvos qualify, *Rambam* determines that mitzvos that are general in nature, which do not command or prohibit specific actions but which rather serve to admonish us to keep all God's commands and be consistent in our service to Him, are not counted in the *Taryag Mitzvos*. *Rambam* is of the opinion that the exhortation to remember the Sinaitic Experience and to make it the basis of the education that we offer our children belongs in this category. There is no substantive difference between him and *Ramban* on any practical level (*Megillas Esther* to the glosses of *Ramban* to *Sefer HaMitzvos* loc. cit.; *Sefer HaChinuch* and *Smag* also do not count this as a mitzvah).]

Halachah encourages us to remember our Sinaitic Experience. *Tur* (*Orach Chaim* §47) notes that *Birchas HaTorah*, the blessing we make daily thanking God for having given us the Torah, provides an opportunity. The *berachah* reads, "Who has chosen us from among all the nations, and given us His Torah." While saying these words, we should bring to mind our national collective memory of having been selected from among all the nations, of having been brought to Sinai, of hearing God's words, and of having been the recipients of His Torah.

Arizal maintains that we are to recall our Sinaitic Experience during the blessing that we recite before *Krias Shema*, when we say the words, "… and You have chosen us from among all the nations … and You, our King, have brought us close to Your great Name to thank You and to proclaim Your unity out of love." These words convey the idea, of which we must be mindful, that by giving us the Torah, Hashem made us special and that, in response to this act of love, we accepted Him as our King (*Shaar HaKavanos, Derush Yotzer*, Jerusalem ed., p. 19b; *Pri Eitz Chaim, Shaar Krias Shema*, Dobrovno ed., p. 39; see *Magen Avraham, Orach Chaim* 60:2).

THE SINAITIC EXPERIENCE IS THE BASIS FOR OUR BELIEF IN THE DIVINE AUTHORSHIP OF THE TORAH

Rambam (*Hil. Yesodei HaTorah* ch. 8) makes clear that we can view the Sinaitic Experience, and only the Sinaitic Experience, as the ultimate proof for the Divine authorship of the Torah. Here is a paraphrase of what he says:

We cannot trust miracles, for they can always be faked. Hence, they can never be taken as proof that a person who performs them is a legitimate messenger from God. Moshe performed the miracles he did, not to validate his authority, but because specific circumstances warranted the act. The Jews had to be saved from the pursuing Egyptians, their hunger had to be assuaged, their thirst quenched and it was essential that Korach's rebellion be quashed. The sea split, the manna descended from Heaven, the rock yielded its bounty and Korach was swallowed up by the earth. None of this would have convinced a skeptical people of Moshe's authenticity as God's prophet.

Whence, then, the source of our unquestioning faith?

It is based on the one form of evidence that can never be impeached. We ourselves, without the help of any intermediary, saw the flames and heard the thunder. We saw Moshe approach the blackness and heard God charging him, "Moshe! Go and tell the Jewish nation such and such."

…The Torah (Shemos 19:9) itself makes the point that the Sinaitic Experience alone is unchallengeable proof of Moshe Rabbeinu's uniqueness as God's prophet. "See, I am about to come to you within the thickness of the cloud, so that the people should hear Me speaking to you, and will therefore believe in you forever." Clearly, had the Revelation at Sinai not taken place, any belief in Moshe Rabbeinu would have been weak and tentative.

Rambam expands upon this thought (loc. cit., 8:3): Again, we paraphrase:

From all that we have said, it is clear, that even if a prophet were to perform miracles and on their basis attempt to persuade us to deny parts of Moshe Rabbeinu's Torah, our certainty of the Sinaitic Experience would

> *lead to uttter rejection of his attempts. We would know, beyond any room*
> *for doubt, that he wrought his "miracles" by means of sorcery. Had we*
> *been convinced of Moshe Rabbeinu's uniqueness on the basis of the mir-*
> *acles he had wrought, then a more astounding set of wonders might over-*
> *come our conviction. Since, however, our belief is based on revelation, it*
> *transcends miracles, and no "tricks" will move us …*

It transpires that, as we stood at Sinai, the Jewish nation in its entirety experienced the prophetic encounter with God in the same manner and at the same level as Moshe Rabbeinu (see, however, below). For those wondrous moments we were no different from him. We, as much as he, were privy to what God said. We *know* absolutely that God communicated with Moshe Rabbeinu. We were there and this knowledge can never be taken from us (see Appendix, note 2).

SOME PROBLEMS AND SOLUTIONS

 ow did God communicate with us at Sinai? Later in this Introduction, we will learn that *Rambam* and *Ramban* disagree. According to *Rambam*, the Jewish people never heard God actually speaking. They heard a voice unbroken into words and had no comprehension of what it conveyed. Moshe Rabbeinu had to interpret the sound for them. *Ramban*, on the other hand, maintains that God spoke the first two *dibros* of the *Aseres HaDibros* to the people in a manner that they *did* comprehend. Moshe Rabbeinu's interpretation was only required for the latter eight *dibros*. [Although the word *dibros* is usually translated as *commandments*, this is not an accurate translation, as there are more than ten commandments — i.e. mitzvos — in the "Ten Commandments." A more accurate translation would be *utterance* or *statement*. We will use the Hebrew *Dibrah* when we are referring to one of the "Ten Statements"; *Dibros* when we are referring to two or more of them.]

However, if Moshe Rabbeinu's interpretation was required for some of the *dibros*, is not much of what we have learned above thrown into question? It would seem that to the extent that any interpretation was necessary, the revelation was incomplete, and could not serve as the basis of an absolute belief. Should we not be plagued by the nagging possibility that the *Aseres HaDibros* represented Moshe Rabbeinu's own understanding of God's Word?

Alshich (Toras Moshe, Devarim 5:4) offers a solution. There is a tradition that when Moshe Rabbeinu spoke his prophecies, he did not use his voice at all. His subordination to his prophetic role was so total that it was the "voice of the *Shechinah* [Divine Presence]" speaking from within his throat that we heard. If that is the case, the answer to our problem is simple. The people recognized the "voice of the *Shechinah*" because they had already heard it, albeit as an undifferentiated sound. Their familiarity with the sound precluded any doubts about the authenticity of Moshe Rabbeinu's interpretation.

CHAPTER 2: FROM WHOM DID THE JEWISH PEOPLE HEAR THE ASERES HADIBROS?

he Rishonim are of different minds about what actually happened at Sinai. From whom did the Jewish people hear the *Aseres HaDibros*? How, precisely, were these communicated to them? Some Rishonim maintain that God Himself spoke *all* the *dibros* to the people. We required no form of intermediary. We all rose to the very highest level of prophetic clarity. We were as much the recipients of the Divine Revelation as was Moshe Rabbeinu.

Other Rishonim differentiate between the first two and the latter eight of the *Aseres HaDibros*. Klal Yisrael apprehended the first two with total clarity as did Moshe Rabbeinu. For the latter eight, things were different. They heard a "voice" but had no comprehension of what it was saying; Moshe Rabbeinu had to act as an interpreter.

A third opinion maintains that the people never shared Moshe Rabbeinu's level of prophecy. They heard the first two *dibros* as an undifferentiated sound, that Moshe Rabbeinu then interpreted for them. They did not hear the last eight *dibros* at all. Hashem communicated these latter eight *dibros* to Moshe alone, who then passed them on to the people.

THE TEXTUAL EVIDENCE AND VARIOUS RABBINIC STATEMENTS CONCERNING THIS ISSUE

t will help to look at the textual sources before we begin our analysis of the Rishonim. First, then, the Scriptural evidence:

A. *What did the Jewish people hear?*

The following verse appears in *Parashas Va'eschanan* (*Devarim* 5:19) immediately following the recording of the *Aseres HaDibros*:

> *Hashem spoke these words to all of you on the mountain. He did this from within the fire, the clouds and the darkness. It was a mighty voice, never to be repeated. He inscribed them upon two stone tablets and gave these to me.*

The phrase *Hashem spoke these words to all of you* indicates that the Jewish people heard the entire *Aseres HaDibros* from God Himself.

In *Parashas Eikev* (*Devarim* 9:10) the Torah says much the same:

> *Hashem gave me the two stone tablets inscribed by God's hand. On these tablets were inscribed a precise record of the words that God had spoken to you on the day when all of us gathered together.*

Then again, a bit further, (*Devarim* 10:4):

> *He wrote upon the tablets precisely what He had written on the earlier occasion. These were the Aseres HaDibros that God had communicated to us, on the mountain from within the fire, on the day when all of us gathered there, and that He then gave to me.*

From all these verses it would seem that Klal Yisrael heard all the *Aseres HaDibros* that Hashem inscribed upon the tablets.

B. *There are significant differences between the wording employed in the first two dibros and that used in the latter eight.*

However, a close reading will show that there are differences between the wording of the first two *dibros* and that of the following eight. The first two use the first person. *I am Hashem, your God* … and, … *before Me* clearly indicates that God Himself is speaking. The latter eight *dibros* uniformly speak in the third person. Thus, *Do not take the Name of Hashem in vain* …, *Hashem made, Hashem blessed, He sanctified it*, and so on.

This change clearly indicates a change in perspective of how both the speaker (God) and the listener (the Jewish nation) are to be viewed. However, the text does not make clear what that difference might be.

C. *Did Moshe Rabbeinu mediate between God and the Jews?*

Several verses appear to affirm that Moshe did indeed play a mediating role in communicating the *Aseres HaDibros* to Klal Yisrael.

Immediately preceding the *Aseres HaDibros* in *Parashas Va'eschanan* (*Devarim* 5:5), the verse cites Moshe as saying:

> *Then I stood between Hashem and you, to pass on God's words to you. [This was necessary because] you were afraid of the fire and did not come up the mountain …*
> In *Parashas Yisro* (*Shemos* 19:9) we have God saying to Moshe:
> … *So that the people should hear Me speaking to you, so that they will forevermore put their trust in you.* And further along (v. 19) it says: *Moshe would speak and God would respond by (giving him) "voice."*

While these verses suggest that Moshe filled a mediating role for all the *Aseres HaDibros*, other verses suggest that his involvement did not occur until *after* the *Aseres HaDibros* were completely communicated. This seems to be the implication of *Shemos*

20:16, where it is reported that Klal Yisrael came to Moshe *after* they had already heard the *Aseres HaDibros*, begging him: *You speak to us so we may listen, rather than God addressing us directly, which will surely result in our deaths.*

The same pattern recurs in *Parashas Va'eschanan* (*Devarim* 5:24) where, *after* the *Aseres HaDibros* had been spoken, the people approached Moshe and begged him: *You draw near and listen to all that Hashem, our God, will say.*

D. *The Medrashim*

This matter is actually the subject of a dispute between Amoraim, in a Medrash (*Shir HaShirim Rabbah* 1:13). R' Yehoshua ben Levi asserts that Klal Yisrael heard only the first two *dibros* from God Himself. He adduces (*Shir HaShirim* 1:2): *Let Him grant me of the kisses of His mouth.* The implication is that God has only bestowed some of the possible kisses. R' Yehoshua ben Levi interprets "kiss" as a metaphor for direct communication. It thus follows that only some of the *dibros* were the subject of such communication. The Sages, however, argue with R' Yehoshua ben Levi. They maintain that the Jews heard *all* the *dibros* from God Himself. They base this upon the verse cited above (*Shemos* 20:9): *You speak to us so we may listen, rather than God addressing us directly, which will surely result in our deaths* — the people only begged Moshe to act as a go-between after *all* the *dibros* had been spoken.

The Medrash then wonders how R' Yehoshua ben Levi would deal with this verse, which seems to stand in oppostion to his position. The Medrash offers two possibilities: Either R' Yehoshua ben Levi could invoke the rule that chronology is not the only criterion by which the Torah organizes its narratives (אין מוקדם ומאוחר בתורה), in which case the verse in question might well describe something that had really happened earlier; or that the people really made their request immediately after the first two *dibros* had been spoken [but the Torah left the account of their request to the end, so as not to interrupt the *Aseres HaDibros*].

The Medrash then provides another source for R' Yehoshua ben Levi's opinion. We have a tradition that the Torah encompasses six hundred and thirteen mitzvos. Now we are told (*Devarim* 33:4) that, תורה צוה לנו משה — *the Torah was commanded to us by Moshe.* The numerical value of the word "תורה" is six hundred and eleven (*taf* = 400; *vav* = 6; *reish* = 200; *heh* = 5). This indicates that of the six hundred and thirteen, Moshe told us only six hundred and eleven. We may deduce that the other two were communicated to us directly by God (this same argument is cited in *Makkos* 23b; see Appendix, note 3).

There are also several Tannaic sources that deal with this issue. *Mechilta* (quoted by *Rashi*, *Shemos* 20:1) teaches as follows: Hashem said all the *dibros* "as one," something entirely beyond human reach. Why then are they recorded separately in the Torah? Because subsequently, each *dibrah* was repeated by itself.

We do not know precisely what "as one" might mean. It seems to mean that the entire passage was communicated miraculously "as one *word*," — i.e. not divided into the distinct utterances that make what we say intelligible. Be that as it may, the *Mechilta* certainly treats the entire passage, that is, *all* of the *Aseres HaDibros*, as one unit (see Appendix, note 4).

Subsequent to that undivided communication, someone unscrambled the message. This could have occurred in one of several ways. [We will first list all the various possibilities and then proceed to associate them with various authorities.]

1. That God Himself spoke all the *Aseres HaDibros* to all the people a second time, this time making them intelligible by differentiating them into words. [This is the simplest way to understand the verses. Accordingly, when the Gemara *(Makkos,* loc. cit.) mentions that we heard *Anochi* (the first *dibrah*) and *Lo Yihyeh* (the second *dibrah*) from God Himself, the Gemara does not intend to preclude the other *dibros* — it merely saw no need to enumerate them all, and stopped after listing two of the ten.]

2. That, on this second round, God spoke only the first two (now intelligible) *dibros* to the people. He spoke the other eight to Moshe Rabbeinu alone, who then passed them along to the people (see Appendix, note 5).

3. That God, on this second round, spoke all the *dibros* to Moshe Rabbeinu only, and that Moshe Rabbeinu then passed all of them along to the people.

4. And, finally, that God did not speak a second time at all. It was Moshe Rabbeinu, who, having understood the original communication, passed all the *Aseres HaDibros* along to the people.

There is another relevant *Mechilta.* It considers *Shemos* 19:19, which states: משה ידבר והאלהים יעננו בקול — *Moshe would speak, and God responded with a voice.* The difficulty here is apparent: If the Torah meant to say that Moshe Rabbeinu conveyed God's words to the people, we would have expected the order to be reversed, i.e. "God responded, etc." Moreover, "respond" would not be the appropriate verb to use (see commentary of *Netziv* to *Mechilta).* How, then, is the verse to be understood?

R' Eliezer suggests that when God taught the *Aseres HaDibros* to Moshe, He would not begin a new segment until Moshe affirmed that the previous one had been accepted and understood by the people. Thus, *Moshe would speak,* means that Moshe would signal that they understood the previous segment, and only then would *God respond with a voice.*

R' Akiva agrees with this. Clearly, it would be unreasonable for God to continue His instruction if the people had not yet understood the previous segments! R' Akiva, however, believes that this is too obvious to mention. The Torah here has something else in mind: Hashem wanted the people to hear precisely what Moshe Rabbeinu had heard when God spoke to him. Accordingly, He infused Moshe Rabbeinu's human voice with all the power and sweetness that inhered in God's speech. *Moshe would speak,* to the people, *and God would respond with a voice;* He would *respond* to Moshe Rabbeinu's effort by lending him the qualities of Divine speech. *Rashi (Shemos* 19:19) adopts the *Mechilta's* second approach, viz., that God spoke only the first two *dibros* to the people. He told the other eight to Moshe alone, who then passed them on to the people (see Appendix, note 6).

Rambam's position

Rambam (Moreh Nevuchim 2:33) maintains that the people heard only the first two *dibros,* and even those they heard as an undifferentiated, unintelligible voice addressing Moshe Rabbeinu. They only comprehended those two *dibros* — along with the latter eight — upon their reiteration by Moshe Rabbeinu.

Rambam's source is the verse *(Tehillim* 62:12): *God spoke "one," but I heard "two."* This implies that God spoke in an undifferentiated "voice" in which no distinct letters or words were discernible. Thus, the verse teaches us that God spoke "one" — i.e. all He said was condensed into one word. Moshe "unpacked" this word into the "two" first *dibros*. (*Rambam* bases his position on *Makkos* 23b-24a; see Appendix, note 7).

Here is an adaptation of an extremely long passage in the *Moreh Nevuchim*:

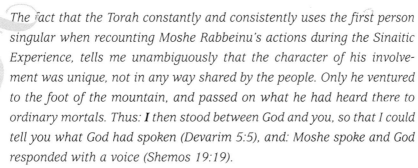

> The fact that the Torah constantly and consistently uses the first person singular when recounting Moshe Rabbeinu's actions during the Sinaitic Experience, tells me unambiguously that the character of his involvement was unique, not in any way shared by the people. Only he ventured to the foot of the mountain, and passed on what he had heard there to ordinary mortals. Thus: **I** then stood between God and you, so that I could tell you what God had spoken (*Devarim 5:5*), and: *Moshe spoke and God responded with a voice (Shemos 19:19)*.
>
> The Mechilta bears this out when it says that Moshe Rabbeinu passed on to the people every communication that he received from God, precisely as he had heard it.
>
> There are several verses that we must understand along these lines. Thus, the verse, … so that the people might hear as I speak to you (*Shemos 19:9*), is to be understood as follows: My speech was only to you; the people only heard the mighty voice, not any distinct words.
>
> The Torah chooses its words carefully. Therefore, the verse reads: You heard a sound of words but saw no image at all. Nothing but a sound (*Devarim 4:12*). Note, "the sound of words," not, "words."
>
> That said, we must still deal with the fact that we find throughout the Medrashic literature statements that the people "heard" the first two dibros from God and that Moshe Rabbeinu had no role in mediating them. This, however, in no way contradicts what we have written. We must recall that God's existence and His singularity — the subject of these two dibros — may be proven philosophically. These principles do not require revelation. Now, in regard to anything that is demonstrable through the application of logic, one who is not endowed with the gift of prophecy is the absolute equal of the prophet. Therefore, these Medrashim maintain that the people "heard" these two dibros. This simply means that Moshe Rabbeinu, who did actually hear these two dibros, had no advantage over the people who did not (see Appendix, note 8).

We can now sum up *Rambam's* position as follows: He accepts the position of R' Yehoshua ben Levi (discussed above) and the Gemara in *Makkos* in the name of R' Hamnuna that the people heard the first two *dibros* from God. They learned the remaining eight *dibros* in precisely the same manner in which they learned all the other mitzvos — from Moshe Rabbeinu and *only* through him (see Appendix, note 9).

Ramban's position

Ramban (*Shemos* 20:1, in the footsteps of *Ibn Ezra*; see also *Ramban* to *Devarim* 5:5) maintains that the verse (*Devarim* 5:19): *Hashem spoke **these words** to **your entire***

community, which follows immediately after the *Aseres HaDibros*, makes *Rambam's* position untenable. In his view, the verse clearly indicates the people heard not only the first two *dibros*, but also the latter eight. He accommodates the Rabbinic sources which differentiate between the first two *dibros* and the eight which followed by postulating that the people not only "heard" but also *understood* the first two *dibros* — thus eliminating any role for Moshe Rabbeinu — while they "heard" the latter eight but did not understand what was being said. Here, it was necessary for Moshe Rabbeinu to mediate (see Appendix, note 10).

Here is a paraphrase of part of *Ramban's* argument:

> I will explain to you how the tradition that our Sages handed down to us is to be understood. There is no doubt that the people "heard" all the *Aseres HaDibros*. The text makes this abundantly clear. However, whereas they understood the first two *dibros* as clearly as did Moshe Rabbeinu, this was not so in the latter eight. For these, they required Moshe Rabbeinu's interpretation (see Appendix, note 11).
>
> All this being so, we can divide the corpus of the six hundred and thirteen mitzvos into three groups. The first two *dibros*, that deal with belief in God and the prohibition against idol worship — together, the very basis upon which Judaism is built — were communicated to the people directly. These required the absolute clarity of prophecy on the highest level. For the subsequent eight *dibros* it was sufficient for the people to hear them being communicated to Moshe Rabbeinu. It did not matter that they could not understand. Moshe Rabbeinu would pass the meaning on to them. For the rest of the mitzvos, their unquestioning belief in Moshe Rabbeinu's prophecy would suffice (see Appendix, note 12).

A careful reading of *Rashi* (which requires the consolidation of two disparate comments) leads to the conclusion that he shares *Ramban's* position. As we have seen, *Rashi* to *Shemos* 19:19 states clearly that they only required Moshe's mediation for the first two *dibros*. God endowed him with a "voice" with which to speak to the people for the latter eight only.

Rashi to *Shemos* 20:1 cites the *Mechilta* which asserts that all the *Aseres HaDibros* were pronounced in one undifferentiated act of communication, which, as we have seen, is something that is utterly beyond human emulation, and that Moshe then unscrambled them. If we are to integrate the two remarks into one consistent approach, we can do so by postulating *Ramban's* position. The people understood the first two *dibros* in their original, undfferentiated form, but required Moshe's interpretation for the rest (see Appendix, note 13).

A Position taken by many other commentators

Many commentators, such as *Maharam Gabbai* (*Avodas HaKodesh* 4:34); *Abarbanel* (to *Shemos* 20:1); *R' Yitzchak Aramaah* (*Akeidas Yitzchak* §89) and *R' Yosef Albo* (*Sefer HaIkkarim* 3:18) reject the idea that the people were somehow less privy to *any* of the *Aseres HaDibros* than was Moshe Rabbeinu. They are of the opinion that statements like the one made by the verse (*Devarim* 5:9): Hashem *spoke* these words *to* your entire community — clarify that everybody heard everything.

But how do these commentators accommodate the various Rabbinic statements that assert that the people heard only the first two *dibros*, but not the latter eight, directly from God?

They offer the following suggestions:

1. The Torah relates mitzvos in very general terms. The details of the precise manner of their fulfillment were normally communicated to them orally by Moshe Rabbeinu. As an example, we might take the first of the *Aseres HaDibros*. Clearly, it obligates us to accept certain beliefs that are implicit in the fact that God took us out of Egypt. However, the Torah text does not tell us what these might be. The same is true of all mitzvos. For example, the Torah tells us to keep Shabbos, but does not tell us how this is to be done. This was not true for the first two *dibros*. Hashem communicated these *dibros* to the people with *all* their details and complexities. For these two, but *only* these two, the people had as complete a picture as did Moshe Rabbeinu for all the other mitzvos (*Avodas HaKodesh*).

2. The first two *dibros* were unique in the sense that they were never to be repeated in the rest of the Torah. [The first *dibrah*, stated by God in the first person, *I am Hashem, your God …,* is unique to the Sinaitic Experience. On the other hand, the prohibitions against idol worship contained in the second *dibrah* are repeated frequently. Elsewhere, however, the prohibitions only forbid the worship of physical phenomena — i.e. objects that are parts of nature, such as the heavenly bodies, or graven images. It is only here, in the second *dibrah,* that nonphysical entities are interdicted.] When the Sages said that the people heard the first two *dibros* directly from God, they meant that they heard them *only* from God, rather than through Moshe Rabbeinu's mediation. On the other hand, the latter eight *dibros* recur throughout the rest of the Torah in one form or another (*Abarbanel*).

3. The Sages' dictum about the unique character of the first two *dibros* refers to the *quality* of the prophecy enjoyed by the people. They understood the first two *dibros* with a greater degree of clarity and comprehension than the others (*Akeidas Yitzchak*; see Appendix, note 14).

4. Although the people *heard* the first two *dibros,* they only *overheard* the latter eight. The first two *dibros* were addressed directly to them, just as they were addressed directly to Moshe Rabbeinu. In the latter eight, God addressed Moshe, while permitting the people to overhear what He was saying (*Maasei Hashem*).

[That given, it is possible that there may be a halachic difference between the first two *dibros* and the latter eight. Since Hashem addressed the first two *dibros* to the people directly, they can never be overridden by a later prophet, even on a temporary basis. The other eight are not subject to this limitation. While no prophet may ever permanently eliminate any of the Torah's commands, he may, if the situation warrants it, override any of them as a *Hora'as Shaah,* a temporary measure. This will hold true for the latter eight *dibros* as it does for all other commands in the Torah (*Sefer HaIkkarim*; see Appendix, note 15).]

———— תר ————

3

CHAPTER 3:

DIFFERENCES BETWEEN THE ASERES HADIBROS OF
פרשת יתרו (דיברות ראשונות) &
פרשת ואתחנן (דיברות אחרונות)

he chart below illustrates the differences between the words and letters that occur in the *Dibros HaRishonos* and those that occur in the *Dibros HaAcharonos*:

פרשת ואתחנן - דיברות אחרונות	פרשת יתרו - דיברות ראשונות
אנכי יהוה אלהיך אשר הוצאתיך מארץ מצרים מבית עבדים:	אנכי יהוה אלהיך אשר הוצאתיך מארץ מצרים מבית עבדים:
לא יהיה לך אלהים אחרים על פני: לא תעשה לך פסל כל תמונה אשר בשמים ממעל ואשר בארץ מתחת ואשר במים מתחת לארץ: לא תשתחוה להם ולא תעבדם כי אנכי יהוה אלהיך אל קנא פקד עון אבת על בנים ועל שלשים ועל רבעים לשנאי: ועשה חסד לאלפים לאהבי ולשמרי מצותו:	לא יהיה לך אלהים אחרים על פני: לא תעשה לך פסל וכל תמונה אשר בשמים ממעל ואשר בארץ מתחת ואשר במים מתחת לארץ: לא תשתחוה להם ולא תעבדם כי אנכי יהוה אלהיך אל קנא פקד עון אבת על בנים על שלשים ועל רבעים לשנאי: ועשה חסד לאלפים לאהבי ולשמרי מצותי:
לא תשא את שם יהוה אלהיך לשוא כי לא ינקה יהוה את אשר ישא את שמו לשוא:	לא תשא את שם יהוה אלהיך לשוא כי לא ינקה יהוה את אשר ישא את שמו לשוא:
שמור את יום השבת לקדשו כאשר צוך יהוה אלהיך ששת ימים תעבד ועשית כל מלאכתך: ויום השביעי שבת ליהוה אלהיך לא תעשה כל מלאכה אתה ובנך ובתך ועבדך ואמתך ושורך וחמרך וכל בהמתך וגרך אשר בשעריך למען ינוח עבדך ואמתך כמוך: וזכרת כי עבד היית בארץ מצרים ויצאך יהוה אלהיך משם ביד חזקה ובזרע נטויה על כן צוך יהוה אלהיך לעשות את יום השבת:	זכור את יום השבת לקדשו: ששת ימים תעבד ועשית כל מלאכתך: ויום השביעי שבת ליהוה אלהיך לא תעשה כל מלאכה אתה ובנך ובתך עבדך ואמתך ובהמתך וגרך אשר בשעריך: כי ששת ימים עשה יהוה את השמים ואת הארץ את הים ואת כל אשר בם וינח ביום השביעי על כן ברך יהוה את יום השבת ויקדשהו:
כבד את אביך ואת אמך כאשר צוך יהוה אלהיך למען יאריכן ימיך ולמען ייטב לך על האדמה אשר יהוה אלהיך נתן לך:	כבד את אביך ואת אמך למען יארכון ימיך על האדמה אשר יהוה אלהיך נתן לך:
לא תרצח	לא תרצח
ולא תנאף	לא תנאף
ולא תגנב	לא תגנב
ולא תענה ברעך עד שוא:	לא תענה ברעך עד שקר:
ולא תחמד אשת רעך ולא תתאוה בית רעך שדהו ועבדו ואמתו שורו וחמרו וכל אשר לרעך:	לא תחמד בית רעך לא תחמד אשת רעך ועבדו ואמתו שורו וחמרו וכל אשר לרעך:

A glance at the chart shows that there are no differences in the first and third *dibros* between the two locations.

There are minor differences in the second *dibrah*. *Parashas Yisro* has the conjunctive *vav* in "וכל תמונה" and *Parashas Va'eschanan* does not. Further in this *dibrah*, this is reversed. *Parashas Va'eschanan* has the conjunctive *vav* in "ועל שלשים"; *Parashas Yisro* does not.

The word אבות is written *malei* ["full," that is, with the *vav*] in *Parashas Va'eschanan*, while *Parashas Yisro* has the deficient, אבת.

The final difference is that the last word, מצותי is written in *Parashas Yisro* precisely as it is pronounced. In *Parashas Va'eschanan* the last letter is a *vav*, although, there too, it is pronounced מצותָי.

By contrast to these relatively minor differences in the second *dibrah*, those in the fourth *dibrah* are striking.

The first and most obvious is that *Parashas Va'eschanan* replaces the first word, זכור, *remember*, with שמור, *guard*.

Parashas Va'eschanan also has an entire phrase that does not occur in *Parashas Yisro* at all. Thus, the first sentence in the *Parashas Va'eschanan* passage reads: שמור את יום **השבת לקדשו כאשר צוך ה' אלהיך**. The *Parashas Yisro* version has the simple: זכור את יום השבת לקדשו.

The reason given for the Shabbos command in *Parashas Yisro* is: *... for Hashem created Heaven and earth in six days, and on the seventh day He rested ...,* which means that Hashem gave us Shabbos to commemorate the Creation, while *Parashas Va'eschanan* has: *You should recall that you were a slave in Egypt and that Hashem took you out of there with a mighty hand and an outstretched arm ...,* indicating that Shabbos is meant to commemorate the Exodus.

Where *Parashas Yisro* states simply that we are to let our animals rest on Shabbos, without listing any particular animals, *Parashas Va'eschanan* specifies: *your ox and your donkey and all your animals.*

The *Parashas Yisro* passage has *... you,* and *your son* and *your daughter, your servant* and *your maidservant,* providing no conjunctive *vav* for *your servant, Parashas Va'eschanan* does provide this conjunctive *vav*.

Parashas Yisro and *Parashas Va'eschanan* also differ substantively in the fifth *dibrah*.

Where *Parashas Yisro* writes simply *Honor your father and your mother so that your days may be lengthened ..., Parashas Va'eschanan* adds כאשר צוך ה' אלהיך, *as Hashem, your God, commanded you,* immediately after, *Honor your father and your mother.* Moreover, *Parashas Va'eschanan* adds למען ייטב לך, *so that it may go well with you,* to *Parashas Yisro*'s promise of lengthened days.

Parashas Va'eschanan adds the conjunctive *vav* to each of the last four *dibros*: ולא תנאף **ולא תגנב, ולא תענה, ולא תחמד**. None of these conjunctions occur in *Parashas Yisro*.

In the ninth *dibrah, Parashas Va'eschanan* changes *Parashas Yisro*'s עד שקר to עד שוא.

In the tenth *dibrah*, there is a change of sequence. Where in *Parashas Yisro, your neighbor's house* precedes *your neighbor's wife,* in *Parashas Va'eschanan,* the wife is mentioned before the house. Moreover, there is also a change in wording. *Parashas Yisro* uses לא תחמד for each of the possessions: *house, wife, servant, maidservant, ox and donkey.*

Parashas Va'eschanan retains this wording for *wife.* However, for the monetary possessions, it uses: לא תתאוה.

In the tenth *dibrah, Parashas Va'eschanan* lists *his field* while *Parashas Yisro* does not.

Are the dibros ha'acharonos a record of what Hashem actually said at Sinai?

ow do we reconcile the various differences between the two sets of *Dibros*? *Teshuvos Maharam Alshekar* (§102), in the name of R' Sherira Gaon and R' Hai Gaon, maintains that God actually pronounced two distinct versions of the *Aseres HaDibros* at Sinai (see Appendix, note 16). Moreover, the two versions were stated simultaneously — as the Gemara states, concerning one of the differences in the fourth *dibrah: Zachor* and *Shamor,* and concerning the difference in the ninth *dibrah: Sheker* and *Shav,* that Hashem miraculously pronounced the two words in one expression (*Rosh Hashanah* 27a; *Shavuos* 20b). This approach rejects the possibility that Moshe Rabbeinu (in his speech as recorded in *Parashas Va'eschanan*) made any changes to what he had actually heard. (see Appendix, note 17).

On the other hand, *Yefei Mareh* (to *Yerushalmi, Nedarim* 4:1) posits that the expansive version of the *Dibros* in *Parashas Va'eschanan* adds explanatory additions made by Moshe Rabbeinu. In this respect, the *Aseres HaDibros* are no different from other mitzvos, many of which are stated concisely in the earlier books, and subsequently elucidated in *Devarim.* This opinion agrees, however, that the words Hashem miraculously pronounced in one expression, such as the word *Shamor* (in *Parashas Va'eschanan*) that was pronounced simultaneously with the word *Zachor* (in *Parashas Yisro*) were part of the *Dibros* given by God at Sinai (see Appendix, note 18).

Can a case be made that both versions were used; the one for the first tablets, the other for the second?

here are two Rabbinic sources which clearly indicate that both versions were used; one for the first tablets, the other for the second. One source, *Medrash Aggadah* (Buber, *Devarim* 5:6) states this explicitly. The other source, in *Bava Kamma* (54b), emerges from a discussion there concerning the text of the fifth *dibrah,* which bids us to honor our parents. Both in *Parashas Yisro* and in *Parashas Va'eschanan* we are promised longevity as a reward for the punctilious observance of this command. *Parashas Va'eschanan,* however, adds another reward: למען ייטב לך — *so that it shall go well with you,* which does not appear in *Parashas Yisro.* Why? The Gemara answers as follows: Hashem, knowing that the first tablets were going to be broken, did not want טוב — *good* (the root word for ייטב) to appear on these tablets, for if "good" were to have been shattered, this might have presaged a cessation of "good" from the Jewish nation. Clearly then, the *Parashas Yisro* version appeared on the first tablets, while the *Parashas*

Va'eschanan version was inscribed on the second tablets. [In spite of these apparently incontrovertible sources, there is some discussion among commentators about what actually happened — see *Ramban* to *Shemos* 20:8 and *Teshuvos Radvaz* 3:649 (see Appendix, note 19).]

WHY ARE THERE TWO VERSIONS OF THE ASERES HADIBROS?

he authorities we have seen until now address specific changes from the first *Dibros* to the second *Dibros*. Other authorities, however, deal with the entire *Aseres HaDibros* as one, indivisible unit. Most of these authorities attribute the changes to the *Cheit HaEgel*, the sin of the worship of the Golden Calf (see *Shemos* ch. 32-33). After that dreadful act, nothing was ever again quite the same (see *Pri Tzaddik, Parashas Bo* §10. See also *Sanhedrei Ketanah* to *Sanhedrin* 56b).

Let us examine this thesis. We will consider the changes which occur in some of the *dibros* and examine whether we can ascribe these changes to the intervening episode of the Golden Calf.

First, the fourth *dibrah*, the commandment to keep Shabbos: (*Shemos* 20:8-11, and *Devarim* 5:12-15)

These five differences require explanation:

1. The opening word in the first *Dibros* is: זכור, *Remember*. In the second *Dibros,* the opening word is: שמור, *Guard* (*against violation*).

2. The rationale assigned to the mitzvah is different in the two versions. *Parashas Yisro* has it recall the fact that God created the world, while *Parashas Va'eschanan* substitutes the Exodus from Egypt.

3. When speaking of the obligation to have one's servants rest on Shabbos, *Parashas Va'eschanan* has the phrase למען ינוח עבדך ואמתך כמוך, *So that your servant and your maidservant might rest as do you. Parashas Yisro* does not have this phrase.

4. *Parashas Yisro* ends the *dibrah* with the words על כן ברך ה' את יום השבת ויקדשהו, *It is for this reason that God blessed the Shabbos day and hallowed it. Parashas Va'eschanan* does not have this phrase.

5. The second version has שמור ... כאשר צוך ה' אלהיך, *Guard ... as Hashem, your God, commanded you.* This phrase does not appear in the *Parashas Yisro* version.

What changed due to the sin of the Golden Calf? The forty-nine days that elapsed from when the people left Egypt were not wasted. During that period, by concerted striving toward goodness and holiness, the people had managed to regain the level of sanctity that Adam had enjoyed before he ate from the forbidden tree (see *Shabbos* 146a.) The nation tumbled from this exalted standing, however, when they made the Golden Calf. After that, they returned to the state of Adam after the sin, when he was consigned to daily toil.

We can readily understand how the episode of the Golden Calf radically altered the very nature of Shabbos. Adam in the Garden of Eden knew nothing of the backbreaking labor required to beat a recalcitrant earth into submission. The curse of having to produce one's bread by the sweat of one's brow still lay in the future. The need for rest, in the sense of a tired body requiring rejuvenation, did not exist. In that state of being, Shabbos has a very different function. It bids us to contemplate the sanctity of a day upon which God withdrew from His creative activity.

Thus, the pre-sin Shabbos of *Parashas Yisro*, bids us, "Think!" (Remember!); while the post-sin Shabbos of *Parashas Va'eschanan*, bids us, "Rest!" (Guard!).

Now we can readily understand the differences between the two versions of the *dibrah*: זכור, *Remember!* Bids us to think about the implications of God's day of rest. שמור, *Guard (against violation)*, tells us to desist from work.

1. *Parashas Yisro* bids us to view Shabbos as a commemoration of Creation. *Parashas Va'eschanan* focuses upon the Exodus because our collective memory of the hard labor in Egypt teaches us the value of Shabbos as a day of rest.

2. Just as we need to rest from our weekday exertions on Shabbos, so do our servants. Hence, *Parashas Va'eschanan* is as concerned for them as it is for us. By contrast, in *Parashas Yisro*, the prohibition against having our servants work on Shabbos is a part of our own need to keep the tranquility of our Shabbos intact (so as to focus our thoughts on our commemoration of Creation).

3. On the Shabbos envisaged by *Parashas Yisro*, we would not want to experience the sanctity of the day because of our own need to rest, but rather in order to tap into that sanctity. Hence, *Parashas Yisro* teaches us precisely what it is that makes Shabbos special. Since, on the other hand, *Parashas Va'eschanan* is focused on Shabbos as a day of rest, it does not teach us about the special sanctity of the day.

4. The phrase: *as Hashem, your God, commanded you,* must refer to an earlier occasion upon which we were told to keep the Shabbos. This can only mean Marah, the place where we camped shortly after having crossed the Yam Suf. Indeed, our Sages relate a tradition that it was there that we received an oral command to keep the Shabbos. Now, this all happened before we came to Sinai and therefore we had not yet achieved the level of Adam before he sinned. Hence, the Shabbos that we received at that time was the Shabbos of *Parashas Va'eschanan*, not that of *Parashas Yisro*. Accordingly, *only* the second *Dibros* are indeed כאשר צוך — since their wording accords with the earlier commandment (see Appendix, note 20).

We now turn to the fifth *dibrah*, which exhorts us to honor our parents. There are two differences between the two versions, and we can readily understand these differences on the basis of our thesis. The first of these, we have already discussed: In the second *Dibros* we have the phrase למען ייטב לך — *so that it shall go well with you*, but not in the first. The second difference is similar to the one we just saw in regard to Shabbos — viz., the second *Dibros* have: כאשר צוך ה' אלהיך — *as Hashem, your God, commanded you.* This phrase does not occur in the first *Dibros*.

According to the Gemara in *Bava Kama* (54b) that we examined earlier, the reason for the omission of למען ייטב לך in the first *Dibros* is the episode of the Golden Calf. Hashem did not want the concept of טוב — *good* to be engraved upon tablets which were fated to be smashed. A broken טוב would not augur well for the people.

That given, it is simple enough to account for the missing: כאשר צוך ה' אלהיך in the first *Dibros*. In our discussion of the same phrase in the fourth *dibrah* (Shabbos), we saw that the meaning is: *as God commanded you [at Marah].* In the case of this *dibrah*, the *mitzvah* as given in Marah would certainly have contained the phrase למען ייטב לך, since at that time the episode of the Golden Calf still lay in the future. Accordingly, the second *Dibros* were indeed כאשר צוך, since the wording accorded with the earlier formulation. However, as we explained in regard to the fourth *dibrah,* the first *Dibros*, which omitted למען ייטב לך, also had to omit "כאשר צוך" — (see Appendix, note 21).

We now move on to the tenth *dibrah*, which forbids us to be jealous of what our neighbor possesses. In *Parashas Yisro* we have only לא תחמוד, which we can translate as: *You shall not covet. Parashas Va'eschanan* adds לא תתאוה, which we can render: *You shall not crave.* Can we use the intervening episode of the Golden Calf to explain the change here as well?

First we need to know the difference between *coveting* and *craving. Rambam* (*Sefer HaMitzvos, Lo Saaseh* §266) explains as follows: We only violate the prohibition against coveting if our jealousy expresses itself in a concrete action. For example, if I subject the owner to intense pressure, if I browbeat or cajole him until I wear him down and he agrees to sell me the object, and then I buy it from him, I have violated the prohibition against coveting.

Craving is a different matter. In *Parashas Va'eschanan*, God asks us to control not only our actions, but also our feelings. We sin by simply *desiring* to pressure another to give up his property (see further in *mitzvah #38*).

That given, we can argue that the episode of the Golden Calf does, indeed, explain this expansion of the prohibition. Our Sages, in *Medrash Tanchuma* (*Ki Sisa* §20), examine the expression ויקמו לצחק — *and they arose to laugh,* that is used to describe the wild abandon of the people who worshipped the Golden Calf. Although צחק normally connotes *laughter,* here it is said to connote immorality. In fact, the Sages (*Sanhedrin* 63b) teach that throughout history, when Jews have worshipped idols, they have never been motivated by actual belief in this or that idol. Rather, the people saw idolatry as opening the doors for wild and public dissoluteness. Thus, the Golden Calf gave them — according to their line of thinking — license to shrug off all their normal inhibitions.

Accordingly, the episode of the Golden Calf can be read as the moment of truth concerning the dangers of harboring strong desires — even if we have not yet acted upon them. We humans apparently cannot be trusted to *limit* our cravings. Once we permit them to gnaw away at our defenses, the step to physical transgression is a small and easy one. Accordingly, after the episode of the Golden Calf, the Torah broadened the prohibitions against jealousy (see *Yismach Moshe* to *Parashas Va'eschanan,* 98b).

ANOTHER THEORY THAT COULD EXPLAIN THE NEED FOR TWO DIFFERENT VERSIONS OF THE ASERES HADIBROS

li Yakar (to *Shemos* 20:8) offers a radically different explanation for the discrepancies between *Parashas Yisro* and *Parashas Va'eschanan*. He maintains that the original version, the one in *Parashas Yisro*, was designed to make it possible for *all* the nations, not only Klal Yisrael, to accept the Torah. Subsequently, when these nations rejected the Torah, God emended the text so that it should reflect the specific *Jewish* interest in these *Dibros*.

Kli Yakar's approach is based upon a Medrashic tradition, that before God gave us the *Dibros*, He offered them to the other nations as well (see *Pesikta Rabbasi* §21; *Pirkei D'Rabbi Eliezer* §41; *Yalkut Shimoni, Vezos HaBerachah* ch. 33 §951). This, in *Kli Yakar's* view, was accomplished by announcing the *Dibros* with a קול גדול — a great *"voice"* (*Devarim* 5:19) which carried from one end of the world to the other, *in every national language* (see *Zevachim* 116a and *Maharasha, Chidushei Aggados* to *Berachos* 88b). Everybody heard the *Aseres HaDibros* and anybody could have come forward and accepted the gift. In the end, the nations could not make peace with the prohibitions against murder, theft and immorality, and refused the Torah. Hence, when God acceded to Moshe Rabbeinu's prayer to give us another chance after the episode of the Golden Calf, there was no one else to whom they would be of interest, and He accordingly worded them specifically for the Jewish nation.

Kli Yakar demonstrates how his theory accounts for the changes between the two versions.

He begins his analysis with the mitzvah of Shabbos. He asserts that the idea of Shabbos — i.e. the recognition of Hashem as Creator — could have had universal application, albeit in a very different form from the one we know today: Such a Shabbos could not have included a prohibition to perform the thirty-nine *melachos* (creative activities) that are manifest in the charge of שמור — *Guard!* of the *Parashas Va'eschanan* version of this *dibrah*. This prohibition is not applicable to non-Jews, because the Gemara (*Sanhedrin* 58b) interprets the provision *They shall not rest day or night* (*Bereishis* 8:22) in the covenant which God made with mankind as *prohibiting* the nations from deliberately desisting from creative activities. On the other hand, the positive aspects of Shabbos — the זכור (*Remember!*) of *Parashas Yisro* — might well have been applicable to everybody.

This explains why the *dibrah* of Shabbos in *Parashas Yisro* speaks of God as Creator, while the *dibrah* in *Parashas Va'eschanan* centers upon the Exodus: Creation is of universal concern; the Exodus from Egypt matters only to us.

Of course, *Kli Yakar* has to deal with the very first *dibrah* — which, already in the *Parashas Yisro* version of the *Aseres HaDibros*, introduces God as the One Who took us out of Egypt. What possible meaning could this have to anyone but the Jews? He explains that this is suggested only as a *sufficient* cause to require us to serve Him. All humanity ought to serve God, the Creator. We Jews have another reason to serve Him; that He took us out of Egypt.

[*Kli Yakar* offers a technical solution to the discrepancy between *Parashas Va'eschanan*, which spells out that *your ox* and *your donkey* are to do no work on Shabbos; and *Parashas Yisro*, which is satisfied with the more general *your animals*. The explication of that solution would take us beyond the scope of this essay (see Appendix, note 22).]

As we have seen, Shabbos and the command to honor our parents have a discrepancy in common; the version in *Parashas Va'eschanan* adds the phrase: *as Hashem, your God, commanded you,* to the *Parashas Yisro* version. *Kli Yakar* suggests that his approach can explain the change: Since we *alone* were given these two mitzvos at Marah, this phrase would therefore have been meaningless to the other nations — an audience the *Parashas Yisro* version wanted to include.

Even more, the inclusion of this phrase in *Parashas Yisro* would have weakened any inclination that the nations might have had to receive the Torah. It would have sent the message: The Jewish nation has already been informed of these mitzvos and you have not. The non-Jews would infer that they would never be more than second-class citizens. That alone would have been sufficient reason for them to reject the Torah.

We have already noted that the *Parashas Va'eschanan* version of the fifth *dibrah*, that bids us to honor our parents, urges us to fulfill this command, *so that it will be good for you* (למען ייטב לך). *Parashas Yisro* omits this phrase and anticipates only that we will merit a long life (למען יארכון ימיך). *Kli Yakar* suggests that *Ibn Ezra's* interpretation of these two phrases can explain the discrepancy.

Ibn Ezra posits that *Parashas Yisro's* promise of longevity may be fulfilled in this world, while the "good" promised in *Parashas Va'eschanan* is to be enjoyed in the next world. This may explain why *Parashas Yisro* preferred to make no mention of this reward: Since the *Parashas Yisro* version was intended for the non-Jewish nations of the time as well, it was better to avoid promises of rewards that other nations, which were unschooled in the concept of the World to Come, might well conclude that such a reward was an empty promise. The non-Jewish nations might suspect, that, as the saying goes: "He who wishes to deceive, will do well to predict matters which lie far in the future."

Kli Yakar then suggests that his approach also explains the changes in the ninth *dibrah*, which deals with bearing false witness. *Parashas Yisro* (that was meant to address both Jews and non-Jews) speaks of עד שקר — *false testimony*, while *Parashas Va'eschanan* (meant for Jews alone) has עד שוא — *useless testimony* (his explanation is based on *Ramban* to *Devarim* 5:17). Both *false* and *useless* describe cases in which the witness is lying. However, when he testifies *falsely*, a witness makes a statement that would have caused someone to be pronounced liable or guilty. On the other hand, when a witness testifies *uselessly*, he is making a statement that would not have caused any practical ramification at all. In short, in the case of useless testimony there is no victim. *Kli Yakar* posits that an interdiction against *useless* testimony would have been too demanding for the non-Jewish people of the time. The prohibition on *useless* testimony demands a level of adherence to truth in consonance with the high degree of sanctity demanded of Klal Yisrael, but would have been beyond any reasonable expectation for people whose lives were lived on a very different level. Even the non-Jews of the time, however, could have been expected to desist from *false* testimony.

Finally, we have the significant change in the wording of the tenth *dibrah*. In *Parashas Yisro* we have לא תחמד, from the root חמד — *to covet*, while *Parashas Va'eschanan* has לא תתאוה from the root תאו — *to crave*.

Now, the English verb, *to covet*, does not really convey the full range of the Hebrew, חמד. *Ibn Ezra* (to *Devarim* loc. cit.) demonstrates from a number of texts that חמד describes craving that expresses itself in action. Indeed, *Rambam* (*Hil. Gezeilah VeAveidah* 1:9) rules that in order to transgress לא תחמד, one must actually acquire the object from its owner. תאוה, on the other hand, describes desire alone. Thus, לא תתאוה prohibits even the simple scheming to obtain another's object, even if this never manifests itself in any actual action.

Clearly then, *Parashas Va'eschanan's* לא תתאוה is much further-reaching than *Parashas Yisro's* לא תחמד. *Kli Yakar* argues that the level of self-control demanded by *Parashas Va'eschanan* would have been ill-suited to the non-Jewish nations of the time. Such mastery over one's impulses would only have been possible for a people who had been trained to make do with very little. Klal Yisrael's centuries of slavery in Egypt effectively trained them to lead lives of modest expectation. Only after the non-Jewish nations of the time had refused the Torah was it possible to expand *Parashas Yisro's* לא תחמד to *Parashas Va'eschanan's* לא תתאוה (see Appendix, note 23).

4

CHAPTER 4:
THE INNER STRUCTURE OF THE ASERES HADIBROS

he division of the *Aseres HaDibros* into two distinct sets of five *dibros*, engraved on separate tablets, makes it clear that, broadly speaking, the *Dibros* comprise two distinct groups. We will deal with this division shortly. Meanwhile, we will consider the order of each set of five.

Chizkuni (*Shemos* 20:14) suggests that each set moves from the obvious to the less obvious, a principle familiar to Gemara students and known as, לא זו אף זו — *Not only this, but even that . . .* Applied to the first set of five *dibros*, this works as follows: The first *dibrah* requires us to accept the Lord Who took us out of Egypt as our God. We are then taught that accepting Him is not enough; we are also forbidden to worship any entity besides Him, something which is not at all implicit in the first *dibrah*. We move on to learn that our intimate relationship with this God forbids us even to take an oath that invokes His Name frivolously. Then, not only are we commanded concerning our relationship with God and our treatment of His Name, but we are also commanded to observe Shabbos, because God desisted from His creative activities on the seventh day. And, finally, not only are we commanded concerning our direct relationship with God, we are also called upon to honor our parents, whose relationship with us is taken as a model of our relationship with God (see below for more on this *dibrah*; see also *Maharal, Tiferes Yisrael* ch. 36).

Thus, the second, third, fourth and fifth *dibros* are all expansions of the first. They assert that a formal acceptance of Hashem as our God is not enough. Once we have formally subordinated ourselves to Him, that relationship must color every aspect of our lives.

We can readily discern this principle at work in the second set, applied here to interpersonal relationships. We start with the prohibition against murder, surely the most heinous violation of another's rights. We move on to the non-bodily encroachment of committing adultery and from there to the lesser encroachment of stealing from him. The next prohibition, which forbids the bearing of false witness, also belongs to this continuum: Indirect damage to our fellow is also interdicted. Finally we have the prohibition against even coveting or desiring our fellow's possessions.

THE FIRST FIVE DIBROS: RELATIONSHIPS BETWEEN MAN AND GOD
THE SECOND FIVE: RELATIONSHIPS BETWEEN MAN AND MAN

e noted earlier that the *Aseres HaDibros* are divided into two distinct groups. The first five deal with *Bein Adam LaMakom* — relationships *between man and God*, while the second five deal with *Bein Adam LeChaveiro*, relationships *between man and his fellow man.*

Nine of the ten *dibros* fit smoothly into this division. The only one that requires some thought is the fifth *dibrah*, the one that commands us to honor our parents. Left to ourselves we would have defined this mitzvah as one that governs human relationships. Why, then, does it belong on the first tablet?

Ramban (to *Shemos* 20:12), however, asserts that our obligation to honor our parents is a function of our obligation to honor God: It is because our parents are, so to speak, partners with God in bringing us into the world, that we are commanded to honor them. Thus, by honoring our parents we also honor God (see also *Sforno* ad loc.; *Malbim* to *Shemos* 20:13-14 and *Maharal, Tiferes Yisrael* loc. cit.).

There are technical differences between the two groups that the dichotomy between *Bein Adam LaMakom* and *Bein Adam LeChaveiro* helps to explain. For example, *Chizkuni* (to *Shemos* loc. cit.) points out that God's Name appears in the first group but not in the second. In addition, *Ramban* (to *Shemos* 20:13-14) notes that in the first group there is occasional mention of reward and punishment. No reward is mentioned in the second group.

The division between *Bein Adam LaMakom* and *Bein Adam LeChaveiro* explains these distinctions. God's Name belongs in the first set of *dibros*, because these are all dedicated to His honor, but not in the second set, where society is the beneficiary. Moreover, because society benefits from adherence to the second set of mitzvos, it is not necessary to promise extrinsic rewards for fulfilling them. The laws that govern human relationships bring their own reward, in that life within a group in which everyone's rights are respected is rewarding and fulfilling in itself (see also *Pesikta Rabbasi* ch. 21).

THE TWO GROUPS OF FIVE DIBROS ARE PARALLEL

echilta (*Parashas BaChodesh* §8; cited in *Rosh* to *Shemos* 20:13 and *Rashi* to *Shir HaShirim* 4:5) points out that the two groups of five are structured so that the *dibros* of each group parallel the *dibros* of the other group. Here is how:

The sixth *dibrah*, the prohibition against murder, parallels the first *dibrah* that mandates belief and acceptance of Hashem as God.

Mechilta illustrates the connection between these two *dibros* in the following manner: The connection between these two *dibros* can be illustrated in the following manner. Let us imagine a king who has plastered pictures of himself, and erected statues depicting his likeness, all over his capital city. We can all agree that if someone were to come and destroy any of these pictures or statues, this would derogate the standing of the king in his city. Now, since God created man in His "image," if someone murders his fellow man, he is, so to speak, derogating Hashem (see *Meiri*, Introduction to *Beis HaBechirah*, for an alternative explanation of the parallel).

The seventh *dibrah*, the prohibition against adultery, parallels the second *dibrah* that interdicts idol worship. The connection is clear. There is an obvious similarity between someone who is disloyal to the Master of the Universe and turns to the worship of idols and a wife who is disloyal to her husband and commits adultery with another.

The eighth *dibrah*, the prohibition against theft, parallels the third *dibrah*, the prohibition against taking a false oath. As *Mechilta* explains, this is because thievery will very likely land the thief in court. Once there, and under examination, it is highly likely that he will have to take one or another oath. He can easily find himself in a situation in which he would feel himself forced to swear falsely (see *Meiri* loc. cit.).

The ninth *dibrah*, the prohibition against bearing false witness, parallels the fourth *dibrah*, the obligation to sanctify the Shabbos. *Mechilta* explains that this fits well with the teaching of our Sages, that by keeping Shabbos in all its details one testifies to the fact that God created the world in six days, while by desecrating the Shabbos one bears false witness against God as Creator (see *Rambam*, end of *Hil. Shabbos* and *Maggid Mishneh* ad loc.).

The tenth *dibrah*, the prohibition against coveting the property of another, parallels the fifth *dibrah*, the obligation to honor parents, as follows: When our children see us being jealous of another person, they draw the conclusion that the other person is better situated, and hence probably more important, than their own parents. In the end, these children will reserve their honor for those people who have an abundance of material goods, and will look down on their own parents who cannot compete in that arena (see *Meiri* loc. cit.; for another alternative explanation, see *Kli Yakar* to *Shemos* 20:13).

CHAPTER 5:
THE ASERES HADIBROS INCLUDE ALL OF THE SIX HUNDRED AND THIRTEEN MITZVOS

rom earliest antiquity it has been accepted as axiomatic that in some way, the *Aseres HaDibros* incorporate all six hundred and thirteen mitzvos. *Ralbag* (to *Parashas Yisro*; see also his commentary to *Melachim* I 8:9) posits that Hashem designed the *Aseres HaDibros* to include all the mitzvos so that the entire Jewish nation might hear all the mitzvos (in an abstract form) directly from Hashem, not through Moshe. As a result of their having heard this "short version" of the mitzvos prophetically, they retained no doubt as to the source of the mitzvos.

Maharam Gabbai (*Avodas HaKodesh* 4:34) makes the same point, and adds that we may view the *Aseres HaDibros* as ten "categories." Every mitzvah in the Torah falls into one of these categories. Thus, we can compare the *Aseres HaDibros* to the roots and trunk of an enormous tree from which branches and twigs — that is, all the other mitzvos — then spread out.

The following paraphrase of R' Yaakov Tzvi Mecklenburg's commentary, *HaKesav VeHaKabbalah* (to *Shemos* 32:16), will clarify this understanding further:

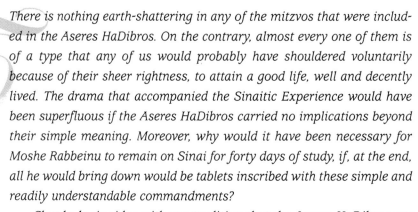

There is nothing earth-shattering in any of the mitzvos that were included in the Aseres HaDibros. On the contrary, almost every one of them is of a type that any of us would probably have shouldered voluntarily because of their sheer rightness, to attain a good life, well and decently lived. The drama that accompanied the Sinaitic Experience would have been superfluous if the Aseres HaDibros carried no implications beyond their simple meaning. Moreover, why would it have been necessary for Moshe Rabbeinu to remain on Sinai for forty days of study, if, at the end, all he would bring down would be tablets inscribed with these simple and readily understandable commandments?

Clearly, logic sides with our tradition that the Aseres HaDibros are really ten categories under which countless other mitzvos, each with its own categories and subcategories with minutiae piled upon minutiae, all as detailed in our Oral Law, are subsumed (see Appendix, note 24).

Here are some sources from which we can see how widely this idea, that the *Aseres HaDibros* somehow include or subsume all six hundred and thirteen commandments, is accepted in our tradition:

In *Shemos* 24:12, Hashem says to Moshe: *Come up to Me upon the mountain and remain there. I will give you the stone tablets, the Torah, and the commandments that I have written, to teach them.* *Targum Yonasan* (ad loc.) renders *the stone tablets, the Torah and the commandments* as follows: The stone tablets upon which the entire Torah is hinted, as are all the six hundred and thirteen mitzvos ... *Rashi* (ad loc.) also had this tradition. He comments: All six hundred and thirteen mitzvos are included in the *Aseres HaDibros*. R' *Saadiah Gaon* has composed a *piyut* [liturgical poem] in which he reviews all the mitzvos and explains to which particular *dibrah* each one belongs.

A Talmudic source also confirms this tradition. The Gemara (*Shabbos* 87a) records the logic that led Moshe Rabbeinu, when he saw the people worshipping the Golden Calf, to conclude that he ought to smash the tablets. His reasoning ran as follows: Since in regard to the *pesach* offering, which is only one of the six hundred and thirteen commandments, the Torah forbids a *mumar* — that is, a person whose actions have estranged him from God — to partake of the offering, then, in the case of the Golden Calf, where the *entire* Torah is being given, and the Jews are all sinning, how much more so are they unfit for it! *Rashi* (ad loc.) explains: "It is correct to describe the tablets upon which the *Aseres HaDibros* were inscribed as "the entire Torah," because the entire Torah is dependent upon these tablets.

Yerushalmi (*Taanis* 4:5) states the matter even more clearly than does *Bavli*: *If someone who is not circumcised is forbidden to partake of the Korban Pesach which is no more than a single mitzvah, then we must certainly distance him from the "Torah"* [the *Aseres HaDibros* — Korban HaEidah] *in which all the mitzvos* are *included.*

The same point is made in *Yerushalmi Shekalim* 6:1. Here is a paraphrase: Chananiah, the nephew of R' Yehoshua, taught: Between each of the *dibros* much Torah was taught. We derive this from *Shir HaShirim* (5:14): *His arms are like rods of gold studded* (lit. *filled in*) *with precious stones.* The *Dibros* were just like a great ocean . . . Just as in a mighty sea many little waves come along between the huge breakers, so too, much Torah was taught between each of the *dibros*. *Rashi*, in his commentary (ad loc.) demonstrates how Chananiah's idea is derived from the text. *His arms* — this refers to the tablets that God gave us with His right hand and that He had wrought with His own hands. *Rods of gold* — these are the *dibros*, concerning which *Tehillim* (19:11) teaches: *They are more desirable than gold. Studded with precious stones* — because the entire Torah is included in the *Aseres HaDibros* (see also *Bamidbar Rabbah* 13:15-16; *Megillah* 15b; *Sefer HaBahir* [*Medrash R' Nechuniah ben HaKanah*] §24; *Zohar*, end of *Parashas Yisro* [93b]).

THE NUMBER OF LETTERS THAT MAKE UP THE ASERES HADIBROS

s with the entire Torah, nothing about the *Aseres HaDibros* is mere coincidence. The very number of letters which comprise the *Dibros* is purposeful and significant.

Indeed, the Medrash (*Bamidbar Rabbah* 13:15) points out that there are altogether 620 letters in the *Dibros* — a number that encompasses two significant groups of letters, the one of 613, and the other, of seven. The first group is, of course, the total number of mitzvos in the Torah, and this correspondence constitutes yet another allusion to the idea that we have just discussed — that, somehow, all the mitzvos are included in the *Aseres HaDibros*.

Commentators offer various explanations for the additional seven letters. The Medrash (ibid.) itself posits that they correspond to the seven days of Creation. This indicates that the Creation, which occurred in seven days, is contingent on our fulfillment of the Torah (see also *Roke'ach*'s commentary on the *Siddur*, on *LaMenatze'ach* [*Tehillim* ch. 20]). Some commentators suggest that the seven letters allude to the seven Rabbinic ordinances: Chanukah, Purim, *Eiruvin, Netilas Yadayim*, the Shabbos candles, the recitation of *Hallel* and the various blessings (*Kesser Torah* [*R' David Vital*]; *Toras HaOlah* [*R' Moshe Issserles*] 3:38; *Shelah* to *Parashas Yisro* and *Shaar HaOsios, Os Beis, Berios* §1; *Megaleh Amukos, Parashas Va'eschanan* §197). Another explanation is that the seven letters allude to the seven Noahide Laws — which are binding upon all humans, not just upon Jews (prohibitions against idol worship, illicit relations, murder, robbery, blaspheming God, eating meat taken from a live animal, and the obligation to avoid anarchy by establishing laws to govern society) — (*Baal HaTurim* to *Shemos* 20:14; see also *Matanos Kehunah* to the Medrash loc. cit. 18:21; see also Appendix, note 25).

HALACHIC CONSEQUENCES OF THE IDEA THAT ALL 613 MITZVOS ARE CONTAINED IN THE ASERES HADIBROS

The Gemara (*Berachos* 23b) teaches that one may not hold anything while praying — even a *Sefer Torah*. A tradition cited by the *Geonim* asserts that in this context the term *"Sefer Torah"* includes even a very small scroll consisting of the *Aseres HaDibros* by themselves, and that such a scroll has the character of a complete *Sefer Torah* because it comprises six hundred and thirteen letters (*Teshuvos HaGeonim, Shaarei Teshuvah* §149; *Aruch*, entry on תפל in the name of *R' Nachshon Gaon*).

Another example involves the *Sefer Torah* of a king. The Gemara (*Sanhedrin* 21b) teaches that a Jewish king must have two *Sifrei Torah*. One is to be kept in his treasury, while the other must be with him constantly, worn on his arm like a bracelet. Since wearing a complete *Sefer Torah* is clearly impossible, *Rosh* (in his Torah commentary to *Parashas Shoftim*; also in *Daas Zekeinim MeBaalei HaTosafos* ad loc.) posits that this "bracelet" *Sefer Torah* contained no more than the *Aseres HaDibros*.

A third example concerns an oath taken on a *Sefer Torah*. There is a Geonic opinion, (that is not, however, accepted as halachah), that an oath taken while holding a *Sefer Torah* can never be nullified. The Geonim make it clear that, in this context, swearing on the *Aseres HaDibros* has the same status as swearing on a complete *Sefer Torah* (*Teshuvos HaGeonim, Shaarei Teshuvah* §141).

In keeping with the idea that the *Aseres HaDibros* encompass all the six hundred and thirteen commandments, many authorities, from the Geonic period onwards, proposed systems that attributed each mitzvah to a corresponding *dibrah*. There were those who felt that logic demanded that all positive commandments belonged with the three positive *dibros* (1, 4 and 5) and all the negative commandments with the other seven (*Rabbeinu Bachya, Kad HaKemach*, entry on שבועות) but others, notably *R' Saadiah Gaon*, did not feel bound to this system (see Appendix, note 26).

Mishnah Berurah (*Orach Chaim* 494:12) suggests that this tradition underlies the widespread custom to eat dairy foods on the festival of Shavuos, which commemorates the Sinaitic Experience. Since Hashem conveyed all the six hundred and thirteen commandments to the Jewish people at Sinai, they would have been hard pressed to serve meat dishes immediately after they returned home. Animals would first have to be slaughtered by the newly required *shechitah* method, for which many preparations were necessary — not least, the careful sharpening of the knife to the high standards that *shechitah* requires. Furthermore, the new prohibition against eating blood would have made it necessary to drain all blood from the meat through the time-consuming salting and washing process. All in all, it was much simpler to eat dairy dishes. Thus, according to this view, our custom to eat dairy foods on Shavuos developed in commemoration of what happened on that first Shavuos in the desert.

KRIAS SHEMA AND THE ASERES HADIBROS

he *Krias Shema* and its attendant blessings form a significant part of our *Shacharis* (morning) and *Maariv* (evening) prayers. *Krias Shema* consists of the three paragraphs, *Shema* (*Devarim* 6:4-9), *Vehayah Im Shamoa* (*Devarim* 11:13-21) and *Vayomer* (*Bamidbar* 15:37-41). *Yerushalmi* (*Berachos* 1:5) notes that, between them, these three paragraphs hint at all ten of the *Dibros* (see *Beis Yosef, Orach Chaim* 61:3 ד"ה יש נוהגים). This is as follows:

1. The first *dibrah*, which requires belief in God, is hinted by the words *Hashem, our God*.

2. The second *dibrah*, which forbids idol worship, is hinted by the words *Hashem is One*.

3. The third *dibrah*, which forbids invoking God's Name in a false oath, is hinted by the words *and you shall love Hashem*… (and therefore not invoke His Name improperly).

4. The fourth *dibrah,* which commands us to keep Shabbos, is hinted by the words *so that you should remember and keep all My mitzvos*.

5. The fifth *dibrah*, which commands us to honor our parents, is hinted by the words *so that your days may be lengthened* (because this *dibrah* promises longevity as the reward for honoring parents).

6. The sixth *dibrah*, which forbids murder, is hinted by the words *you will speedily be lost* … (since one who murders will himself be lost — i.e. killed).

7. The seventh *dibrah*, which forbids adultery, is hinted by the words *you shall not stray [after your eyes]* (lest you be tempted and commit adultery).

8. The eighth *dibrah*, which forbids robbery, is hinted in the words *you shall gather your harvest* (i.e. yours, and not someone else's).

9. The ninth *dibrah*, which forbids bearing false witness, is hinted by the words *I, Hashem, your God, am the true God.* [This is because God considers a false witness as if he testified that God did not create Heaven and Earth.]

10. The tenth *dibrah,* which forbids us to covet our neighbor's possessions, is hinted by the words *[You should write them] upon the doorposts of your house.* (This indicates that your friend's house is out of bounds for you.)

Mishnah Berurah (*Orach Chaim* 61:2) sums up the opinion of various codifiers, as follows: [Since all the *Aseres HaDibros* are referenced in *Krias Shema,*] when one recites the *Shema* he should contemplate the *Dibros,* so as to make sure that he does not violate any of them (see also *Avudraham, Dinei Krias Shema* ד"ה גרסינן בירושלמי and *Kol Bo* §10 ד"ה וטוב להרהר).

THE INCLUSION OF THE ASERES HADIBROS AS A FORMAL PART OF KRIAS SHEMA AND ITS BLESSINGS

hortly after the destruction of the Second Temple, the Sages of the Mishnah compiled the tractate of *Tamid* to preserve a record of how the Divine Temple service was conducted. The Mishnah takes us through a typical day of the service, detailing how, where and when all the steps of the sacrificial service took place. Mishnah 5:1 describes the somewhat abbreviated *Shacharis* (morning) service which was conducted in the Temple. It records that the *Aseres HaDibros* were part of the daily prayer service and that they were recited immediately before the *Shema.* *Rambam,* in his commentary to the Mishnah, explains that it was because the *Aseres HaDibros* are the very basis of the Torah, the starting point from which everything else develops, that they were included in the service.

Over the years, it was often suggested that the *Aseres HaDibros* be made a formal part of our daily prayers. Why, it was argued, should their recital be limited to the Temple service? (See *Tiferes Yisrael* ad loc. §3 and *Teshuvos Igros Moshe, Orach Chaim* §22.) However, this suggestion was never implemented — and for good reason. The rationale is recorded in *Berachos* (12a): There was always the danger that this would result in people harboring the heretical belief that only these mitzvos, that we reiterate on a daily basis, are truly part of the Torah. Therefore, the Sages were loath to ascribe special significance to any particular group of mitzvos (see *Yerushalmi Berachos* 1:5 and *Avudraham* loc. cit.; see also *Bechor Shor* to *Berachos* 12a).

Still, the Gemara's interdiction left certain potential loopholes unexplored. For example, it could be argued that only the inclusion of the *Aseres HaDibros* together with *Krias Shema,* as was done in the Temple, was banned. Perhaps reciting them at a less central point in the service would not be objectionable. Moreover, there was the possibility that only communal recitation was forbidden. Might it not be possible that a person who felt inspired by such a recitation and wanted to make it a part of his daily prayers, could do so?

Thus, several hundred years later, *Rashba* (*Teshuvos HaRashba* §184) was asked whether it might not be possible to include the *Aseres HaDibros* in the daily service. In view of the interdiction of the Gemara cited above, *Rashba* replied in the negative.

Nevertheless, *Siddur R' Amram Gaon* (*Seder Maamados*) and *Tur* (*Orach Chaim* §1) do recommend the recitation of the *Aseres HaDibros* (along with *Parashas HaAkeidah* [the binding of Yitzchak] and the *Parashas HaMan* [the heavenly manna which provided Klal Yisrael with food during their trek through the Wilderness]). Why do these authorities dispute *Rashba's* ruling, which seems to accord with the Gemara?

Maharshal (*Teshuvos Maharshal* §64) — who insisted in his synagogue that the *Aseres HaDibros* be recited in public, at the beginning of services, prior to *Baruch SheAmar* — argued that *Rashba* (and the Gemara) — meant only to forbid the inclusion of the *Aseres HaDibros* as a part of *Krias Shema* and its blessings. The public reading before *Baruch SheAmar* was therefore perfectly acceptable, and it was such reading that *Tur* permitted. *Maharshal* maintained that this is a great mitzvah, as in reviewing God's commandments we indicate that we cherish them, and thus honor Hashem.

Beis Yosef (to *Tur* loc. cit.) disagrees, and rules that any *public* recitation of the *Aseres HaDibros* is forbidden. He asserts that *Tur's* recommendation is only meant for *individuals*. An individual who wishes to give daily voice to his identification with the Sinaitic Experience can bring great blessing upon himself, so long as he recites the *Dibros* privately (see *Bach* and *Derishah* ad loc.). *Arizal* goes further, and takes the Gemara's interdiction as absolute. He seems to forbid the recitation of the *Aseres HaDibros* at *any* point of the service (see *Shaar HaKavanos* [R' Chaim Vital], *Derush Birchos HaShachar* p.1c). *Chida* (*Teshuvos Tov Ayin* §10), however, posits that *Arizal's* ruling was meant only to forbid the recitation of the *Dibros* at any point *during* the service. He rules that it is permissible to recite the *Dibros* after the conclusion of *Shacharis*. *Mishnah Berurah* (1:16; from *Olas Tamid* and *Artzos HaChaim*) also rules that it is permissible to recite the *Dibros* after the prayer service is concluded, and the *Aseres HaDibros* are indeed printed at that point in many *siddurim*. [*Elyah Rabbah* §239 cites *Shelah* (to *Maseches Chullin, Inyan Krias Shema DeLailah*) who recommends reciting the *Aseres HaDibros* as they appear in *Parashas Va'eschanan* (where they include the word *tov* — good) in conjunction with the *Shema* that we recite before going to bed at night (see Appendix, note 27).]

THE CUSTOM TO STAND WHEN THE ASERES HADIBROS ARE BEING READ IN THE SYNAGOGUE

Through the ages, the prevailing custom of the congregation to stand when the *Aseres HaDibros* are read in the synagogue (in *Parashas Yisro* and *Parashas Va'eschanan*, and on Shavuos), has occasioned much discussion. The Gemara's interdiction against reciting the *Dibros* during prayer may be interpreted broadly, and hence as prohibiting any singularization of the *Aseres HaDibros*, including selectively standing for its reading. Nevertheless, the custom has staunch defenders. *Teshuvos Dvar Shmuel* (§276), for example, argues eloquently in favor of the custom. He posits that since there is an obligation to arise when a Torah scholar enters a room, the Divine Presence certainly deserves no less respect. It was for that reason that when the Divine Presence descended upon *Har Sinai* to give us the *Aseres HaDibros*, the entire nation stood to greet Him (*Shemos* 19:17). Since we regard the reading of the *Aseres HaDibros* in the synagogue as a reenactment of that unforgettable moment, when we rise, we are not showing particular respect to a specific passage of the Torah, but to Hashem, who "came down" to give us the Torah. In his opinion, this show of respect is so obviously appropriate that there is no apprehension that someone may misconstrue the sign of respect as a statement that only this part of the Torah is important (see also *Teshuvos Tov Ayin* §11 and Appendix, note 28).

CHANTING THE ASERES HADIBROS IN THE SYNAGOGUE

he cantillations [the melodic notations for chanting the Torah, known in Hebrew as *Taamei HaMikrah* ("Notations of the Scripture") or *taamim* (singular: *taam*), and in Yiddish as *trop*] are more punctuation marks than they are musical notes. Thus, there are two categories of *taamim*: those that indicate that a word or phrase is connected to the next word or phrase, and those that indicate a pause between one word or phrase and the next one. In each of these categories, there is a hierarchy of stronger and weaker *taamim*. In this way, the *taamim* punctuate verses, much as commas, semi-colons, colons and periods all indicate different degrees of separation within a sentence.

However, while punctuation marks do not usually affect the way words are pronounced, as we shall see, the *taamim* determine the correct vocalization of given words. Now, there are two possible ways of reading and punctuating the *Aseres HaDibros*. When we are simply reading the *Aseres HaDibros* as a part of the regular *Krias HaTorah* [Torah reading] the status of these verses as the *Aseres HaDibros* will not determine their punctuation. However, when we are interested in reenacting the Sinaitic Experience, each *dibrah* should be distinct from the others, yet at the same time it should be unified internally. Such a reading will be very different from a normal sentence structure. It leads to very short sentences on the one hand, and very long sentences on the other hand. Through the years, the *Dibros*-determined system of *taamim* became known as *Taam Elyon* ("Superior Notation"); while the regular system of *taamim* became known as *Taam Tachton* ("Inferior Notation").

Let us take, for example, the sixth, seventh and eighth commandments. These are the prohibition against murder, adultery and robbery. Each is made up of only two words — viz., לא תרצח, לא תגנוב, לא תנאף. Now, normally, a verse in the Torah cannot have less than three words. Therefore, if we were to ignore their status as separate *dibros* we would read all of them together in one sentence. When, however, the *dibrah* status of each commandment is the determining factor, then they must be punctuated as three distinct verses.

On the other hand, let us look at the first two *dibros*. When they are punctuated in the "normal" manner, they are read as five distinct verses. However, when we treat them as *dibros,* then, since at Sinai, these two were said "as one" (as we have seen earlier), we must read the entire section as one long verse.

As so often happens, in actual practice there are different customs concerning the *taamim*. Some differentiate between the Torah reading of Shavuos, which commemorates the Sinaitic Experience, and that of *Shabbos Parashas Yisro* and *Shabbos Parashas Va'eschanan,* when the *Aseres HaDibros* are simply another part of the text. Accordingly, on Shavuos it is the *dibrah* status of each section that is the determining factor, and, therefore, *Taam Elyon* is appropriate. However, at all other times *Taam Tachton* is more appropriate. A conflicting view maintains that *Taam Elyon* should be used for *every* public reading — that is, not only for Shavuos, but also for the Torah reading of *Shabbos Parashas Yisro* and *Shabbos Parashas Va'eschanan.* Accordingly, it is only when an individual reads the Torah in private that *Taam Tachton* holds sway. [Both opinions are cited in *Magen Avraham, Orach Chaim* §494, the former in the name of *Teshuvos Masas Binyamin* §6 and *Chizkuni* to *Shemos* 20:14. This is the Ashkenazic custom. The latter opinion is that of *Ohr Torah* to *Shemos* 20:14 in the name of *Mahari ben Chaviv,* the *"Kosev"* in *Ein Yaakov* to *Shekalim* 6:30. It is also the opinion of *Shulchan Aruch HaRav. Shaarei Tefillah* writes that this is the Sephardic custom. For a lengthy discussion of the issues of *Taam Elyon* and *Taam Tachton,* see *Beur Halachah* to *Orach Chaim* §494 ד"ה מבחדש השלישי.]

OTHER CUSTOMS CONCERNING THE READING OF THE ASERES HADIBROS

We have already seen that it is the prevailing custom for the congregation to rise and stand when the *Aseres HaDibros* are read in the synagogue, not out of respect for a specific passage of the Torah, but for Hashem, Who "came down" to give us the Torah. Another aspect of this special regard is the widespread custom to honor the rabbi of the congregation with the aliyah in which the Aseres HaDibros are read (see *Magen Avraham, Orach Chaim* 428:8; *LiDavid Emes* [*Chida*] 2:4 and *Chaim BeYad* [*R' Chaim Palagi*] §62).

Another example of our special regard for the *Aseres HaDibros* does not affect us today, but was significant in the times of the Mishnah. While it has become universally accepted that everyone who is called to the Torah makes a blessing before and after his portion has been read, it was not always so. In the times of the Mishnah, an opening blessing was recited by the first person to be called up, and a closing blessing was recited by the last person to receive an *aliyah.* None of the people called for the *aliyos* in between recited blessings (see *Megillah* 21a-b). Even in the times of the Mishnah, however, the person who was called up for the *Aseres HaDibros* recited his own opening and closing blessings (*Maseches Sofrim* 12:5-6; *Yerushalmi, Megillah* 3:7; see Appendix, note 29).

SWEARING BY THE ASERES HADIBROS

From antiquity it has been customary to place one's hand upon some sacred object when swearing, thereby lending greater gravity to the trust that the oath is meant to inspire (see *Bereishis* 24:2). Most frequently, the sacred object was a *Sefer Torah.* [Perhaps this was done to signify that the person swearing affirmed that the oath was as true as the *Sefer Torah* he was holding.] According to *Shulchan Aruch* (*Yoreh Deah* 237:7), an oath made while holding the text of the *Aseres HaDibros* is identical in its gravity to one made holding a *Sefer Torah.* Moreover, *Shach* (*Yoreh Deah* 237:13) and *Beur HaGra* (ad loc.) both rule that although, strictly speaking, the gravity of the oath is only enhanced if one actually holds the *Sefer Torah* or *Aseres HaDibros* in hand, by custom, it suffices making the connection verbally (i.e. swearing *by* the *Sefer Torah* or *Aseres HaDibros*); physical contact is not necessary (see Appendix, note 30).

OTHER "TENS" THAT CORRESPOND TO THE TEN OF THE ASERES HADIBROS

e come across the number ten in the context of one Jewish practice or another quite frequently. Often, however, the practice itself presents no obvious intrinsic reason that would explain why this particular number, rather than another, was chosen. In such cases, the number ten in question was frequently chosen as a reflection of the **Aseres** *HaDibros*. For example, the law that all Torah readings (other than the *Krias HaTorah* of Shabbos morning) must consist of a minimum of ten verses between the three *aliyos* is based on the correspondence to the *Aseres HaDibros* (*Maseches Sofrim* 21:7; *Megillah* 21b).

Another example is found in the *Mussaf* prayer for Rosh Hashanah. In the *Amidah* (*Shemoneh Esrei*) of that *Mussaf,* we add three sections that have as their subjects the main themes of the day of judgment: *Malchuyos, Zichronos* and *Shofaros. Malchuyos* affirms God's Kingship, *Zichronos* recognizes Him as Judge of the world, and *Shofaros* examines the idea of the *shofar.* Each of these sections is built around a series of three verses relating to that section's subject, from each of the three parts of the Bible (*Torah, Neviim, Kesuvim*). The law, however, is that an additional verse must be added so that ten verses in total are included. The Gemara (*Rosh Hashanah* 32a) states that the number ten is required so as to correspond to the *Aseres HaDibros*.

Yet another example is found in the *Kaddish* prayer. *Shibolei HaLeket* (cited in *Elyah Rabbah, Orach Chaim* §56) points out that the *Kaddish* contains ten expressions of our aspirations for Hashem's Name. These aspirations are divided into two sets; in the first paragraph there is a set of two: *Yisgadal VeYiskadash* [May His great Name grow exalted and sanctified]; while the second paragraph contains the other eight: *Yisbarach, VeYishtabach, VeYispoar, VeYisromam, VeYisnasei, VeYis'hadar, VeYisaleh, VeYis'hallal* [Blessed, praised, glorified, exalted, extolled, mighty, upraised and lauded be the Name of the Holy One]. He explains that these ten expressions correspond to the *Asarah Maamaros* — the Ten Statements — by which God created the world (*Avos* 5:1). Hence, since the *Kaddish* focuses upon God as the Creator of the world (*BiAlma DiBera KiReusei*), it contains ten expressions, corresponding to the *Asarah Maamaros*.

Shibolei HaLeket then explains why these expressions are divided into the two sets of two and eight. A widespread perspective links the "ten" of the *Asarah Maamaros,* which established the physical world, to the *Aseres HaDibros,* which established the spiritual world of mitzvos. As we have seen, the *Aseres HaDibros* may be categorized as two sets. The first set, consists of the two *dibros* that *Klal Yisrael* heard from God Himself; the second set, of the other eight they heard from Moshe Rabbeinu. It was in correspondence to this dichotomy, that the ten expressions of the *Kaddish* were distributed accordingly. [We have seen that according to all authorities — even those who do not ascribe the division to this precise reason — there is some distinction between the first two *dibros* and the last eight.]

— יב —

עשרת הדברות

———— 🙠 ————

THE TEN COMMANDMENTS

———— 🙠 ————

Mitzvos 25-38

Mitzvah 25

מִצְוַת הָאֱמוּנָה
בַּשֵּׁם יִתְבָּרַךְ

פרשת יתרו

TO BELIEVE IN THE EXISTENCE OF HASHEM

THE MITZVAH:

MITZVAH
25

מְצְוַת הָאֱמוּנָה
בַּשֵׁם יִתְבָּרַךְ (עֲשֵׂה)

TO BELIEVE IN THE EXISTENCE OF HASHEM

מצוה
כה

SOURCE

אָנֹכִי ה' אֱלֹהֶיךָ שמות (פרשת יתרו) כ:ב
"I am Hashem, your God"

THE MITZVAH

We are obligated to know[1] that there is a Prime Be-ing[2] Who brought all existence into being,[3] and con-tinually sustains its existence.[4] We must further know that this Being, to Whom we refer as Hashem, is the Lord of the Universe[5] and runs it with His limitless power.[6]

LAWS

1 One must also be aware of the following truths:

A. That Hashem always ex-isted, that He will exist forever, and that prior to Creation, nothing else ex-isted aside from Him.[7]

B. That everything in exis-tence is dependent on Hashem for its continued existence, but Hashem's existence is not depend-ent on anything.[8]

C. That Hashem has no corpo-real body (*guf*) or form.[9]

2 To know that Hashem ex-ists is one of six mitzvos that are incumbent upon a Jew

every moment of his life.[10]

3 It is praiseworthy for one to be constantly engaged in a process of deepening one's awareness and understanding of Hashem's existence.[11]

4 This mitzvah applies to both men and women, in all places and at all times.[12]

5 One who denies the exis-tence of Hashem is termed a *min* (sectarian), and forfeits his share in the World to Come.[13]

NOTES: For the prohibition to be-lieve in any other gods, see *mitzvah #26.*[14] For the mitzvah to know that Hashem is One, see *mitzvah #417.*[15]

A REASON

Being aware of Hashem as the sole source and sustainer of all existence is the foundation of all knowledge, the first and es-sential step toward understanding, and toward living a life on the path of Torah and mitzvos.

1. *Rambam, Hil. Yesodei, HaTorah* 1:1.

Rambam expresses this mitzvah as an obligation *leida* (לֵידַע), *to know*, from the Hebrew root יָדַע, a root used consistently throughout the Torah to imply not merely abstract intellectual cognition (as the word *knowledge* gen-erally implies in English), but rather an intimate, connected awareness. For example, the verse states, *And Adam knew his wife* (Bereishis 4:1), using the verb *knew* (יָדַע) as a syn-onym for marital relations; another verse states ... *because I know him* ... (ibid. 18:19), where the word *know* refers to Hashem's love for and close-ness to Avraham, (see *Rashi* ad loc.); in yet another verse, Hashem states, ... *because I have known [My nation's] pain* (Shemos 3:7), which *Rashi* (ad loc.) interprets to mean that Hashem focused His attention and awareness, so to speak, on their suffering, and did not "cover His eyes." *Rambam* himself uses the term *dei'os*, also from the root יָדַע, to refer to character traits, such as anger and patience, which are expressions of the way one mentally views and *connects* to the world, expressions of a mental map which determines the way one acts and responds (see *Hil. Dei'os* 1:1).

In light of this understanding of the root, יָדַע, *Rambam's* description of this mitzvah as an obligation *to know* [לֵידַע] (see *Ramban* to *Shemos* 20:2 and *Sefer HaChinuch* §25, both of whom also use the term יְדִיעָה, *knowl-edge* in describing what this mitzvah requires) implies that it is not fulfilled through a one-time intellectual event of learning that Hashem exists; rather, it is fulfilled through a perpet-ual and developing *state of awareness* (*da'as*) of the fact of His existence and all that it implies, a connected aware-ness that impacts one's life at all times because it defines the entire

AN EXPANDED TREATMENT

mental context within which one lives. This understanding of the mitzvah is echoed by the *Chinuch*, who states that "all the days of a person's life he is obligated *to maintain this state of awareness* [of Hashem's existence]" (כל ימי האדם חייב להיות במחשבה זו). Consequently, the *Chinuch* defines it as a "perpetual mitzvah" (*mitzvah temidi*), i.e. one of six mitzvos that are incumbent upon a Jew every moment of his life (see Law 2). [Furthermore, the *Chinuch* states that the mitzvah requires one to "*ingrain into his mind* that [the belief] is true and cannot be otherwise," which also implies an ongoing process involving a developing awareness, as opposed to simply holding a belief that is not part of an ongoing awareness] (see *Hirsh, Chorev,* Vol. I, Section 1:1; there are commentators who understand the word ידיעה, *knowledge*, as referring to that which one intellectually understands and verifies through cognitive proofs [see *Beis HaLevi,* end of *Parashas Bo* and *Shelah, Asara Maamaros, Maamar* §1]; see, however, *Hil. Teshuvah* 5:5, which seems to indicate that, according to *Rambam,* a fact can be referred to as a ידיעה even if it is known purely through tradition without actually being verified through proof).

2. To describe the Entity of Whom we must know, *Rambam* (ibid.) speaks simply of a *Being* (מצוי, from the root מצא, and meaning literally something *found* or *extant*). Hashem's essential nature (if we may use such a term in passing and only because language fails us) is entirely beyond comprehension, so that the only appropriate description is one that offers just the fact of His existence (see *Peirush* ad loc.; *Moreh Nevuchim* 1:58). Even the term *Being* is not adequate, because

His existence is qualitatively different from that of the beings He created (*Moreh Nevuchim* 1:57; *Sefer HaIkkarim* 2:1; *Derech Hashem* I 1:5; see also Law 1B). When attempting to convey an idea of Hashem's essence, we are limited to detailing what He *is not* (*Moreh Nevuchim* 1:60), but we can never define what He *is.* All we can say is that He is perfect in every possible way and free of any conceivable deficiency (*Sefer HaChinuch* §25; *Derech Hashem* I 1:2). *Rambam (Hil. Yesodei HaTorah* ibid.) refers to Hashem as the **Prime** *Being* (מצוי ראשון) because He existed before all else, i.e. nothing created Him or preceded Him, or even existed alongside of Him prior to Creation (*Peirush* ibid.; see also *Hil. Teshuvah* 3:7 and next note). Furthermore, Hashem is called *Prime Being* because He is the ultimate reality upon which all else is contingent (see Law 1B).

[It should be noted that the Names by which we refer to Hashem are not descriptions of the true nature of His existence but rather of the way we observe Him relating to the world (i.e. His "actions"); these Names are all derived from words used with reference to humans, except for the Tetragrammaton (יהוה), which is used exclusively to refer to Hashem and alludes to a certain aspect of His Existence (see *Moreh Nevuchim* 1:61).]

3. *Rambam, Hil. Yesodei HaTorah* ibid.; *Sefer HaChinuch* §25; *Smak* §1; *Ramchal, Derech Hashem* 1:1.

The fact that all four sources cited here chose to use the expression "brings (or brought) all existence into being" (ממציא כל הנמצא) underscores that we are dealing here [not with the formation of the specific things that comprise our universe, but rather with the bringing into being of a new type

of existence (i.e. qualitatively different to and dependent upon His existence) out of which the details of our universe would be formed (see *Peirush, Hil. Yesodei HaTorah,* ibid. and *Moreh Nevuchim* 2:13). This idea is fundamental to the Torah's concept of Creation, namely, that it was a creation *ex nihilo,* that is, of "something from nothing" (יש מאין). In other words, prior to the act of Creation, only Hashem existed, and He brought existence as we know it into being from non-existence (*Moreh Nevuchim* ibid.; *Rabbeinu Bachya, Bereishis* 2:3). This concept differs from the various philosophies and religions throughout history which proposed that God formed our universe using some form of matter which had existed alongside Him eternally (see also *Rambam, Hil. Teshuvah* 3:7 with *Kessef Mishneh*).

4. We are not referring here to Hashem's sustaining of the *functioning* of the universe, but rather to His sustaining of its very *existence.* Both *Rambam* (*Hil. Yesodei HaTorah,* ibid.) and *Ramchal* (ibid.) use the present tense in describing Hashem as One Who "*brings* all existence into being," as opposed to simply One Who originally *brought* existence into being, seemingly to teach that Hashem continually wills existence into being at every moment (*Hil. Yesodei HaTorah* 1:1; see Law 1B).

5. *Rambam, Hil. Yesodei HaTorah* 1:5; *Ramchal* ibid.

[The verse (*Shemos* 20:2) states: *I am Hashem, your* **God (Elokecha)** which teaches that the mitzvah is not only to know that Hashem exists, but also that He is the *Eloka* (Lord)]. The word *Eloka* comes from the Hebrew root which implies authority, power and control, and derivations of it are used throughout the Torah to refer to

מִצְוֺת הָאֱמוּנָה
בַּשֵׁם יִתְבָּרֵךְ (עשה)

TO BELIEVE IN THE EXISTENCE OF HASHEM

מצוה
כה

SOURCE

אָנֹכִי ה' אֱלֹהֶיךָ   שמות (פרשת יתרו) כ:ב

"I am Hashem, your God"

THE MITZVAH

We are obligated to know[1] that there is a Prime Being[2] Who brought all existence into being,[3] and continually sustains its existence.[4] We must further know that this Being, to Whom we refer as Hashem, is the Lord of the Universe[5] and runs it with His limitless power.[6]

LAWS

1 One must also be aware of the following truths:

A. That Hashem always existed, that He will exist forever, and that prior to Creation, nothing else existed aside from Him.[7]

B. That everything in existence is dependent on Hashem for its continued existence, but Hashem's existence is not dependent on anything.[8]

C. That Hashem has no corporeal body (*guf*) or form.[9]

2 To know that Hashem exists is one of six mitzvos that are incumbent upon a Jew every moment of his life.[10]

3 It is praiseworthy for one to be constantly engaged in a process of deepening one's awareness and understanding of Hashem's existence.[11]

4 This mitzvah applies to both men and women, in all places and at all times.[12]

5 One who denies the existence of Hashem is termed a *min* (sectarian), and forfeits his share in the World to Come.[13]

NOTES: For the prohibition to believe in any other gods, see *mitzvah #26*.[14] For the mitzvah to know that Hashem is One, see *mitzvah #417*.[15]

A REASON

Being aware of Hashem as the sole source and sustainer of all existence is the foundation of all knowledge, the first and essential step toward understanding, and toward living a life on the path of Torah and mitzvos.

DEDICATED BY THE KEST FAMILY
LOS ANGELES, CALIFORNIA

rulers and judges (see *Rashi* on *Bereishis* 6:4 and *Peirush, Hil. Yesodei HaTorah* ibid.). Thus, referring to Hashem as "Lord of the Universe" indicates that He did not just bring existence into being and leave it to its own devices, but rather maintains control over it as its absolute and only

Master (see *Moreh Nevuchim* 2:30 [end] and 2:33; *Kad HaKemach,* entry on *Emunah; Chareidim* 9:1; *Sefer HaIkkarim* 3:18; *Chizkuni* to *Bereishis* 1:1 ד"ה אלהים; *Rambam* (ibid.) also describes Hashem as אדון כל הארץ, *Master of the Earth*).

According to some authorities,

since the verse states **your** Lord, rather than **the** Lord, part of the mitzvah is to know that Hashem not only is Lord of the Universe, but also supervises and guides the Jewish nation as part of a unique relationship (see *Ramban* to *Shemos* 20:2).

6. *Rambam, Yesodei HaTorah* 1:5.

This mitzvah is unique in the sense that it is not derived from a verse that states an explicit command, such as "You shall know that there is a God," but rather, from a declaration made by Hashem to every Jew standing on *Har Sinai,* namely, *I am Hashem, your God.* The reason that Hashem's declaration is seen as a specific mitzvah is that the word "I am" (*Anochi*) is a declaration of the fact of His Existence; it is as if He stated: *Know that the Universe has a God* (*Sefer HaChinuch* 25; see also *Ramban, Sforno, Daas Zekeinim* and *Rabbeinu Bachya* to *Shemos* 20:2). The Jews, with whom Hashem communicated at *Har Sinai,* directly perceived the truths about His Existence that this mitzvah requires one to know (*Ramchal* ibid. 1:2; see also below, note 15).

Now, the verse which begins with the words *I am Hashem, your God,* continues with the clause, *Who has taken you out of the land of Egypt.* Some Rishonim hold that this second clause serves not merely to identify Hashem, but is actually part of the mitzvah. Thus, we are required to know not only that Hashem exists but also that Hashem redeemed us (miraculously) from slavery in Egypt (*Sefer HaChinuch* ibid.; *Smag* §1; *Smak* §1), which implies that He is autonomous, potent, able to suspend natural law (implying in turn that natural law is itself His creation), and that He constantly supervises the world that He created (*Ramban* to *Shemos* loc. cit.; *Sefer HaChinuch* ibid.).

Since the words, *I am Hashem,*

your God, open the Revelation at Sinai, a number of Rishonim add that the mitzvah further requires us to know that Hashem gave us the Torah, as though the verse read, *I, the Being Who at this moment is giving you the Torah, am Hashem, your God* (*Sefer HaChinuch*; see *Derashos HaRan* §9, p. 363 in the *Mosad HaRav Kook* ed.).

Halachos Gedolos (*Bahag*) does not enumerate knowledge of God's existence among the 613 mitzvos. *Ramban* to *Sefer HaMitzvos* (*Aseh* §1) explains that this is because the mitzvos are Hashem's *decrees*, some of which command us to engage in certain activities (מצוות עשה), while others prohibit us from engaging in certain activities (מצוות לא תעשה). Knowledge of the existence of Hashem, however, is the underlying principle that necessarily *precedes* these decrees, the foundation upon which they all are based. Therefore, maintains *Bahag*, this knowledge should not be listed as one of the mitzvos (see *Megillas Esther* and *Lev Sameach* ad loc.; see also *Shaarei Yosher* 5:2; see *Sefer HaIkkarim* 1:14).

7. *Sefer HaChinuch* §25; *Kad HaKemach*, מציאות ה׳; *Chareidim* §1; *Ramban* to *Shemos* ibid; see also *Ramban* to *Bereishis* 1:1 and to *Sefer HaMitzvos*, omitted prohibitions הראשונה; *Rambam, Commentary to the Mishnah*, Introduction to the Tenth Chapter of *Sanhedrin*, first and fourth principle; *Ramchal* ibid. 1:1-3).

Although *Hil. Yesodei HaTorah* 1:1 is not entirely explicit in stating that we are obligated by the present mitzvah to know that Hashem is eternal, such knowledge is implied by the designation of Hashem as the *Prime Being* (see *Peirush* ibid. and above, note 2). Moreover, according to *Yesodei HaTorah* 1:11, the precept of Hashem's eternity is a logical consequence of His incorporeality (discussed below, note 9).

Knowledge of Hashem's eternity is basic to the concept of His sovereignty. For not only is Hashem eternal, but He *alone* is eternal; all else is finite and must have a beginning in time. Neither matter nor spirit, nor the natural laws that govern them, nor the very dimensions of time and space, had antecedents in any previous reality, but all were *created* — willed into existence out of utter nothingness — by Hashem, the single timeless Being Who preceded the universe. Natural law is therefore changeable and subject to Hashem's control (see *Ramban* loc. cit.; see also *Hasagos HaRaavad, Hil. Teshuvah* 3:7; see also *Kuzari* 1:67). As we saw earlier (note 3), stating that prior to Creation only Hashem existed comes to exclude other philosophies throughout history which proposed that God formed our universe using some form of matter which had existed alongside Him eternally.

8. Thus, were one to imagine that He does not exist, then on that premise nothing at all could exist, however, if nothing else were to exist, or if everything else would cease to exist, His own existence would be unaffected. Hence, the prophet, Yirmiah states: ה׳ אלקים אמת, *Hashem, the Lord, is reality* (*Yirmiah* 10:10), in other words, He alone is [absolute] reality (*emes*), and nothing else is of a reality comparable to His. Furthermore, the Torah states: אין עוד מלבדו, *There is none other than He* (*Devarim* 4:35), which is to say, there is no other existing entity that is real in the sense that He is (*Rambam, Hil. Yesodei HaTorah* 1:1-4; see also *Rambam, Commentary to the Mishnah*, ibid. first principle and *Ramchal* ibid. 1:4).

9. *Rambam, Hil. Yesodei HaTorah* 1:5, 7; *Sefer HaChinuch*; *Rambam, Commentary to the Mishnah*, ibid. third principle.

Rambam states:

It is clear from the Torah and the Neviim that Hashem is neither body nor corpus. For the verse says (*Devarim* 4:39), *… because Hashem is God in the Heavens above and on the earth below*, whereas a body cannot be [simultaneously] in two places. And the verse says (*Devarim* 4:15), *for you saw no image [on the day Hashem spoke to you at Chorev* etc.]. And the verse [also] says (*Yeshayah* 40:25), *To whom can you compare Me that I shall be likened?* [*says the Holy One*]; but if He were a body, He could be compared [in some sense] to other bodies. What, then, does the Torah mean when it says, *and under His legs* (*Shemos* 24:10); *written by the Lord's finger* (ibid. 31:18); *the hand of Hashem* (ibid. 9:3); *the eyes of Hashem* (*Devarim* 11:12); *the ears of Hashem* (*Bamidbar* 11:1), and similar expressions? All these are suited to the understanding of humans, who are familiar only with bodies. For the Torah speaks in the language of humans, but [in truth] these expressions are all metaphors (*Hil. Yesodei HaTorah* 1:8-9).

Rambam (ibid. 1:11-12) proceeds to elaborate some consequences of Hashem's incorporeality:

Once we have determined that Hashem is neither body nor corpus, it becomes apparent that none of the occurrences that affect bodies affect Him (i.e. that no quality or state associated with matter can apply to Him): neither connection nor separation; neither place nor quantity; He neither ascends nor descends; He has neither right nor left, neither front nor back; He neither stands nor sits; He does not exist within time (for time itself is His creation), and hence has no beginning, end, or age; He never undergoes change, for there is nothing that can cause Him to change (nothing can affect Him); He has no death, nor even life comparable to the life of a live

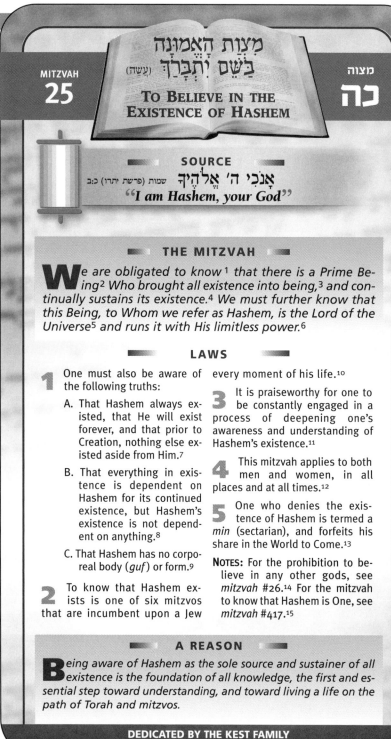

MITZVAH 25

מצוה כה

מִצְוַת הָאֱמוּנָה
בְּשֵׁם יִתְבָּרַךְ (עֲשֵׂה)

TO BELIEVE IN THE EXISTENCE OF HASHEM

■ SOURCE ■

אָנֹכִי ה' אֱלֹהֶיךָ שמות (פרשת יתרו) כ:ב
"I am Hashem, your God"

■ THE MITZVAH ■

We are obligated to know[1] that there is a Prime Being[2] Who brought all existence into being,[3] and continually sustains its existence.[4] We must further know that this Being, to Whom we refer as Hashem, is the Lord of the Universe[5] and runs it with His limitless power.[6]

■ LAWS ■

1 One must also be aware of the following truths:

A. That Hashem always existed, that He will exist forever, and that prior to Creation, nothing else existed aside from Him.[7]

B. That everything in existence is dependent on Hashem for its continued existence, but Hashem's existence is not dependent on anything.[8]

C. That Hashem has no corporeal body (*guf*) or form.[9]

2 To know that Hashem exists is one of six mitzvos that are incumbent upon a Jew

every moment of his life.[10]

3 It is praiseworthy for one to be constantly engaged in a process of deepening one's awareness and understanding of Hashem's existence.[11]

4 This mitzvah applies to both men and women, in all places and at all times.[12]

5 One who denies the existence of Hashem is termed a *min* (sectarian), and forfeits his share in the World to Come.[13]

NOTES: For the prohibition to believe in any other gods, see *mitzvah #26*.[14] For the mitzvah to know that Hashem is One, see *mitzvah #417*.[15]

■ A REASON ■

Being aware of Hashem as the sole source and sustainer of all existence is the foundation of all knowledge, the first and essential step toward understanding, and toward living a life on the path of Torah and mitzvos.

was angered at times, and joyous at times, that would entail change. All such qualities are to be found only in lowly, lightless bodies, confined in shells of matter, formed of elemental dust. Whereas He, may He be Blessed, is raised and exalted above all this!

See also the third of *Rambam's Thirteen Principles*, where he stresses (as does *Sefer HaChinuch*) that Hashem neither has a material form *nor* is He a force or spirit that resides in any material form. That is, unlike the human soul for example, which animates the body and forms a compound entity — a living person — *with* the body, Hashem is a wholly transcendent Being, Who although He sustains and controls the world, is not of the world.

10. There are six mitzvos that are not dependent on any particular time, place or circumstance (unlike, for example, *mitzvah #325, to live in a succah*, which applies only during the Succos festival, or *mitzvah #588, to pay a worker on the same day [that he completes his work]*, which one never fulfills unless one hires an employee), and which require no tools other than one's own consciousness. They are incumbent upon a person always (see *Sefer HaChinuch, Hakdamah*). The six, known as the *mitzvos temidios* (perpetual commandments) are:

Mitzvah #25: To know that Hashem exists.

Mitzvah #26: Not to believe that another god exists aside from Hashem.

Mitzvah #417: To know that Hashem is One.

Mitzvah #418: To love Hashem.

Mitzvah #432: To fear Hashem.

Mitzvah #387: Not to be led astray by one's thoughts or eyes.

(*Sefer HaChinuch*, end of *Seder U'Minyan HaMitzvos* and the final paragraphs of *mitzvos #25, #417,*

body; no folly, nor even wisdom like the wisdom of a wise man; no sleep or awakening; no anger or laughter; no joy or despondency; no silence, nor speech like the speech of a person. Thus said the Sages (*Chagigah* 15a): Above there is no standing nor sitting, no separation nor connection. Now

since this is so, any attributions of emotions to Hashem in the Torah and the Neviim are all metaphors and figures of speech ... Hence the verse asks [rhetorically] (*Yirmiah* 7:19; see *Radak* ad loc.): *Can they anger Me?* Why, [another] verse says (*Malachi* 3:6): *I, Hashem, have never changed,* and if He

#418 and #432; see *Beur Halachah* §1, (ד"ה הוא כלל גדול). The mitzvah to know that Hashem exists is considered a perpetual mitzvah because, as we saw earlier (note 1), it is fulfilled by maintaining a perpetual state of awareness of Hashem's existence at all times.

11. As we mentioned earlier (note 1), the *Sefer HaChinuch* states that one should "*ingrain into his mind* that [the knowledge required by this mitzvah] is true and cannot be otherwise." Now, one fulfills this mitzvah simply by believing that the concepts are true, even though one does not understand *why* they are true. However, the *Chinuch* goes on to state that if "he merits to grow in levels of wisdom, and his mind understands and his eyes see absolute proof that the beliefs he holds are clearly true, he will then be fulfilling this mitzvah in the most desirable manner (*mitzvah min ha'muvchar*)."

Rambam advocates a similar approach. The knowledge required by this mitzvah actually encompasses the first four of his thirteen fundamental principles, and after defining the thirteen fundamentals, *Rambam* writes: Know them … review them many times, contemplate them deeply, and if your mind fools you into thinking that you have grasped their implications after [studying them] one time, or even ten times, Hashem knows that your mind has lied to you; therefore do not rush [your] reading [of them] … (*Rambam Comm.*, Introduction to the Tenth Chapter of *Sanhedrin*).

Now, as we saw earlier (note 6), the truths that this mitzvah requires one to know were actually perceived directly by every member of the Jewish nation through the Revelation at *Har Sinai*. They taught these truths to their children, and they were then passed down from generation to gen-

eration, as the Torah commands: *You shall not forget the things you saw with your own eyes [at Sinai] … and you shall make them known to your children and grandchildren.* However, these truths can also be logically deduced through an understanding of what we observe in the physical world (*Ramchal, Derech Hashem* 1:2). In fact, *Rambam* (*Hil. Avodas Kochavim* 1:3) writes that our forefather Avraham discovered Hashem's existence along with all its implications, purely through an observation of the world around him. Deepening one's belief through attentiveness to physical and biological details is referred to as *bechinah* (examination), and is the subject of *Chovos HaLevavos, Shaar HaBechinah* (see also *Chazon Ish, Emunah U'Bitachon* §1).

Some Rishonim recommend that one study the philosophical proofs of Hashem's existence as presented in the relevant metaphysical treatises. (*Emunos VeDei'os, Hakdamah; Chovos HaLevavos, Hakdamah; Moreh Nevuchim* 3:54; *Sefer HaChinuch* §25). Such philosophical inquiry is called *chakirah* (investigation), and forms the subject of *Chovos HaLevavos, Shaar HaYichud*. Other authorities disallow *chakirah* because the issues are subtle and one may easily slip into error (*Shiltei HaGiborim* §1 *to Avodah Zarah*, fol. 5b, citing *Riaz; Teshuvos Chavos Yair* §219). Some advise that one should never engage in *chakirah* until one has studied the entire Talmud, and even then only to learn how to respond effectively to heretics (see *Teshuvos HaRashba* 1:414-417, *Teshuvos HaRivash* §45; *Teshuvos Chavos Yair* §124; *Moreh Nevuchim, Hakdamah* and 1:32-33).

12. As a rule, both men and women are obligated in those positive commandments which are not dependent on time (see *Kiddushin* 29a).

Later authorities discuss whether this mitzvah applies to non-Jews as well. On the one hand, a command like *I am Hashem, your God, Who took you out of the land of Egypt*, can hardly be addressed to non-Jews, whom Hashem never redeemed from Egypt. On the other hand, how can non-Jews be commanded to uphold their Seven Noahide Laws (listed in note 17 to *mitzvah* #27) unless they are expected to believe in the Lawgiver? See *Seder Mishnah, Yesodei HaTorah* 1:7 1; *Divrei Yirmiyahu* ibid. 1:6; *Sefer Mitzvos Hashem* 1:36 ff., and in *Dinei Bnei Noach* mitzvah §25.

13. *Rambam, Hil. Teshuvah* 3:6,7; *Chareidim* 9:1; see *Rosh Hashanah* 17a.

For a discussion regarding what classifies a person as a *min* and what consequences are involved, see *Iyunim.*

14. That prohibition is derived from the verse, *You shall not recognize other gods before Me* (*Shemos* 20:3). Now, the declaration, *I am Hashem, your God,* the source of the present mitzvah, can be understood to imply: *Know that I **alone** am God* (*Shemos Rabbah, Parashah* 29:1-2; see *Mechilta* to *Yisro* ad loc.). Hence, according to some, included in this mitzvah is the requirement to know not only that Hashem exists and is the Lord of the Universe, but that there is no other god aside from Him (*Sefer HaChinuch* §25; *Sforno* to *Shemos* ibid; *Smak* §1). The verse, *I am Hashem your Lord*, can therefore be viewed as an *issur aseh* (a prohibition implied by an imperative) that proscribes belief in other gods (*Kinas Sofrim, aseh* §1; see *Rashi* to *Horayos* 8a ד"ה איזו היא, cited by *Kinas Sofrim* and *Lev Same'ach; Sefer HaIkkarim* 3:18). One who harbors idolatrous beliefs violates *mitzvah* #26 by commission, and *mitzvah* #25 by *omission*, i.e. by failure to believe in Hashem exclusively.

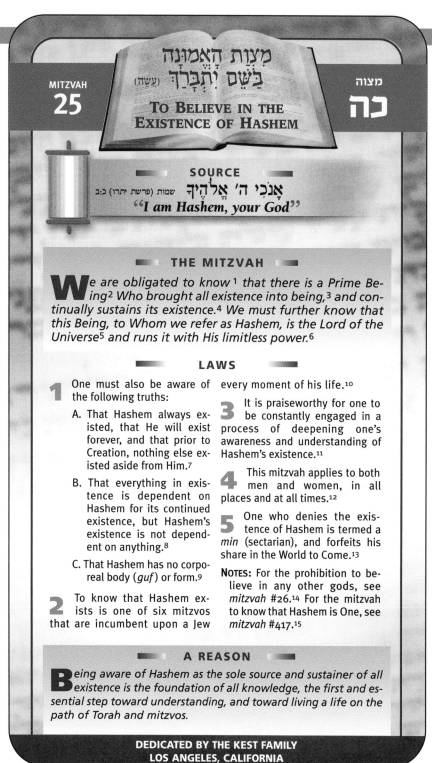

מִצְוַת הָאֱמוּנָה בְּשֵׁם יִתְבָּרֵךְ (עֲשֵׂה)

MITZVAH 25 — מצוה כה

TO BELIEVE IN THE EXISTENCE OF HASHEM

▬ SOURCE ▬

אָנֹכִי ה' אֱלֹהֶיךָ שמות (פרשת יתרו) כ:ב

"I am Hashem, your God"

▬ THE MITZVAH ▬

We are obligated to know [1] that there is a Prime Being [2] Who brought all existence into being, [3] and continually sustains its existence. [4] We must further know that this Being, to Whom we refer as Hashem, is the Lord of the Universe [5] and runs it with His limitless power. [6]

▬ LAWS ▬

1 One must also be aware of the following truths:

A. That Hashem always existed, that He will exist forever, and that prior to Creation, nothing else existed aside from Him. [7]

B. That everything in existence is dependent on Hashem for its continued existence, but Hashem's existence is not dependent on anything. [8]

C. That Hashem has no corporeal body (*guf*) or form. [9]

2 To know that Hashem exists is one of six mitzvos that are incumbent upon a Jew every moment of his life. [10]

3 It is praiseworthy for one to be constantly engaged in a process of deepening one's awareness and understanding of Hashem's existence. [11]

4 This mitzvah applies to both men and women, in all places and at all times. [12]

5 One who denies the existence of Hashem is termed a *min* (sectarian), and forfeits his share in the World to Come. [13]

NOTES: For the prohibition to believe in any other gods, see *mitzvah #26*. [14] For the mitzvah to know that Hashem is One, see *mitzvah #417*. [15]

▬ A REASON ▬

Being aware of Hashem as the sole source and sustainer of all existence is the foundation of all knowledge, the first and essential step toward understanding, and toward living a life on the path of Torah and mitzvos.

Comm. ibid. second principle; *Ramchal, Derech Hashem* 1:5). Furthermore, not only is He an absolute unity, but He is also "One" in the sense of being *unique*. It is impossible for two beings to exist with the qualities described in Law 1 (*Rambam, Hil. Yesodei Hatorah* ibid and *Ramchal*, ibid. 1:6).

Although *Rambam* and *Sefer HaChinuch* count knowledge of Hashem's oneness as a separate mitzvah (#417), any conception of Hashem that fails to acknowledge His oneness would be utterly fallacious, and hence could also never fulfill what *mitzvah* #25 requires one to know. Moreover, Hashem's oneness is linked intrinsically to concepts that are assuredly encompassed by *mitzvah* #25. *Rambam* demonstrates in *Hil. Yesodei HaTorah* (1:7) that besides being a Scriptural precept, Hashem's oneness is an inescapable logical consequence of His incorporeality (see law 1C; see also *Moreh Nevuchim* 1:35; *Sefer HaIkkarim* 1:15). Furthermore, Hashem's sovereignty and mastery (see note 5 above) are predicated on His oneness, because true sovereignty must be total and unopposed (*Sefer HaChinuch* §417; see *Emunos VeDei'os* §2, ד"ה ואומר תחלה).

---

15. We derive that mitzvah from the verse שמע ישראל ה' אלקינו ה' אחד, *Hear O Israel, Hashem is our God, Hashem is One* (*Rambam*, ibid. 1:7). It requires one to know that Hashem's unity is unlike any unity found in the universe. He is not unified like a particular species, such as humanity, which comprises many individual entities, nor is He unified like a single body which has different parts and dimensions; rather, he is an absolutely simple unity without any structure or additional qualities (*Rambam, Hil. Yesodei HaTorah*, 1:7; *Rambam*,

עיוני	# A BROADER LOOK AT THE LAWS

1 *The definition of a min*

The term *min*, which literally means a [separate] *kind* or *species* (but in this context refers to a *sectarian*) is a term used throughout the Talmud (e.g. Mishnah, *Berachos* 9:5 and Mishnah *Rosh Hashanah* 2:1) to refer to certain heretics who organized themselves into sects distinct from the main body of Jewry. According to *Rambam* (*Hil. Teshuvah* 3:7), the term properly applies only to heretics who advocate a false conception of God, specifically those who deny His existence, oneness, incorporeality or that He pre-existed the universe and brought all existence into being from nothingness (see *Kessef Mishneh* ad loc.). Also included in *Rambam's* definition of a *min* is one who worships an imagined god (*eloha*) as an intermediary (*meilitz*) between himself and Hashem. Heretics who admit the transcendence of God but deny that He heeds or communicates with mankind are referred to by their own term, *apikorsim*. Those who deny the Divine origin of the Written Torah or of the Oral Law, or who claim that the Torah has been superseded, are called *kofrim* (ibid. 3:8).

Minim, *apikorsim* and *kofrim* do not share in the fundamental beliefs that unify the Jewish People and (barring the exceptions discussed in the following paragraph) are consequently regarded as outside the fold, thereby relinquishing their claim to the brotherhood and courtesies that Jews normally owe one another (*Rambam, Hil. Avodah Zarah* 2:5 and *Hil. Mamrim* 3:2, and *Commentary to the Mishnah*, end of Introduction to the Tenth Chapter of *Sanhedrin*; *Sefer HaChinuch*; see *Hil. Avodah Zarah* 10:1 and *Hil. Rotze'ach U'Shemiras Nefesh* 4:10; *Chazon Ish, Yoreh Deah* 2:16). Futhermore, these individuals forfeit their share in the World to Come (see Law 5). However, if they repent, even in their final hours and even if they never publicly repudiate their former heresy, they regain a share in the World to Come (*Rambam, Hil. Teshuvah* 3:14).

People who hold heretical beliefs are not all equally culpable. According to *Rambam* (*Hil. Mamrim* 3:3), only those who, as adults, have led themselves astray through their own corrupted thinking are held fully responsible, whereas the children and grandchildren of such sectarians, who have been indoctrinated with false beliefs since childhood, are not held responsible. According to others, those who wholeheartedly accept the truth of the Torah and its principles, but have come to mistaken conclusions about what the Torah actually means to communicate regarding Hashem (e.g. by taking anthropomorphic references to Him literally) are not classified as *minim*. In their view, only those who understand what the Torah means, yet deny the principles it teaches, are defined as *minim* (see *Hasagos HaRaavad* to *Hil. Teshuvah* 3:7 and *Sefer HaIkkarim* 1:2; cf. *Rosh Amanah* ch. 12, p.14a, Koenigsberg ed.; *Kovetz He'aros, Dugma'os* 12:8 quoting *R' Chaim Soloveitchik of Brisk*).

Question:

Several authorities have dealt with the number of core beliefs prescribed by the Torah. Foremost among them was *Rambam* (*Commentary* to the *Mishnah*, Introduction to *Perek Chelek*), who lists thirteen primary principles of belief. He states that only a person who believes in these thirteen principles is fully included in the Jewish Nation. It is a mitzvah to love such a person, and to display mercy toward him. Even if that person has sinned and violated many laws, other Jews remain obligated with regard to him to fulfill all the duties that a person must fulfill toward his fellow. On the other hand, a person who rejects any one of these principles is a heretic. Are there, indeed, thirteen principles, and why are they the minimal set of beliefs that a person must possess to be fully included in the Jewish Nation?

Answer:

A. The principles:

Rambam's thirteen principles are universally accepted. Some people recite an abbreviated version of the principles (the *Ani Maamin* statements) after their morning prayers. Many people recite the liturgical poem, *Yigdal*, which is also a synopsis of the thirteen principles (see the discussion in *Tikkun Tefillah* [in *Siddur Otzar HaTefillos* ad loc.] concerning the identity of the author of *Yigdal*).

In brief, the thirteen principles require one to believe: 1. In the existence of God; 2. In the unity of God; 3. That God is totally nonphysical; 4. That God's existence is absolutely eternal; He preceded and will outlast everything; 5. That God is the only One Whom we may serve, pray to, and praise; 6. In the existence of prophecy; 7. That Moshe was superior to all other prophets; 8. That the Torah given to us by Moshe originated from God; 9. That

the Torah is God's permanent word, and it will not and cannot be changed; 10. That God knows all that men do; 11. That God rewards those who obey the commandments of the Torah and punishes those who violate its prohibitions; 12. That *Mashiach* will come; 13. That God will resurrect the dead.

An earlier source for this number of principles may be found in the text of an ancient prayer attributed to the Amora R' Tavyomi, in which it says: *And You have bestowed grace upon me, and I know You by Name, with the straightforwardness of the thirteen principles. And You directed the radiance of Your Presence toward me. Dwell with me, and bestow upon me peace from those who reject these thirteen* (see *Teshuvos Chasam Sofer, Yoreh Deah* §356). *Shelah* (*Shaar HaOsios*) suggests that the thirteen principles correspond to the thirteen attributes of God's mercy (see *Shemos* 34:6-7), the first principle corresponding to the first attribute, etc.

B. R' Yosef Albo's three principles:

R' Yosef Albo (fifteenth century) wrote his classic work, *Sefer HaIkkarim*, on the topic of the primary principles. He counts as primary principles only those core beliefs that are indispensable — i.e. those principles whose absence would undermine the character and practice of Judaism. For example, let us suppose a person lacked belief in the coming of *Mashiach* and in the resurrection of the dead (Principles 12 and 13). Lacking these principles, his practice of Judaism would remain essentially unchanged — so long as he retained his belief in reward and punishment (Principle 11). *Sefer HaIkkarim* maintains that, in fact, only three principles are truly indispensable — namely, belief in: 1. God; 2. The Torah's Divine origin; 3. Reward and punishment. If any one of these principles were to be eliminated, the character and practice of Judaism would be without basis, and therefore untenable; however, if one maintains these three principles, his Judaism is based on firm and solid foundations.

Sefer HaIkkarim (1:4) finds an allusion to the three primary principles in the *Mussaf* service of Rosh Hashanah. The Sages of the Great Assembly (*Anshei Kenesses HaGedolah*) formulated three sections, each containing ten verses, to include in this service: *Malchuyos* — Kingship, *Zichronos* — Remembrance, and *Shofaros* — Shofar. *Malchuyos* corresponds to the first principle, belief in God, in that its theme is God's Kingship. Following this theme, it includes the *Al Kein Nekaveh* prayer (the second paragraph of *Aleinu*), which expresses our hope that all the world's inhabitants will come to recognize and know God. *Zichronos* corresponds to the third principle, belief in reward and punishment, in that its theme is God's recollection of each human being to judge him, and to reward and/or punish him. *Shofaros* corresponds to the second principle, the Torah's Divine origin, in that when God transferred the Torah from the Divine realm in which it originated to this world, the sound of the *shofar* accompanied the process. In the spirit of this theme, the section opens with a description of the giving of the Torah at *Har Sinai*. *Sefer HaIkkarim* posits that if a person accepts these three primary principles, then God judges him favorably on Rosh Hashanah.

Abarbanel (*Rosh Amanah* ch. 17) frames the dispute between *Rambam* and *Sefer HaIkkarim*: According to *Sefer HaIkkarim*, we define a primary principle as one that is an essential and indispensable foundation of Judaism. According to *Rambam*, however, *any* major and fundamental concept in Judaism is considered a primary principle.

C. Belief in God: A primary principle or a mitzvah?

Rambam counts several of his primary principles as specific mitzvos. Indeed, the first principle, belief in God, is also the very first mitzvah that *Rambam* enumerates in his count of the 613 mitzvos in *Sefer HaMitzvos*. R' Chisdai Crescas (*Ohr Hashem* ch. 1, cited in *Rosh Amanah,* ch. 4) asks: How can we count a primary principle — a part of the foundation of Judaism that must therefore precede the fulfillment of the mitzvos — as a mitzvah?

Many authorities, however, note that the language of the standard Hebrew translation of *Sefer HaMitzvos* — *The first mitzvah is the command that He commanded us to believe [in] the Deity* — is not a

precise translation of the Arabic original. The Arabic word translated as *believe* is more precisely translated as *know*. In fact, in the brief count of the mitzvos that appears at the beginning of *Rambam's Mishneh Torah*, and in the first law (*Hil. Yesodei HaTorah* 1:1), the Hebrew word that *Rambam* himself wrote is לידע — *to know*. Thus, write these authorities, while the *primary principle* is belief, the mitzvah is to reach complete knowledge and conviction, through the many various approaches (see above, note 11) by which one may enhance his rudimentary belief, until he attains full and true knowledge of God's existence (*Maaseh Roke'ach* to *Hil. Yesodei HaTorah* 1:1; *Metzudas David* [*Radvaz*] mitzvah §1; *Ohr HaNe'erav* [*R' Moshe Cordevero*] 2:1; see *Sefer HaMitzvos*, R' Chaim Heller ed., mitzvah §1, with note §1, and *Sefer HaMitzvos*, Frankel ed., *Tziyunim* to mitzvah §1).

D. Abarbanel's opinion that there are no primary principles:

Abarbanel (*Rosh Amanah* ch. 23) and *Radvaz* (*Teshuvos Radvaz* 1:344) maintain that it is not possible to isolate primary principles. They note that the existence of primary principles would imply that other principles are not primary, and therefore neither as important nor as significant as the primary ones. They assert that even the "lesser" mitzvos embody fundamental concepts (although we may not perceive them). Therefore, everything written or transmitted in both the Written and the Oral Laws (תורה שבכתב ותורה שבעל פה) is of equal importance. We cannot say that some matters are more significant and some are less significant. *Abarbanel* suggests that *Rambam* only compiled the Thirteen Principles to provide simple people — who cannot comprehend complex and profound issues of belief — with a short, simplified list of tenets that even they might understand and accept (see also *Teshuvos Chasam Sofer, Yoreh Deah* §356).

E. The distinction between the primary principles and the rest of the Torah:

On the other hand, *R' Chaim Soloveitchik* of Brisk (cited in the *Shaarei Torah* Torah journal), defends

Rambam's distinction between the primary principles and the rest of the Torah and its mitzvos. It is true that a person who consciously and deliberately *rejects* even the smallest part of the Torah is a heretic. He has *chosen* to estrange himself from Judaism. Yet, a person who *does not know* a part of the Torah is certainly *not* a heretic, and is fully included in the Jewish Nation. But a person who is unaware of any one of the primary principles is incapable of full participation in the Jewish Nation. His ignorance of any of these principles will inevitably lead him to false conclusions and wrong attitudes. Thus, such a person [unfortunately] remains estranged from Judaism (see *Rambam, Hil. Mamrim* 3:3, for a discussion of the halachic status of a *tinok shenishbah* — "a captured child").

This distinction between the primary principles and the rest of the Torah and its mitzvos also serves to explain why *Rambam* lists separately concepts that other principles obviously include. For example, if one accepts the principle that the Torah is of Divine origin, he automatically accepts that God communicates with prophets, whether he is consciously aware of that acceptance or not — since that is how we received the Torah, through Moshe Rabbeinu. *Rambam* nevertheless splits these concepts into two principles to show that ignorance — even unconscious ignorance — of the specific belief embodied in this principle estranges a person from Judaism. It is not enough for one not to reject these principles. He must become aware of them and know them.

THE BLESSING FOR THE MITZVAH

he Sages did not institute a blessing for the mitzvah of believing in Hashem. This is just one of a number of positive commandments for which the Sages did not institute a blessing. Various rules have been suggested to account for the absence of a blessing for these mitzvos, some of which also explain why no blessing was instituted for the mitzvah of believing in Hashem.

A. *It is a mitzvah which applies at all times.*

Blessings are recited only for mitzvos whose obligation is restricted to a specific time. Examples of these are *tzitzis, tefillin, succah* and the like. A blessing is not called for in the case of mitzvos whose obligation is always in effect, and from which one is never exempt; for example, the mitzvah of believing in Hashem and fearing Him, the mitzvah of honoring one's parents, etc. This is because a blessing expresses the love one feels for the mitzvah, and one does not feel the same fondness for mitzvos he is always obligated to perform as he does for mitzvos that he is able to perform only at intervals. Thus, no blessing is recited for them (*Ohr Zarua*, I:40).

B. *It is a mitzvah which requires no action.*

The Sages did not institute a blessing for mitzvos that require no action; for example, the mitzvah of relinquishing loans during *shemittah* (*Teshuvos* of *Ri ben Pelet*, cited by *Rashba* in his *Teshuvos* 1:18 and *Teshuvos HaMeyuchasos L'Ramban* [attributed to *Ramban*, but actually authored by *Rashba*] §189; *Abudraham, Shaar* §3; *Orchos Chaim* of *R' Aharon MiLuneil, Hil. Berachos* §72; *Rabbeinu Manoach* in his commentary to *Rambam, Hil. Berachos* 11:2; see also *Beis Yosef, Orach Chaim* §432,

who explains that this is the reason no blessing is recited for the mitzvah of nullifying *chametz*). Since one fulfills the mitzvah of believing in Hashem in his mind, without any physical action on his part, the Sages did not institute a blessing for it.

C. *It is a mitzvah which demonstrates acceptance of Hashem's sovereignty.*

Some Rishonim explain that the reason no blessing is recited before performing the mitzvah of reciting the *Shema* is that the purpose of reciting a blessing before performing a mitzvah is to demonstrate that by performing the mitzvah we are subjugating ourselves to Hashem's rulership [by fulfilling His commandments]. The first verse of the *Shema* embodies the concept of accepting Hashem's sovereignty, so a blessing for this mitzvah would be superfluous (*Abudraham,* commentary to *Tefillas Shacharis — Krias Shema;* see also *Ritva Pesachim* 7b). Similarly, any mitzvah which by its very nature demonstrates Hashem's sovereignty does not require a blessing. Since to believe in Hashem is to accept His sovereignty, the Sages did not institute a blessing for this mitzvah.

D. *It is a mitzvah which has no limits.*

Some explain that the reason the Sages did not institute a blessing for the mitzvah of honoring one's parents (*mitzvah #33*) is that if one were to recite a blessing for any specific act of honoring his parents, he would be tempted to feel that he has fulfilled his obligation for the moment. In reality, however, he has not even come close to fulfilling the Biblically mandated measure of this mitzvah. As the Gemara says regarding R' Tarfon and his elderly mother: Although [R' Tarfon] would place his hands beneath [his mother's] feet for her to walk upon as she went to bed, the Sages, when told of this incident, responded that he had not yet done even half of what the Torah requires for honoring a parent

(*Kiddushin* 31b; see also *Yerushalmi, Kiddushin* 1:7). Were a person to recite a blessing before performing an inadequate act of honoring his parent, he would not be blessing [Hashem], but disgracing Him! The Sages understood that few people merit to perform this mitzvah properly, so they did not institute a blessing for it (*Maharit Algazy*, cited in *S'dei Chemed, Asifas*

Zekeinim, Maareches Berachos 1:16; see *mitzvah #33* at length). The mitzvah of believing in Hashem also has no limit, for the more we contemplate the reality of Hashem's existence, the greater our understanding of His existence becomes (see *Rambam, Hil. Yesodei HaTorah* 1:9-10). For this reason, this mitzvah is not subject to a blessing.

ILLUMINATIONS OF THE MITZVAH
Suggested Reasons & Insights

I. EMUNAH: THE ESSENCE OF THE MITZVAH IMPERATIVE

Fundamental to the recognition of man's true vocation in life is the conviction that the affairs of this world are controlled and guided by the One Who created it. The call for *emunah,* faith, is by no means an isolated mitzvah; it is the bedrock of the entire structure of Torah and wisdom. *Emunah* is to recognize the existence of a Being that predates the created world; that it was He Who brought all things, in Heaven and earth, into being; and that there is not, anywhere in the universe, a creation that can for a moment remain in existence without the continued supply of His creative sustenance (*Rambam, Hilchos Yesodei HaTorah* ch. 1). To be deficient in these tenets of *emunah* is to lose most privileges due to a member of the Jewish people (see *Chinuch* §25. See also *Chovos HaLevavos,* preface to *Sha'ar HaYichud*).

The central importance of *emunah* lies in the fact that man's entire relationship to the mitzvos is grounded in it (*Abarbanel, Shemos* 20:2). Only after one is certain that there exists a Creator Who continues to manage and sustain the life of all the world's creatures, will he be compelled to conclude that he is duty-bound to accept the sovereignty and bend to the will of the One to Whom he owes his very existence. God said to Yisrael [before introducing the mitzvos]: 'I am Hashem your God. You have accepted My sovereignty; now accept My decrees' (*Mechilta, Yisro* §6).

I am Hashem, your God. The meaning of this verse is as follows:

I am Hashem; the reality of My existence [*I am*], and the fact that I have granted you, and all else, the gift of existence [the connotation of Hashem's Four-Letter Name] should become axiomatic to you.

...Your God; you should then accept Me as your God, and devote yourself to My service (*Mefaresh* to the *Rambam* ad loc. §6).

Another insight — I, the Lord, am *your* God means I am your Creator, your Lawgiver, your Judge; the Director of your thoughts, your feelings, your words and your actions. Every one of your internal and external possessions has come to you from My hand; every breath of your life has been apportioned to you by Me. Look upon yourself and all that is yours as My property, and devote yourself wholly to Me ... Be the instrument of My will ... and so join freely the choir of creation as My creature, My servant ... (*Chorev* 1:4).

II. EMUNAH: THE BULWARK IN MAN'S STRUGGLE AGAINST HIS INCLINATION TO EVIL

Aside from serving as the basis for our duty to observe the mitzvos, a deep reservoir of *emunah* also provides the moral fortitude that is constantly needed to overcome the innumerable challenges that a Jew will inevitably face in his effort to remain faithful to the service of God. A person who can remain cognizant of God's world-filling presence, of His all-seeing eye, scrutinizing man's every action and thought, and of his own comparative insignificance and impotence, is not very likely to fall into sin (*Derech Pikudecha, Mitzvos Aseh* §25, *Cheilek HaDibbur* §3; *Reishis Chochmah, Sha'ar HaAhavah* §12. See *Pri HaAretz, Parshas Lech Lecha,* who writes that *emunah* brings about the suppression of the physical desires).

Six hundred and thirteen mitzvos were given to Yisrael, but along came Chavakuk (2:4) and summed them all up in just one: *The righteous lives by his faith* (*Makkos* 24a). *Emunah* is more than just an individual mitzvah; if a person can succeed in developing a deeply rooted faith in God, experiencing heartfelt joy in having found in this faith the purpose of his existence, he will, buoyed by this joy, scale all obstacles on the way to his complete fulfillment of all the rest of the mitzvos (*Likutei Amarim-Tanyah* §33).

III. EMUNAH: ITS ROLE IN THE ABILITY TO GIVE ONE'S LIFE TO SANCTIFY GOD'S NAME

 Jew is obliged to develop a faith of such strong conviction that it cannot be shaken even by a threat to his life (*Chinuch* §25). The determination Jews have displayed in their willingness to forfeit their lives to defend the integrity of the Jewish concept of One Unique God is a trait that was planted forever, deep into the Jewish consciousness, by the tremendous force of the Divine declaration, *I am Hashem your God* (*Derech Pikudecha, Mitzvos Aseh* §25, *Cheilek HaMachshavah* §3). For the people who heard this declaration, as they stood at *Har Sinai,* it became second nature to believe in its truth (*Pri Tzaddik, Rosh Hashanah* §15; see *Sefas Emes, Shevuos* 5646).

Even among Jews who have long renounced their allegiance to mitzvah observance, when put to the test, many find the strength to offer their life, or suffer torture and punishment, for the sake of their faith. This moral courage will often not even be the product of conscious deliberation, of logical thinking, but a Jewish soul's intuitive reflex, that a Jew must not — cannot — deny the existence or Oneness of Hashem our God (*Likutei Amarim-Tanyah* §18).

IV. EMUNAH: EMBODYING ALL THE MITZVOS

 ust as true faith provides a person with the ability to clear all hurdles obstructing his progress in pursuit of Torah and mitzvos, there is, conversely, a process by which the involvement in mitzvah observance serves to build and intensify that very *emunah*. Every mitzvah performed, for no other reason than one's belief in God and the law of His Torah, in turn drives that conviction all the more deeply into his consciousness. This idea is expressed by the verse (*Tehillim* 119:86) *All Your mitzvos are faith* (*Yismach Moshe, Parashas Terumah*).

As a result, it emerges that with each mitzvah one observes out of a belief in the One Who gave that command, the person has at the same time heeded the mitzvah to have *emunah* (*Derashos Rabbeinu Yonah*). And not only in the active performance of a mitzvah, or in the abstention from a possible active transgression, but even by merely contemplating the performance of a mitzvah, or pushing out of mind a forbidden thought — all because of the compelling awareness of God and His Torah — one has fulfilled the commandment, *I am Hashem, your God* (*Degel Machaneh Efraim, Parashas Bereishis* ד"ה או).

This, indeed, is the underlying aim of all the mitzvos — to rarefy the individual by enabling him to tap into the wellspring of faith that lies deep within his heart. For this reason, the Sages have said (*Avos* 2:1), *Be as scrupulous with a minor mitzvah as with a major one.* Every mitzvah is to be treasured, because with each one a person acknowledges God, and the ultimate goal of all the mitzvos is that we come to believe in our God and give thanks to the One Who created us (*Ramban, Shemos* 13:16). This, then, is another way by which *emunah* embraces the totality of mitzvah observance, revealing an additional layer of meaning in the aforementioned verse from *Tehillim, All Your mitzvos are faith* (*Maharsha, Chidushei Aggados, Makkos* 24a. See there at length, 23b-24a).

V. THE EXODUS: PREAMBLE TO THE TORAH; FOUNDATION OF EMUNAH

 ntil this point, the focus has been on the first half of the commandment to believe in the existence of God: *I am Hashem, your God.* But the verse continues, further identifying the One Who is about to call us into His service: ...*Who took you out of the land of Mitzrayim, from the house of bondage.* Many commentators express surprise at the choice of this form of introduction. We might have thought that a more compelling opening would be, "I am Hashem your God, Who created the Heavens and the earth" (*Ibn Ezra, Shemos* 20:2, quoting *Rabbi Yehudah HaLevi*; *Kuzari* 1:25). Or, perhaps, "I am the One Who formed you and brought you to life. I fed you and provided you with all your needs; in My hands reside life and death, reward and punishment. You are forever indebted to Me, obliged to heed My every command and to serve Me with all your heart" (*R' Yosef Bechor Shor, Shemos* ad loc.).

A number of insights have been offered to resolve this question:

A. *Yetzias Mitzrayim — the decisive factor in the Jewish nation's obligation to accept the Torah*

The Torah, along with the awesome responsibility that its acceptance entailed, was not given to all the world's inhabitants; its yoke was placed exclusively on the shoulders of the Jewish people. If this one nation, among seventy others, was to be convinced that it was incumbent upon them to accept this responsibility, one obvious question, that was sure to be asked, had to be addressed. Why us, and nobody else? After all, the entire human race owes its existence to the original creation of Heaven and earth, and all, as a result, equally belong to the Creator. So God did not see fit to invoke the Creation in His call to the Jewish people. Instead, He reminded them of the debt that they alone owed for the unparalleled care and love that He showed for them in Egypt, when He came forward *to take for Himself, a nation from amidst a nation, with challenges, with signs, with wonders, with war, with a strong hand, and with an outstretched arm* (*Devarim* 4:34), the likes of which He has never done for another nation (*R' Yosef Bechor Shor,* ibid.; *Chizkuni, Shemos,* ad loc. See *Ibn Ezra, Shemos,* ad loc.).

We have therefore become indebted to Him beyond the debt owed by all His other creatures, for He has taken us to be His servants, bestowed upon us a reflection of His glory, and has called us "His children" and "a kingdom of nobles." We are

thus bound to acknowledge His kingship and obey His decrees, whether as servants or children, and to devote body, soul, and possessions to the sanctification of His name, fulfilling His will in any way we can (*Eileh HaMitzvos* §25; see *Abarbanel, Shemos,* ad loc.).

B. *Yetzias Mitzrayim — a concept within everyone's grasp*

The Exodus was an event that was personally experienced by everyone who stood at the foot of *Har Sinai.* It was thus easier for them to connect to that revelation of God's omnipotence than to the ancient history of the world's origin (*Kuzari* 1:25). In addition, the Exodus was an event they had witnessed firsthand, and was for them a living reality that could not be challenged. On the other hand, the Creation of the world involves obscure concepts that are not well understood by all levels of the population, and, if one were to argue against the truths of Creation, many would be at a loss to respond. God began, then, with the words *I am Hashem, your God*; the full significance of which could be appreciated only by the very wise, and then continued, *...who took you out of Mitzrayim,* by which He addressed the public at large (*Ibn Ezra, Shemos,* ad loc.; see *Kuzari* ibid. §12-25).

C. *Yetzias Mitzrayim — the first step in accepting God's sovereignty*

While yet in Egypt, inspired by the wonders they had witnessed, the Jews had submitted to the Kingship of God, and the subsequent bestowal of the Torah at *Har Sinai* was predicated on that acceptance. For this reason the Exodus was mentioned as an introduction to *Mattan Torah.* This can be compared to a king, who, upon his entry into a new province, was petitioned by his subjects, "Decree laws for us to obey!" He replied, "No! First you must acknowledge my sovereignty. Otherwise I will not issue any decrees, for on what other basis will you be sure to comply?" In this fashion, God appeared to the *Bnei Yisrael,* and said, *I am*

Hashem, your God, who took you out of Mitzrayim. Do you acknowledge that I am He Whose sovereignty you accepted, as a result of the Exodus? Yes, came the reply. If so, God continued, you can proceed to receive My decrees. In this way, the commandments hinged on what had occurred in Mitzrayim (*Avodas HaKodesh, Sisrei Torah* §38, cited also in *Shelah, Pesachim, Torah Ohr* §18).

D. *Yetzias Mitzrayim — a source of reassurance to the people*

Citing the precedent of *Yetzias Mitzrayim* was, in effect, a way of reassuring the nation accepting the Torah that this was a gift being granted to them out of love, and the observance of its laws would bring them great benefit. "True, the performance of the mitzvos will not be without difficulty, but you may rest assured, that I, Who rescued you lovingly from the grip of Mitzrayim, would not instruct you to do anything unless it promotes your well-being and protects you from harm" (*Derashos Rabbeinu Yonah,* ibid.).

E. *Yetzias Mitzrayim — a crucial element of complete faith in God*

Belief in the veracity of the Torah's account of the Exodus is, in fact, inseparable from true faith in God. For it is not sufficient to be convinced of God's existence. The mitzvah of *emunah* includes also the call to believe in the Divine Providence that was so clearly revealed by *Yetzias Mitzrayim.* A Jew is expected to rely on God with all his heart, and to believe in His Providence. So that the true concept of Unity may reside in one's heart, one must believe that God's eyes penetrate every part of the world, and take notice of all of man's actions and thoughts. One who does not accept the full significance of the words, ... *Who took you out of the land of Egypt,* cannot claim to subscribe to *I am Hashem, your God.* This idea forms the foundation of the entire Torah (*Orchos Chaim* of the *Rosh,* Day 1).

THROUGH THE EYES OF THE SAGES
Stories, Parables & Reflections

I. AVRAHAM: FATHER OF FAITH

*A*s *alluded to in Scripture and elaborated upon in the works of our Sages, our ancestor Avraham, on the strength of his own observations and reasoning, arrived at an awareness of the world's Creator. He then dedicated his existence — even agreeing to surrender his life — demonstrating to others the truth about the uniqueness of God, teaching that none but He should be revered and worshipped. Avraham bequeathed this legacy of monotheism to his progeny, thus enlightening mankind to this very day.*

As an introduction to the laws of idolatry in his halachic code Mishneh Torah, Rambam traces the history of polytheistic philosophy and Avraham's efforts to dispel its fallacies:

The birth of paganism

In the days of Enosh, mankind fell prey to a grievous misconception that led to the emergence of idol worship. The people reasoned that it was proper to pay tribute to the Heavenly bodies as God's emissaries to the world, just as a king expects his ministers to be treated with honor by those subject to his rule. Over time, these demonstrations of honor led to genuine worship as the popular conception of the celestial forces graduated from subordinate proxies to independent deities. Idols were fashioned to represent the gods, and the images themselves became objects of veneration and worship. The simple masses perceived nothing beyond the monuments and statues of wood and stone, and even the more sophisticated among them, who knew that the idols were merely symbols of metaphysical powers, imagined that divinity was limited to the stars and other Heavenly bodies. The existence of a Creator was virtually unknown, and the

Name of Hashem became forgotten to mankind, aside from a precious few individuals, such as Chanoch, Mesushelach, Noach, Shem and Ever. In this manner civilization declined until the birth of the "pillar of the world" — our forefather Avraham. [See further in *mitzvah #26*.]

------ ✥ ------

The advent of Avraham

This great personality was yet a child when he began to apply his mind to the mysteries of the world around him. He wondered: How is it possible that the orbiting bodies maintain their course without a being that moves and guides them? Surely they cannot move on their own! Surrounded as he was by primitive pagans in his native Ur Casdim, there was no one to teach him and answer his questions, so he searched for insight with his own faculties until he finally discovered the truth: There exists just one God Who is the Creator of all, and it is He Who conducts the orbiting bodies. Avraham then realized that the entire world was in error.

------ ✥ ------

Beacon of faith

Avraham then began to broadcast his findings and debate with his countrymen to show how they had strayed from the truth. He destroyed idols and preached to the people that the world has only one God Whom they should exclusively worship, and he advocated the destruction of all the carved images to prevent further error. His compelling arguments won him many adherents, until the local ruler (Nimrod) attempted to put him to death. Avraham was saved by a miracle, and he fled to Charan, where he increased his efforts to propagate his message of monotheism all over the world. He traveled from city to city and country to country, addressing gatherings and giving individualized instruction, converting in the process many of his listeners to the path of truth. Eventually, he brought his teaching to the land of Canaan, as it is written (*Bereishis* 21:33), *And there he proclaimed the Name of Hashem,*

God of the Universe. Many thousands gathered around him, and they were referred to as "the men of Avraham's house" (ibid. 17:33). He instilled in them his doctrine of faith in God, and he also authored books on the subject.

———— ৭৫ ————

৩ *Providing for posterity*

Avraham transmitted his teachings to his son Yitzchak, who himself became a teacher and a guide. Yitzchak trained his son Yaakov and appointed him to teach others as well; Yaakov established a following whom he taught and provided for. He schooled all of his sons and singled out Levi to head a yeshiva, through which he might disseminate the ways of God and preserve the traditions of Avraham. Yaakov provided for Levi's descendants to maintain the role of teachers in Israel, and thus the creed of Avraham continued to thrive among the children of Yaakov and others who joined them; the world was at last witnessing the formation of a nation that had an awareness of God. However, as Israel's sojourn in Egypt stretched out over many years, the Jews became influenced by the ways of their neighbors and they began to imitate their worship of idols. Only the tribe of Levi held fast to the principles of their forefathers; never did they engage in idolatry. The doctrine established by Avraham was close to being uprooted, as Yaakov's descendants drifted back to the misguided practices of the world at large. It was only out of the love God has for us and His fidelity to the oath He had made to Avraham, that He raised up Moshe Rabbeinu, the master of all prophets, and sent him to draw Israel back to become God's inheritance, to be granted His mitzvos, and to be taught how to serve Him (*Rambam, Hil. Avodas Kochavim* ch. 1).

———— ৭৫ ————

৩ *Three years old*

R' Ami bar Abba taught: At the age of three Avraham came to know his Creator, as it is said

(*Bereishis* 26:5), *Because* (עקב) *Avraham hearkened to My voice.* The numerical value of "עקב" is 172 (indicating that he obeyed God's voice for 172 of the 175 years of his life) (*Nedarim* 32a; *Bamidbar Rabbah* 18:21; *Bereishis Rabbah* 30:8, see there [with commentary of *Maharzav*] for another opinion; see also there 64:4, 95:3; *Shir HaShirim Rabbah* 6:1; et al.)

———— ৭৫ ————

৩ *Seeking out his Creator*

Who inspired [the one] from the east? (*Yeshayah* 41:2). R' Yehudah explained: This refers to Avraham, whose inspiration to discover God came from the east. At first, when Avraham observed the sun rising from the east, he concluded, "That must be the king that created me," and he worshipped the sun throughout that day. But then evening came and the sun went down; the moon began to shine in its place. He declared, "Apparently, this being rules over the one that I worshipped all day, for the light of the first has been extinguished." Avraham worshipped the moon throughout the night. The morning then dawned, the darkness dispersed, and the eastern horizon became bathed in light. Avraham concluded, "Both of these powers must be ruled by a king who has control over them!" God took note of Avraham's longing to discover Him, so He revealed Himself and spoke to him, as it is written (ibid.) *Righteousness called him near* (*Zohar* I, 86a).

———— ৭৫ ————

৩ *An imposing edifice*

R' Yitzchak taught: Avraham's experience is analogous to a traveler on the road who caught sight of a mansion gleaming with light. He mused: Could it be said that this mansion does not have a master? The owner set his gaze upon him, and said, "I am its master." In the same way, Avraham said, "Is it possible that this world is without a Director?" God gazed upon him and said, "It is I, the Master of the world" (*Bereishis Rabbah* 39a).

———— ৭৫ ————

✧ *Spreading knowledge of God*

[A]vraham] planted an "eshel" in Beer-sheva
(*Bereishis* 21:33). Reish Lakish explained:
He established an orchard, planting all types of
delicacies (to serve to wayfarers — *Rashi*). R'
Yehudah and R' Nechemiah disputed the matter.
One said it was an orchard, while the other maintained it was an inn. [The word *eshel* (אשל) is an
acronym for the words אכילה, *eating*; שתייה, *drinking*; and לוייה, *escorting*, as Avraham fed his guests
and then accompanied them as they went on their
way — *Rashi*.] The term *planted* can refer to erecting a structure, as it is written (*Daniel* 11:45), *He
will pitch [lit. plant] the tents of his palace ... And
there he proclaimed the Name of Hashem, God of the
universe* (*Bereishis* ibid.). Reish Lakish taught: Do
not read it וקרא (And he proclaimed); rather, read
it ויקריא (And he caused it to be proclaimed).

Avraham placed God's Name in the mouth of
every traveler. How so? After they had finished their
food and drink, they arose to bless him. He would
say to them: "Was it *my* food that you ate? It was all
the property of the God of the world!" They would
then thank, praise and bless the One Who decreed
the world into existence. [As recorded in the
Medrash Tanchuma: He would say to them, "You
should bless the Proprietor Who provides sustenance to all the creatures and grants them life."
They would inquire, "Where can He be found?" And
he would answer, "He rules over the Heavens and
earth; He puts to death and brings to life; He strikes
down and heals; He forms a fetus inside the womb
of its mother and then draws it out into the world;
He causes plants and trees to grow; He lowers [peo-
ple] into the grave and then raises [them] up."
Upon hearing that, the guests would ask, "How can
we bless Him and express our gratitude?" He would
instruct them to recite, "Blessed be God, Who is
Blessed forever and ever. Blessed be the One Who
grants bread and nourishment to all flesh," and he
would teach them about the blessings and doing
charitable deeds. This is what is meant by the verse
(*Bereishis* 12:5) *And the souls they had made in Charan*. R' Alexandri wondered: What can be meant by

"the souls they had made"? Even if all the world's
creatures were to combine all their efforts, they still
would not be capable of making as much as a gnat!
Rather, it means that Avraham and Sarah taught
them the fear of Heaven and instructed them in the
Torah. (Scripture thus treats them as if they had created them, for they brought them to the life of the
World to Come — *Eitz Yosef*.) God declared to Avraham: "You distributed charity and made Me known
in the world; you shall receive your reward," as it is
said (ibid. 15:1), *Your reward is very great*. (*Sotah*
10a-b; *Bereishis Rabbah* 43:7, 54:6; cf. ibid. 84:4;
Tanchuma, Lech Lecha 12; *Zohar,* Omissions to Section I, 264b).

———— ✧ ————

✧ *Partner in creation*

[G]od declared: My Name was unknown to My
creatures and you familiarized them with Me; I
hereby consider you My partner in the creation of
the world (*Bereishis Rabbah* 43:7; cf. *Bamidbar Rabbah* 14:2).

———— ✧ ————

✧ *Wellsprings of faith*

[A]vraham dug this well of faith, for he taught the
people of the world to enter into the service of
God; once he had dug the well, he caused it to surge
with a stream of water that shall never cease. But
once Avraham died, what do we find? *All the wells
that his father's servants had dug in the days of Avraham ... the Philistines stopped up, and filled them with
earth* (*Bereishis* 26:15). That the Philistines filled in
the wells alludes to the fact that the populace reverted to the worship of idols, and the world became desolate, for there was no one to recognize
God. Once Yitzchak arrived, however, what does it
say? *Yitzchak dug anew the wells of water which they
had dug in the days of Avraham, his father* (ibid. v.
18). Yitzchak returned the world to its proper state;
he taught the populace to recognize God. In this
vein, it is said (ibid. 25:11), *Yitzchak settled near the*

well *LaChai-Ro'i.* What did this well consist of? The waters on which all life of the upper and lower worlds depend (*Zohar,* Addendum to Section 3, 302a; *Zohar Chadash* I, 45b).

II. Dialogues on faith in God

Moshe Rabbeinu confronts Pharaoh

hey said to Pharaoh, "So said Hashem, the God of Israel, 'send out My people that they may celebrate for Me in the Wilderness'" (*Shemos* 5:1). R' Chiya bar Abba taught: That day was a day of international tribute to Pharaoh; all the kings came to render their homage, bringing crowns as gifts to confirm his sovereignty over the entire world. They also brought their idols with them. Once they had crowned him, Moshe Rabbeinu and Aharon arrived at the entrance of Pharaoh's palace. The servants reported that two elderly men were standing at the entrance. Pharaoh bid them to enter. As they came before him, the king waited expectantly for them to proffer a crown, or to present a scroll extolling his praises. But they did not even greet him. He asked, "Who are you? What do you seek?" They responded, "We are messengers of God. So said God, 'Send out My people that they may celebrate for Me in the Wilderness.'" With that, Pharaoh grew angry. He said, "Who is God that I should listen to His voice, to send out Israel? Does He not know to send me a crown? It is only with idle talk that you come to me! I do not know God; nor will I send out Israel!" He said to them, "Wait for me; I will consult my manual." He immediately went into his palace and read through the list of the nations and their deities. He returned and announced, "I conducted a search in my library and could not find your God." [This explains the two verses: At first, Pharaoh asked, "Who is God?" But after checking his sources, he asserted decisively, "I do not know God!" — *Maharzav.*]

R' Levi taught: To what can this be compared? To a Kohen who possessed a dull-witted servant. The servant entered a cemetery in search of his master. The passersby asked him, "Isn't your master a Kohen?" He answered affirmatively. They said to him, "Fool! Who ever saw a Kohen in a cemetery?" This is precisely what Moshe Rabbeinu and Aharon answered to Pharaoh. "Fool! Can the living be expected to be found among the dead? Ours is a Living God; the deities you searched through are dead. Ours is the Living God, the King of the world."

He said to them, "Is He youthful or aged? How old is He? How many cities has He conquered? How many provinces has He captured? For how long has He reigned?" They answered, "The power and strength of our God fills the world. He existed before the world was created, and He will continue to exist when the world reaches its end. He formed you and breathed life into you."

Pharaoh pressed on, "What has He accomplished?" They answered, "He stretches out the Heaven and establishes the foundation of the earth. His voice cleaves with flames of fire, shatters mountains and smashes rock. His bow is fire; His arrows are flames; His spear is a torch. The clouds are His shield, the lightning His sword. He forms the mountains and hills; He blankets the mountains with grass; He sends down rain and dew; He causes vegetation to grow. He forms a fetus inside the womb of its mother, and then draws it out into the world. He deposes kings and crowns kings."

Pharaoh said to them, "Your words are false from the start, for I am the lord of the world; I created myself along with the Nile — *Mine is my river, and I have made myself* (*Yechezkel* 29:3). At that point, Pharaoh assembled all the wise men of Egypt, and said to them: "Have you heard of the God of these men?" They replied, "We have heard that He is the son of wise men and a descendant of the kings of yore." God interjected, "Yourselves you call wise men, and Me the *son* of wise men!?" Thus it is said (*Yeshayah* 19:11), *Pharaoh's wisest advisers offer boorish counsel. How can you tell Pharaoh I am the son of wise men, descendant of the kings of yore?* At this, God declared, "By your lives, [I swear] that I will stamp out your wisdom," as it is said, *The wisdom of its wise men will be lost, and the understanding of its sages will be concealed* (*Yeshayah* 29:14).

Pharaoh brought the word back to Moshe Rabbeinu and Aharon. "I do not know of your God. Who is God that I should listen to His voice?" God replied, "Wicked one! You dare question My existence with the words 'Who (מי) is God'? You will be correspondingly struck with the two letters of 'מי'." The letter 'מ' equals forty, and the letter 'י' equals ten, for a total of fifty, the number of plagues God brought upon the Egyptians at the *Yam Suf*. For concerning the plagues in Egypt, the Torah states (*Shemos* 8:15), *The magicians said to Pharaoh, "It is the finger of God."* But of those at the Sea, it is said (ibid. 14:31), *Israel saw the great hand with which God acted against Egypt.* How many plagues did they receive with the finger? Ten. Now reckon ten plagues for each finger of the "great hand"; the result is fifty plagues.

Another approach: Pharaoh said "מי ה'" — "Who is God?" Reverse the letters of "מי" to read "ים" — the sea. "The Sea [of Reeds] will introduce you to God" (*Shemos Rabbah* 5:14; *Tanchuma, Va'eira* §5; *Medrash Mishlei* (*Buber*) 27:17).

———— ৺৶ ————

❧ *R' Yehoshua ben Chananiah and Hadrian of Rome*

The Roman Emperor Hadrian asked R' Yehoshua, "Is there really a Master of the universe?" R' Yehoshua responded, "Is this, then, a world of disorder?" "So who created the Heaven and earth?" asked Hadrian. R' Yehoshua answered, "The Holy One, Blessed is He, as it is said (*Bereishis* 1:1), *In the beginning God created the Heavens and the earth.* Hadrian asked, "Why does He not reveal Himself two times a year so that people may see and become imbued with His fear?" R' Yehoshua answered, "Because the world could not endure His radiance, as it is said (*Shemos* 33:20), *For no human can behold Me and live.* Hadrian insisted, "If you do not show Him to me, I refuse to believe it." So R' Yehoshua brought him out into the midday sun. He instructed, "Gaze into the sun and you will be able to see Him." Hadrian

protested, "Who is able to stare at the sun?" R' Yehoshua countered, "Don't your ears hear what your mouth is saying? If to the sun, which is just one of the myriads of servants attending God, no man can hold his gaze, how much more so in regard to God, Whose radiance is such that it fills the World! When, then, will He reveal His Glory? When the false deities will be removed from the world, as the Torah states (*Yeshayah* 2:18), *The false gods will perish completely,* after which *God alone will be exalted on that day* (ibid. 17). And, elsewhere, it is written (ibid. 40:5), *The glory of God will be revealed, and all flesh together will see that the Mouth of God has spoken* (*Yalkut Shimoni, Ki Sisa* §396; cf. *Chullin* 59b-60a).

———— ৺৶ ————

❧ *A lion's roar*

Hadrian challenged R' Yehoshua ben Chananiah: "Your God is likened to the lion, as it is written (*Amos* 3:8), *A lion has roared; who will not fear?* What distinction is that? A mighty warrior can overcome a lion!" [Hadrian called into question the Omnipotence of God. He argued that just as a lion's power can be checked by man, God's will, too, can be contravened by the pagan gods — *Maharsha*.] R' Yehoshua replied, "The allegory does not refer to that kind of lion, but to the fearsome lion from the forest of Bei Ila'i." The emperor said, "I would like you to show it to me." Answered the Sage, "You could never behold it." Hadrian persisted, so R' Yehoshua interceded with Heaven, and the lion set out from its place, progressing toward Rome. When it reached a distance of four hundred *parsah* it let out one roar, at which all the pregnant women miscarried, and the walls of Rome fell. At a distance of three hundred *parsah,* it roared once again, shaking out all the men's teeth, and toppling the emperor himself from his throne to the ground. Hadrian pleaded with R' Yehoshua, "Please pray for mercy, and have it return to its place." R' Yehoshua complied, sending the beast back to its place (*Chullin* 59b).

———— ৺৶ ————

✍ *A repast for God*

The Emperor proposed to R' Yehoshua ben Chananiah, "I would like to prepare a banquet for your God." [Hadrian thus indicated his denial of God's incorporeality — *Maharsha.*] R' Yehoshua replied, "You could not possibly do it." "Why not?" "Because His retinue is too large." But Hadrian insisted, so the Sage instructed, "Go and prepare a feast on the bank of the river Rabisa, where there is ample space for His many retainers. Hadrian labored throughout the six summer months to make the arrangements, and a wind came along, sweeping it all into the sea. He repeated the effort throughout the six winter months, and then came a rainstorm, washing it all out to sea. The emperor returned to R' Yehoshua, and asked, "What is the meaning of this?" Answered the Sage, "The gusts of wind were the attendants charged with sweeping the floors, and the rains were the servants who moisten the ground so as to hold down the dust. Those two companies alone have completely consumed all the food you have prepared." Hadrian concluded, "If His legions are truly so vast, then I am not capable of accommodating them" (ibid. 60a).

III. THE CENTRAL IMPORTANCE OF FAITH

✍ *A prerequisite for receiving the Torah*

 ou shall not recognize other gods before Me. Why was this said? Because it was previously said, *I am Hashem, your God.* An analogy can be drawn to a human king who, upon his entry into a new province, was petitioned by his subjects, "Decree laws for us to obey!" He replied, "Only when the populace acknowledges my sovereignty, will I agree to issue any decrees, for if they will not acknowledge my rule, they will surely not abide by my laws." In this fashion God appeared to Israel and said, *I am Hashem, your God …* Do you acknowledge that I am the One Whose sovereignty you accepted in Egypt? "Yes," came the reply. "If so," God continued, "You have accepted My rule;

now accept My decree: *You shall not recognize other gods before Me"* (*Mechilta, Yisro*).

———— ✌ ————

✍ *The core of the mitzvos*

R' Simlai expounded: Six hundred and thirteen mitzvos were communicated to Moshe Rabbeinu … David came along and summed them up in eleven … Yeshayah arose and summed them up in six … Michah later reduced that number to three … Yeshayah reconsidered and condensed the mitzvos into two … and then along came Chavakuk (2:4), who summed them all up in just one: *The righteous lives by his faith* (*Makkos,* 24a; *Tanchuma, Shoftim* §9).

———— ✌ ————

✍ *Branches of faith*

All the mitzvos are appendages that are designed as expressions of the secret of faith (*Zohar* II, 165b; cf. ibid. 162b).

———— ✌ ————

✍ *Expansive embrace*

To *know that Hashem, He is the God* (*Devarim* 4:35). This is the essence of the entire secret of faith, the sum of the Torah, and of what is above and below (*Zohar* II, 161b; cf. *Rai'a Meheimna,* ibid. 25a).

IV. THE FRUITS OF FAITH

✍ *Reaping its benefits*

 reat is the power of the faith that Israel has in the One Who decreed the world into existence. In reward for this faith, the Divine Inspiration rested upon them as they sang the Song at the Sea, in accord with the verse (*Shemos* 14:31-15:1), *They had faith in God, and in Moshe, His servant. Then Moshe and the Children of Israel sang this song to God …*

———— ✌ ————

⮑ Avraham

Our forefather Avraham inherited this world, as well as the next, only in the merit of his faith in God; it is thus written (*Bereishis* 15:6), *[Avram] believed in God, and He counted it for him as righteousness.*

—— ⛬ ——

⮑ The Exodus

It was in the merit of the Jews' faith that they were redeemed from Egypt, as it is said (*Shemos* 4:31), *And the people believed;* And (*Tehillim* 31:24): *God safeguards the faithful.*

—— ⛬ ——

⮑ Prayer

When praying to God, it is advantageous to cite the faith of our ancestors, as we find (*Shemos* 17:12): *Aharon and Chur supported [Moshe Rabbeinu's] hands … and his hands remained faithful until the sun set.* This is an indication that Moshe Rabbeinu recalled in his prayers the faithfulness of the Forefathers.

—— ⛬ ——

⮑ Access to God

This is the gate of God; the righteous shall enter through it (*Tehillim* 118:20). Which of the righteous may enter? The stalwarts of faith, as is evident from the following verse (*Yeshayah* 26:2): *Open the gates, so the righteous nation, guardian of faith, may enter!*

—— ⛬ ——

⮑ Song of the future

It is good to thank God, and to sing praise to Your Name … to relate Your kindness in the morning and Your faith in the nights … For You have gladdened me, God, with Your deeds; at the work of Your hands I sing glad song (*Tehillim* 92:2-3,6). Only as a result of the "faith in the nights," the faith of our ancestors in the dark night of this world, did we earn our place in the "morning" of the World to Come, to join in "glad song" as we behold "the work of God's hands."

—— ⛬ ——

⮑ Success in battle

The king Yehoshaphat exhorted his people [as they marched out to war] (*Divrei HaYamim* II, 20:20), *Have faith in Hashem, your God, and show yourselves loyal; have faith in the prophets and be successful.*

—— ⛬ ——

⮑ Return of the diaspora

It is only in reward for Israel's faith that the in-gathering of the exiles will occur, as it is written (*Shir HaShirim* 4:8), *With Me will you be exiled from Levanon [the Temple], O bride, with Me from Levanon until you return; you will then behold the fruits of your faith … Also (Hoshea 2:21): I will betroth you to Me forever; and I will betroth you to Me [on account of your] faith* (*Mechilta, Beshalach; Tanchuma* ibid. §10; cf. *Shemos Rabbah* 22:3, 23:5).

—— ⛬ ——

⮑ Redemption — past and future

In reward for the fear that our saintly ancestors Avraham, Yitzchak and Yaakov had of God, and in reward for the faith that Israel had in their Creator while still in Egypt, they were redeemed from Egypt, and the Sea was split for their sake. The same is true of the future: God will come and retrieve Israel from among the nations, and He will bring the era of Mashiach and the era of redemption (*Tanna D'vei Eliyahu Rabbah* 25:11).

—— ⛬ ——

⮑ Immortality

God said to Israel: If you would have fulfilled the injunction, *I am Hashem, your God,* then you would have remained immortal, as it is said (*Tehillim* 82:6), *I said, 'You are angelic, sons of the Most High are you all.'* But now that you have transgressed it [through the worship of the Golden Calf] you will be subject, instead, to the latter words of the verse (ibid. 7): *But like men you shall die* (*Tanna D'vei Eliyahu Rabbah* 26:3; cf. *Avodah Zarah* 5a).

———— ᴣᴘ ————

❧ *Pillar of the universe*

Rav Huna prefaced his discourse with the following teaching in the name of Rav Acha: The verse states (*Tehillim* 75:4): *The earth and all its inhabitants are melting, but I* (אנכי) *have firmly established its pillars forever.* The world would have been destroyed, but, in the merit of Israel's acceptance of the commandment, אנכי ה' אלקיך, I stabilized forever the pillars of the world (*Bereishis Rabbah* 66:2; *Shir HaShirim Rabbah* 1:15, 7:1; *Pesikta Rabbasi* 21:21; et al).

———— ᴣᴘ ————

❧ *Levels of faith*

The Sages taught: Yisro gave legitimacy to the pagan deities, as it is said (*Shemos* 18:11),

Hashem is greater than all the gods (implying that the gods are great, only Hashem is yet greater). Naaman acknowledged God's majesty, but incompletely, for he declared (*Melachim* II, 5:15), *Now I know that there is no god anywhere on earth, except in Israel.* (He conceded God's dominion over the earth, but not over the Heavens.) Rachab went further, placing God in Heaven and earth, as she avowed (*Yehoshua* 2:11), *For Hashem, your God, He is God in the Heavens above and on the earth below.* Moshe Rabbeinu, however, proclaimed the entire expanse of the universe as His exclusive domain, for he called on his people to *know this day and take to your heart that Hashem, He is the God, in Heaven above and on the earth below — there is none other* (*Devarim* 4:39). R' Oshaya taught: In response, God declared (*Mishlei* 31:31), *Give her* (i.e. Moshe Rabbeinu) *the fruits of her hands.* You attested on My behalf that there exists none besides Me; in like manner I will attest about you (*Devarim* 34:10), *Never again has there arisen in Israel a prophet like Moshe Rabbeinu* (*Devarim Rabbah* 2:28; cf. *Mechilta,* beginning of *Yisro; Medrash Shmuel* §9; *Yalkut Shimoni, Yisro* §269, *Yehoshua* §10).

IS BELIEF IN HASHEM ONE OF THE 613 COMMANDMENTS?

lthough *Rambam* (*Sefer HaMitzvos, Aseh* §1), *Chinuch* (§25) and others count the requirement to believe in Hashem as one of the 613 commandments, many others do not include it in their list of the 613 (see *Bahag, R' Saadiah Gaon, R' Eliyahu HaZakein, R' Y. Albargeloni, Yere'im, Zohar HaRakia*).

A. *Reasons why belief in Hashem should not be counted as one of the 613 commandments.*

Several approaches have been suggested to explain why belief in Hashem should not be counted as one of the 613 commandments.

1. ***The verse does not embody a commandment, but rather is a statement of fact.***

The verse, *I am Hashem, your God*, was not intended as a commandment, but as a statement of fact. The Torah refers to Hashem's sovereignty at the beginning of the Ten Commandments because it is the prerequisite to the commandments that follow. Our obligation to fulfill Hashem's decrees is derived from the fact that He is our sovereign (*Hasagos HaRamban* to *Sefer HaMitzvos, Aseh* §1). [It should be noted that *Ramban* himself maintains that belief in Hashem *is* one of the 613 commandments;

see *Hasagos HaRamban, Lo Saaseh* §5.] The fact that this statement was not issued in the imperative form (e.g. "*Know* that I am Hashem your God," or, "*Accept* that I am Hashem your God") supports the contention that it is not intended as a commandment, but as an *introduction* to the Ten Commandments (see *Lev Same'ach* to *Sefer HaMitzvos* ibid. ד״ה ומ״מ).

2. ***The obligation to believe in Hashem is the basis for all the other commandments.***

Even if this statement was intended as a commandment to accept Hashem's sovereignty and not merely as a statement of fact, it cannot be counted as one of the 613 commandments. The 613 commandments are expressions of Hashem's will; the fundamental obligation to *heed* His will derives from our acceptance of His sovereignty. Without an obligation to accept Hashem's authority, there can be no obligation to fulfill His commands. Belief in Hashem and acceptance of His sovereignty, then, is the prerequisite of the obligation to observe all the other commandments. The fundamental nature of the commandment of believing in Hashem places it in a separate category from the other commandments; it cannot be counted as one of the 613, for it is the very *foundation* of all the commandments (*Ramban* ibid.; see also *R' Chisdai Crescas, Sefer Or Hashem*, cited in

מפתח למוני המצוות

THE COUNT OF THE MITZVAH

Baal Halachos Gedolos / —
— / בה״ג

R' Saadiah Gaon / —
— / רס״ג

R' Eliyahu HaZakein / —
— / ר׳ אליהו הזקן

Rashbag / —
— / רשב״ג

R' Yitzchak El-Bargeloni / Asin 1
ר״י אלברג׳לוני / עשין א

Maamar HaSechel / Dibbur Rishon 1
מאמר השכל / דיבור ראשון א

Sefer Yere'im / —
— / יראים

Rambam, Sefer HaMitzvos / Aseh 1
רמב״ם / עשה א

Sefer Mitzvos Gadol (Smag) / Aseh 1
סמ״ג / עשה א

Sefer Mitzvos Katan (Smak) / 1
סמ״ק / א

Zohar HaRakia / —
— / זוהר הרקיע

Tefillah L'Moshe to *Tehillim* 62:12; *Zohar HaRakia* §11).

3. The obligation to believe in Hashem is counted together with the commandment to recite the Shema.

The essence of this commandment is to accept Hashem's sovereignty as the One and Only God. This concept is embodied in the first verse of the *Shema*, which states: *Hear, O Israel, Hashem is our God, Hashem is the One and Only* (*Devarim* 6:4). The Torah requires us not only to accept Hashem's sovereignty in our hearts, but to make a verbal declaration to that effect; hence, the commandment to recite the *Shema* twice daily (*mitzvah #420*). The recitation of the *Shema*, then, is the means by which we fulfill the obligation to believe in Hashem. Therefore, these two commandments — the mitzvah to believe in Hashem and the mitzvah to recite the *Shema* — are counted as only one of the 613 (*Commentary of R' Yeruchem Fishel Perla* to *Sefer HaMitzvos L'Rasag, Aseh* §3-4).

4. One cannot be commanded to believe.

Only those commandments whose fulfillment depends on choice are included in the count of 613. Belief, however, is not a matter of choice. One cannot *choose* to believe in Hashem; one either believes in Hashem or he does not. Therefore, the commandment of belief is not counted as one of the 613 commandments (*R' Chisdai Crescas*, ibid.).

B. Possible proofs to each side of this question:

1. The Gemara in *Makkos* (23b-24a) states: Rav Simlai expounded: Six hundred and thirteen commandments were related to Moshe … Rav Hamnuna said: Which verse [teaches this] (i.e. what is the Scriptural source for the concept of 613 commandments)? *Moshe commanded us the Torah as a heritage* (*Devarim* 33:4). The numerical value [גמטריא, *gematria*] of the word "Torah" [תורה] is six hundred and eleven. [Thus, the verse teaches that Moshe transmitted 611 commandments.] The passages, *I am Hashem, your God* etc., and, *You shall not recognize other gods before Me* etc. were heard directly from Hashem [and these passages account for two additional commandments, for a total of 613]. This Gemara seems to clearly state that the verse, *I am Hashem, your God*, the source of the obligation to believe in Hashem, is counted as one of the 613 commandments, one of two the Jews received directly from Hashem.

However, some explain that the Gemara does not mean that the passage of *I am Hashem, your God* contains a commandment. The Gemara merely states that two of the 613 commandments are contained in the passages the Jews heard directly from Hashem. In fact, though, both are contained in the passage *You shall not recognize other gods before Me*, etc. This passage is also the source for the prohibition against making idols (*mitzvah #27*) and the prohibition against worshipping idols (*mitzvah #28*). The passage of *I am Hashem, your God* etc., however, contains no commandment (*Hasagos HaRamban* ibid.; see, however, *Megillas Esther* there, who rejects *Ramban's* explanation).

2. Elsewhere, the Gemara would seem to imply that the obligation to believe in Hashem is *not* counted as a mitzvah. The Gemara in *Horayos* (8b) states that the first commandment stated to the Jews was the commandment related to idol worship. This is an apparent reference to the passage of *You shall not recognize other gods before Me* in the Ten Commandments,

which is the source for the prohibition against idol worship (see *Rashi* there ד"ה למן היום, see, however, *Be'er Sheva, Horayos* ibid. who interprets the Gemara as referring to the prohibition against idol worship that was given to Adam [see *Sanhedrin* 56b]; see also *Seder Mishnah, Hil. Yesodei HaTorah* 1:6:3). Evidently, the Gemara does not consider belief in Hashem to be a commandment; otherwise, it would have counted that commandment as the first of the Ten Commandments, for the passage, *I am Hashem, your God*, is written before the passage of *You shall not recognize other gods before Me* (*Zohar HaRakia* ibid.; see also *Teshuvos Tashbetz*, I:139).

However, some reject this proof, pointing out that *Rashi* explains that the Gemara refers to the passage of *I am Hashem, your God* as well as the passage of *You shall not recognize other gods before Me*. The obligation to believe in Hashem is also defined as a commandment related to idol worship, for belief in Hashem is the antithesis of idol worship (see *Lev Same'ach* ibid.; *Eshel Avraham* to *Hasagos HaRamban, Sefer HaMitzvos, Aseh* §1; for a different explanation as to why that Gemara does not prove that belief in Hashem is *not* a commandment, see *Rosh Amanah* ch. 18 and *Chidushei Mahardam* to *Sefer HaMitzvos* ibid.).

Mitzvah 26

אִסוּר הָאֱמוּנָה בֶּאֱלוֹהוּת אַחֶרֶת מִלְבַד הַשֵׁם

פרשת יתרו

NOT TO ATTRIBUTE DIVINITY TO ANY ENTITY OTHER THAN HASHEM

THE MITZVAH:

MITZVAH 26

אִסוּר הָאֱמוּנָה בֶּאֱלוֹהוּת אַחֶרֶת מִלְבַד הַשֵּׁם (לֹא תַּעֲשֶׂה)

NOT TO ATTRIBUTE DIVINITY TO ANY ENTITY OTHER THAN HASHEM

מצוה כו

SOURCE

לֹא יִהְיֶה לְךָ אֱלֹהִים אֲחֵרִים עַל פָּנָי שמות (פרשת יתרו) כ:ג

"You shall not recognize other gods before Me"

▰▰ THE MITZVAH ▰▰

We are forbidden to believe that another "god" (eloha) exists aside from Hashem.

▰▰ LAWS ▰▰

1 This prohibition is violated simply by *believing* that another god exists.[1] If one acts upon such a belief and actively *serves* the imagined god, then, depending on the manner of his service, he violates either *mitzvah #28*,[2] *mitzvah #29*,[3] or both.[4]

2 The definition of a "god" in this context is an entity which possesses, at minimum, the free will to make independent choices and the governing power to implement them.[5]

3 One violates this prohibition even if one believes that Hashem has ultimate authority over that which one believes is a god.[6]

4 This prohibition is one of six mitzvos that are incumbent upon a Jew every moment of his life.[7]

5 This mitzvah applies to both men and women, in all places and at all times.[8]

6 One who believes in the existence of another god rejects the fundamental tenet of Judaism (*kofer ba' ikkar*) upon which all else hinges.[9] He is not, however, punishable by human courts.[10]

NOTE: One who maintains that Hashem Himself is a compound entity (i.e. consists of different parts or aspects), violates *mitzvah #417, To know that Hashem is One.*[11]

▰▰ A REASON ▰▰

It is only possible to remain faithful to the Torah when one recognizes Hashem as the sole God of the world. Once one believes other gods exist, one becomes obliged to obey their wishes as well, inevitably at the expense of Torah observance.

1. *Rambam* distinguishes between the present mitzvah, which prohibits the mere *belief* in the existence of another god, and *mitzvos #28* (*You shall not bow to them*) and *#29* (*nor shall you serve them*), which prohibit actually *worshipping* the imagined god (see *Sefer HaMitzvos, Lo Saaseh* §1, 5, and 6; *Hil. Yesodei HaTorah* 1:6 and *Hil. Avodah Zarah* 3:2-3). Some commentators explain that the language of the verse itself implies that it prohibits belief exclusively; the phrase לא יהיה לך — which we have translated *You shall not recognize*, but which literally means *There shall not exist **for** you* — suggests that the object of the prohibition is something reserved for *oneself*, namely an unexpressed belief (*Beurei Maharshal* to *Smag, Lo Saaseh* §1; *Or HaChaim* to *Shemos* 20:3; see *Medrash HaGadol* to *Devarim* 5:7). Of such unspoken heresies the prophet said (*Yechezkel* 14:5): *Thereby the House of Israel shall be seized for [the thoughts of] their hearts* (*Or HaChaim* ibid.; see *Kiddushin* 39b with *Rashi* ד"ה למען and *Meiri*; cf. *Rosh* to *Rosh Hashanah* 1:5, who understands the passage in *Kiddushin* differently).

According to *Ramban* (*Sefer HaMitzvos, Lo Saaseh* §5; *Shemos* 20:3), however, the commandment not to *"recognize other gods"* does not pertain to mere belief that another god exists, but rather to outward *acknowledgment* of such a god by active worship or by a verbal declaration of fidelity. Moreover, and unlike *Rambam*, *Ramban* holds that there are no additional mitzvos forbidding various modes of idol worship. Rather, *You shall not recognize,* etc. is a general prohibition against all forms of idol worship, whether by verbally accepting the entity upon oneself as a god [מקבל עליו באלוה] (saying, *You are my god* to the idol; see *mitzvah #28*), or

AN EXPANDED TREATMENT

by performing a service for the idol. The entire passage, from לא יהיה לך in verse 3 through verse 6, and including verse 5 (*You shall not bow to them, nor shall you serve them, etc.*), is thus a single commandment in his view. *Sefer HaChinuch* defines the present mitzvah according to *Rambam* (*not to* **believe** *in any god other than Hashem*), yet proceeds in his treatment of it to elaborate the laws regarding active idol worship, apparently following *Ramban*. See also *Sefer HaChinuch* to mitzvah #28, and his conclusion to mitzvah #29.

A third opinion interprets לא יהיה לך אלהים אחרים to mean, *You shall not* **have** *other gods*, i.e. idols. Accordingly, this specific verse serves to prohibit not belief in other gods, nor active idol worship, but rather *possession* of an idol [which most Rishonim include under mitzvah #27; see our treatment there] (*R' Saadiah Gaon, Lo Saaseh* §1 with the commentary of *R' Yerucham Fishel Perla* ad loc.; *Smak* §61; see *Mechilta DeRashbi* to *Shemos* 20:3; *Vayikra Rabbah* 24:5; see also *Sifra, Kedoshim* 1:12; *Zohar HaRakia, Lo Saaseh* §7; *Yereim HaShalem* §243; *Smag, Lo Saaseh* §1). According to this opinion, the prohibition against belief in other gods would have to be derived from a different source. One such source is the verse, *You shall not make with Me gods* (idols) *of silver* (*Shemos* 20:20), which can be taken to mean that we may not believe in any additional divinity together with Hashem, the one true Divinity (*R' Saadiah Gaon*, quoted by *R' Avraham ben HaRambam* in his commentary to *Shemos*, and cited in *Otzar HaGeonim* to *Sandhedrin* 63a).

2. Not to serve an *avodah zarah* in one of the ways that Hashem is served in the *Beis HaMikdash*. See our treatment of *mitzvah #28*.

3. Not to serve an *avodah zarah* in the manner practiced by its devotees, or to display reverence for an *avodah zarah*. See our treatment of *mitzvah #29*.

4. If a particular *avodah zarah* is customarily served in a manner that parallels one of the services performed in the *Beis HaMikdash*, then a worshipper who performs that service for that *avodah zarah* violates both *mitzvah #28* and *mitzvah #29*.

5. This basic definition has been gleaned from the statements of various Rishonim (cited in this note), none of whom deal directly with the question of what makes something a "god" vis-a-vis this prohibition. The verse itself forbids specifically the belief in the existence of other **elohim,** a word which implies authority, power and control (see *Rashi* on *Bereishis* 6:2; *Peirush, Hil. Yesodei HaTorah* ibid.; *Kuzari,* beginning of *Maamar* §4; see also *Rambam, Commentary to the Mishnah, Sanhedrin* 10:1, fifth principle, which states that it is not worth serving any entity other than Hashem, because no other entity possesses *free will* [אין משפט ולא בחירה אלא לו לבדו השי"י]; see *Rivash* cited by *Kessef Mishneh, Hil. Avodah Zarah* 3:6 regarding idolaters' false belief that their gods can independently harm or benefit humans [יש לה כח להרע או להטיב], and *Meiri* to *Sanhedrin* 61b, who cites the misconception that idols can respond to prayers; see also *Ran* to *Sanhedrin* ibid. and *Ramban* to *Shemos* 20:3).

6. We are forbidden to believe not only that Hashem's sovereignty is shared, but even that as Lord Most High (*Bereishis* 14:20), He delegates independent control to subordinate deities (*Sefer HaChinuch* §26; *Beur Halachah, Orach Chaim* §1 ד"ה הוא כלל גדול; see also *Sforno, Shemos* 20:3 and *Sefer HaIkkarim* 3:18) [For example, we may not believe that Hashem is comparable to the chief of staff in an army, who is the supreme commander, but who has generals and officers serving under him, all of whom have the freedom to make independent choices and implement them within their own designated area of command].

There are in truth *no* supernatural entities independent in the slightest degree from Hashem. Even angels are mere agents compelled to perform no more and no less than the exact tasks that Hashem appoints for them (*Rambam, Commentary to the Mishnah*, ibid.; *Hil. Avodah Zarah* 2:1; *Ramban* to *Shemos* 20:3; see also *Sefer HaIkkarim* 2:28. cf. *R' Sherira Gaon, Teshuvas HaGeonim Harkavy* §373, and *Or Hashem* II, 2:1, who maintain that angels possess a measure of autonomy — they may sometimes choose how best to fulfill a particular mission, but cannot overstep the parameters of the mission; see the references cited in *Shome'a Tefillah* p. 285; see also *Moreh Nevuchim* 2:7 for a similar approach. All agree, however, that no angel can ever independently harm or benefit a person, so that even according to *R' Sherira* et al. angels are not truly autonomous, and certainly do not in any way diminish Hashem's absolute dominion).

Because Hashem does not relegate His authority, but rather holds our lives and destinies in His own hands, as it were, it is both pointless and forbidden to pray to angels, or even to petition them to mediate between ourselves and Hashem by supplicating Him on our behalf. Rather, we must turn our hearts and prayers directly to Hashem (*Commentary to the Mishnah* ibid.; *Hil. Avodah Zarah* 2:1; *Sefer HaIkkarim* 3:18; *Rosh Amanah* §12, ד"ה ועל הספק השני; see *Sanhedrin* 38b and *Yerushalmi Berachos* 9:1).

MITZVAH 26

אִסּוּר הָאֱמוּנָה בֶּאֱלֹהוּת
אַחֶרֶת מִלְּבַד הַשֵּׁם (לֹא תַעֲשֶׂה)

NOT TO ATTRIBUTE DIVINITY TO ANY ENTITY OTHER THAN HASHEM

מצוה כו

SOURCE

לֹא יִהְיֶה לְךָ אֱלֹהִים אֲחֵרִים עַל פָּנַי שמות (פרשת יתרו) כ:ג

"You shall not recognize other gods before Me"

THE MITZVAH

We are forbidden to believe that another "god" (eloha) exists aside from Hashem.

LAWS

1 This prohibition is violated simply by *believing* that another god exists.[1] If one acts upon such a belief and actively *serves* the imagined god, then, depending on the manner of his service, he violates either *mitzvah #28*,[2] *mitzvah #29*,[3] or both.[4]

2 The definition of a "god" in this context is an entity which possesses, at minimum, the free will to make independent choices and the governing power to implement them.[5]

3 One violates this prohibition even if one believes that Hashem has ultimate authority over that which one believes is a god.[6]

4 This prohibition is one of six mitzvos that are incumbent upon a Jew every moment of his life.[7]

5 This mitzvah applies to both men and women, in all places and at all times.[8]

6 One who believes in the existence of another god rejects the fundamental tenet of Judaism (*kofer ba'ikkar*) upon which all else hinges.[9] He is not, however, punishable by human courts.[10]

NOTE: One who maintains that Hashem Himself is a compound entity (i.e. consists of different parts or aspects), violates *mitzvah #417, To know that Hashem is One.*[11]

A REASON

It is only possible to remain faithful to the Torah when one recognizes Hashem as the sole God of the world. Once one believes other gods exist, one becomes obliged to obey their wishes as well, inevitably at the expense of Torah observance.

For a discussion regarding certain liturgical poems and prayers that are seemingly addressed to angels, see *Iyunim* §1.

7. There are six mitzvos that are not dependent on any particular time, place or circumstance (unlike, for example, *mitzvah #325, to live in a succah*, which applies only during the Succos festival, or *mitzvah #588, to pay a worker on the same day [that he completes his work]*, that is never incurred unless one hires an employee), and which require no tools other than one's own consciousness. They are incumbent upon a person always (see *Sefer HaChinuch, Hakdamah*). The six, known as the *mitzvos temidios* ("perpetual commandments") are:

Mitzvah #25: To know that Hashem exists.

Mitzvah #26: Not to believe that another god exists aside from Hashem.

Mitzvah #417: To know that Hashem is One.

Mitzvah #418: To love Hashem.

Mitzvah #432: To fear Hashem.

Mitzvah #387: Not to be led astray by one's thoughts or eyes.

(*Sefer HaChinuch*, end of *Seder U'Minyan HaMitzvos* and the final paragraphs of *mitzvos #25, #417, #418* and *#432*; see *Beur Halachah* §1, ד"ה הוא כלל גדול).

8. *Sefer HaChinuch* §26. A Mishnah in *Kiddushin* 29a teaches that all the prohibitions of the Torah (excepting two specified there) apply equally to men and women.

9. *Hil. Yesodei HaTorah* 1:6; *Charedim* 21:1; see also *Sefer HaChinuch* ibid.

Rambam's language (ibid.) is "whoever believes that there is another god (*eloha*) aside from Hashem ... denies the *fundamental tenet* (כופר בעיקר), for *this* is the great fundamental tenet (עיקר הגדול) upon which all else hinges." [This implies that the fundamental tenet being rejected here is the belief that Hashem is the only God, an assertion supported by the fact that *Rambam* refers to that belief elsewhere (*Hil. Avodah Zarah* 1:3) using the same term: "[Avraham] began ... to teach [all the people] *that there is one God* (E-l-o-h-a) for the entire universe ... and he implanted this *great fundamental tenet* (עיקר הגדול) into their minds ..."] (cf. *Peirush, Yesodei HaTorah* 1:6; see *Sanhedrin* 38b, where the term

כופר בעיקר is applied to worshipping false gods, and the same is true in *Hil. Avodas Kochavim* 2:6; see also *HaEmunos VehaDei'os* §2, where *R' Saadiah Gaon* demonstrates at length that belief in a multitude of gods is incompatible with belief in a sovereign omnipotent Creator; in a similar vein, the Sages state: "Whoever acknowledges a false god denies the entire Torah" [*Sifri* to *Devarim* §54; see *Sifri* to *Bamidbar* §111. *Rambam, Hil. Avodah Zarah* 2:4 cites both passages from *Sifri* combined as a single statement; cf. *Sefer HaIkkarim* 1:14]).

10. As explained above (Law 1 and note 1), the present mitzvah is violated by thought rather than by action, and thoughts are never subject to retribution at human hands (*Minchas Chinuch* ד"ה שלא; see also *Sefer HaChinuch* §387; cf. *Rambam Hil. Avodah Zarah* 2:3). However, there is punishment inflicted from Heaven (*Minchas Chinuch* ibid.). If the heretic puts his belief into practice and serves the imagined god, then he is liable to execution, as detailed under *mitzvos* #28 and #29.

Due to the severity attached to any conception of multiple gods, the Sages prohibited the seemingly innocent repetition of certain expressions in prayer, lest one seem to be addressing two different divinities. For example, we are forbidden to say *modim anachnu lach* (we acknowledge You) twice in succession during the *Shemoneh Esrei* or its repetition, even though in doing so we mean to address Hashem alone (see *Berachos* 33b; *Rambam, Hil. Tefilah* 9:4; *Tur* and *Shulchan Aruch, Orach Chaim* 121:2). Similarly, when reciting the *Shema*, a person may not say *shema, shema* (hear, hear), lest he appear to be declaring allegiance to multiple entities (*Berachos* ibid.; *Rambam, Hil. Krias Shema* 2:11; *Tur* and *Shulchan Aruch, Orach Chaim* 61:9). [Authorities dispute whether the prohibition is to

repeat the single words *modim* or *shema*, or to repeat the entire clause *modim anachnu lach* and the entire verse *Shema Yisrael,* etc. (see *Rashi* ad loc. ד"ה מילתא and *Tosafos* ad loc. 34a ד"ה אמר פסוקא).]

Furthermore, some maintain that it is forbidden to respond *"Amen, Amen"* upon hearing a blessing, for that repetition too may appear to refer to two gods (*Sefer Ohel Moed*, cited in *Beis Yosef, Orach Chaim* §61; *Rama, Orach Chaim* 61:12; see *Yerushalmi, Megillah* 4:10 and *Beur HaGra, Orach Chaim* 61:22). Others hold, however, that one may respond *Amen, Amen*, citing as evidence the verse (*Tehillim* 89:53): *Blessed is Hashem forever, Amen and Amen* (*Beis Yosef* loc. cit.; *Magen Avraham* 61:10). [For a justification of the custom to repeat *Hashem hu HaElohim* (Hashem is the Lord) seven times following the *Ne'ilah* prayer that closes the Yom Kippur service, see *Tosafos* and *Shulchan Aruch Orach Chaim* loc. cit.; see also *Taz, Orach Chaim* 61:4 regarding the repetition of *baruch shem kevod,* etc. (Blessed is the Name of the Glory of His majesty forever and ever), also during *Ne'ilah*.]

11. That mitzvah is derived from the verse: *Hear O Israel, Hashem is our God, Hashem is One!* (*Devarim* 6:4). [From *Hil. Yesodei HaTorah* 1:6-7, the following distinction seems to emerge between the present prohibition, *Do not recognize other gods,* etc., and *mitzvah* #417, *To know that Hashem is One.* *Mitzvah* #417 speaks of the Entity Who *Rambam* calls the *manhig* (controller or guide), the God on High Who sustains the cosmos and directs the stars and planets in their revolutions. One violates this mitzvah by believing that rather than being directed by Hashem alone, the cosmos is controlled by a partnership (if one imagines there are two gods) or a committee (if one imagines that there are three or more) of deities. It is to

this concept that *Rambam* refers when he states (ibid. 1:7): This God is One, He is not two, and not more than two … (see also, *Ramchal, Derech Hashem* 1:6). *Mitzvah* #417 thus requires us to know that Hashem, the world's single Guide, is not composed of parts or aspects, but is an absolute indivisible unity. Failure to fulfill *mitzvah* #417 is a failure to accept the second of *Rambam*'s *Thirteen Principles* (*Commentary to the Mishnah* ibid.) — the oneness of Hashem — and renders a person the second kind of *min* listed by *Rambam* in *Hil. Teshuvah* 3:7. The present mitzvah, however, speaks to those who may already accept that the universe as a whole is sustained by a single supreme God, but who may nevertheless mistakenly imagine that there can be another, lesser, deity controlling his own sector or aspect of reality. The very language of the verse, *You shall not recognize other gods before Me*, assumes a distinction already in the mind of the listener between *Me*, the supreme God, and any other imagined deity, which could only be *another* god. Belief in subordinate deities is the heresy that most idolaters subscribe to, for even while worshipping their parochial divinities, they call Hashem "God over the gods" (*Menachos* 110a). However, other Rishonim maintain that one who believes in a partnership or committee of gods violates *mitzvah* #26 as well. For further discussion, see *Commentary of R' Y. F. Perla* to *Sefer HaMitzvos L'Rasag, Aseh* §3 and §4.]

[One who attributes divinity only to a single created entity (such as the sun), so that he recognizes no more than one god, nevertheless violates *mitzvah* #26, because the entity he venerates cannot be the Creator, and is therefore by definition *another* god, a (false) deity other than the true Deity. One who knows Hashem by another name, however, violates no mitzvah].

A BROADER LOOK AT THE LAWS

1 Liturgical Requests Directed Toward Angels:

The phrasing of several liturgical poems (*piyutim*) and prayers seems to indicate that they are directed to angels, beseeching them to bring our prayers before Hashem. For example, the *Selichos* include such supplications as, "Those who bring in pleas for mercy, bring our pleas for mercy before the Master of mercy"; and "Angels of mercy, servants on High, please entreat Hashem"; and "Attribute of mercy, devolve upon us, and before your Maker cast our appeals." Many authorities have questioned such phrasing, as we are forbidden (end of note 6) to pray to angels (see *Maharal, Nesivos Olam, Nesiv HaAvodah* ch.12; *Teshuvos Chasam Sofer, Orach Chaim* §166; *Korban Nesanel, Rosh Hashanah*, end of the first chapter, §3.) Even the liturgical poem *Shalom Aleichem*, recited in virtually every Jewish household before the Friday night *kiddush*, has been called into question on account of the stanza, "Bless me with peace, angels of peace" (*barchuni leshalom malachei hashalom*; see *Siddur HaYaavetz, Hanhagas Leil Shabbos* §10 [p. 150a in the Lemberg edition]; see also *Kesser Rosh* §93, who writes that *R' Chaim of Volozhin* would omit this stanza).

Some authorities indeed suggest that it is better not to recite such poems (*Teshuvos Chasam Sofer* loc. cit.; *Korban Nesanel* loc. cit.; *Siddur HaYaavetz* loc. cit.). Others advise that the wording of such poems and prayers should be changed so that they can be read as addressing Hashem, not the angels. For example, instead of saying, "Those who bring in pleas for mercy, *bring* our pleas for mercy before the Master of mercy," which seems to address a request to the angels themselves, one should say, "Those who bring in pleas for mercy *should bring* our pleas for mercy before the Master of mercy," which is a plea addressed to Hashem, asking Him

to cause the angels to collect our prayers and present them before Him (*Maharal* loc. cit., second approach; see *Teshvos Yehudah Yaaleh, Orach Chaim* §21, in the name of *Maharam Bennet*). Other authorities offer various justifications for the problematic phrasing:

A. *Maharal* (loc. cit., first approach) suggests that the angels are adjured by Hashem to bring our prayers before Him. The liturgical poems therefore do not actually beseech the angels (as such requests are unnecessary in any event), but rather direct them to carry out their designated function (see also *Pachad Yitzchak* [Lampornati], ד״ה צרכיו).

B. *Teshuvos Mahari Bruna* (§275) suggests that these poems and prayers are not, in fact, directed toward the angels, but, rather, to Hashem. Why, then does the wording of the poems sound like a request from the angels? He explains this through a parable: When a servant is too fearful to approach the king directly, he loudly states his case to the king's councilors, so that the king may overhear the conversation and grant the petition. So too, we phrase certain prayers as if they were addressed to angels, not because we imagine that angels can fulfill our requests, but rather in the hope that *Hashem* will "overhear" our prayers and grant our requests. [See the preface to *Siddur Otzar HaTefillos* at length; see also *Rosh Amanah* ch. 12 concerning Yaakov's blessing to Menasheh and Efraim: *May the angel who redeemed me from all evil bless the youths* (*Bereishis* 48:16).]

2 Invoking Hashem and Another Entity in a Single Statement:

One may not, when speaking, juxtapose the Name of God with any other entity, even if it is clear that the speaker does not regard that other entity as a divinity. For example, it is forbidden to take an oath in the name of both Hashem and something else, or even to express gratitude to Hashem and to a person in the same sentence (see *Succah* 45b; *Tosafos* to *Sanhedrin* 63a ד"ה כל; *Rambam, Hil. Shavuos* 11:2; *Smag, Lo Saaseh* §1). For this reason, some authorities maintain that a person, in thank-ing a friend for a favor, should not say: "Hashem and you [together] did me this great favor" (*Bnei Yissaschar, Tishrei* 11:12 in the note, cited in *Darchei Teshuvah, Yoreh Deah* 147:17).

שיח הלכה SITUATIONS IN HALACHAH

Question:
Is it proper to pray at the gravesite of a deceased *tzaddik*?

Answer:
There are several reasons why prayers that are uttered at a *tzaddik's* final resting place are more readily accepted:

A. The gravesite of a *tzaddik* is sacred, and prayers uttered in a sacred place are more readily accepted (*Maharil, Hil. Rosh Hashanah* §63).

B. The merit of a *tzaddik* lends support to one who prays at his gravesite, and this facilitates the acceptance of his prayers (see *Levush*, end of §579; *Maavar Yabok*; *Imrei Noam* §41).

C. Divine blessing flows down to the world in the merit of *tzaddikim*, and this continues to be the case even after they pass away. By praying at the *tzaddik's* gravesite, one may more easily tap into that flow (*Derashos HaRan* §8 ד"ה ויראה לי עוד).

A verse in the Torah may be adduced as the source of the practice of praying at the gravesite of a *tzaddik* (*Bamidbar* 13:22; see *Rashi* ad loc.): *And they* [the spies (*meraglim*) sent by the *Bnei Yisrael* to scout out Eretz Yisrael] *came up through the Negev, and they came to Chevron*. The Gemara (*Sotah* 34b) explains that the verse means that Calev the son of Yefuneh went to the tomb of the Patriarchs in Chevron, to pray that he be saved from the evil counsel of the spies. Thus, we see that as early as the time of the Exodus from Mitzrayim, it was customary to go to the graves of *tzaddikim* to pray. [Other sources may be adduced as well (e.g. *Taanis* 16a and *Rashi* to *Bereishis* 48:7); see, however, *Iggeres HaGra*, who discourages visits to cemeteries.]

Question:
Is it permissible to make requests of the deceased in one's prayers?

Answer:
Because Hashem is unique in His capability to fulfill requests and to bestow good or to inflict evil, one may only pray to Hashem, and not to any other entity. One who does pray to any other entity is in violation of this prohibition, *You shall not recognize other gods*

before Me — which forbids attribution of Divine prerogatives to any other entity. Thus, while one may pray to Hashem at a *tzaddik's* gravesite, one may *not* direct his prayer to the *tzaddik* who is interred there — e.g. to ask the *tzaddik* to provide him with salvation. Such prayer would indicate that the person who is praying believes that another entity possesses divine power (*Maharil, Hil. Taanis* §18).

[Aside from the prohibition of *You shall not recognize other gods before Me*, a person who prays to a deceased person may also be in violation of the prohibition of seeking communication with the dead (see *mitzvah #515*).]

Question:

May one ask the deceased to serve as an advocate before Hashem?

Answer:

According to some authorities, not only is it forbidden to request salvation from the deceased, but it is even forbidden to ask the deceased person to transmit prayers uttered at his gravesite to Hashem. Moreover, these authorities maintain that it is even forbidden to ask the deceased to serve as one's advocate before the Heavenly Tribunal. Thus, when a person prays at a gravesite, he may not address the deceased at all. The person may only supplicate Hashem and ask that his prayers be accepted and salvation granted in the merit of the *tzaddik* buried there (see *Pri Megaddim, Orach Chaim* 581:16; *Mishnah Berurah* 581:27 and *Chayei Adam* §138).

However, several Talmudic sources seem to indicate that it is even permissible to make requests of the deceased (*Taanis* 23b, concerning R' Mani; *Chagigah* 22b, concerning R' Yehoshua; *Berachos* 18b, concerning Zeiri, et al.). Indeed, in the case of Calev (cited above), he is said to have prayed as he stood before the tomb of the Patriarchs: "My Fathers, supplicate on my behalf that I should be saved from the [evil] counsel of the spies."

Accordingly, some authorities maintain that it is permissible to ask the deceased to serve as one's advocate before the Heavenly Tribunal. They explain that this type of request does not violate the prohibition of *You shall not recognize other gods before Me*, because it does not indicate a belief that the deceased is capable of granting the request. On the contrary, asking the deceased to serve merely as an advocate before Hashem indicates that one believes that the deceased is *not* capable of granting a request. Accordingly, it is only forbidden to request salvation directly from the deceased (see *Pri Megadim* loc. cit; *Teshuvos Minchas Elazar, Orach Chaim* §68 at length; and *Gesher HaChaim* 2:26). [With regard to prayers that appear to be directed at angels, see *Iyunim* §1.]

Teshuvos Maharam Schik (*Orach Chaim* §293) suggests how one may enlist either a live or a deceased *tzaddik* to serve as one's advocate. The proper manner in which to do so is by describing one's troubles to the *tzaddik*. The *tzaddik* (whether alive or deceased), sensing the anguish of the person and feeling his pain, suffers together with that person, and *on his own initiative* supplicates Hashem on behalf of the suffering person. Hashem, in turn, in order to alleviate the suffering of the *tzaddik*, removes the troubles of the person who came to the *tzaddik*. [For evidence that R' Chaim of Volozhin held it permissible to make requests of deceased *tzaddikim,* see *Siddur Otzar HaTefillos, Mavo*, ch. 3; for further explanation of the efficacy of a (live) *tzaddik's* prayer on someone else's behalf, see *Teshuvos Chasam Sofer, Orach Chaim* §166.]

ILLUMINATIONS OF THE MITZVAH
Suggested Reasons & Insights

I. "THERE IS NONE OTHER THAN HIM"

o complement the first commandment calling for belief in God as the Creator and Guiding Force of the world, the second commandment introduces the prohibition of idolatry, defined in this context as the belief in the existence of a deity other than God (*Smag, Lo Saaseh* §1). It is not sufficient to simply believe in God's existence; a Jew must also realize that God is the sole Master of the world, and outside of Him there is no power or moving force, and only then can one's faith in God be complete. But as long as one is persuaded that there can be a force or forces parallel to and independent of those emanating from God, he cannot be said to believe in God, because his conception of God and His role in the universe are incorrect. This is why the Sages say that *"Anochi"* and *"Lo yiheyeh lecha,"* the first two commandments, were uttered [by God] simultaneously (*Yalkut Shimoni, Yirmiyah* §266), because they are interdependent; the fulfillment of one is inconceivable without the other (*Akeidas Yitzchak, Shemos* §45).

The repudiation of "other gods" involves not only denying that any forces can exist independently of God, but also the refusal to acknowledge that they have any degree of power outside of what they draw from God. These articles of faith are corollaries of the elementary principle that "God is One," which means many things: He is the only Being that *must*, by definition, exist; He is the only Creator, the only source of existence, the only Ruler, the world's only guiding force. He alone monitors, to the last detail, everyone and everything; nothing can stand before His will; nothing can interfere with what He does, nothing can occur due to blind chance, natural law, or the influence of Heavenly bodies and forces. He alone is the Judge of the world; and all that happens is a result of His decree, whether here on earth or above in Heaven (*Daas Tevunos* §36).

Inasmuch as the mitzvah to reject other deities serves to complement the mitzvah of *emunah*, it becomes a part of the foundation of faith on which the entire body of Torah and mitzvos must rest. Unqualified acceptance of the mitzvos hinges on a fully developed belief in the Unity of God. So long as there is room in one's mind for a deity other than God, the compelling nature of the Torah is lost, for the dictates of God are bound to conflict with those of the other (*Commentary* of *Maharan Zak* to *Smag, Lo Saaseh* §1). Therefore, say *Chazal* (*Sifrei, Devarim* §54), Anyone who gives legitimacy to the worship of idols has, in effect, denied the entire Torah (*Chinuch* §26).

II. TRUST IN GOD ALONE

ncluded in this mitzvah to believe in One God to the exclusion of any other is the demand that one place his reliance uniquely and solely on that One God, in recognition of the fact that He is the sole source of life and sustenance, and that all the vicissitudes of life come about under His watchful eye and as a result of His Providence.

For this reason the commandment is worded, "לא יהיה לך **אלהים אחרים**," as the name *"Elokim,"* in reference to Hashem, denotes the Omnipotent Master of all the world's powers. A person who looks elsewhere to satisfy his needs or to achieve his ambitions gives the object of his worship the credit of being "**אלהים אחרים**," as possessing the independent ability to influence events in this world. Yes, it is true that a Jew is enjoined to invest, in the pursuit of his needs, the degree of effort required by the laws of nature, but he must never place his confidence in the efficacy of those efforts. He has only to look Heavenward, to the one true Power to Whom the laws of nature belong, Who will provide his needs through whatever medium He chooses (*Derech Pikudecha, Lo Saaseh* §26-29, *Cheilek HaMachshavah* §7).

In the same vein, when a person becomes involved in some activity to which he applies his intelligence, talents, and abilities, he must remain aware that it is God Who granted him these traits (*Tzidkas HaTzadik* §232). These ideas are alluded to by the sequence of the verses, *I am Hashem, your God, Who took you out of Mitzraim. You shall not recognize other gods before Me.* This to say: "After I have demonstrated, in the miraculous way by which I took you out of Egypt, My complete mastery over the laws of nature, is it conceivable for you to turn away from Me and place your trust in natural forces that are completely subject to My control?" (*Abarbanel, Shemos* 20:3).

This is actually a wondrous device which one can use to completely neutralize any harmful designs of others who may be plotting against him. He should firmly establish in his heart the notion that God is the only true source of power in this world, and that the Unity of God encompasses all that exists, thereby negating in his mind all other forces. He should accordingly devote all his thoughts to the contemplation of the sole Master of the World, and God will respond by defeating all the forces that may threaten him, rendering them completely powerless to act against him (*Nefesh HaChaim* 3:12).

III. SERVICE OF GOD — FOR THE SAKE OF GOD

Another element of this mitzvah is the admonishment that a person, while involved in Torah and mitzvos, should have no purpose in mind other than to serve his Maker. For if one puts some other selfish motivation, such as prestige or financial gain, alongside the will of God as the goal of his activity, it is tantamount to dividing his devotion between two deities; in addition to his loyalty to the One Whose command he obeys, he also worships the material possessions that he craves, or the people by whom he expects to be honored (*Derech Pikudecha, Lo Saaseh* §26-29, *Cheilek HaMachshavah* §5). It emerges, then, that this commandment's influence is felt in the proper fulfillment of every other mitzvah (*Derashos Rabbeinu Yonah*). In a way, a person who blends self-interest into his service of God is worse than an idolater, for the latter has only one other object of worship, while the former knows no limit (*Chovos HaLevavos, Shaar Yichud HaMa'aseh* §4).

THROUGH THE EYES OF THE SAGES
Stories, Parables & Reflections

I. THE DEVELOPMENT OF POLYTHEISM

n his introduction to the laws of idolatry, Rambam (Hil. Avodas Kochavim) describes the process by which an error in judgment eventually led to the spread of polytheistic theory and heathen practice.

———— ✒ ————

❧ The generation of Enosh

It was in the days of Enosh that mankind fell prey to a serious mistake; one that ensnared even the wise men of the era, including Enosh himself. This was their error: It was observed that God had created the stars and other heavenly bodies to conduct the affairs of the world, giving them the distinction of residing in Heaven and attending to His will. As such, they reasoned that it would be proper, and in accordance with the Divine will, to pay tribute to them, just as the subjects of a human king are expected to honor the royal ministers, as an extension of their reverence for the king himself. With this idea in mind, the people began to build temples to the stars, recite their praises, offer sacrifices and bow down before them — all in fulfillment of what they understood to be the will of the Creator. This was the essence of star worship, and its knowledgeable adherents would explain it as such; they would never profess that a particular star was the sole god in existence. To this the prophet referred in his exclamation (*Yirmiah* 10:7-8), *Who would not fear You, O King of the nations? For kingship befits You; for among all the wise men of the nations and in all their kingdoms [it is known] that there is none like You. The vain idols for which they are punished are uniformly foolish and stupid; they are [but] wood.* They are well aware that You, God, are unique, but

they are convinced that this nonsense conforms with Your will.

———— ✒ ————

❧ Pagan worship develops

With the passage of time, there arose false prophets who claimed that they were in contact with God and had been given a message to convey to the people: "There is a specific star (or the stars in general) that you must worship; sacrifice to it and pour it libations; build it a temple and fashion its image, so that the masses — men, women and children — will prostrate themselves before it." They would describe its image as it allegedly appeared in their prophetic vision. In this way, there began the practice of making all kinds of images, in temples, under trees, and atop mountains and hills, and people would congregate and bow down before them. They would be told that the image held the power to help, as well as harm, and it was thus worthy of their reverence and worship. The priests would determine exactly which form of worship was the optimal way to bring success and prosperity. Other charlatans appeared on the scene, claiming that a star, an angel, or another heavenly body had communicated directly with them, giving specific instructions on how it was to be served. These conventions proliferated throughout the world in a wide variety of forms.

———— ✒ ————

❧ Deification ensues

After a great many years, the awesome Name of God became forgotten by mankind. The more sophisticated and learned, though they knew that the images were merely symbols of metaphysical forces, were convinced that these forces represented the crest of divinity; in their minds no god was superior to them. As for the masses, they perceived nothing at all beyond the monuments and statues of wood and stone that they were trained from youth to revere and worship. By this time, the existence of a Creator was virtually unknown, outside of a precious few individuals, such as Chanoch,

Mesushelach, Noach, Shem and Ever. This is how the world progressed, until the birth of that "pillar of the world" — our forefather Avraham (see *mitzvah #25*).

II. DIALOGUES ON DIVINITY

❧ *Avraham and Nimrod*

erach, the father of Avraham, manufactured idols and sold them for worship. It happened once that Terach left his shop, and he had Avraham take his place. Soon a man came, seeking to purchase an idol. Avraham asked him for his age, and upon learning he was fifty, he exclaimed, "Woe to a man of fifty who is prepared to worship a statue just a few days old." The man turned around and walked off in shame. Once, a woman came carrying a plateful of flour. She said, "Here, take this flour and offer it to the idols." Instead, Avraham rose up, grabbed a club, and smashed all the statues. He then placed the club in the hands of the largest of them. When his father returned, he demanded to know who was responsible. His son replied, "What do I have to hide? A woman came with a plateful of flour and asked me to offer it before the idols. So I placed it before them. Then one statue said, "I will eat first," to which another one countered, "No, I will eat first." At that, this large one here picked up the stick and broke them to pieces." Said Terach, "Why do you mock me? Are these statues capable of doing such things?" Avraham responded, "Let your ears hear what your mouth is saying! (If you know they are impotent, why do you venerate them?)" Terach seized his son and delivered him to Nimrod. The ruler reasoned with Avraham, "True, the statues are lifeless. But let us worship fire instead." Avraham replied, "In that case we should rather bow down to water, which can extinguish a fire." Nimrod said, "Indeed, let us deify water!" Avraham was not satisfied. "But, if so, we must revere the clouds, which bear the water aloft." Again, Nimrod agreed. Avraham persisted, "Better yet, let us worship the wind, for the wind is able to disperse the clouds! Then

again, it follows that we should deify the human being, who has the ability to contain the wind (i.e. the spirit of life, which remains inside the human body, despite its many openings)." Nimrod now interrupted, "This is all idle talk! I declare for the worship of fire. Into a fire, then, I shall have you thrown; let the God you venerate come and save you from it!" (*Bereishis Rabbah* 38:13; *Yalkut Shimoni, Noach* §62).

———— ❧ ————

❧ *Avraham: merchant turned priest*

When Rosh Hashanah arrives, the ministering angels say before God, "Why do you show such favor to this nation [of Israel]?" God answers, "I do it because of the devotion of their forefather Avraham. For when his father Terach gave him many idols to sell, Avraham smashed them. He went and discredited all the idols in the marketplace and sanctified My Name before the world."

It is said of Avraham, that when his father entrusted him with a few baskets full of idols to sell on the market, a person came along in search of a deity. He said, "I am strong, so give me a strong one." [The prevailing theory was that the image of a particular star could draw down to this world some of that star's capabilities. Thus an idol representing a star of valor could be expected to bestow of its might upon its worshippers — *Me'orei HaEish*.] Avraham selected an idol that was standing above all the rest. [His practice was to place the idols representing weakness on top, so that the simple-minded would not be led to believe that the strong ones had used their superior strength to choose for themselves the most prominent place — ibid.] The customer was dubious. "Is this deity, then, mighty like me? Fool! You haven't yet learned the system of the gods!" Avraham retorted, "It is you who is foolish! If this god was not the strongest of the lot, it could not have perched itself on top of the others! But I will not speak with you further until you pay me its value." The shopper gave him the money and took the idol. As he was leaving, Avraham asked, "How old are you, then?" He answered,

"Seventy years old." Said Avraham, "If so, you are older than your god. How could you, born seventy years ago, prostrate yourself before this god, which was just now formed by the blows of a hammer?" The customer immediately threw away the image into the basket, took back his money, and went on his way.

Next came a woman whose husband had died. She said, "I am a poor widow. Give me a god that is poor like me (and would thus be satisfied with minimal offerings of bread and water)." Avraham pulled out a statue from below all the rest. The woman protested, "This one is too demanding for me, and I could never afford to satisfy its needs." Avraham exclaimed, "Fool! If it was not the lowliest one of the lot, it would not be sitting beneath all the rest! But it will not agree to budge from its place until you pay me the price in full." She gave him the money and collected the idol. As she turned to leave, Avraham said, "How old are you?" She answered, "Many years old." Avraham exclaimed, "Let this woman's soul be blown away! You, who have been in existence for many years, are set to prostrate yourself before a god who was created just yesterday under my father's hammer!?" Upon hearing these words, the woman returned the idol, took back her money, and went on her way.

Avraham then took all the statues and brought them back to his father. Terach's other sons said, "This Avraham must not be adept at selling idols; let us, instead, make him a priest." Avraham asked, "What does a priest do?" They told him, "He sweeps before the idols and moistens the floor [to hold down the dust], and serves them their food and drink." So Avraham went and brought the idols their food and drink. He told them, "Partake of the food, and have a drink, and then you may help other people for my sake, for it is I who have fed you." But not one responded, or took any food. Avraham began to say, *They have a mouth, but cannot speak; they have eyes but cannot see. They have ears, but cannot hear … Their hands — they cannot feel; their feet — they cannot walk* (*Tehillim* 115:5-7). What, then, did he do? He took a club and smashed all the

statues and threw them into a blazing fire; he then sat down, and watched them burn.

In the meantime, Nimrod came in and saw what he had done. He said to him, "Don't you know that I am the lord of all the world's creatures, and the sun, moon and stars all march to my orders? So why have you destroyed my deity?" At that point, God granted insight to Avraham, and he replied to Nimrod, "My master, the king! It has been the custom since the day of creation that the sun comes out from the east and sets in the west. I propose that tomorrow you direct the sun to rise from the west and set in the east, at which time I will acknowledge you as the lord of all creatures. In addition, if it is true as you said, that you are the Master of all that exists, surely none of the world's secrets are hidden from you. So, tell me, what am I thinking and what will I do in the future?" With that the wicked Nimrod began to stroke his beard and ponder thoughtfully. Avraham interrupted him. "You have no need to ponder, for you are not the lord of this world. You are merely a son of Cush. If you were really the lord of this world, why could you not save your father from death? Just as you were powerless to save him from death, you will be no more capable of saving yourself" (*Tanna D'vei Eliyahu* 25:5-8).

———— ❧ ————

✒ *Yirmiah the prophet*

The prophet Yirmiah addressed the people (*Yirmiah* 10:11): *Tell them this: The gods who did not make the heavens and earth shall vanish from the earth and from under these heavens.* R' Eliezer explained: *"Tell them this…"* If the nations of the world attempt to persuade you to worship their heathen gods, say this to them: If their gods can remove the heavens and earth, we will accept their divinity; if not, they shall vanish from the earth. R' Yehoshua said: This you should tell them: If they can create their own heaven and earth, we will worship them. If not, they shall vanish from the earth. Rabbi Akiva taught: Answer them thus: If they are able to remove the heavens and earth, and then create replacements of a different hue, we will worship them. If not, they shall vanish from the earth (*Tanchuma, Shoftim* 12).

———— ❧ ————

❧ *Hadrian of Rome*

After the Roman Emperor Hadrian had subjugated the entire world, he returned to Rome. He called together the members of his palace. "I ask of you to declare me a god, for I have vanquished the entire world." They replied, "But you have yet to capture the city and Temple of the Jewish God." So Hadrian went off, and, with the assistance of Heaven, succeeded in destroying the Temple and banishing the Jews of the land. He returned once again to Rome and renewed his claim. "I have now destroyed the Jewish God's Temple, burned His [Temple] Hall and exiled His people. Declare me a god." R' Berechiah taught: Hadrian had three philosopher (advisers). The first one responded: One does not rebel against a king in the king's own palace. First leave the confines of His palace and only then can you be proclaimed as god. The second one warned: You will not succeed, for He has already conveyed through His prophet (*Yirmiah* 10:11): *Tell them this: The gods who did not make the heavens and earth shall vanish from the earth and from under these heavens.* Finally, the third one spoke urgently, "I beg you, please come to my aid at this critical time." "What is the matter?" queried the Emperor. "I have a ship that is out at sea more than three *mil* away; it is caught in a storm and is in danger of sinking. All my treasures are on board that ship!"

The Emperor offered, "I will send my legions and ships to its rescue." The adviser said, "Your Majesty, why must you bother with legions and ships? Simply send a little gust of wind in the proper direction — that will suffice to save it." Said the Emperor, "And from where am I to get a gust of wind?"

The philosopher replied, "If you are incapable of producing some wind, how can you expect to be proclaimed a deity? Of God it is said (*Yeshayah* 42:5), *Thus said the God, Hashem, Who created the heavens and stretched them forth; Who firmed the earth and its produce, Who gave a soul to the people upon it, and a*

spirit [רוח, lit. wind] *to those who walk on it.* The Emperor, defeated, went home sadly. His wife told him, "Those men misled you. You can surely become a god; you are a great and mighty king, and everything is in your power. But one thing you need to do: Return His deposit and you can become a god." Said he, "What is His deposit?" She replied, "Your soul." "But if my soul is gone, what am I to do?" Countered his wife, "If over your own spirit you have no dominion — as, indeed, it is said (*Koheles* 8:8), *Man is powerless over the spirit — to restrain the spirit; nor is there authority over the day of death —* how can you consider becoming a god?" (*Tanchuma, Bereishis* §7; see also *Tanchuma* to *Shoftim* §12).

———— ❧ ————

❧ *Miriam and her seven sons*

It is related of a righteous woman named Miriam, that she was taken captive with her seven sons. They were delivered to the [Roman] Caesar, who placed them in the innermost of seven rooms. He summoned the eldest son before him and ordered, "Prostrate yourself before this idol!" He responded, "God forbid! I shall not bow down before an idol." The ruler prodded, "Why not?" The lad replied, "For it is written in our Torah (*Shemos* 20:2), *I am Hashem, your God.* With that, the boy was taken out and killed.

[After the refusals and slayings of the first six sons (as is recounted in this section of *mitzvah* #28-29)], the seventh and last was brought in. The ruler said, "Prostrate yourself before this idol, and I will be good to you." The boy protested, "God forbid! Our Torah says (*Devarim* 4:39), *You are to know this day and take to your heart that Hashem, He is the only God in the heavens above and on the earth below; there is no other.* Not only that, but we have sworn to God that we would not exchange Him for another God, just as He took an oath that He would never exchange us for another people, as it is written in our Torah (*Devarim* 26:17-18): *You have designated Hashem today [to be your God], and Hashem has designated you to be His people.*"

The Caesar said, "Listen, my son. Your brothers had their fill of good years and life, but you are yet young; bow down to this statue, and I will bestow favors upon you." The lad replied, "It is written in our Torah (*Shemos* 15:18), *God shall reign forever and ever,* and it is also said (*Tehillim* 10:16), *God is King forever; the nations have perished from His land.* You will become obsolete along with all the rest of His enemies. A mortal being is alive today and dead tomorrow; wealthy one day and a pauper the next; but God lives and endures forever and ever." The ruler inquired, "Is there truly a God in this world?" The boy answered, "Woe to you, Caesar! Do you behold a world of anarchy?" The Caesar asked, "Has your God a mouth?" Answered the boy, "In regard to your gods it is written (*Tehillim* 115:5), *They have mouths, but cannot speak.* But as for our God we find (ibid. 33:6), *By the Word of God were the heavens made.*" "Does your God have eyes?" He answered, "Regarding your gods it is written (ibid. 115:5), *They have eyes, but cannot see.* But in connection with our God, it is said (*Zechariah* 4:10), *The Eyes of God — they scan the whole world.*"

Finally, the Caesar asked, "If all these attributes are found in your God, why doesn't He save you from me just as he rescued Chananiah, Mishael, and Azariah from the hands of Nevuchadnezzar?" Answered the boy, "Chananiah, Mishael and Azariah were upstanding Jews, and Nevuchadnezzar was a king who was worthy of being the agent of a miracle. But you are unworthy, and, as for ourselves, the Heavenly Court has found us deserving of death. If you do not slay us, the Omnipresent has many agents to kill us — bears, wolves, lions, snakes, leopards, scorpions, that can strike and kill us. Nevertheless, God will someday exact vengeance from you on account of our blood…" (*Eichah Rabbah* 1:50).

III. QUESTIONS OF FAITH; THE SAGES RESPOND

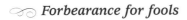 *Forbearance for fools*

he Sages in Rome were asked the following question: If God truly disapproves of idolatry, why does He not destroy all the idols? They replied: If the pagans had deified things that the world does not need, God would have indeed eradicated them. But what do they venerate? The sun and the moon, the stars and constellations. Should the entire world be destroyed on account of these fools? The heathens retorted: In that case, let God annihilate those objects of worship that are of no cosmic value, and spare those that are! The Sages responded: Such a policy would bolster the claims of those who worship the latter. They would say: We have proof that our gods are truly divine: They were not erased along with the others (*Avodah Zarah* 54b).

------ ❦ ------

The dog and the dead

A [non-Jewish] philosopher once asked Rabban Gamliel: It is written in your Torah (*Devarim* 4:24): *For Hashem, your God — He is a consuming fire, a jealous God.* Why does He exact revenge from the worshippers and not from the worshipped? Rabban Gamliel replied: I will offer a parable. There was a human king who had a son. The boy raised a pet dog which he named after his father. Whenever he swore, he would say, "By the life of Father the dog." When the king learned of this, at whom was he angry? At the boy or the dog? Obviously, at the boy. In the same way, God's wrath is reserved for the people who refer to their idols as gods; He ignores the idols themselves. The philosopher countered: Dare you call our idol a dog? It really has substance! Rabban Gamliel responded: What did you see that convinced you of this? He answered: One time there was a conflagration that burned down our whole town, save for the temple, which was the only thing spared. Rabban Gamliel answered: I will answer you with an analogy. There was a king against whom a province rebelled. When the king went to battle against them, did he wage war with the living, or with the dead? The answer is plain: He waged his war with the living. The philosopher rejoined: You called our idol a dog, and now you call it a corpse. If you are right, then let God destroy it! The Jewish

Sage answered: If the pagans would deify things that the world does not need, God would indeed eradicate them. But what do they venerate? The sun and the moon, the stars and constellations, the springs and the valleys. Should the entire world be erased on account of some fools? So it is written (*Tzefaniah* 1:2-3, as rendered by *Rashi*): *Shall I destroy everything upon the face of the land? said God. Shall I destroy man and animal? Shall I destroy the bird of the sky and the fish of the sea — all the things that cause the wicked to stumble?* Why, they are even capable of worshipping man: *Shall I destroy man from the face of the land?* (ibid. 54b-55a).

——— ❧ ———

❧ *A jealous God*

The General Agrippa (a non-Jewish army general who lived during the rule of King Agrippa — *Rashi*) asked Rabban Gamliel: It is written in your Torah (*Devarim* 4:24), *For Hashem, your God is a consuming fire; a jealous God.* Is a wise man ever jealous of any but a wise man; a warrior of any but a warrior; a rich man of any but a rich man? Rabban Gamliel replied: I will draw an analogy. To what can this matter be compared? To a man who takes an additional wife. If the second wife is of superior rank, the first wife will not take so much offense and hate her husband for it. But if the second is of inferior stock, the first wife will take offense and feel hatred toward her husband (*Avodah Zarah* 55a, as rendered by *Rashi*).

——— ❧ ———

❧ *Miraculous cures*

A Jew named Zunin remarked to Rabbi Akiva: You and I know that there is no substance to idol worship. But then we see handicapped people embarking [on a pilgrimage to their deities] and coming back healthy and whole. How can this be explained? Rabbi Akiva answered: I will offer a parable. There was a trustworthy person in town, with whom all of the townsfolk would deposit their valuables without resort to witnesses. There was one man, however, who always insisted on witnesses,

until it happened one time that he forgot to take this precaution. The wife of the custodian said to him, "Let us now take advantage and deny the transaction!" He retorted, "Because this one fool acted improperly, shall we violate our faithfulness?" It is the same with our subject. When Heaven sends suffering upon a person, the angels appointed over the suffering are made to take an oath that they will visit them upon the victim only on a certain day, and remain there only until a certain day at a specified hour (in the event that the person had not yet repented), through the hand of a certain doctor and a specified medication. Now [in the case we are discussing], when the appointed time for the end of his suffering had come, the idolater went to pray at his house of worship. It is a result of his failure to repent that he was influenced to go there this very day in order to lead him further astray. The angels charged with removing the suffering declare, "Truly we should not leave!" But then they say, "Because this fool acted improperly, shall we forfeit our fidelity to the oath that we took?"

Indeed, this was the meaning of R' Yochanan when he declared: What is meant by the Scriptural phrase (*Devarim* 28:59), *... evil and faithful illnesses*? The illnesses are evil in their mission to torment one's body, while faithful to their oath (*Avodah Zarah* ibid., with *Maharsha*).

——— ❧ ———

❧ *Deliverance from drought*

Rava, son of Rav Yitzchak, said to Rav Yehudah: What shall we say about the pagan temple in our locale? When the area needs rain, the deity appears to its devotees in a dream, saying, "Sacrifice a human to me and I will bring rain." Lo and behold, they offer the sacrifice, and it begins to rain! Rav Yehudah answered: If I had died before now, I would not have had the opportunity to relate the following teaching. So taught Rav: What is meant by the verse (*Devarim* 4:19), *Lest you raise your eyes to the Heaven and you see the sun, and the moon, and the stars — the entire legion of heaven — and be drawn astray and bow to them and worship them, which Hashem your God* **has apportioned to all the peoples** *under the entire heaven!?* We are to infer from here that God deliberately misleads the idolatrous nations, so as to banish them from the world.

This is also the intent of a statement by Reish Lakish: What is the intent of the verse (*Mishlei* 3:34) *To the scoffers, He will scoff, and to the humble, He will bestow favor?* If one aspires to depravity, they [in Heaven] show him the way, and if one seeks purity, they offer assistance (ibid; a similar passage appears in *Zohar Chadash, Bereishis* 14b).

———— ❧ ————

❧ *The pagan majority*

R' El'asha related: A certain idolater asked R' Yehoshua ben Karchah, "Your Torah states (*Shemos* 23:2), *Be disposed toward the majority.* Well, we are more numerous than you. Why don't you align yourselves with us in our worship of idols?" The sage responded, "Do you have any sons?" The idolater answered, "Oh, you've reminded me of my troubles! I actually have many sons, but when they sit together to a meal at my table, the first recites his blessings to one deity, and the second to another, and so on, and before they have risen from the table they are hitting one another on the head!" R' Yehoshua asked, "And so have you had them make common cause?" "No," was the answer. "Well, before you attempt to have us agree with you, go and create agreement among your own children." The idolater, rebuffed, went on his way. R' Yehoshua's disciples then spoke up. "Rabbi, him, you pushed off with a broken reed, but what answer do you have for us?" He replied, "Regarding Eisav, although only six souls are mentioned, we find that the plural form is used, as in this verse (*Bereishis* 36:6): *And Eisav took his wives, his sons, and his daughters and all the* **souls** *(nafshos) of his household.* Whereas, in connection with Yaakov, where there were seventy souls, the singular form is preferred, as it is written (*Shemos* 1:5), *"And all the* **soul***[s] (nefesh), descendants of Yaakov, were seventy* **soul***[s].* This must be attributed to the fact that the family of

Eisav was divided by their worship of multiple deities, while the descendants of Yaakov were united in their devotion to one God. [This refuted the idolater's challenge, for factionalized pagans do not constitute a majority, as they do not represent a unified opinion — *Maharzav*] (*Vayikra Rabbah* 4:6).

IV. HEATHEN DECEIT IN PROMOTING THEIR IDOLS

❧ *The Baal's devotees at Mount Carmel*

hey took the bull that [Eliyahu] gave them and prepared it, and called out in the name of the Baal from morning until noon, saying, 'O Baal, answer us!' But there was no sound or response; and so they danced by the altar that **he** *had made* (*Melachim* I, 18:26). Was *he* (Eliyahu) the one who made the altar? Was it not *they* who had made it? Rather, this alludes to the endeavor of Chiel (one of the priests of Baal) to make an altar that was hollow. His fellows placed him inside it holding a flame. They told him: When you hear the loud calling, stoke the flame in your hand and kindle a fire from underneath. Chiel stood ready, but God dispatched a snake that bit him; he immediately died (*Yalkut Shimoni, Melachim* I, 214; alluded to also in *Shemos Rabbah* 15:15; see *Maharzav* there).

———— ❧ ————

❧ *Priestly avarice*

What is meant by the verse (*Hoshea* 13:2), *They have made for themselves a molten image … those who slaughter man; they shall kiss the calves*? The priests would set their eyes on men of great wealth, and would place their likeness beside the feeding-trough of the [idolized] calves. When rich men would approach, the calves would be led toward them. The animals, recognizing their faces and being reminded of food, would run after them, nudging them expectantly. The priests would declare: "The deity desires you. Come and sacrifice yourself to it!" (*Sanhedrin* 63b).

———— ❧ ————

✧ Nebuchadnezzar and Daniel

The Sages related: Nebuchadnezzar went to great lengths to convince Daniel to prostrate himself to his statue. He would say, "Come and see what it is able to do, and you will bow down to it of your own volition." What did that wicked man do? He took the head-plate of the [Jewish] High Priest and placed it inside the statue's mouth. He then gathered various musicians, who sang praises before it, and the statue would speak: "I am Hashem, your God." When Daniel saw this, he said, "Will you allow me to kiss your idol on its mouth?" "Why on the mouth?" asked the king. "Because it utters such wonderful words." Permission was immediately granted, so Daniel approached it and adjured the head-plate, saying, "I am a flesh-and-blood agent of God. Beware of causing the desecration of God's Name. I now decree upon you to follow after me." He drew near to kiss it, and extracted the head-plate. [This fulfilled the verse (*Yirmyah* 51:44), *I will deal with [the deity] Bel in Babylonia and remove from his mouth what he has swallowed.*] Once he descended, the musicians resumed their praises, but there was no response from the idol. At that point a gust of wind came and toppled the statue.

When the nations of the world witnessed the miracles God wrought for Chananiah, Mishael and Azariah in saving them from the fiery furnace, they grabbed their idols, smashed them to pieces and fashioned the shards into bells that they hung around the necks of their donkeys and dogs. They would jingle the bells and announce: "See what it is that we worshipped." This brought to fulfillment the prophecy (*Yeshayah* 46:1), *Bel is kneeling; Nebo is doubled over. Their idols were made over to the beast and animal* (*Shir HaShirim Rabbah* 7:9; cf. *Zohar* II, 175a, and, for a broader treatment, *Tikunei Zohar, Tikun* 69, 97a-b).

——— ✧ ———

✧ A great feast for Bel

It happened that Darius celebrated a holiday for Bel, the deity of Babylon. The king prepared a sacrifice to offer to Bel: One bull, ten rams, one hundred pigeons, one hundred sheep, seventy loaves of bread, and ten barrels of wine. This was the daily offering in the temple of Bel. An elaborate table was arranged in front of the idol, and the king said to Daniel, "Would that you believed in the glory of our great god Bel, who is about to consume the spread on this table!" Daniel replied, "Please do not be deceived in this matter, for the idol Bel is impotent and worthless; it is merely the creation of craftsmen — how shall it eat or drink? I tell you it is the priests who eat from its table. If you will grant me authority over its priests, I will lay bare their devious practices by which they seduce you to worship a nonentity." The king replied, "So be it."

So Daniel gave orders to close off all the entrances to the temple, except for the gateway reserved for the king, and had a layer of ashes strewn all over the floor of the hall. Darius and Daniel then left the hall through the king's gate, locking the doors and applying both of their seals. They retired to the palace for the night, and in the morning they returned to the gate and found the seals intact. They removed the locks and opened the doors, and they beheld the table, completely cleared of its burden of bread, meat and wine. The king, profoundly moved by this sight, fell to the ground before Bel, and proclaimed, "Great is your name, Bel! Who can compare to your power among all the gods of the nations!" Daniel responded, "Do not speak so! Look down upon the ashes that we spread on the floor, and behold the footprints around the table. To whom do they belong? They are the ones who have partaken from the table of Bel! The king turned to look, and he discerned the footprints of men, women, youths, and babes. He sent for the arrest of the seven priests, the attendants of Bel, and forced upon them an oath: "If you fail to tell me the truth, be advised that you will be put to death!" They admitted the truth and showed the king the concealed passageways which they used to enter Bel's hall at night and feast at his table. Being apprised of their deviousness, Darius gave the command and the temple of Bel was razed to the ground (see *Yosifun*, chapter 3).

V. The severity of the sin

❧ Key to the Torah

he issue of idolatry is a serious one, for one who denies the validity of idols is reckoned as if he acknowledged the whole of the Torah. [And conversely one who accepts their validity is reckoned as if he denied the whole of the Torah (*Sifrei*)] (*Nedarim*, 25a; *Kiddushin* 40a, *Shevuos* 29a; *Chullin* 5a; *Sifrei, Re'eh* §54; see also *Horayos* 8a.)

Whoever accepts the validity of idolatry has denied the Ten Commandments, and all that Moshe was commanded by God, the prophets were commanded by God, and the forefathers were commanded by God. Whoever denies idolatry acknowledges the whole Torah (*Sifrei, Shelach* §111; see there for other sources).

———— ❧ ————

❧ Intentions and deeds

A good intention is counted by God as a deed: If a person intended to perform a mitzvah and he was then prevented from following through, he is nevertheless considered as having done it. An evil intention, however, is not reckoned as a deed. And what is the meaning of the verse (*Yechezkel* 14:5), *...In order to seize the house of Israel for what is **in their hearts***, which indicates that they are punished even for unexpressed thoughts? Answered Rav Acha bar Yaakov: That verse is discussing the sin of idolatry, of which it has been taught: The issue of idolatry is a serious one, for one who rejects idols, is considered to have acknowledged the whole of the Torah [and it is thus a sin so grave that even the mere intention to commit is treated as the deed] (*Kiddushin* 40a).

———— ❧ ————

❧ Wicked in thought

If one betroths a woman conditionally, upon the stipulation that he is a *rasha* — a wicked man, and he is known to be thoroughly righteous, there still are grounds for concern that the betrothal may have taken effect. It is possible that he entertained in his mind an idolatrous thought [which alone is enough to characterize him as a wicked man] (*Kiddushin* 49b).

VI. Repudiating idolatry: Past and future

❧ Precondition for the Exodus

n Egypt, the Jews clung stubbornly to their worship of idols, as it is said (*Yechezkel* 20:8), *[They] did not cast away the detestable [idols] of their eyes, and they did not forsake the idols of Egypt.* God said to Moshe: As long as Israel continues to worship the deities of Egypt, they will not be redeemed. Go and tell them to abandon their evil ways and renounce the worship of idols. This is the meaning of the command, (*Shemos* 12:21), *Draw and take for yourselves a sheep and slaughter the Passover [offering].* In other words, "draw" yourselves away from idolatry and set aside a sheep, the deity of Egypt, to be slaughtered for the Passover offering (*Shemos Rabbah,* 16:2).

———— ❧ ————

❧ The Paschal Lamb

When God told Moses to prepare the Passover sacrifice, Moses responded, "Master of the world! How can I possibly do such a thing? Do You not know that the sheep is the deity of Egypt? So it is stated: *Behold, if we were to slaughter the deity of Egypt in their sight, will they not stone us?* (*Shemos* 8:22). Answered God, "By your life, [I swear that] the Jews will not leave Egypt until they have slaughtered the god of Egypt before their eyes, so that I may have them know that their god is naught." Indeed, on the night that Egypt's firstborn were slain, while the Jews sacrificed and partook of their Passover offerings, the Egyptians looked on but could do nothing. Thus it is said (*Bamidbar* 33:4), *The Egyptians were burying those among them whom*

God had struck, every firstborn, and on their deities God inflicted punishments (ibid. v. 3).

——— ৵ ৶ ———

৵৹ *The future moment of truth*

The time will come in the future when God will gather the deities of the nations and grant them spirit and soul. He will say: Let each nation with its idol march across the bridge of *Gehinnom* (hell). They will then begin traversing the bridge, and when they reach the middle, the bridge will narrow to the breadth of a thread, at which point the idols and their followers will fall into *Gehinnom* (*Tanna D'vei Eliyahu Zuta* 21:3).

——— ৵ ৶ ———

৵৹ *The deities will serve*

Humiliated will be all who worship idols, who pride themselves in worthless gods (*Tehillim* 97:7). R' Yudan taught in the name of Rav Nachman: In the future God will breathe life into the pagan idols, which will come and prostrate themselves before Him, and they will then humiliate the people who worshipped them. R' Pinchas taught: God in the future will give the idols the power of speech, and they will berate their devotees, saying, "Woe to you, who spurned the Creator, the true Source of life, and bowed down instead to lifeless forms." On this, R' Yochanan commented: Do not be amazed; there is a precedent for this. When God descended onto Mount Sinai, He granted vitality to the idols and they bowed down to Him. Rav Tachlifa added: Scripture supports this assertion, as it is written (ibid.), *All the powers* (i.e. the sun, moon, etc.) *bowed down to Him.* It does not read, 'they *will* bow', for they already bowed in the past — at Sinai (*Medrash Tehillim* §31; *Yerushalmi, Avodah Zarah* 4:7; cf. *Tanchuma, Tetzaveh* §10).

ambam, in his *Sefer HaMitzvos*, derives four negative commandments from the passage in the Ten Commandments that deals with idolatry (*Shemos* 20:3-7): 1) a prohibition against believing in idols (*Lo Saaseh* §1); 2) a prohibition against making or possessing idols (*Lo Saaseh* §2); 3) a prohibition against bowing down to idols (*Lo Saaseh* §5); and 4) a prohibition against worshipping an idol in a manner unique to that idol (*Lo Saaseh* §6). *R' Saadiah Gaon* also derives these four prohibitions from this verse (see *Sefer HaMitzvos of R' Saadiah Gaon, Lo Saaseh* 1-4).

The view that this passage refers to multiple negative commandments, however, is problematic, for the Gemara in *Makkos* (23b-24a) indicates that it is the source for only *one* commandment. The Gemara states: Rav Simlai expounded: Six hundred and thirteen commandments were related to Moshe... Rav Hamnuna said: Which verse [teaches this] (i.e. what is the Scriptural source for the concept of 613 commandments)? *Moshe commanded us the Torah as a heritage* (*Devarim* 33:4). The numerical value (*gematria*) of the word "Torah" [תורה] is six hundred and eleven. [Thus, the verse teaches that Moshe transmitted 611 commandments to the Jewish Nation.] The passages *I am Hashem, your God* etc., and *You shall not recognize other gods before Me* etc. were heard directly from Hashem (and each of these passages contains one commandment, for a total of 613).

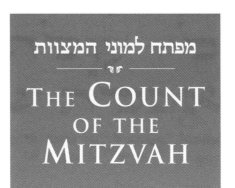

מפתח למוני המצוות
§
THE COUNT
OF THE
MITZVAH

Baal Halachos Gedolos / Lavin 26
בה"ג / לאוין כו

R' Saadiah Gaon / Lavin 1
רס"ג / לאוין א

R' Eliyahu HaZakein / Amud 35
ר' אליהו הזקן / עמ' 35

Rashbag / Lo Saaseh Os 7
רשב"ג / לא תעשה אות ז

R' Yitzchak El-Bargeloni / Lavin 26
ר"י אלברג'לוני / לאוין כו

Maamar HaSechel / Dibbur Sheini 1
מאמר השכל / דיבור שני א

Sefer Yere'im / 243
יראים / רמג

Rambam, Sefer HaMitzvos / Lo Saaseh 1
רמב"ם / לא תעשה א

Sefer Mitzvos Gadol (Smag) / Lo Saaseh 1
סמ"ג / לא תעשה א

Sefer Mitzvos Katan (Smak) / 61
סמ"ק / סא

Zohar HaRakia / Lavin 1
זוהר הרקיע / לאוין א

According to *Rambam* and *R' Saadiah Gaon*, however, the Jews actually heard *five* commandments directly from Hashem — one in the passage of *I am Hashem, your God,* etc., and four in the passage of *You shall not recognize other gods before Me* etc. — and only 608 from Moshe!

[Note: *Bahag* (as explained by *Ramban* in his *Hasagos* to *Rambam's Sefer HaMitzvos, Aseh* §1) cites this passage as the source for two negative commandments: 1) a prohibition against making or possessing idols (*Lavin* §26); and 2) a prohibition against worshipping idols (*Niskalin* §8). However, the aforementioned Gemara presents no difficulty according to him, for he does not derive any commandment from the passage of *I am Hashem your God* (*Bahag* does not count the obligation to believe in *Hashem* as one of the 613 commandments; see above, *mitzvah* #25 at length). Thus, the two commandments contained in the passage of *You shall not recognize other gods before Me* (according to *Bahag*) account for both commandments that the Jews heard directly from *Hashem* (see *Hasagos HaRamban* ibid.).]

Several other approaches have been suggested to resolve this difficulty according to *Rambam* and *R' Saadiah Gaon*:

A. *The Jews heard only one of the four commandments in the passage directly from Hashem.*

The Gemara does not mean that the Jews heard the *entire passage* relating to idolatry directly from Hashem, but that they heard the *verse* of *You shall not recognize other gods before Me*, which contains the prohibition against believing in idols. The commandments contained in the remaining verses in the passage, however, were transmitted to them by Moshe (*Megillas Esther* and *Lev Same'ach, Aseh* §1).

B. Commandments that are repeated elsewhere in the Torah are counted as having been transmitted by Moshe.

Three of the four commandments contained in this passage are repeated elsewhere in the Torah. The prohibition against making or possessing idols is stated again in *Devarim* 4:16 (*Lest you act corruptly and make yourselves a carved image*); the prohibition against bowing down to idols is repeated in *Shemos* 34:14 (*You shall not bow down to an alien god*); and the prohibition against worshipping an idol in a manner unique to that idol is stated again in *Devarim* 12:30 (*Beware... lest you seek out their gods, saying, How did these nations worship their gods, and I will do the same*). The additional references to these three prohibitions, like the entire Torah (with the exception of the first two passages of the Ten Commandments), were transmitted to the Jews by Moshe. Thus, although the Jews originally heard these commandments directly from Hashem, they are counted as part of the 611 commandments that were transmitted to them by Moshe (*Maayan HaChochmah, Lo Saaseh* §14; see also *Bris Moshe* to *Semag, Lo Saaseh* §17).

C. The Gemara does not mean that the Jews heard commandments directly from Hashem, but that they comprehended certain commandments on their own.

Rambam (*Moreh Nevuchim* 2:32) has a novel interpretation of the Gemara in *Makkos*. Rambam explains that the Jews did not actually hear *any* commandments directly from Hashem. They heard the Voice of Hashem as He uttered the Ten Commandments, but they were not able to grasp the content of His speech. However, as a result of the awesome revelation to which they were witness, they arrived at the realization that there is an obligation to believe in Hashem and that it is forbidden to believe in idols. Thus, they did not require Moshe to transmit these commandments to them. According to *Rambam*, the Gemara does not mean that they *heard* two commandments from Hashem, but that they comprehended two commandments *because they heard the Voice* of Hashem. Interpreted in this manner, the Gemara does not contradict *Rambam's* view that the passage of *You shall not recognize other gods before Me* contains four separate prohibitions. For it was only the first of these commandments, the prohibition against believing in idols, that the Jews comprehended on their own. The other three prohibitions required transmission from Moshe, and are therefore included in the 611 commandments heard from Moshe (*Meshech Chochmah, Shemos* 20:3).

Mitzvah 27

אִסוּר עֲשִׂיַּת פֶּסֶל

פרשת יתרו

Not to Make
an Idol

THE MITZVAH:

אִסוּר עֲשִׂיַת פֶּסֶל
(לֹא תַעֲשֶׂה)

MITZVAH 27

NOT TO MAKE AN IDOL

מצוה כז

SOURCE

לֹא תַעֲשֶׂה לְךָ פֶסֶל וְכָל תְּמוּנָה שמות (פרשת יתרו) כ:ד

"Do not make for yourself an idol or any image[1]"

THE MITZVAH

One is forbidden to make or commission someone else to make idols or images for one's own worship.[2]

NOTE: One who makes an idol or image for someone else violates mitzvah #214: Not to make an object of idolatry for oneself or for others.[3]

LAWS

1 This prohibition forbids the making[4] of any idol or image intended for worship.[5] The nature of the intended worship is the topic of *mitzvos* #28 and #29.

2 A person violates this prohibition either by making idols (i.e. sculptures) and images (i.e. pictures, portraits, or engravings) himself, or by commissioning others to make them for him.[6]

3 The prohibition is violated when the idol or image is completed, even if it is not eventually worshipped.[7]

4 Although it is forbidden to derive benefit from idolatry (see *mitzvah* #429), it is permitted to derive benefit from payment given for making an idol or image.[8]

5 One who violates this prohibition in front of witnesses, after having been warned,[9] receives *malkos* (lashes).[10]

6 One must give up one's life rather than violate this prohibition.[11]

7 This prohibition applies to both men and women, in all places and at all times.[12] These acts are forbidden to non-Jews as well, as idolatry is prohibited by one of the Seven Noahide Laws.[13]

NOTE: For the positive mitzvah to destroy idols and images, see *mitzvah #436: To destroy idolatry and its accompaniments.*

A REASON

The Torah forbids pagan and idolatrous worship. We are forbidden to make idols and images intended for worship, lest we come to serve them.

1. This prohibition forbids a person to make idols and images himself, and also prohibits one to commission others to make idols and images (see, however, below note 6). However, as suggested by the phrasing of the verse: *Do not make for "yourself" an idol*, it only forbids a person to make an idol or image (or to commission others to make an idol or image) that he intends to worship himself. A person who makes an idol or image, or commissions others to make idols or images, for anyone other than himself (e.g. for sale) does not violate *this* prohibition (see *Rambam, Hil. Avodas Kochavim* 3:9 and *Sefer HaMitzvos, Lo Saaseh* §2-3). [*Minchas Chinuch* (27:5), however, suggests that *Sefer HaChinuch* (loc. cit.) disagrees, and maintains that even a person who commissions others to make idols and images for sale or for a third party *does* violate this prohibition.]

According to *Ramban*, only the *worship* of any idol or image is prohibited here, and a separate prohibition in *Vayikra* (19:4) forbids the *making* of idols (*Ramban, Hasagos* to *Sefer HaMitzvos, mitzvah* §5 and *Megillas Esther* ad loc.; see also *Sefer HaChinuch* §27).

The Rabbis also expound the verse: *Do not make for yourself an idol or image* as if it read: *Do not make of yourself an idol*, thus deriving that a person is forbidden to attempt to convince other people to worship *him* idolatrously (*Sanhedrin* 61a). Thus, the prohibition to make an idol or image covers any manner in which a person causes an object of idolatrous worship to come into existence (see below, note 4) — even if that "object" is his own self. [It should be noted that although one who violates this prohibition by making or commissioning others to make an actual idol or image

AN EXPANDED TREATMENT

is punished by *malkos* (see below, note 10), a person who is successful in getting other people to worship him is liable to the death penalty, just as is anyone who subverts others to worship idols (*Sanhedrin* ibid., *Rambam, Hil. Avodas Kochavim* 5:5; see also *mitzvah #462*).

2. This prohibition only applies to the making of idols or images with the intent to worship them. It does not apply to the making of idols or images that one does not intend to worship — for example, images that are decorative in nature (see *Sefer HaMitzvos, Lo Saaseh* §2; §4). However, while one who makes forms for decorative purposes does not violate this prohibition, under certain circumstances he *does* violate *mitzvah #39: Not to make forms, even for decorative purposes* (see below, *mitzvah #39*).

3. In addition to violating this prohibition, the person who makes the idol or image also violates *mitzvah #214: Not to make an object of idolatry for oneself or for others* (see *Vayikra* 19:4; see, however, next note). There are two distinctions between these prohibitions. First, *mitzvah #214* only prohibits a person to make idols and images *himself*, while this mitzvah also forbids a person to commission others to make them. Second, *mitzvah #214* forbids the making of idols or images whether one intends to worship them himself or not, while this mitzvah only forbids the making of idols and images for one's *own* worship (whether by making the idols and images himself or by commissioning others to make them). See also next note.

4. Although, as we have explained (notes 1-3 above), the Torah here seems to be forbidding specifcally the *making* of an idol, *Rambam* (*Sefer HaMitzvos, Lo Saaseh* §3) explains that

this mitzvah comes to forbid the acquisition and possession *as well as* the making of an idol or image (see also *Igros Moshe, Yoreh Deah* II §55). [Other authorities hold that one who keeps an idol or image in his possession, although he has no intent to worship it, violates *mitzvah #26: You shall not have other gods before Me* (*Semag, Lavin* §1 and *Sefer Yereim* §243 (§63 in the older edition); see above, *mitzvah #26*).] See further, *Iyunim* §1.

5. *Rambam* (*Hil. Avodas Kochavim* 3:9) writes that this prohibition is violated by: "One who makes *an object of idolatry* for himself;" while in 3:10 (in the context of *mitzvah #39*) he writes: "It is forbidden to make *forms* for decorative purposes." Thus, although the word *pesel* usually refers to a sculpture, and the word *temunah* usually refers to an image, in fact, our prohibition forbids the making of *anything* with the intent to worship it. These parameters emerge from *Mechilta* to *Shemos* 20:4, which brings to bear on this prohibition over a dozen verses found throughout the Torah that discuss the making of various idolatrous objects. *Mechilta* thus derives that making a sculpture, image, or symbol from any kind of substance that represents *anything* is included in this prohibition. [*Mechilta* specifically mentions representations of foreign gods, all sorts of living creatures, all sorts of celestial bodies, all sorts of angelic creatures, the depths, the darkness, and even one's own reflection in water.] *Mechilta* concludes that the Torah teaches explicitly that the prohibition applies to all these representations to leave no room for error. In the *Mechilta*'s words: *To such lengths Hashem pursued the Evil Inclination* (explicitly forbidding every possible form of idol or image) *so as not to allow any room for one to find any excuse*

to permit [*any type of idolatry*] (cf. *Sefer HaMitzvos, Lo Saaseh* §3 and *Megillas Esther* ad loc.; see also *Minchas Chinuch* 27:3 and *Malbim, HaTorah VeHaMitzvah* to *Shemos* 20:4).

6. Some sources imply that when one orders another to make an idol, the prohibition is violated only by the person making the idol or image (see *Minchas Chinuch* 27:1 in explanation of *Rambam, Hil. Avodas Kochavim* 3:9; see *Midrash HaGadol* to *Devarim* (5:8); see also *Sefer HaMitzvos, Lo Saaseh* §2; *Semag, Lavin* §20). Other sources imply that one who commissioned the making of an idol or image violates this prohibition by the acquisition of the idol or image that emerges from his commission (*Midrash HaGadol* to *Vayikra* 19:4, *Sefer HaMitzvos, Lo Saaseh* §2-3, *Beurei Maharshal, Semag, Lavin* §20). *Minchas Chinuch* (27:6) himself, however, suggests that the person who commissioned the idol or image to be made only violates this prohibition if he supplies raw materials of his own from which the craftsman then makes the idol or image; if the craftsman uses his own material, neither one has violated this prohibition (for the purchaser has not made the idol, and the craftsman has not made it for his own worship. However, the craftsman will have violated *mitzvah #214*; see above, note 3). See further *Iyunim*, §1.

7. Although it is not forbidden to derive benefit from an idol or image that belongs to a Jew until it is actually worshipped (see next note), the prohibition to *make* an idol or image has already been violated at the time of the idol's manufacture (see *Minchas Chinuch* 27:4; *Ridvaz* to *Yerushalmi Avodah Zarah* 4:4; see also *Pnei Moshe* ad loc.).

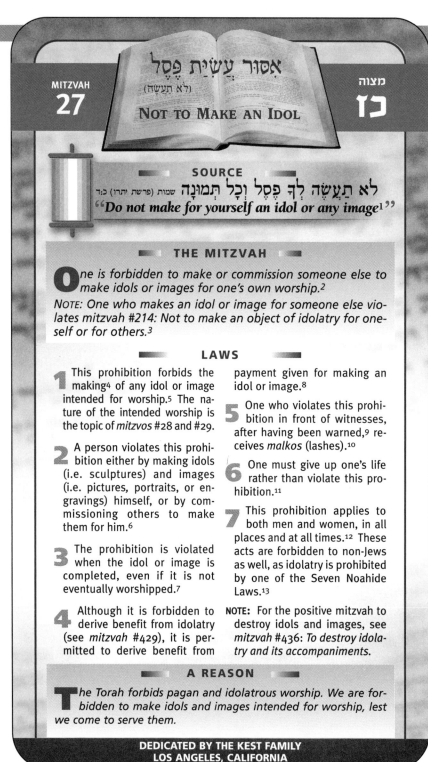

אָסוּר עֲשִׂיַּת פֶּסֶל
(לֹא תַעֲשֶׂה)

MITZVAH 27

NOT TO MAKE AN IDOL

מצוה כז

SOURCE

לֹא תַעֲשֶׂה לְךָ פֶסֶל וְכָל תְּמוּנָה שמות (פרשת יתרו) כ:ד

"*Do not make for yourself an idol or any image*[1]"

THE MITZVAH

One is forbidden to make or commission someone else to make idols or images for one's own worship.[2]

NOTE: One who makes an idol or image for someone else violates mitzvah #214: Not to make an object of idolatry for oneself or for others.[3]

LAWS

1 This prohibition forbids the making[4] of any idol or image intended for worship.[5] The nature of the intended worship is the topic of *mitzvos* #28 and #29.

2 A person violates this prohibition either by making idols (i.e. sculptures) and images (i.e. pictures, portraits, or engravings) himself, or by commissioning others to make them for him.[6]

3 The prohibition is violated when the idol or image is completed, even if it is not eventually worshipped.[7]

4 Although it is forbidden to derive benefit from idolatry (see *mitzvah #429*), it is permitted to derive benefit from payment given for making an idol or image.[8]

5 One who violates this prohibition in front of witnesses, after having been warned,[9] receives *malkos* (lashes).[10]

6 One must give up one's life rather than violate this prohibition.[11]

7 This prohibition applies to both men and women, in all places and at all times.[12] These acts are forbidden to non-Jews as well, as idolatry is prohibited by one of the Seven Noahide Laws.[13]

NOTE: For the positive mitzvah to destroy idols and images, see *mitzvah #436: To destroy idolatry and its accompaniments.*

A REASON

The Torah forbids pagan and idolatrous worship. We are forbidden to make idols and images intended for worship, lest we come to serve them.

**DEDICATED BY THE KEST FAMILY
LOS ANGELES, CALIFORNIA**

8. The halachah follows the Tannaic view that a worker or craftsman is owed his wages as he completes each increment of his labor or of the manufacturing process. [This is the principle of יֶשְׁנָה לִשְׂכִירוּת מִתְּחִלָּה וְעַד סוֹף — *the wage is accrued from the beginning to the end of the service for which a worker is* paid. A second Tannaic view (see *Kiddushin* 48a-b and 63a) disputes this, and maintains that a hired worker is not legally owed his wages until the completion of his work (אֵינָה לִשְׂכִירוּת אֶלָּא לַבַּסוֹף); but the halachah does not accept this view.] Accordingly, even if an idol or image is completed and

worshipped immediately upon completion (see above, note 7), most of the craftsman's wage was accrued incrementally *before* the idol or image was completed and became forbidden as idolatry — and that part of the wage is therefore permitted. Moreover, even the final increment — that which turned the unfinished form into a finished idol or image of worship — is insignificant, since it is worth less than a *perutah*. Thus, none of the wages are prohibited (see *Avodah Zarah* 19b with *Rashi* and *Tosafos* there; *Rosh* there 1:19; *Ran* to *Avodah Zarah*, fol. 5b ד"ה ואם; see also *Avodah Zarah* 51b-52b; *Rambam, Hil. Avodas Kochavim* 7:4-5 and 9:11; and *Sefer HaMitzvos, Lo Saaseh* §2). However, some authorities maintain that it is [Rabbinically] forbidden to derive benefit from the wages (see *Rif* and *Ran* to *Avodah Zarah*, fol. 5b and *Tur* and *Shulchan Aruch, Yoreh Deah* 143:2), see *Bach* ad loc. ד"ה ומ"ש and *Shach* §4 who offer different reasons for this. *Taz* ad loc. (§3) suggests that even those Rishonim who do not mention that it is permissible to derive benefit from the payment that someone received for making an idol or image concede that the strict letter of the law permits such benefit. However, to distance people from idolatry, the Sages did not publicize this leniency.

9. As in all cases of *malkos*, the punishment may only be imposed if a warning was given (to the person who was about to violate the prohibition) immediately before the violation (see *Sanhedrin* 8b, *Makkos* 20b et al.; see *mitzvah #594). Minchas Chinuch* (27:4; see also 27:8) is uncertain whether the prohibition is violated only upon *completion* of the idol, in which case [he maintains that] the warning would have to be issued immediately before completion; or whether the entire act of manufacture is forbidden, so that warning at any stage of the process would be sufficient (and multiple warnings could conceivably result in liability to multiple sets of *malkos*). *Yerushalmi* (*Avodah Zarah* 4:4) however, states: *He is warned on each hammer [blow], and when he finishes, is administered lashes* (see *Tal Torah* ad loc.).

10. As mentioned above (note 3), apart from this prohibition — that is, *not to make an idol or image* — a person who makes an idol or image also violates *mitzvah* #214: *Not to make idolatry, for oneself or for others* (see *Vayikra* 19:4). Therefore, one who makes an idol or image for his own worship receives two sets of *malkos*, one for each prohibition [if he was warned about both prohibitions] (*Rambam, Hil. Avodas Kochavim* 3:9; see *Sefer HaMitzvos, Lo Saaseh* §2-3 from *Sifra*; *Sefer HaChinuch* §214; *Minchas Chinuch* 27:2). [For the parameters of the punishment of *malkos*, see *mitzvah* #594.]

11. The mitzvah to sanctify Hashem Name (*mitzvah* #296) requires a Jew to give up his or her life rather than violate the prohibitions against idolatry, illicit relationships (*arayos*) or bloodshed (ייהרג ואל יעבור — *he must let himself be killed and not violate*; see *mitzvah* #296; see also *Sanhedrin* 74a; *Sefer HaChinuch* §296, *Rama, Yoreh Deah* 157:1). Although violating an ancillary prohibition of idolatry does not incur the death penalty (as we have seen, the penalty for violating the prohibition against *making* an idol is *malkos*, not death), some authorities maintain that the rule that one must give up one's life rather than violate the prohibition applies to ancillary prohibitions of idolatry as well. In their view, one would be required to give up one's life rather than make an idol (*Sefer HaChinuch* loc. cit.; *Rama* loc. cit.; see *Minchas Chinuch* 296:15). Other authorities disagree, maintaining that one may violate ancillary prohibitions of idolatry if not doing so will cost him his life (*Tosafos* to *Avodah Zarah* 27b ד"ה שאני; *Nimukei Yosef* to *Bava Kamma* fol. 40a, ד"ה אמר המחבר).

12. This is in conformance with the general rule that men and women are equated by the Torah with regard to prohibitions (see Mishnah, *Kiddushin* 29a, and the Gemara there, 35a).

13. The Gemara in *Sanhedrin* (56a) lists seven mitzvos that were given to non-Jews (the reference to Noahide Laws reflects the fact that all of mankind descended from Noah, whose family were the sole survivors of the Flood). [For the full list, see note 13 to *mitzvah* #29.] One of these mitzvos is a prohibition against idolatry (see ibid. 56b, where the Gemara derives this from Scripture). Since the prohibition against making an idol falls under the general category of idolatry, it is also forbidden to non-Jews (see *Sanhedrin* 56b where the prohibition to make an idol or image is categorized as idolatry; see also *Rambam, Hil. Melachim* 9:2, who writes that even ancillary prohibitions of idolatry which do not carry the death penalty are also forbidden to non-Jews; see also *Minchas Chinuch* 27:7 and *Mitzvas Hashem* [*R' Yonasan Steif*] §6).

A BROADER LOOK AT THE LAWS

1 What is the forbidden action in the case of a person who commissions someone else to make an idol?

As mentioned above (note 6), the authorities disagree as to when a person who commissions someone else to make an idol or image violates this prohibition. Some authorities maintain that it is the actual *making* of the idol or image that is the forbidden action, and that the violation is attributed to the person who issued the commission via the mechanism of agency [שליחות] (*Sefer HaChinuch* §27 in explanation of *Rambam, Hil. Avodas Kochavim* 3:9; this would also seem to be the simple understanding of the phrasing of *Lechem Mishneh* ad loc.; see further below, *Iyunim* §2). Other authorities maintain that it is the *issuance of the commission* to make the idol or image that is the forbidden action in such a case (*Mishnas Chachamim, Hil. Avodah Zarah* §17, *Yavin Shemuah* §3; *Minchas Chinuch* 27:1); the principle of agency is thus not required to render the person issuing the commission liable. Still other authorities maintain that the forbidden action takes place when the person who issued the commission acquires and takes possession of the idol or image (*Megillas Esther* to *Sefer HaMitzvos, shoresh* §9; *S'dei Chemed* vol. 4, *Maareches Lamed* §12 in the name of *Mirkeves HaMishneh* [Alfandri]; see *Rambam* in *Sefer HaMitzvos, Lo Saaseh* §3 who writes: *that he acquired idolatry "and it came to him"*; see above, note 4).

2 Why does a person who commissions someone else to make an idol or image receive lashes, even though he has violated a prohibition without performing an action?

We learned above (Law 2) that a person who commissions someone else to make an idol or image receives *malkos* (*Rambam, Hil. Avodas Kochavim* 3:9

and *Sefer HaMitzvos, Lo Saaseh* §2). Since verbal expression is not considered an action (*Sanhedrin* 65b), this law seems to contradict the rule that a person who violates a prohibition that does not involve action [לאו שאין בו מעשה] does not receive *malkos* (*Makkos* 2b). The authorities suggest various resolutions of this issue:

A. Although normally verbal expression is not considered an action, since in this case the expression resulted in an action (the making of the idol), it is deemed an action. Therefore, one who commissions someone to make an idol or image receives *malkos* (*Mishnas Chachamim* loc. cit.; *Minchas Chinuch* 27:1 in explanation of *Lechem Mishneh* to *Rambam* ad loc.).

B. The person who commissioned the idol or image does not receive *malkos* for issuing the commission. Rather, it is for the acquisition and taking possession of the idol or image that he is punished (*S'dei Chemed* loc. cit.; *Nimukei Maharai* cited in *Sefer HaLikkutim* [Frankel] to *Rambam, Hil. Avodas Kochavim* 3:9).

C. Since it is *possible* to violate this prohibition through an action (e.g. if the person himself makes the idol), the prohibition is considered to be inherently one that is violated through an action, and therefore *any* violation of the prohibition, even through a verbal command, renders a person liable to *malkos* (*S'dei Chemed* loc. cit. from *Mareh Nogah* to *Rambam, Hil. Avodas Kochavim* loc. cit.).

D. The Torah was stringent with regard to idolatry, and subjected a person who violates its prohibitions to *malkos* even though he did not violate the prohibition through an action (*Minchas Chinuch* loc. cit.; *S'dei Chemed* loc. cit. ד"ה וגם, based on *Sefer HaChinuch* §86; see *Minchas Chinuch* 86:1; see also *Kessef Mishneh* to *Hil. Avodas Kochavim* 5:11).

E. The craftsman who makes the idol or image is an agent of the person who commissioned him to do so. Therefore, through the vehicle of agency, the person who commissioned the idol or image to be made is treated as if he himself actually made the idol or image (a simple understanding of the phrasing of *Lechem Mishneh* loc. cit.; cf. *Minchas Chinuch* loc. cit.).

This final explanation, however, requires further analysis, for it would seem to contradict the principle that there can be no agent for an act of transgression (אין שליח לדבר עבירה; see *Kiddushin* 42b and *Sefer HaChinuch* §27, who poses the question).

One possible resolution is that the Torah only attributes the violation to a person who issued a commission in cases where there *can* legally be an agent for an act of transgression, such as a case in which the agent was unaware that he was violating a prohibition [and thus the *reason* that there is no agency for transgressions — namely, that the agent should not have heeded his sender's instructions — does not apply, allowing his agency to *be* effective] (see *Bava Metzia* 10b, and *Tosafos* to *Kiddushin* 42b ד"ה אמאי. For further exceptions to this rule, see *Minchas Chinuch* 27:6 and *Maharam Schick* on the mitzvos ad loc.). Alternatively, it is possible that since this prohibition is in the category of idolatry, the Torah was stringent in its regard and therefore made it an exception to the rule that there can be no agent for an act of transgression (*Mikneh Avraham*, cited in *S'dei Chemed*

loc. cit. ד"ה ועל מה שהקשה; see there for further discussion of this view).

3 Why is this prohibition not deemed a "generalized prohibition" (לאו שבכללות)?

Since this prohibition forbids the making of all sorts of idols and images, it would seem that it should be deemed a "generalized prohibition" (לאו שבכללות — an umbrella injunction that covers several specific prohibitions). Since the law is that one does not incur *malkos* for transgressing a generalized prohibition (see *Pesachim* 41b and *Rashi* ad loc.; see also *Rambam, Sefer HaMitzvos shoresh* §9 ד"ה ומה שראוי and *Hasagos HaRamban* ad loc.), *Raavad* (to *Hil. Avodas Kochavim* 3:9 based on *Sanhedrin* 63a) questions how a person can receive *malkos* for violating this prohibition. He answers that a prohibition is only classified as a generalized prohibition if it forbids several distinct acts under an umbrella prohibition. [For example, the prohibition against eating the *korban pesach* "any way other than roasted" (כי אם צלי אש) is a generalized prohibition, because it forbids both cooking the *pesach* in water and eating it raw.] This prohibition, however, forbids only one act — the making of an idol. The fact that many types of idols are included does not render this a generalized prohibition.

SITUATIONS IN HALACHAH

שיח הלכה

Question:

How could Aharon have agreed to make the *Eigel HaZahav* (Golden Calf), contrary to the prohibition against crafting a graven image?

Answer:

We learned above (note 3) that the manufacture of an idol is forbidden even if the maker does not intend to worship it himself. The manufacture of the *Eigel*, then, aside from leading to pagan worship, apparently involved two infractions of Torah law simply by virtue of its production. The *Bnei Yisrael*, who commissioned Aharon to make the statue, transgressed *mitzvah #27*, *Do not make for yourself an idol or image*, while Aharon himself, for his part in making it for his fellow Jews, was apparently in violation of *mitzvah #214*, *not to make an object of idolatry for oneself or for others*.

Many of the commentators are troubled by this assessment. How could Aharon, the Kohen chosen by God, have willingly complied with the demand of the masses to take action contrary to the law of the Torah?

❧ *Why Aharon did not forfeit his life*

The Medrash (*Shemos Rabbah* 41:7; *Vayikra Rabbah* 10:3; see also *Sanhedrin* 7b), in its account of the events leading up to the creation of the Golden Calf, adds detail to the account related in *Shemos*: At first, the people approached Chur, son of Miriam, and said, "Arise, and make a god for us!" When he refused to cooperate, they set upon him and killed him. They next approached Aharon, demanding, "Arise, and make a god for us!" When Aharon heard that, he became afraid. [This is alluded to in the verse (*Shemos* 32:5) which states: וירא אהרן ויבן מזבח לפניו, *And Aharon saw, and he built an altar before it*. The words וַיַּרְא אַהֲרֹן, *and Aharon saw*, can be vowelized as וַיִּירָא אַהֲרֹן, *and Aharon was*

afraid; and the words וַיִּבֶן מִזְבֵּחַ לְפָנָיו, *and he built an altar before it,* can be vowelized as וַיָּבֶן מִזְבָּחַ לְפָנָיו, *and he understood* (the danger he was in) *from the slaughtered one* (Chur) *who lay before him.*] Aharon understood, then, that he faced the same fate as his nephew Chur; his life was in danger. He therefore agreed to make the *Eigel*. This, however, is still problematic. Idol worship is one of the three sins for which one is required to sacrifice his life rather than transgress, so Aharon, like Chur, seemingly should have resisted the crowd, even if it would have cost him his life! (see *Ramban* to *Shemos* 32:21).

Some commentators (see *Or HaChaim* to *Shemos* ad loc.) answer that only the actual *worship* of a pagan symbol — a capital crime — is counted among the three sins. But one is not required to give up his life to avoid being forced into *making* an idol, a transgression that does not carry the death penalty. Accordingly, Aharon was permitted to produce the Golden Calf to avert his death at the hands of the multitude.

This solution, however, is subject to dispute. According to many authorities, *all* prohibitions relating to idol worship, regardless of the penalty they carry, must be avoided even at the cost of one's life (see above, note 11). Some commentators go so far as to say that this applies to even the mere provision of support to another Jew's idol worship (*R' Yosef Engel*, in *Beis HaOtzar* §52 and *Lekach Tov* §1). If so, the question remains: Why didn't Aharon forfeit his life rather than construct the *Eigel*?

Moreover, even according to the opinion that the making of a graven image is not categorized as one of the three sins, a difficulty still remains. The Rishonim (see *Nimukei Yosef* to *Sanhedrin*, fol. 18a ד״ה המקדש) write that when a distinguished personality, known for his piety, observes that his contemporaries are excessively lax in a specific mitzvah, it is appropriate for him to persist in his fulfillment of that mitzvah, even at the cost of his life, so that his generation may learn proper fear of Hashem from his example. A precedent for this is found in the story of Chananyah, Mishael, and

Azaryah, who preferred to be cast into a blazing furnace rather than to prostrate themselves before a statue of Nevuchadnezzar, even though the tyrant had only his honor in mind, and not genuine worship. In light of this, it would seem that Aharon HaKohen, who was surrounded by a populace deficient in their understanding of the Torah's prohibition of idolatry, might have recognized just such an opportunity to sanctify Hashem's Name and give up his life for the sake of the mitzvah.

It has been suggested that Aharon did, in fact, consider this option, but determined that it must not be taken. He feared that if his brethren would indeed kill him, the devastating consequences for the nation would be irreversible. A parallel incident occurred many years later, when the prophet Zechariah was slain by his fellow Jews, who did not accept his words of rebuke. This tragedy is cited as one of the factors that led to the eventual destruction of the first *Beis HaMikdash*, and resulted in the slaughter of hundreds of thousands of Jews (see *Sanhedrin* 96b). So Aharon, in the interest of *Klal Yisrael's* ultimate welfare, declined to sacrifice his life, something he would otherwise have willingly done (see *Pardes Yosef*, and *Sanhedrin* 7b).

Or HaChaim (ibid.) offers another solution; he states that Aharon's conduct did not technically violate any prohibition. For Aharon did not actively fashion the image of the calf; he merely cast the gold into the flames, and it spontaneously emerged in the shape of a calf. Since he did not actively make the *Eigel*, there was nothing that he was required to sacrifice his life to avoid doing. *Megillas Sefer* (to *Shir HaShirim* 1:2) goes even further: In his view, Aharon had no intention of creating an image of any kind with his action. Having perceived that the primary factor in the Jews' present moral failure was the abundance of wealth in their possession — as the prophet (*Hoshea* 2:10) complained, *I lavished silver upon her, and gold, which they used for the Baal* — Aharon proceeded to collect their golden jewelry and threw it into the fire; his objective was to destroy it all in the flames. But, alas, the Satan intervened, and the image of a calf emerged from the flames.

Yet another solution proposed (see *Minchas Chinuch* 27:3; see also *Pnei Yehoshua* to *Rosh Hashanah* 24b) is that the Jews did not have any idolatrous designs in mind when they produced the *Eigel*. They were looking for nothing more than a substitute leader to serve in place of the missing Moshe Rabbeinu [which, while incorrect behavior, would not be true idol worship]. However, once the calf emerged from the flames, the [non-Jewish] "mixed multitude," who had ascended from Mitzrayim with the Jews, went further and deified the calf in consonance with their old practices, and then drew the rest of the masses astray into worship of the image. At the time of its casting, though, the calf was in no way intended to represent a deity, and thus Aharon was not required to sacrifice his life to avoid making it.

ILLUMINATIONS OF THE MITZVAH
Suggested Reasons & Insights

I. A SAFEGUARD AGAINST IDOLATRY

The making of idols and carved images was forbidden by the Torah to preserve the law against idol worship (see *Chinuch* §27), for "once he creates it, he may bow down to it, and from there he will progress to genuine worship" (*Rabbeinu Bachya, Shemos* 20:4). This concern is reminiscent of the opening verse in *Tehillim*: *Fortunate is the man who has not walked in the counsel of the wicked, who has not stood in the pathway of the sinful, and has not sat in a session of scoffers.* The Gemara (*Avodah Zarah* 18b) asks: If one has not even walked in the path of the sinful, surely he didn't stand there. And given that he has not even stood, how would he come to sit? Rather, answer the Sages, the point of this verse is that if one will allow himself to walk by, he will find himself stopping, if only to stand. And once he has stood, he will eventually sit, joining the company of indolent scoffers; before long, he will himself become an active participant in their mockery.

The road to idol worship is no different. If one wishes to avoid stumbling into true veneration of idols, he must not even tread in its path. But once the figure has been made, the first step has been taken. As the Torah here says, *You shall not make for yourselves a graven image … You shall not bow down to them and you shall not serve them.* For if you will make it, you will eventually bow. And once you have bowed, you will inevitably serve (*Rabbeinu Bachya* ibid.).

[It is forbidden to fashion a carved image even for a pure-minded purpose; for example, to memorialize a miracle wrought by God through the agency of the force depicted in that image. One may believe that he is actually furthering God's will by dedicating a lasting testimonial to the miraculous intervention by which God came to our aid. Isn't it true — he would be tempted to reason — that there are several mitzvos ordained by the Torah to serve just such a purpose? The *sukkah* is lived in for seven days, "so that your generations shall know that I settled you in *sukkos* when I took you out of the land of Mitzrayim" (*Vayikra* 23:43). On Pesach, the *korban pesach* is brought to remind us how God "passed over" our ancestors' dwellings, sparing their firstborn from the effects of the plague. And matzah is eaten in commemoration of the unleavened dough with which our forefathers hurried out of the land of Mitzrayim. Why shouldn't an idol, too, follow those precedents in bearing testimony to the divinity and power of our merciful God? To counter such logic and to prevent such an error, the Torah teaches us a categorical prohibition against crafting a sculpted image, even if the subject is an agent of God (*Rabbeinu Bachya,* ibid.).]

II. "TO WHOM DARE YOU COMPARE GOD?"

Beyond creating images to represent deities or the controlling forces of the universe, the Torah prohibits carving an image even when it is meant as a symbol of God Himself. One must not believe that it is desirable, in the cause of enhancing our awareness of God, to designate something concrete and visible as a representation of the Invisible God. Such a notion is liable to obscure one of the foundations of the Jewish concept of God — the fact that the Creator has neither body nor physical form, and a physical being cannot possibly behold His essence at all. As the Torah itself explains: *For you did not see [at Har Sinai] any image on the day God spoke to you* (*Devarim* 4:15). What physical image, then, can one propose to make, to represent a Being that has no form? Or, in the words of the prophet (*Yeshaya* 40:18), *To whom do you compare God?* (R' Y. Bechor Shor, *Shemos* 20:4; *Chizkuni* ad loc.).

III. "GODS OF SILVER AND GODS OF GOLD YOU SHALL NOT MAKE FOR YOURSELVES."

The abstract "idolization" of silver and gold, which draws men into the relentless pursuit of material wealth, is also warned against by this mitzvah. Just as the reverence of a pagan symbol inevitably dilutes one's dedication to the service of God, it is likewise impossible to invest time and effort into one's spiritual calling while being consumed by the scramble for possessions and wealth. At some point, these icons of the modern-day form of idolatry will, in the minds of such men, supplant their God in Heaven as the focus of their lives, their source for hope and security. To warn against such folly comes the verse (*Shemos* 20:20): *Gods of silver and gods of gold you shall not make for yourselves* (*Akeidas Yitzchak* §45).

One who does find himself in possession of wealth and property must endeavor to guard himself from placing his reliance on them, for to do so is equivalent to denial of God, as the verse states (*Devarim* 8:11,17): *Be heedful lest you will forget Hashem your God ... and you will say in your heart, 'My strength, and the power of my hand, have made for me all this wealth'* (*Derashos Rabbeinu Yonah, Shemos* ad loc.).

THROUGH THE EYES OF THE SAGES

Stories, Parables & Reflections

I. THE GOLDEN CALF

In Parashas Ki Sisa the story of the Golden Calf is told. Moshe had been atop Mount Sinai for forty days and forty nights, and when he did not return at the expected time, the people assumed that he had died. They sought to replace him with a new leader of a godly nature, and Aharon was called on to create it for them. Aharon proceeded to collect their jewelry, and he threw the gold into a fire. Out of the flames emerged a golden calf, which became for some an object of pagan worship.

On the morrow Moshe finally descended from the mountain with the Divine gift of two Tablets in hand, only to be greeted by the raucous sounds of his brethren celebrating around a graven image. Immediately, he threw down the holy Tablets, shattering them before the eyes of the nation. He destroyed the calf and punished those who had deified it, but the lofty level attained by the nation as a whole with the Revelation at Sinai was lost.

Moshe reascended the mountain to pray for forgiveness on behalf of his people, and in time God yielded and pledged not to destroy them. Instead, His retribution would be meted out piecemeal; whenever Israel's sins would necessitate punishment, some measure of this debt would be collected as well. After forty days Moshe came down and then went back up a third time, this time to receive a new set of Tablets in place of the first set.

A sampling of the Sages' comments on this episode follows:

────── ✌ ──────

✌ Hope for Penitents

In reality, Israel was not suited to commit such a sin, just as, in a later time, King David was not suited to act as he did with Bathsheva. Why did this

episode occur? To give hope to penitent sinners. If a whole community stumbles, they will be encouraged by the precedent set by the Golden Calf, and if an individual sins, he need only study the example of David (*Avodah Zarah* 4b-5a).

────── ✌ ──────

✌ A tragic mistake

Scripture relates that Moshe was *boshesh, delayed*, in descending the mountain. This word can be read as *ba'u shesh*, meaning *six hours have passed.* Moshe was scheduled to return after forty days, as the sixth hour began. When forty days had passed, the Satan came and said to the Jews: The sixth hour is gone and your teacher Moshe has not returned! [In reality, there was one day remaining, because the forty days did not begin with the day of his departure, but with the first full day Moshe spent in Heaven — *Rashi.*] The Jews paid the Satan no heed, but then he showed them an image of a bier carrying Moshe to Heaven. It was to this image that the people referred when they said to Aharon (*Shemos* 32:1), *For **this** man Moshe who brought us up from the land of Egypt — we do not know what became of him* (*Shabbos* 89a; cf. *Shemos Rabbah* 41:7; *Tanchuma, Ki Sisa* §19).

────── ✌ ──────

✌ Aharon's role

Originally, it was Chur, the son of Miriam, who was asked to help create a replacement for Moshe; when he refused to cooperate, he was assailed and killed. The people then proceeded to Aharon, who understood what was at stake, and thus feared to defy them. The words וַיַּרְא אַהֲרֹן וַיִּבֶן מִזְבֵּחַ לְפָנָיו — *And Aharon saw, and he built an altar before him* (*Shemos* 32:5) — can also be read: וַיִּירָא אַהֲרֹן וַיָּבֶן מִזְבֵּחַ לְפָנָיו — *And Aharon feared, and understood from the slaughtered man in front of him* (cf. *Maharzav* to *Shemos Rabbah*). Aharon reasoned, "If they kill me too, this would fulfill the verse (*Eichah* 2:20), *Should a Kohen and prophet be slain in God's sanctuary?* And in that case, they will be sentenced to immediate exile (and the resulting damage to the world would be irreparable)."

Another approach: *And Aharon saw* … What did he see? He realized that if he left the work to the people, they would all contribute and the graven image would be completed at once. But if he himself undertook to do it, he could delay until Moshe returned. Moreover, if he would make it himself, he could do so in the Name of God, as indeed it is written (*Shemos* 32:5), *Aharon proclaimed and he said, "A festival for God tomorrow!"*

Alternatively, Aharon said to himself: "If the people build it, they will bear the blame. Better I should be blamed in their stead." This can be compared to the son of a king, who, in a moment of arrogance, reached for a sword to attack his father. The prince's mentor intervened and said to his charge, "Don't bother yourself; I will do it for you." The king gazed at him and finally said, "I understand your intention. Rather you should bear responsibility than my son. I swear by your life that you shall not be sent away from the palace; rather you will eat from my table, and receive twenty-four gifts." Similarly, Aharon was told, in his role as *Kohen Gadol* (*Vayikra* 21:12), *From the sanctuary he shall not go out* (even when in mourning, the *Kohen Gadol* is not disqualified from performing the Temple Service); he was given the privilege of eating the remaining portions of the sacrificial offerings; and was presented, on behalf of all other *Kohanim* (the priestly descendants of Aharon) with　twenty-four gifts. God said to Aharon (*Tehillim* 45:8), *You loved righteousness and abhorred wickedness;* you loved maintaining the innocence of My children, and you hated to see them incur any punishment. *It is for this that Hashem, your God, has anointed you* — thus did God say to Aharon: "By your life, from the entire tribe of Levi, only you have been chosen for the role of High Priest" (*Vayikra Rabbah* 10:3; cf. *Sanhedrin* 7a; *Shemos Rabbah* 41:7; *Bamidbar Rabbah* 15:21; *Tanchuma, Tetzaveh* §10, *Ki Sisa* §19, *Beha'aloscha* §14; *Pirkei D'Rabbi Eliezer* §45).

———— 🙠 ————

🙠 Molding the Calf

Forty thousand of the "mixed multitude" that had joined the Exodus gathered around Aharon; among them were two Egyptian sorcerers, by the names of Yonus and Yombrus, who had performed before Pharaoh in Egypt. Aharon reluctantly threw the gold into the fire, and the sorcerers stepped forward and worked their magic. Some say the one who did this was Michah, who, as an infant, was squeezed by the Egyptians into the wall of a building (in place of a brick), and was saved by Moshe himself. Michah now took the tablet Moshe had crafted in Egypt to retrieve the coffin of Yosef, on which was written "Rise up, Ox!" and he threw it into the furnace amid the rings. A calf then emerged, leaping and grunting, prompting the crowd to exclaim (*Shemos* 32:4), *This is your god, O Israel* (*Tanchuma, Ki Sisa* 19; cf. *Rashi, Sanhedrin* 103b. See also *Zohar* II, 191a-192b, at length).

Another source says that Aharon had found among the rings a headplate of gold that had the Holy Name [of God] written on it, along with an engraving depicting a calf, and it was that alone that he threw into the furnace. Therefore, it is said, *I threw **it** (not them) into the fire, and this calf came out.* The calf came out grunting, for the Satanic angel Samael infiltrated it and made grunting noises to lead Israel astray (*Pirkei D'Rabbi Eliezer*).

———— 🙠 ————

🙠 A shameful betrayal

Israel's impudence in making the Golden Calf was analogous to a bride who betrays her husband in the midst of her wedding. Regarding this it is said (*Shir HaShirim* 1:12), *While the king was yet at his table [Sinai], my nard [malodorous deed — the Golden Calf] gave forth its scent* (*Shabbos* 88b; *Gittin* 36b).

In regard to the Golden Calf, it is said (*Daniel* 9:7), *The righteousness is Yours, O God, and the shamefacedness is ours.* After all that Israel did in making the Golden Calf, the supply of manna should have been curtailed; instead, it is written (*Nechemiah* 9:17-18, 20), *You did not forsake them, even when they made themselves a molten calf ... You did not withhold Your manna from their mouths ...* Moreover, the worshippers of the calf actually took some manna and presented it as an offering before their idol, and the manna still rained down the following day. Indeed, the righteousness is God's, while shamefacedness is ours.

Alternatively, as Israel stood down below, engraving an idol and angering their Creator, God, at that very moment, was sitting on High, engraving the Tablets with which to grant them true life. Concerning this it was said, *The righteousness is Yours, O God, and the shamefacedness is ours* (*Shemos Rabbah* 41:1; *Tanchuma, Ki Sisa* §14, *Re'eh* §16; *Pesikta D'Rav Kahana* 10:8; cf. *Medrash Tehillim* 3:3).

───── ❧ ─────

❧ *Varying punishments*

A wise woman once asked R' Eliezer: Why were the idolaters who worshipped the calf not all punished in the same manner? [Some were killed by the swords of the Leviim (*Shemos* 32:28), others died in a Heaven-sent plague (ibid. v. 35), and a third group died after drinking from water mixed with the ashes of the calf (ibid. v. 20), similar to an adulterous wife who is tested with the bitter waters of the *sotah*.] Rav and Levi gave differing answers. One said: Those who slaughtered sacrifices or burned incense were killed by the sword; those who embraced or kissed the statue died in the plague, and those who were inwardly glad died from distension of the stomach (brought on by the potion they drank). The other said: Those who were seen and warned by witnesses (and could be punished by the court), were killed by the sword; those who were seen but not warned, died in the plague; and those who were neither seen nor warned, died from distension of the stomach (*Yoma* 66b; cf. *Bamidbar Rabbah* 9:48; *Tanchuma, Ki Sisa* §26; *Pesikta Rabbasi* §10).

───── ❧ ─────

❧ *Eminence Lost*

When the Jews proclaimed, *We will do and we will listen,* signifying their unquestioning acceptance of God's law, sixty myriads of ministering angels came, and adorned each one with two crowns [of Divine radiance — *Rashi*], one corresponding to *we will do* and the other to *we will listen.* But now that Israel had sinned, one hundred and twenty myriads of destructive angels came down to remove them, as is stated (*Shemos* 33:6): *The Children of Israel were stripped of their jewelry from Mount Chorev.* However, in the future God will restore them, as it is said (*Yeshayah* 35:10): *And the redeemed of God will return, and they will come to Zion with song, and eternal joy will be upon their heads.* This alludes to a joy that was long ago on their heads [i.e. the crowns they received at Sinai] (*Shabbos* 88a; *Sifrei, VeZos HaBrachah* §356; *Eichah Rabbah, Pesichah* §24; *Pesikta Rabbasi* 10:6, 34:10; et al.).

───── ❧ ─────

❧ *Foreign domination and death*

Israel received the Torah so that no other nation could ever dominate them, as it says (*Devarim* 5:26): *... so that it should be good for them and their children forever.* Rabbi Yose taught differently: Israel received the Torah so that the Angel of Death could not hold sway over them as it is written (*Tehillim* 82:6): *And I had said, you are angelic, sons of the Most High, are you all.* But, alas, you corrupted your deeds with the Sin of the Calf, and henceforth *like men you shall die ...* How does the first opinion explain this verse? The death it refers to is poverty (*Avodah Zarah* 5a; *Mechilta, Yisro;* cf. *Tanchuma, Shelach* §13, *Eikev* §8; *Shemos Rabbah* 32:1, 41:7, 51:8; *Shir HaShirim Rabbah* 8:6; *Zohar* II, 45b; et al.).

───── ❧ ─────

❧ *Perpetual suffering*

At this time, an edict was passed that Israel be destined to study the Torah amidst suffering, servitude, expulsions, confusion, oppression, and hunger. However, God will eventually reward them for their suffering — in the Messianic Era and in the World to Come, as it is said (*Yeshayah* 40:10), *Behold, God will come with force, and His power shall rule for Him; behold His reward is with Him, and His wages are there before Him* (*Tanna D'vei Eliyahu Zuta* §4).

———— ❧ ————

❧ The Temple's destruction

R' Yitzchak said: There is no punishment that comes to the world that does not include a minute amount of retribution for the sin of the Calf, as it is said (*Shemos* 32:34): *On the day that I make My account, I shall bring their sin to account against them.* R' Chanina said: After twenty-four generations (in the generation of Tzidkiah, which was witness to the Temple's destruction) this accounting was made, as it is said (*Yechezkel* 9:1): *And He called in my ears with a great voice, saying: The city's accounts draw near, each man with his weapon of destruction in hand* (see *Sanhedrin* 102a; cf. *Yerushalmi, Taanis* 4:5; *Eichah Rabbah* 1:28, 2:3).

II. THE IDOL OF MICHAH

n the book of *Shoftim, chapters 17-18, the incident of Michah's idol is related in detail. Michah's mother, from Mount Ephraim, made a molten idol for him, and he set up around it a house of idol worship complete with an ephod and icons which would reveal the future by means of sorcery. He hired as a priest a lad from the tribe of Levi who was in need of a livelihood; this priest Yonasan was a grandson of none other than Moshe Rabbeinu himself.*

After some time, the tribe of Dan overtook the shrine and appropriated the idol with its accessories, and they retained the Levi to continue as priest. The Danites went on to conquer the city of Layish and settle there. They brought to Layish the idol of Michah, and there it remained, under the care of the Levi and his sons, for many years.

———— ❧ ————

❧ Michah and Moshe

Why was he called *Michah*? Because he was pressed [*nismachmech*] into a building in Egypt, instead of a brick. Moshe complained to God, *Why have You brought harm to this nation?* — now, when there is a shortage of bricks, they place Jewish children into the building! God answered, "It is merely thorns that they are destroying; it is known to Me that if these children were to live, they would grow up to be thoroughly wicked. If you wish, you may make an experiment and take one of them out. Moshe went and took out one of the babies, who grew up to be that infamous Michah (see *Sanhedrin* 101b with *Rashi* there).

———— ❧ ————

❧ The idol's history

R' Leizer taught: A graven image (this was the idol of Michah — *Sifrei* and *Mechilta*) crossed the Sea of Reeds together with Israel, as it is said (*Samuel* II, 7:23): *…before Your nation, whom You have redeemed for Yourself from Egypt, nations and their **gods**…* (*Yerushalmi Succah* 4:3; *Mechilta, Bo*; *Sifrei, Beh'aloscha* 84; et al; see also *Sanhedrin* 103b).

———— ❧ ————

❧ Crossing in shame

R' Yose said: There is something even more shameful — The Jews crossed the split Sea with the idol of Michah in their possession, as it is said (*Zechariah* 10:11), *A rival crossed through the sea.* Nevertheless, the sea split for their sake. Concerning this it was said (*Daniel* 9:7), *The righteousness is Yours, O God, and the shamefacedness is ours* (*Tanchuma, Ki Sisa* §14, *Re'eh* §16; *Shemos Rabbah* 41:1; *Pesikta D'Rav Kahana* 10:8; cf. *Bamidbar Rabbah* 16:26; *Medrash Aggadah, Bamidbar* 1:15).

———— ❧ ————

❧ Michah's merit

Why is Michah not counted among those who lost their portion in the World to Come? Because his bread was always available for travelers (cf. *Shoftim* 17:8; 18:2). R' Nassan taught: There was a distance of three *mil* between Gerav (Michah's hometown — *Rashi*) and Shiloh (then the site of the Tabernacle), and the smoke of the Tabernacle's Altar would intermingle with the smoke of the sacrifices offered to Michah's idol. The ministering angels sought to push Michah aside [i.e. to destroy him], but the Holy One, Blessed is He, said to them, "Leave him be, for his bread is always available to travelers" (*Sanhedrin* 103b).

——— ✻ ———

✎ Grandson of Moshe

And [the Danite men] turned there and said [to Yonasan]: *Who brought you here (halom), and what are you doing here (bazeh), and what is there here (poh) for you?* (*Shoftim* 18:3). They were saying to him: Are you not a descendant of Moshe, regarding whom it is written (*Shemos* 3:5): *Do not approach any closer (halom)?* Are you not a descendant of Moshe, regarding whom it is written (ibid. 4:2): *What is this (mazeh) in your hand?* Are you not a descendant of Moshe, regarding whom it is written (*Devarim* 5:28): *And you stand here (poh) with Me?* How could you become a priest of idol worship? He replied to them: I have received a tradition from the house of my grandfather (Moshe): Let one hire himself out to the service of idols rather than come to need the gifts of others. [Yonasan thought that Moshe literally meant the service of idols, *avodah zarah*. He was mistaken; Moshe actually meant a job that is foreign (*zarah*), i.e. unfitting to him. As Rav said to Rav Kahana, "Flay carcasses in the marketplace, and receive your wage, and do not think, 'I am a great man; this is beneath my dignity.'"] Later, when King David saw that money was very dear to [Yonasan], he lured him away with an appointment to oversee the royal houses of treasure, as it is said (*Divrei HaYamim* I, 26:24): *And Shevuel, the son of Gershom, the son of Moshe, was overseer of the treasure houses.* Was his name, then, really Shevuel? Wasn't it Yonasan? R' Yochanan taught:

He was so called for he returned (*Shav*) to God (*El*) with all his heart (*Bava Basra* 110a).

R' Shmuel bar Nachman was asked: But isn't it written (*Shoftim* 18:30), *And Yonasan, son of Gershom, son of Menasheh, he and his descendants were priests for the Danite tribe until the people of the Land were banished* (indicating that he and his family remained at this post well beyond the reign of King David)? He answered: After David died, Shlomo arose and replaced all the royal officers, after which Yonasan reverted to his ruinous ways (*Yerushalmi, Sanhedrin* 11:5, *Berachos* 9:2. In *Berachos*, the *Yerushalmi* adds that he was the fraudulent prophet described in *Melachim* I, 13:11).

——— ✻ ———

✎ Unfaithful service

R' Shmuel bar Nachman was asked by his colleagues: How did a priest for an idol (i.e. Yonasan, who, as noted above, was still living during King David's reign) merit so long a life? He answered: This was due to his begrudging attitude toward the idol in his care. If one would come with an offering of a bull, sheep, or goat with which to appease the deity, this priest would dissuade him, saying, "Why? What good will it do you? It does not eat or drink, and it cannot help nor harm!" The supplicant would counter, "What, then, should I do?" To which the priest would answer, "Go and bring me a plateful of fine flour along with ten eggs, and I will appease the idol for you." After the worshipper left, Yonasan would eat the offering himself. It happened one time, upon hearing the priest's disparaging remarks about the idol, that a clever pilgrim retorted, "If this fetish is worthless, then why are you here?" He answered, "For the sake of my livelihood" (*Yerushalmi, Sanhedrin* 11:5, *Berachos* 9:2. A different version is found in *Shir HaShirim Rabbah* 2:18, where he is recorded as customarily asking the supplicant for his age, after which he would admonish the petitioner for stooping to worship a statue so much "younger" than himself).

III. THE CALVES OF YERAVAM

mong the incidents of idolatry that appear in Tanach, the calves of Yeravam are noteworthy in that they represent the first occurrence of officially promoted idol worship involving a significant portion of the Jewish nation. Yeravam is therefore seen as the classic proponent of idolatry among the kings of Israel (cf. *Melachim* I, 15:34, 16:19, et al); even Achav, whose later outrages made Yeravam's sins pale in comparison (*Sanhedrin* 102b), is nevertheless described as having gone "in the ways of Yeravam" (cf. *Melachim* I, 16:31). Thus said the Sages: Every upstanding king was attributed to David, and every wicked king was attributed to Yeravam (*Sifrei Zuta, Bamidbar* 27:1).

After the Ten Tribes seceded from the kingdom of Yehudah and crowned Yeravam, son of Nevat, as king, Scripture relates the following:

> *Yeravam then thought, "Now the kingship may revert to the house of David. If the people will go up to bring offerings in the Temple of God in Jerusalem, the heart of this people will return to their lord, to Rechavam, king of Yehudah, and they will kill me ...*
>
> *The king took counsel, and he made two golden calves; and he said to [the people], "It is too far for you to go up to Jerusalem. These are your gods, O Israel, who brought you up from the land of Egypt!" He placed the one in Beth-el and the [other] one in Dan. This matter became a sin, and the people traveled to Dan [to worship] before one. He also made a temple of high places, and he appointed priests from the commoners of the people, who were not of the children of Levi.*
>
> *Yeravam also innovated a holiday in the eighth month, on the fifteenth day of the month, in imitation of the holiday in Yehudah, and brought offerings on the altar ... (Melachim I, 12:28-32).*

——— ✻ ———

∽ *The sin at its root*

Rav Nachman taught: Yeravam's arrogance drove him out of the world, as it is said, *Yeravam then*

thought: *Now the kingship may revert to the house of David. If this people will go up to bring offerings in the Temple of God in Jerusalem, the heart of this people will return to their lord, to Rechavam, king of Yehudah, and they will kill me ...* He reasoned: Now, there is a law received by tradition from Moshe at Sinai that no one may sit in the Temple Courtyard except a king of Davidic descent. When the people will see Rechavam sitting, while I stand, they will conclude, "This one is a king, and that one is a subject." And if I sit, I will be judged to have committed an act of rebellion against the king, and I will be killed. With that, *the king took counsel, and he made two golden calves; and he said to [the people], "It is too far for you to go up to Jerusalem ..." (Sanhedrin* 101b).

——— ✻ ———

∽ *Mysterious powers*

Elisha [the prophet] came to Damascus (*Melachim* II, 8:7). What business did he have in Damascus? R' Yochanan taught: He went to persuade Gechazi, his erstwhile attendant, to return to the fold. He said to him, "Repent!" but Gechazi declined, saying, "This tradition I have received from you: A sinner who also led others to sin is not allowed the opportunity to repent!" What, then, had Gechazi done? According to one opinion, he hung a magnet over 'the sin of Yeravam' [the calves], causing them to be suspended in mid-air (to create the impression that they had supernatural powers). Others say that he carved a Divine Name into the mouths of the calves, and they would call out the words of the Ten Commandments: I am Hashem, your God; You shall not recognize other gods... (ibid. 107b).

——— ✻ ———

∽ *Deceiving the leaders*

The king took counsel, and he made two golden calves... R' Yehuda taught: Yeravam would seat the wicked and righteous together, and presented his plan to set up statues in Beth-el and Dan. He said, "Are you ready to sign on to whatever I do?" They agreed. He then said, "I would like to be king." "Yes," they answered. "Will you do as I say?" "Yes." "Even to worship an idol?" At that point, the righteous one interjected, "God forbid!" His wicked companion said to him, "Do you really think that a great man like Yeravam (as he was known to be at that time — see *Sanhedrin* 102a) would engage in idolatry? He is only testing our loyalty!" In this way, all the righteous men were tricked into affixing their signatures, including the prophet Achiyah the Shilonite, and they could not thereafter retract their endorsements (ibid. 101b with *Rashi* there).

——— ᴡ ———

ᴄ⸱ *Corrupting other Jews*

Anyone who brings merit to the public will not become an agent of sin; anyone who causes others to sin is not given the opportunity to repent. Moshe was meritorious and caused the public to gain merit, so the merit of the nation was attributed to him, as it is said (*Devarim* 33:21), *The righteousness of God he performed, and His laws, together with Israel.* Yeravam sinned and led the public to sin, so the misdeeds of the public are attributed to him, as it is written (*Melachim* I, 15:30), *For the sins of Yeravam, who sinned and caused Israel to sin* (*Avos* 5:18).

Those who sinned and induced others to sin, such as Yeravam, son of Nevat, and his kind, descend into *Gehinnom* and are punished there for all generations (*Rosh Hashanah* 17a).

And Yeravam pushed Israel away from God; he caused them to commit a great sin (*Melachim* II, 17:21). R' Chanin said: Like two sticks that strike one another [just as when a person strikes one stick on another, propelling it to fly some distance away, so too, Yeravam shoved Israel away from God, against their will] (*Sanhedrin* 102a with *Rashi* there).

——— ᴡ ———

ᴄ⸱ *The effect on Avraham*

And he pursued [the four kings] until Dan (*Bereishis* 14:14). Once the righteous Avraham reached Dan, his strength was sapped, for he foresaw that in Dan his descendants would worship idols, as it is

said, *And he placed one in Beth-el, and one he placed in Dan.* Our Sages have taught: Idol worship causes harm before its time as well as after its time. How so? Yeravam had yet to make the calf and set it up in Dan, but already we find (*Bereishis* 14:15): *And [Avraham] struck them and chased them until Chovah.* We searched through all the sources and did not find mention of a place called Chovah. This indicates that Dan was called Chovah [literally: demerit] in anticipation of the idol that was one day to stand there (*Tanchuma, Lech Lecha* §13; cf. *Sanhedrin* 96a; *Bereishis Rabbah* 43:2; *Pirkei D'Rabbi Eliezer* §27).

——— ᴡ ———

ᴄ⸱ *Yaakov's dismay*

When Yosef began drawing his sons close to Yaakov so that he might bless them, God said, "Should I not inform Yaakov about who is destined to arise from these children — Yeravam, son of Nevat, who stems from Ephraim? *And Yaakov saw Yosef's sons and he said, "Who are these?"* (*Bereishis* 48:8). [Did Yaakov not know them? Did he not sit with them in the study of Torah, day in and day out? (*Tanchuma*).] Rather, with the word *these* Yaakov alluded to the Golden Calf, regarding which it was said, **These** *are your gods, Israel,* a pronouncement paraphrased by Yeravam in regard to his calves, as it is written, *The king took counsel, and he made two golden calves; and he said to [the people], ... "Behold, Israel, your gods that brought you out from the land of Egypt!"* As soon as Yaakov brought Yeravam to mind, God withdrew the Holy Inspiration from him (*Pesikta Rabbasi* §3; *Tanchuma, Vayechi* §6; *Pesikta Zutrasa, Bereishis* 48:5; *Zohar* I, 227b-228a).

——— ᴡ ———

ᴄ⸱ *Tragic consequences*

The sons of my mother [אמי] *incited* [נחרו] *against me* (*Shir HaShirim* 1:6). That is to say, the members of my people [אומתי] — Yeravam, son of Nevat, caused God to be filled with wrath [חרון] against me, because *they made me a keeper of the vineyards* to care for Yeravam's two calves, and *my own vineyard I did not keep;* I did not observe the rotating watches of Kohanim and Leviim in the Holy Temple (*Shir HaShirim Rabbah* 1:6).

R' Oshaya said: Until Yeravam, Israel was already suckling from one calf (that is, suffering the damaging impact of the one Calf that was made in the Desert); from Yeravam on, they suckled from another two (*Sanhedrin* 102a with *Rashi* there).

How long did the effects of the sin of the Golden Calf last? Until the calves of Yeravam, son of Nevat. This is the intent of the verse (*Hoshea* 7:1), *When I would have healed Israel, the iniquity of Ephraim became revealed, along with the evils of Samaria.* God said, "I was ready to heal Israel from the sin of the Golden Calf, but then the evils of Samaria became revealed" (*Eichah Rabbah* 2:3).

⤴ Invitation to repent

After this matter, Yeravam failed to repent from his evil ways (*Melachim* I, 13:33). After what matter? R' Abba answered: After God grabbed Yeravam by his cloak, and said to him, "Repent! And then I, you, and [David] the son of Yishai will stroll together in *Gan Eden*." Said Yeravam, "But who will lead?" God answered, "The son of Yishai will lead." "If so," said Yeravam, "I am not interested" (*Sanhedrin* 102a).

⤴ Yeravam's fate

Thus said Hashem, God of Israel: Inasmuch as I elevated you from the midst of the people and emplaced you as ruler over My people, Israel, and I tore away the kingship from the House of David and gave it to you, but you were not like My servant David, who kept My commandments and who went after Me with all his heart, to do only what is proper in My eyes. But you have acted more wickedly than any who were before you, and you went and made for yourself the gods of others and molten images to anger Me, and you have cast Me behind your back. Therefore, behold — I

am bringing evil upon the house of Yeravam, and I shall eliminate every male offspring from Yeravam and all property, whether hidden or public, in Israel. And I shall consume the house of Yeravam, as one completely consumes food until it is waste. Anyone of the house of Yeravam who dies in the city, the dogs will eat; and whoever dies in the field, the birds of the heavens will eat — for God has spoken (*Melachim* I, 14:7-11).

⤴ The prophecy materializes

Nadav, son of Yeravam, became king over Israel in the second year of Asa, king of Yehudah, and he reigned over Israel for two years. He did evil in the eyes of God; he went in the path of his father and his sins, by which he caused Israel to sin. Baasa, son of Achiyah of the house of Issachar, conspired against him, and Baasa struck him down at Gibbeson of the Philistines, while Nadav and all of Israel were besieging Gibbeson. Baasa killed him in the third year of Asa, king of Yehudah, and reigned in his place. It happened that when he became king he struck down the entire house of Yeravam; he did not leave a soul in the house of Yeravam, until he annihilated it, according to the word of God, which he had spoken through the hand of Achiyah the Shilonite, on account of the sins of Yeravam that he had committed and caused Israel to commit, with his provocations by which he angered Hashem, God of Israel (ibid. 15:25-30).

IV. THE IDOL OF MENASHEH

enasheh was twelve years old when he became king, and he reigned for fifty-five years in Jerusalem. He did what was evil in the eyes of God, like the abominations of the nations that God had driven out before the Children of Israel. He rebuilt the high places that his father Chizkiah had broken down. He erected altars to Baal. He made asheirah trees; and he bowed down to the entire host of the heavens and worshipped them. He built altars in the Temple of God … He built altars to the entire host of the heavens in the two courtyards of the Temple of

God ... [and] was profuse in doing what was evil in the eyes of God, to anger Him. He placed the graven image that he had made in the Temple of God ...

Menasheh led Yehudah and the inhabitants of Jerusalem astray to do more evil than the nations that God had destroyed from before the Children of Israel.

God spoke to Menasheh and his people, but they did not listen. So God brought against them the officers of the king of Assyria's army, and they captured Menasheh with hunting hooks, bound him in chains and led him off to Babylonia. But in his distress he beseeched Hashem, his God, and he humbled himself greatly before the God of his fathers. He prayed to Him, and He was entreated by him and heard his supplication, and He returned him to Jerusalem, to his kingship. Then Menasheh realized that Hashem is God.

After this ... he removed the strange gods and the image from the Temple of Hashem and all the altars that he had built on the Mountain of the Temple of God and in Jerusalem, discarding them outside the city. He rebuilt the Altar of God and slaughtered peace-offerings and thanksgiving offerings on it, and he commanded Yehudah to worship Hashem, the God of Israel. (*Divrei HaYamim* II, 33).

------ ✿ ------

✿ A four-faced image

In connection to Menasheh's idol, the verse originally refers to it as "a graven image" in the singular, but then later refers to a number of "graven images." R' Yochanan thus taught: At first Menasheh had made one face on it, but he later fashioned four, so that it would face the Divine Presence in every direction and infuriate God (*Sanhedrin* 103b; see *Eichah Rabbah, Pesichah* §22, for a description of how idolatry gradually made inroads into Israel until matters came to a head with Menasheh).

The endeavor of the righteous brings life (*Mishlei* 10:16). Everything that David and Shlomo accomplished enhanced the life of Israel. But *the*

produce of the wicked brings sin; with Menasheh's one entry into the Holy of Holies (to study the form of the *keruvim,* after which he modeled his statue), he brought sin to Israel, for he made an image with four faces and brought it into the hall of the Temple. Why four faces? They alluded to the four angels that bear aloft the Throne of God. Alternatively, the four faces corresponded to the four directions of the world. Menasheh proclaimed, "Anyone who comes from any of the four directions should prostrate himself before this image" (*Devarim Rabbah* with *Maharzav* there 2:20; cf. *Tanna D'vei Eliyahu Zuta* 9:3).

------ ✿ ------

✿ Menasheh's origins

In those days Chizkiah became ill to the point of death, and Yeshayah the prophet came to him and said to him, So said God, "Direct your household, for you will die and not live" (*Melachim* II, 20:1; *Yeshayah* 38:1). What does it mean, *You will die and not live?* In this world you will die, and in the World to Come you will not live. Chizkiah asked, "For what am I being punished so severely?" Answered Yeshayah, "Because you did not attempt to have any children." Chizkiah countered, "But that is because I foresaw through Divine Inspiration that I am destined to bear unworthy children." Yeshayah replied, "Why must you interfere with the private matters of God? You ought to do what you are commanded to do, and allow God to act as *He* wishes." Chizkiah proposed, "Give me, then, your daughter in marriage; perhaps my merit and yours will cause my offspring to be worthy." Answered Yeshayah, "But the decree has already been issued; it is too late." Chizkiah responded, "Complete your prophecy, and then leave! I possess a tradition from my grandfather's (king David; cf. *Shmuel* II, 24:15-17) house: Even if a sharp-edged sword is placed on your neck, do not despair of pleading for mercy (*Berachos* 10a; *Yerushalmi, Sanhedrin* 10b; see *Hagahos HaBach* to *Berachos* ibid. for the rest of the narrative).

------ ✿ ------

⤺ *Instant repercussions*

He overlaid the Temple with precious stones for splendor, and the gold was Parvayim gold (*Divrei HaYamim* II, 3:6). What is *Parvayim* gold? Reish Lakish said: It has a reddish tint, reminiscent of the blood of an ox [*par*]. Some say: It is gold that produces fruit [*peiros*]. For when Shlomo built the Temple, he fashioned golden trees of various types, and when the trees of the field would bear fruit, their counterparts in the Temple would produce fruit as well. The golden fruit would fall off the tree and would be collected and saved to pay for the Temple's maintenance. But once Menasheh installed an idol in the Temple Hall, those trees all dried up; this is what is meant by the verse (*Nachum* 1:4), *The blossom of Levanon [the Temple] was devastated.* However, in the future God will rejuvenate them, as it is said (*Yeshayah* 35:2), *It will blossom abundantly and rejoice ... the glory of Levanon has been given to it.*

───── ⤩ ─────

⤺ *Forfeiture of the Temple and Kingdom*

When God foretold the destruction of the Temple and the loss of Jewish independence with the call to *Remove your turban* [the priesthood], *lift off the crown* [of the exiled king Tzidkiyah]! (*Yechezkel* 21:31), the ministering angels protested to God, "Master of the world! Is **this** to be the fate of Israel, who submitted to You with the declaration, 'We shall do,' even before they said, 'We will hear'? God replied, "Should **this not** be the fate of those who have demeaned the exalted and exalted the demeaned by erecting an idol in the Temple Hall?" (*Gittin* 7a, this exchange between God and the angels corresponds to the continuation of the aforementioned verse: *This, not this? The degraded exalt, and the exalted degrade*).

──────────

For what reason was the Temple razed? Because they left no place devoid of idol worship, as it is said (*Yeshayah* 5:8), *... until there was no more place.* At first they worshiped in secret, and

idolatry gradually gained acceptance, until they introduced it into the Holy of Holies, as it is written (*Yechezkel* 8:5), *The image of provocation was in the entryway [of the Temple]* (*Eichah Rabbah, Pesichah* §22. See *Yerushalmi, Taanis* 28b, where one opinion asserts that the erection of Menasheh's idol in the Temple was one of the tragic events over which the Fast of the Seventeenth of Tamuz was established).

───── ⤩ ─────

⤺ *The prototypical idolater*

Yonasan, son of Gershom, son of Menasheh, he and his sons were priests for the tribe of Dan (*Shoftim* 18:30). Was Gershom, then, the son of Menasheh? He was the son of Moshe, as it is written (*Divrei HaYamim* I, 23:15), *The sons of Moshe were Gershom and Eliezer.* Rather, because Yonasan did an act that was reminiscent of the sin of Menasheh (by serving as priest for the idol of Michah; see above), the Scripture associates him with Menasheh (*Bava Basra* 109b).

───── ⤩ ─────

⤺ *Menasheh's repentance*

God spoke to Menasheh and his people, but they did not take heed. So God brought upon them the generals of the Assyrian army, and they captured Menasheh ... R'Levi taught: They devised a copper pot and put him inside, and they kindled a fire below it. Once Menasheh realized that he was in serious trouble, he invoked the names of every pagan deity known to the world; not one was left out.

After that did not help him, he said to himself, I remember my father teaching me this verse in school: *When you are in distress and all these things have befallen you ... you will return to Hashem, your God, and hearken to His voice. For Hashem, your God, is a merciful God; He will not abandon you nor destroy you, and He will not forget the covenant of your forefathers that He swore to them* (*Devarim* 4:30). I will call out to Him, then. If He responds, very well. But if not, then they are all the same!

The ministering angels began closing the windows of Heaven to prevent the ascent of Menasheh's prayer. They pleaded to God, "Master of the Universe! A person who engaged in idolatry and erected a statue in the Temple Hall, You are prepared to receive in repentance?" Answered God, "If I do not accept his contrition, I will thereby discourage others from repenting." What did God do for him? He excavated a tunnel underneath His throne (a place where the angels had no jurisdiction — *Medrash Rus Rabbah*) and accepted his prayer. This is alluded to in the verse *He prayed to Him, and He allowed Himself to be entreated by him* [ויעתר]. For in Arabia, they call a tunnel עתרתא [a cognate of ויעתר].

And God returned him [וישיבהו] *to his kingship in Jerusalem.* How was he returned? God brought him back with a gust of wind [produced by the wings of the angels — *Targum*], as we are accustomed to saying (in the *Shemoneh Esrei* prayer): משיב הרוח, *God makes the wind blow* (The words וישיבהו and משיב share the same root).

At that point Menasheh declared, "There is, indeed, justice, and the world has a Judge" (*Yerushalmi, Sanhedrin* 10:2; *Devarim Rabbah* 2:20; *Rus Rabbah* 5:6; *Pesikta D'Rav Kahana* §24; cf. *Sanhedrin* 101b and 103a; *Vayikra Rabbah* 30:3; *Pirkei D'Rabbi Eliezer* §43; *Zohar* I, 136a).

An insincere prayer

Three people came forth with a persuasive argument (i.e. they came not with a prayerful request, but with an argument that could not be countered): Kayin, Eisav, and Menasheh ... In the case of Menasheh, he began by calling to the many pagan gods, and ended by calling to the God of his ancestors [as if to say: If You do not save me, of what use is my call to You any more than the other deities?] (*Sanhedrin* 101b with *Rashi* there).

Menasheh in the World to Come

Three kings and four commoners have no share in the World to Come ... Yeravam, Achav, and Menasheh. R' Yehudah says: Menasheh does have a portion in the World to Come, for it says: *And he prayed to Him ... and He heard his plea, and He returned him to Jerusalem to his kingdom.* The Sages replied: God returned him only to his kingdom, but not to the life of the World to Come. (*Sanhedrin* 90a).

Rabbi Yochanan said: Whoever says that Menasheh has no place in the World to Come demoralizes the repentant. For a Tanna taught before R' Yochanan: Menasheh repented after thirty-three years (ibid. 93a).

THE PROHIBITION AGAINST MAKING IDOLS: HOW MANY COMMANDMENTS?

A. *The view of Rambam*

ambam and *Chinuch* list two separate negative commandments relating to making idols: (1) making an idol for one's own worship (*Rambam, Sefer HaMitzvos, Lo Saaseh* §2; *Chinuch* §27) and (2) making an idol for *others* to worship (*Rambam* ibid. *Lo Saaseh* §3; *Chinuch* §214).

Some question *Rambam's* count based on his list in *Hil. Sanhedrin* 19:4 of all the negative commandments for which the penalty is *malkos* [lashes; see *mitzvah* #594]. There, *Rambam* lists the prohibition against making idols for worship as only one negative commandment (#1), not two commandments as he maintains in *Sefer HaMitzvos*! (*Lechem Mishneh, Hil. Sanhedrin* ibid.).

Some answer that in *Hil. Sanhedrin, Rambam* does not refer to the *specific commandments* for which a transgressor is penalized with *malkos*, but rather to *general categories* of prohibitions that are punishable with *malkos*, grouped by the acts these prohibitions forbid. The two commandments related to making idols constitute one such category, since they both forbid essentially the same act — making idols — even though they differ in details. Thus, *Rambam*

Baal Halachos Gedolos / —
בה"ג / —

R' Saadiah Gaon / Lavin 2
רס"ג / לאוין ב

R' Eliyahu HaZakein / Amud 64
ר' אליהו הזקן / עמ' 64

Rashbag / Lo Saaseh Os 8
רשב"ג / לא תעשה אות ח

R' Yitzchak El-Bargeloni / —
ר"י אלברג'לוני / —

Maamar HaSechel / Dibbur Sheini 3
מאמר השכל / דיבור שני ג

Sefer Yere'im / —
יראים / —

Rambam, Sefer HaMitzvos / Lo Saaseh 2
רמב"ם / לא תעשה ב

Sefer Mitzvos Gadol (Smag) / Lo Saaseh 20
סמ"ג / לא תעשה כ

Sefer Mitzvos Katan (Smak) / 161
סמ"ק / קסא

Zohar HaRakia / Lavin 2
זוהר הרקיע / לאוין ב

counts them as one in his list of prohibitions to which *malkos* applies (*Mirkeves HaMishneh* to *Rambam, Hil. Sanhedrin* ibid.; *Aruch HaShulchan HeAsid, Sanhedrin* 61:3; see also *Derech Mitzvosecha*, part 3 ד"ה כתב הרמב"ם).

B. *The view of Bahag*

In his count of the negative commandments, *Bahag* list one commandment related to idolatry, *You shall not recognize other gods before Me* (#26), an apparent reference to the prohibition against worshipping idols. He does *not* list a separate commandment not to *make* idols, which would indicate that he does count this prohibition as one of the 613 commandments.

Some say that *Bahag* does count the prohibition against making idols as a separate negative commandment, and that his reference to the commandment of *You shall not recognize other gods before Me* actually refers to a prohibition against *possessing* idols (of which the prohibition against *making* idols is a corollary). [This interpretation of the commandment is supported by *Mechilta*. These authorities point out that *Bahag* already lists the prohibition against worshipping idols in his count of the prohibitions whose penalty for transgression is stoning (*niskalin* #8). The prohibition he lists in his section of negative commandments, then, must not be referring to worshipping idols, but to a *different* prohibition, *possessing* idols

(*Ramban, Hasagos* to *Sefer HaMitzvos* of *Rambam, Aseh* §1).]

[Note: This explanation is untenable according to *Rambam's* understanding of *Bahag*. *Rambam* (*Sefer HaMitzvos, shoresh* §14) maintains that mitzvos *Bahag* classifies by order of punishment do not refer to actual prohibitions, but rather to the mitzvah incumbent upon *Beis Din* to administer punishment the Torah specifies for each prohibition. The actual prohibitions are listed in *Bahag's* list of negative commandments. According to *Rambam's* understanding, *Bahag* lists only one commandment concerning idols — *You shall not recognize other gods before Me* — and this likely refers to the prohibition against worshipping idols. *Ramban*, on the other hand, contends that mitzvos *Bahag* lists in the sections categorized by punishment *do* refer to actual prohibitions (see *hasagos* to *Sefer HaMitzvos* ad loc. ד"ה וכתב עוד). According to *Ramban*, then, the prohibition *Bahag* lists in his section of negative commandments is a *second* commandment related to idols, and can be understood as referring to a prohibition against possessing (or making) idols.]

C. The view of Ramban

Ramban (*Hasagos* to *Sefer HaMitzvos* of *Ramban, Lo Saaseh* §5) maintains that the entire passage in the Ten Commandments relating to idols is counted as a single negative commandment, which includes prohibitions against: a) verbally deifying an idol; b) performing one of the four services (i.e. bowing down, slaughtering a sacrifice, pouring a libation, or burning an offering) for an idol; and c) worshipping an idol in the manner in which it is customarily worshipped. According to *Ramban*, this commandment does *not* include a prohibition against *making* an idol. That prohibition is derived from the verse (*Vayikra* 19:4) which states: *Do not turn to the idols, **and molten gods you shall not make for yourselves**.* [However, in

Ramban's count of the negative commandments omitted by *Rambam* (see *Hasagos HaRamban* at the end of *Rambam's* list of negative commandments), he does not include the verse in *Vayikra* as the source for a commandment, for which reason] some conclude that *Ramban* does not count the prohibition against making idols as one of the 613 commandments (see *Dina D'Chayei* to *Smag, Lavin* §20, citing his brother, the author of *Mishmeres HaMitzvos*). Others, however, maintain that *Ramban does* count this prohibition as one of the 613 [and presumably does not include it in his list because *Rambam* agrees that it is a commandment, although he derives it from a different source] (*Dina D'Chayei* ibid.). These authorities bring the following proofs to support their view:

1. In his list of negative commandments (ibid. ד"ה וכן), *Ramban* states that two of the prohibitions connected to idolatry that *Rambam* lists as separate commandments are, in his (*Ramban's*) opinion, not counted as separate commandments. Now, from his comments to *Rambam's Lo Saaseh* §5 (cited above), it is evident that *Ramban* is referring to the prohibitions related to worshipping idols (i.e. performing one of the four services and worshipping an idol in its customary manner), which, he maintains, are included in the commandment not to believe in idols. Clearly, then, he does *not* disagree with *Rambam's* view that the prohibition against making idols is a separate commandment.

2. *Ramban* (*Hasagos* ibid.) argues that *Rambam* should have counted the prohibition against displaying reverence for an idol (see *mitzvah* #29, Law 2) as a separate commandment. This prohibition, argues *Ramban*, is not included in the commandments against worshipping idols (*mitzvos* #28 and #29), since it is derived from a separate source and, moreover, is not subject to the same punishment (execution) as those prohibitions (see *mitzvah*

#28, Law 6, and *mitzvah* #29, Law 5). Now, these reasons for defining a prohibition as a separate commandment also apply to the prohibition against making idols; it is derived from a different source than the other prohibitions related to idol worship (as noted above), and the punishment for making an idol (*malkos*; see above, Law 5) is different from the punishment which applies for idol worship (execution). According to *Ramban's* criteria, then, this prohibition must be counted as a separate commandment.

Mitzvah 28

אִסּוּר הִשְׁתַּחֲוָאָה לַעֲבוֹדָה זָרָה

פרשת יתרו

Not to
Bow Down to
an Avodah Zarah

THE MITZVAH:

MITZVAH 28 מצוה כח

NOT TO BOW DOWN TO AN AVODAH ZARAH

אִסּוּר הִשְׁתַּחֲוָאָה לַעֲבוֹדָה זָרָה (לֹא תַעֲשֶׂה)

■ SOURCE ■

לֹא תִשְׁתַּחֲוֶה לָהֶם שמות (פרשת יתרו) כ:ה

"You shall not bow down to them"

■ THE MITZVAH ■

We are prohibited from bowing down to any idol, object or entity, as well as from serving it in any one of the other ways that Hashem is served in the Beis HaMikdash.[1]

■ LAWS ■

1 This prohibition applies even if one believes that Hashem is the Supreme Deity, and intends to honor him by worshipping one of His creations.[2]

2 This prohibition encompasses four specific services:[3] (a) Bowing down to the idol;[4] (b) Sacrifice — slaughtering an animal as an offering to the idol;[5] (c) Libation — pouring any liquid, or sprinkling blood of a sacrifice, as an offering to the idol;[6] (d) Burning food or incense as an offering to the idol.[7]

3 One who serves an idol in one of these four ways is liable even if that idol is not customarily served in that manner.[8]

4 These services are prohibited whether performed in the presence of the idol or not.[9]

5 One who serves an idol is liable even if he never explicitly declared the idol his deity.[10] Conversely, one who declares an idol his deity is liable even without serving it actively.[11]

6 Deliberate transgression of this commandment is punished by execution (stoning).[12] An inadvertent transgressor must offer a *chatas.*[13]

7 One must refuse to practice idolatry even at the cost of his life.[14]

8 This commandment applies to both men and women, in all places and at all times.[15]

9 These acts are forbidden for non-Jews as well, as idolatry is one of the Seven Noahide Laws.[16]

■ A REASON ■

The Creator of the world is the one true God, without any equal in Heaven or on earth. How can one render the honor due Him to any other being?

1. One may not serve an angel, a star or other celestial body, a geological feature such as a mountain or lake, any creature, plant, element, or substance, or any fabricated object (*Rambam, Hil. Avodah Zarah* 2:1; see *Rosh HaShanah* 24b). One may not even serve an object that is itself not considered a deity, but that is adored by devotees as a palpable representation of a deity (such as a statue of a mythological divinity, or an icon imagined to depict the "true" form of a star [see *Rambam*, ibid. 1:2]). Although the verse refers here only to *bowing down*, the intent is to prohibit any form of adoration by which Hashem is worshipped. Such homage must be reserved for Hashem and never directed toward any other, entity (*Rambam, Sefer HaMitzvos Lo Saaseh* §5, citing *Mechilta* ad loc., and *Hil. Avodah Zarah* 3:3; *Sefer HaChinuch* §28; see also *Sanhedrin* 60b).

This prohibition is distinct from *mitzvah #29, nor shall you serve them,* in that this prohibition forbids serving *any avodah zarah* in one of four specific ways (listed in Law 2), whereas *mitzvah #29* prohibits serving an *avodah zarah* in the particular manner practiced by its devotees [regardless of what this entails] (*Sanhedrin* ibid.; *Rambam* ibid. 3:2-3). See further in our treatment of *mitzvah #29.*

Simply believing in a deity other than Hashem, without worshipping it in any way, is a violation of *mitzvah #26, You shall not recognize other gods before Me* (*Rambam, Hil. Yesodei HaTorah* 1:6; *Sefer HaMitzvos, Lo Saaseh* §1; *Sefer HaChinuch* §26; cf. *Ramban* in *Hasagos to Sefer HaMitzvos, Lo Saaseh* §5.)

2. *Rambam* maintains that serving celestial bodies as a way to honor Hashem was actually the original and primary form of idol worship (which is why idolatry in general is

AN EXPANDED TREATMENT

often referred to as "star worship" in the Talmud [see *Berachos* 54a and 57b]). He explains that very early in human history people fell prey to the misconception that it was proper to pay tribute to the heavenly bodies as God's emissaries to the world, just as a king expects his ministers to be treated with honor by those subject to his rule. Over time, these demonstrations of honor led to genuine worship as the popular conception of the celestial forces graduated from subordinate, non-divine agents to independent deitites (*Hil. Avodah Zarah* 1:1,2; for a more detailed account of the history of idolatry, see *Chazal* section, *mitzvah* #25; for other misconceptions held by idolaters regarding their objects of worship, see *Ramban* to *Shemos* 20:3).

3. As will be seen, all four of these are *inner services*, services performed within the *Beis HaMikdash* for Hashem (*Sanhedrin* 60b, as apparently understood by *Rambam* in *Sefer HaMitzvos, Lo Saaseh* §5, and *Hil. Avodah Zarah* 3:3; cf. *Hasagos HaRamban* to *Sefer HaMitzvos* ibid.; *Meiri* to Mishnah *Sanhedrin* ibid.; see end of note 7). Furthermore, all four are mentioned in the Torah as forms of worship that were improperly directed toward idols (see *Rashi* to *Sanhedrin* ibid., ד"ה ולחשוב).

4. Mishnah, *Sanhedrin* 60b; *Rambam, Hil. Avodah Zarah* 3:3. As used in Scripture, השתחואה (from the root שחה), which we have translated as *bowing down*, usually connotes prostration, i.e. laying oneself face down upon the ground with arms and legs outstretched, in a posture of utter submission (see *Megillah* 22b with respect to *mitzvah* #349, *Do not emplace in your land a flooring stone upon which to prostrate yourself*; see also

Rambam, Hil. Tefillah 5:13). Prostration was in fact the obeisance commonly performed before Hashem in the *Beis HaMikdash* (see *Shavuos* 16b; *Tiferes Yisrael* to *Tammid*, 6:4). With respect to this prohibition, however, the definition of השתחואה is more expansive. Thus, as soon as one kneels to an idol and bends so that his face comes in contact with the ground, he has transgressed the prohibition against bowing down and is liable to the penalties detailed in Law 3, even if he did *not* outstretch his limbs (*Rambam, Hil. Avodah Zarah* 6:8 and *Hil. Shegagos* 14:2; *Tashbetz* 3:315, adducing *Horayos* 4a; *Minchas Chinuch* 28:2; *Or Same'ach, Hil. Avodah Zarah* ibid.; *Chazon Ish, Sanhedrin* 21:6; *Turei Even* to *Megillah* ibid.; *Chasdei David, Tosefta Sanhedrin* 10:2; for further explanation, see *Maharam Schik, Taryag Mitzvos* 28:2).

Some authorities add that merely kneeling to an idol, or bowing from the waist, renders the worshipper liable, even if he never presses his face to the ground (*Or Same'ach* ibid.; see also *Chazon Ish* ibid.). Others distinguish between idols whose devotees customarily bow down to them (even if that bowing normally takes the form of full prostration), and idols to which devotees do not normally bow. If one kneels or bends at the waist to one of the former idols he is liable, whereas one is not liable for bowing down to one of the idols in the second group unless he bends so far as to press his face to the ground (*Tzafnas Pane'ach, Mahadura Tinyana, Hil. Avodah Zarah* 6:6, resolving a possible contradiction between *Rambam's* ruling in *Hil. Avodah Zarah* and his ruling in *Hil. Shegagos*). Others rule still less stringently. While they, too, make a distinction between idols to which devotees customarily prostrate

themselves and idols that are not usually served in this manner, they maintain that even if one bends to an idol of the former category he is not liable until he touches his face to the ground, whereas bowing down to an idol in the latter category never renders the worshipper liable unless he prostrates himself fully, with arms and legs outstretched (*Commentary of R' Yerucham Fishel Perla* to *Sefer HaMitzvos L'Rasag, Lo Saaseh* §1, 4:3, in explanation of *Rambam*).

Certain idols are customarily served not reverentially, but in an ignominious and degrading manner. The idol *Markolis*, for example, would be stoned; devotees of *Baal Pe'or* would expose themselves to the idol (see further in *mitzvah* #29). Although bowing down is a show of deference and certainly no insult, one who bows even to such an idol is nonetheless liable (this is derived from Scripture's repetition of the prohibition against bowing down; see *Sanhedrin* 63a with *Rashi*).

One may bow (or prostrate himself) to a person out of deference or fear, so long as that person is not venerated as a deity (*Sanhedrin* 61b, with *Yad Ramah*).

5. Mishnah, *Sanhedrin* 60b; *Rambam, Hil. Avodah Zarah* 3:3. This applies to any animal fit as an offering to Hashem, whether by a Jew on the Altar in the *Beis HaMikdash*, or by a non-Jew on a private altar he may erect (a '*bamah*'). Therefore, if an animal has one of the minor physical blemishes (enumerated in *Vayikra* 22:17-25) that disqualify it from being brought as an offering in the *Beis HaMikdash*, one who sacrifices that animal to an idol is nevertheless liable, because a blemished animal is still fit to be offered by a a non-Jew on

MITZVAH 28 / מצוה כח

אִסוּר הִשְׁתַּחֲוָאָה לַעֲבוֹדָה זָרָה (לֹא תַעֲשֶׂה)

NOT TO BOW DOWN TO AN AVODAH ZARAH

SOURCE

לֹא תִשְׁתַּחֲוֶה לָהֶם שמות (פרשת יתרו) כ:ה

"You shall not bow down to them"

THE MITZVAH

We are prohibited from bowing down to any idol, object or entity, as well as from serving it in any one of the other ways that Hashem is served in the Beis HaMikdash.[1]

LAWS

1 This prohibition applies even if one believes that Hashem is the Supreme Deity, and intends to honor him by worshipping one of His creations.[2]

2 This prohibition encompasses four specific services:[3] (a) Bowing down to the idol;[4] (b) Sacrifice — slaughtering an animal as an offering to the idol;[5] (c) Libation — pouring any liquid, or sprinkling blood of a sacrifice, as an offering to the idol;[6] (d) Burning food or incense as an offering to the idol.[7]

3 One who serves an idol in one of these four ways is liable even if that idol is not customarily served in that manner.[8]

4 These services are prohibited whether performed in the presence of the idol or not.[9]

5 One who serves an idol is liable even if he never explicitly declared the idol his deity.[10] Conversely, one who declares an idol his deity is liable even without serving it actively.[11]

6 Deliberate transgression of this commandment is punished by execution (stoning).[12] An inadvertent transgressor must offer a *chatas*.[13]

7 One must refuse to practice idolatry even at the cost of his life.[14]

8 This commandment applies to both men and women, in all places and at all times.[15]

9 These acts are forbidden for non-Jews as well, as idolatry is one of the Seven Noahide Laws.[16]

A REASON

The Creator of the world is the one true God, without any equal in Heaven or on earth. How can one render the honor due Him to any other being?

**DEDICATED BY THE KEST FAMILY
LOS ANGELES, CALIFORNIA**

---

his private altar (*Avodah Zarah* 51a; see *Minchas Chinuch* 26:2). If, however, the animal lacks a limb, rendering it unfit to be offered to Hashem even by a non-Jew on a private altar, one who sacrifices that animal to an idol is not liable (*Avodah Zarah* ibid.,

see *Rambam, Hil. Avodah Zarah* 3:4). [Note the following qualification: As mentioned above (note 1), if one serves an idol in the manner that that idol is customarily served, he has violated *mitzvah #29* — regardless of whether he is also in violation of

mitzvah #28. Therefore, if a particular idol is customarily offered animals lacking limbs, a worshipper who sacrifices a limbless animal to that idol is liable for transgression of *mitzvah #29*. See *Rambam, Hil. Avodah Zarah* ibid.]

A similar logic pertains regarding species. Five kinds of beasts and birds are fit to be offered in the *Beis HaMikdash*: cattle, sheep, goats, pigeons, and doves. Furthermore, a non-Jew may also privately offer Hashem any clean (*tahor*) beast or bird (*Zevachim* 115b; see *Mishneh LaMelech, Hil. Maaseh HaKorbanos* 19:16), such as an antelope or deer, chicken or goose (the clean species are identified in *Vayikra* ch. 11 and *Devarim* ch. 14). Therefore, a worshipper who sacrifices any clean beast or bird to an idol is liable (*Minchas Chinuch* 26:2). One is *not* liable for sacrificing any insect (including the permitted edible grasshoppers listed in *Vayikra* 11:22; see below), fish, or unclean creature (based on *Rambam Hil. Avodah Zarah* 3:4; cf. *Raavad* ad loc.; see also *Rada* ad loc.; see further, *Iyunim* §4).

The method of slaughter prescribed for offerings of animals to Hashem is *shechitah* — severing the throat with a knife or other sharp instrument (see *Vayikra* 1:5; Mishnah *Chullin* 1:1-4). Therefore, because the services prohibited by the present mitzvah parallel those services performed for Hashem in the *Beis HaMikdash*, one is not liable for sacrifice to an idol unless he slaughtered the animal by *shechitah* (see *Minchas Chinuch* 26:3, ד"ה והנה נראה דזובה). For this reason as well, one cannot be liable for sacrificing an insect, as insects lack an animalian throat enclosing an esophagus, windpipe, and blood-carrying arteries (see *Avodah Zarah* 51a with *Rashi* there ד"ה מר סבר). [Again, this applies only to idols to which insects are not customarily sacrificed. If a particular idol is customarily offered insects, one who sacrifices an insect to that idol is liable for transgressing *mitzvah* #29 (*Rambam* ibid.).]

Bird sacrifices offered in the *Beis HaMikdash* are slaughtered by *me-likah*, severing the neck of the bird using the thumbnail (see *Chullin* 20a; *Rambam, Hil. Maaseh HaKorbanos* 6:23). Some authorities hold that idolatrous *melikah* is analagous to idolatrous *shechitah*: both are included under sacrificial slaughter. One who slaughters a bird to an idol by *melikah* is therefore liable (*Kessef Mishneh* and *Mishneh LaMelech, Hil. Avodah Zarah* 3:3; see also *Ran* to *Sanhedrin* 60b). Others maintain that the category of forbidden slaughter does *not* include *melikah*, because the Torah never mentions *melikah* in connection with idolatry (*Meiri* to Mishnah *Sanhedrin* ibid.; see note 3). A worshipper is therefore not liable for slaughtering a bird to an idol by *melikah*.

Meal offerings (*menachos*) in the *Beis HaMikdash* are readied by a procedure called *kemitzah*. The Kohen gathers a fistful of the meal which is then burned on the Altar, after which the remainder is later consumed by the Kohanim within the *Beis HaMikdash* courtyard (see *Vayikra* ch. 2; Mishnah *Menachos* 72b; *Rambam, Hil. Maaseh HaKorbanos* 13:12-14). *Kemitzah* is like *shechitah* in that both separate from the body of the offering a portion designated for the Altar: the fistful of meal, and the blood that spews from the incision to be sprinkled on the Altar, respectively. *Tosafos* (*Yoma* 63b, ד"ה זריקת, cited by *Mishneh LaMelech, Hil. Avodah Zarah* 3:3) therefore maintain that a worshipper who performed *kemitzah* on meal offered to an idol is liable as though he sacrificed an animal. [According to *Tosafos*, the same would presumably be true of *melikah*.]

Some additional practices may be

considered "corollaries" of sacrifice and render a worshipper liable. See *Iyunim* §4.

6. Mishnah, *Sanhedrin* 60b; *Rambam, Hil. Avodah Zarah* 3:3. Libations of wine are poured on the Altar in the *Beis HaMikdash* as accompaniments to certain animal sacrifices (see *Rambam, Hil. Maaseh HaKorbanos* ch. 2). Furthermore, an individual may voluntarily offer a wine libation independent of any sacrifice (Mishnah, *Menachos* 104b; *Rambam* ibid. 14:1 and 17:12). One is therefore liable for offering a similar libation to an idol. [No libation in the *Beis HaMikdash* was less than three *lugim* (a liquid measure equal in volume to approximately six eggs). Nevertheless, none of the earlier authorities mention that to be liable for idol worship one must offer at least three *lugim*, and it therefore appears that one is in fact liable for pouring even a minuscule amount (*Minchas Chinuch* 26:4).]

The lifeblood of animals and birds sacrificed in the *Beis HaMikdash* is sprinkled or smeared on the Altar. Sprinkling is analagous to libation, and is in fact referred to as libation in *Tehillim* 16:4 (Gemara, *Sanhedrin* ibid.). A worshipper who sprinkles or tosses blood toward an idol, or who smears blood on the idol or on the idol's altar, is liable (*Rambam* ibid. simply notes that one who sprinkles is liable, but does not describe the act of sprinkling).

Thus far we have spoken of wine and blood. However, the Gemara in *Avodah Zarah* (50b-51a) suggests that one is liable for a sprinkling or pouring of anything "that fragments," meaning anything liquid enough to scatter on impact like droplets of blood. The Gemara counts "oil and flour" as examples of this category. In fact, a Baraisa in *Avodah Zarah* 50b (accepted as halachah by *Rambam, Hil. Avodah Zarah* 3:4), states: If [a

worshipper] stuffed feces (as an offering) into [the mouth of an idol (see *Rashi* to *Avodah Zarah* ibid., ד"ה ספת; cf. *Tosafos*, ד"ה ספת)], or if he poured a libation of urine before [the idol], he is liable. Idolatrous libations and sprinklings can apparently consist of any fluid or semisolid, even the foulest. See *Iyunim* §4.

7. Mishnah, *Sanhedrin* 60b; *Rambam, Hil. Avodah Zarah* 3:3. In the *Beis HaMikdash*, incense was burned daily on the inner Altar, and designated parts of certain animal, bird, and meal offerings were burned on the outer Altar. A worshipper who similarly serves an idol is in violation of this prohibition. There is no minimal amount he must burn to be liable (*Minchas Chinuch* 26:4).

Thus far, we have followed *Rambam* in *Sefer HaMitzvos, Lo Saaseh* §5, and in *Hil. Avodah Zarah* 3:3, and *Sefer HaChinuch* §28, who all maintain that bowing down is categorized as a service (see *Rambam, Hil. Bias Mikdash* 2:4 with *Kessef Mishneh*; *Tzafnas Pane'ach, Hil. Avodah Zarah* 6:8), and can therefore be used by the Torah as an example of this prohibition, which actually prohibits all four services (see notes 1 and 3). Others, however, disagree, and maintain that *You shall not bow down to them* speaks only of bowing. Sacrifice, as well as libation and burning, are forbidden by the verse (*Vayikra* 17:7), *Let them no longer sacrifice to the demons,* etc. (*Tosafos* to *Sanhedrin* 61a, ד"ה מנין, as explained by *Malbim* to *Shemos* 20:5; see *Rashi* to *Sanhedrin* 60b, ד"ה לפי שיצאה), or by the clause (*Shemos* 20:5), *nor shall you serve them* (*Hasagos HaRamban* to *Sefer HaMitzvos*; *Smag, Lo Saaseh* §17). According to these Rishonim, bowing down needs its own prohibition because although bowing down is a form of adulation, it is *not* a service, and would not be forbidden by a verse that speaks of service or of

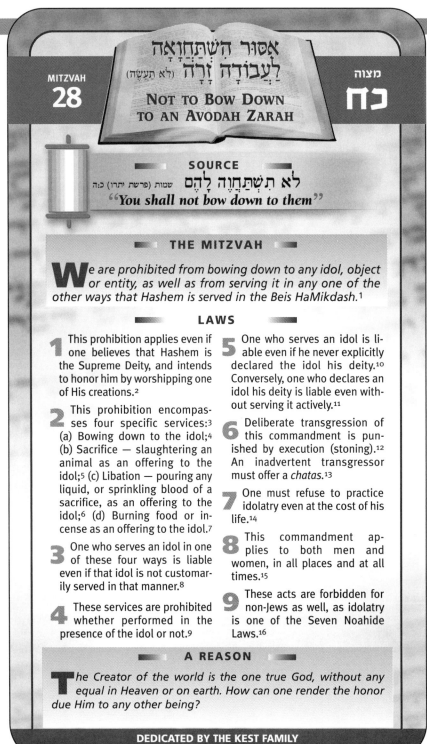

MITZVAH 28 — מצוה כח

אִסּוּר הִשְׁתַּחֲוָאָה לַעֲבוֹדָה זָרָה (לֹא תַעֲשֶׂה)

NOT TO BOW DOWN TO AN AVODAH ZARAH

SOURCE

לֹא תִשְׁתַּחֲוֶה לָהֶם   שמות (פרשת יתרו) כ:ה

"You shall not bow down to them"

THE MITZVAH

We are prohibited from bowing down to any idol, object or entity, as well as from serving it in any one of the other ways that Hashem is served in the Beis HaMikdash.[1]

LAWS

1 This prohibition applies even if one believes that Hashem is the Supreme Deity, and intends to honor him by worshipping one of His creations.[2]

2 This prohibition encompasses four specific services:[3] (a) Bowing down to the idol;[4] (b) Sacrifice — slaughtering an animal as an offering to the idol;[5] (c) Libation — pouring any liquid, or sprinkling blood of a sacrifice, as an offering to the idol;[6] (d) Burning food or incense as an offering to the idol.[7]

3 One who serves an idol in one of these four ways is liable even if that idol is not customarily served in that manner.[8]

4 These services are prohibited whether performed in the presence of the idol or not.[9]

5 One who serves an idol is liable even if he never explicitly declared the idol his deity.[10] Conversely, one who declares an idol his deity is liable even without serving it actively.[11]

6 Deliberate transgression of this commandment is punished by execution (stoning).[12] An inadvertent transgressor must offer a *chatas*.[13]

7 One must refuse to practice idolatry even at the cost of his life.[14]

8 This commandment applies to both men and women, in all places and at all times.[15]

9 These acts are forbidden for non-Jews as well, as idolatry is one of the Seven Noahide Laws.[16]

A REASON

The Creator of the world is the one true God, without any equal in Heaven or on earth. How can one render the honor due Him to any other being?

sacrifice (*Rashi* ibid. and *Ramban* ibid.).

8. *Sanhedrin* 60b; *Rambam, Hil. Avodah Zarah* 3:3. As we have already noted, according to *Rambam* a defining feature of this prohibition is that it applies to *any* idol. If this prohibition had forbidden bowing down only to idols customarily served in such a manner (as well as sacrifice, libation, or burning only for idols customarily served by sacrifice, libation, or burning), it would have been redundant, because serving an idol in its customary manner is prohibited in any case by *mitzvah* #29.

9. *Minchas Chinuch* 26:5, citing *Tosafos* to *Chullin* 40a ד"ה לפני עבודת כוכבים. Although idolatry is prohibited even where no idol is present, with respect to liability the following condition applies: No person is subject to retribution at the hands of a human court unless it is indisputable that he intended to commit, and then actually committed, the transgression with which he is charged. If one prostrates himself at the feet of an idol, or if he leads an animal into the idol's presence and slaughters it before the idol, he is condemned by his actions: he can be judged indubitably to have acted in honor of the idol, and thereby to have incurred death by stoning. But where no idol is present, we cannot presume that anyone who bows down or slaughters an animal, does so as an act of idolatry. Therefore, in the absence of an idol (or at a distance from the idol) no service is assumed to be idolatrous unless the worshipper explicitly professed that the service he was about to perform was indeed in worship of an idol (see *Tosafos* ibid.).

In neither case is the worshipper liable to death unless he is warned immediately beforehand that by his act he would incur *sekilah*, and unless he immediately acknowledged the warning by replying that he would transgress in spite of the warning (see *Sanhedrin* 40b-41a with *Rashi* to 40b, ד"ה קיבל עליו and ד"ה התיר עצמו; see also *Chullin* 41a).

10. Mishnah *Sanhedrin* 60b. Regarding a worshipper who claims that he does not consider the idol divine, but that he serves it for other motives (such as fear of the idol's devotees or a desire to ingratiate himself with them), see *Iyunim* §5.

11. Mishnah ibid.; *Rambam, Hil. Avodah Zarah* 3:4. *Shemos* 32:8 reads: *They have strayed quickly from the path that I commanded them; they have made* themselves a calf cast [of gold], and have bowed to it and sacrificed to it and said, This is your god, O Israel, who brought you up from the land of Egypt. According to Sanhedrin 63a, the declaration This is your god is juxtaposed to the depiction of active worship (and [they] sacrificed to it) to draw an implicit comparison: such a declaration, like sacrifice, is an act of idolatry, and is punished with equal severity.

Rambam (Sefer HaMitzvos, Lo Saaseh §5) lists declaring an idol one's deity as one of the acts prohibited by this prohibition, possibly because such a declaration, like bowing, sacrifice, libation, and burning, carries liability when directed to *any* idol. Moreover, verbal deification, like the four services, is a form of homage that we owe Hashem (see *mitzvah* #25), and that must never be misdirected (see note 1). *Ramban* (Hasagos to Sefer HaMitzvos, ibid.), however, includes deification — as he does all forms of idol worship — under the commandment, *You shall not have other gods before Me* (see *mitzvah* #26). *Tosafos* to *Sanhedrin* 60b, ד"ה מנין לרבות, maintain that deification of an idol always carries liability not because deification is naturally akin to bowing and sacrifice, but because deification is in fact a native form of worship for any and every idol. Accordingly, the prohibition of declaring an idol one's deity would be included in *mitzvah* #29.

The forbidden declaration may take several forms. The example given in the Mishnah is of a worshipper who says, directing his words toward a present idol, "You are my god!" *Rambam* (Hil. Avodah Zarah ibid.) cites that example and adds that the law applies as well to any similar assertion. *Meiri* (to Mishnah ibid.) writes that where the idol is absent and a worshipper cannot address or indicate it directly, he incurs liability for declaring, "I accept such-

and-such idol as my deity!" In this, however, opinions vary somewhat. Some maintain that saying "Such-and-such idol is my deity!" regarding an absent idol is sufficient to incur liability, as if one said, "You are my deity!" in the presence of an idol (*Tiferes Yisrael* to *Sanhedrin* 7:54; see also *Rashi* to *Sanhedrin* ibid., ד"ה והמקבלו). Others hold, however, that in the absence of an idol one incurs no liability unless he expressly declares his intent to serve the idol, by saying for example, "Such-and-such idol is my deity, and I shall go and serve it!" (*Maharshal, Sanhedrin* ibid. in explanation of *Rashi*).

Additional points relevant to deification are treated in *Iyunim* §5.

12. *Devarim* 17:5; Mishnah *Sanhedrin* 53a; *Rambam, Hil. Avodah Zarah* ibid. *Sekilah*, execution by stoning, is one of four methods of capital punishment mandated by the Torah for different transgressions. According to the accepted Tannaic opinion, *sekilah* is the harshest of the four (Mishnah, *Sanhedrin* 79b; *Rambam, Hil. Sanhedrin* 14:4; the Sages are quoted in the Mishnah as adducing that *sekilah* must be the severest punishment because it is meted out to persons guilty of idolatry, the severest sin). The procedure for *sekilah* is detailed in Mishnayos *Sanhedrin* 6:1-4 and *Rambam, Hil. Sanhedrin* 15:1. It should be noted that unlike most other sinners liable to *sekilah*, whose sentence is carried out at the gates of the town where they were condemned, idolaters are stoned at the gates of the town where they practiced their idolatry (*Kesubos* 45b; *Rambam* ibid. 15:2).

Following his execution, the corpse of an idolater, like that of a blasphemer, is hung momentarily atop a wooden pole, but is then immediately taken down and buried.

If one violated this commandment deliberately, but there were no

witnesses, or he did not receive proper warning, he is punished with *kares* (*Bamidbar* 15:31: Mishnah, *Kereisos* 2a; *Sanhedrin* 64b with *Rashi* ד"ה אחת שלא כדרכה; *Rambam Hil. Avodah Zarah* 3:1 and *Hil. Shegagos* 1:1,3). *Kares*, literally *severance*, is the severest of heavenly penalties, and, although its exact nature is disputed, involves the death of either body or soul, or both. For a summation of the various opinions, see *Abarbanel* to *Bamidbar* 15:22.

13. Mishnah, *Kereisos* 2a; *Rambam, Hil. Shegagos* 1:3. A *chatas*, or *sin-offering* (pl. *chataos*) is an animal offered by a sinner to atone for his guilt. The *chatas* is slaughtered in the *Beis HaMikdash* and its blood placed on the corners of the Altar. Designated sacrificial parts (known as *emurin*) are burned upon the Altar, and the meat is consumed by the Kohanim within the *Beis HaMikdash* compound (see *Vayikra* ch. 4; *mitzvah* #121). For any prohibition whose deliberate transgression is punished by *kares*, the inadvertent transgressor incurs an obligation to bring a *chatas* offering. The one exception is blasphemy, because *chataos* are incurred only for forbidden *actions*, and speech is not considered an act (Mishnah ibid. and *Rambam* ibid. 1:2).

The *chatas* mandated for idolatry differs from other *chataos* in the following respect. For most transgressions punishable by *kares,* the Torah stipulates that the inadvertent sinner offer a female goat or ewe if he is a commoner, a he-goat if he is the king, or an ox if he is the *Kohen Gadol* (in which case the meat of the ox is not eaten, but is burned, together with its hide, outside the *Beis HaMikdash*). An inadvertent idolater, however, no matter his status, must offer a female goat (*Vayikra* ibid.; *Bamidbar* 15:27, with *Rashi*; *Rambam* ibid. 1:4).

["Inadvertent," in this context, means that the worshipper was

MITZVAH 28

אִסוּר הִשְׁתַּחֲוָאָה לַעֲבוֹדָה זָרָה (לֹא תַעֲשֶׂה)

NOT TO BOW DOWN TO AN AVODAH ZARAH

מצוה כח

■ SOURCE ■

לֹא תִשְׁתַּחֲוֶה לָהֶם   שמות (פרשת יתרו) כ:ה
"You shall not bow down to them"

■ THE MITZVAH ■

We are prohibited from bowing down to any idol, object or entity, as well as from serving it in any one of the other ways that Hashem is served in the Beis HaMikdash.[1]

■ LAWS ■

1 This prohibition applies even if one believes that Hashem is the Supreme Deity, and intends to honor him by worshipping one of His creations.[2]

2 This prohibition encompasses four specific services:[3] (a) Bowing down to the idol;[4] (b) Sacrifice — slaughtering an animal as an offering to the idol;[5] (c) Libation — pouring any liquid, or sprinkling blood of a sacrifice, as an offering to the idol;[6] (d) Burning food or incense as an offering to the idol.[7]

3 One who serves an idol in one of these four ways is liable even if that idol is not customarily served in that manner.[8]

4 These services are prohibited whether performed in the presence of the idol or not.[9]

5 One who serves an idol is liable even if he never explicitly declared the idol his deity.[10] Conversely, one who declares an idol his deity is liable even without serving it actively.[11]

6 Deliberate transgression of this commandment is punished by execution (stoning).[12] An inadvertent transgressor must offer a *chatas*.[13]

7 One must refuse to practice idolatry even at the cost of his life.[14]

8 This commandment applies to both men and women, in all places and at all times.[15]

9 These acts are forbidden for non-Jews as well, as idolatry is one of the Seven Noahide Laws.[16]

■ A REASON ■

The Creator of the world is the one true God, without any equal in Heaven or on earth. How can one render the honor due Him to any other being?

Hil. Shegagos 7:1). Furthermore, even if the worshipper knew that idolatry is prohibited, but was unaware that transgression is punishable by *kares*, his service is deemed inadvertent and he must offer a *chatas* (see *Shabbos* 69a; *Rambam, Hil. Shegagos* 2:2). If, however, the very act of idolatry was inadvertent — that is, if the worshipper did not intentionally direct his devotions to an idol — he incurs no liability at all. For example: If one believes himself to be in a synagogue, and bows down in honor of Hashem, but later discovers that he is actually standing before an idol in a pagan temple, since he never intended to bow down to the idol, he is not liable to a *chatas* (*Kereisos* 3a; *Shabbos* 72b; *Sanhedrin* 62a-b).

14. *Sanhedrin* 74a; *Pesachim* 25a; *Rambam, Hil. Yesodei HaTorah* 5:2; *Tur* and *Shulchan Aruch, Yoreh Deah* 157:1. If an idolater threatens to kill a Jew unless he bows to or otherwise serves an idol, the Jew must forfeit his life rather than submit. Futhermore, if a Jew is mortally ill and his cure depends on an act of idolatry, he must foreswear the cure rather than practice idolatry. This issue will be elaborated under *mitzvah #296, to sanctify the Name of Hashem*.

The other two prohibitions that one may not transgress even to save his life are those prohibiting murder and illicit relations. [These are actually classes of prohibitions, as the prohibitions of idolatry include more than a single mitzvah. Similarly, adultery and other various incestuous unions are prohibited each by their own mitzvah.]

15. *Sefer HaChinuch* §28. Generally, women are obligated in all negative commandments (see *Kiddushin* 29a).

16. This mitzvah is included in the prohibition against idolatry that applies to

---

unaware that idolatry is prohibited, or was unaware at least that the prohibition applied in all its stringency to his particular circumstances, or to the particular form of service that he practiced. If, for example, a worshipper believed that one may sacrifice to

idols that are not customarily served by sacrifice, and did so, he must bring a *chatas*. So, too, a worshipper who served an idol of wood or clay under the mistaken belief that only idols of gold or silver are prohibited, must bring a *chatas* (*Kereisos* 3b; *Rambam,*

non-Jews (*Sefer HaChinuch*; see *Sanhedrin* 56a; *Tosefta, Avodah Zarah* ch. 8; *Rambam, Hil. Melachim* 9:1-2; see also *Sefer Mitzvos Hashem* [R' Yonasan Steif] 2:6, 3:46 and *Seder Mishnah* to *Hil. Yesodei HaTorah* 1:6:4). The Gemara in *Sanhedrin* (56a) lists seven mitzvos that were given to non-Jews (the reference to Noahide Laws reflects the fact that all of mankind descended from Noach, whose family were the sole survivors of the Flood). They are (1) the requirement to establish a system of civil laws (see *Rambam, Hil. Melachim* 9:14); (2) a prohibition against blasphemy (euphemistically referred to as "blessing" the Name of Hashem); (3) a prohibition against idolatry; (4) a prohibition against illicit relations (see *Sanhedrin* 57a); (5) a prohibition against murder; (6) a prohibition against theft; and (7) a prohibition against eating a limb torn from a live animal (אבר מן החי). The Gemara (ibid. 56b) derives these mitzvos from a verse in *Bereishis* (2:16), which speaks of Hashem's commands to *Adam HaRishon*. With respect to this prohibition, the verse states *And Hashem, God, commanded* (*Bereishis* 2:16); the Gemara expounds this to teach a prohibition against idolatry (*Sanhedrin* 56b).

The עיונים, טוב טעם, and מאוצרות חז"ל sections of Mitzvos #28 and #29
have been combined, as the two mitzvos embody many common concepts.

A BROADER LOOK AT THE LAWS

1 Avoiding an appearance of idol worship

Not only is actual idolatry forbidden, but one may not even *appear* to venerate an idol. Hence, if one happens to be standing in front of an idol and a thorn enters his foot or he drops a coin, he may not immediately bend to remove the thorn or retrieve the coin, lest he seem to be bowing to the idol (*Avodah Zarah* 12a). Rather, he should first sit down (*Rambam Hil. Avodah Zarah* 3:7), or turn to face backwards or sideways, and only then grasp the object (*Tur* and *Shulchan Aruch, Yoreh Deah* 150:2). Similarly, one may not bend to drink water from a stream that flows before an idol (*Avodah Zarah* ibid. and *Tur* ibid.).

Furthermore, if a fountain of water spouts from the mouth of a statue, one may not put his lips in contact with those of the statue to drink directly from the fount, lest he appear to be kissing an idol (*Avodah Zarah* 12a; kissing an idol is one of the forbidden displays of reverence addressed in Mitzvah #29, Law 2). *Rambam* (*Hil. Avodah Zarah* 3:8) and *Shulchan Aruch* (*Yoreh Deah* 150:3) apparently maintain that this restriction applies only to statues that are actual idols or that serve as ornaments before idols. *Tur* (ibid.) makes no such qualification, and accordingly, one may not drink from the mouth of even the most innocuous statue, lest the statue be mistaken for an idol that the drinker is kissing (*Smak* §65 states this explicitly; see *Bach* to *Tur* ibid.). *Bach, Shach,* and *Taz* (ibid.) decide that while, strictly speaking, the halachah here follows *Rambam* and *Shulchan Aruch,* one is praiseworthy if he complies with the more stringent opinion.

Some Rishonim go so far as to rule that just as one may not practice actual idolatry even at the cost of his life, so must one forfeit his life to avoid appearing idolatrous. Thus, one may not bend to drink from the aforementioned stream even if he is dying of thirst (*Rashba* and *Ran* [first explanation] to *Avodah Zarah* ibid. and *Tur* ibid., from the simple understanding of the Gemara there; see also *Tosafos* to *Yoma* 82a, end of ד"ה מה). Others hold that when confronted with mortal danger, one need not give up his life to avoid the appearance of idolatry. Therefore, one may bend to drink from the stream. The danger, however, must be imminent. A person who is not yet dangerously thirsty, but who wishes to continue traveling and worries that he may not find water when he grows thirsty later, may *not* drink from the stream (*Ran* ibid., second explanation; *Teshuvos HaRosh,* 19:17; *Rama, Yoreh Deah* 150:3). [The dispute may stem from different understandings of the obligation to avoid idolatrous appearances. According to the lenient view (*Rosh* et al.), such appearances are apparently proscribed by the more general Rabbinic obligation to avoid even a suspicion of transgression (מראית עין). This obligation is not specific to idolatry: One may not, for example, drink fish blood that has been gathered in a bowl, lest he appear to be drinking the Biblically prohibited blood of animals (*Kereisos* 21b with *Rashi,* ד"ה שכנסו; *Yoreh Deah* 66:9). Where life is endangered, the obligation does not stand — whether the suspicion to be avoided is of idolatry or of any other transgression. But according to the stringent view (*Rashba* et al.), appearing to venerate an idol is prohibited for reasons specific to idolatry: either because even the *appearance* of veneration does honor to the idol, or because a person who engages in apparent veneration of an idol may eventually find himself drawn to actually worship it (see *Ran* ibid. and *Tosafos* to *Pesachim* 25a, ד"ה חוץ;

see also *Sefer HaChinuch* §28). Apparent veneration of an idol is thus one of the transgressions 'peripheral' to actual worship (אביזרייהו דעבודה זרה), and as such is encompassed under the commandment to sanctify Hashem's name by dying rather than practicing idolatry (see *mitzvah #296*).]

Rama (*Yoreh Deah* ibid.) suggests that the dispute also applies as well to situations where even if the apparent idolatry were real idolatry, no penalty of death would be incurred; for example, drinking water from the mouth of a statue and thereby appearing to kiss an idol — an act which would violate a prohibition but would not render the violator liable to execution. See also *Rashi* to *Avodah Zarah* 12b, ד"ה פרצופות; see, however, *Mishnas Chachamim* cited in *Minchas Chinuch* 28:3.

Acting in a manner that seems idolatrous is prohibited even where there is no observer present (*Avodah Zarah* ibid.; *Perishah* and *Shach, Yoreh Deah* 150:1).

2 Bowing before a monument

Statues are often erected in the likeness of the local ruler or king. As long as such a statue remains purely monumental and no divinity is attached to it, one may bow toward the statue in honor of the king (see *Sanhedrin* 61b-62a with *Rashi* and *Meiri*). *Chamra VeChayei* (ibid.) suggests, however, that this is true only if the king decreed that all passersby bow before his monument. In such a case, bowing does not even create an appearance of idol worship since it is evident to any observer that the person bowing, like all others who pass before the monument, means simply to fulfill the decree. Where there is no decree and one bows to a statue on his own initiative, he may engender a suspicion that his bow is idolatrous. See also *Tosafos* to *Kesubos* 33b, ד"ה אילמלי.

3 Playing music in service of an idol

Communal sacrifices in the *Beis HaMikdash* are attended by Leviim singing to the accompaniment of instrumental music (see *mitzvah #394*). Some commentators therefore consider singing as well as playing instruments components of sacrificial service, and hold a worshipper who sang or played before an idol liable for violation of the prohibition against sacrifice to an idol — even if the idol he sang to was not customarily worshipped with song (*Meiri* to Mishnah *Sanhedrin* 60b; see *Tzafnas Pane'ach, Hil. Avodah Zarah* 3:3).

4 Primary categories and corollaries of idol worship

The Gemara (*Sanhedrin* 62a) teaches that bowing, sacrifice, libation, and burning are primary categories (*avos*, literally *fathers*) that may have corollaries (*tolados*, literally *offspring*, but in the present context, *derivates* or *corollaries*), idolatrous practices that share a defining feature with one of the four services and therefore render a worshipper liable as if he had practiced one of the four. The Gemara's example is "breaking a stick before [and in honor of] an idol," which is, as *Rashi* (ד"ה שבר) explains, a corollary of sacrifice because "[breakage] is similar to sacrifice in that sacrifice [also] breaks (i.e. cuts) the neck [of the animal]." That is, both sacrifice and breakage sunder an object and thereby commit it irreversibly to the idol. The example of stick breaking is an allusion to *Avodah Zarah* 50b, where Rav Yehudah rules in the name of Rav: "If an idol is worshipped with sticks, then if one broke a stick before [the idol] he is liable, [but] if he threw the stick to [the idol] he is not liable." *Rashi* (ad loc. ד"ה שבר) comments that Rav speaks of an idol not normally served by the breaking or throwing of sticks (if one threw a stick to such an idol he *would* be liable, for violation of *mitzvah #29*; see note 1), but in whose service sticks are otherwise employed, for example, to beat upon drums. A worshipper who broke a stick as an offering to the idol is liable as though he sacrificed an animal, whereas a worshipper who threw a stick as an offering cannot be deemed to have practiced a form of libation or sprinkling, because the stick remains whole, while a sprinkling must scatter on impact (as Rava explains in *Avodah Zarah* ibid.), like the blood that was offered on the Altar in the *Beis HaMikdash* (see note 6). Below, we will address why Rav Yehudah qualifies his ruling by speaking of an idol worshipped in some way with sticks.

Several other statements in Tractate *Avodah Zarah* seem either to corroborate or contradict the principle that corollaries of the four services incur liability. According to a Baraisa also on 50b, "If one stuffed excrement (as an offering) into [the mouth of an idol], or if he poured a libation of urine before [the idol], he is liable," presumably because although stuffing excrement and pouring urine are certainly not the primary forms of sprinkling and libation, they can nevertheless be corollaries (the Baraisa speaks of excrement moist enough to scatter on impact; see Gemara ibid. 51a). On the other hand, in a second Baraisa on 51a, we find Tannaim contesting whether a worshipper is liable for sacrificing a grasshopper to an idol: "R' Yehudah holds him liable, whereas the Sages exempt him [because a grasshopper is dissimilar from the animal sacrifices offered Hashem]." Thus the Sages, at least, refuse to consider sacrificing a grasshopper a corollary to animal sacrifice. [The Gemara does observe that the Sages cannot be reconciled with Rav, who considers even stick breaking a corollary of sacrifice, but notes no contradiction between the Sages and the Baraisa that deems stuffing excrement and pouring urine forms of idolatrous libation.] Moreover, R' Avahu (later on 51a) cites a derivation by R' Yochanan that exempts an idolater who sacrificed to an idol if the animal lacked a limb, because such animals are invalid as offerings to Hashem (see note 5). How then can one be liable for pouring urine or breaking a stick to honor an idol, yet incur no liability for sacrificing a grasshopper or even slaughtering an animal that merely lacks a limb?

The Rishonim suggest various solutions. *Raavad* (*Hasagos* to *Hil. Avodah Zarah* 3:4) maintains that Tannaim disagree whether the four services indeed are primary categories that have corollaries, and that the dispute concerning grasshoppers between R' Yehudah and the Sages

hinges on this question. According to R' Yehudah, corollaries of the services incur liability, so an idolater is liable for sacrifice of a grasshopper as though he slaughtered an animal fit to be offered to Hashem; the Sages reject the very concept of corollaries to the primary forms of idolatry, so they exempt an idolater who offers a grasshopper. The Sages would similarly exempt one who stuffs excrement or pours urine or any liquid other than those that may be offered Hashem (blood, wine, and possibly water; see note 6 and the end of next paragraph), or who sacrifices an animal that lacks a limb. R' Yochanan rules with the Sages. Rav, however, rules with R' Yehudah, and therefore holds an idolater liable for breaking a stick in honor of any idol, even an idol in whose worship sticks play no part. Why, then, did Rav speak of "an idol worshipped with sticks"? Only to stress that for *throwing* a stick one is never liable, even if the customary worship of the idol somehow involves sticks (unless of course the customary worship is to actually throw the sticks). Also in accordance with R' Yehudah and Rav is the Baraisa that finds an idolater liable for stuffing excrement or pouring urine. The halachah follows Rav. Thus, an idolater incurs liability for breaking a stick, stuffing excrement or pouring urine, as well as for sacrificing a grasshopper or an animal lacking a limb.

Ramban (*Avodah Zarah* 50b-51a) agrees that Rav and R' Yehudah on the one side, against R' Yochanan and the Sages on the other, argue whether corollaries of the four services incur liability. But contrary to *Raavad*, *Ramban* maintains the halachah follows R' Yochanan. Accordingly, an idolater is *not* liable for breaking a stick, stuffing excrement, or pouring urine, nor for sacrificing a grasshopper or an animal lacking a limb (except where these are native forms of worship). *Ramban* notes, however, an exceptional case where liability is incurred for a practice that, while not constituting actual sacrifice, is related to sacrifice. An idolater who harvests grain or grapes as an offering to an idol is liable (see *Avodah Zarah* 51a), because grain and grapes are offered in the *Beis HaMikdash*: grain as *menachos* (meal offerings), and grapes in *bikkurim* (the offering of first produces; see *mitzvah* #91). Since sundering the fruit from the vine or the grain from its stubble is akin to slaughter (*Rashi* ad loc. ד"ה שבצרן), *and* results, moreover, in a product of a kind that can be offered to Hashem, the harvest is idolatrous service that parallels inner service. See also *Ritva* and *Ran* to *Avodah Zarah* ad loc.

Unlike *Raavad* and *Ramban*, *Tosafos* (ibid., ד"ה חייב), see no dispute between Rav and R' Yochanan. They maintain that offerings cannot be corollaries of sacrificial slaughter or libation unless the idol served is normally professed to harbor interest in the things being offered (see also *Rashi* to 50b, ד"ה שבר). Thus, Rav holds an idolater liable for breaking a stick only if the idol is, in fact, somehow "worshipped with sticks." The Baraisa that renders an idolater liable for stuffing excrement or pouring urine should be similarly understood to speak only of idols in whose worship excrement or urine play some customary part. R' Yehudah, too, means that if the worship of a particular idol involves grasshoppers, then an idolater who sacrifices a grasshopper to that idol is liable. [Rav rules in accordance with R' Yehudah]. R' Yochanan, though, who exempts sacrifice to an idol of an animal lacking a limb, speaks of an idol whose worship normally involves no animals. Hence, an idolater is liable for breaking a stick, sacrificing grasshoppers or animals lacking limbs, or stuffing excrement or pouring urine only if the idols he served were customarily worshipped somehow with sticks, grasshoppers, animals, feces, and urine, respectively. Otherwise he is not liable except for sacrifices of whole-bodied animals or birds, or for sprinklings and libations of blood or wine. [And possibly of water as well, because water is offered as a libation on the Altar every day of the Succos festival. See *Minchas Chinuch* 26:4; *Tzafnas Pane'ach*, Hil. Avodah Zarah 3:3; see also *Rechush HaYam*, cited by *Minchas Yitzchak* V. 4, 1:5.]

Rambam (Hil. Avodah Zarah 3:4) seemingly endorses a middle position. His interpretation of Rav's ruling on sticks is enigmatic; *Kessef Mishneh* submits that where an idol is worshipped in some way with sticks, *Rambam* maintains, based on an alternate version of Rav's statement recorded in *Avodah Zarah* 51a, that a worshipper who broke a stick before the idol *and* one who threw a stick to the idol are both liable. Indisputable, however, is that *Rambam* decides that an idolater is not liable for sacrificing a grasshopper or an animal lacking a limb, yet asserts unconditionally that an idolater *is* liable for stuffing his idol with excrement or pouring it urine. Here again is our original contradiction: "It does not stand to reason," as *Raavad* objects, "that sacrificing a grasshopper or an animal that lacks a limb should be less [severe] than stuffing excrement or pouring urine!"

Some commentators answer that, paradoxically, the closer an idolatrous service approaches in form the service of Hashem, the more significant small discrepancies grow. Thus, writes *Kessef Mishneh*, stuffing excrement and pouring urine, *because* they have no counterparts in the *Beis HaMikdash*, more nearly resemble inner service than does sacrifice of grasshoppers or of animals lacking limbs, whose approximate counterparts — whole-bodied cattle, sheep, goats, pigeons, and doves — *are* offered in the *Beis HaMikdash* and thereby highlight how grasshoppers and animals lacking limbs diverge from valid offerings (see also *Pri Chadash*; *Chazon Ish* to *Yoreh Deah* 56:4). Other commentators (*Arba'a Turei Even* et al.), however, consider this proposal logically insupportable. See further, *Or Same'ach* to Hil. Avodah Zarah ibid.

5 *Service motivated by love or fear*

The Gemara in *Sanhedrin* (61b) records the following Amoraic dispute: "If one serves an idol for love or fear, Abaye says he is liable, but Rava says he is not liable." That is, for intentional service out of love or fear one does not incur the penalty of death, and for inadvertent service out of love or fear (e.g. where the worshipper was unaware that service motivated by fear is prohibited) he does not offer a *chatas* (as evident from *Sanhedrin* 62a and *Shabbos* 72b; see *Yad Ramah* and *Ran* to *Sanhedrin* 61b; *Pri Chadash* to *Hil. Avodah Zarah* 3:6; cf. *Kessef Mishneh* ibid.; *Maharsha* to *Tosafos, Sanhedrin* 64a ד"ה אע"ג). *Rashi* explains "love or fear" to mean that the worshipper served the idol to impress a devotee whom the worshipper loved, or to avoid the wrath of a devotee whom the worshipper feared, all the while denying in his heart that the idol was in any way divine. He is not liable because his service was a mere charade, performed not for the idol but for the benefit of onlookers. The halachah follows Rava, as it does in almost all his disputes with Abaye (see *Kiddushin* 52a with *Rashi* ד"ה יע"ל קג"ם).

The "fear" we speak of here was not of mortal danger. Rather, the worshipper feared that unless he served the idol, devotees would harm his property. If, however, the worshipper feared for his life, then even Abaye would agree he is not liable. See *Rambam Hil. Yesodei HaTorah* 5:4; *Ramban* and *Ritva* to *Shabbos* 72b; *Rivash* cited by *Kessef Mishneh, Hil. Avodah Zarah* 3:6; cf. *Rabbeinu Dovid* quoted by *Ran* to *Sanhedrin* 61. See also *mitzvah* #296, regarding whether a person is ever punishable by human courts for transgressing a prohibition under duress of life.

Rambam (*Hil. Avodah Zarah* ibid.) understands Rava differently. "If one serves an idol for love, i.e. he was enamored of a particular statue because of its unusually beautiful workmanship (and believing, as devotees do, that the idol was alive, he desired to please it, as he might desire to please an especially handsome human), or if he served [the idol] out of fear lest it harm him — [imagining] as devotees imagine that an idol can help or harm — then if he served it in its customary manner, or by one of the four services (that normally render one liable no matter what idol they are performed for) ... he is not liable." Credence that an object is alive and autonomous and supernaturally able to help or hinder is certainly sufficient to render one guilty of idolatrous beliefs (see *Ran* and *Meiri* to *Sanhedrin* 61b; *Rivash* cited by *Kessef Mishneh, Hil. Avodah Zarah*

3:6). Nevertheless, *Rambam* apparently maintains, a worshipper is *liable* only for service that reflects not just admiration for the idol's form or apprehension of the idol's potency, but also a conviction that the idol is genuinely worthy of homage (see *Hil. Avodah Zarah* 1:1 and 2:1; note that according to 1:2, homage of idols historically preceded belief in the *potency* of idols). Service predicated on conviction, rather than rote obedience driven by expectation of reward or fear of retribution, is what we owe Hashem (see *Hil. Teshuvah* 10:1-2), and it is of such service that *Shemos* 22:19 says, *Whosoever sacrifices to the gods shall be condemned — only to Hashem alone!* One who serves an idol without conviction is therefore exempt from punishment by human hands (see also *Rach* and *Ramban* to *Shabbos* 72b; *Yad Ramah* to *Sanhedrin* 61b; cf. *Hasagos HaRaavad* ad loc.).

Rambam concedes, however, that if a worshipper declared an idol to be his deity he is liable, even if the declaration was motivated by love or fear of the idol. Unlike active services, which may be born of conviction but may also easily be expressions of love or fear, declaring an idol one's deity is *inherently* a reflection of conviction — because one's "deity," by definition, is the entity one holds worthy of homage. The declaration may be honest — if the worshipper truly believes the idol deserves homage, or it may be dishonest — if the worshipper imagines he is lying to the idol to purchase its good graces. But in either case the declaration remains a kind of idolatry that *expresses* conviction, and is therefore penalized. [See *Tosafos* to *Yoma* 82a, end of ד"ה מה; see also *Rabbeinu Dovid* quoted by *Ran* to *Sanhedrin* 61b.]

The Rishonim raise the following difficulty: Even where an idolater threatens to kill a Jew unless he serves an idol, the Jew must transcend his fear and forfeit his life rather than practice idolatry (see Law 7 and note 14). How then can Rava exempt one from punishment for idolatry motivated by "fear" (including fear of mere monetary harm), or even by "love" (where no danger at all threatens the worshipper)? *Tosafos* (*Sanhedrin* 61b and *Shabbos* 72b

ד"ה רבא אמר, first explanation) answer that although one must refuse to serve an idol even if he fears for his life, he is nevertheless not punishable after the fact if he does serve the idol. The Torah sets penalties only for genuine idol worship, whereas service "for love or fear" is no more than a pretense. Still, engaging in the motions of idolatry is also a form of idolatry, and as such it is encompassed by the obligation to avoid idolatry even at the cost of one's life (*Ran* to *Sanhedrin* ibid.; see *mitzvah* #296). Alternatively: Rava never exempted a person who worshipped an idol that devotees consider divine. One must indeed forfeit his life rather than serve such an idol, and if one served such an idol "for love or fear (of non-mortal harm)" he is liable to the penalties for idolatry. Rava speaks only of an idol that *no one* serves except "for love or fear." An example of this would be a king who declares himself a god, whose subjects, none of whom truly believe in their king's divinity, nevertheless all bow to him on pain of his displeasure. Rava maintains that one need not forfeit his life to avoid bowing to such a king, nor is one punished for doing so (*Tosafos* ibid., last explanation; *Yereim* §270, cited by *Smag, Lo Saaseh* §17; *Minchas Chinuch* 26:1 suggests that *Rambam* is of a similar opinion, but most other commentators agree that *Rambam*'s wording cannot support such an interpretation). See also *Tosafos* to *Shabbos* (ibid.) second explanation; *Rabbeinu Dovid,* quoted by *Ran* to *Sanhedrin* 61b.

Another seeming contradiction to Rava arises from *Sanhedrin* 64a, where the Gemara infers from the Mishnah (60b) that if one bared himself to *Pe'or,* or stoned *Markolis,* he is liable even if his intent was to deride the idol. How can service "for love or fear" be exempt from penalty because the worshipper did not venerate the idol in his heart, while an attempt to scorn an idol, without even a pretense of veneration, *is* penalized? According to the second explanation presented in the previous paragraph, there is actually no difficulty, because Rava does in fact penalize service "for love or fear" except where the idol served is venerated by no one (*Tosafos* to *Sanhedrin* 61b and *Shabbos* 72b ד"ה רבא אמר). If,

however, Rava exempts "service for love or fear" even where performed for idols whose devotees consider them divine, a resolution is necessary. Several possibilities are offered:

A. When the Mishnah teaches that one is liable for baring himself to *Pe'or* derisively or stoning *Markolis* derisively, it speaks of a worshipper who meant to *serve* the idols by shaming them — because he believed, as do devotees of *Pe'or* and *Markolis,* that these idols crave humiliation. If, however, his intent was purely to desecrate the idols and embarrass their devotees, he, no less than one who served an idol "for love or fear," is not liable (*Tosafos* ibid.; see *Yad Ramah* to *Sanhedrin* ibid.).

B. One who worships "for love or fear" denies that the service of the idol is worthy in itself; he simply sees himself compelled to serve to achieve entirely different ends. This is not the worship born of conviction for which the Torah renders an idolater liable; whereas a person who, in his zeal against idolatry, derisively bares himself to *Pe'or* or stones *Markolis,* willingly carries out what he believes is a moral imperative. In this, paradoxically, he resembles the idol's devotees: though he realizes that all idols are contemptible, while they imagine that *Pe'or* and *Markolis* crave humiliation and are entitled to have their cravings satisfied, both they *and* he act on a heartfelt conviction that *Pe'or* and *Markolis* deserve to be derided! When this person learns that *Pe'or* and *Markolis* are worshipped in the manner that he inadvertently practiced, he must offer a *chatas* (*Rivash* in explanation of *Rambam,* cited by *Kessef Mishneh* ad loc.; moreover, if the person knew that devotees of *Pe'or* and *Markolis* claim that their idols desire shame, then his actions cannot be considered purely derisive, and if he was forewarned, he is therefore liable to execution — see *mitzvah* #29, note 7).

See also *Kessef Mishneh* to *Hil. Avodah Zarah* 3:6; cf. *Yad Ramah* and *Ran* to *Sanhedrin* 61b; *Pri Chadash* to *Hil. Avodah Zarah* ibid.

Unless circumstances indicate otherwise, worship is presumed to be sincere. A deliberate and forewarned idolater therefore cannot claim that in his heart he did not venerate the idol, and he is executed — unless he declared before the fact that the service he was about to perform would be "for love or fear" (*Yad Ramah* ibid.; see also *Tosafos* to *Shabbos* 72b ד"ה רבא אמר).

6 Idolaters liable to more than one chatas

If one performed, inadvertently and in the course of a single *he'eleim* (literally *unawareness,* a period of time during which one remained continuously ignorant of a particular prohibition or of its applicability to particular circumstances), the same service for five different idols, he is liable to offer only one

chatas, because he is guilty of only one error — unawareness that the specific idolatry he practiced was forbidden (*Rambam, Hil. Shegagos* 6:2). If, however, he performed several dissimilar services, e.g. he bared himself to *Pe'or* and also stoned *Markolis,* then the number of *chataos* he is obligated to bring depends on the nature of the error (or errors) that led him to sin. If he was unaware that idolatry of any kind is prohibited, and therefore served both *Pe'or* and *Markolis* each in its peculiar manner, he is guilty of a single error and must therefore bring a single *chatas.* If, however, he was aware that idolatry is prohibited, but was unaware that to bare oneself to *Pe'or* is a form of idolatry, and was also unaware that to stone *Markolis* is idolatry, he is guilty of two distinct errors. He must therefore bring two *chataos* (based on *Hil. Shegagos* 7:1).

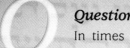

SITUATIONS IN HALACHAH

> ### Question:
> In times past, it was the practice when greeting a person of stature to bow or doff one's hat. May a Jew greet a person in this manner if the person is displaying an idolatrous icon?

Answer:

As we have explained (*Iyunim* §2), the Sages prohibited numerous activities because they *appear* to violate the prohibition against bowing before an idol. For example, a person standing in the vicinity of an idol may not bend down to drink water from a stream, or remove a thorn that lodged in his foot, or retrieve a coin he dropped, lest it appear to an observer that he is bowing before the idol (see *Avodah Zarah* 12a; *Rambam, Hil. Avodas Kochavim* 3:7).

According to some Rishonim, this prohibition applies in our scenario. Accordingly, if a Jew encounters someone [even an influential, powerful person whose displeasure could have negative consequences] wearing an idolatrous ornament, he may not honor him by bowing or doffing his hat. Although the Jew's intention is not to honor the idol but the person, he *appears* to be honoring the idol. Therefore, the act is forbidden (*Terumas HaDeshen* I:196, cited in *Rama, Yoreh Deah* 150:3; *Chamra V'Chayei, Sanhedrin* p. 307).

However, other Rishonim maintain that the case of a person of stature differs from those in which the Sages enacted their decree. In those cases, the observer does not know why the person is bowing; therefore, he is likely to interpret the act as veneration of the idol. Here, however, it is obvious that the person's intent is to honor the powerful individual he has just met. Since no one will construe his act as one of venerating the idol, it is permitted. However, even these authorities agree that if possible, one should refrain from bowing in this situation (*R'*

Yitzchak of Oppenheim, cited in *Terumas HaDeshen* ibid. and *Rama* ibid.). [This argument is apparently undermined by the fact that the Rabbis apply their decree to one who bends down to drink. In that case, an observer can easily discern the person's true purpose; yet, the act is forbidden. For discussion of this point, see *Terumas HaDeshen* ibid.; *Beur HaGra, Yoreh Deah* ibid. §5.]

According to some Rishonim, the stringent view is reflected in an incident recounted in Scripture, in which Mordechai, leader of the Jews in the Persian diaspora, refused to prostrate himself before the king's minister Haman, notwithstanding a royal edict to that effect (see *Esther* 3:1-5). According to one opinion in the Gemara, the reason he refused to bow was that Haman had declared himself a deity, and it is forbidden to bow before a false god (Abaye in *Sanhedrin* 61b). However, others maintain that since those who bowed before Haman did so only out of fear, but did not accept his divinity in their hearts, bowing before him was permitted (Rava, *Sanhedrin* ibid., as explained by *Tosafos* there, second approach). According to the latter view, it is not clear why Mordechai did not bow before Haman. *Tosafos* (ibid.) explain that Mordechai refrained because Haman wore a garment embroidered with idolatrous images (see *Esther Rabbah* 7:5), and Mordechai did not wish to prostrate himself before them. Now, had Mordechai consented to bow, it would have been apparent to any observer that his intent was not to honor the idol, but to honor Haman himself. Yet, he refused to bow. We see that it is forbidden to show honor to a person displaying an idolatrous image (*Terumas HaDeshen* ibid.; *Chamra V'Chayei* ibid. p. 302; *Beur HaGra* ibid. §5). [For deflections of this proof, see *Maharam Al-Shakar*, appendices, §76; *Magen Giborim, Orach Chaim* 113:3. For a different explanation of why Mordechai did not bow, see *Tosafos* ibid.]

Support for the lenient view is found in another Scriptural incident concerning our forefather Avraham and the three wayfarers he welcomed into his home. Avraham instructed the three guests to wash the dust from their feet (see *Bereishis* 18:4). The Sages explain that the wayfarers (who were actually angels) appeared before Avraham in the guise of Arabs, whose custom it was to worship the dust upon their feet. So as not to allow an idol into his home, Avraham bade them wash before entering (*Rashi ad loc.*, from *Bava Metzia* 86b). Yet, an earlier verse (ibid. v. 2) states that when Avraham first greeted the wayfarers, he bowed low before them, notwithstand-

ing the idolatrous dust upon their feet. This would seem to indicate that one is *permitted* to honor a person displaying an idolatrous object, in accordance with the lenient view (*Maharam Al-Shakar* ibid.; *Pri Chadash, Orach Chaim* 113:5). [See *Maharam Al-Shakar* for deflections of this proof as well.]

Rama (ibid.) rules that a person faced with this situation should preferably follow the stringent view and refrain from bowing.

———— ✌ ————

Question:
Is a person permitted to burn incense in his home, or does this resemble an act of idolatry?

Answer:
Some Rishonim maintain that one who burns incense to demons commits an act of idolatry. This is true not only where the person attributes divinity to the demons and burns the incense as a form of worship, but even where his purpose in burning the incense is merely to summon demons to his service. Although he attributes no divinity to the demons in that case, he has committed idolatry (*Beis Yosef, Yoreh Deah,* end of §179, and in *Shulchan Aruch, Yoreh Deah* 179:19).

Others maintain that where one's objective is not to worship the demons but merely to summon them, he has committed not idolatry, but sorcery; specifically, the sorcerous conjuration known as *Ov* [prohibited in *Devarim* 18:11; see *mitzvah* #513] (*Rabbeinu Yerucham,* cited in *Beis Yosef* ibid.; see *Shach, Yoreh Deah* ibid. §22; *Beur HaGra* there §30).

Based on the prohibition of demon worship, the Sages issued a decree forbidding a person to burn fragrant incense in his home, lest it appear that he is offering incense before demons. They permitted such burning only where there is an unpleasant odor in the house, for it is then evident that he is burning the incense to dispel the odor, and not as

an act of demon worship (*Beis Yosef* ibid. with *Shach* §21).

———— ✌ ————

Approximately 150 years ago, there arose among the Jews of Turkey and the Arabian lands, primarily amongst their womenfolk, the belief that all misfortune that befell people was the handiwork of demons. As a result of this belief, the women of these lands would respond to misfortune — for example, illness — with rites intended to appease and pacify the demons. They would banish all residents of the sick person's home for a period of days, leaving only the patient himself and a woman to perform the rites. All holy books and *mezuzos* were removed from the house, so as not to impede the conjuration of the demons. After surrounding the patient's bed with various foods and delicacies, the woman would break eggs, kneel upon the floor, and say to the demons: "Here is an offering for you; cease tormenting So-and-so." Sometimes, the woman would burn incense as an offering to the demons. Throughout the period of these rites, the patient was forbidden to utter blessings or to pray, for fear that the holy words would anger the demons.

Many Rabbinic leaders of the era objected to these practices, on the grounds that they constituted demon worship, and were therefore prohibited as idolatry. [The objections were detailed in the work *K'nesiah L'Shem Shamayim,* written by *R' Menasheh Sithon,* a Syrian rabbi of the period.] However, some wished to permit these practices, based on the words of *Riaz* (cited in *Shiltei HaGiborim, Avodah Zarah,* fol. 8b), who writes that according to those who hold that summoning demons is *not* idolatry, but is prohibited only as *Ov*-sorcery, the prohibition applies *only* if the demons are summoned as a means of contacting the dead [which is the purpose of the *Ov* conjuration]. From *Riaz* we may conclude that according to the lenient view, burning incense to demons is forbidden only if (a) the person accepts the divinity of the demon and wishes to worship it, or (b) he summons the demons in order to contact the dead. Based on this reasoning, some argued that these customs were permissible, since they involved neither accepting the divinity of the demons nor contacting the dead (see *Knesiah L'Shem Shamayim* p. 52).

The authorities offer several responses. Firstly, they point out that although some rule that summoning demons is not idolatry, the *Beis Yosef* in *Shulchan Aruch* (ibid.), whose ruling is authoritative, states clearly that it *is* idolatry. Thus, *Riaz's* reasoning is halachically irrelevant. Secondly, they argue that since there are some who attribute divinity to demons and worship them, all actions that resemble such worship are forbidden, even if they themselves are not intended as demon worship. Finally, the authorities assert that notwithstanding their denials, the women who perform these rites actually relate to the demons as deities; thus, all agree that their actions are prohibited (see *Knesiah L'Shem Shamayim* ff. 7a-10b).

ILLUMINATIONS OF THE MITZVAH
Suggested Reasons & Insights

I. "THERE IS NONE LIKE OUR GOD"

n view of the fact that the Creator is the One true God, without any equal in Heaven or on Earth, the Torah prohibits prostration and other forms of worship to pagan deities. The reason is spelled out by the Torah (*Shemos* 20:5): *For I am Hashem, your God;* meaning to say, "You already possess a godly Master; do not, then, turn to others" (*Chizkuni, Shemos* ibid.). Moreover, once Hashem created a person and sustains his life, how can that person give the honor due Him to some other, who, in any case, cannot help nor harm? (*Ibn Ezra, Shemos* ibid.).

The verse continues: *For I am Hashem, your God, a vengeful God* (*Shemos* ibid.): There is no parallel between Me and any other being, and it is therefore fitting that I should avenge My honor when it is inappropriately applied to another (*Sforno, Shemos* ibid. §5).

II. AN ACT OF TREACHERY TOWARD GOD

here is a unique relationship between God and the people of Israel. God established an everlasting covenant with us, binding us to become for Him "a kingdom of priests and a holy nation" (*Shemos* 19:6), devoted to carrying out His will. For His part, He will forever associate His Holy Name with the Jewish people. When a person directs his worship toward a pagan deity, he has thus broken this pact and rebelled against God.

The verse states: *Do not bow down to them or worship them, for I am Hashem, your God, a **vengeful** God.* The concept of vengeance is used by the Torah in reference to God only in the context of idol worship. Since Israel has been consecrated as God's treasured nation from among all others,

much as a wife to a husband, God's reaction to a Jew's defection to the worship of foreign gods is described in the terms of a husband avenging the treachery of his unfaithful wife. This is why this term is not — and could not — be used in relation to the pagan worship of other peoples, who do not enjoy the intimate relationship with their Creator that is unique to Israel (*Ramban, Shemos* 20:3; see also *Abarbanel,* ad loc.; *Akeidas Yitzchak* §88 and §45). In fact, in all the words of condemnation that the prophets have had for the nations of the world, there is not one mention of the sin of idolatry (*Rabbeinu Bachya, Shemos* 20:5).

In light of the treachery that idolatry entails, we can begin to appreciate the singular gravity the Torah associates with this sin. No other transgression, as much as it may contradict the will of God, repudiates entirely the special relationship between God and Israel as much as idolatry (*Pachad Yitzchak, Chanukah*).

III. TO WORSHIP GOD, AND NOT HIS SERVANTS

t is possible for the veneration of an idol to grow out of the misguided belief that the Creator, after bringing the world into existence, found it beneath His dignity to devote His attention to the management of this mundane world. According to this view, the affairs of the world were left completely in the hands of the celestial functionaries and controlling forces, such as the sun, the moon, and the Heavenly hosts. Adherents of this philosophy believe that God is too exalted and removed from the world to even take notice of the lowly human's worship of Him; it is only the stars and zodiacal constellations that can be reached by our worship (*Derashos HaRan* §9). Others, in a variant of this error, contend that God Himself desires that people worship these forces, in the manner of a king who would like to see his royal officials being treated honorably by his subjects; it is an extension of his own honor. Neither of these notions are close to the truth. The Creator of the world, *though He is enthroned on high, deigns to look far down, into the Heavens and the earth* (*Tehillim* 113:5-6), and takes an interest in even the lowliest of creatures, guiding their fate and providing their needs. It is to Him alone, the source of all power, that one should direct his worship. The sundry forces that impact the world are merely conduits through which God channels His power; they are not to be perceived as deities in their own right to whom we ought to subordinate ourselves, whether in theory or in practice (*Ramban, Shemos* 20:3; see also the *Ramban's Derashas Torah Temimah*. *Rabbeinu Bachya* (*Shemos* ad loc.) adds that this explains why idols are termed "other gods," for they have no innate power; any abilities they may exhibit are perforce drawn from a source "other" than themselves.

THROUGH THE EYES OF THE SAGES
Stories, Parables & Reflections

Idolatry: Its Appeal, Its Severity, Its Consequences

I. THE EVIL INCLINATION FOR IDOL WORSHIP IN ANCIENT TIMES

*I*n the days of old, the world's lone monotheistic people were confronted on all sides with an intellectual challenge presented by the widely held belief in the supernatural powers of pagan deities. But aside from that, we find that people were also driven by an innate desire to engage in the worship of idols. People would experience a spiritual thrill in performing the rituals of sacrifice, prostration, and other forms of devotion that varied from one deity to another. Since the Sages of the Great Assembly succeeded in extinguishing this idolatrous passion, the attraction that idol worship held in the eyes of the ancients is to our minds incomprehensible. But in its prime, this urge combined with the perception that idols held the key to all kinds of material blessings to form a potent temptation that ensnared even the greatest of people.

The Talmud (*Sanhedrin* 63b) does, however, record an opinion that the people of Israel were well aware that the idols were worthless, and were not initially attracted to idolatry per se. Rather, they embraced pagan practices only to unburden themselves of the restraining yoke of the Torah, thus freeing themselves for a life of abandon. But even according to this approach, in due course the desire for idol worship was kindled within them, and it eventually raged to the point where even young children would give their lives for its sake (see below).

——— ৵৶ ———

৵ *A powerful desire*

*N*ow they (the Ten Tribes) continued to sin, and they have made themselves a molten image from

their silver, in the shape of idols (*Hoshea* 13:2). Each person made for himself an image of his idol that he could keep in his pocket. When he would be reminded of it, he would pull it out to hug it and kiss it. The Sages related: Eliyahu the Prophet was seeking the bloated victims of hunger in the streets of Jerusalem. It happened once that he found a young boy lying in a heap of rubbish, swollen from hunger. He said to him, "What family are you from?" The boy answered, "I am from the family of So-and-so, and am the only one left." Eliyahu offered, "If I will teach you something that will ensure that you live, are you willing to learn?" The child agreed. Eliyahu instructed, "Simply say every day, *Hear O Israel, Hashem is our God; Hashem is One!* But the child protested. "Quiet! Do not make mention of the name of Hashem," for his father and mother had never taught it to him. With that, the boy brought out his idol and began to cuddle and kiss it, until his belly split. The figurine fell to the ground and he fell lifelessly upon it, in fulfillment of the Biblical warning (*Vayikra* 26:30), *I will cast your carcasses upon the carcasses of your idols* (*Sanhedrin* 63b. See also ibid. 102b, where it is said that even the greatest of the Amoraic sages would have succumbed to the urge for this sin had they lived in an earlier era).

——— ৵৶ ———

৵ *Abolishing the lure of idolatry*

*T*hey cried out in a great voice to Hashem, their God (*Nechemiah* 9:4). What did they say? "Alas, alas, this evil inclination [for idol worship] is what destroyed the Temple and burned its Hall; it killed the righteous, and exiled Israel from its land; should it now continue to frolic among us? Did You plant it within us for any other reason than that we might earn our reward [by conquering it]? Well, we would rather not have the desire; we will give up the reward!" … They spent three days in fasting and prayer, and a note fell down from Heaven, bearing the single word *Emes,* "Truth." R' Chanina said: We have thus received the approval of the Holy One, Blessed is He, for 'truth' is His seal."

With that, a flame of fire in the form of a lion cub was seen exiting the Holy of Holies. The prophet (Zechariah, son of Ido — *Rashi* to *Yoma*) explained to the Jews: That was the [representation of the] passion for idolatry (*Sanhedrin* 64a; *Yoma* 69b. Cf. *Zohar Chadash, Tikunim* 166a. See also below and *Shir HaShirim Rabbah* 7:8 for other opinions on who was responsible for the eradication of the ardor for pagan worship).

———— ৯৫ ————

৯৫ *A great source of merit*

The entire congregation that had returned from the captivity made succos and dwelt in succos, something the Children of Israel had not done since the days of Yehoshua, son of Nun ... and there was very great joy (Nechemiah 8:17). Is it conceivable that David arose and the people did not build *succos*, until the time of Ezra? Rather, the verse refers to the fact that Ezra had pleaded successfully for the abolition of man's desire for idolatry, and the merit thereof sheltered the people like *succos*. [This achievement, long overdue, was unprecedented, and] the verse criticizes Yehoshua for not having done it himself, in his time. Thus Yehoshua's name, which is everywhere spelled יהושע, is in this case missing a letter, being rendered ישוע. For it is understandable that Moshe did not attempt to pray for this, because he lacked the merit of settling in the Land of Israel. But as for Yehoshua, who brought the Jews into the Land and did have this merit, why did he not petition for God's mercy in regard to this matter? (*Arachin* 32b).

———— ৯৫ ————

৯৫ *One inclination, two rewards*

The Creator introduced two passions into His world: the desire for idolatry and the lust for immorality. The desire for idolatry has since been uprooted; only man's physical urges remain. God proclaimed: If one succeeds in withstanding immoral temptation, I will view him as having overcome both of these urges. This can be compared to

a snake-hunter who pursued two poisonous snakes. He himself captured the larger snake and left over the smaller one, declaring, "Whoever can catch this one will be considered as if he captured them both" (*Shir HaShirim Rabbah* 7:8).

II. THE SEVERITY OF THE PROHIBITION

৯৫ *The key to upholding the Torah*

hat mitzvah is equivalent to all the other *mitzvos*? It is the prohibition of idol worship (*Horayos* 8a).

When a man from among you brings an offering to God ... (Vayikra 1:2). 'From among you,' but not from all of you. An offering from an apostate may not be accepted. The Sages thus taught: We may accept offerings from the [impenitent] sinners in Israel, so that they may be moved to repent, with these exceptions: one who habitually pours wine libations for an idol, and one who publicly desecrates Shabbos. From this it can be learned that a sinner in regard to idol worship is treated as an apostate regarding the entire Torah (*Chullin* 5a; *Eiruvin* 69b; *Vayikra Rabbah* 2:9; *Tanna D'vei Eliyahu Rabbah* 6:12).

———— ৯৫ ————

৯৫ *Retreat of the Divine Presence*

When Yitzchak grew old and his eyes became too weak to see (Bereishis 27:1). What happened before this [that brought on his blindness]? *Eisav was forty years old and he took as a wife Judith ... the Hittite, and Basmas ... the Hittite, and they were a source of spiritual bitterness to Yitzchak and Rivkah* (ibid. 26:34-35). Before, the Divine Presence had resided in Yitzchak's home. But when Eisav brought in his Canaanite wives, they would burn incense to their pagan gods, and the Divine Presence withdrew. Yitzchak looked on in distress. God declared: I will cause his eyesight to fade so that he will not see and he will suffer no more (*Tanchuma, Toldos* §8; cf. *Mechilta, Yisro* §9).

III. THE IDOLATER'S PUNISHMENT

❧ Tzaraas

leven things can cause a person to become afflicted with *tzaraas* (a condition resembling leprosy): Idolatry … From where is it derived that idolatry can bring one *tzaraas*? We find that when the Israelites made the Golden Calf they were smitten with *tzaraas*, as it is said, *And Moshe saw that the nation was exposed* [פרוע] (*Shemos* 32:25). And in connection with *tzaraas* we find: *And the hair of his head shall be unshorn* [פרוע] (*Vayikra* 13:45) (*Tanchuma, Metzora* §4; *Zohar, Bamidbar* 206a. Cf. *Bamidbar Rabbah* 7:5).

———— ❧ ————

❧ In this world and the next

There are four things for which a person is penalized in this world while the principal [of the punishment] remains for him in the World to Come. They are: Idol worship, illicit relations, and murder — and slanderous speech is equal to all three combined. From where is it known that this is true of idolatry? For it is said in regard to idolatry (*Bamidbar* 15:31, see *Rashi* to v. 32), *That soul will be utterly cut off; its sin is upon it.* What is meant by 'its sin is upon it'? This phrase is intended to teach that though the person is removed from this world, he remains with this sin in the next world (*Yerushalmi, Pe'ah* 1:1; *Tosefta*, ibid. 1:2).

———— ❧ ————

❧ Disinherited in the World to Come

Anyone who worships idols, whether in his youth or old age, and dies without repenting—even if he is [otherwise] suited for the High Priesthood — he has no share in the World to Come. So it is said (*Amos* 8:14): *Those who swear by the idol of Samaria … they will fall and not rise again* (*Tanna D'vei Eliyahu Rabbah* 3:8).

———— ❧ ————

❧ An unparalleled punishment

There is no punishment more severe than that meted out for idol worship. For God acts with vengeance (exacting punishment unforgivingly — *Rashi* to the following verse) only with concern to idolatry, as it is said (*Shemos* 20:3,5), *You shall not recognize other gods before Me … for I am Hashem, your God, a jealous God.* And similarly (*Devarim* 4:23-24): *Beware for yourselves lest you forget … and you make for yourselves a carved image, a likeness of anything … for Hashem, your God, is a consuming fire, a jealous God.* (*Devarim Rabbah* 2:18, as explained by *Maharzav*).

For strong till the death is the love, hard as the grave is the vengeance (*Shir HaShirim* 8:6). The love that God has for the Jewish nation is strong till the death; regarding this it is written (*Malachi* 1:2), *I have loved you, says God.* But hard as the grave is the vengeance with which God reacts when they provoke His jealousy with their worship of idols, as it is said (*Devarim* 32:16), *They would arouse His jealousy with strangers.*

———— ❧ ————

❧ Under God's watchful eye

R' Avahu taught: Three sins are never obscured by the "curtain" [that separates the Divine Presence from the Heavenly host; that is, God does not divert His attention from the perpetrators until He exacts retribution — *Rashi*]: Cheating another, robbery, and idolatry … As for idolatry, it is written (*Yeshayah* 65:3), *The people who anger Me are before Me always, those who sacrifice in the gardens and burn incense on the bricks* (*Bava Metziah* 59a).

IV. COMMUNAL CONSEQUENCES

❧ The flood in Enosh's generation

When were the pagan objects of worship first called gods (a name hitherto reserved for the only true God)? It came to pass in the days of Enosh, son of Sheis, as it is said (*Bereishis* 4:26), *To*

Sheis as well, a son was born, and he called his name Enosh. It was then begun to call [others] *in the Name of God.* In those times the oceans rose and deluged a third of the world. God declared: You have done something novel by calling yourselves by My Name; I will likewise do something novel and I will call *Myself* by My name (i.e. I will demonstrate that I am truly Master of the world, and uniquely worthy of My Name). So it is written (*Amos* 9:6): *Who calls to the waters of the sea and pours them upon the face of the earth; Hashem is His Name* (*Tanchuma, Yisro* 16; *Bereishis Rabbah* 23:7; *Sifrei, Eikev* §43; et al.).

———— ৰ৴ ————

৩ *Drought and hunger*

In the days of [King] David there was a famine for three years, year after year (*Shmuel* II, 21:1). In the first of these years King David said to his people, "Perhaps there are idol worshippers among you, for the rain of the heavens is only withheld when Israel is guilty of idolatry, as it is said (*Devarim* 11:16-17: *...Lest your heart be seduced ... and you will serve other gods and bow down to them ... and He will hold back the Heavens so that there will be no rain ...* (*Yevamos* 78b; *Bamidbar Rabbah* 8:4; *Medrash Shmuel* §28; *Yerushalmi, Kiddushin* 4:1, *Sanhedrin* 6:7, et al.).

———— ৰ৴ ————

৩ *The famine proclaimed by Eliyahu the prophet*

Yehoshua adjured the people at that time, saying, 'Cursed before God be the man who shall arise and rebuild this city of Yericho. With [the death of] his firstborn he will lay its foundation, and with [the death of] his youngest he will set up its gates* (*Yehoshua* 6:26). The Sages taught: One may neither rebuild Yericho under a different name, nor may one build a different city and name it Yericho. For it is written (*Melachim* I, 16:34), *In the days [of Achav], Chiel of Beth-el built Yericho; with [the death of] Aviram his firstborn he laid the foundation, and with [the death of] Seguv he set up its gates ...* (And Chiel did not rebuild the original Yericho, but a different city under that name — *Rashi*.)

King Achav was Chiel's close friend, and he and Eliyahu came to extend their condolences as Chiel sat in mourning ... Achav mused, "Even the curse of Moshe never came to fruition. Moshe forewarned, *And you will serve other gods ... and God's wrath will be kindled and He will hold back the Heavens ...* But here is a man like myself, who has erected idols in every high place, and there is such an abundance of rain that I am prevented from going to worship them (because the roads are too muddy — *Rashi*). So is it possible, then, that his disciple Yehoshua's curse should be fulfilled? Upon hearing these words, Eliyahu declared before Achav (ibid. 17:1), *As Hashem, God of Israel, lives... [I swear] that there will not be dew nor rain during these years, except by my word* (*Sanhedrin* 103a; *Yerushalmi*, ibid. 10:2; *Tanna D'vei Eliyahu Zuta* 8:3).

———— ৰ৴ ————

৩ *Haman's decree*

The disciples asked of R' Shimon bar Yochai: Why were the Jews of that generation [of Achashveirosh] deserving of obliteration? He countered: Offer an answer yourselves. They suggested: Because they partook of Achashveirosh's feast. R' Shimon rejoined: If so, then only the Jews of Shushan should have been threatened! ... Rather, it was because they bowed down before the statue of Nevuchadnezzar. Asked the disciples: In what merit, then, were they miraculously saved? He answered: They only outwardly committed the deed (due to their fear of the tyrant), so God as well only dealt with them outwardly [with a decree that caused fear, but was not to be implemented] (*Megillah* 12a; cf. *Shir HaShirim Rabbah* 7:8).

———— ৰ৴ ————

৩ *Destruction and exile*

On account of illicit relations, idolatry, and the failure to observe the Shemittah and Yovel years, exile comes to the world. The Jews' enemies banish them and others come to settle in their place ... As for idolatry, it is written (*Vayikra* 26:30): *I will cast your carcasses upon the carcasses of your idols* (indicating people who sinned through idolatry) … *I will make your sanctuaries desolate, and you I will scatter among the nations* (prescribing as punishment the Temple's destruction and the nation's exile) … *Your enemies who dwell [in your land] will become desolate* (predicting that our enemies will take over our land — Rashi) (*Shabbos* 33a; cf. *Avos* 5:9; *Bamidbar Rabbah* 7:10).

Why was the First Temple destroyed? Because of the three sins that were prevalent then: Idolatry, illicit relations, and murder (*Yoma* 9a; *Bamidbar Rabbah* 7:10).

— ⚜ —

ᘒ *Foreign domination*

As a result of the sin of idolatry, Israel was reduced to a flour-like powder, as it is written (*Yeshaya* 47:2), *Take a millstone and grind flour.* God then strewed them among the nations as if by a gale of wind, as it is said (*Zechariah* 7:14), *I will cause them to be storm-tossed among all the nations* (*Bamidbar Rabbah* 9:44).

— ⚜ —

ᘒ *Delaying the redemption*

R' Yose ben Chalafta taught: Anyone who knows for how many years the Jews worshiped idols also knows when Mashiach will come. I have three different verses to support this assertion. First (*Hoshea* 2:15): *And I will repay her for all the days of the Baalim to which she burns incense* — according to the days of [their worship of] the Baalim. The second one (*Zechariah* 7:13): *Just as [God] had called and they did not listen, so* (for that amount of time — *Matnos Kehunah*) *will they call out and I will not listen.* And third (*Yirmiah* 5:19): *When they will say, 'Why has Hashem, our God, done all these things to us?' you shall say to them, 'Just as you deserted Me and worshipped alien gods in your land, so will you serve foreigners in a land not your own* (*Eichah Rabbah, Pesichah* §21; see there for more Scriptural sources).

Sanctifying God's Name

The annals of Jewish history are replete with the stories of repeated attempts by the pagan nations around us to persuade, often by force, the Jews in their midst to follow their example and worship their deities. The Jewish people, however, have always stood firm in the face of coercion, and countless Jews have willingly surrendered their lives to defend the integrity of their pure Torah faith. Following is a selection from our Sages' accounts of two such episodes.

I. CHANANIAH, MISHAEL, AND AZARIAH

The narrative of three Jews in the royal service of the Babylonian ruler Nebuchadnezzar appears at length in the Book of Daniel (ch. 3). Nevuchadnezzar erected a statue of gold in the valley of Dura, and gathered together representatives of the many nations under his rule to celebrate its dedication. A royal edict laid down that, at the sound of the music that was to be played, all had to prostrate themselves before the statue; whoever failed to do so would be thrown into a fiery furnace.

Three Jewish nobles, Chananiah, Mishael, and Azariah (or, by their Babylonian names, Shadrach, Meishach and Abed Nego), who had been appointed over the province of Babylon, were present at the ceremony but refused to bow down. When Nevuchadnezzar was told of this, he summoned the men, who declared that, as servants of God, they could never bow down to the statue. An incensed Nevuchadnezzar ordered them bound with ropes and thrown into a furnace heated to seven times its normal level. After they were tossed inside, the three could be seen strolling freely among the flames, accompanied by a fourth figure of angelic appearance, and neither they nor their clothing were harmed by the fire. Nevuchadnezzar, awed by the miracle, called for them to come out, sanctioned their further devotion to God, and threatened that anyone who uttered disparaging words about their God would be punished with death.

— ⚜ —

❧ *Their response to the king*

I counsel you: Obey the command of the king, but on a matter that is subject to an oath [that you took before] God, do not panic before him; do not persist in an evil thing (Koheles 8:2). God instructed Israel: "I adjure you — if the government [of the nations] passes harsh decrees upon you, do not violate any of them — *Obey the command of the king.* But if it requires you to negate the Torah and *mitzvos,* do not take heed."

This is how Chananiah, Mishael, and Azariah reacted when Nevuchadnezzar unveiled his statue (Daniel 3:16-18): [They] said to the king, Nevuchadnezzar, we are not worried about replying to you about this matter. Behold, our God whom we worship is able to save us; He will rescue us from … your hand, O king. But if He does not, let it be known to you, O king, that we do not worship your god, and to the golden statue that you have set up we will not prostrate ourselves. They pointedly did not address him as king in this part of the verse. They said to him, "If it is in regard to levies and taxes, or other such laws, we are obliged to obey the command of the king, and we will recognize you as our ruler. But if you demand of us to deny our God, you are merely Nevuchadnezzar, and we are bound to act only *in accordance with [our] oath to God.* Upon hearing these words, Nevuchadnezzar was filled with fury and the form of his face became contorted toward [them] (ibid. v. 19) (Tanchuma, Noach §10, Beha'aloscha §9; Bamidbar Rabbah 15:14; Medrash Tehillim §28. See Vayikra Rabbah for an elaborate record of the exchange between them).

❧ *Pure-minded sacrifice*

Chananiah, Mishael, and Azariah, having been chosen to represent Israel at the dedication of Nevuchadnezzar's statue, turned to Daniel in search of advice. "What do you say; shall we bow down, or not?" Daniel replied, "You have a prophet to consult; take your question to him." So they called on the prophet Yechezkel, who cited a

tradition received from his mentor Yeshayah (Yeshayah 26:20): Hide for a brief moment, until the wrath has passed. The three protested, "Do you want the people (who will not notice our absence) to say that every nation bowed down to the statue? Let us, instead, denigrate the statue by showing our presence and not bowing down. This way, it will be reported that all the nations except Israel worshipped the statue." Yechezkel replied, "If that is your intent, wait for me while I seek God's advice." Of this meeting it is written (Yechezkel 20:1): Men from among the Elders of Israel came to inquire of God, and they sat before me …

Yechezkel spoke before God, "Chananiah, Mishael, and Azariah seek to give up their lives for the sanctification of Your Name. Will You save them or not?" God answered, "I will not save them." When the prophet returned to the three with God's negative reply, they responded, "Whether He will save us or not, we shall give our lives to sanctify His Name." After they took leave from Yechezkel, God reappeared to the prophet and said, "Do you truly think that I would not save them? Surely I will! But leave them be and say not a word; I wish to let them proceed in their innocence (so that their reward will be greater — Matnos Kehunah). The three went to the ceremony and spread themselves among the crowd (to become more conspicuous — see Radal; Yafeh Kol).

This is why people customarily swear by the "One Who props up the world on three pillars." There are those who say that these pillars are Avraham, Yitzchak and Yaakov, but others maintain that they are Chananiah, Mishael, and Azariah (Shir HaShirim Rabbah 7:8).

❧ *The rationale for their action*

Todus of Rome expounded: What did Chananiah, Mishael, and Azariah reason when they submitted themselves to the fiery furnace for the sake of God's Name? They cited the precedent set by the frogs of Mitzrayim. If the frogs, who were never commanded to sanctify God's Name, nevertheless climbed inside hot ovens and crawled into the Egyptians' dough while it baked, then we, who are obliged to sanctify God's Name, are surely expected to do no less (*Pesachim* 53b).

———— ◦ ————

⤳ *The making of a miracle*

When the wicked Nimrod cast our forefather Avraham into a fiery furnace, the angel Gavriel said before God, "Master of the Universe! Allow me to go down and cool off the fire, so as to rescue the righteous one from the heat of the flames." God replied, "I am One in My world, and he is unique in his world; it is befitting for the Lone One to save the lone one." But since God never withholds the reward of any creature, He promised the angel: You will have the merit of saving three of his descendants.

R' Shimon the Shilonite expounded: When the wicked Nevuchadnezzar cast Chananiah, Mishael, and Azariah into the fiery furnace, Yorkemo, the angel appointed over ice, presented himself before God and said, "Master of the Universe! Allow me to go down and cool off the fire, so as to save these righteous men from the heat of the flames." Gavriel interjected, "The might of God will not become evident this way, for you are the Minister of Ice, and everyone knows that water can extinguish a fire. Rather I, the Minister of Fire, shall go down and chill the fire from inside the furnace and, at the same time, magnify its heat outside the furnace (so that the men who threw the three into the fire were incinerated, as related in *Daniel* [ibid. v. 22] — *Rashi*). I will thereby effect a miracle within a miracle." At that, God ordered Gavriel to proceed. Gavriel then exclaimed (in recognition of the fact that God was fulfilling His longstanding promise that He would one day save Avraham's descendants — *Rashi*), *God is true forever* (*Tehillim* 117:2) (*Pesachim* 118a-b. In *Medrash Tanchuma*, however, it is said that God Himself descended to save them, as it were).

———— ◦ ————

⤳ *A Day of many miracles*

The Sages taught: Six miracles were wrought on that day: 1) The underground furnace rose up to ground level so as to become visible to all; 2) Part of the furnace's walls were breached to expose its interior; 3) Its foundation caved in; 4) Nebuchadnezzar's golden statue was overturned on its face; 5) Four royal contingents (who had been instrumental in condemning Chananiah, Mishael, and Azariah to the fire) were burned to death; 6) Yechezkel resurrected the dead in the plain of Dura [see *Yechezkel* ch. 37] (*Sanhedrin* 92b, following *Rashi*; *Tanchuma, Noach* §10; *Shir HaShirim Rabbah* 7:9; see also *Tanchuma, Tzav* §2).

———— ◦ ————

⤳ *The public reaction*

When Chananiah, Mishael, and Azariah emerged from the flames, the people of the gentile nations came and struck the Jews on their faces , saying: You have a God of this caliber and yet you prostrate yourselves before a statue !? [This apparently follows the opinion cited in *Shir HaShirim Rabbah* (7:8) that there were additional Jewish delegates at the statue's dedication who did, in fact, bow down to the statue.] They immediately broke out and exclaimed (*Daniel* 9:7): *Yours, O God, is the righteousness, and ours is the shamefacedness.*

Yours, O God, is the righteousness ... R' Elazar quoted Rebbi as saying: Chananiah, Mishael, and Azariah were the ones who declaimed this verse. For *the satraps, the nobles, the governors and the ministers of the king assembled and saw these men over whose bodies the fire had no effect* ... (ibid. 3:27). These noblemen went and spat in their faces, and said, "You knew that your God is of such a stature, and still you (that is, the Jews of the First Temple era) worshipped idols, and caused the destruction of His Temple, the burning of His [Temple] Hall, and the ongoing exile of your people?" The three lifted their gaze toward Heaven and exclaimed, *Yours, O God, is the righteousness* (expressing their acceptance of God's judgment) *and ours is the shamefacedness* [for

You tolerated for so long our vexatious behavior] (*Tanchuma, Re'eh* §16, *Ki Sisa* §14; *Pesikta D'Rav Kahana* 10:8; see *Sanhedrin* 93a).

——— ✒ ———

∽ *Preventing a flood*

After the deluge, Noach built an altar and offered sacrifices to Hashem. *And God smelled the pleasing aroma, and [He] said … I will never again smite every living being as I have done* (*Bereishis* 8:21). The aroma was that of our forefather Avraham emerging from the fiery furnace. *And He smelled* — the aroma of Chananiah, Mishael, and Azariah ascending from the fiery furnace. This is analogous to a devoted friend of a king who paid tribute to him with a beautiful gift. The friend's son never sent any tribute, but when a grandson arose, he did. The king exclaimed, "How similar is your gift to that of your grandfather!" [So too, after Avraham cast himself into the fiery furnace for the sake of God's Unity, no one followed suit until Chananiah, Mishael, and Azariah came forth. God then exclaimed, "This act is akin to that of your ancestor Avraham!" — *Rashi*.] (*Bereishis Rabbah*).

——— ✒ ———

∽ *The woman and her seven sons*

For your sake we are killed continually; we are considered as sheep for slaughter (*Tehillim* 44:23). This verse is personified by the woman (identified in some Medrashim as Miriam bas Tanchum) and her seven sons. Her first son was brought before the Caesar and was ordered to prostrate himself before an idol. He refused, quoting the verse of the Torah (*Shemos* 20:2) *I am Hashem, your God.* They carried him off and executed him. The second son was brought and was told: Worship this idol! He refused, explaining: Our Torah commands us (ibid. 3), *You shall not recognize other gods before Me.* He was taken away and put to death. They then brought in the third son, who quoted the verse (ibid. 22:19), *One who makes a sacrifice to the gods shall be destroyed,* and he was

summarily killed. The fourth son made reference to the Torah's admonishment (ibid. 34:14), *Do not bow down to another god.* The fifth son protested, "But it says in our Torah (*Devarim* 6:4), *Hear O Israel, Hashem is our God, Hashem is One!* The sixth son based his refusal on the Scriptural verse (*Devarim* 4:39), *You are to know this day and take to your heart that Hashem, He is the only God in the Heavens above and on the earth below; there is no other.* They were all executed in turn.

Finally, the seventh son was brought in. He was commanded: Bow down to this idol! The boy said: We have already sworn to God that we would not exchange Him for another God, just as He took an oath that He would never exchange us for another people, as it is written in our Torah (*Devarim* 26:17-18): *You have designated Hashem today [to be your God], and Hashem has designated you to be His people.* The Caesar then offered, "I will throw my signet ring [which bears my image] down before you, and you bend over to pick it up, so that it can be reported that you submitted to my royal authority." Said the boy, "Pity on you, O Caesar! Pity on you! If regarding your own honor you are so particular, how much more so must you be with the honor of God!"

As they were taking him away to put him to death, his mother pleaded, "Give him to me so that I may kiss him a bit." She said, "My sons! Bring this message to our forefather Avraham: You bound [a sacrifice on] one altar, while I have bound seven." Once her last son was killed, she climbed to the roof and fell off and died. A voice emanating from Heaven was then heard to say, *A glad mother of children* [*Tehillim* 113:9] (*Gittin* 57b; *Eichah Rabbah* 1:50; *Eichah Zuta* 1:21; *Tanna D'vei Eliyahu Rabbah* 30:16-17; *Pesikta Rabbasi* §43. A lengthy debate about faith in God that took place between the seventh son and the potentate, recorded in *Tanna D'vei Eliyahu Rabbah* and *Eichah Rabbah,* is quoted above in this section of *mitzvah* #26. The same two sources give the age of the seventh boy as just over two and a half years).

מפתח למוני המצוות
ﬡ
THE COUNT
OF THE
MITZVAH

Baal Halachos Gedolos / —
בה"ג / —

R' Saadiah Gaon / Lavin 4
רס"ג / לאוין ד

R' Eliyahu HaZakein / —
ר' אליהו הזקן / —

Rashbag / —
רשב"ג / —

R' Yitzchak El-Bargeloni / —
ר"י אלברג'לוני / —

Maamar HaSechel / Dibbur Sheini 4
מאמר השכל / דיבור שני ד

Sefer Yere'im / 270
יראים / רע

Rambam, Sefer HaMitzvos / Lo Saaseh 5
רמב"ם / לא תעשה ה

Sefer Mitzvos Gadol (Smag) / Lo Saaseh 19
סמ"ג / לא תעשה יט

Sefer Mitzvos Katan (Smak) / 64
סמ"ק / סד

Zohar HaRakia / —
זוהר הרקיע / —

Mitzvah 29

אִסּוּר עֲבוֹדָה לֶאֱלִילִים

פרשת יתרו

NOT TO SERVE AN AVODAH ZARAH

THE MITZVAH:

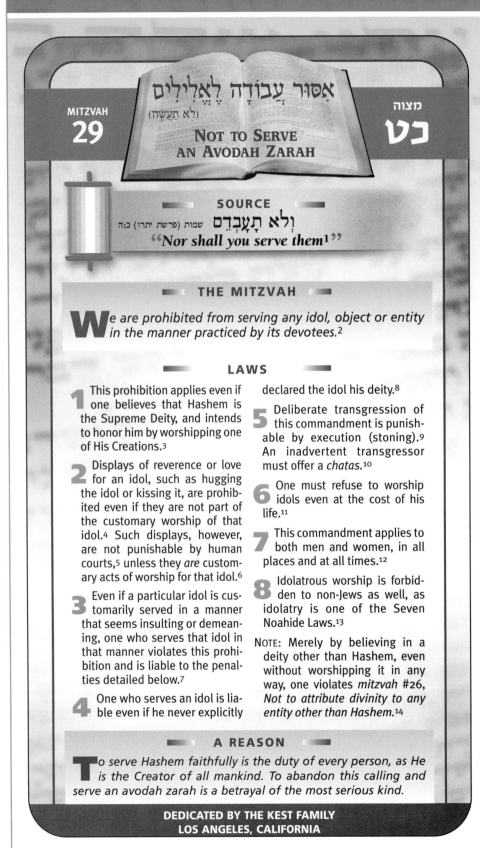

MITZVAH 29

אִסּוּר עֲבוֹדָה לֶאֱלִילִים
(לֹא תַעֲשֶׂה)

NOT TO SERVE AN AVODAH ZARAH

מצוה כט

SOURCE

וְלֹא תָעָבְדֵם שמות (פרשת יתרו) כ:ה
"Nor shall you serve them¹"

THE MITZVAH

We are prohibited from serving any idol, object or entity in the manner practiced by its devotees.²

LAWS

1 This prohibition applies even if one believes that Hashem is the Supreme Deity, and intends to honor him by worshipping one of His Creations.³

2 Displays of reverence or love for an idol, such as hugging the idol or kissing it, are prohibited even if they are not part of the customary worship of that idol.⁴ Such displays, however, are not punishable by human courts,⁵ unless they *are* customary acts of worship for that idol.⁶

3 Even if a particular idol is customarily served in a manner that seems insulting or demeaning, one who serves that idol in that manner violates this prohibition and is liable to the penalties detailed below.⁷

4 One who serves an idol is liable even if he never explicitly declared the idol his deity.⁸

5 Deliberate transgression of this commandment is punishable by execution (stoning).⁹ An inadvertent transgressor must offer a *chatas*.¹⁰

6 One must refuse to worship idols even at the cost of his life.¹¹

7 This commandment applies to both men and women, in all places and at all times.¹²

8 Idolatrous worship is forbidden to non-Jews as well, as idolatry is one of the Seven Noahide Laws.¹³

NOTE: Merely by believing in a deity other than Hashem, even without worshipping it in any way, one violates *mitzvah #26, Not to attribute divinity to any entity other than Hashem.*¹⁴

A REASON

To serve Hashem faithfully is the duty of every person, as He is the Creator of all mankind. To abandon this calling and serve an avodah zarah is a betrayal of the most serious kind.

**DEDICATED BY THE KEST FAMILY
LOS ANGELES, CALIFORNIA**

1. This clause follows the verse's opening clause, *You shall not bow to them,* which is the source for *mitzvah #28.*

2. Mishnah, *Sanhedrin* 60b as explained by the Gemara there; *Rambam, Hil. Avodah Zarah* 3:2-3 and *Sefer HaMitzvos, Lo Saaseh* §6; *Sefer HaChinuch* §29; *Ramban* to *Devarim* 12:30. One may not serve an angel, a star or other celestial body, a geological feature such as a mountain or lake, any creature, plant, element, or substance, or any fabricated object (*Rambam, Hil. Avodah Zarah* 2:1; see *Rosh Hashanah* 24b). One may not even serve an object that is itself not considered a deity, but that is adored by devotees as a palpable representation of a deity (such as a statue of a mythological divinity, or an icon imagined to depict the "true" form of a star [see *Rambam,* ibid. 1:2]).

The present mitzvah is distinct from *mitzvah #28* in that this mitzvah prohibits serving an entity in whatever manner that particular idol is customarily served, whereas *mitzvah #28* prohibits serving *any* entity in one of four specific ways (bowing, sacrifice, libation, burnt offerings). *Rambam* explains:

Various modes of worship were established by idolaters for each idol and each icon, and the worship of one is unlike the worship of another. For example, *Pe'or* is worshipped by people who expose themselves to it, while *Markolis'* worship is that people throw rocks to it or clear rocks from before it (see note 7). Many [differing] modes of worship were similarly established for the other idols... *Beis Din* is therefore required to be familiar with the [various] manners of worship [so that they know what acts are punishable]. For

AN EXPANDED TREATMENT

[*Beis Din*] does not stone (see Law 2 and note 5) [an idolater] who practiced a particular form of worship unless it knows that that is the customary manner of worship [for the idol that he served] (*Rambam, Hil. Avodah Zarah* 3:2).

Another form of native worship offered as an example in *Sefer HaMitzvos* and *Sefer HaChinuch* is "shaving one's hair for *Kemosh*" (god of the Moabites; see *Bamidbar* 21:29 and *Shoftim* 11:24 et al.; see *R' Chaim Heller*'s footnote 18 to his edition of *Sefer HaMitzvos* ibid.). [One other particular form of worship has its own prohibition; a person who passes his child through the fire in worship of the idol called *Molech* has transgressed *mitzvah* #208, *Do not give your offspring to be passed* (through fire) *for Molech.* See there for details of this law.]

We have followed *Rambam* and *Sefer HaChinuch* in ascribing the proscription against serving an idol in its peculiar manner to the clause, *nor shall you serve them.* Others maintain that this prohibition derives from the passage (*Devarim* 12:30-31), *Beware ... lest you inquire after their gods, saying, 'How* (i.e. in what manner) *do these peoples serve their gods; let me do the same!' Do not do so...* (*Rashi* to *Devarim* ad loc. and to *Sanhedrin* 60b, ד"ה אחד; see however ד"ה עובר בלא תעשה, with *Maharshal* and *Maharsha*). See also *Hasagos HaRamban* to *Sefer HaMitzvos, Lo Saaseh* §5.

3. *Rambam* maintains that serving celestial bodies as a way to honor Hashem was actually the original and primary form of idol worship (which is why idolatry in general is often referred to as "star worship" in the Talmud [see *Berachos* 54a and 57b]). He explains that very early in human

history people fell prey to the misconception that it was proper to pay tribute to the heavenly bodies as God's emissaries to the world, just as a king expects his ministers to be treated with honor by those subject to his rule. Over time, these demonstrations of honor led to genuine worship as the popular conception of the celestial forces graduated from subordinate, non-divine agents to independent deities (*Hil. Avodah Zarah* 1:1,2; for a more detailed account of the history of idolatry, see *Chazal* section, *mitzvah* #25; for other misconceptions held by iodolaters regarding their objects of worship, see *Ramban* to *Shemos* 20:3).

4. In addition to hugging and kissing, the Mishnah (*Sanhedrin* ibid.) lists "sweeping or tamping down [the floor before the idol], bathing [the idol] or rubbing it with oil," as well as "dressing or shoeing" the idol. *Rambam* (*Hil. Avodah Zarah* 3:6) adds "any similar act of reverence." This category thus includes both shows of affection and the kinds of personal service that a servant would perform for his master.

5. Concerning a worshipper who engages in such displays of reverence, the Mishnah teaches that while he is not liable to execution, he does transgress a prohibition. According to *Rambam* (*Commentary to the Mishnah* ad loc. and *Hil. Avodah Zarah* ibid.; *Sefer HaMitzvos* does not mention "hugging or kissing" and the like), the relevant commandment is the present mitzvah, *nor shall you serve them* (see *Mechilta DeRashbi* to *Shemos* 20:4; cf. *Rashi* to *Sanhedrin* 60b ד"ה עובר, and 63a ד"ה אבל המגפף, who, while offering dissimilar suggestions in the two places, consistently differs from *Rambam*'s understanding in

holding that displays of reverence are prohibited by their own separate commandment; see also *Hasagos HaRamban* to *Sefer HaMitzvos, Lo Saaseh* §5). "Serve," in the context of idolatry, apparently supports two connotations. The primary meaning is to worship in the manner customary to a particular idol, as evidenced by the verse (*Devarim* 12:30), *Beware ... lest you inquire after their gods, saying, 'How* (i.e. in what manner) *do these peoples* **serve** *their gods; let me do the same!'* (see *Sanhedrin* 61a and *Rambam, Hil. Avodah Zarah* 2:2). Of such worship, a verse later in *Devarim* states (17:2-5), *Should there be found among you... a man or woman who commits evil ... and goes and* **serves** *false gods or bows to them..., remove that man or that woman... and pelt them with stones so that they die* (see *Rashi* to *Sanhedrin* 60b; *"or bows to them"* renders liable to death those who engage in the forms of idolatry encompassed by *mitzvah* #28). A secondary meaning of *"serve"* in the clause *nor shall you serve them* is to display reverence by embracing, grooming, or performing menial tasks for an idol. Displays of reverence, even those not customarily practiced by devotees of a particular idol, are therefore prohibited. No verse, however, sentences a worshipper to execution for engaging in such displays. [He may nonetheless be liable to death at the hand of Heaven; see *Tosefta Sanhedrin* 10:2; *Yoma* 66b as explained by *Meshech Chochmah* to *Shemos* 32:27 and *Chazon Yechezkel* to *Tosefta* ibid.; cf. *Tos. Yeshanim* to *Yoma* ibid. on 68a).]

Such a worshipper also will not receive *malkos.* Although *malkos* are the usual penalty for active transgression of a prohibitory commandment (see *mitzvah* #594), they are

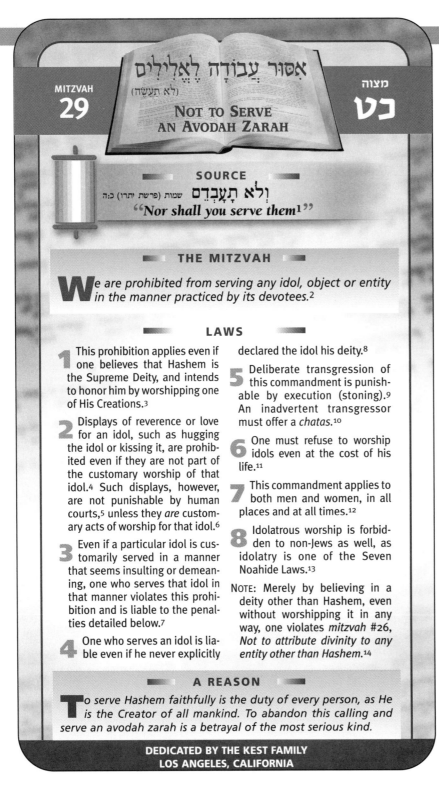

MITZVAH 29

אִסוּר עֲבוֹדָה לָאֱלִילִים
(לֹא תַעֲשֶׂה)

NOT TO SERVE AN AVODAH ZARAH

מצוה כט

SOURCE

וְלֹא תָעָבְדֵם
שמות (פרשת יתרו) כ:ה

"Nor shall you serve them[1]"

THE MITZVAH

We are prohibited from serving any idol, object or entity in the manner practiced by its devotees.[2]

LAWS

1 This prohibition applies even if one believes that Hashem is the Supreme Deity, and intends to honor him by worshipping one of His Creations.[3]

2 Displays of reverence or love for an idol, such as hugging the idol or kissing it, are prohibited even if they are not part of the customary worship of that idol.[4] Such displays, however, are not punishable by human courts,[5] unless they *are* customary acts of worship for that idol.[6]

3 Even if a particular idol is customarily served in a manner that seems insulting or demeaning, one who serves that idol in that manner violates this prohibition and is liable to the penalties detailed below.[7]

4 One who serves an idol is liable even if he never explicitly declared the idol his deity.[8]

5 Deliberate transgression of this commandment is punishable by execution (stoning).[9] An inadvertent transgressor must offer a *chatas*.[10]

6 One must refuse to worship idols even at the cost of his life.[11]

7 This commandment applies to both men and women, in all places and at all times.[12]

8 Idolatrous worship is forbidden to non-Jews as well, as idolatry is one of the Seven Noahide Laws.[13]

NOTE: Merely by believing in a deity other than Hashem, even without worshipping it in any way, one violates *mitzvah #26, Not to attribute divinity to any entity other than Hashem.*[14]

A REASON

To serve Hashem faithfully is the duty of every person, as He is the Creator of all mankind. To abandon this calling and serve an avodah zarah is a betrayal of the most serious kind.

DEDICATED BY THE KEST FAMILY
LOS ANGELES, CALIFORNIA

kissing the idol or one of the other displays of reverence is the customary form of worship for this idol, it is, of course, treated no less stringently than other customary services, and is penalized as such.

7. Two examples are given by the Mishnah, *Sanhedrin* 60b and *Rambam, Hil. Avodah Zarah* 3:2. Devotees of *Pe'or*, or *Ba'al Pe'or*, would expose themselves to the idol as though intending to defecate before it (*Yad Ramah* ibid.), and would sometimes even do so (*Sanhedrin* 64a). *Markolis* was an imagined divinity represented by three hewn stones, two as a base and the third atop the others (*Rashi to Sanhedrin* 60b, ד"ה מרקוליס, from *Avodah Zarah* 50a). Adherents would throw rocks toward the idol and even aim to hit it (*Sanhedrin* 64a), or would clear some of the rocks already thrown to make room for more (ibid. and *Rambam, Hil. Avodah Zarah* ibid.). The growing pile of rocks was seen as an enlargement of the *Markolis* (*Avodah Zarah* 51a with *Rashi*, ד"ה כמגדל). Although baring oneself in this manner and stoning are both demeaning and insulting acts, one who engages in the native worship of either idol is liable. If one bares himself to *Markolis*, however, or stones *Pe'or*, he is not liable, because while both idols professedly share a taste for offensive worship, in neither case did he serve the idol as it is customarily served (*Sanhedrin* 61a and *Rambam* ibid.).

One may not bare himself to *Pe'or* or stone *Markolis* even if he intends no idolatry but rather means to heap scorn on the idol (*Sanhedrin* 64a). One who does so while unaware that he is actually engaging in the customary act of worship for *Pe'or* or *Markolis* is deemed to have inadvertently practiced idolatry, and must offer a *chatas* (*Rambam, Hil. Avodah Zarah* 3:5). A person who *does* know how *Pe'or* or *Markolis* are customarily

administered only for violations of the explicit, primary meaning of a commandment. That displays of reverence are forbidden, however, is merely the derivate, secondary meaning of *nor shall you serve them* (*Sanhedrin* 63a, as understood by *Rambam* in his *Commentary to the*

Mishnah and in *Hil. Avodah Zarah* 3:6; see *Ran to Sanhedrin* ibid.; cf. *Rashi to Sanhedrin* ibid., ד"ה לאו שבכללות; *Raavad to Hil. Avodah Zarah* 3:9).

6. *Rashi to Sanhedrin* 60b, ד"ה אבל המגפף and ד"ה אחד העובד; *Rambam, Hil. Avodah Zarah* 3:6. Where embracing or

served, however, cannot avow that in exposing himself to *Pe'or* or in stoning *Markolis* he merely meant to deride the idol, because the fact remains that he deliberately served the idol in the manner that the idol supposedly desires. Therefore, if one was informed that his intended act of derision was in fact a customary act of worship, and was moreover forewarned that the penalty for intentional idolatry is *sekilah*, yet nevertheless proceeded to bare himself to *Pe'or* or to stone *Markolis*, he is liable to execution (*Rambam* as understood by *Kovetz*, cited in *Sefer HaLikutim* to *Rambam*, Frankel edition; *Rada*; *Mikra'ei Kodesh*; see also *Meiri* to Mishnah 60b; cf. *Kessef Mishneh* ad loc. and to *Hil. Yesodei HaTorah* 5:4). [*Tosafos* to *Sanhedrin* 64a ד"ה אע"ג) apparently disagree, maintaining that so long as a person's intent was to deride the idol, he never incurs the death penalty, even if he was aware that his act of derision would be considered an act of worship by the idol's devotees (see *Maharsha* ad loc.; cf. *Maharam*; *Tosafos* to 61b ד"ה רבא second explanation, cited by *Gilyon HaShas* to 64a, disagree with *Tosafos* to 64a; see further, *Iyunim* §5). Only if he intended to *worship* the idol by shaming it — because he believed, as do the devotees of *Pe'or* and *Markolis* — that the idol craves humiliation, does he incur death. See also *Rashi*, ד"ה ואע"ג.]

8. Mishnah, *Sanhedrin* 60b. Regarding a worshipper who declared an idol his deity but did not serve it actively, see *mitzvah* #28. Regarding one who claims that he does not consider the idol divine, but rather serves it for ancillary motives (such as fear of the idol's devotees or a desire to ingratiate himself with them), see *Iyunim* §5.

9. *Devarim* 17:5; Mishnah, *Sanhedrin* 60b; *Rambam, Hil. Avodah Zarah* ibid. *Sekilah*, execution by stoning, is one

of four methods of capital punishment mandated by the Torah for different transgressions. According to the accepted Tannaic opinion, *sekilah* is the harshest of the four (Mishnah, *Sanhedrin* 79b; *Rambam, Hil. Sanhedrin* 14:4; the Sages are quoted in the Mishnah as adducing that *sekilah* must be the severest punishment because it is meted out to persons guilty of idolatry, the severest sin). The procedure for *sekilah* is detailed in Mishnayos *Sanhedrin* 6:1-4 and *Rambam Hil. Sanhedrin* 15:1. It should be noted that unlike most other sinners liable to *sekilah*, whose sentence is carried out at the gates of the town where they were condemned, idolaters are stoned at the gates of the town where they practiced their idolatry (*Kesubos* 45b; *Rambam* ibid. 15:2).

Following his execution, the corpse of an idolater, like that of a blasphemer, is hung momentarily atop a wooden pole, but is then immediately taken down and buried.

If one violated this prohibition deliberately, but there were no witnesses, or he did not receive proper warning, he is punished with *kares*. (*Bamidbar* 15:31; Mishnah, *Kereisos* 2a; *Sanhedrin* 64b with *Rashi* ד"ה אחת שלא כדרכה; *Rambam, Hil. Avodah Zarah* 3:1 and *Hil. Shegagos* 1:1,3). *Kares*, literally *severance*, is the severest of heavenly penalties, and, although its exact nature is disputed, involves the death of either body or soul, or both. For a discussion of the various opinions, see *Abarbanel* to *Bamidbar* 15:22.

10. Mishnah *Kereisos* 2a; *Rambam Hil. Shegagos* 1:3. A *chatas*, or *sin-offering* (pl. *chataos*), is an animal offered by a sinner to atone for his guilt. The *chatas* is slaughtered in the *Beis HaMikdash* and its blood placed on the corners of the Altar. Designated sacrificial parts (*emurim*) are burned

upon the Altar, and the meat is consumed by the Kohanim within the *Beis HaMikdash* compound (see *Vayikra* chapter 4; *mitzvah* #121). For any prohibition whose deliberate transgression is punished by *kares*, the inadvertent transgressor incurs an obligation to bring a *chatas*. The one exception is blasphemy, because *chataos* are incurred only for forbidden *actions*, and speech is not considered an act (Mishnah ibid. and *Rambam* ibid. 1:2).

The *chatas* mandated for idolatry differs from other *chataos* in the following respect: For most transgressions punishable by *kares*, the Torah stipulates that the inadvertent sinner offer a female goat or ewe if he is a commoner, a he-goat if he is the king, or an ox if he is a *Kohen Gadol* (in which case the meat of the ox is not eaten, but burned together with the skin outside the *Beis HaMikdash*). An inadvertent idolater, however, no matter his status must offer a female goat (*Vayikra* ibid.; *Bamidbar* 15:27, with *Rashi*; *Rambam* ibid. 1:4).

"Inadvertently" in this context means that the worshipper was unaware that idolatry is prohibited, or was unaware that the prohibition applied in all its stringency to his particular circumstances or to the particular form of service that he practiced. If, for example, a worshipper served an idol of wood or clay under the mistaken belief that only idols of gold or silver are prohibited, he must offer a *chatas* (*Kereisos* 3b, *Rambam, Hil. Shegagos* 7:1). So too, a person who bared himself to *Pe'or* or stoned *Markolis* intending to deride them, unaware that his actions were actually customary modes of worship for these idols is liable to a *chatas* (*Rambam, Hil. Avodah Zarah* 3:5; see note 7 above). Furthermore, even if a worshipper knew that idolatry is prohibited, but was unaware that this transgression is punishable

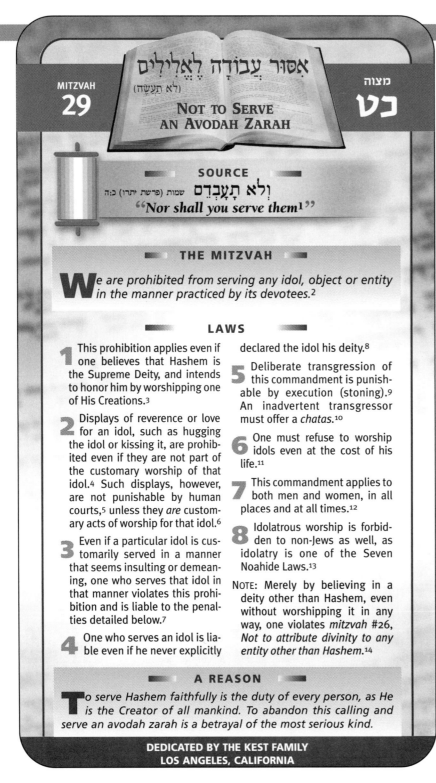

MITZVAH 29

אִסּוּר עֲבוֹדָה לָאֱלִילִים
(לֹא תַעֲשֶׂה)

NOT TO SERVE AN AVODAH ZARAH

מצוה **כט**

SOURCE

וְלֹא תָעָבְדֵם שמות (פרשת יתרו) כ:ה
"Nor shall you serve them[1]"

THE MITZVAH

We are prohibited from serving any idol, object or entity in the manner practiced by its devotees.[2]

LAWS

1 This prohibition applies even if one believes that Hashem is the Supreme Deity, and intends to honor him by worshipping one of His Creations.[3]

2 Displays of reverence or love for an idol, such as hugging the idol or kissing it, are prohibited even if they are not part of the customary worship of that idol.[4] Such displays, however, are not punishable by human courts,[5] unless they *are* customary acts of worship for that idol.[6]

3 Even if a particular idol is customarily served in a manner that seems insulting or demeaning, one who serves that idol in that manner violates this prohibition and is liable to the penalties detailed below.[7]

4 One who serves an idol is liable even if he never explicitly declared the idol his deity.[8]

5 Deliberate transgression of this commandment is punishable by execution (stoning).[9] An inadvertent transgressor must offer a *chatas*.[10]

6 One must refuse to worship idols even at the cost of his life.[11]

7 This commandment applies to both men and women, in all places and at all times.[12]

8 Idolatrous worship is forbidden to non-Jews as well, as idolatry is one of the Seven Noahide Laws.[13]

NOTE: Merely by believing in a deity other than Hashem, even without worshipping it in any way, one violates *mitzvah #26, Not to attribute divinity to any entity other than Hashem.*[14]

A REASON

To serve Hashem faithfully is the duty of every person, as He is the Creator of all mankind. To abandon this calling and serve an avodah zarah is a betrayal of the most serious kind.

by *kares*, his service is deemed inadvertent and he must offer a *chatas* (see *Shabbos* 69a; *Rambam, Hil. Shegagos* 2:2). If, however, the very act of idolatry was inadvertent — that is, if the worshipper's act was not intentionally directed toward an idol — he incurs no liability at all. [See the example provided in note 13 to *mitzvah #28.*]

11. *Sanhedrin* 74a; *Pesachim* 25a; *Rambam, Hil. Yesodei HaTorah* 5:2; *Tur* and *Shulchan Aruch, Yoreh Deah* 157:1. If an idolater threatens to kill a Jew unless he serves an idol, the

Jew must forfeit his life rather than submit. Furthermore, if a Jew is mortally ill and can be cured only by an act of idolatry, he must foreswear the cure rather than practice idolatry. This issue will be elaborated under *mitzvah #296, to sanctify the Name of Hashem.* Regarding forms of idolatry that are proscribed by a prohibitory commandment but are not punishable by execution, such as displays of reverence for an idol (see Law 5 and note 10), see *Rama, Yoreh De'ah* 157:1 (with *Be'ur HaGra* 14), who rules that they too may not be violated even at the cost of one's life; cf. *Nimukei Yosef* to *Bava Kamma,* fol. 40a; see also *Avodas HaMelech* to *Hil. Yesodei HaTorah* 5:6.

The other two prohibitions that one may not transgress even to save his life are those prohibiting murder and illicit relations. [These are actually classes of prohibitions, as the prohibitions on idolatry include more than a single mitzvah. Similarly, adultery and each of various incestuous unions are prohibited by its own mitzvah.]

12. *Sefer HaChinuch* §29; see Mishnah, *Kiddushin* 29a and Gemara there, 35a.

13. This mitzvah is included in the prohibition against idolatry that applies to non-Jews (*Sefer HaChinuch* §29; see *Sanhedrin* 56a; *Tosefta, Avodah Zarah* ch. 8; *Rambam, Hil. Melachim* 9:1-2; see also *Sefer Mitzvas Hashem* [R' Yonasan Steif] 2:6, 3:46; and *Seder Mishnah* to *Hil. Yesodei HaTorah* 1:6:4). The Gemara in *Sanhedrin* (56a) lists seven mitzvos that were given to non-Jews (the reference to Noahide Laws reflects the fact that all of mankind descended from Noach, whose family were the sole survivors of the Flood). They are (1) the requirement to establish a system of civil laws (see *Rambam, Hil. Melachim* 9:14); (2) a prohibition against blasphemy (euphemistically referred to as "blessing" the

Name of Hashem); (3) a prohibition against idolatry; (4) a prohibition against illicit unions (see *Sanhedrin* 57a); (5) a prohibition against murder; (6) a prohibition against theft; and (7) a prohibition against eating a limb torn from a live animal (אבר מן החי). The Gemara (ibid. 56b) derives these mitzvos from a verse in *Bereishis* (2:16), which speaks of Hashem's commands to Adam HaRishon. With respect to this prohibition, the verse states *And Hashem, God commanded* (*Bereishis* 2:16); the Gemara understands this as a prohibition against idolatry (*Sanhedrin* 56b).

Under the prohibition of idol worship, non-Jews may not act reverently toward idols even in ways that do not constitute customary service for those idols (see Law 5 and note 10). Like Jews, however, non-Jews are not executed for such displays of reverence (*Sanhedrin* 56b as apparently understood by *Rambam, Hil. Melachim* 9:2; cf. *Sefer Hachinuch* §26; see *Minchas Chinuch* 26:18).

14. *Rambam, Hil. Yesodei HaTorah* 1:6; *Sefer HaMitzvos, Lo Saaseh* §1; *Sefer HaChinuch* §26; cf. *Ramban* in *Hasagos to Sefer HaMitzvos, Lo Saaseh* §5.

The עיונים, טוב טעם, and מאוצרות חז"ל sections of Mitzvos #28 and #29 have been combined, as the two mitzvos embody many common concepts.
They are to be found with our presentation of *mitzvah #28*.

Question:

If a person says to an idol, "You are my god," but performs none of the acts with which this idol is usually worshipped, has he violated the prohibition of ולא תעבדם, *nor shall you serve them?*

Answer:

One who believes in the divinity of an idol, whether or not he expresses his faith orally, violates the prohibition (*mitzvah #26*) of לא יהיה לך אלהים אחרים על פני, *You shall not recognize other gods before Me* (see *Minchas Chinuch* 26:6; *Tzafnas Pane'ach* to *Rambam, Hil. Avodas Kochavim* 3:4; *Tosafos, Kereisos* 7b ד"ה מגדף).

The commandment of *nor shall you serve them*, however, is directed not toward one's *belief* in an idol, but toward one's *worship* of it. One violates this prohibition through an act of worship. Nevertheless, if a person says to an idol, "You are my god," he has

violated the prohibition of *nor shall you serve them*, even though he performs none of the acts with which the idol is normally worshipped. The Rishonim explain that an oral statement accepting an idol as one's deity constitutes an act of worship, and is therefore prohibited by this commandment (*Tosafos, Sanhedrin* 60b ד"ה מניין, as explained by *Minchas Chinuch* ibid.; *Sefer HaEshkol, Avodah Zarah,* fol. 192a; *Maharam, Sanhedrin* 61a ד"ה רמי).

Although this statement is in any case forbidden under the prohibition of לא יהיה לך (*mitzvah #26*), its prohibition under לא תעבדם has a practical ramification with regard to witnesses who issue a warning to a transgressor. Although the warning must identify the precise prohibition being violated, it is valid no matter which of these prohibitions it mentions, since the person's statement violates *both* prohibitions (see *Minchas Chinuch* ibid.). [As a rule, punishment for Biblical infractions is administered only if the perpetrator is forewarned. According to some Rishonim, the warning must identify precisely which prohibition the person is violating (*Rashi, Shevuos* 20b ד"ה ואזהרתיה וד"ה אכלתי; cf. *Rambam, Sanhedrin* 12:2).] See further above, *mitzvah #28*, note 11.

WORSHIPPING AN IDOL IN A REVERENT MANNER

s noted above (see Law 2), it is forbidden to display reverence toward an idol (e.g. hugging or kissing it), even if this is not the manner in which the idol is customarily worshipped. Some authorities count this prohibition as a separate commandment (*Smag, Lavin* §18; *Smak* §62), in addition to the commandment not to worship an idol in its customary manner, and the commandment not to perform any of four specific services for it [i.e. bowing, slaughtering a sacrifice, burning a sacrifice, and pouring a libation; see *mitzvah* #28]. Others, however, do not list this prohibition in their count of the 613 commandments (see *Rambam, Sefer HaMitzvos,* et al.). This seems difficult to understand, for this prohibition is clearly not a corollary of those other prohibitions, as is evident from the fact that a specific derivation is required to teach this prohibition (see above, note 5), and that one who reveres idols is not subject to the punishment to which one is subject for violating those other prohibitions [one who reveres an idol is not liable to any court-imposed punishment (see Law 2), whereas one who violates those other prohibitions is liable to execution (see ibid. Law 5 and *mitzvah* #28, Law 6)] (*Hasagos HaRamban* to *Sefer HaMitzvos of Rambam, Lo Saaseh* §5).

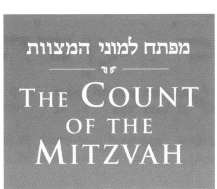

Baal Halachos Gedolos / —
בה"ג / —

R' Saadiah Gaon / Lavin 3
רס"ג / לאוין ג

R' Eliyahu HaZakein / —
ר' אליהו הזקן / —

Rashbag / —
רשב"ג / —

R' Yitzchak El-Bargeloni / —
ר"י אלברג'לוני / —

Maamar HaSechel / Dibbur Sheini 6
מאמר השכל / דיבור שני ו

Sefer Yere'im / 270
יראים / רע

Rambam, Sefer HaMitzvos / Lo Saaseh 6
רמב"ם / לא תעשה ו

Sefer Mitzvos Gadol (Smag) / Lo Saaseh 17
סמ"ג / לא תעשה יז

Sefer Mitzvos Katan (Smak) / 63
סמ"ק / סג

Zohar HaRakia / —
זוהר הרקיע / —

Several approaches have been suggested to explain why *Rambam* and others do not count this prohibition as a separate commandment.

A. *Two prohibitions derived from the same verse are counted as only one commandment of the 613*

According to *Rambam* (*Commentary to the Mishnah, Sanhedrin* 7:6; *Hil. Avodah Zarah* 3:6), the prohibition against displaying reverence toward an idol is derived from the same verse that states the prohibition against worshipping an idol in the manner that it is customarily worshipped — *nor shall you serve them* (*Shemos* 20:4; see above, note 5). Some authorities, including *Rambam*, maintain that two prohibitions derived from the same verse are counted as a single commandment [unless the verse states a separate prohibitory phrase for each prohibition] (see *Rambam, Sefer HaMitzvos, shoresh* §9). According to this view, it is clear that the prohibition against displaying reverence toward an idol is not counted as a separate commandment. Rather, it is included in the commandment not to worship an idol in the customary manner (*Dina D'Chayei* to *Smag, Lo Saaseh* §18; *Lev Same'ach* to *Sefer HaMitzvos* of *Rambam, Lo Saaseh* 5:1; *Mishnah Chachamim* §14-15, *Yavin Shemuah* §2).

B. *This prohibition is considered a "generalized prohibition"*

Some Rishonim maintain that the source for the prohibition against displays of reverence to an idol is the phrase *do not worship them* in *Shemos* 23:24 (part of a verse which states: *Do not prostate yourself to their gods, **do not worship them,** and do not act according to their practices*). This verse is not needed to teach a prohibition against serving idols in their customary manner, for that is derived from the phrase *nor shall you serve them* in the Ten Commandments. Therefore, it is understood as forbidding one to engage in displays of reverence toward an idol (see *Rashi, Sanhedrin* 60b ד"ה עובר בלא תעשה).

Now, the Gemara (*Sanhedrin* 63a) states that one does not receive *malkos* for violating this prohibition because it is a "generalized prohibition" [לאו שבכללות; i.e. a general prohibition which includes several specific prohibitions (see *Pesachim* 41b)]. The Rishonim explain that although, according to the aforementioned view, the source for this prohibition — the phrase *do not worship them* — teaches only the specific prohibition against displaying reverence toward an idol, it is considered a "generalized prohibition" because according to its *simple* meaning, the verse deals with the same prohibition as taught in the phrase *nor shall you serve them* in *Shemos* 20:4 — not to worship idols in the customary manner (the prohibition against displays of reverence toward idols is expounded from the *superfluity* of the verse). Thus, the phrase *do not worship them* refers to multiple prohibitions, and

is therefore a "generalized prohibition" (*Chidushei HaRan, Sanhedrin* 63a).

According to this explanation, it is understandable that the prohibition against displaying reverence toward an idol is not counted as a separate commandment. Many authorities maintain that the specific prohibitions included in a "generalized prohibition" are not counted as separate commandments (see *Rambam, Sefer HaMitzvos, shoresh* §9). Since the prohibition against displaying reverence toward idols is treated like a "generalized prohibition," it, too, is not counted as a separate commandment (*Mishnas Chachamim* §14-15, *Yavin Shemuah* §2 ד"ה והאמת; *Maharam Schik* §29; *Chidushei Mahardam to Sefer HaMitzvos of Rambam, Lo Saaseh* §6; see *Lechem Mishneh, Hil. Maachalos Assuros* 9:2; see also *Rambam, Commentary to the Mishnah, Sanhedrin* 7:6).

[Note: *Rambam* (*Commentary to the Mishnah, Sanhedrin* ibid.) writes that the reason one does not receive *malkos* for engaging in acts of reverence toward an idol is because this prohibition is not explicitly mentioned in the verse that is the source for the prohibition (according to *Rambam*, this is *Shemos* 20:5, as noted above). Although the Gemara seems to give another reason, namely because the prohibition is a "generalized" prohibition, *Rambam* evidently understands that these two reasons are actually the same; the reason one does not receive *malkos* for violating a "generalized prohibition" is *because* the specific prohibitions included in it are not referred to explicitly in the verse.]

Mitzvah 30

אִסוּר שְׁבוּעָה לַשָּׁוְא

פרשת יתרו

NOT TO MAKE A VAIN OATH IN HASHEM'S NAME

THE MITZVAH:

MITZVAH
30

אִסּוּר שְׁבוּעָה לַשָּׁוְא
(לֹא תַעֲשֶׂה)
**NOT TO MAKE A VAIN
OATH IN HASHEM'S NAME**

מצוה
ל

SOURCE

לֹא תִשָּׂא אֶת שֵׁם ה' אֱלֹקֶיךָ לַשָּׁוְא שמות (פרשת יתרו) כ:ז
"You shall not take the Name of Hashem, your God, in vain"

THE MITZVAH

It is forbidden to make a vain oath in Hashem's Name.[1] This prohibition applies to an oath made in any language[2] (for the separate prohibition to make a false oath, see mitzvah #227).

LAWS

1 The purpose of an oath is: (a) to create a binding obligation or prohibition (e.g. "I swear to do [or not to do] such and such..."); or (b) to attest to the truth of a statement.[3] A vain oath thus includes any oath which serves neither of these purposes, either because it creates an impossible obligation, or because it attests to a fact that does not require verification.

2 The four types of vain oaths are: (a) An oath contradicting an obvious fact, e.g. swearing that a stone is gold;[4] (b) An oath attesting to an obvious fact, e.g. that a stone is a stone;[5] (c) An oath not to perform a mitzvah, e.g. not to put on *tefillin*;[6] (d) An oath to do something impossible.[7]

3 An oath is created through an oral declaration.[8] Answering "Amen" to an oath expressed by others on one's behalf is equivalent to expressing the oath itself.[9]

4 The prohibition applies to both men and women,[10] in all places and at all times.

5 The consequence for violating this prohibition deliberately is *malkos*,[11] even though it is a prohibition that does not involve an action.[12]

A REASON

The greatness of God transcends all existence, and His Name should be uttered only amid feelings of awe, and strictly for matters of the utmost importance. To invoke His Name for a needless oath is thus a serious affront to the honor of God.

1. One violates this prohibition whether one uses one of Hashem's actual Names (such as the one we pronounce as *A-don-ai*), or whether one swears using one of the terms that describe His attributes (each referred to as a כינוי [*kinui*]), such as *Merciful One* (רחום) or *Slow to Anger* (ארך אפים). Even making a vain oath using a reference to Hashem in a different language (e.g. God) is a violation of the prohibition (*Rambam, Hil. Shevuos* 2:2-4 with *Kessef Mishneh* and *Rabbi Akiva Eiger* there [Frankel ed.]; see also *Hil. Yesodei HaTorah* 6:2, 5 for a list of Hashem's Names and the *Kinuyim*; see also below, end of note 3, for the dispute as to the function of Hashem's Name in creating a binding oath).

Swearing in Hashem's Name is in essence equating the truth of the oath with the truth of Hashem's existence. In other words, one who swears to perform a particular act is obligating himself to unswervingly fulfill his commitment, just as Hashem's existence is unchanging and eternal. Thus, violating such an oath is tantamount to denying the truth and eternity of His Name (*Chinuch, Ibn Ezra, Shemos* 20:7 and *Targum Onkelos* on *Bereishis* 21:23 and *Vayikra* 5:4).

The primary prohibition stemming from the verse: *You shall not take the Name of Hashem, your Lord, in vain* (*Shemos* 20:7) is that of using Hashem's Name to make a vain *oath*. However, the prohibition, according to some, is not limited solely to oaths. The Torah's choice of the more general expression, *Lo Sisa*, meaning *do not **take** [Hashem's Name ... in vain]*, rather than *Lo Sishava, do not **swear***, serves to leave open the possibility of extending the prohibition beyond oaths, and incorporating other activities which involve taking Hashem's Name in vain, such as

AN EXPANDED TREATMENT

making an unnecessary blessing (see further, *Iyunim* §1).

Making a vain oath is not only a violation of the prohibition against taking Hashem's Name in vain, but also a violation of the positive mitzvah to fear Hashem (*mitzvah* #432), which includes treating His Name with reverence and not mentioning it in vain (*Temurah* 4a and *Rambam, Hil. Shevuos* 12:11).

2. The general rule is that any word in any language which, in a given location, implies that one is making an oath, has the power to create a valid oath in that location (*Rambam* ibid. 2:5; see also *Tosafos* to *Nedarim* 2a ד"ה כל; *Shulchan Aruch, Yoreh Deah* §237 with *Beur HaGra* and *Rema,* ibid. §207 with *Hagahos Rabbi Akiva Eiger*).

3. The Torah gives a person the power to create new and legally binding obligations and prohibitions through the instrument of an oath. Thus, a person who swears to perform an act becomes Biblically obligated to do so, and liable to punishment if he does not perform it. [Aside from an oath, there is another type of legal declaration called a *neder* (vow), which, like the oath, is capable of creating new prohibitions (see *mitzvos* #407 and #575). One general difference between an oath and a *neder* in terms of creating a new prohibition is that through an oath one prohibits *oneself* from performing an act (for example, eating an apple), whereas through a *neder* one prohibits an *object,* in this case, the apple, to oneself (*Rambam, Hil. Nedarim* 3:7).]

In addition to assigning it the power to create obligations and restrictions, the Torah also establishes the oath as an instrument to attest to the truth of a statement. Although a person may choose to make such an

oath at any time, there are a number of oaths which are imposed by the court (*shevuos hadayanim* — שבועות הדיינים), some based on Biblical law, others enacted by the Rabbis. For example, in certain circumstances, a defendant is given the opportunity to swear that he is telling the truth and thereby free himself of the claim lodged against him (see *Rambam, Hil. Shevuos,* ch. 11). It is a mitzvah to swear in Hashem's Name when the Torah obligates one to do so (*Rambam,* ibid. 11:1; see *mitzvah* #435).

The Torah not only warns against *vain* oaths, but also against *false* oaths, based on the verse: *You shall not swear falsely in My Name* (*Vayikra* 19:12; see note 4 for the difference between *vain* and *false* oaths). Now, the consequences for making a false oath vary depending on the type of oath one makes. Aside from vain oaths, there are three other categories of oaths in the Torah, each of which carries a unique penalty for swearing falsely. These other categories are: (a) *Shevuas Bitui* [*Oath of Utterance*] (*Vayikra* 5:4; *Rambam, Hil. Shevuos* 1:1-3; see *mitzvos* #123 and #227) (b) *Shevuas HaPikadon* [*Oath of Deposit*] (see *Vayikra* 5:20-26; *Rambam,* ibid. 1:8; see *mitzvos* #129 and #226) and (c) *Shevuas HaEidus* [*Oath of Testimony*] (*Vayikra* 5:1; *Rambam,* ibid., 1:12; see *mitzvos* #123 and #227).

There is a major dispute among the commentators as to the role of Hashem's Name in creating an oath. Some authorities rule that if Hashem's Name is not mentioned in the oath, none of the consequences of swearing falsely (or in vain) would apply in any of the four categories of oaths mentioned above. Others differentiate between the four categories, ruling that mention of Hashem's Name is required for certain categories but not

for others [i.e. in order for the consequences of swearing falsely to apply] (see *mitzvah* #227 for sources and explanations of the various approaches).

Although the verse: *You shall not take the Name of Hashem, your Lord, in vain* (*Shemos* 20:7) primarily warns against using Hashem's Name to make a *vain* oath, the verse also functions, according to some, as a general warning against making a *false* oath, because swearing falsely also constitutes taking His Name in vain. [See *Radvaz,* IV:154, who states that this is implied by the declaration made by judges to frighten a defendant when he is about to swear (to deter him from swearing falsely). They tell the defendant: "Know that the entire world shook when the Holy One, Blessed is He, stated at Sinai: *You shall not take the Name of Hashem, your God, in vain*" (*Shevuos* 37a).] Thus, we see that the verse which prohibits making a vain oath is also used to deter someone from making a false oath in court. A further indication that the verse functions as the source for both prohibitions is the following statement made by the Gemara: "[When the Ten Commandments were declared, the warnings against] vain [oaths] and false [oaths] were said simultaneously; something that the ear cannot hear, and the mouth cannot say..." (*Yerushalmi, Shevuos* ch. 3:8).

4. Another example of an oath in this category is swearing that a certain man is a woman, or a certain woman is a man (see Mishnah, *Shevuos* 29a; *Rambam,* ibid. 1:4; *Tur,* ibid. 236:4)

An oath that contradicts an obvious fact is not only vain, it is a lie. As stated earlier (note 3), there is a separate prohibition in the Torah against making a *false* oath (*mitzvah* #227), and there are those who rule that one whose

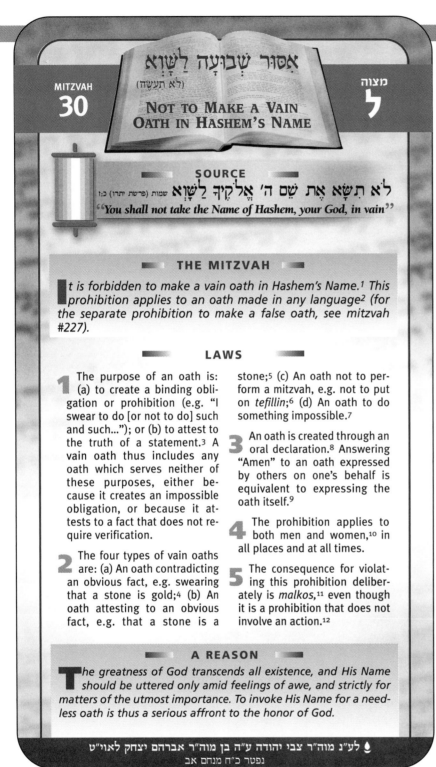

MITZVAH 30 — מצוה ל

אִסוּר שְׁבוּעָה לַשָּׁוְא
(לֹא תַעֲשֶׂה)

NOT TO MAKE A VAIN OATH IN HASHEM'S NAME

SOURCE

לֹא תִשָּׂא אֶת שֵׁם ה' אֱלֹקֶיךָ לַשָּׁוְא   שמות (פרשת יתרו) כ:ז

"You shall not take the Name of Hashem, your God, in vain"

THE MITZVAH

It is forbidden to make a vain oath in Hashem's Name.[1] This prohibition applies to an oath made in any language[2] (for the separate prohibition to make a false oath, see mitzvah #227).

LAWS

1. The purpose of an oath is: (a) to create a binding obligation or prohibition (e.g. "I swear to do [or not to do] such and such…"); or (b) to attest to the truth of a statement.[3] A vain oath thus includes any oath which serves neither of these purposes, either because it creates an impossible obligation, or because it attests to a fact that does not require verification.

2. The four types of vain oaths are: (a) An oath contradicting an obvious fact, e.g. swearing that a stone is gold;[4] (b) An oath attesting to an obvious fact, e.g. that a stone is a stone;[5] (c) An oath not to perform a mitzvah, e.g. not to put on *tefillin*;[6] (d) An oath to do something impossible.[7]

3. An oath is created through an oral declaration.[8] Answering "Amen" to an oath expressed by others on one's behalf is equivalent to expressing the oath itself.[9]

4. The prohibition applies to both men and women,[10] in all places and at all times.

5. The consequence for violating this prohibition deliberately is *malkos*,[11] even though it is a prohibition that does not involve an action.[12]

A REASON

The greatness of God transcends all existence, and His Name should be uttered only amid feelings of awe, and strictly for matters of the utmost importance. To invoke His Name for a needless oath is thus a serious affront to the honor of God.

לע"נ מוה"ר צבי יהודה ע"ה בן מוה"ר אברהם יצחק לאוי"ט
נפטר כ"ח מנחם אב

matters which, although proven false, *might* have been true, whereas an oath contradicting an obvious fact is clearly false from the outset (see *Rambam, Hil. Shevuos* 1:2-3).

[It should be noted that in order for the fact contradicted through an oath to be considered "obvious," it has to be known by at least three people (*Shevuos* 29a; see also *Yerushalmi, Shevuos* 3:8). Furthermore, these three people must be members of the general population (i.e. laymen); however, if the fact is known only by highly educated people or experts in a particular field, it is not considered an "obvious" fact regarding the prohibition against making a vain oath. For example, if a person living during medieval times swore that the sun is smaller than the earth, it would not have constituted a vain oath, even though the statement was known to be false. The reason is that during that period of history, the falsity of this statement was known only to the educated elite. Thus, the person might have been basing his oath on the fact that to the naked eye, the sun *does* seem smaller than the earth (*Rambam, Hil. Shevuos* 5:22; see *Radvaz* there, who rules that even if a highly educated person had made the oath, it would not have been considered contradicting an obvious fact, because, although he himself knows the truth about the size of the sun, those hearing the oath do not, and he was making the oath with their understanding in mind).]

5. *Pesikta Rabbasi, Parashah* 22; *Yerushalmi, Shevuos* 3:8; *Rambam, ibid.* 1:5.

Other examples within this category include swearing that "the sky is the sky" or that "the number two is two." Although this type of oath states the truth, it is nevertheless considered vain, because it attests to facts which are obvious to any normal person and

oath contradicts an obvious fact has not only made a vain oath, but has also violated the prohibition against making a false oath; and, in certain circumstances, would be liable to two sets of lashes (see *Minchas Chinuch* 30:2). However, others rule that one

would violate only the prohibition against vain oaths, not the one against false oaths (*Yerushalmi, Shevuos* 3:8 with *Pnei Moshe* there). According to this approach, one way to distinguish between the two categories is that the prohibition against *false* oaths involves

thus do not require verification through an oath (*Rambam* ibid.).

There are those who hold that an oath attesting to the truth of an obvious fact is not a violation of the *Biblical* prohibition against making a vain oath; rather, it is a *Rabbinic* prohibition. [However, this is the minority view] (see *Ritva, Shevuos* 29a and *Mechilta De'Rashbi, Shemos* 20:7).

6. Just as swearing *not to* perform a mitzvah is considered a vain oath, so too is swearing *to* perform a prohibited act, for example, swearing to eat non-kosher meat or to physically hurt another person (*Rambam*, ibid. 5:12 and 5:16).

An oath not to fulfill a mitzvah (whether positive or negative) does not take effect; i.e. one is not bound by it. [Since one is not bound by the oath, one is not allowed to fulfill it, because doing so would of necessity entail a violation of a mitzvah.] Any oath that one is prohibited from fulfilling is considered vain, just as an oath that is physically impossible to fulfill is considered vain (*Ritva, Nedarim* 15a; *Rashi, Shevuos* 26a, ד"ה מאי and 29a, ד"ה שבועה).

The reason that an oath not to fulfill a mitzvah does not take effect is as follows: The Nation of Israel made a collective oath at Mount Sinai committing themselves and future generations to fulfill the mitzvos of the Torah. Every individual Jew, for all generations, is considered eternally bound by that oath (מושבע ועומד מהר סיני) [as if he had made the oath himself]. Now, one of the principles of the laws of oaths is that an oath regarding a certain matter cannot take effect if another oath has already been made concerning that same matter (אין שבועה חלה על שבועה). Therefore, an oath not to fulfill a mitzvah cannot take effect, because one is already bound by the oath at Sinai to perform it (see *Rambam* ibid. and *Hil.*

Nedarim 3:7-8). Alternatively, an oath not to fulfill a mitzvah does not take effect because the Torah did not assign an oath the power to uproot a person's Torah obligation (see *Ran, Nedarim* 16b ד"ה הא, and *Rosh* there, ד"ה אמר אביי).

Although all agree that swearing not to fulfill a positive *Biblical* mitzvah is considered a vain oath, there is a dispute as to whether the same applies to an oath not to perform a *Rabbinic* mitzvah (such as lighting candles on Chanukah). Some rule that an oath not to perform a Rabbinic mitzvah is not vain because, in contrast to one regarding a Biblical mitzvah, it *does* take effect, and thus the person who made the oath would be obligated to fulfill it by not performing the mitzvah. According to this approach, the reason that the oath takes effect in this case is that Rabbinic mitzvos were instituted *after* the revelation of the Torah at Mount Sinai, and thus are not included in the oath made by the nation at that time. However, there are those who rule that an oath not to perform a Rabbinic mitzvah does not take effect, and is thus considered a vain oath (see *Tur, Orach Chaim* §570; *Beis Yosef*, ibid. §418 in explanation of *Rambam's* view; see also *Mahralbach* §104).

Although a person is already bound by the oath at Mount Sinai to perform the mitzvos, it is permissible to make an oath to perform a positive mitzvah (e.g. to put on *tefillin*), in order to strengthen one's resolve. This is based on the verse in *Tehillim* 119:106: *I swore, and I will fulfill* [*my oath*]*, to keep Your righteous laws* (*Nedarim* 8a; *Rambam* ibid. 11:3; *Shulchan Aruch, Yoreh Deah* 203:6). However, where one failed to perform the mitzvah about which one swore, there is a dispute as to whether the oath would retroactively be considered vain (see *Radvaz* to *Hil. Shevuos* 5:16; *Meiri, Nedarim* 8a; *Afikei Yam*, I:36). There is also a dispute

among the Rishonim as to whether swearing not to transgress a prohibition (e.g. "I swear not to eat non-kosher food") is considered a vain oath (see *Rambam*, ibid. 5:11 and 5:16, and *Radvaz* there; *Ritva, Nedarim* 15a and *Makkos* 22a; *Meiri, Nedarim* 8a; *Afikei Yam*, I:36)

7. *Shevuos* 25a and *Rashi* there ד"ה מלקין; *Rambam,* ibid. 1:7. Another example of an oath in this category is swearing not to eat or drink for seven consecutive days.

An oath regarding something that is not in one's power to fulfill is considered a vain oath, even though it is possible that it will be fulfilled. For example, saying to a friend: "I swear that I will never know anything regarding which I will need to testify on your behalf" is a vain oath, even though the prediction might come true, because one cannot control what one will know in the future (*Rambam,* ibid. 5:15).

Swearing that another person will (or will not) perform a particular action is also considered by some to be a vain oath, because one cannot control another's actions, and thus, like the oath discussed in the previous paragraph, this is not in one's hands to fulfill. Others, however, rule that it is not a vain oath, because the person about whom one swore may hear about the oath, and choose to go ahead and fulfill it. Among those who do consider it a vain oath, there is also a dispute as to whether one would incur *malkos* for it or not (see *Rashi, Shevuos* 25a ד"ה ליתיה, *Rambam*, ibid. 5:2 and *Rivash* §387; *Tur, Yoreh Deah* §236 and *Bach* there; *Shulchan Aruch, Yoreh Deah* 236:2 and *Shach* there §4-5).

When a person swears in order to bolster an exaggerated claim, if it is considered a vain oath depends upon if his exaggeration is a commonly used one or not. One who swears, for example, that he saw a camel flying

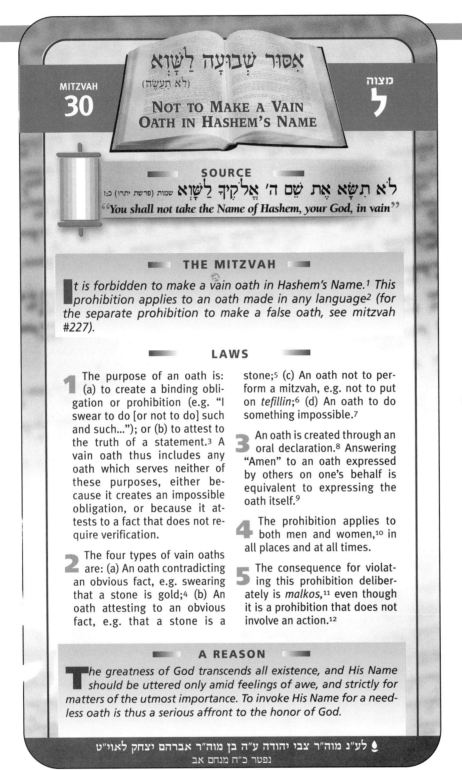

אִסוּר שְׁבוּעָה לַשָּׁוְא
(לֹא תַעֲשֶׂה)

MITZVAH 30

NOT TO MAKE A VAIN OATH IN HASHEM'S NAME

מצוה ל

SOURCE

לֹא תִשָּׂא אֶת שֵׁם ה' אֱלֹקֶיךָ לַשָּׁוְא שמות (פרשת יתרו) כ:ז

"You shall not take the Name of Hashem, your God, in vain"

THE MITZVAH

It is forbidden to make a vain oath in Hashem's Name.[1] This prohibition applies to an oath made in any language[2] (for the separate prohibition to make a false oath, see mitzvah #227).

LAWS

1 The purpose of an oath is: (a) to create a binding obligation or prohibition (e.g. "I swear to do [or not to do] such and such..."); or (b) to attest to the truth of a statement.[3] A vain oath thus includes any oath which serves neither of these purposes, either because it creates an impossible obligation, or because it attests to a fact that does not require verification.

2 The four types of vain oaths are: (a) An oath contradicting an obvious fact, e.g. swearing that a stone is gold;[4] (b) An oath attesting to an obvious fact, e.g. that a stone is a stone;[5] (c) An oath not to perform a mitzvah, e.g. not to put on tefillin;[6] (d) An oath to do something impossible.[7]

3 An oath is created through an oral declaration.[8] Answering "Amen" to an oath expressed by others on one's behalf is equivalent to expressing the oath itself.[9]

4 The prohibition applies to both men and women,[10] in all places and at all times.

5 The consequence for violating this prohibition deliberately is *malkos*,[11] even though it is a prohibition that does not involve an action.[12]

A REASON

The greatness of God transcends all existence, and His Name should be uttered only amid feelings of awe, and strictly for matters of the utmost importance. To invoke His Name for a needless oath is thus a serious affront to the honor of God.

through the air has made a vain oath, even if he later claims that he really saw a bird, but referred to it as a camel due to its massive size. The reason we do not accept his claim is that people do not generally refer to anything as a camel except for a camel itself. Even if

the person claims that he himself always refers to large birds as camels, he still receives *malkos* for making a vain oath, because with respect to the laws of oaths, we rule according to the way the general population speaks (לשון בני אדם) (*Rambam*, ibid. 5:21 and *Radvaz*

there). However, a person who swears that he saw something that could not possibly have occurred, but it is clear that he is exaggerating and does not intend for people to take his words literally, has not made a vain oath. For example, swearing that one saw a group of people equal in number to the group of Jews that were led out of Egypt by Moses (about 3 million), is not considered a vain oath, since people generally use that expression to describe a very large group (see *Nedarim* 24b). The same applies to other expressions commonly used as exaggerations (see *Ramban, Shevuos* 29a in the name of *Rabbeinu Tam; Ritva, Shevuos* ibid.; *Ran, Nedarim,* ibid.; *Rama, Yoreh Deah* 236:5 and *Beur HaGra* there §18).

8. See *Shevuos* 26b; *Rambam,* ibid., 2:10. The Torah describes an oath specifically in terms of an oral declaration, as we see from the following verse in *Vayikra* 5:4: *Or if a person swears by uttering with [his] lips to cause harm or good.* However, some commentaries rule that an oath expressed in writing is valid, even though it was never expressed orally. They explain that the Torah's description of an oath as an oral declaration is not intended to exclude all other oaths, but rather to teach that an oath can be created only through a *physical act,* such as speech, and not through a mental commitment to make an oath. Therefore, an act of writing also has the power to create a binding oath (*Chavos Ya'ir* §194; *Shevus Yaakov,* I:56). However, there are those who rule that an oath can be created by means of an oral declaration only, and therefore, a written oath is not valid (*Shav Yaakov, Yoreh Deah* §49; see also *Tumim* 96:5; *Teshuvos Rabbi Akiva Eiger, Mahadura Kamma* §29; *Teshuvos Chasam Sofer, Yoreh Deah* §227; *Minchas Chinuch* 30:17, and 86:4).

Only that which a person expressed in words is considered part of his oath, even if it is clear (for example, through his own allusions) that he intended to include other things in it (Shach, Choshen Mishpat, 73:27; Har Tzvi, Yoreh Deah, §186).

9. Mishnah, Shevuos 29b and Rashi there ד"ה מפי עצמו; Rambam, ibid. 2:1; Tur, Yoreh Deah 237:2). The principle that answering "Amen" is the equivalent of expressing the oath itself is derived from the oath made by a sotah (suspected adulteress) to attest to her innocence. In the procedure outlined by the Torah, a Kohen pronounces the oath, and the sotah simply answers "Amen" (see Bamidbar 5:11-31).

Even if one answers "Amen" to an oath expressed on one's behalf by someone who is unfit to swear himself (e.g. a minor), one is nevertheless bound by the oath, because by answering "Amen," it is as if he repeated the oath himself (Rambam, ibid.). Even answering the equivalent of "Amen," such as simply saying "yes" or "I am obligated to fulfill this oath," or "I accept this oath upon myself," or any similar expression, in any language, is considered the equivalent of expressing the oath itself (Rambam, ibid.; see Shevus Yaakov, I:56, who rules that even a non-verbal sign of commitment to an oath expressed by others [such as nodding one's head] is sufficient).

10. Mishnah, Shevuos 29b. See also Mishnah, Kiddushin 29a, and the Gemara there on 35a, which equates men and women regarding prohibitions in the Torah.

An oath made by a minor (קטן) in the year before the age of adulthood is considered a valid oath. For a male, the year before adulthood begins when he is twelve years and one day old, whereas for a female, it begins when she is eleven years and one day old. However, a minor during that year must be questioned first in order to

verify that he understands exactly what he is doing. If he shows understanding, his oath is valid; if not, his words are meaningless (prior to that year, however, a minor's oath is never valid, even if he claims to understand).

The oath of a minor who has reached the age of adulthood (thirteen for a male, twelve for a female), is valid even if he claims not to understand what he is doing, and even if he has not produced the physical signs of puberty required to be considered a full legal adult (Rambam, Hil. Nedarim 11:1; see also mitzvos #227 and #575).

Even though a minor's oath is valid in certain circumstances, if he does make a vain oath, he is exempt from punishment, because minors are exempt from punishment for all transgressions (Minchas Chinuch 30:10. Regarding the principle that a minor is exempt from all mitzvos, see Chagigah 3a and Rambam, Hil. Chagigah 2:4).

11. Mishnah, Shevuos 29a and Rambam, Hil. Shevuos 1:7. One who is guilty of making a vain oath is not required to bring an offering under any circumstances. This is in contrast to each of the other three categories of oaths (see above, note 3), where an offering is required in certain circumstances for swearing falsely (Mishnah, Shevuos 27b; Rambam, Hil. Shevuos 1:7; Mechilta, Shemos 20:7; Shevuos 26a מאי מיעט מיעט מצוה and Rashi there).

12. In general, prohibitions that do not involve an action (לאו שאין בה מעשה) are not subject to the penalty of malkos. Now, although speech is not considered an "action" with regards to this principle, making a vain oath is one of a few speech-oriented prohibitions which do incur malkos, even though no action is involved. Some of the other exceptions are: making a false oath [shevuas sheker — see mitzvah #227], cursing another person using one of Hashem's Names [mitzvah

#231), and verbally substituting a different animal for an already consecrated sacrificial animal [temurah — תמורה — see mitzvah #351] (see Shevuos 21a with Tosafos ד"ה חוץ (both); Rambam, Hil. Sanhedrin 18:2; see also Meshech Chochmah, Shemos 20:7 and Rabbeinu Yonah, Sha'arei Teshuvah, 3:45).

Taking Hashem's Name in vain through a vain or false oath is a unique prohibition in the sense that it is the only one regarding which the Torah declares; Hashem will not absolve (לא ינקה) (Shemos 20:7). Many interpret this verse to mean that although other transgressions are fully atoned for through receiving the appropriate punishment imposed by the Torah (e.g. malkos), taking Hashem's Name in vain is not fully atoned for in this way. In other words, a person who makes a vain oath does not achieve full atonement through receiving malkos alone, but rather must endure extra retribution inflicted by Hashem Himself. For when one takes Hashem's Name in vain, he has not only violated a Torah prohibition, but has also desecrated Hashem's Name (חלול השם) in the process. The extra retribution is required to atone for the desecration of the Name. The Rishonim emphasize that considering the extreme severity of taking Hashem's Name in vain, one should be more cautious of it than of any other transgression (Rambam, Hil. Shevuos 12:1 with Lechem Mishneh, and 11:16; see also Hil. Teshuvah 1:2 and 4; cf. Hasagos HaRa'avad to Hil. Shevuos 12:1).

It should be noted that a penalty imposed by the Torah for committing a transgression, whether it be bringing an offering, malkos, or capital punishment, cannot provide full atonement unless it is accompanied by sincere repentance (תשובה) and verbal confession (וידוי) (see Rambam, Hil. Teshuvah 1:1).

עיונים

A BROADER LOOK AT THE LAWS

1 The prohibition extends beyond oaths:

As mentioned above (note 2), although the primary prohibition stemming from the verse, *You shall not take the Name of Hashem, your Lord, in vain* (Shemos 20:7), is that of using Hashem's Name to make a vain *oath,* the prohibition, according to some, is not limited solely to oaths. The Torah's choice of the more general expression *Lo Sisa,* meaning *You shall not **take,*** rather than *Lo Si'shava, You shall not **swear,*** serves to leave open the possibility of extending the prohibition beyond oaths, and incorporating other activities which involve taking Hashem's Name in vain. Some examples are:

∽ Mentioning Hashem's Name in vain

According to some, even mentioning Hashem's Name in vain *without* making an oath is considered a violation of the prohibition of *Lo sisa* (Zohar, Shemos 88a, She'iltos §53; Bahag, Hilchos Shevuos, §52; Ramban to Shemos 20:7; Rabbeinu Bachya, Shemos ibid., Sefer HaChinuch). However, the Gemara in *Temurah* (4a) implies that it is not a violation of *Lo sisa,* but rather a violation of only the positive mitzvah (#432) to fear Hashem, which is based on the verse: *You shall fear Hashem, your God* (Devarim 6:13). Many Rishonim concur with this approach (Tosafos, Rosh Hashanah 33a הא ד"ה; Ran, Nedarim 7b השומע ד"ה; see also Rambam, Hil. Shevuos 12:11; Sha'alos U'Teshuvos R' Akiva Eiger, Mahadura Kamma §25; Nishmas Adam, Klal §5; see also Birchei Yosef, Choshen Mishpat 34:17, who cites additional Rishonim). [For an explanation of how those who rule that it is also a violation of *Lo sisa* would understand the Gemara in *Temurah* 4a, see Sd'ei Chemed, Ma'areches 2, Klal §115 [p. 74]; Commentary of R' Y.P. Perla to Sefer HaMitzvos L'Rasag, Aseh §1 [p. 42].

∽ Making an unnecessary blessing

The Gemara in *Berachos* (33a) states that one who recites an unnecessary blessing has violated the prohibition of *Lo sisa.* Now, there are those who interpret the Gemara as referring to an actual violation of the Biblical prohibition, thereby equating making an unnecessary blessing with making a vain oath (She'iltos §53; Rambam, Hil. Berachos 1:15 and Hil. Shevuos 12:9; Sha'alos U'Teshuvos HaRambam [Blau ed.] §124, see Shulchan Aruch, Orach Chaim 215:4 and Magen Avraham there §6; Sha'alos U'Teshuvos R' Akiva Eiger, Mahadura Kamma §25; Sefer HaMenuchah LeRabbeinu Manoach, Hilchos Krias Shema 2:13, cited in Beis Yosef, Orach Chaim 67; see Pri Chadash there).

Others, however, rule that reciting an unnecessary blessing is a violation of only a Rabbinic prohibition, and the Gemara (ibid.) simply mentions the prohibition of *Lo Sisa* as a Scriptural allusion (asmachta) but did not mean that one would actually be violating a Biblical prohibition (Tosafos, Rosh Hashanah 33a, הא ד"ה; Rosh, Kiddushin 1:49; Ritvah, Berachos 33a; Terumas HaDeshen §37; Minchas Chinuch 30:8; see also Nishmas Adam, Klal 5:1, who writes that even Rambam, cited in the previous paragraph as support for the other approach, holds that making an unnecessary blessing violates only a Rabbinic prohibition).

∽ Chillul Hashem

The word תשא, *take,* in the verse, לא תשא את שם ה' אלקיך לשוא, *You shall not take the Name of Hashem, your Lord, in vain,* comes from the root נשא, which can also mean to "raise up" or "carry." Thus, one could read the verse as a warning not to *carry* the Name of Hashem in vain. When does one carry the Name of Hashem? When one wears *tefillin,* for example, which have the Name of Hashem written inside them, or even when wearing a *tallis,* because it is clear to all that one who wears it represents Hashem's Name. Thus, the verse can be understood as a warning not to commit transgressions while wearing one's *tallis* and *tefillin* [for that too is considered using Hashem's Name falsely] (*Pesikta Rabasi, Parashah 22* and *Meiri, Shabbos* 49a). In a similar vein, one could understand the verse as a warning not to "raise oneself up" falsely through Hashem's Name; for example, by accepting a position of authority when one is not fit for the position (*Pesikta Rabasi*, ibid.), or acting as if one is extremely strict regarding the Torah, when one is not truly on that level (*Medrash Aggadah* [Buber ed.], *Shemos* 20:7; see also *Or HaChaim, Shemos* ibid.).

SITUATIONS IN HALACHAH

Question:
In a case of doubt, should one think, rather than say, a blessing?

Answer:
We have learned (see above, *Iyunim* §1) that the prohibition of *Lo Sisa* extends beyond oaths, and that the Gemara in *Berachos* (33a) states that one who recites an unnecessary blessing has violated the prohibition of *Lo Sisa*.

In fact, R' Akiva Eiger (*Teshuvos Mahadura Kamma* §25) asks why the law says that one who is unsure whether he has recited the blessings after bread (*Birchas HaMazon*) must recite them now (even thought he may have recited it before). Should the person not be concerned that he is reciting the blessings in vain, thus violating *Lo Sisa*? R' Akiva Eiger responds that since in "repeating" the blessings one is following the principle that one must be stringent when unsure if he has fulfilled a Biblical obligation (*safek d'Oraisa l'chumrah*), the blessings are not considered in vain, and hence *Lo Sisa* is not violated (see also *Tzlach* to *Berachos* 20b, and *Pri Megadim, Eishel Avraham, Orach Chaim* 185:1).

We also learned above (see *Iyunim* ibid.) that there is a difference of opinion as to whether the Gemara (loc. cit.) that links the recitation of unnecessary blessings to the prohibition of *Lo Sisa* is referring to an actual violation of the Biblical prohibition, or only to a violation of a Rabbinic prohibition. In any event, authorities infer the parameters of unnecessary blessings from the parameters of vain oaths. Therefore, since in regard to vain oaths, the Gemara (*Shavuos* 26b; see *Tos.* ad loc., end of ד"ה גמר בלבו) rules that one does not violate *Lo Sisa* by *thinking* a vain oath (see also *Rambam, Hil. Shavuos* 2:10,12; *Hil. Nezirus* 1:5-6 and *Hil. Nedarim* 2:2), if one is unsure whether he is obligated to make a blessing or not, he should *think* the blessing (*Tzlach* and *Pri Megadim* loc. cit.; *Chida* in *Pesach Einayim* to *Berachos* 20b, from *Ginas Veradim, Orach Chaim* 1:43). [*Shelah HaKadosh* seems to maintain that thinking an unnecessary blessing *does* violate *Lo Sisa*. Most authorities, however, reject his position.]

Thus, for example, if one is unsure whether he made a blessing over food he would like to eat, he may think the blessing and proceed to eat the food. *Teshuvos Maharam Schik* (*Orach Chaim* §42) explains that thinking the blessing in such a case of doubt is sufficient because it is deemed a double doubt (*sfek sfeika*): Perhaps he is not required to make the blessing, and even if he is required to make the blessing, perhaps thinking a blessing is tantamount to reciting it. *Maharam Schik* asks, however: If one can fulfill a requirement to make a blessing in thought alone while at the same time not violating *Lo Sisa*, why is there a principle (regarding all blessings other than *Birchas HaMazon*) that when one is unsure whether he is required to make a blessing, that he should refrain from reciting the blessing (*safek berachos lehakel*)? It would be better to think the blessing! He suggests that perhaps this principle indeed only teaches us that in a case of doubt one is not *required* to recite the blessing, but it would indeed be correct (although not mandatory) to think the blessing. *Teshuvos Ksav Sofer* (§12-13) goes further, and writes that in a case of doubt one is *required* to think the blessing. [*Shiyarei Knesses HaGedolah* to *Orach Chaim* §85, and *Leket HaKemach, Hil. Berachos* write only that it is best to be stringent and think the blessing.]

ILLUMINATIONS OF THE MITZVAH
Suggested Reasons & Insights

I. SWEARING IN VAIN: A DEROGATION OF GOD'S HONOR

he primary reason for this prohibition is that an oath invokes the Name of God, and if the oath — even if it be true — serves no purpose, the Name of God has been uttered in vain, showing a frivolous disregard for the honor of God. We are thus given the message that we are not to treat lightly the honor of the Creator, and not to disparage it in either speech or thought (*Abarbanel, Shemos* 20:7). Even a king of flesh-and-blood would not tolerate the use of his name for pointless oaths; all the more so the King of kings (*Shelah, Yisro, Torah Ohr* §2). By taking care to obey this commandment, people will develop an awareness that the existence of the timeless God in Heaven transcends all other existence, and that His Name should be invoked, in connection with our words and deeds, only amidst feelings of awe and trepidation, and not in the trivial manner that people speak of mortal humans and other subjects of transient existence (*Chinuch* §30).

[The law against trivializing God's Name does not apply only to oaths; it is forbidden in general to mention His Name in vain, as in making needless blessings (see *Berachos* 33a), or in everyday speech (see *Zohar* II, 88a, et al.; *Rambam, Hil. Shevuos* 12:1). Even in a permitted context, one should be cautious not to allow the Holy Name to be brought to his lips in a frivolous way (*Commentary of R' Avraham ben HaRambam, Shemos* 20:7); rather, a person should tremble with fear when he is about to utter God's Name (*Chayei Adam* 5:1). "How can a person but approach with special care, throughout the prayers and various blessings, the utterance of the Ineffable Name, or any of God's other holy Names, so that it may be accompanied with the most intense concentration?" (*Yesod V'Shoresh HaAvodah,* 2:2)]

Regarding the penalty in store for those who defy this prohibition and swear in vain, the Sages have said, *Wild beasts come upon the world on account of vain oaths and the desecration of God's Name* (*Avos* 5:11). This punishment corresponds to the sins that incur it, as it is well established that the natural fear that animals have for humans derives from the fact that a human being reflects the image of God. However, unfaithfulness toward the service of God, especially by way of a sin which directly degrades God's exalted stature in man's eyes, results in the effacement of the Divine image in man, and — "measure for measure" — his own stature is degraded in the eyes of his fellow creatures, and the beasts of prey lose the fear of man they once had (*Mirkeves HaMishnah, Avos* ad loc.; see also *Derech Chaim* ad loc.).

II. SWEARING IN VAIN: AMONG THE MOST GRIEVOUS OF SINS

ransgressing the prohibition of swearing in vain can, in a sense, be more serious than the worst of sins, because of the ease with which it can be repeated again and again. It can become so habitual that a person may constantly swear and remain oblivious to what he is doing. In contrast, such grave sins as murder or adultery are not likely to be repeated with such reckless abandon, for fear of the consequences. In addition, people who engage in sinful behavior generally do so with a specific objective in mind. The murderer thirsts for revenge, the adulterer pursues pleasure, the thief seeks personal gain. But a person who develops the habit of swearing is wont to do so reflexively, without cause or gain; it has simply become for him a manner of speech. To display such wanton disregard for the Divine Will is nothing less than a public desecration of the Name of God (*Ibn Ezra, Shemos* 20:7; see *Shaarei Teshuvah* 1:7-8; *Derashos Rabbeinu Yonah*; *Shemiras HaLashon* §9).

So severe is the sin of taking an oath in vain, that the Torah here makes the unique statement that *God*

will not absolve one who takes His Name in vain (Shemos 20:7). In the Sages' measured phraseology, a vain oath is specifically described as a "serious" transgression (see *Yoma* 85b), and the Rishonim have stated that had this been the only sin widespread in Israel, it would still have sufficed to extend the exile and perpetuate our suffering (*Ibn Ezra* ibid.).

In light of the deprecation of God's honor engendered by one who takes an oath in vain, this sin is likened to worship of idols. So commented the Sages: The Ten Commandments begin with *I am Hashem, your God* [teaching faith in God], continue with *You shall not have other gods* [forbidding idolatry], and the third is *You shall not take the Name of Hashem, your God, in vain.* How does the last of this trio belong with the others? This placement is meant to instruct us that one who habitually takes false or vain oaths is considered to have worshipped idols. [For just as it behooves us to fear God and to refrain from applying the honor due Him to another in idol worship, so also must we treat His Name with reverence, and one who takes His Name in vain profanes that Name, as it is written (*Vayikra* 19:12), *You shall not swear falsely in My Name, and thereby profane the Name of your God (Ramban, Shemos* 20:7).] One who regularly violates this mitzvah withholds the satisfaction that God derives from those who fulfill His will, and he rejects a full-fledged acceptance of the yoke of Heavenly rule. By contrast, anyone who resists the habit of making false or vain oaths brings satisfaction to God, and fully subordinates himself to the yoke of Heavenly rule (*Tanna D'vei Eliyahu Rabbah* 26:14; see *Sefer Ikkarim* 3:26).

A person who has truly accepted God as his Master will always be hesitant to utter His Name; he will do so only for spiritual matters, and even then sparingly. It goes without saying that he would not invoke it for insignificant or nonsensical matters (*Akeidas Yitzchak* §45).

There is more. In one respect, the act of making a false or superfluous oath is even worse than idolatry. For by invoking His Name to attest to a matter whose verification is of no consequence, the swearer intimates that God Himself is of no import

or benefit to existence. This notion is even more objectionable than the belief of one who enters another deity into a partnership with God for control of the world (*Ralbag, Shemos* 20:7).

This sin can be seen as being worse than idolatry — worse even than denying entirely the existence of God — from another perspective as well. None of the other sins, as much as they represent defiance of God, serve to distort the *nature* of God's reality. But when one acknowledges God, yet associates His Name with falsehood, he has done just that, and has profaned His honorable Name. An analogy can be drawn to a king of a country in which two cities rebelled against him. One city proceeded to crown another man as king, while the other did not take that step, but dishonored their erstwhile king by repudiating his legitimacy and labeling him an impostor. Now, the first city did not, by transferring their allegiance to another ruler, directly impinge on the king himself. There was change only on the receiving end; the subjects took for themselves a different king. The second city, on the other hand, did not substitute another sovereign, but they directly assaulted the king's honor by impugning the veracity of his claim to the throne. This sheds light on why this mitzvah has been singled out among all the others, as in this teaching of the Sages: "The entire world shuddered when God spoke, *'You shall not take the Name of Hashem, your God, in vain.'*" Inasmuch as this sin undermines the honor of God, it contrives in turn to unsettle the world, because the world is nothing more than an embodiment of the honor of God (*Maharal, Tiferes Yisrael* §39).

III. SWEARING IN VAIN: TRIVIALIZING THE CONCEPT OF AN OATH

 n addition to slighting the honor of God, one who takes an oath in vain debases the sacred nature of an oath. An oath that invokes the name of God is an extraordinary matter, and depreciating it by swearing in vain is correspondingly a sin of considerable gravity. When a person swears, he invests his word with a sacred quality, and assumes full responsibility for what he says. Woe to the person who would toy with such a weighty matter! "Taking an oath means submitting yourself and your entire, visible, material world to the authority of the Invisible One; that is, to His punishing judgment, in the event that the statement regarding which you swear is not true" (*R' Samson R. Hirsch, Bereishis* 21:23). Hence "swearing without object or cause is simply playing with the most solemn of all solemn acts of man; namely, the submission of one's words and deeds to the judgment of God, Who decides and fixes his future and fate" (ibid., *Shemos* 20:7).

IV. SWEARING IN VAIN: AN ASSAULT ON THE WORLD'S EXISTENCE

wearing in vain not only shows contempt for a venerable concept, but also undermines the foundation of the world's survival. The reality of God's existence is what sustains all the worlds, and to invoke His Name in a trivial way or to reinforce a lie is to deny the truth of His existence, for implicit in an oath in the Name of God is the assertion that the truth of the statement in question is equal to the truth of God's existence. Thus, if the statement turns out to be false, the equation results in a denial of God's reality. This reveals another facet to the Sages' teaching, cited above, that the entire world shuddered when this commandment was spoken by God at Sinai, because the very source of the world's existence was at stake (*Beis Elokim, Shaar HaYesodos* §31).

[This idea is allegorized in the language of the commandment, *You shall not lift up* (לא תשא) *the Name of Hashem, your God, in vain.* This can be compared to one who lifts a tree by its trunk; the branches will obviously rise up as well. Similarly, all the world's creatures are dependent on God's Name, and one who "raises" God's Name on his lips brings with it all the "branches" that adhere to it; it is no surprise, then, that the abuse of God's Name affects all the world's creatures, and the punishing consequences will be felt throughout. Accordingly, the verse continues, ... *for*

God will not absolve one who takes (*lifts*) *His Name in vain.* Why is this so? Now the answer is clear. God stands ready to forgive a sinner only for sins between man and God, but not for those between man and his fellow. So how can God forgive the person who lays his hand on the "trunk" of the holy tree, causing all the world's inhabitants that branch out from that tree to suffer as a result? Can the culprit seek out all the casualties of his misdeed to gain their forgiveness? Can he travel to the ends of the universe to appease the denizens of Heaven and earth, all of whom felt the effects of his deed? It is therefore said that God will not wipe away a sin such as this; it is unforgivable (*Kli Yakar, Shemos* 20:7).]

There is another way in which swearing in vain cripples the world: The continued existence of the world relies on the oath taken by God to never again repeat the flood that destroyed the world in the time of Noach (see *Bereishis* 8:21 and *Rashi* there), as the verse states (*Yeshaya* 54:9): *As I swore that the waters of Noach would never again pass over the earth.* A person who allows himself to make vain or false oaths demonstrates his contempt for the solemnity of an oath, and effectively declares that God's oath, as well, is devoid of meaning and is not really binding. He thus, in effect, releases God from His obligation, freeing Him to do what He promised He would not. This notion, of course, spells disaster for the world; we are thus provided with yet another understanding of the Sages' statement that, as this commandment was being issued at Sinai, the entire world shook, for the world's very survival hinges on it (*Akeidas Yitzchak* §45).

This is why the Targum's Aramaic translation for the word "swear" is "קיים," a term that also denotes survival. The existence of the world depends on the inviolability of an oath; people who swear and then make good on their oaths reinforce this inviolability and perpetuate the world, while those who swear and go back on their word are considered to have contributed to the world's demise (*Toras HaMinchah, Shemos* §24).

THROUGH THE EYES OF THE SAGES
Stories, Parables & Reflections

I. THE SEVERITY OF THE SIN

∽ Quaking in fear

he entire universe shuddered when God warned at Sinai, *You shall not take the Name of Hashem, your God, in vain* (*Shevuos* 39a; see *Illuminations of the Mitzvah* for an understanding of this phenomenon).

———— ⚜ ————

∽ Akin to idolatry

The Ten Commandments begin with *I am Hashem, your God*, and *You shall not recognize other gods before Me*. Immediately following is the commandment, *You shall not take God's Name in vain*. We are thus taught that a person who regularly takes vain and false oaths is considered as if he has engaged in the worship of idols. He withholds from God the satisfaction He derives from those who fulfill His will, and he rejects a full-fledged acceptance of the yoke of Heavenly rule. By contrast, anyone who resists the habit of making vain or false oaths brings satisfaction to God, and fully subordinates himself to the yoke of Heavenly rule (*Tanna D'vei Eliyahu Rabbah* 26:14).

———— ⚜ ————

∽ An unforgivable sin

One who breaks faith with his oath denies God's existence and is never forgiven, as it is said (*Shemos* 20:7), *For God will not absolve one who takes His Name in vain* (*Tanchuma, Mattos* §1).

II. CONSEQUENCES OF TRANSGRESSION

∽ Loss of one's children

od said to the Jews: Why would you see fit to swear vainly in My Name? This sin results in the death of your children, as it is said (*Yirmiyah* 2:30), *[Because you swore] in vain I struck your children* (*Otzar HaMedrashim, Medrash Aseres HaDibros*).

———— ⚜ ————

∽ Impoverishment

Someone who induces his fellow to take a false oath will eventually be divested of all his wealth … R' Yonah taught: This is true even if the oath conforms to the truth [but is not truly necessary — see *Matnos Kehunah* and *Radal*] (*Vayikra Rabbah* 6:3).

———— ⚜ ————

∽ Drought, famine and exile

You shall not take [God's Name in vain]. If you would have upheld this commandment, you would have beheld the fulfillment of the oath that God Himself took (*Yeshayah* 62:8): *God has sworn by His right hand, and by the arm of His strength, I will no longer give away your grain as food for your enemies, and strangers will not drink the wine for which you have toiled.* But now that you have transgressed it, you will become the subject of a different prophecy (*Devarim* 11:17): *The wrath of God will blaze forth against you; He will hold back the Heavens so that there will be no rain, and the ground will fail to yield its produce. You will then quickly perish from the land that God is giving you* (*Tanna D'vei Eliyahu Rabbah* 26:5).

———— ⚜ ————

∽ Ravaging beasts

Beasts of prey come upon the world on account of vain oaths and the desecration of God's Name (*Avos* 5:9).

———— ⚜ ————

❧ Depopulation

As a result of vain and false oaths, the desecration of God's Name, and Shabbos desecration — beasts of prey proliferate, domestic animals perish, the human population dwindles, and the roads become desolate. That improper oaths can be responsible for all this is evident from the verse (*Vayikra* 26:23): *If with these* (אלה) *you will not be chastened toward Me …* Read not "אֵלֶּה" but "אָלָה" — [in regard to] oaths. And what form of chastisement is described there (ibid. v. 22)? *I will incite the beasts of the field against you and they will kill your children, decimate your livestock, and reduce your numbers; and your roads will be deserted* (*Shabbos* 33a).

——— ❧ ———

❧ The cities of Yehudah

There were twenty-four major cities in Yehudah, and they were all destroyed on account of oaths made in vain, even though they were not false (*Yerushalmi, Nedarim* 3:2, *Shevuos* 3:8; *Pesikta Rabbasi* §22).

——— ❧ ———

❧ The King's Mountain

It is related that on Har HaMelech ('The King's Mountain') there once stood two thousand cities, and they all were destroyed on account of vain oaths, although they were true. How so? A person would [casually] say to his fellow: I swear that I will now go to such-and-such place and I will eat and drink. He would indeed go and make good on his oath; even so, all the cities were razed (*Tanchuma, Vayikra* §7, *Mattos* §1; *Bamidbar Rabbah* 22:1; *Medrash Aggadah, Vayikra* §5).

——— ❧ ———

❧ Disowned in the future

Anyone who habitually makes vain and false oaths does not inherit the life of the World to Come (*Tanna D'vei Eliyahu Rabbah* 26:17).

——— ❧ ———

❧ Causing another to swear

I have brought out this curse, said God … and it shall enter the house of the thief and the house of he who swears falsely in My Name; it shall lodge inside his house and destroy it, along with its wood and its stones (*Zechariah* 5:4). *I have brought out the curse* — for immediate use. *It shall enter the house of the thief* — this refers to a thief who steals deviously. He makes a claim against someone who, in fact, owes him nothing, and compels him to swear in order to reinforce his denial. [Although he swears to the truth, the oath's cause is unjustified] (*Shevuos* 39a; *Tosefta, Sotah* 7a, *Tanna D'vei Eliyahu Rabbah* 26:15).

———

When a defendant declares his readiness to take the oath required by *Beis Din* in order to deny his obligation, all who are present turn and say to each other, *Turn away from the tents of these wicked men* (*Bamidbar* 16:26). Why, though, is the plural form used? Granted, the one taking the oath is acting improperly, but the plaintiff, who is merely demanding the oath — why should he be referred to as wicked? R' Shimon ben Tarfon explained: The Torah stipulates (*Shemos* 22:10), *An oath of God shall be between both of them.* This teaches that both litigants will be punished as a result of the oath [even the plaintiff, who was remiss in entrusting his money to an untrustworthy person and thus brought about the desecration of God's Name — *Rashi*] (*Shevuos* 39b).

III. Uttering God's Name in Vain

Because the gravity of making vain or false oaths derives from the sanctity of God's Name which is irreverantly invoked by the oath — as indicated by the language of the commandment, "You shall not take the Name of Hashem your God in vain" — the Sages have taught that the trivialization of God's Name in any form, even outside the context of swearing, is included in this prohibition. One example is to make mention of God's Name without cause or purpose, a sin which the Sages have cast *in the most serious light, as is demonstrated by the following quotations.*

———— ❧ ————

❧ Poverty and excommunication

Rav Chanin taught in the name of Rav: If one hears his fellow uttering God's Name in vain, he is obliged to excomminicate him. If he fails to do so, he himself is subject to excommunication. For wherever the careless mention of God's Name is prevalent, impoverishment is bound to be found, and poverty is likened to death (*Nedarim* 7b; *Medrash Sechel Tov, Bereishis* §44).

———— ❧ ————

❧ Removal from the world

Anyone who pronounces God's Name in vain is uprooted from the world (*Pesikta Zutrasa, Bereishis* 1:1).

———— ❧ ————

❧ Unjustified existence

It is forbidden for a person to utter the Name of God for no purpose; anyone who does so would be better off had he never been born (*Zohar, Shemos* 87b).

———— ❧ ————

❧ Retribution after death

You shall not take the Name of Hashem, your God, in vain. One may not pronounce the Holy Name without valid purpose; it is sanctioned only in prayer and blessings. One who utters God's Name outside of the context of prayer and blessings is destined to be punished when his soul departs, at which time vengeance will be exacted, as the verse states, *For God will not absolve one who takes His Name in vain* (ibid. 88a).

———— ❧ ————

mong those who count the prohibition against swearing falsely as one of the 613 commandments is *R' Saadiah Gaon* (*Lo Saaseh* §31). This, however, presents a difficulty. According to *R' Saadiah Gaon*, any commandment which we are required to observe anyway, on account of a different commandment, is not counted as one of the 613 commandments. Thus, for example, *R' Saadiah Gaon* does not count the commandment of *You shall love the convert* (*Devarim* 10:19; see *mitzvah* #431) as one of the 613, since we are obligated to love him even without this specific commandment, because of the commandment of *You shall love your fellow as yourself* (*Vayikra* 19:18; see *mitzvah* #243), which applies to Jews in general (see *R' Yeruchem Fischel Perla, Introduction to Sefer HaMitzvos of R' Saadiah Gaon, shoresh* §9 ד"ה אלא). Now, one who swears falsely also transgresses the commandment to fear Hashem (*mitzvah* #432), which forbids taking Hashem's Name in vain (see *Iyunim* §1). Thus, even without a specific prohibition against swearing falsely it is forbidden to do so. Why, then, does *R' Saadiah Gaon* count the prohibition against swearing falsely as a separate commandment of the 613?

Some answer that there are cases in which one transgresses the prohibition against swearing falsely, yet he does not violate the injunction not to take Hashem's Name in vain. It is on account of these scenarios that *R' Saadiah Gaon*

counts the prohibition as one of the 613 (*Commentary of R' Yeruchem Fischel Perla to Sefer HaMitzvos L'RaSag, Aseh* §1, pg. 35 ff, pg. 49 ff). These cases include the following scenarios:

A. *Making a false oath without mention of Hashem's Name*

Some Rishonim maintain that an oath is valid even if it contains no mention of Hashem's Name (see *mitzvah* #225). According to this view, if one swears a false oath without mentioning Hashem's Name, he would be guilty only of swearing falsely, but not of taking Hashem's Name in vain (see, however, *R' Perla* ibid., who notes that *R' Saadiah Gaon* seems to subscribe to the view that an oath is not valid unless it mentions Hashem's Name).

B. *Making a false oath using one of the "subordinate names" [כינויים] of Hashem*

An oath which mentions one of Hashem's "subordinate names" (*kinuyim* — i.e. terms that are not actual Names of Hashem but are used to refer to Him; e.g. the Compassionate One, the Merciful One) is a valid oath (Mishnah, *Shevuos* 35a; *Rambam, Hil. Shevuos* 2:2,3; see *mitzvah* #227). These *kinuyim*, however, do not have the sanctity of actual Names of Hashem, and it is not forbidden to utter them without reason, as it is forbidden to utter the actual Names of Hashem. Thus, one who swears falsely using one of Hashem's *kinuyim* transgresses the prohibition against

מפתח למוני המצוות

THE COUNT OF THE MITZVAH

Baal Halachos Gedolos / Lavin 27
בה"ג / לאוין כז

R' Saadiah Gaon / Lavin 31
רס"ג / לאוין לא

R' Eliyahu HaZakein / Amud 62
ר' אליהו הזקן / עמוד 62

Rashbag / Lo Saaseh Os 10
רשב"ג / לא תעשה אות י

R' Yitzchak El-Bargeloni / Lavin 27
ר"י אלברג'לוני / לאוין כז

Maamar HaSechel / Dibbur Shlishi 1
מאמר השכל / דיבור שלישי א

Sefer Yereim / 244
יראים / קמד

Rambam, Sefer HaMitzvos / Lo Saaseh 32
רמב"ם / לא תעשה לב

Sefer Mitzvos Gadol (Smag) / Lo Saaseh 238
סמ"ג / לא תעשה רלח

Sefer Mitzvos Katan (Smak) / 129
סמ"ק / קכט

Zohar HaRakia / Lavin 9
זוהר הרקיע / לאוין ט

swearing falsely, but is not guilty of taking Hashem's Name in vain.

C. *Agreeing to make a false oath*

The prohibition against swearing falsely forbids not only actually making a false oath, but even *accepting upon oneself* to make an oath one knows to be false (*Mechilta* to *Shemos* 20:7; *Shaarei Teshuvah* 3:45). Clearly, though, one is not guilty of taking Hashem's Name in vain simply for agreeing to make a false oath containing the Name of Hashem. [Note: *Rambam, Tur* and *Shulchan Aruch* do not write the law that it is forbidden to agree to make an oath one knows to be false; for possible reasons for this omission, see *Mirkeves HaMishneh* to *Mechilta* ibid.]

Mitzvah 31

מִצְוַת קִדּוּשׁ
הַשַׁבָּת בִּדְבָרִים
פרשת יתרו

To Sanctify
the Shabbos
with Speech

THE MITZVAH:

MITZVAH 31

מצות קדוש הַשַּׁבָּת בִּדְבָרִים (עֲשֵׂה)

TO SANCTIFY THE SHABBOS WITH SPEECH

מצוה לא

◼ SOURCE ◼

זָכוֹר אֶת יוֹם הַשַּׁבָּת לְקַדְּשׁוֹ שמות (פרשת יתרו) כ:ח

"Remember the day of Shabbos to sanctify it"

◼ THE MITZVAH ◼

One is obligated to sanctify Shabbos by reciting declarations that describe its unique and holy qualities[1] upon its commencement (kiddush) and at its conclusion (havdalah).[2]

◼ LAWS ◼

1 One must recite *kiddush* on Friday evening.[3] If one began Shabbos early, he may recite *kiddush* before nightfall.[4]
   If one did not recite *kiddush* on Friday night, he can do so the following day.[5]

2 One must recite *havdalah* at the conclusion of Shabbos.[6] If one did not do so, he may recite it before Tuesday evening.[7]

3 Biblically, one can fulfill this mitzvah with any declaration that contains praises of Shabbos.[8] However, the Rabbis established specific texts for *kiddush* and *havdalah*.[9]

4 One must mention the Exodus from Egypt in *kiddush*.[10]

5 One fulfills his obligation by hearing *kiddush* or *havdalah*

recited by someone else, provided that both have intent to fulfill the listener's obligation.[11]

6 *Kiddush* and *havdalah* should be recited over a cup of wine;[12] one must drink some of the wine.[13]

7 One must recite *kiddush* where he intends to eat the Shabbos meal, and should begin the meal right after *kiddush*.[14]

8 In addition to the Biblically required *kiddush* on Friday night, the Rabbis instituted *kiddush* on Shabbos day.[15]

9 One must recite *kiddush* and *havdalah* on Yom Tov as well.[16]

10 This mitzvah applies to both men and women, in all places and at all times.[17]

◼ A REASON ◼

Kiddush and havdalah inspire us to reflect upon the greatness of Shabbos. In kiddush, we affirm that God created the world, thereby implanting this belief deep in our hearts. We include wine in the ritual to create a joyous mood, for the faith articulated in these prayers affects us most deeply when expressed in an atmosphere of joy.

IN MEMORY OF ABRAHAM PARKOFF
אברהם בן יצחק דב הכהן ע"ה

---

1. See *Shabbos* 119a, as explained by *Teshuvos HaRashba*, IV:295; *Rambam, Hil. Shabbos* 29:1.

One sanctifies Shabbos in *kiddush* by expressing the holiness of the day and its exalted status; we also mention the Exodus from Egypt [which is cited in the Torah (*Devarim* 5:15) as a reason for the commandment to make Shabbos holy]. The recital of *havdalah* sanctifies Shabbos by highlighting the difference between the holy Shabbos and the other days of the week (*Rambam, Sefer HaMitzvos, Aseh* §155). In addition, the fact that we refrain from any weekday activity until after reciting *havdalah* underscores the sanctity of Shabbos (see *Migdal Oz* to *Rambam, Hil. Shabbos* 29:1). See further below, notes 9 and 10.

Although when the term "remember" is used in Scripture, it often refers to remembering in one's mind, the Torah's directive to "*remember* the day of Shabbos" is understood as commanding us to remember Shabbos with a *verbal* declaration extolling its virtues. A different commandment (*Devarim* 5:12) requires us to always bear the sanctity of Shabbos in mind, stating, "*Guard the day of Shabbos to sanctify it*" — so the commandment to *remember* the day of Shabbos can only be referring to a *verbal* remembrance (*Toras Kohanim, Vayikra* 26:3; see, however, *Pri Megadim, Orach Chaim, Eishel Avraham* 271:2, who suggests that perhaps one *can* fulfill this obligation with a mental remembrance; see also *Shaagas Aryeh* §13).

2. *Pesachim* 106a; *Rambam, Hil. Shabbos* 29:1; *Tur, Orach Chaim* 271:1 and 294:1.

Not all Rishonim agree that *havdalah* is a Biblical obligation. Although many Rishonim maintain that *havdalah* is part of the same Biblical obligation

AN EXPANDED TREATMENT

as *kiddush* (*Rambam, Sefer HaMitzvos, Aseh* §155; *Chinuch* §31; *Smag, Aseh* §29; see also *Mefaresh [Rashi]* to *Nazir* 4a ד"ה והרי), others take the view that *havdalah* is a Rabbinic obligation (see *Rosh* to *Nazir* 4a ד"ה אלימא; *Orchos Chaim, Hil. Shabbos* §18 in the name of *Rash*, cited in *Beis Yosef, Orach Chaim* §296 ד"ה כתוב בארחות חיים; see also *Tosafos* to *Pesachim* 106a ד"ה זוכרהו and *Shevuos* 20b ד"ה נשים, as explained by R' Akiva Eiger in his glosses to *Orach Chaim* 296:4). See *Iyunim* §4.

3. The verse (*Shemos* 20:8) commands us to sanctify Shabbos through verbal declaration; this implies that the declaration should be made when the holiness of Shabbos first arrives [on Friday night] (see *Pesachim* 106a with *Rashbam* and *Ran* there; *Rambam, Hil. Shabbos* 29:1; *Tur, Orach Chaim* 271:1 see *Shulchan Aruch* ibid. with *Magen Avraham* §1).

4. *Berachos* 27b. *Shulchan Aruch, Orach Chaim* 267:2, writes that one may accept upon himself the observance of Shabbos even before nightfall (see *Yoma* 81b), and he may then eat the Shabbos meal. It follows that one may recite *kiddush* before nightfall, for once one begins his observance of Shabbos, one may not eat before reciting *kiddush*. [Although the period before nightfall has the status of Shabbos only on a Rabbinic level, one can nevertheless discharge his Biblical obligation of *kiddush* then (*Mordechai, Megillah* §798). Alternatively, the time that one can accept Shabbos upon himself Rabbinically is close enough to Shabbos to allow fulfillment of the Biblical *kiddush* obligation at that time (*Pri Megadim, Orach Chaim, Mishbetzos Zahav* 271:1). Others maintain that this period is indeed considered Shabbos even on a Biblical level (*Ritva, Berachos* 27a

ד"ה אומר קדושה and 27b ד"ה מדרב צלי *Or Zarua*, vol. II §14).]

Other authorities are of the opinion that *kiddush* is not dependent on the start of Shabbos. They maintain that one can sanctify Shabbos by declaring its praises even *before* Shabbos begins. In their view, one can fulfill his *kiddush* obligation before nightfall even if he did not already accept Shabbos upon himself (*Rambam, Hil. Shabbos* 29:11; *Tos. HaRosh, Berachos* ibid.; *Pri Megadim, Orach Chaim, Mishbetzos Zahav* 271:1; see *Minchas Chinuch* 31:8 and *Pri Megadim* ibid.).

However, some Rishonim disagree completely with the view that one may recite *kiddush* before nightfall. They argue that the Gemara in *Berachos* (27b), which is the source for this view, reflects the view of the Tanna R' Yehudah, who maintains that one may *daven Maariv* from *plag haminchah* [an hour and a quarter before sunset] onward (see ibid. 27a). The custom, however, is not to *daven Maariv* before nightfall, in acceptance of the view of the Rabbis who argue with R' Yehudah. Therefore, they maintain, one should not recite *kiddush* before nightfall either (*Ritz Geios*, cited by *Tur, Orach Chaim*, end of §293; see *Beis Yosef, Orach Chaim* §267 ד"ה ומ"ש רבינו and *Magen Avraham* 267:1; see also *Rif* and *Ran, Pesachim* fol. 21b, who imply that one should not recite *kiddush* before twilight; also see *Shiltei Gibborim* there §2).

5. *Mechilta D'Rabbi Shimon bar Yochai, Shemos* 20:8; see *Pesachim* 105a; *Rambam, Hil. Shabbos* 29:4; *Tur* and *Shulchan Aruch, Orach Chaim* 271:8. However, if one recites the *kiddush* during the Shabbos day, he does not recite the verses of *"Vayechulu"* (*Bereishis* 2:1-3; see below, note 9), as those verses pertain specifically to

Hashem's completion of Creation before the onset of Shabbos (*Orchos Chaim* [R' Aharon MiLunei] *Hil. Kiddush HaYom* §3, citing *Tosafos;* see *Rama*).

The authorities disagree as to the exact nature of this law. Some explain that the obligation to recite *kiddush* extends throughout the entire Shabbos. Thus, although it is *proper* to discharge the *kiddush* obligation as soon as Shabbos begins, if one did not do so, he can fulfill his obligation on Shabbos day as well (*Siddur Rav Amram Gaon* vol. II:15, as explained by *Bach, Orach Chaim* §271). Others maintain that one can fulfill the *kiddush* obligation only on Friday night. However, the Torah allows one to *compensate* for his failure to fulfill the mitzvah by reciting *kiddush* during the day [similar to the law that allows one to compensate for not praying the *Shemoneh Esrei* of *Shacharis* by praying the *Minchah Shemoneh Esrei* twice (see *Shulchan Aruch, Orach Chaim* 108:1)] (*Rambam* ibid., as explained by *Bach* ibid.). [See *Iyunim* §2 for the practical ramifications of this dispute.] Yet others suggest that one who does not recite *kiddush* on Friday night can no longer fulfill the Biblical obligation of *kiddush*. According to this view, the requirement to recite *kiddush* the next day is a Rabbinic innovation, but does not compensate for one's failure to fulfill the mitzvah of *kiddush* on Friday night as mandated by Torah law (see *Minchas Chinuch* 31:9). [Regarding *havdalah*, see below, note 7.]

6. *Rambam, Hil. Shabbos* 29:1.

The Gemara in *Berachos* (27b) states that in cases of necessity, one may recite *havdalah* even before Shabbos has ended. However, many Rishonim maintain that one should recite *havdalah* before the end of Shabbos only if he will not be able to

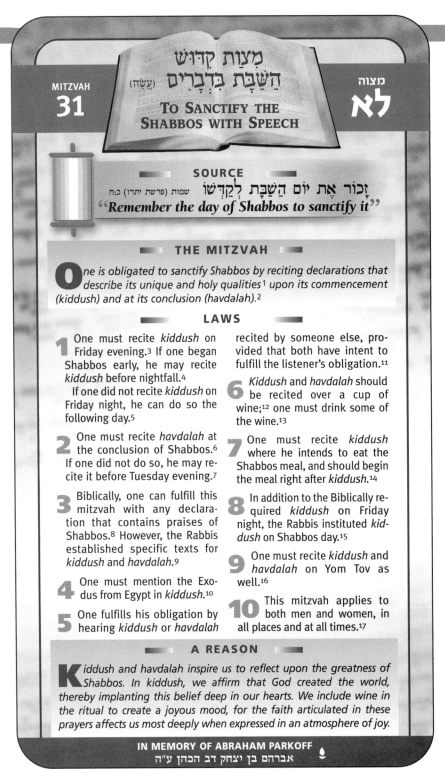

IN MEMORY OF ABRAHAM PARKOFF
אברהם בן יצחק דב הכהן ע"ה

Of course, reciting *havdalah* before nightfall does not remove any of the Shabbos restrictions. These remain in effect until Shabbos has ended (see *Tosafos, Berachos* ibid. ד"ה צלי; *Shulchan Aruch, Orach Chaim* 293:3).

In practice, the Poskim write that one should not recite *havdalah* before nightfall, because it is a custom which appears strange in the eyes of the masses. Moreover, it may lead to the premature performance of activities that are forbidden on Shabbos (see *Maharshal's* glosses to *Tur, Orach Chaim* §293 regarding praying the *Maariv* of Saturday night before nightfall, cited by *Bach, Orach Chaim* ibid., *Magen Avraham* ibid. §4 and *Mishnah Berurah* ibid. §9).

7. The first three days of each week are considered connected to the Shabbos that precedes them, while the period beginning with the fourth day is considered connected to the upcoming Shabbos. Therefore, it is appropriate to say *havdalah* only until (but not on) Tuesday night (*Pesachim* 106a [see also ibid. 107a with *Tosafos* ד"ה אמימר]; *Rambam, Hil. Shabbos* 29:4; *Tur* and *Shulchan Aruch, Orach Chaim* 299:6).

This ruling is not unanimously accepted. Some Rishonim rule that one can recite *havdalah* only until *Sunday* evening (*Rif, Pesachim* fol. 21b, as understood by *Ran* there ד"ה מי שלא הבדיל and *Maggid Mishneh, Hil. Shabbos* 29:4 [see *Chidushei Anshei Shem* to *Rif* ibid. §1, who explains the *Rif* differently]; *Bahag, Hil. Kiddush, Siddur Rav Saadiah Gaon* p. 126; *Ritz Geios* vol. I p.18, in the name of *R' Saadiah Gaon* and *R' Natranai Gaon*, cited by *Tur* ibid.; see also *Shulchan Aruch* ibid.). A third view, cited in *Yerushalmi* (*Berachos* 5:2), maintains that one can recite *havdalah* through *Thursday*.

The same dispute regarding the nature of the law that one who did not recite *kiddush* on Friday night can recite it on Shabbos day (see above,

recite it after Shabbos; for example, if he must travel immediately after Shabbos to perform a mitzvah. Ideally, however, one should not recite *havdalah* until nightfall (*Tosafos, Berachos* ibid. ד"ה צלי; *Rav Hai Gaon* cited by *Hagahos Mordechai, Berachos* §90 and *Tur, Orach Chaim* §293; see also *Rosh* to *Berachos*

4:6). Indeed, it is a mitzvah to extend Shabbos, with all its restrictions, even *past* nightfall (see *Yoma* 81b; *Shulchan Aruch, Orach Chaim* 261:2). Other Rishonim, however, apparently maintain that one may even initially recite *havdalah* before the end of Shabbos (see *Rambam, Hil. Shabbos* 29:11).

note 5) also applies to the law that one can recite *havdalah* through Tuesday (or Sunday) evening. Some maintain that although it is *proper* to recite *havdalah* at the conclusion of Shabbos, the obligation actually extends into the week (see *Maharam Mi-Rothenburg*, cited by *Rosh, Berachos* 3:2 and as explained by *Taz, Yoreh Deah* 396:2). Others are of the opinion that the *havdalah* obligation applies only on *Motza'ei Shabbos*, but that one can compensate for his failure to fulfill this mitzvah by reciting *havdalah* later (see *Rosh* ibid., as explained by *Taz* ibid.). According to a third view, one who does not recite *havdalah* on *Motza'ei Shabbos* has lost the opportunity to fulfill the Biblical mitzvah, but is required by Rabbinic enactment to recite *havdalah* even afterward (*Minchas Chinuch* 31:9; see there at length regarding this issue).

The *havdalah* one recites during the week differs somewhat from that which is recited on *Motza'ei Shabbos*. During the week, one does not recite the blessing over fire which is part of the *Motza'ei Shabbos havdalah* (*Pesachim* 106a; *Rambam, Hil. Shabbos* 29:4; *Tur* and *Shulchan Aruch, Orach Chaim* 299:6). We recite this blessing to commemorate the creation of fire, which took place on the first *Motza'ei Shabbos* (see below, note 9); thus, there is no reason to recite it during the week (*Rashbam, Pesachim* ibid. ד"ה אבל). Similarly, one does not recite a blessing over spices when making *havdalah* during the week (*Tur* and *Shulchan Aruch* ibid.), because the reasons we smell spices during *havdalah* (see below, note 9) apply only on *Motza'ei Shabbos* (*Beis Yosef, Orach Chaim* ibid.).

8. For the verse does not specify a specific text of remembrance (see *Rambam, Sefer HaMitzvos, Aseh* §155 and *Chinuch* 31; *Teshuvos HaRashba*,

IV:295). See further below, notes 9 and 10.

Mechilta (*Shemos* 20:12) states that *kiddush* must consist of a blessing (cited in *Rambam, Sefer HaMitzvos* ibid.; see also *Ritva, Nedarim* 13b). Some maintain that one does not fulfill his Biblical *kiddush* obligation unless the declaration he recites in praise of Shabbos is in the form of a blessing [i.e. it must include the words, "Blessed are You, Hashem, Who sanctifies the Shabbos"] (*Pri Megadim, Orach Chaim* §271, *Mishbetzos Zahav* §1). Others, however, are of the opinion that a declaration in *any* form suffices under Biblical law, and that it is *Rabbinic* law which requires that this declaration take the form of a blessing (*Teshuvos HaRashba* ibid.; *Teshuvos R' Akiva Eiger, Mahadura Kamma* §7; see also *R' Akiva Eiger's* glosses to *Shulchan Aruch, Orach Chaim* 271:2). Even according to the opinion that it was the Rabbis who instituted that the text of *kiddush* must consist of a blessing, it is possible they also decreed that one who does not follow this Rabbinic enactment does not fulfill even his *Biblical* obligation (*Minchas Chinuch* 31:3, based on *Pri Megadim, General Introduction to Orach Chaim*, third section, §8).

9. The Gemara in *Berachos* (33a) states that the *Anshei Knesses HaGedolah* (the group of one hundred and twenty Sages who were the leaders of the Jewish people at the beginning of the Second Temple Era; this group included Ezra, Mordechai, and the prophets Chaggai, Zechariah, and Malachi) established texts for *kiddush* and *havdalah* (see *Meiri* there, and *Teshuvos HaRashba* IV:295). See *Rambam, Hil. Shabbos* 29:2.

It is customary to begin *kiddush* with the first three verses of *Bereishis* ch. 2 [ויכלו השמים וכו'] (*Rambam, Hil. Shabbos* 29:7; *Tur* and *Shulchan*

Aruch, Orach Chaim 271:10). The reason for this practice is that one is required to say these verses as part of the Friday night prayer (see *Shabbos* 119b). By reciting these verses at *kiddush*, one discharges the obligation of those members of his household (e.g. his wife and children) who did not pray the Friday night *Maariv* (*Tosafos* to *Pesachim* 106a ד"ה זוכרהו; *Rosh, Pesachim* 10:15; *Tur, Orach Chaim* §271). The text the Rabbis instituted for *kiddush* includes a mention of the creation of the world [the words זכרון למעשה בראשית, *A remembrance of Creation*]. The Rabbis inserted this reference to Creation into *kiddush* because Shabbos attests to Hashem's creation of the world [it is because Hashem rested on the seventh day of Creation that we are commanded to refrain from work on Shabbos, the seventh day of the week] (*Ramban* to *Devarim* 5:15; *Ravyah,* II:508; see also *Tuv Taam* §1).

The text of *kiddush* also describes Shabbos as תחלה למקראי קדש, *the prologue to the holidays*. This refers to the fact that in *Vayikra* ch. 23, the commandment to observe Shabbos is stated before the commandment to observe the holidays (*Ravyah* ibid., first explanation; *Tur, Orach Chaim* §271). Alternatively, Shabbos is referred to as *the prologue to the holidays* because Shabbos was sanctified during the Seven Days of Creation, whereas the holidays were not sanctified until later (*Ravyah* ibid., second explanation).

Our text of *havdalah* consists of a selection of Scriptural verses, followed by four blessings — one each on wine, spices, and fire, and the *havdalah* blessing itself [see further below] (*Shulchan Aruch, Orach Chaim* 296:1). The Scriptural verses follow a common theme — each speaks of the fact that Hashem is our Savior and guards us from harm. As Shabbos ends and the pressures and challenges of the

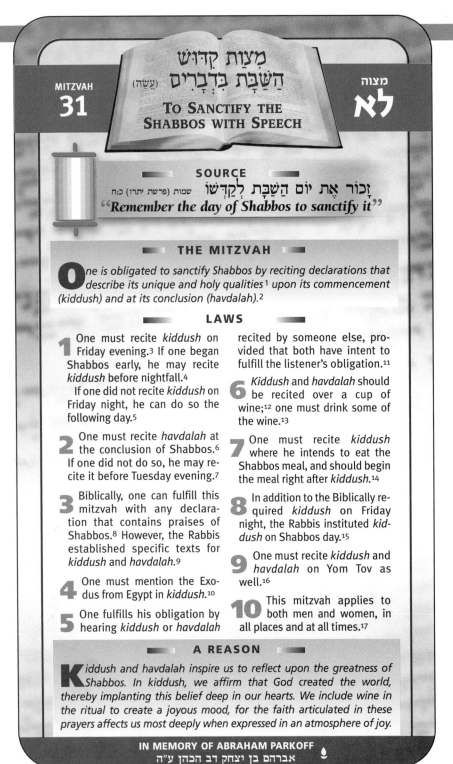

MITZVAH
31

מִצְוַת קִדּוּשׁ
הַשַּׁבָּת בִּדְבָרִים (עשה)

מצוה
לא

To Sanctify the Shabbos with Speech

SOURCE

זָכוֹר אֶת יוֹם הַשַּׁבָּת לְקַדְּשׁוֹ   שמות (פרשת יתרו) כ:ח

"Remember the day of Shabbos to sanctify it"

THE MITZVAH

One is obligated to sanctify Shabbos by reciting declarations that describe its unique and holy qualities[1] upon its commencement (*kiddush*) and at its conclusion (*havdalah*).[2]

LAWS

1 One must recite *kiddush* on Friday evening.[3] If one began Shabbos early, he may recite *kiddush* before nightfall.[4]
If one did not recite *kiddush* on Friday night, he can do so the following day.[5]

2 One must recite *havdalah* at the conclusion of Shabbos.[6] If one did not do so, he may recite it before Tuesday evening.[7]

3 Biblically, one can fulfill this mitzvah with any declaration that contains praises of Shabbos.[8] However, the Rabbis established specific texts for *kiddush* and *havdalah*.[9]

4 One must mention the Exodus from Egypt in *kiddush*.[10]

5 One fulfills his obligation by hearing *kiddush* or *havdalah*

recited by someone else, provided that both have intent to fulfill the listener's obligation.[11]

6 *Kiddush* and *havdalah* should be recited over a cup of wine;[12] one must drink some of the wine.[13]

7 One must recite *kiddush* where he intends to eat the Shabbos meal, and should begin the meal right after *kiddush*.[14]

8 In addition to the Biblically required *kiddush* on Friday night, the Rabbis instituted *kiddush* on Shabbos day.[15]

9 One must recite *kiddush* and *havdalah* on Yom Tov as well.[16]

10 This mitzvah applies to both men and women, in all places and at all times.[17]

A REASON

Kiddush and havdalah inspire us to reflect upon the greatness of Shabbos. In kiddush, we affirm that God created the world, thereby implanting this belief deep in our hearts. We include wine in the ritual to create a joyous mood, for the faith articulated in these prayers affects us most deeply when expressed in an atmosphere of joy.

coming week loom, we strengthen our faith by declaring that Hashem watches over us constantly.

The *havdalah* blessing itself, which is the essence of *havdalah*, was instituted to highlight the "separation" of Shabbos and its holiness (see above, note 2). In this vein, the blessing notes

several "separations" (*havdalos*) that are mentioned in the Torah. They are: (1) the separation between the sacred and the non-sacred (*Vayikra* 10:10); (2) the separation between light and darkness (*Bereishis* 1:4); and (3) the separation between *Klal Yisrael* and the nations [*Vayikra* 20:26] (*Orchos Chaim*,

Hil. Seder Tefillas Motza'ei Shabbos §3). See further, *Pesachim* 103b.

As part of *havdalah*, the Rabbis instituted that one recite a blessing over spices and smell them (*Berachos* 51b; *Rambam, Hil. Shabbos* 29:24; *Tur* and *Shulchan Aruch* 296:1 and 297:1). The reason for smelling spices during *havdalah* is to assuage our sadness at the departure of Shabbos (*Rambam, Hil. Shabbos* 29:29; *Tur* §297), or at the departure of the "additional soul" [נשמה יתרה] that we are granted for the duration of Shabbos [see *Beitzah* 16a] (*Rashbam, Pesachim* 102b ד"ה ושמואל; *Tosafos, Pesachim* ibid. ד"ה רב; *Shibbolei HaLeket* §130, *Orchos Chaim, Hil. Havdalah* §3). Alternatively, the sweet smell of the spices counteracts the foul smell of the fires of *Gehinnom*, which begin to burn on *Motza'ei Shabbos* after having been extinguished for the duration of Shabbos (*Shibbolei HaLeket* ibid., in the name of *Rabbeinu Yaakov bar Yakar; Orchos Chaim,* ibid.; see *Tosafos, Beitzah* ibid.).

The Rabbis also instituted that one make a blessing over fire as part of *havdalah* (*Berachos* ibid.; *Rambam; Hil. Shabbos* 29:24; *Tur* and *Shulchan Aruch, Orach Chaim* 296:1 and 298:1). Most Rishonim explain that the Rabbis instituted this blessing to commemorate the creation of [man-made] fire, which took place on the first *Motza'ei Shabbos* after Creation [see *Pesachim* 54a] (*Ramban, Berachos* 52b; *Rosh, Berachos* 8:3; *Orchos Chaim, Hil. Havdalah* §12 and §16, first explanation; *Tur, Orach Chaim* §298). Others say that we recite this blessing because it was forbidden to light a fire during Shabbos, and now it is permitted (*Orchos Chaim* ibid., second explanation).

10. This is derived through a *gezeirah shavah* that links the verse which commands us to recite *kiddush* (*Shemos* 20:8) with another verse that commands us to remember the Exodus

(*Devarim* 16:3). Both verses use the term זכירה, remembrance (see *Pesachim* 117b with *Rashbam* there; see also *Rambam, Hil. Shabbos* 29:2; for reasons why the Exodus must be mentioned in *kiddush*, see *Tosafos* to *Pesachim* ibid. ד"ה למען, and *Ramban* to *Devarim* 5:14, cited by *Tur, Orach Chaim* §271).

Some say that mentioning the Exodus during *kiddush* is a Biblical requirement (see *Rashbam, Pesachim* ibid. ד"ה צריך שיזכיר; *Minchas Chinuch* 31:5; see also *Rambam, Sefer HaMitzvos, Aseh* §155 [Frankel ed.]). Others imply that it is a requirement instituted by the Rabbis (see *Teshuvos HaRashba* IV:295).

The mention of the Exodus found in the text of *kiddush* reads: *For that day* [i.e. Shabbos] *is the prologue to the holidays, a memorial to the Exodus from Egypt. Rambam* explains that the words *a memorial to the Exodus* refer to Shabbos, which commemorate the Exodus [as it says in *Devarim* 5:15: *And you shall remember that you were a slave in the land of Egypt, and Hashem, your God, has taken you out from there … therefore Hashem, your God, has commanded you to make the day of Shabbos holy*] (*Moreh Nevuchim* part 2 ch. 31; see also *Ramban* to *Devarim* ad loc., cited by *Tur, Orach Chaim* §271). Another opinion maintains that this phrase refers to the holidays; i.e. Shabbos is the prologue to the holidays, which are memorials to the Exodus (*Ravyah*, II:508; *Tur* ibid.).

11. See *Tur* and *Shulchan Aruch, Orach Chaim* 273:4.

This law is based on the principle known as "listening is like responding" [שומע כעונה]; that is, hearing someone else recite a text is the equivalent of reciting that text oneself. See *Rosh Hashanah* 29a-b; *Rambam, Hil. Berachos* 1:10-11; see *Succah* 38b for the Scriptural source for this law. This principle is effective only if

the one listening to the recitation intends to discharge his obligation by listening to the text, *and* the one reciting the text intends to discharge the obligation of the listener (see *Rosh Hashanah* 29a with *Rashi* ד"ה איכוון and *Tos. HaRosh*; *Rambam, Hil. Berachos* 1:11; *Shulchan Aruch, Orach Chaim* 213:3).

The rule of "listening is like responding" applies only if the one reciting the text is himself obligated to recite it. However, in cases like those of *kiddush* and *havdalah*, one can fulfill his obligation by hearing the text recited by another even if that person already discharged his own obligation (see *Rosh Hashanah* ibid.; *Rambam, Hil. Berachos* 1:10). This is because every Jew is obligated to enable other Jews to fulfill their mitzvah obligations, based on the principle that *all Jews are responsible for one another* [כל ישראל ערבין זה בזה]. Thus, even one who already recited *kiddush* is deemed obligated to recite *kiddush* by virtue of the second person's need to perform the mitzvah (see *Rashi* to *Rosh Hashanah* ibid. ד"ה אע"פ). [There is much debate among the authorities regarding whether this principle holds men "responsible" for the mitzvah performance of women. If it does not, then a man would seemingly not be able to discharge the *kiddush* obligation of a woman if he already fulfilled his own obligation. For discussion of this issue, see *Rosh, Berachos* 3:13; *Dagul Me'Rivavah, Orach Chaim* §271, on *Magen Avraham* §2; *Teshuvos R' Akiva Eiger, Mahadura Kamma* §7.]

12. See *Tur* and *Shulchan Aruch, Orach Chaim* 271:10 and 294:1.

The Gemara in *Pesachim* (106a) cites *Shemos* 20:8 as the source for this requirement, expounding the verse: *Remember the day of Shabbos to sanctify it* to mean, *Remember it over a cup of wine*. [The term זכור, *remembering*, is associated with wine in several

verses (*Hoshea* 14:8, *Shir HaShirim* 1:4). Therefore, we interpret the command to "remember" as referring to reciting *kiddush* over wine (*Tosafos, Pesachim* ibid.). In addition, wine is the beverage designated by the Torah as being the most fitting to accompany praises of Hashem — see *Berachos* 35a.] Although this would seem to indicate that the requirement to recite *kiddush* over a cup of wine is of Biblical origin, most Rishonim maintain that it is, in fact, a Rabbinic enactment (*Rambam, Hil. Shabbos* 29:6; *Chinuch* §31) and the Gemara's exposition is merely an *asmachta*, a Scriptural allusion to the Rabbinic edict (*Tosafos, Nazir* 4a ד"ה מאי; *Tosafos* to *Shevuos* 20b ד"ה נשים and to *Pesachim* 106a ד"ה זוכרהו, first explanation; *Ramban* to *Shemos* ad loc.). Others, however, maintain that Biblical law does require that *kiddush* be recited over a cup of wine, as the Gemara's exposition would seem to imply (*Tosafos, Pesachim* ibid. and *Shevuos* ibid. second explanation; *Mefaresh [Rashi], Nazir* 4a ד"ה והרי; see also *Sefer HaPardes, Hil. Havdalah, Shibbolei HaLeket* §130; see also *Rashba, Shabbos* 23b ד"ה הא דאמר, *Ran, Shabbos* fol. 10a ד"ה אמר רבא, and *R' Akiva Eiger* to *Orach Chaim* 271:1). Regarding *havdalah*, the Gemara states in *Berachos* (33a) that it was originally recited as part of the *Maariv* prayer recited at the end of Shabbos (in the form of the prayer "*Atah Chonantanu*" which is inserted into the fourth blessing of *Shemoneh Esrei*). When the financial means of the nation improved, the Sages enacted that it be recited upon wine (in the form described above; see note 9). The Gemara relates that in later times, the situation of the Jews deteriorated once again, and the Sages reverted to requiring *havdalah* during prayer. To avoid constantly having to revise their decree, they then enacted that *havdalah* should always be recited during

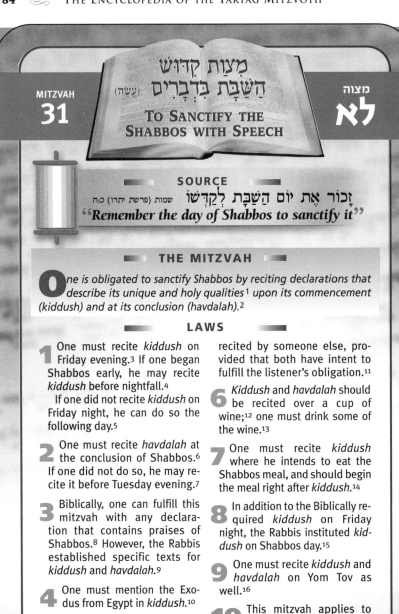

MITZVAH 31

מצות קדוש השבת בדברים (עשה)

TO SANCTIFY THE SHABBOS WITH SPEECH

מצוה לא

SOURCE

זָכוֹר אֶת יוֹם הַשַּׁבָּת לְקַדְּשׁוֹ שמות (פרשת יתרו) כ:ח

"Remember the day of Shabbos to sanctify it"

THE MITZVAH

One is obligated to sanctify Shabbos by reciting declarations that describe its unique and holy qualities[1] upon its commencement (kiddush) and at its conclusion (havdalah).[2]

LAWS

1 One must recite *kiddush* on Friday evening.[3] If one began Shabbos early, he may recite *kiddush* before nightfall.[4]

If one did not recite *kiddush* on Friday night, he can do so the following day.[5]

2 One must recite *havdalah* at the conclusion of Shabbos.[6] If one did not do so, he may recite it before Tuesday evening.[7]

3 Biblically, one can fulfill this mitzvah with any declaration that contains praises of Shabbos.[8] However, the Rabbis established specific texts for *kiddush* and *havdalah*.[9]

4 One must mention the Exodus from Egypt in *kiddush*.[10]

5 One fulfills his obligation by hearing *kiddush* or *havdalah*

recited by someone else, provided that both have intent to fulfill the listener's obligation.[11]

6 *Kiddush* and *havdalah* should be recited over a cup of wine;[12] one must drink some of the wine.[13]

7 One must recite *kiddush* where he intends to eat the Shabbos meal, and should begin the meal right after *kiddush*.[14]

8 In addition to the Biblically required *kiddush* on Friday night, the Rabbis instituted *kiddush* on Shabbos day.[15]

9 One must recite *kiddush* and *havdalah* on Yom Tov as well.[16]

10 This mitzvah applies to both men and women, in all places and at all times.[17]

A REASON

Kiddush and havdalah inspire us to reflect upon the greatness of Shabbos. In kiddush, we affirm that God created the world, thereby implanting this belief deep in our hearts. We include wine in the ritual to create a joyous mood, for the faith articulated in these prayers affects us most deeply when expressed in an atmosphere of joy.

IN MEMORY OF ABRAHAM PARKOFF

אברהם בן יצחק דב הכהן ע"ה

---

which no one has drunk) and still others to the manner in which the cup is held when reciting the blessing (e.g. in the right hand). For details, see *Berachos* 51a, *Rambam, Hil. Shabbos* 29:7,16; and *Tur* and *Shulchan Aruch, Orach Chaim* 271:10. A "cup of blessing" must also contain at least a *revi'is ha'log* (a quarter of a *log*) of wine. There are various opinions regarding the measure of a *revi'is*; the most common opinions range, in modern units, from 2.9 ounces (86 ml.) [*R' Chaim Noeh*] to 5.07 ounces (150 ml.) [*Chazon Ish*].

Some Rishonim maintain that if one cannot obtain wine, or if he prefers bread to wine, he may recite *kiddush* over bread (*Rashi, Pesachim* 114a ד"ה מברך, *Rashbam* ibid. 106b ד"ה דחביבא; see also *Beis Yosef, Orach Chaim* 172:9). Others, however, contend that bread cannot be used for *kiddush* (*Rabbeinu Tam*, in *Tosafos, Pesachim* 106b ד"ה מקדש). All agree that *havdalah* cannot be recited over bread.

The Rishonim also disagree as to whether one can recite *kiddush* over *chamar medinah* [חמר מדינה, lit. *wine of the country*; this refers to the most popular beverage in a given locale, which the populace drinks instead of wine] (*Tur* and *Shulchan Aruch, Orach Chaim* 272:9). All agree, though, that *chamar medinah* is suitable for *havdalah* (*Tur* and *Shulchan Aruch* ibid. 296:2). See further in *Siach Halachah* section.

13. See *Pesachim* 107a; *Rambam, Hil. Shabbos* 29:7; *Tur* and *Shulchan Aruch, Orach Chaim* 271:13. If the one who recited *kiddush* or *havdalah* does not drink the wine himself, but gives it to one of the listeners to drink, this also suffices (see *Rashbam, Pesachim* 105b ד"ה וש"מ המברך צריך שיטעום and 107a ד"ה וטעם; *Tur* and *Shulchan Aruch, Orach Chaim* 271:14; but see *Tur* and *Shulchan Aruch* ibid. for the dissenting opinion of the *Geonim*).

---

prayer, and, whenever possible, over a cup of wine as well (see *Rashba* to *Berachos* ibid., and *Shulchan Aruch HaRav* 294:2).

The cup of wine over which one recites *kiddush* or *havdalah* is referred to as "the cup of blessing" [כוס של ברכה; i.e. a cup over which a blessing is recited]

(see *Maggid Mishneh, Hil. Shabbos* 29:7). There are several laws regarding a "cup of blessing"; some pertain to the condition of the cup (e.g. it cannot be chipped or cracked, and must be washed inside and out before use to ensure that it is clean), others relate to the wine (e.g. it must be wine from

If neither the reciter nor the listeners drink the wine, they have not fulfilled their *kiddush* or *havdalah* obligations, and must repeat *kiddush* or *havdalah* again (see *Pesachim* 107a; see also *Tur* and *Shulchan Aruch* ibid.). Among those who are of the opinion that reciting *kiddush* over wine is a Biblical requirement (see previous note), some maintain that drinking some of the wine is also required by Biblical law (see *Sefer HaPardes, Hil. Kiddush; Mefaresh [Rashi], Nazir* 4a ד"ה הרי; *Shibbolei HaLeket* §130). Others contend that it is only a Rabbinic requirement (*Tosafos* to *Pesachim* 106a ד"ה זוכרהו, and to *Shevuos* 20b ד"ה נשים).

Although the cup of *kiddush* and *havdalah* must contain at least a *revi'is* of wine (see previous note), one is not required to drink more than a "cheekful" [מלא לוגמיו] (*Pesachim* 107a; *Rambam, Hil. Shabbos* 29:7; *Tur* and *Shulchan Aruch, Orach Chaim* 271:13); this measurement is equivalent to the majority of a *revi'is* (*Tur* and *Shulchan Aruch* ibid.).

14. See *Pesachim* 101a; *Rambam, Hil. Shabbos* 29:8; *Shulchan Aruch, Orach Chaim* 273:3 with *Rama*. [This requirement is known as קידוש במקום סעודה; see *Tosafos* to *Pesachim* ibid., who cites as a source the verse (*Yeshayah* 58:13): וקראת לשבת עונג, *and you shall proclaim Shabbos a delight. Tosafos* understand the verse as teaching that the "delight" of Shabbos (i.e. the Shabbos meal) must occur in *the place* where the proclamation was made.] If one does not eat in the place where he made *kiddush* (for example, he made *kiddush* in one house and then went to another house to eat the Shabbos meal), he has not fulfilled his obligation and must repeat *kiddush*.

Some Rishonim maintain that this requirement is a Rabbinic edict. Thus, one who does not fulfill this requirement has nevertheless discharged his

kiddush obligation on the *Biblical* level (*Rabbeinu Yonah*, cited by *Rosh, Pesachim* 10:5). Others contend that *Biblical* law requires that one eat in the place he recited *kiddush*, and that one who does not do so does not fulfill even his Biblical *kiddush* obligation (*Rosh* ibid., as understood by *R' Akiva Eiger* [glosses to *Orach Chaim* 263:1]; however, *Pri Megadim* [*Orach Chaim, Mishbetzos Zahav* 269:1] explains that *Rosh* actually subscribes to the view of *Rabbeinu Yonah* that the *Rabbis* enacted this requirement, but argues that as part of this edict the Rabbis decreed that one who does not fulfill this requirement has not discharged even his *Biblical* obligation).

15. See *Pesachim* 106a; *Rambam, Hil. Shabbos* 29:10; *Tur* and *Shulchan Aruch, Orach Chaim* 289:1; see also *Rambam* to *Shemos* 20:8.

The daytime *kiddush* is known as *Kiddusha Rabbah*, "the Great Kiddush" (*Pesachim* ibid., for explanations of this name, see *Rashbam* and *Ran* ibid.). In contrast to the nighttime *kiddush*, the Rabbis did not establish a text for *Kiddusha Rabbah*; one need merely recite the appropriate blessing for drinking wine [*borei pri hagafen*], and drink some of the wine (*Pesachim* ibid.). It is customary, however, to recite various Scriptural verses related to Shabbos before the *borei pri hagafen* blessing; many recite all or part of the passage in *Shemos* that commands us to remember Shabbos (*Shemos* 20:8-11); others add the passages in *Shemos* pertaining to the observance of Shabbos that are mentioned together with the commandment to build the *Mishkan* (*Shemos* 31:16-17), and still others begin with passages mentioning the reward in store for those who observe Shabbos (*Yeshayah* 58:13-14). There are Rishonim (*Talmidei Rabbeinu Yonah, Berachos* 36b ד"ה וברכת; see *Tur* and *Beis Yosef, Orach Chaim* 291:4) who

maintain that according to *Rambam* (*Hil. Shabbos* 30:9), one must also recite this *kiddush* before *seudah shlishis*, the third meal eaten on Shabbos. However, *Tur* (*Orach Chaim* 291) and *Beis Yosef* (there ד"ה וכתב הרמב"ם) cite many Rishonim who maintain that there is no *kiddush* for the third meal, and *Shulchan Aruch* (291:4) concurs with their view.

The Rishonim suggest various explanations for why the Rabbis enacted a requirement to recite a blessing over wine on Shabbos day. Some explain that by reciting a blessing over wine — the beverage designated for singing the praises of Hashem (see *Berachos* 35a) — before beginning the Shabbos meal, we distinguish this meal from those of the weekdays, thus honoring the Shabbos (*She'iltos* of *R' Achai Gaon* §54; *Rashbam* to *Pesachim* ibid. ד"ה אמר; see also *Chidushei Rabbeinu Dovid* and *Maharam Chalavah* ibid.). [Thus, although the daytime *kiddush* makes no mention of Shabbos, it actually fulfills the same function as the Friday night *kiddush*, demonstrating the uniqueness of Shabbos (*Ran* to *Pesachim*, fol. 22a ד"ה זכרהו, second explanation).] Others say that this blessing over wine corresponds to the blessing over wine recited as part of the Friday night *kiddush*. They explain that the Rabbis considered it appropriate to enact a *kiddush* obligation for the day, similar to the Biblical obligation of Friday night. However, they deemed it sufficient to institute an abridged version of the Friday night *kiddush*, consisting only of the first blessing of that text, which is the blessing over wine (*Ran* to *Pesachim* ibid., first explanation).

16. See *Pesachim* 104a and 105a; *Tosefta, Berachos* 3:12; *Rambam, Hil. Shabbos* 29:18; *Tur* and *Shulchan Aruch, Orach Chaim* 473:1; 643:1.

Most authorities maintain that the *kiddush* and *havdalah* obligations

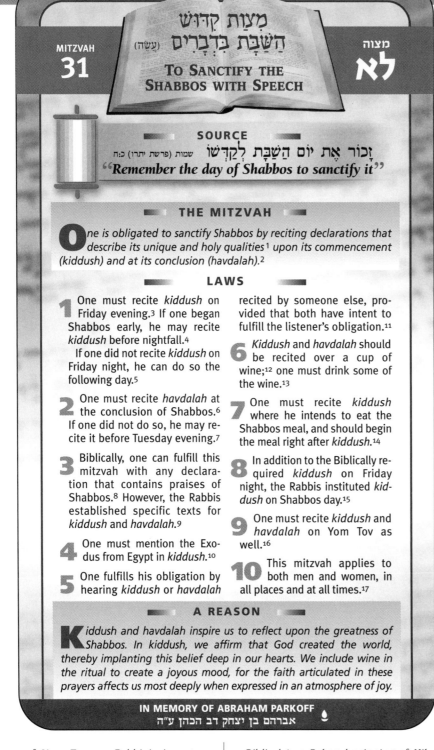

מצות קדוש
הַשַּׁבָּת בִּדְבָרִים (עֲשֵׂה)

מצוה **לא**

TO SANCTIFY THE SHABBOS WITH SPEECH

SOURCE

שמות (פרשת יתרו) כ:ח זָכוֹר אֶת יוֹם הַשַּׁבָּת לְקַדְּשׁוֹ

"Remember the day of Shabbos to sanctify it"

THE MITZVAH

One is obligated to sanctify Shabbos by reciting declarations that describe its unique and holy qualities[1] upon its commencement (kiddush) and at its conclusion (havdalah).[2]

LAWS

1 One must recite *kiddush* on Friday evening.[3] If one began Shabbos early, he may recite *kiddush* before nightfall.[4]
If one did not recite *kiddush* on Friday night, he can do so the following day.[5]

2 One must recite *havdalah* at the conclusion of Shabbos.[6] If one did not do so, he may recite it before Tuesday evening.[7]

3 Biblically, one can fulfill this mitzvah with any declaration that contains praises of Shabbos.[8] However, the Rabbis established specific texts for *kiddush* and *havdalah*.[9]

4 One must mention the Exodus from Egypt in *kiddush*.[10]

5 One fulfills his obligation by hearing *kiddush* or *havdalah*

recited by someone else, provided that both have intent to fulfill the listener's obligation.[11]

6 *Kiddush* and *havdalah* should be recited over a cup of wine;[12] one must drink some of the wine.[13]

7 One must recite *kiddush* where he intends to eat the Shabbos meal, and should begin the meal right after *kiddush*.[14]

8 In addition to the Biblically required *kiddush* on Friday night, the Rabbis instituted *kiddush* on Shabbos day.[15]

9 One must recite *kiddush* and *havdalah* on Yom Tov as well.[16]

10 This mitzvah applies to both men and women, in all places and at all times.[17]

A REASON

Kiddush and havdalah inspire us to reflect upon the greatness of Shabbos. In kiddush, we affirm that God created the world, thereby implanting this belief deep in our hearts. We include wine in the ritual to create a joyous mood, for the faith articulated in these prayers affects us most deeply when expressed in an atmosphere of joy.

specific period of time (see *Kiddushin* 29a). *Kiddush*, though, is an exception to this rule; although it certainly qualifies as a time-bound positive mitzvah, women are Biblically obligated in *kiddush* just as men are. This is derived from the commandment in *Devarim* 5:12 to "*guard* the day of Shabbos to sanctify it," which parallels the commandment in *Shemos* 20:8 to "*remember* the day of Shabbos to sanctify it," the source for the *kiddush* obligation. The commandment to "guard the day of Shabbos" is a negative commandment, which forbids the performance of various activities on Shabbos. As such, it applies equally to men and women. The Gemara expounds: Whoever is included in the commandment to "guard the day of Shabbos" is also included in the parallel commandment to "remember the day of Shabbos" [by reciting *kiddush*] (*Berachos* 20b; see *Rambam, Hil. Avodah Zarah* 12:3; *Tur* and *Shulchan Aruch, Orach Chaim* 271:2; see *Iyunim* §4 regarding whether women are Biblically obligated in *havdalah* as they are in *kiddush*).

There is some question as to whether women are similarly obligated in the *kiddush* of Yom Tov. For discussion of this issue, see *Ravyah* I:61; *Minchas Chinuch* 31:18; *Teshuvos R' Akiva Eiger, Mahadura Kamma,* addendum to §1; *Teshuvos Yad Eliyahu (Rav Eliyahu Rogoler), Pesakim* §17; and *Shulchan Aruch HaRav, Orach Chaim* 271:5.

of Yom Tov are Rabbinic in nature (*Maggid Mishneh, Hil. Shabbos* 29:18, cited by *Magen Avraham* 271:1 and *Mishnah Berurah* 271:2; see also *Shaagas Aryeh* §13, who writes that this is also the view of *Rashi*). However, based on *Mechilta* (*Shemos* 20:12), some say that these obligations are

Biblical (see *Bahag,* beginning of *Hil. Kiddush V'Havdalah; Shitah Mekubetzes, Beitzah* 4b ד"ה והא; see also *Minchas Chinuch* 31:16 regarding the view of *Rambam*).

17. Women are normally exempt from positive mitzvos that are tied to a

A BROADER LOOK AT THE LAWS

1   *Does one fulfill his kiddush obligation with the Maariv prayer of Friday night?*

As mentioned above (Law 3; see note 8), according to Biblical law any declaration extolling the virtues of Shabbos suffices to fulfill the mitzvah of *kiddush*. The requirement to follow a specific text for *kiddush* is a Rabbinic enactment. Similarly, most Rishonim maintain that Biblical law also does not require that *kiddush* be recited over a cup of wine (see Laws, note 12). Nor, according to some Rishonim, does Biblical law mandate that one eat the Shabbos meal in the place he recited *kiddush* (see ibid. note 14). Accordingly, there are those who maintain that one fulfills his *kiddush* obligation, at least on the Biblical level, by praying the Friday night *Maariv Shemoneh Esrei*, which contains numerous references to the holiness and uniqueness of Shabbos (*Magen Avraham, Orach Chaim* 271:1; *Pnei Yehoshua to Berachos* 51b ד"ה במשנה; see also *Dagul Me'Rivavah to Magen Avraham,* 271:2). [Indeed, some say that one fulfills his Biblical *kiddush* obligation simply by saying "Good Shabbos" (glosses of *R' Akiva Eiger to Magen Avraham* ibid. ד"ה וכן משמע).]

Many authorities, however, disagree with this assertion. These authorities offer several reasons why one does not fulfill his *kiddush* obligation with the Friday night *Shemoneh Esrei*:

A. Many Rishonim rule that מצות צריכות כוונה, *mitzvos require intent*; i.e. in order to discharge an obligation imposed by the Torah, one must specifically intend to fulfill that mitzvah when he performs the mitzvah act (*Bahag, Hil. Berachos* ch. 2; *Rosh, Rosh Hashanah* 3:11; *Ramban* in *Milchemes Hashem, Rosh Hashanah* fol. 7a ד"ה ועוד; see also *Shulchan Aruch, Orach Chaim* 60:4, who rules in accordance with this view). If so, one does not discharge his *kiddush* obligation by praying *Maariv*, because [presumably] he does not intend to fulfill the mitzvah of *kiddush* at this

time (*Minchas Chinuch* 31:11; *Mishnah Berurah* 271:2).

B. Moreover, even those Rishonim who rule that *mitzvos do **not** require intent* (see *Rashba to Rosh Hashanah* 28b; *Geonim*, cited by *Beis Yosef, Orach Chaim* §589 ד"ה וצריך) agree that if one intends to fulfill a *different* mitzvah with this act, he does not fulfill the mitzvah for which he does not have intent (*Ran to Rosh Hashanah* fol. 9b ד"ה ואין). Since the intent one has when praying is to fulfill the mitzvah of prayer, not of *kiddush*, he does not discharge his *kiddush* obligation (*Minchas Chinuch* ibid.; see also *Teshuvos Chasam Sofer, Orach Chaim* §21).

C. Many Rishonim maintain that according to Biblical law, one must mention the Exodus from Egypt as part of *kiddush* (see Law 4 with note 10). The Friday night *Shemoneh Esrei* contains no mention of the Exodus. Therefore, it does not satisfy even the Biblical requirements for *kiddush* (*Minchas Chinuch* 31:5; see *Beur Halachah* to 271:1, who also raises this difficulty with the view of *Magen Avraham* et al., and suggests possible resolutions). [Note: This reason does not suffice when Yom Tov falls out on a Shabbos, because the *Shemoneh Esrei* of Yom Tov does refer to the Exodus.]

D. Even if the Friday night *Shemoneh Esrei* does fulfill all the Biblical requirements of *kiddush*, once the Rabbis enacted that one must fulfill the mitzvah in a specific manner and with a specific text, one cannot fulfill even his *Biblical* obligation if he does not follow the Rabbinically mandated form of *kiddush* (*Minchas Chinuch* 31:3, based on *Tosafos to Succah* 3a ד"ה דאמר and to *Berachos* 11a ד"ה תני; *Pri Megadim, Orach Chaim, Eishel Avraham* 271:1, *Mishbetzos Zahav* 269:1 and in his *General Introduction* 3:8).

2   *Reciting kiddush on Shabbos day or havdalah after Motza'ei Shabbos*

As noted above, the authorities disagree as to the nature of the law that one who did not recite *kiddush* on Friday night may recite it during Shabbos day

(Law 1). Some explain that the obligation to recite *kiddush* extends throughout the entire Shabbos, and not just on Friday night. Others say that one can fulfill the mitzvah of *kiddush* only on Friday night, and liken the law that one can recite it during Shabbos day to the law that one who did not pray *Shacharis* can compensate for his failure to fulfill his prayer obligation by praying *Minchah* twice (see note 5). This same dispute applies to the law that one who did not recite *havdalah* can recite it until the following Tuesday evening (Law 2; see note 7). Following are some of the practical ramifications of this dispute:

A. If one was exempt from mitzvos on *Motza'ei Shabbos* (for example, a minor, or an אונן, *onen* [one who suffered the loss of one of his close relatives that day]; an *onen* is not obligated in positive commandments), but not by the following Tuesday — According to those that hold the *havdalah* obligation extends until Tuesday evening, this person is obligated to recite *havdalah*. If, however, the obligation lasts only through *Motza'ei Shabbos*, he is not obligated (nor may he) recite *havdalah*. Since he was not obligated on *Motza'ei Shabbos*, so there is no requirement for him to compensate for a failure to fulfill a mitzvah from which he was exempt (see *Rosh, Berachos* 3:2; *Taz, Yoreh Deah* 396:2; see *Rosh, Taanis* 4:40 regarding years when *Tishah B'Av* falls on Sunday, in which case one cannot recite *havdalah* [as Rabbinically mandated, over a cup of wine] on *Motza'ei Shabbos*).

B. If one deliberately refrained from reciting *kiddush* on Friday night or *havdalah* on *Motza'ei Shabbos* — The concept of "compensating" for not fulfilling a mitzvah applies only to one whose failure to perform the mitzvah was unintentional; i.e. either he forgot to fulfill the mitzvah, or he was unable to do so due to circumstances beyond his control. One who *deliberately* refrains from fulfilling a mitzvah, however, cannot compensate for his failure to fulfill the mitzvah (see *Berachos* 26a; *Rambam,*

Hil. Tefillah 3:8; *Tur, Orach Chaim* 108:1,7 and *Shulchan Aruch* there). Thus, if reciting *kiddush* on Shabbos day, or *havdalah* after *Motza'ei Shabbos*, is a means of compensating for one's failure to fulfill these obligations, one who intentionally neglected to recite *kiddush* or *havdalah* in its proper time would not be able to recite it later. If, however, these obligations extend past Friday night and *Motza'ei Shabbos* respectively, even one who deliberately refrained from fulfilling his obligation when he should have done so can still fulfill it later (*Bach, Orach Chaim* §271; see also *Teshuvos Chasam Sofer, Orach Chaim* §17).

3   *The law when one did not recite havdalah on Motza'ei Yom Tov*

The authorities disagree as to the law that applies if one did not recite *havdalah* on *Motza'ei* Yom Tov. Some maintain that he can no longer recite *havdalah*. They explain that the reason one can recite the Shabbos *havdalah* until Tuesday evening is that the three days following Shabbos are still related to that Shabbos. [The *fourth* day ushers in the approach of the *following* Shabbos, and is not connected with the Shabbos that just passed (see *Gittin* 77a, and *Rashbam* to *Pesachim* 106a ד"ה עד רביעי).] This is not the case with Yom Tov; thus, one who does not recite *havdalah* at the conclusion of Yom Tov cannot recite it later (*Chochmas Shlomo, Orach Chaim* 299:6; *Teshuvos Zera Emes*, III:51). Others maintain that the law regarding the Yom Tov *havdalah* is the same as the law regarding the Shabbos *havdalah,* and one can recite *havdalah* up to three days after Yom Tov (*Teshuvos She'eilas Yaavetz*, I:168; see also *Teshuvos Chasam Sofer, Yoreh Deah* §203). A third view is even more lenient regarding the Yom Tov *havdalah* than regarding the *havdalah* of Shabbos. This view allows reciting the Yom Tov *havdalah* the entire week, until the following Shabbos (see *Birkei Yosef, Orach Chaim* §491; see also *Teshuvos Binyan Shlomo*, addendum §18).

4　Are women obligated in havdalah?

One of the ramifications of the dispute as to whether *havdalah* is a Biblical or a Rabbinic obligation (see above, note 1) concerns whether or not women are obligated in *havdalah*. As noted above (Law 10), women are obligated in *kiddush* even though it is a mitzvah which is tied to a specific time (Shabbos), and women are generally exempt from such time-bound commandments (see note 17). According to those who maintain that *havdalah* is part of the Biblical commandment to "remember the day of Shabbos," which is the source of the *kiddush* obligation, women are thus obligated in *havdalah* just as they are obligated in *kiddush* (*Maggid Mishneh, Hil. Shabbos* 29:1; *Meiri, Berachos* 20b, first view). However, if *havdalah* is a Rabbinic obligation, there are those who maintain that women are exempt, just as they are exempt from most time-bound commandments (*Orchos Chaim* ibid. as explained by *Bach, Orach Chaim* end of §296). [Others maintain, however, that even if *havdalah* is a Rabbinic obligation, the Rabbis patterned it on the Biblical *kiddush* obligation, and decreed that women are obligated in *havdalah* (*Ritva* to *Pesachim* 54a; *Meiri* to *Berachos* ibid., second view).] *Shulchan Aruch* (*Orach Chaim* 296:8) cites both the view that women are obligated in *havdalah* and the view that they are exempt (see *Mishnah Berurah* there §34).

SITUATIONS IN HALACHAH

Question:

If a person has no wine or is unable to drink wine, how should he fulfill the mitzvah of *kiddush*?

Answer:

As we have explained (Law 6), the Sages decreed that *kiddush* and *havdalah* must be recited over a cup of wine or grape juice. If a person has no wine or cannot drink wine (because it makes him ill — see *Mishnah Berurah* 272:32, with *Beur Halachah* ד"ה ואם יין), his law is as follows:

On Friday night: He recites the *kiddush* over bread [even if all he has is part of a loaf — see *Mishnah Berurah* 274:2] and simply substitutes the blessing of *hamotzi* for the usual *hagafen* blessing. The other segments of the *kiddush* recitation are unchanged (see *Shulchan Aruch, Orach Chaim* 272:9). [For details on how one performs the recitation of *kiddush* over bread, see *Mishnah Berurah* 271:41, 272:28.]

If the person has no bread, he recites the Friday night *kiddush* over *chamar medinah*, literally, *wine of the country*, which is the beverage (other than water) that serves as the predominant drink of that place (*Shulchan Aruch* ibid. 272:9, with *Mishnah Berurah* §24-25, 27 and *Beur Halachah* there). As its name implies, the *chamar medinah* designation varies according to one's country of residence. That which is considered *chamar medinah* in one place might not possess this status in another. When using *chamar medinah*, one recites the blessing of *shehakol* instead of the *hagafen* blessing. [The precise definition of *chamar medinah* is not entirely clear; see *Mishnah Berurah* ibid.; *Beur Halachah* ibid.; *Mishnah Berurah* 296:9 and 483:11; see also *Igros Moshe, Orach Chaim* II:75, who states that the beverage must be one that one would serve in honor of an esteemed guest. One who wishes to recite *kiddush* over a beverage other than wine or grape

juice should consult a Rabbinic authority to determine whether the beverage in question is considered *chamar medinah*.]

If the person has neither wine, bread, nor *chamar medinah*, his law is as follows: If he knows he will eventually be able to obtain something suitable for *kiddush*, he must wait until he obtains the necessary item; he may not taste food or drink until he recites *kiddush*. If he feels too weak to go without food for that length of time, or if he knows he will not be able to obtain the item before midnight (*chatzos*), he is not required to wait, and may eat at once. When he does obtain wine or bread [or *chamar medinah*] later that night, he recites the *kiddush* and eats at least an olive's volume (a *kezayis*) of bread or other baked goods [e.g. cake, cookies] (*Mishnah Berurah* 289:10).

On Shabbos day: One substitutes a *chamar medinah* beverage for wine. If one has no *chamar medinah*, he may use bread (*Shulchan Aruch* ibid.). One simply recites *hamotzi* over the bread [even if all he has is part of a loaf] and eats his meal. Until then, one is forbidden to eat or drink. If one has neither wine, *chamar medinah*, nor bread, one may eat the meal without *kiddush* (*Mishnah Berurah* ibid.). [Although we customarily recite certain Scriptural verses before Shabbos morning *kiddush* (see *Mishnah Berurah* 289:2), these should not be recited when *kiddush* is made over bread. Since they are not mandatory, they constitute an interruption between the washing of one's hands and the *hamotzi* blessing.]

It emerges that on Friday night, bread is preferable to *chamar medinah*, whereas on Shabbos day, *chamar medinah* is preferable to bread. The authorities explain that all things being equal, bread is a better choice for *kiddush* than *chamar medinah*. This is because bread is the main component of the Shabbos meal, which is eaten in honor of Shabbos. It stands to reason that the Shabbos *kiddush* [which proclaims the honor of Shabbos] should be recited over a food that is eaten in honor of Shabbos (*Tur* §272; *Mishnah Berurah* ad loc. §27). Furthermore, bread is itself a necessary part of *kiddush*, whose validity depends upon its being followed immediately by the Shabbos meal. Therefore, where there is no wine, the *kiddush* is recited over bread (*Mishnah Berurah* 296:7; see Law 7 and note 14). Why then is *chamar medinah* preferred on Shabbos day? It is because the *kiddush* of Shabbos morning has no special blessing; rather, we simply recite the usual blessing for the food or beverage being used — i.e. *hagafen, shehakol* or *hamotzi.* When wine is used, it is immediately evident that the *hagafen* blessing serves also as a *kiddush* recitation, because one would not ordinarily drink wine just prior to a meal. Where, however, one substitutes bread for wine, it is not immediately evident that the blessing over the bread serves a *kiddush* purpose too, since bread is *always* eaten as part of one's meal. To ensure that the *kiddush* recitation would be noticed, the Sages instituted *chamar medinah* as the first choice to substitute for wine. Because the beverage precedes the meal, it is clearly intended as a fulfillment of the *kiddush* obligation (*Shulchan Aruch* ibid. 272:9). The Friday night *kiddush,* by contrast, contains a special blessing formulated specifically for *kiddush.* One who recites *kiddush* over bread recites this blessing along with the *hamotzi* blessing. Although the bread is eaten as part of one's meal, this blessing ensures that its *kiddush* aspect will be recognized. Therefore, on Friday night, bread is given preference over *chamar medinah* (ibid.).

Another reason to differentiate between the *kiddush* of Friday night and that of Shabbos day is that some Rishonim maintain that *chamar medinah* is altogether invalid for the Friday night *kiddush.* Out of concern for this view, the Poskim rule that if possible, it is better to use bread on Friday night (*Mishnah Berurah* 272:27).

The measure required for *chamar medinah* is the same as for wine. Thus, one who recites *kiddush* over a *chamar medinah* beverage must use a minimum of one *revi'is* of the beverage, and must drink the equivalent of one cheekful (see *Mishnah Berurah* ibid. §30). For discussion of the measure required when reciting *kiddush* over whiskey on Shabbos morning, see *Teshuvos Maharsham,* vol. 1, §175; *Eishel Avraham, Orach Chaim* §272, to *Magen Avraham* §6; *Mishnah Berurah* ibid.

Question:

How should one who has no wine fulfill the mitzvah of *havdalah*?

Answer:

One who has no wine may recite *havdalah* over a *chamar medinah* beverage (*Shulchan Aruch* ibid. 296:2, with *Mishnah Berurah* §8). If he has no such beverage, his law depends upon the following variables: If he knows that he will be able to obtain *chamar medinah* before midday (*chatzos*) on Sunday, he must wait until then to recite *havdalah.* In that case, he must refrain from eating or drinking until his midday recitation, as consumption of food and drink is forbidden before *havdalah* (*Shulchan Aruch* ibid. 299:1). If, however, he knows that he will be unable to obtain a *chamar medinah* beverage before midday on Sunday, or if he is weak and cannot wait until then to eat, he may eat immediately, since he has in any case recited *havdalah* in the *Maariv* prayer [אתה חוננתנו] (ibid. 296:3, with *Mishnah Berurah* §17). If he manages to obtain wine or *chamar medinah* later in the week, he must recite *havdalah* then (*Mishnah Berurah* ibid.), provided it is not yet Tuesday night (*Shulchan Aruch* ibid. 299:6). *Havdalah* may never be recited over bread (*Shulchan Aruch* ibid. 296:2).

THE BLESSING FOR THE MITZVAH — ברכת המצוה

he Sages did not institute a blessing to be recited before performing the mitzvah of *kiddush* as they did for most positive commandments. Although this mitzvah differs from most other mitzvos in that it only entails reciting a text, this cannot be the reason why the Sages did not institute a blessing for it; for there are a number of mitzvos that consist only of reciting words, such as the mitzvah of *Sefiras Ha'Omer* or that of reciting *Hallel*, and yet require blessings. [The same question may be asked regarding the mitzvah of *havdalah*, which, according to *Rambam* and *Chinuch,* is included in the mitzvah of *kiddush*.] There are several explanations why no blessing is recited before this mitzvah; some of which were suggested to account for the absence of blessings in the case of certain other mitzvos, and apply here as well.

A. The blessing of kiddush itself serves as the blessing for the mitzvah:

Some Rishonim maintain that there is, in fact, a blessing for the mitzvah of *kiddush*. They consider the text of *kiddush*, which the Sages formulated as a blessing, to also be the blessing for this mitzvah (see *Meiri, Pesachim* 7a ד"ה ודברים). [This contention is supported by the version of *kiddush* cited by the Gemara (*Pesachim* 117b), which includes the words: "Who has sanctified us with His mitzvos, and commanded us, etc., the standard form of blessings recited before performing a mitzvah." [Our version of *kiddush* does not contain these words. However, *Meiri* (ibid.) explains that this is only because these words are part of the formula for a "short blessing" [ברכה קצרה] (i.e. a blessing which begins but does not end with the phrase, "Blessed are You, Hashem"), and *kiddush* consists of a "lengthy blessing" [ברכה ארוכה] (i.e. one which

both begins and ends with the phrase, "Blessed are You, Hashem").]

B. Hashem's Name is mentioned in kiddush:

Some Rishonim explain that the reason no blessing is recited before performing the mitzvah of reciting the *Shema* is that the purpose of reciting a blessing before performing a mitzvah is to demonstrate that by performing the mitzvah we are subjugating ourselves to Hashem's rulership [by fulfilling His commandments]. Since the first verse of the *Shema* embodies the concept of accepting Hashem's sovereignty, a blessing for this mitzvah would be superfluous (*Abudraham, Commentary to Tefillas Shacharis — Krias Shema;* see also *Ritva, Pesachim* 7b). Similarly, any mitzvah which by its very nature demonstrates Hashem's sovereignty does not require a blessing. By the same token, a mitzvah which entails mentioning Hashem's Name does not require a blessing, since the very mention of Hashem demonstrates that we are performing the mitzvah to fulfill His will. For this reason, no blessing is required for the mitzvos of recounting the story of the Exodus from Egypt [which proves Hashem's omnipotence] and *Birchas HaMazon* [the text of which contains numerous mentions of Hashem's Name] (*Teshuvos D'var Moshe, Orach Chaim* III:6; *Simchas HaRegel* [*Chida's* commentary to *Haggadah shel Pesach*]). Since the text of *kiddush* also contains Hashem's Name, the Sages did not institute an additional blessing to be recited for fulfilling the mitzvah.

C. We do not recite a blessing for the mitzvah of reciting a blessing:

Some Acharonim suggest that the reason the Sages did not institute blessings for the mitzvos of recounting the story of the Exodus and *Birchas HaMazon* is that these mitzvos themselves contain blessings, and the Sages did not institute a blessing for any mitzvah which is itself performed by reciting a blessing. Had they not established this rule, they would have been compelled to institute a blessing for the mitzvah of reciting a blessing for a mitzvah (reciting a blessing for a mitzvah is itself a Rabbinic mitzvah), and an additional blessing for the mitzvah of reciting *that* blessing, resulting in an endless number of blessings (*Maaseh Nissim* [*R' Yaakov MiLisa's* commentary to *Haggadah shel Pesach*] p. 7; *Beis David, Orach Chaim* §83). This also explains why the Sages did not institute a blessing for the mitzvah of *kiddush*, since the text of *kiddush* contains a blessing.

D. *It is a mitzvah which requires no action:*

Although the Sages did institute a blessing for mitzvos which only require the act of speech, they did not institute a blessing for mitzvos which require no action whatsoever, such as the mitzvah of relinquishing loans during *shemittah* (*Teshuvos* of *Ri ben Pelet*, cited by *Rashba* in his *Teshuvos* 1:18 and *Teshuvos HaMeyuchasos LaRamban* [attributed to *Ramban* but actually authored by *Rashba*] §189; *Abudraham, Shaar* 3; *Orchos Chaim* of *R' Aharon MiLunei, Hil. Berachos* §72; *Rabbeinu Manoach* in his commentary to *Rambam, Hil. Berachos* 11:2; see also *Beis Yosef, Orach Chaim* §432, who explains that this is the reason no blessing is recited for the mitzvah of nullifying *chametz*). Although most Rishonim imply that one can fulfill the mitzvah of *kiddush* only by reciting the words of the text, some Acharonim maintain that even thinking the words of *kiddush* suffices to fulfill one's Biblical obligation (*Pri Megadim, Orach Chaim, Eishel Avraham* 271:2; *Kaf HaChaim, Orach Chaim* 271:10; see also *Teshuvos Shaagas Aryeh* §13). According to this view, *kiddush* is a mitzvah which requires no action, so the Sages did not institute a blessing for it.

ILLUMINATIONS OF THE MITZVAH
Suggested Reasons & Insights

I. INSTILLING FAITH IN THE WORLD'S CREATION

habbos is a testimonial to the fact that *for six days God made the Heavens and the earth, the sea and all that is in them, and He rested on the seventh day* (Shemos 20:11). Accordingly, the Torah prescribes the recital of *kiddush* as a way to give expression to the concept of Shabbos, arouse contemplation of the day's significance and establish in our hearts belief in the world's Creation (*Sefer HaChinuch* §31), for an idea that is repeatedly articulated is not easily forgotten (*Radvaz, Ta'amei HaMitzvos* §91; cf. *Derashos HaRan* §5). The words are recited over a cup of wine, for wine gladdens the heart, making one more receptive to the meaning of this ritual (*Chinuch* ibid.; see also above, note 12).

[It is customary to preface the *kiddush* with the Scriptural passage beginning with "*Vayechulu*" (*Rambam, Hilchos Shabbos* 29:7). The basis for this practice is the Talmudic statement (*Shabbos* 119b) that "anyone who prays on Friday night and recites *Vayechulu* is reckoned as having become a partner in the work of Creation" (cf. *Maggid Mishneh* ad loc.). This is so because by repeating this passage with its account of creation, a person demonstrates his unwavering confidence in its veracity, as if he himself was witness to it, and had actually taken a part in God's work (*Kol Bo* §35). Indeed, the recital of *Vayechulu* is treated as a formal testimony to the fact that God created the world, which is called for by the precept *Remember the day of Shabbos to sanctify it,* and should therefore be said standing. One who withholds this affirmation is reckoned as if he testifies to the falsehood that the world is not God's,

which borders on a denial of His very existence (*Akeidas Yitzchak*).

The doctrine that the world did not always exist, but was brought into being at a definite point in time, is of central importance to all the Torah's principles, and so we call to mind, on one day each week, the truth of the fact that Hashem created the world in six days and rested on the seventh (*Sefer HaChinuch* §32). Every basic article of faith needs to be enshrined in some concrete symbolization, just as was done for the Exodus from Egypt. Certainly, the reality of the world's creation from nothing (*ex nihilo*) is an idea so fundamental that it calls for a weekly reminder to preserve its place of prominence in our hearts and minds. To this end we were given Shabbos, with its attendant charge to *Remember the day of Shabbos to sanctify it* (*Eitz HaChayim* 29:30).

II. PREVENTING SHABBOS DESECRATION

he Torah directs us to attest, through *kiddush,* to the holiness of Shabbos, not merely to promote awareness of the world's creation, but also to serve notice to ourselves that the seventh day, with all its laws and restrictions, has begun; and we will thus be protected from inadvertent performance of forbidden work (*Ralbag, Shemos* §20). [*Ralbag* further explains that it is for this reason that the mitzvah of *kiddush,* in contrast to most time-related (positive) commandments, applies to women as well as men, for both are equally subject to the negative commandments that regulate work on Shabbos.]

The prohibition against performing work on Shabbos is particularly in need of a strong verbal reminder, because the activities forbidden are routine features of everyday life, and the force of habit can easily lead to their unintentional performance on Shabbos. This idea is borne out by the progression of the verses in the passage concerning Shabbos, as follows: *Remember the day of Shabbos* [by reciting *kiddush*, in order] *to sanctify it* [by observing its laws. And why only in regard to this mitzvah, among so many others, is a reminder required? Because on the other] *six days you may labor and accomplish all your work,* [and only] *on the seventh day it is Shabbos,* [dedicated] *to Hashem, your God; do not do any work* (*Ben Ish Chai, Year* II, *Parshas Yisro*).

III. A STATEMENT OF PURPOSE IN REGARD TO THE CESSATION OF WORK

he mitzvah of *kiddush* was intended not only to remind one of the injunction to rest, but also to declare the purpose for this abstention from work. The *kiddush* proclaims that purpose to be the Divinely ordained sanctity of Shabbos, as opposed to simply a dearth of chores to be done.

[This explanation gives added meaning to the Sages' comment on the change in the wording of this mitzvah from the first set of *luchos* [Tablets] to the second. The first version reads: *Remember* [זכור] *the Shabbos day* (through the recitation of *kiddush*) *to sanctify it*. On the second *luchos,* we were instructed instead to *Safeguard* [שמור] *the Shabbos day* (from desecration by work) *to sanctify it*. The two injunctions, say *Chazal,* were actually uttered simultaneously by God at Sinai. The implication is that these two precepts are interrelated. In light of the above, the connection lies in the fact that our rest on Shabbos safeguards its sanctity only when we make clear, through *kiddush,* the reason for the cessation of activity (*Gur Aryeh, Devarim* 5:12; cf. *Toras Moshe/Chasam Sofer,* ad loc.).

IV. BRINGING TO LIGHT THE SANCTITY OF SHABBOS

he recitation of *kiddush* also has the function of a dedication formally sanctifying the day as Shabbos. This parallels the Torah-mandated dedication of the *Yovel* year (see

mitzvah #332), which consists of a formal announcement ("It is sanctified; it is sanctified") in a court of Torah law (*Ramban, Shemos* 20:8). Although Shabbos is inherently holy, we are still enjoined to consecrate it by an act of our own, in much the same way that the owner of a kosher animal is bidden to sanctify its firstborn offspring, despite the fact that it is automatically holy from the moment of birth (see *Moshav Zekeinim* [Paris], cited in *Tosafos HaShalem al HaTorah, Bereishis* 2:3).

That we are called upon to personally sanctify Shabbos is laden with meaning. It is true that Shabbos is innately holy, but its full potential for holiness can be reached only through the participation of the Jewish people. For the purpose of Shabbos, and the source of its holiness, is the role it plays in testifying to the creation of the universe as the work of God. But the revelation of Godliness in the world is the central function of the Jewish nation, as it is said (*Yeshayah* 43:12), *You are My witnesses, says Hashem, and I am God*. To the extent that the Jewish people bear witness to His existence, His Divinity unfolds to the world, and this adds, in turn, to the holiness of Shabbos (*Sefas Emes, Yisro* 5650; see there further, *Shevuos* 5638).

Human input is necessary to bring out the sublime qualities inherent in Shabbos, for its holiness becomes manifest only to the extent that it is perceived and experienced by the human heart. This is the aim of the recitation of *kiddush* — to help attune one's heart and faculties to properly receive the holiness of the day, which in turn serves to augment the sanctity of Shabbos (*Pri Tzaddik, Ma'amar Kedushas Shabbos* §2).

V. HONORING THE SHABBOS QUEEN

habbos is likened to a queen, and we are obliged accordingly to render her honor in various ways. Thus, there was a custom among some of the Talmudic Sages (*Shabbos* 119; *Bava Kamma* 32a b) to dress in their finery and herald the onset of Shabbos with the call, "Come, let us go forth to greet the Shabbos Queen." In this vein we were given the mitzvah of *kiddush,* with which we may honor and glorify the Shabbos day (*Teshuvos HaRashba* IV:295). Indeed, the *kiddush* recited as Shabbos commences has been compared to a ceremony of welcome for a visiting king, while the *havdalah* bids farewell and accompanies the royal guest as he leaves (cf. *Pesachim* 103a).

VI. BETROTHAL OF SHABBOS TO ISRAEL

habbos has been described as the bride of the Jewish people. The Sages relate that Shabbos complained before God, "Each of the other six days has its own counterpart. All except me, for I have no mate." The Holy One, Blessed is He, replied, "The Jewish people shall be your mate." (*Bereshis Rabbah* 11:8) The match was thus made between Shabbos and the Jewish nation, and each week it is renewed as Shabbos begins. The *kiddush* confirms the act of betrothal, just as the groom consecrates his bride as she joins him under the wedding canopy (*Maharsha, Chidushei Aggados, Bava Kamma* 32b; cf. *Avudraham, Maariv shel Shabbos,* where he writes the opening phrase of the Shabbos evening prayer, "You have consecrated the seventh day…," is reminiscent of the formula used for the consecration of the bride by her groom). [See also *Sefer HaKaneh* for a discussion of the inner meanings of *kiddush* and *havdalah,* and *Sifsei Kohen, Parshas Ki Sisa.*]

THROUGH THE EYES OF THE SAGES
Stories, Parables, & Reflections

I. THE GREAT REWARD FOR FULFILLING THE MITZVAH OF RECITING KIDDUSH AND HAVDALAH

n many places, *Chazal* relate the bountiful rewards that will be given to one who is diligent in observing the mitzvah to recite *kiddush* and *havdalah* over wine every Shabbos. A sampling of these rewards follows:

➣ *Wealth, longevity, and Olam Haba*

The Gemara in *Shabbos* (23b; see *Maharsha* there) states: A person who takes care to recite the Shabbos *kiddush* over wine will merit to fill up many barrels with wine.

———

The Gemara in *Megillah* (27b) relates: R' Zakkai's disciples asked him, "In what merit have you attained longevity?" R' Zakkai responded to them, "In all of my days … I never neglected the Shabbos *kiddush* (i.e. I was always careful to recite it over wine — see *Rashba*). I had an elderly mother: Once [when I could not afford to purchase wine], she sold the veil that was upon her head and bought me wine for *kiddush* [with the proceeds of that sale]." A Baraisa taught: When [R' Zakkai's mother] passed away, she left him [an inheritance of] three hundred barrels of wine; when [R' Zakkai himself] passed away, he left his children three thousand barrels of wine. *Tosafos* (ibid.) note that this reward is the one mentioned in the Gemara in *Shabbos* (cited above) given to one who is diligent in always reciting *kiddush* on wine.

———

The Gemara there (*Megillah* ibid.) also relates the following story: Rav Huna was once wearing a belt made of woven grass as he stood before [his teacher] Rav. Rav asked him, "What is this? Why are you not wearing your regular belt?" Rav Huna answered: "I did not have [wine for] *kiddush*, so I borrowed money and gave my belt as collateral, and with that money obtained wine for *kiddush*." Rav said to him, "May it be the will of God that you be swathed in silk as a reward!"

One who is diligent in observing the mitzvah of *kiddush* will receive more than mere wealth. *Pirkei D'Rabbi Eliezer* (ch. 18) states: Whoever recites the blessing of *kiddush* over wine on Shabbos, his days and his years in this world will be lengthened, and he will be granted more years of life in *Olam Haba* (the World to Come).

——— ⌇ ———

➣ *Partnership in Creation; atonement of one's sins*

As part of the Friday night *kiddush*, we recite the passage of *Vayechulu* (*Bereishis* 2:1-3), which states that Hashem finished creating the world in six days, and rested on Shabbos. [This passage is also recited in the Friday night *Maariv Shemoneh Esrei*.]

———

The Gemara in *Shabbos* (119b) describes the great power of reciting the passage of *Vayechulu*. Rav Hamnuna said: Anyone who prays on the eve of the Shabbos and says *Vayechulu* on Friday night is considered by Scripture as if he had become a partner with the Holy One, Blessed is He, in the act of Creation, as the verse states: *Vayechulu* [*and they* — the Heavens and the earth — *were finished*]. Do not pronounce [this word] *Vayechulu* [*and they were finished*], but rather *Vayechalu*, which means: *and they* — the Creator and one who recites His praise and the praise of Shabbos — *finished* (see *Rashi* there). R' Elazar said: From where is it known that speech is tantamount to an action with respect to the world's creation, so that simply reciting *Vayechulu* (which describes the Creation) can be reckoned as if one actually took part in the act of Creation? For it says (*Tehillim* 33:6): *By the Word of Hashem, the Heavens were made*. Since the world itself was created through speech, as it were, one can be considered to be a participant in Creation even through mere speech. Rav Chisda said in the name of Mar Ukva: Anyone who says *Vayechulu* on Friday night merits that the two ministering angels that escort a person [home from *shul* on Friday night — see further below] rest their hands upon his head and tell him (*Yeshayah* 6:7): *Your iniquity will depart and your sin will be atoned* (see *Maharsha* ad loc.; see also *Zohar* II 207b, which states that if one recites *Vayechulu* intently during the Friday night *kiddush*, he will receive atonement for his sins).

——— ❧ ———

❧ Reward for reciting havdalah: Blessings and belovedness

R' Tzaddok says: Whoever does not recite *havdalah* over wine at the departure of Shabbos, or does not at least hear *havdalah*, will never see even the harbinger of blessing. But whoever does hear others reciting *havdalah*, or recites *havdalah* himself over wine, the Holy One, Blessed is He, acquires that person as His cherished treasure, as the verse (*Vayikra* 20:26) states: *You shall be holy people for Me, for I Hashem am holy; and I have separated (va'avdil) you from the nations to be Mine.* And it says elsewhere (*Shemos* 19:5-6): *You shall be to Me a cherished treasure from among all the nations … You shall be to Me a kingdom of Kohanim and a holy nation* (*Pirkei D'Rabbi Eliezer* ch. 20; see *Yalkut Shimoni, Bereishis* §34, and *Tur, Orach Chaim* §296). We see that reciting *havdalah* brings one Hashem's blessings, as well as a special closeness to Him.

——— ❧ ———

❧ The life of the World to Come

The Gemara in *Pesachim* (113a) states in the name of R' Yochanan that there are three who will inherit the World to Come. One of them is he who recites *havdalah* over wine at the departure of Shabbos. *Rashbam* (ibid.) explains this to mean

that he leaves over [wine] from *kiddush* for *havdalah* (i.e. he has only a small quantity of wine, and he restrains himself from drinking more than necessary for *kiddush*, so that he will have enough wine left over for *havdalah*).

II. HONORING THE SHABBOS AND DELIGHTING IN IT

he essence of the mitzvah of *kiddush* is the utterance of words, as *Chinuch* (§31) defines the mitzvah: "Speaking of the greatness of Shabbos, its qualities and its superiority to the other days before and after … so that this endeavor should inspire us to remember the day's greatness and to help us establish in our hearts a permanent belief in Hashem's creation of the universe." Additionally, there is also an element of *honoring* Shabbos in the recital of *kiddush*, as can be seen in the metaphor the Sages used to describe *kiddush*: Going out to render honor to royalty (see *Pesachim* 103a). The Prophet commands us, as a central part of observing Shabbos, to *delight* in Shabbos, as it says (*Yeshayah* 58:13): *You shall proclaim Shabbos "a delight" [oneg], and the holy [day] of Hashem, "honored."* One delights physically on Shabbos by partaking of fine food and drink, dressing in fine clothing, resting and the like (see *Mechilta D'Rabbi Shimon bar Yochai* 20:8 and *Tanna D'vei Eliyahu Rabbah* 26:20). These serve the same purpose as *kiddush*, as *Radak* (*Yeshayah* ibid.). states: "By enhancing [that day] over other days, one will recall the act of Creation, and that God made it from nothingness (*ex nihilo*) and rested on the seventh day." Furthermore, by delighting in Shabbos, one honors Shabbos with deeds, in addition to honoring it with words [i.e. the recitation of *kiddush*] (see *Metzudas David* loc. cit.). The following section illustrates the importance the Sages accorded to honoring and delighting in Shabbos, and the tremendous reward that awaits those who fulfill this mitzvah properly.

——— ❧ ———

According honor to Hashem

Whoever delights in Shabbos is considered as if he honored the Holy One, Blessed is He, as the verse states (*Yeshayah* 58:13): *You shall proclaim Shabbos "a delight," and the Holy One, Hashem, "honored."* This teaches that if you proclaim Shabbos a delight, then the Holy One, Hashem, will be honored (*Tanna D'vei Eliyahu Rabbah* 26:20).

When mortal man merits to observe the honor of Shabbos perfectly, as we have discussed, the Holy One, Blessed is He, declares about him (*Yeshayah* 49:3): *He said to me: "You are My servant, Israel, in whom I glory"* (*Zohar* II, 209a).

Like receiving a queen or a bride

You shall call Shabbos a delight (*Yeshayah* 58:13): What is the meaning of the word, *"v'karasa"* — *You shall call*? That one should invite Shabbos as one would invite a guest, with a set table, a home in proper order, and appropriate foods and beverages, superior to [what is served on] other days (*Zohar* II, 47a).

One must "add from the mundane to the holy" in all things relevant to Shabbos, whether in regard to his food and drink, his clothing, or even how he reclines [while dining]. He should prepare for himself a pleasant spot to recline, furnished with embroidered pillows and beddings from all those available in his house, similar to the manner in which people prepare a beautiful canopy for a bride, because Shabbos is both a queen and a bride. For this reason the Sages of the Mishnah would go out toward the eve of Shabbos in order to meet the Shabbos queen on the way, and they would say, "Come, O bride! Come, O bride!" (see below, "Receiving the holy Shabbos"). One must stir up song and gladness at the Shabbos table … one must receive the queen [i.e. Shabbos] with the profuse light of candles and with delicacies and beautiful clothes; the house should be prepared with multiple vessels for the needs of Shabbos, and an attractive place to recline should be readied for every member of the household (*Zohar* III, *Raya Meheimna* 272b. See also *Tikkunei Zohar, tikkun* §21, 57a and *tikkun* §48, 85b; *Zohar* II, 204b; *Zohar Chadash, Rus* 42b–43a).

Heaven repays the expenses one incurs for honoring the Shabbos

The Holy One, Blessed is He, said to the Jewish nation: "My children! Borrow on My account and sanctify the holiness of Shabbos (i.e. borrow in order to pay for the expenses of Shabbos), and trust in Me to repay your loans" (*Beitzah* 15b).

Rav Tachlifa, the brother of Ravna'i Chozaah, taught in a Baraisa: A person's yearly income is fixed between Rosh Hashanah and Yom Kippur, with the exception of expenditures for Shabbos and Yom Tov, and expenditures to pay for the Torah learning of one's children. There is no fixed amount granted for these expenses; whatever he spends will be returned to him. If he decreases his expenditures, he will receive less, and if he increases his expenditures, he will receive more (*Beitzah* 15b-16a). Indeed, the repayment will exceed the expenditure. For it is written (*Koheles* 8:15): *And I praised gladness, for there is nothing better for a man to do beneath the sun than to eat, drink, and be glad, and this will accompany him (vehu yilvenu) in his toil, during the days of his life that God has given him beneath the sun.* Now, the words *vehu yilvenu* can be expounded as if they read, *vehu yalvenu*, and he shall lend him. To whom does the verse refer when it states: *vehu yilvenu*? To the mortal man who eats, drinks, and rejoices on Shabbos and Yom Tov: He is giving the Holy One, Blessed is He, a loan, as it were, and the Holy One, Blessed is He, shall return to him many times what he spent on this account. By doing two mitzvos, one is reckoned as if he lends to the Holy One, Blessed is He: When he has pity on the poor and when he spends on behalf of Shabbos and Yom Tov (*Zohar* II, 255a).

———— ✎ ————

✿ Reward for honoring and delighting in the Shabbos is guaranteed

R' Tanchum bar R' Chiya said in the name of R' Yochanan: It is written (*Yechezkel* 20:20): *Sanctify My Shabbosos.* How do you sanctify Shabbos? With food, drink, and a clean garment. What is written concerning the fulfillment of this mitzvah? *And Shabbos shall be a sign between Me and you, for you to know that I am Hashem, your God* (ibid.). When the verse states in closing: *I am Hashem,* it is to say that Hashem tells those who sanctify Shabbos: "I can be trusted to reward you well" (*Bamidbar Rabbah* 10:1; *Shir HaShirim Rabbah* 6:1:4).

———— ✎ ————

✿ Better than fasting

Honoring the Shabbos is superior to a thousand fast days (*Tanchuma Bereishis* §3).

———— ✎ ————

✿ Angelic blessings

A Baraisa teaches: R' Yose bar Yehudah says: On the eve of Shabbos, two ministering angels escort a person home from shul, one good angel and one bad angel. If he comes home and finds the lamp lit, the table set, and his bed made, the good angel says, "May it be Hashem's will that it should be the same way next Shabbos," and the bad angel is forced to answer, "Amen." But if the house is not prepared for Shabbos, the bad angel says, "May it be Hashem's will that it should be the same way next Shabbos," and the good angel is forced to answer, "Amen" (*Shabbos* 119b).

———— ✎ ————

✿ The blessing of wealth

The Gemara in *Shabbos* relates: Rebbi inquired of R' Yishmael bar R' Yose: Through what [worthy practice] do the wealthy people in Eretz Yisrael merit such great wealth? R' Yishmael bar R' Yose answered him: Because they tithe their crops faithfully, as it says (*Devarim* 14:22): *Tithe, you shall tithe.* (*Aseir, t'aseir*). This double expression is expounded to teach us: *Aseir bishvil shetis'asheir*: "Tithe (*aseir*), so that you shall become rich (*shetis'asher*)". Rebbi asked further: And those in Babylonia, who have no Biblical obligation to tithe the crops growing there, through what do they merit their riches? He replied to him: Because they honor the Torah. Rebbi asked a final time: And those in other lands, through what do they merit their riches? He said to him: Because they honor Shabbos.

————

The Gemara illustrates this last answer with a personal account from a later Sage: R' Chiya bar Abba said: Once I was the guest of a homeowner in Ludkaya, and when it was time to serve the meal they brought before him a golden table so heavy it required sixteen people to carry it. And there were sixteen silver chains anchored to it, as well as plates, cups, pitchers, and flasks set upon it, and upon the table were all varieties of foods and all sorts of delicacies and aromatic spices. When they placed the table down before him, they recited (*Tehillim* 24:1): *To Hashem is the earth and its fullness,* etc. (i.e. we are not permitted to benefit from all this until we bless His Name through the blessing over the bread — see *Rashi* there). And when they removed the table, they recited (*Tehillim* 115:16): *As for the Heavens, the Heavens are Hashem's, but the earth He has given to humans,* and we have enjoyed all this good only through His beneficence. I said to [this homeowner], "My son, through what good deed did you merit all this?" He said to me, "I used to be a butcher, and from every animal of superior quality I said, 'Let a portion of this be for Shabbos.'" I said to him, "Fortunate are you that you have merited all this; Blessed is the Omnipresent Who has bestowed this upon you" (*Shabbos* 119a; see also *Bereishis Rabbah* 11:4 and *Pesikta Rabbasi* §23).

———— ✎ ————

✒ *The story of Yosef Mokir Shabbei*

There was a certain non-Jew in the neighborhood of Yosef Mokir Shabbei (Yosef who honors Shabbos) whose possessions were extremely abundant. The astrologers told him, "All your possessions will pass to Yosef Mokir Shabbei." In an attempt to avoid this fate, the wealthy man liquidated all his possessions and bought an extremely valuable pearl. He made for himself a felt hat with gold settings studded with pearls, and placed this extremely valuable pearl among them. In this way, he planned to safeguard his wealth at all times. One day, as he was passing over a river crossing, a wind blew his hat off and cast it into the water. A fish came and swallowed the valuable pearl. Fishermen caught this fish and brought it ashore on Friday afternoon, by which time most people had already concluded their purchases for Shabbos. They said, "Who will buy this fish now, at this late hour?" They were told, "Go, bring it to Yosef Mokir Shabbei, for he always buys any prize item for the honor of Shabbos." They brought it to him and he bought it. When he cut the fish open, he discovered the pearl inside, and later sold it for thirteen attics full of gold *dinars*. [This is an exaggeration; the Gemara means that he sold it for an enormous sum of money (*Rashi*; see also *Tosafos*).] A certain elder encountered him and said, "He who borrows [on behalf of] Shabbos, Shabbos repays him" (*Shabbos* 119a; *Pesikta Rabbasi* §46).

———— ✒ ————

✒ *A boundless heritage*

R' Yochanan said in the name of R' Yose: Whoever delights in Shabbos is given a boundless heritage, as the verse states (*Yeshayah* 58:13-14): *If you proclaim Shabbos a delight … then you shall delight in Hashem, and I shall mount you upon the high places of the earth; and I will sustain you with the heritage of your forefather, Yaakov.* The Prophet emphasizes that the heritage will be like that of Yaakov; not like [that of] Avraham, about whom it is written

(*Bereishis* 13:17): *Arise, walk within the land, through its length and its breadth, for to you I will give it* (which implies, this land, but no other land); and not like the heritage of Yitzchak, about whom it is written (*Bereishis* 26:3): *For to you and your descendants will I give all these lands* (which implies, but no more than *these* lands); rather, your heritage will be like that of Yaakov, about whom it is written (*Bereishis* 28:14): *And you shall burst forth west and east and north and south,* without any boundary (see *Bereishis Rabbah* 69:5). [This reward is measure for measure: If one disperses his money without limits for the honor of Shabbos, he is likewise rewarded with a heritage without limits (*Beis Yosef, Orach Chaim* §242).] Rav Nachman bar Yitzchak said: He is spared from the subjugation of the rest of the Jewish people in the various exiles. [This reward, too, is measure for measure: Since he accepts upon himself the yoke of Shabbos, the yoke of the nations' governments is removed from him (*Beis Yosef, Orach Chaim* ibid.).] This is derived as follows: It is written here, regarding one who delights in Shabbos: *And I shall mount you upon the high places of the earth,* and it is written there (*Devarim* 33:29): *Your enemies will attempt to deceive you, but you will trample upon their high and mighty ones.* The similar wording in these two passages (**high** *places*, **high** *and mighty ones*) links them, and teaches that one who delights in the Shabbos is spared from the oppression of his enemies (see *Shabbos* 118a-b).

———— ✒ ————

✒ *Granting the wishes of one's heart*

Rav Yehudah said in the name of Rav: Whoever delights in the Shabbos will be granted the wishes of his heart, as it says (*Tehillim* 37:4): *Delight in Hashem and He will grant you the wishes of your heart.* Now, I do not know what is meant by *delight* here; however, when it says (*Yeshayah* 58:13): *You shall proclaim the Shabbos a delight,* I may conclude that the first verse also refers to the delight of Shabbos (*Shabbos* 118b; *Medrash Tannaim, Devarim* 5:15).

———— ✒ ————

～ *Rewards in this world and the next*

Fortunate in his portion is he who merited to honor Shabbos; fortunate is he in this world and in the World to Come (*Zohar* II, 64a and 207a).

___

Perhaps you think that I have given you Shabbos for your detriment, forbidding you from earning a livelihood? No, I have given Shabbos to you only for your benefit! How so? R' Chiya bar R' Abba said: You sanctify Shabbos through food, drink, and a clean garment, giving yourself pleasure, and I reward you for this! From where do we know this? Because it is written (*Yeshayah* 58:13): *You shall proclaim Shabbos a delight,* etc. What is written further (ibid.)? *Then you shall delight in Hashem.* And what is this delight? As the verse states elsewhere (*Tehillim* 37:4): *You shall delight in Hashem and He will grant you the wishes of your heart.* The Jewish nation said to the Holy One, Blessed is He: But when will You give us the reward for the mitzvos that we do? The Holy One, Blessed is He, replied to them: For the mitzvos you do, you will enjoy the "interest" of the reward right now; but their true reward I will give you only at the time of *eikev* (literally, *heel* — this is a reference to the end of time). From where do we know that reward will come at the time of *eikev*? From what we read here (*Devarim* 7:12): *And it shall be because (eikev) when you hearken [to these laws ... and He shall bless you and increase you]* (*Devarim Rabbah* 3:1).

___

Great is the delight of Shabbos (*oneg Shabbos*), for whoever delights in Shabbos merits to sit in the Heavenly academy, as the verse states (*Yeshayah* 58:13-14): *You shall proclaim Shabbos a delight ... then you shall delight in Hashem.* In addition, his prayer is listened to, as it says (*Iyov* 22:26-27): *Then you will delight in the Almighty, and you will raise your face to God; you will entreat Him and He will listen to you* (*Medrash Tannaim, Devarim* 5:15).

___

It is written (*Koheles* 8:15): *And I praised gladness, for there is nothing better for a man to do beneath the sun than to eat, drink, and be glad, and this (vehu) will accompany him in his toil during the days of his life that God has given him beneath the sun.* [The verse begins:] *And I praised gladness;* now, would Shlomo HaMelech really praise gladness arising from material pleasures?! Rather, the phrase *And I praised gladness* refers to gladness of the Holy King, Hashem, during the times that He shows His authority in this world; namely on Shabbos and Yom Tov. That is to say, from all the good deeds a person does, there is nothing better for a man to do beneath the sun than to eat, drink and to exhibit gladness on Shabbos and Yom Tov, so that he will have a portion in the World to Come. The verse continues: *And this (vehu) will accompany him in his toil.* The word *vehu* is expounded to mean, *and He ...,* referring to the Holy One, Blessed is He; He will accompany him in order to elevate him to the World to Come (*Zohar* II, 255a).

III. HOW THE SHABBOS WAS HONORED IN PRACTICE BY THE SAGES OF THE TALMUD

～ *They prepared numerous dishes of fine quality for Shabbos*

Rabbah bar Rav Huna traveled to the home of Rabbah bar Rav Nachman. They brought before him three *se'ah* [a very large volume] of fried wafers brushed with oil, a great delicacy. Rabbah bar Rav Huna said to the members of the household in surprise, "Did you know that I was coming, that you prepared this lavish course in my honor?" They said to him, "Are you any more precious to us than Shabbos? We did not know you were coming; we prepared the wafers in honor of Shabbos" (*Shabbos* 119a).

___

R' Abba would buy meat from thirteen butchers for thirteen half-*dinars,* in order to be sure that he would have the tastiest meat available to sample on Shabbos. He would bring each purchase to his house, and would tell his cooks, "Be energetic and hurry! Be energetic and hurry! Quickly prepare this meat, before I bring back my next purchase" (*Shabbos* 119a).

———————

R' Chiya the Great went to the south and was hosted by R' Yehoshua ben Levi on a weekday. They brought before him twenty-four dishes. R' Chiya the Great said to his host, "If this is what you do on a weekday, what do you do on Shabbos?" R' Yehoshua ben Levi answered, "On Shabbos, we double the number of dishes!" (*Eichah Rabbah* 3:4).

——— ৵৶ ———

◈ Personal efforts in preparing for Shabbos

The Gemara in *Shabbos* (119a) relates how many Amoraim would involve themselves personally in the preparation for Shabbos:

- ◈ R' Abahu, who was a prominent and wealthy man, would sit upon a seat of ivory while he fanned the fire used to cook for Shabbos.

- ◈ Rav Anan would wear a black smock on Fridays, so he would not desist from helping with Shabbos preparations for fear of soiling his clothes.

- ◈ Rav Safra would singe the head of the animal being prepared for Shabbos [to remove the hair before cooking].

- ◈ Rava would salt the *shibbuta* fish.

- ◈ Rav Huna would light lamps.

- ◈ Rav Pappa would twist the wicks to be lit.

- ◈ Rav Chisda would chop up the beets finely.

- ◈ Rabbah and Rav Yosef would split wood to be used for cooking.

- ◈ R' Zeira would light the kindling to start the fire.

- ◈ Rav Nachman bar Yitzchak would go in and out of his house constantly on Fridays bringing in bundles of Shabbos supplies, such as furniture, bedding, and delicacies. He acted as a person might if he were receiving his teacher in his home, and showing the teacher that his presence was so cherished that he was scrambling to exert himself in his honor and enhance his stay (see *Rashi* ibid.). He said: If R' Ami and R' Assi (who were his teachers) were to visit me, would I not go in and out [bringing in bundles] in front of them? Certainly, I should do no less for Shabbos! Some say that it was R' Ami and R' Assi who went in and out bringing in bundles, and they said: If R' Yochanan (who was *their* teacher) were to visit us, would we not bring in bundles before him?

——— ৵৶ ———

◈ Receiving the holy Shabbos

R' Yehudah bar Il'ai would conduct himself as follows: On the eve of Shabbos, they would bring him a basin full of hot water, and he would wash his face, hands, and feet. He would wrap himself in linen cloaks to which *tzitzis* had been attached, and sit and wait to receive Shabbos as if he were going out to greet the king, and he resembled an angel of Hashem, the Lord of Hosts (*Shabbos* 25b).

———————

R' Chanina would wrap himself in fine clothing and stand as Shabbos would approach. He would say, "Come, let us go to greet the Shabbos queen." R' Yannai would don his Shabbos clothes on the eve of Shabbos and say, "Come, O bride! Come, O bride!" (*Shabbos* 119a).

lthough the Gemara (*Berachos* 20b; *Shevuos* 20b) clearly states that *kiddush* is a Biblical obligation, some Rishonim do not list the requirement to recite *kiddush* in their counts of the 613 mitzvos (see *Bahag, R' Yitzchak Bargeloni; Yereim*). Two approaches have been suggested to explain why, in the opinion of these Rishonim, *kiddush* is not counted as one of the 613 mitzvos.

A. *The kiddush obligation is only a Rabbinic requirement.*

Although there are *sugyos* in the Gemara that state that *kiddush* is a Biblical obligation (see above), the Gemara in *Nazir* 3b-4a can be understood as disputing this view. The Gemara there derives from Scripture that a *nazir,* who (in addition to several other restrictions) is forbidden to drink wine (see *mitzvah* #368) — is forbidden to drink even mitzvah wine (i.e. wine whose consumption is Biblically mandated). The Gemara, as understood by many Rishonim (see *Tosafos* there 4a ד"ה אילימא; *Rosh* ד"ה מאי היא), comments that this derivation is not needed to teach that a *nazir* is forbidden to drink the wine of *kiddush* and *havdalah,* for such wine is not considered mitzvah wine, as it is only Rabbinically mandated. These Rishonim understand the Gemara to mean that the obligation to recite *kiddush* is Biblical, but

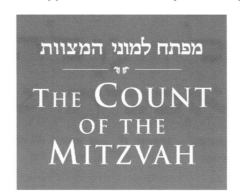

מפתח למוני המצוות

THE COUNT OF THE MITZVAH

Baal Halachos Gedolos / —	בה"ג / —
R' Saadiah Gaon / Asin 33	רס"ג / עשין לג
R' Eliyahu HaZakein / Amud 17	ר' אליהו הזקן / עמ' 17
Rashbag / Asin Os 31	רשב"ג / עשין אות לא
R' Yitzchak El-Bargeloni / Asin 155	ר"י אלברג'לוני / עשין קנה
Maamar HaSechel / Dibbur Revi'i 1	מאמר השכל / דיבור רביעי א
Sefer Yereim / —	יראים / —
Rambam, Sefer HaMitzvos / Aseh 155	רמב"ם / עשה קנה
Sefer Mitzvos Gadol (Smag) / Aseh 29	סמ"ג / עשה כט
Sefer Mitzvos Katan (Smak) / 281	סמ"ק / רפא
Zohar HaRakia / Asin 47	זוהר הרקיע / עשין מז

that the requirement to recite it over wine is only Rabbinic. However, the Gemara can also be understood as meaning that the wine of *kiddush* is not considered mitzvah wine because the very obligation to recite *kiddush* (and not just the requirement to recite it over wine) is Rabbinic in nature. Possibly, those who do not list the *kiddush* obligation in their counts of the 613 mitzvos interpret that Gemara in the second manner, and rule in accordance with this Gemara rather than those *sugyos* that hold the *kiddush* obligation to be Biblical in nature (*Bris Moshe* to *Smag, Aseh* 29:1) [Note: Other Rishonim interpret that Gemara in a diametrically opposite way; according to their interpretation, the Gemara asserts that even the requirement to recite *kiddush* over wine is Biblical; their view is noted above, note 12.]

[It should be noted that this answer does not suffice to explain why *Bahag* does not include the *kiddush* obligation in his list of 613 mitzvos, for he states explicitly that *kiddush* is a Biblical obligation (see *Bahag, Hil. Kiddush V'Havdalah*). Moreover, *Bahag* does include Rabbinic commandments in his list of 613 mitzvos; for example, the mitzvah of lighting lights on Chanukah (see *Bahag, Aseh* §139). Thus, his failure to include the mitzvah of *kiddush* cannot in any case be explained as reflecting a view that *kiddush* is a Rabbinic obligation.]

B. *The kiddush requirement is included in the commandment to refrain from work on Shabbos (mitzvah #32).*

Some explain that although *kiddush* is Biblically mandated, it is not counted as one of the 613 mitzvos because it serves as the blessing for the mitzvah of refraining from work on Shabbos (see *mitzvah #32*). As such, it is not considered a separate mitzvah, but as part of that mitzvah (*R' Yeruchem Fishel Perla,* commentary to *Sefer HaMitzvos of R' Saadiah Gaon,* end of *Aseh* §33; see further, *mitzvah #419,* for a similar explanation as to why many Rishonim do not list in their counts the requirement to recite a blessing before studying Torah, despite the fact that most Rishonim maintain that it is a Biblical requirement).

Mitzvah 32

אִסּוּר עֲשִׂיַּת מְלָאכָה בְּשַׁבָּת

פרשת יתרו

NOT TO PERFORM FORBIDDEN LABOR ON SHABBOS

THE MITZVAH:

MITZVAH
32

אִסּוּר עֲשִׂיַּת מְלָאכָה
בְּשַׁבָּת (לֹא תַעֲשֶׂה)
NOT TO PERFORM
FORBIDDEN LABOR
ON SHABBOS[1]

מצוה
לב

SOURCE

לֹא תַעֲשֶׂה כָל מְלָאכָה שמות (פרשת יתרו) כ:י
" ... You shall not do any melachah[2] "

THE MITZVAH

On Shabbos,[3] a Jew is forbidden to perform any of the thirty-nine melachos (labors) that were performed during the construction of the Tabernacle (Mishkan),[4] or any melachah that resembles one of the thirty-nine.[5]

LAWS

1 By Biblical law, only a "calculated" act violates Shabbos,[6] meaning: (a) It is the act one intended to perform;[7] (b) It serves a constructive purpose;[8] (c) It is an enduring act;[9] (d) It is performed for its inherent purpose;[10] (e) It is performed in the usual manner.[11]

2 *Melachah* requires direct action. One who indirectly causes a *melachah* to occur has not transgressed the Biblical prohibition.[12]

3 One who deliberately performs *melachah* on Shabbos is liable to execution by stoning.[13] If he was not forewarned, he is liable to *kares*.[14] One who transgresses inadvertently must bring a *chatas* offering.[15]

4 Some *melachos* require a specific minimum measure. Performing less than the required measure is forbidden, but carries no penalty.[16]

5 It is forbidden to instruct a non-Jew to perform *melachah* on one's behalf on Shabbos.[17]

6 The Sages forbade numerous activities that resemble or might lead to *melachah*.[18]

7 This prohibition applies to both men and women, in all places and at all times.[19]

NOTE: This prohibition is more serious than almost any other. Violating the Shabbos is a very grave transgression; the Gemara equates it to violating the entire Torah.[20]

A REASON

It is a tenet of our faith that God created the world in six days and rested on the seventh. We refrain from labor each Shabbos in remembrance of Creation; this ensures that the existence of the Creator will remain forever in our thoughts.

1. In addition to this prohibition, there is also a *positive* commandment to abstain from forbidden labor on Shabbos — see *mitzvah #85*.

2. The prohibition against performing *melachah* on Shabbos appears also in *Devarim* 5:14, in the Torah's second listing of the Ten Commandments, and in *Vayikra* 23:3, as part of a passage that teaches the laws of the festivals. The prohibition is repeated there to teach that observing the festivals is as important as observing Shabbos (*Rashi* ad loc.).

Our verse continues as follows: אתה ובנך ובתך עבדך ואמתך ובהמתך, *you and your son and your daughter, your slave and your maidservant, and your animal*. This phrase is a prohibition against allowing one's children and Canaanite slaves to violate Shabbos, and against directing an animal to perform *melachah* on Shabbos (see *Shabbos* 153b-154a, *Ramban, Shemos* 20:9; *Rambam, Hil. Shabbos* 20:14). These prohibitions are discussed at greater length in *Iyunim* §6.

3. I.e. from sunset on Friday until nightfall on Saturday (see *Mechilta, Shemos* 20:10).

4. A. *The Mishkan and Shabbos:* The Torah states that "work" is prohibited on Shabbos, but does not define precisely what constitutes work. Of the many *melachos* that are prohibited on Shabbos, very few are singled out for mention in the Torah (see *Iyunim* §2). The others are known through a Scriptural analogy drawn between Shabbos and the *Mishkan* (Tabernacle). In *Shemos* 35:2, the Torah commands us to observe the Shabbos. That command is immediately followed with discussion regarding the building of the *Mishkan*. By placing these seemingly unrelated matters next to one another, the Torah indicates that they

AN EXPANDED TREATMENT

are to be compared; the analogy teaches that the *melachos* of Shabbos are the very ones that were performed during the construction of the *Mishkan*. Thus, no act is forbidden on Shabbos unless it or a similar act was performed in the course of building the *Mishkan* (see *Shabbos* 49b, 73b-74b, with *Rashi* to the Mishnah on 73a and to 5a (ד"ה לדגלי מדבר). For example, the *Mishkan* was covered with cloth and hides that were dyed in various colors. Because building the *Mishkan* included an act of dyeing, this act is prohibited on Shabbos. [For another Scriptural juxtaposition of Shabbos and the *Mishkan*, see *Shemos* 31:1-17, with *Rashi, Baal HaTurim* and *Daas Zekeinim MiBaalei HaTosafos* to v. 13.]

Shulchan Aruch HaRav (*Orach Chaim* 301:1) illuminates this teaching with another, stating that the reason the Torah mentioned Shabbos in passages concerning the *Mishkan* was to inform the Jews that the *Mishkan* was not to be built on Shabbos. Even during its construction, the laws of Shabbos remained in force (see *Rashi* to *Shemos* 31:13; 35:2). From this we infer that the labors performed while building the *Mishkan* are forbidden on Shabbos.

There is some question as to whether the *melachos* of Shabbos were derived solely from acts performed during *construction* of the *Mishkan*, or whether they were based also on acts performed during the *offering of sacrifices* in the *Mishkan*. See *Rashi, Shabbos* 92a ד"ה שכן משא; *Meiri, Shabbos* 73a; see also foreword to *Eglei Tal* at length.

B. *The thirty-nine melachos:* There are thirty-nine primary *melachos* (*avos melachos*) of Shabbos. They represent thirty-nine categories of forbidden work. The thirty-nine *melachos* are

listed in a Mishnah in Tractate *Shabbos* (73a), and in *Rambam* (*Hil. Shabbos* 7:1). [For a full listing, see below, *The Count of the Shabbos Melachos.*] The number thirty-nine emerges from the analogy between Shabbos and the *Mishkan,* which equates the *avos melachos* and the labors of the *Mishkan.* The Sages calculated the number of significant labors performed in building the *Mishkan* and arrived at thirty-nine; it follows that there are thirty-nine *avos melachos* (see *Shabbos* 49b with *Rashi* ד"ה כנגד עבודות). Others arrive at the number thirty-nine by expounding various Scriptural verses (see *Shabbos* ibid. and 70a with *Rashi* ד"ה דברים). See *Iyunim* §1 for discussion of the latter view.

The Mishnah emphasizes the number thirty-nine to teach that even if a person inadvertently performs every possible *av melachah,* including those that are not among the thirty-nine (see following note), he is not liable to bring more than thirty-nine *chatas* offerings (see *Shabbos* 73b). This is because there is no *av melachah* that does not fall into one of the thirty-nine categories. For example, the *av melachah* of נוטע, *planting a seedling,* which is not listed in the Mishnah, is similar to the *melachah* of זורע, *sowing a seed,* which *is* listed in the Mishnah. The same is true of all the primary *melachos* that were omitted from the Mishnah. Since all *melachos* fall into one of the thirty-nine categories, one who performed every possible *av melachah* brings only thirty-nine *chatas* offerings, even though his sum total of forbidden acts may be more than thirty-nine (see *Ritva, Shabbos* ibid.; see following note).

5. These are the *tolados,* or "derivative *melachos,*" which are acts that bear

some similarity to the *avos melachos* of the *Mishkan.* An example is chopping vegetables into tiny pieces. This act is similar to grinding in that it aims to transform an object into many small segments; therefore, it is a *toladah* of the primary *melachah* of טוחן, *grinding* (*Rambam, Hil. Shabbos* 7:5; see there for further details of this law). *Tolados* are prohibited on Shabbos by Biblical law (see *Shabbos* 70a-b, from *Vayikra* 4:2).

In addition to the *tolados,* there are *melachos* that so closely parallel the primary *melachos* that they too are considered primary *melachos.* An example of this is the *av melachah* of נוטע, *planting a seedling.* This act was not performed in the *Mishkan;* however, it bears a close similarity to one that *was* performed there — namely, the *av melachah* of זורע, *sowing a seed.* Because the purpose of planting a seedling is precisely the same as that of sowing a seed — to cause an object to grow — it too is considered an *av melachah* (*Rambam* ibid. 7:2-3; see also *Shabbos* 73b with *Rashi* ד"ה כולן מלאכה אחת הן).

The general rule in differentiating between *avos* and *tolados* is as follows: A *melachah* that closely resembles an *av* is itself an *av,* while one that is only somewhat similar to an *av* is a *toladah* (*Maggid Mishneh, Shabbos* 7:4; cf. *Kessef Mishneh* there §2). See further, *Iyunim* §3.

With regard to their prohibition and their penalty, primary *melachos* and *tolados* are exactly the same. One who performs a *toladah* on Shabbos, like one who performs an *av melachah,* violates the prohibition of לא תעשה כל מלאכה, *you shall not do any work,* and is liable to a *chatas* offering for an inadvertent transgression, and to death or *kares* for a deliberate one [see Law 3] (see *Bava Kamma* 2a;

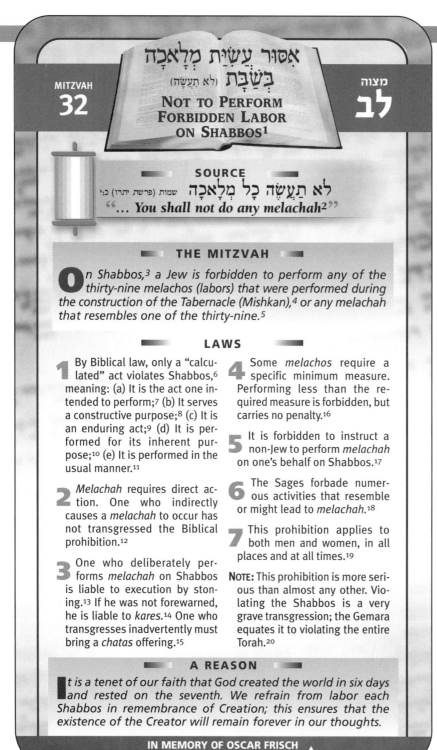

SOURCE

לֹא תַעֲשֶׂה כָל מְלָאכָה שמות (פרשת יתרו) כ:י

"... You shall not do any melachah[2]"

THE MITZVAH

On Shabbos,[3] a Jew is forbidden to perform any of the thirty-nine melachos (labors) that were performed during the construction of the Tabernacle (Mishkan),[4] or any melachah that resembles one of the thirty-nine.[5]

LAWS

1 By Biblical law, only a "calculated" act violates Shabbos,[6] meaning: (a) It is the act one intended to perform;[7] (b) It serves a constructive purpose;[8] (c) It is an enduring act;[9] (d) It is performed for its inherent purpose;[10] (e) It is performed in the usual manner.[11]

2 Melachah requires direct action. One who indirectly causes a melachah to occur has not transgressed the Biblical prohibition.[12]

3 One who deliberately performs melachah on Shabbos is liable to execution by stoning.[13] If he was not forewarned, he is liable to kares.[14] One who transgresses inadvertently must bring a chatas offering.[15]

4 Some melachos require a specific minimum measure. Performing less than the required measure is forbidden, but carries no penalty.[16]

5 It is forbidden to instruct a non-Jew to perform melachah on one's behalf on Shabbos.[17]

6 The Sages forbade numerous activities that resemble or might lead to melachah.[18]

7 This prohibition applies to both men and women, in all places and at all times.[19]

NOTE: This prohibition is more serious than almost any other. Violating the Shabbos is a very grave transgression; the Gemara equates it to violating the entire Torah.[20]

A REASON

It is a tenet of our faith that God created the world in six days and rested on the seventh. We refrain from labor each Shabbos in remembrance of Creation; this ensures that the existence of the Creator will remain forever in our thoughts.

av melachah and *its own toladah,* he is liable to only a single offering. For example, if a person grinds wheat (an *av melachah*) and chops vegetables (a *toladah*) in a single lapse of awareness, he brings only one offering, since both transgressions violate a single category of *melachah* (grinding). Thus, in order to determine the number of offerings that a transgressor must bring, we must identify precisely which labors are *avos melachos* in their own right, and which are *tolados* of *avos melachos* (see *Shabbos* 73b; *Bava Kamma* ibid.; see *Teshuvos Maharalbach* §23).

There is no specific number of *tolados;* a single *av melachah* can have numerous derivatives (*Sefer Yereim* §274). However, *Yerushalmi* (*Shabbos* 7:2) relates that in the three and one-half years that R' Yochanan and Resh Lakish spent studying the *melachos* of Shabbos, they identified thirty-nine *tolados* for each *av melachah.*

The fact that a given *melachah* is classified as a *toladah* does not mean that it was not performed in the *Mishkan*. On the contrary, the Gemara mentions several *tolados* that *were* performed in the *Mishkan* (see *Maharshal* to *Bava Kamma* 2a). How, then, did the Sages determine which of the *melachos* are *avos* and which are *tolados*? This was their criterion: Any *melachah* that was important in the *Mishkan* they classified as an *av,* while any *melachah* that was not important in the *Mishkan* they classified as a *toladah* (see *Bava Kamma* ibid. with *Tosafos* ד"ה ה"ג). [The Rishonim offer varying interpretations of this rule; see *Tosafos* ibid. with *Piskei Tosafos* §3; *Tosafos, Shabbos* 96b ד"ה ולרבי; *Rabbeinu Chananel, Bava Kamma* ibid.; *Ramban, Shabbos* ibid. and 49b; *Maharshal* and *Maharam* to *Bava Kamma* ibid.]

6. This refers to the requirement of מלאכת מחשבת, *calculated* (or *purposeful*) *labor,* which is a fundamental

Shulchan Aruch HaRav 301:1). The purpose of identifying and differentiating between *avos melachos* and their *tolados* is for cases in which a person inadvertently performs two *melachos* in a single lapse of awareness. [That is, he forgets that these acts are prohibited, and remains unaware of the

prohibition throughout the entire period of transgression.] If the *melachos* he performed were from two different categories of *melachos,* then whether they were two *avos,* two *tolados,* or one of each, he is liable to two *chatas* offerings, one for each transgression. If, however, the two *melachos* were an

tenet of Shabbos law. This principle, like so much concerning the *melachos,* is derived from the building of the *Mishkan.* In describing the labors performed there, Scripture employs the term מלאכת מחשבת (*Shemos* 35:33). Since the Shabbos *melachos* are analogous to the labors of the *Mishkan,* it follows that they too must possess these characteristics of purposefulness and design (see *Beitzah* 13b and *Chagigah* 10b, with *Rashi;* see also *Rambam, Hil. Shabbos* 1:9). All the criteria that follow fall under this general requirement.

In the requirements detailed below, the principle of "calculated labor" acts to exclude various actions from being considered *melachos.* Sometimes, though, this principle can serve to *include* specific acts in Shabbos liability. One example is the *melachah* of זורה, *winnowing,* in which a person throws grain into the air so that the wind will carry off the chaff. In other legal contexts — e.g. tort law — a person is not responsible for an act performed in concert with an external force. In the context of Shabbos law, however, this sort of act renders one liable. For Shabbos liability is predicated on an act being performed in a calculated, purposeful manner; since his calculated use of the wind fulfills his purpose, he is liable (see *Bava Kamma* 60a, with *Rashi* ד"ה מלאכת מחשבת). In this case, the principle of calculated labor endows an inferior act with the status of a Shabbos *melachah.* For another example of this, see *Or Zarua* vol. 1, §715; *Ran, Shabbos,* fol. 37b ד"ה גרסי' בגמ'.

7. The requirement of "intent" excludes two types of unintentional *melachah:*

The first is מתעסק, *an unwitting act.* This refers to a case in which a person intends to perform one act, but unwittingly performs a different act; for example, he intends to pick figs on Shabbos, but his hand slips and he picks grapes instead. Although the latter act is also forbidden, it was not the act he intended to perform. Therefore, it is not a "calculated" act, and does not violate the Shabbos (see *Sanhedrin* 62b; *Kereisos* 19a-b; *Rambam, Hil. Shabbos* 1:8,9).

Some maintain that this exclusion applies also where a person intends to perform an entirely permissible act and it transpires that the act he intended to perform was forbidden — e.g. he intends to pick up a plant that he believes is not attached to the ground, and it turns out to be attached, so that he inadvertently performs an act of reaping. Although he intended to pick up this very plant, he did not intend to uproot it; therefore, he has not performed a calculated act, and so has not transgressed the Shabbos (see *Rambam, Hil. Shegagos* 2:7, 7:11; *Meiri, Shabbos* 73a). Others rule that since the act he performed — picking up the plant — was the one he intended to perform, it is considered a calculated act (see *Tosafos, Sanhedrin* 62b ד"ה להגביה and *Shabbos* 72b ד"ה נתכוון). [However, even according to this view, he is not liable to a *chatas* offering, on account of a general Scriptural exemption that limits the *chatas* obligation to cases in which a person is cognizant of performing the sinful act at the time he performs it (see *Tosafos, Sanhedrin* ibid.).]

The second type of *melachah* excluded under the requirement of intent is אינו מתכוון, *an unintentional act.* This is a prohibited act that comes as an unintended consequence of a permitted act. An example would be the unintentional gouging of a furrow in the earth while dragging a chair across a field. Dragging the chair is a permitted act; gouging the furrow violates the primary *melachah* of חורש, *plowing.*

This scenario is the subject of a Tannaic dispute (*Shabbos* 29b; *Beitzah* 23b). R' Shimon holds that although the person is aware that dragging the chair might create a furrow, since this is not his intention, it is not a "calculated" act, and is therefore permitted (*Tosafos, Shabbos* 110b ד"ה תלמוד; *Ritva, Yoma* 34b; cf. *Tosafos, Kesubos* 5b ד"ה את"ל). But R' Yehudah rules that because he is aware that the act might create a furrow, it is forbidden. According to some Rishonim, R' Yehudah considers this a calculated act, in which case it is forbidden by Biblical law (see *Ramban, Shabbos* 75a; *Rashba, Shabbos* 133a). According to others, he agrees that it is not a calculated act, and prohibits it by Rabbinic law only (see *Rashi, Shabbos* 121b ד"ה דילמא; *Tosafos, Shabbos* 41b ד"ה מיחם). The halachah accords with the view of R' Shimon; see *Shulchan Aruch, Orach Chaim* 337:1.

Although R' Shimon permits a person to perform an unintentional *melachah* on Shabbos, he too agrees that if the forbidden act is an *inevitable* consequence of the permitted act, it is forbidden (see *Shabbos* 75a). For example, one who severs the head of an animal or bird on Shabbos cannot claim that he merely wished to take the head but did not intend the creature's death. Since it is inevitable that the bird will die, he is considered to have killed it intentionally. This example provides the name by which this principle is popularly known: פסיק רישיה ולא ימות, which translates as: *Its head is cut off and it will not die?* (*Rashi, Succah* 33b ד"ה מודי ר"ש; *Rambam, Hil. Shabbos* 1:6).

8. By Biblical law, destructive acts are not considered *melachah,* and do not violate the Shabbos (Mishnah, *Shabbos* 105b; *Rambam, Hil. Shabbos* 1:17). This is because of the requirement of מלאכת מחשבת, *purposeful labor,* which is labor that serves a constructive purpose (see *Rashi, Shabbos* 31b ד"ה לעולם and *Sanhedrin* 84b ד"ה מקלקל; see

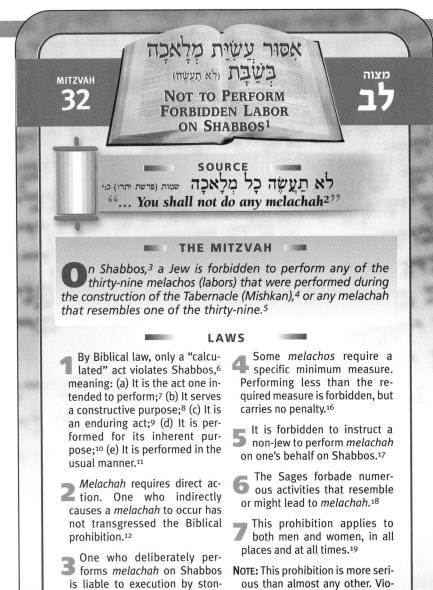

אִסוּר עֲשִׂיַת מְלָאכָה
בְּשַׁבָּת (לֹא תַעֲשֶׂה)

MITZVAH 32

NOT TO PERFORM FORBIDDEN LABOR ON SHABBOS[1]

מצוה לב

SOURCE

לֹא תַעֲשֶׂה כָל מְלָאכָה שמות (פרשת יתרו) כ:י

"*... You shall not do any melachah[2]*"

THE MITZVAH

On Shabbos,[3] a Jew is forbidden to perform any of the thirty-nine melachos (labors) that were performed during the construction of the Tabernacle (Mishkan),[4] or any melachah that resembles one of the thirty-nine.[5]

LAWS

1 By Biblical law, only a "calculated" act violates Shabbos,[6] meaning: (a) It is the act one intended to perform;[7] (b) It serves a constructive purpose;[8] (c) It is an enduring act;[9] (d) It is performed for its inherent purpose;[10] (e) It is performed in the usual manner.[11]

2 Melachah requires direct action. One who indirectly causes a melachah to occur has not transgressed the Biblical prohibition.[12]

3 One who deliberately performs melachah on Shabbos is liable to execution by stoning.[13] If he was not forewarned, he is liable to kares.[14] One who transgresses inadvertently must bring a chatas offering.[15]

4 Some melachos require a specific minimum measure. Performing less than the required measure is forbidden, but carries no penalty.[16]

5 It is forbidden to instruct a non-Jew to perform melachah on one's behalf on Shabbos.[17]

6 The Sages forbade numerous activities that resemble or might lead to melachah.[18]

7 This prohibition applies to both men and women, in all places and at all times.[19]

NOTE: This prohibition is more serious than almost any other. Violating the Shabbos is a very grave transgression; the Gemara equates it to violating the entire Torah.[20]

A REASON

It is a tenet of our faith that God created the world in six days and rested on the seventh. We refrain from labor each Shabbos in remembrance of Creation; this ensures that the existence of the Creator will remain forever in our thoughts.

IN MEMORY OF OSCAR FRISCH
יהושע בן חיים דוב בער ע"ה

leads to a positive benefit in some other area. An example would be inflicting a wound upon a person to obtain blood to feed an animal, which is a destructive act with respect to the person, but a constructive act with respect to the animal. For discussion of this and similar cases, see *Rashi* and *Tosafos* to *Shabbos* 106a; see also *Ramban* there at length.

There are a number of *melachos* that are inherently destructive, such as סותר, *demolishing*, and קורע, *tearing*. Under Biblical law, *melachos* of this sort are prohibited *only* if performed for a constructive purpose, as, for example, when one demolishes a structure in order to build another in the same place (see *Shabbos* 31b; *Rambam, Hil. Shabbos* 1:18) or tears a garment in order to re-sew it (see *Shabbos* 73a).

Destructive labor, although Biblically permitted, is forbidden by Rabbinic decree; see *Tosafos, Kesubos* 5b ד"ה אם תמצא לומר [א], and other Rishonim there.

9. One is liable for performing a Shabbos *melachah* only if its level of completion is such that it can be left to endure as it stands, and requires no further improvement (Mishnah, *Shabbos* 102b, with *Rashi* ד"ה כל העושה; see *Avnei Nezer, Orach Chaim* §249).

Alternatively, the point of this requirement is that the *melachah* must be able to endure for a length of time (see *Rambam, Hil. Shabbos* 9:13, with *Maggid Mishneh*; *Avnei Nezer* ibid.). According to some, it must be able to endure indefinitely; according to others, only until the end of the Shabbos day (see *Ritva, Shabbos* ibid.; *Shaar HaTziyun* 303:68). Some authorities maintain that the question is not how long the *melachah* is *able* to endure, but how long it is *intended* to endure. According to this view, if on Shabbos one builds a structure of a type that is generally dismantled after a short

Chagigah 10a-b). [For possible exceptions to this rule, see *Shabbos* 106a; see, however, *Rambam* ibid.]

A destructive act performed for a constructive purpose, such as erasing words written on paper in order to create a blank sheet to write on, is considered a constructive act, and is

therefore forbidden on Shabbos (see Mishnah, *Shabbos* ibid.). It is not clear, however, whether this rule applies only where the destructive act is itself beneficial, as in the above example, or whether it applies even where the destructive act is not in and of itself beneficial, but merely

time, he is not liable, even if the structure, if left alone, would last for a great length of time. See *Avnei Nezer* ibid. §210 for discussion.

This requirement emerges from the law of מלאכת מחשבת. An incomplete act, or one that cannot endure, does not qualify as "purposeful labor" (*Rashba* and *Ritva* to *Shabbos* 115b).

Although an act that does not endure is permitted under Biblical law, it is forbidden by Rabbinic decree (see Mishnah, *Shabbos* 104b with *Ritva* ד"ה והא דתנן כתב במשקים; see *Shulchan Aruch, Orach Chaim* 340:4).

10. מלאכה שאינה צריכה לגופה, *a melachah performed not for its inherent purpose,* does not violate the Shabbos. There are two views regarding the definition of "a *melachah* performed not for its inherent purpose":

A. It describes a case in which the person's intention in performing the *melachah* does not conform to the *melachah's* essential purpose, as defined by the purpose it served in the *Mishkan.* For example, digging a hole in order to plant something in the ground is forbidden under the *melachah* of חורש, *plowing,* while digging one for storage is forbidden under the *melachah* of בונה, *building.* In both cases, the *purpose* of the *melachah* is the same as it was in the *Mishkan* — to transform the ground by creating a hole. Therefore, it represents a violation of the Shabbos. However, here a person is *not* concerned with transforming the ground, and has no need for a hole, but digs with some other purpose in mind — such as to obtain earth — he has not performed the *melachah* "for its inherent purpose." Therefore, he has not violated the Shabbos (see *Tosafos* to *Chagigah* 10b ד"ה מלאכת, and *Shabbos* 94a ד"ה רבי שמעון).

B. It is a case in which a person performs a *melachah* not because of any

constructive purpose inherent in the act, but in order to prevent or rectify a problem. The Mishnah (*Shabbos* 93b) offers the example of a person who carries a corpse out of his house into a public domain on Shabbos. Ordinarily, one who carries an item from place to place *needs* the item in the second location. Hence, the transfer is purposeful in and of itself; therefore, it violates the Shabbos. Here, however, the person has no need for the corpse, and no interest in bringing it to a specific place, but simply wishes to remove it from the house. Because the transfer is not necessary in and of itself, and is performed only to rectify an undesirable situation, it is regarded as "a *melachah* performed not for its inherent purpose"; therefore, it does not violate the Shabbos (see *Rashi* to *Shabbos* 93b ד"ה ור' שמעון, and 31b ד"ה אפילו בפתילה; *Tosafos* ibid., explaining *Rashi*).

According to the first approach, this type of *melachah* is excluded from the Shabbos prohibition because its purpose differs from the purpose it had in the *Mishkan* (*Tosafos* to *Yoma* 34b ד"ה הני מילי, *Chagigah* ibid., and *Shabbos* 94a ד"ה רבי שמעון). According to the second approach, it is excluded because it does not fit the criterion of מלאכת מחשבת, for an act that lacks an inherently constructive purpose does not qualify as "purposeful labor" (see *Rashi, Shabbos* 93b ibid.; *Chagigah* 10b ibid.).

The exclusion of a *melachah* performed not for its inherent purpose is actually a matter of Tannaic dispute. R' Shimon holds that one who performs this sort of *melachah* is exempt; R' Yehudah rules him liable (see *Shabbos* 105b et al). There is some disagreement as to which view is accepted as halachah (see *Shulchan Aruch, Orach Chaim* 316:8 and 334:27; *Rambam* and *Raavad, Hil. Shabbos*

1:7); however, even R' Shimon, who permits this sort of *melachah* by Biblical law, agrees that it is forbidden by Rabbinic decree (see *Shabbos* 94a; see also previous note).

11. By Biblical law, one violates Shabbos *only* by performing *melachah* in the usual manner, which is determined by the common practice of the majority of people (see *Shabbos* 92a; *Rambam, Hil. Shabbos* 12:14). Thus, one who carries an object from a private to a public domain by grasping it with his foot or by holding it in his mouth has not performed a *melachah* (Mishnah, *Shabbos* ibid.). Similarly, one who writes with a pen held in his foot, mouth or armpit has not performed a *melachah* (Mishnah ibid. 104b). Since these acts were not performed in the usual manner, they do not meet the requirement of מלאכת מחשבת, *purposeful labor* (see *Pri Chadash, Even HaEzer* §123 ד"ה ולכתחלה יכתוב, and *Chelkas Mechokeik* there §5).

Although *melachah* performed in an unorthodox manner is not Biblically prohibited, it is forbidden by Rabbinic decree. This is known from the wording of the Mishnayos cited above, which state that one who performs these unusual acts is פטור, *exempt.* As a rule, when a Mishnah rules a person "exempt" for performing a particular act on Shabbos, it means that he is exempt from punishment, but the act is forbidden (*Shabbos* 3a).

Some Rishonim apply the principle of מלאכת מחשבת to teach yet another rule; namely, that only a significant act violates the Shabbos. For example, one who carries food measuring less than the volume of a dried fig from a private to a public domain on Shabbos is not liable (see *Shabbos* 76a). *Rashbam* (*Bava Basra* 55b ד"ה במסכת שבת) explains that the transfer of so small a volume of food is not a significant act; therefore, it

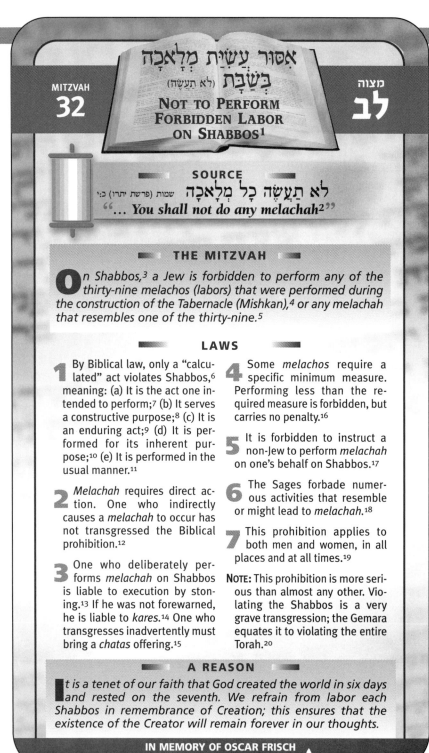

MITZVAH 32 / מצוה לב

אִסּוּר עֲשִׂיַּת מְלָאכָה בְּשַׁבָּת (לֹא תַעֲשֶׂה)

NOT TO PERFORM FORBIDDEN LABOR ON SHABBOS[1]

SOURCE

לֹא תַעֲשֶׂה כָל מְלָאכָה שמות (פרשת יתרו) כ:י

" ... You shall not do any melachah[2] "

THE MITZVAH

On Shabbos,[3] a Jew is forbidden to perform any of the thirty-nine melachos (labors) that were performed during the construction of the Tabernacle (Mishkan),[4] or any melachah that resembles one of the thirty-nine.[5]

LAWS

1 By Biblical law, only a "calculated" act violates Shabbos,[6] meaning: (a) It is the act one intended to perform;[7] (b) It serves a constructive purpose;[8] (c) It is an enduring act;[9] (d) It is performed for its inherent purpose;[10] (e) It is performed in the usual manner.[11]

2 Melachah requires direct action. One who indirectly causes a melachah to occur has not transgressed the Biblical prohibition.[12]

3 One who deliberately performs melachah on Shabbos is liable to execution by stoning.[13] If he was not forewarned, he is liable to kares.[14] One who transgresses inadvertently must bring a chatas offering.[15]

4 Some melachos require a specific minimum measure. Performing less than the required measure is forbidden, but carries no penalty.[16]

5 It is forbidden to instruct a non-Jew to perform melachah on one's behalf on Shabbos.[17]

6 The Sages forbade numerous activities that resemble or might lead to melachah.[18]

7 This prohibition applies to both men and women, in all places and at all times.[19]

NOTE: This prohibition is more serious than almost any other. Violating the Shabbos is a very grave transgression; the Gemara equates it to violating the entire Torah.[20]

A REASON

It is a tenet of our faith that God created the world in six days and rested on the seventh. We refrain from labor each Shabbos in remembrance of Creation; this ensures that the existence of the Creator will remain forever in our thoughts.

Another instance where performance of a melachah does not result in liability (though not related to the requirement of "calculated labor") is when two people perform a melachah together.

This law applies in two cases: (a) where two people act in concert to perform a melachah; for example, they take hold of an object together and carry it from a private domain to a public domain; (b) where each performs half of a melachah and their individual actions combine to form a complete melachah; for example, one person removes an object from a private domain, and a second places it into a public domain (see Mishnah, Shabbos 2a). In both cases, the participants are exempt from punishment, but their actions are prohibited (see Shabbos 92b-93a; Rambam, Hil. Shabbos 1:15). With regard to whether the prohibition is Biblical or Rabbinic, see Responsa of Chacham Tzvi §82; Mekor Chaim to Maginei Eretz §266; Be'er Yitzchak, Orach Chaim §14.

This exemption is limited to cases in which each participant could have accomplished the melachah on his own. Where, however, neither was capable of this (as in the case of a large beam, which cannot be carried by less than two people), their combined act renders both liable [to a chatas offering for inadvertent transgression, and to death or kares for deliberate transgression (see Law 3)]. Where one of the participants is capable of performing the melachah on his own and the other is not, the one who is capable is liable, and the other is exempt (Rambam ibid.1:16; see Shabbos ibid.).

This exemption is known from a verse in Vayikra (4:27): ואם נפש אחת תחטא בשגגה ... בעשתה אחת ממצות ה' אשר לא תעשינה, and if one person ... shall sin inadvertently by transgressing it — one of the commandments of

---

does not qualify as מלאכת מחשבת, "purposeful labor."

In a different illustration of this rule, the Gemara in *Beitzah* (13b) states that a person is permitted to peel barley kernels on Shabbos because this is not a מלאכת מחשבת. [Usually, separating husks from kernels of grain is prohibited on Shabbos, under the *melachah* of מפרק, *separating*, which is a *toladah* of דש, *threshing*.] *Rashi* (there) explains that peeling barley kernels is unskilled labor. This implies that unskilled, insignificant work does not meet the criterion of מלאכת מחשבת, "purposeful labor."

Hashem that may not be done. This verse is part of the passage that obligates a person to bring a *chatas* offering upon transgressing a prohibition. The phrase *by transgressing it* implies that a *chatas* is brought only if one transgresses "it" — i.e. the *entire* sin. Thus, those who transgress only part of a sin are not liable to a *chatas* offering (see *Shabbos* ibid. and 3a). The Sages extended the exemption to the other Shabbos penalties of stoning and *kares* as well.

Although this verse is stated regarding the *general* law of *chatas* offerings, it is expounded only with regard to Shabbos *melachah*. If two people join to commit some other prohibition, they are liable to punishment (see *Teshuvos HaRashba*, vol. 1, §28; *Pnei Yehoshua* to *Shabbos* 93a; cf. *Mekor Chaim* ibid.).

12. The Torah states לא תעשה כל מלאכה, *you shall not do any work.* "You shall not *do*" implies direct action; thus, we derive that one who indirectly causes a *melachah* to occur does not violate the Shabbos. For example, one is permitted to surround a blaze with barrels filled with water, so that the fire will destroy the barrels, and the water they contain will in turn extinguish the fire. Although extinguishing is forbidden on Shabbos, this is an act of indirect causation, and is therefore permitted (see *Shabbos* 120b; see *Iyunim* §5).

According to some opinions, indirect causation of a Shabbos *melachah* is always permitted (see *Taz, Orach Chaim* 514:6; *Shaar HaTziyun* there §31). Others hold that it is generally forbidden (by Rabbinic law), and is permitted only where it will prevent a monetary loss (as in the case of barrels used to extinguish a fire). The halachah follows the latter view (see *Mordechai, Shabbos* §399; *Rama, Orach Chaim* 334:22, with *Hagahos R' Akiva Eiger* there).

13. In *Shemos* 31:15, the Torah prescribes the death penalty for a Shabbos violator: כל העושה מלאכה ביום השבת מות יומת, *whoever does work on the day of Shabbos shall surely die.* This is repeated in *Shemos* 35:2: כל העושה בו מלאכה מות יומת, *whoever does work on [the Shabbos day] shall die.*

In *Bamidbar* 15:35, the Torah identifies the manner of execution as stoning. The verse states, regarding the punishment meted out to one who violated the Shabbos during Israel's wilderness sojourn: רגום אתו באבנים כל העדה מחוץ למחנה, *Let the entire congregation pelt him with stones outside the encampment* (see *Rashi, Shabbos* 6b ד"ה אי נמי).

The death penalty is prescribed only where the transgressor was forewarned. For details concerning the content of the warning, and the form it must take, see *mitzvah* #555.

Some Rishonim hold that a warning given to a potential transgressor must always explicitly identify the relevant prohibition (*Rashi, Shevuos* 20b ד"ה ואזהרתיה וד"ה אכלתי; cf. *Rambam, Hil. Sanhedrin* 12:2). Thus, a warning administered for transgressing Shabbos must identify the precise *av melachah* in question (*Tos. Rid, Shabbos* 138a). However, others hold that it need only identify the general Shabbos prohibition — namely, לא תעשה כל מלאכה, *you shall not do any work* — but not the specific *melachah* (*Keren Orah, Zevachim* 78a ד"ה הפיגול, in explanation of *Tosafos, Shabbos* 73b ד"ה משום). [With regard to whether a warning administered for a *toladah* must identify the relevant *av melachah* or only the *toladah*, see *Shabbos* 138a; *Moed Katan* 2b; *Tos. Rid* ibid.; *Tosafos, Shabbos* ibid. and to *Bava Kamma* 2a ד"ה ולר"א.]

14. This is known from the following verse (*Shemos* 31:14): מחלליה מות יומת כי כל העושה בה מלאכה ונכרתה הנפש

ההיא מקרב עמה, *And you shall keep the Shabbos, for it is holy to you, those who violate it shall surely die; for anyone who does work on [the Shabbos], that person shall be excised from among his nation.*

The verse refers to the penalty of *kares*, excision, which is manifested through the dual punishments of premature death and (according to some views) the loss of one's children (see *Moed Katan* 28a; *Rashi, Shabbos* 25b ד"ה כרת; *Tosafos, Shabbos* 25a ד"ה כרת).

15. It is a general rule that any prohibition whose deliberate transgression is punishable with *kares* requires a *chatas* offering for its inadvertent transgression (*Shabbos* 69a; see *mitzvah* #121).

A transgression is considered to be "inadvertent" if the person is unaware (a) that *melachah* is forbidden on Shabbos, (b) that it is the Shabbos day, or (c) that the particular act he is performing is a Shabbos *melachah*.

If a person inadvertently performs the same *melachah* many times on one Shabbos day, all in a single lapse of awareness [e.g. he forgets that it is Shabbos, and remains unaware of that fact throughout the day], he is liable to only a single *chatas*. If, however, he becomes [even momentarily] aware of the prohibition between each transgression, he must bring a separate *chatas* for each occasion of sin (see *Mishnah, Shabbos* 68a; *Rambam, Hil. Shegagos* 7:5; see above, note 5).

If one inadvertently performs several *different* Shabbos *melachos,* the law depends on the following variables:

A. If he was entirely unaware that it is forbidden to work on Shabbos, he is liable to only a single *chatas,* even if he violated numerous Shabbosos (*Shabbos* 67b-68a; *Rambam* ibid. 7:2).

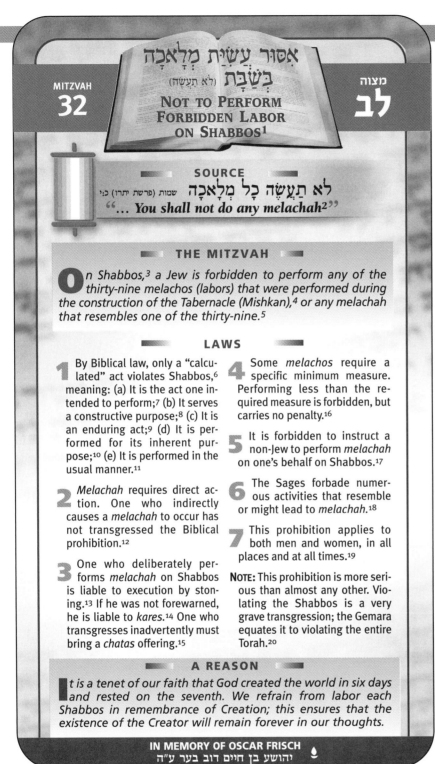

MITZVAH 32 — מצוה לב

אִסּוּר עֲשִׂית מְלָאכָה בְּשַׁבָּת (לֹא תַעֲשֶׂה)

NOT TO PERFORM FORBIDDEN LABOR ON SHABBOS[1]

SOURCE

לֹא תַעֲשֶׂה כָל מְלָאכָה שמות (פרשת יתרו) כ:י

"... You shall not do any melachah[2]"

THE MITZVAH

On Shabbos,[3] a Jew is forbidden to perform any of the thirty-nine melachos (labors) that were performed during the construction of the Tabernacle (Mishkan),[4] or any melachah that resembles one of the thirty-nine.[5]

LAWS

1 By Biblical law, only a "calculated" act violates Shabbos,[6] meaning: (a) It is the act one intended to perform;[7] (b) It serves a constructive purpose;[8] (c) It is an enduring act;[9] (d) It is performed for its inherent purpose;[10] (e) It is performed in the usual manner.[11]

2 Melachah requires direct action. One who indirectly causes a melachah to occur has not transgressed the Biblical prohibition.[12]

3 One who deliberately performs melachah on Shabbos is liable to execution by stoning.[13] If he was not forewarned, he is liable to kares.[14] One who transgresses inadvertently must bring a chatas offering.[15]

4 Some melachos require a specific minimum measure. Performing less than the required measure is forbidden, but carries no penalty.[16]

5 It is forbidden to instruct a non-Jew to perform melachah on one's behalf on Shabbos.[17]

6 The Sages forbade numerous activities that resemble or might lead to melachah.[18]

7 This prohibition applies to both men and women, in all places and at all times.[19]

NOTE: This prohibition is more serious than almost any other. Violating the Shabbos is a very grave transgression; the Gemara equates it to violating the entire Torah.[20]

A REASON

It is a tenet of our faith that God created the world in six days and rested on the seventh. We refrain from labor each Shabbos in remembrance of Creation; this ensures that the existence of the Creator will remain forever in our thoughts.

B. If he was aware of the prohibition to work on Shabbos, but was unaware that it was Shabbos, he is liable to a separate chatas for each Shabbos he violated. Each of the chataos atones for all the melachos he performed on the Shabbos in question (Shabbos ibid.; Rambam ibid.).

C. If he was aware of the Shabbos prohibition, and knew that it was Shabbos, but was unaware that the melachos he performed are prohibited, he is liable to a separate chatas offering for each category of melachah he performed (Shabbos 67b, with Rashi ד"ה היודע שהוא שבת; Rambam ibid. 7:3).

A person does not become liable to a chatas offering until he becomes aware that he sinned. In the case of a Shabbos transgression, he must become aware of precisely which melachah he violated (see Kereisos 19a; Rambam, Hil. Shegagos 8:2; see Aruch LaNer to Kereisos ibid.).

16. For example, one transgresses the melachah of weaving only upon weaving two threads, and the melachah of sewing only upon sewing two stitches. One who weaves or sews less than these measures is not liable to punishment (Mishnah, Shabbos 73a). Conversely, the melachah of building has no measure at all; therefore, one who builds even the minutest amount of a structure on Shabbos is liable to punishment (Mishnah, Shabbos 102b).

There are various explanations offered for why different melachos require a particular measure. Rashbam (Bava Basra 55b ד"ה במסכת שבת) writes that specific measures are given for transporting foods between domains because transfer of a small volume of food is not a significant act, and does not qualify as מלאכת מחשבת, "purposeful labor" (see above, note 11). Rashi explains that the two-letter measure given for the melachah of writing is derived from the Mishkan, whose beams were marked with two letters (see Shabbos 75b with Rashi ד"ה כתב; see also Ran there, fol. 32b ד"ה כתב). Others maintain that the measures of Shabbos melachos, like all other Torah measures, are known through הלכה למשה מסיני, an Oral Law taught to Moshe at Sinai (see Kiryas Sefer, Shabbos ch. 18; see also Eruvin 4a-b).

Although one who performs only part of a melachah's requisite measure — e.g. he sews only one stitch — is not liable to punishment, the act is forbidden by Biblical law, as is any other part-measure of a sinful act [e.g. consuming less than an olive's volume of forbidden food] (see *Ritva, Shabbos* 74a ד"ה וכי מותר; *Rashi* there ד"ה בורר (לאפות פחות). Alternatively, part-measures of Shabbos *melachos,* unlike those of other sins, are forbidden by Rabbinic decree only (see *Agudah, Shabbos* beginning of ch. 8; *Ramban, Shabbos* 74a, *Kiryas Sefer* ibid.; *Totza'os Chaim* 8:1; see also *Minchas Chinuch* 32:4).

One who performs two part-measures of *melachah* even at widely-separated intervals on the same Shabbos (e.g. he inscribes one letter in the morning and another in the afternoon) is liable for transgressing the Shabbos (see Mishnah, *Shabbos* 105a with *Tosafos* ד"ה ורבנן; however, see *Rashi* there ד"ה אחת שחרית). [If, however, the two part-measures are performed on *different* Shabbosos, he is exempt (*Pri Megadim, Introduction to Hil. Shabbos* ד"ה טוחן).]

17. See Mishnah, *Shabbos* 121a, with *Rashi* ד"ה אין אומרים; *Rambam, Hil. Shabbos* 6:1.

This is a Rabbinic enactment. The Rabbis decreed that the non-Jew is to be treated as the agent of the Jew; hence, when the non-Jew performs *melachah,* it is as if it was performed by the Jew himself (see *Rashi, Shabbos* 153a ד"ה מאי טעמא; *Hagahos Maimonios* §2, to *Rambam* ibid.; see *Sfas Emes, Shabbos* ibid.). The Rabbis enacted this decree because they feared that allowing such instruction would cause Jews to make light of the Shabbos prohibitions, and could result in Jews performing *melachah* themselves (*Rambam* ibid.; see *Shulchan Aruch HaRav* 243:1). Alternatively, instructing a non-Jew to perform *melachah* is prohibited under the Rabbinic decree forbidding mundane speech on Shabbos (*Rashi, Avodah Zarah* 15a ד"ה כיון דזבנה; see *Avnei Nezer, Orach Chaim* 43:6). See further, *Siach Halachah* section.

Mechilta derives this prohibition from *Shemos* 12:16, which states regarding festivals: כל מלאכה לא יעשה בהם, *All melachah shall not be done on them.* The verse employs the passive voice (*shall not be done*) to teach that even if the *melachah* is performed by others — i.e. non-Jews — it is forbidden (*Malbim* ad loc.). However, *Mechilta* does not mean to say that this is a Biblical prohibition; rather, the verse is intended as an אסמכתא, *a Scriptural support to a Rabbinic decree* (*Ramban* ad loc.). See, however, *Smag, Lo Saaseh* §75 and *Yereim HaShalem* §304, who suggest that this is actually a Biblical prohibition.

This prohibition applies in the following cases: (a) Where a Jew instructs a non-Jew *on* Shabbos to perform *melachah* either on or after Shabbos (*Rambam* ibid.; *Aruch HaShulchan, Orach Chaim* 243:4). (b) Where a Jew instructs a non-Jew *before* Shabbos to perform *melachah* on Shabbos (*Rambam* ibid.; *Rosh, Shabbos* 1:36; *Mordechai* there §249; see *Aruch HaShulchan* ibid.; *Avnei Nezer, Orach Chaim* 43:6).

18. By Biblical law, one could conceivably busy himself on Shabbos with all types of work and business without ever transgressing the Shabbos. Consider: Under purely Biblical law, one is permitted to weigh and measure produce, and buy and sell merchandise on Shabbos. In a walled city, one is permitted to carry his merchandise to the market, or to load it upon his animal and lead the animal there. Marketplaces could remain open for business on Shabbos, merchants and moneychangers would ply their trades, and laborers could hire themselves out for permitted work. To prevent this from occurring, the Sages forbade numerous activities which are not themselves *melachos,* but

which resemble *melachos,* or could lead people to perform *melachos.*

These decrees were based on the following verse (*Shemos* 23:12, 34:21): וביום השביעי תשבות, *and on the seventh day, you shall rest.* The phrase *you shall rest* conjures a vision of Shabbos as an interval of serenity and calm. As we have demonstrated, this vision cannot be realized by merely refraining from *melachah.* Thus the Rabbis issued enactments which preserved the unique sanctity of this day, and allowed the Torah's vision of Shabbos to come to full flower (*Rambam, Hil. Shabbos* 21:1; see *Maggid Mishneh* and *Lechem Mishneh* there; *Ramban, Vayikra* 23:24).

Enactments of this type are commonly referred to as שבות. The word shares a common root with לשבות, *to rest;* thus, the name represents the origins of these decrees (*Rav MiBartenura, Beitzah* 5:2).

Several other verses are offered as the Scriptural basis of the Rabbinic decrees. For various possibilities, see *Mechilta D'R' Shimon bar Yochai* to *Shemos* 35:2 and 12:16; *Mechilta D'R' Yishmael* to *Shemos* 23:13; *Rashi, Yoma* 74a ד"ה שבתון.

19. *Sefer HaChinuch* §32. This follows the usual rule, whereby women are included in all Biblical prohibitions (see *Kiddushin* 29a).

Non-Jews are forbidden to observe the Jewish Shabbos — see *Sanhedrin* 58b; *Rambam, Hil. Melachim* 10:9.

20. Deliberate, public violation of Shabbos is tantamount to idolatry, and is viewed as a violation of the entire Torah. A Jew who intentionally violates Shabbos in public is a heretic, and is treated as an idolater in all matters of Jewish law (*Rambam, Hil. Shabbos* 30:15, from *Eruvin* 69b and *Chullin* 5a).

A BROADER LOOK AT THE LAWS

1 Scriptural sources for the number of melachos

We have explained (note 4) that some derive the count of thirty-nine *melachos* from an analogy between Shabbos and the *Mishkan,* while others arrive at this number through exposition of various Scriptural verses.

One such exposition focuses on a verse that prefaces the Shabbos obligation (*Shemos* 35:1): אלה הדברים אשר צוה ה', *these [i.e. the Shabbos melachos] are the things that Hashem commanded.* The plural דברים, *things,* indicates two *melachos;* the ה of הדברים, which represents the definite article, *the,* is expounded to teach an additional *melachah.* These, plus the numerical value of אלה (36), total thirty-nine (see *Shabbos* 70a; 97b). Thus, the verse alludes to thirty-nine Shabbos *melachos.*

Alternatively, the relevant verse is לא תעשה כל מלאכה, *you shall not do any work.* The phrase "any work" refers to the number of times that the word מלאכה, *work,* appears in the Torah. As it happens, the word (in various forms) appears thirty-nine times. Each represents another *melachah;* we are commanded to refrain from all thirty-nine (*Shabbos* 49b, with *Rashi* ד"ה שבתורה). [Although the Torah actually contains more than thirty-nine mentions of מלאכה, not all are included in this count. For discussion of which are omitted and why, see *Shabbos* ibid. with *Rashi; Rabbeinu Chananel,* cited in *Ramban, Rashba* and *Ritva* ad loc.; *Tos. Yom Tov* to *Shabbos* 7:2; *Sefer Raavan, Shabbos* §350; *Yefei Einayim* to *Shabbos* 49b.]

Despite these teachings, the analogy between Shabbos and the *Mishkan* remains necessary, for it is the means by which we identify which *melachos* are included in the thirty-nine — namely, the *melachos* of the *Mishkan.* However, the analogy alone does not suffice, for although it is effective in teaching that *melachos* performed in the *Mishkan* are prohibited on Shabbos, it does not specify a certain number of Shabbos *melachos.* Without a specific number, one could argue that other non-*Mishkan* acts are *also* included in the prohibition, in which case the count of *melachos* would exceed thirty-nine, or that two similar *Mishkan melachos* are actually a single *melachah* (see *Shabbos* 73b-74a), in which case the count would be less than thirty-nine. These arguments are precluded by the above expositions, which establish the number of *melachos* as precisely thirty-nine — namely, thirty-nine acts that were performed in the *Mishkan* (see *Shabbos* 74a; *Ramban, Rashba* and *Ritva* to *Shabbos* 49b; however, see *Tosafos* 49b ד"ה כנגד).

2 Melachos singled out for mention in the Torah

Most *melachos* are known through the general comparison of Shabbos and the *Mishkan.* However, there are four *melachos* that are specifically mentioned in the Torah. They are:

A. הוצאה מרשות לרשות, *transferring an object from a private domain* (רשות היחיד) *to a public domain* (רשות הרבים). This is known from a verse in which Moshe Rabbeinu commanded *Bnei Yisrael* to stop bringing donations for the work of the *Mishkan* (*Shemos* 36:6). The Sages teach that he issued this command on Shabbos, because the Levite camp (in which he resided) was a public domain, and the people were bringing their contributions from a private domain. Moshe Rabbeinu warned them that this is forbidden (*Shabbos* 96b).

The *melachah* of transferring between domains was singled out for special mention because it is a מלאכה גרועה, *an inferior melachah,* and would not otherwise have been derived through the comparison to the *Mishkan.* It is inferior because the physical act of transferring an object from one location to another is not *intrinsically* forbidden. Rather, its prohibition derives from external factors; namely, the location from which the object is taken, and the place to which it is transferred.

To illustrate: It is entirely permissible to carry an item from place to place within a private domain, such as from one room of a house to another. Yet, it is absolutely forbidden to carry that same item from the house into a public street. The act of carrying is the same in both instances, yet, in one it is permitted, and in the other forbidden. In the case of other *melachos,* by contrast, the act is inherently undesirable, and is therefore prohibited regardless of one's location.

Because transferring is an inferior *melachah,* we would not have known to include it in the Shabbos-*Mishkan* analogy. Therefore, the Torah must make specific mention of this *melachah* (*Rashba, Shabbos* 2a; *Tosafos* there ד"ה פשט; see also *Chasam Sofer* there ד"ה כיצד).

B. הבערה, *kindling a fire.* The prohibition against lighting a fire on Shabbos is stated explicitly in Scripture, in *Shemos* 35:3: לא תבערו אש בכל משבתיכם ביום השבת, *You shall not kindle a fire in all your dwellings on the Shabbos day.* R' Yose states that this *melachah* is singled out to teach that it alone, among all Shabbos *melachos,* is punishable not with death or *kares* (see Law 3), but with lashes (*malkos*). R' Nasan disagrees. He holds that kindling, like all other *melachos,* is punishable with death. Why then is it singled out? To teach that one must bring a separate *chatas* offering for each *melachah* one performs on Shabbos.

Without this verse, we might have assumed that one who inadvertently performs several *melachos* is liable to only a single offering, to atone for the general sin of לא תעשה כל מלאכה, *you shall not do any work.* By separating kindling from the others, the Torah teaches that every *melachah* carries a separate and distinct prohibition; therefore, each requires its own *chatas* offering (see *Shabbos* 70a; *Rashi, Pesachim* 5b ד"ה וש"מ). [R' Yose also agrees that one is liable to a separate offering for each *melachah;* however, he derives this from another verse (*Shabbos* ibid.).] The halachah follows R' Nasan; therefore, one who kindles a fire on Shabbos is subject to death or *kares* (*Rambam, Hil. Shabbos* 7:1).

C. חריש, *plowing,* and קציר, *reaping.* The verse states (*Shemos* 34:21): ששת ימים תעבד וביום השביעי תשבות בחריש ובקציר תשבות, *Six days you shall work and on the seventh day you shall rest; at the plowing and at the reaping you shall rest.* R' Yishmael understands the phrase *at the plowing and at the reaping* to be referring to plowing and reaping on Shabbos (as indicated by the verse's first clause, *on the seventh day you shall rest*). But R' Akiva holds that this phrase refers not to Shabbos, but to the *shemittah,* or Sabbatical year (*Rosh Hashanah* 9a).

According to R' Yishmael, the Torah mentions these two *melachos* to teach that just as the plowing prohibited by this verse is discretionary (for there is no instance in the Torah of an obligation to plow), so too is the reaping prohibited by this verse discretionary. It follows that where there is an obligation to reap — as in the case of the *omer* offering — it may be done even on Shabbos.

[To explain: The *omer* offering (brought on the second day of Pesach) is made of flour from barley that must be reaped the night before the offering. The verse teaches that if the second day of Pesach falls on Shabbos, the barley may be reaped on Friday night. The obligation to reap the barley overrides the Shabbos prohibition (*Rosh Hashanah* ibid., with *Rashi*).]

3   *An act resembling an av melachah: When is it an av and when a toladah?*

As mentioned above (note 5), a *melachah* that bears a close similarity to an *av melachah* is itself an *av melachah,* while one of lesser similarity is a *toladah. Tiferes Yisrael* (*Kilkeles Shabbos* §1) explains how we determine whether a given *melachah* resembles an *av* closely enough to be considered an *av* in its own right. Firstly, *av melachah* status is reserved for a *melachah* whose purpose is identical to that of an *av.* Thus, planting a seedling or grafting a branch onto a tree is considered an *av melachah,* for its purpose — to cause something to grow — is identical to that of the *av melachah* of זורע, *sowing a seed* (see *Rambam, Hil. Shabbos* 7:3).

However, similarity of purpose alone does not suffice to endow a *melachah* with the status of an *av,* as is evident from the *melachah* of watering plants, whose purpose is to cause something to grow, but which is nevertheless only a *toladah* (see *Rambam* ibid. 8:2). Rather, in order to be deemed an *av,* a *melachah* must also be performed in the same manner as the *av,* or, at the very least, upon the same object as the *av.*

Consider the *melachah* of grafting a branch onto a tree. In addition to sharing the purpose of זורע, grafting is also performed in the same manner, for both acts are performed by inserting a movable object (the seed or branch) into a stationary object (the ground or tree). Therefore, grafting too is an *av melachah.* Or, consider the act of removing a mound of earth to level a field. This act, which is intended to improve the ground in preparation for planting, is similar in purpose to the *av melachah* of חורש, *plowing.* Although it is not performed in the same manner as plowing, it is performed upon the same object (the ground); therefore, it too is an *av melachah.* By contrast, the *melachah* of watering plants is not performed in the same manner as planting, and it is performed on a different object (the water, as opposed to the seed); therefore, it is a *toladah,* not an *av.*

Similarly, if an act resembles an *av melachah* only in the manner of its performance, but not in its purpose, it is a *toladah.* For example, the *melachah* of grinding iron to dust is similar in form to the primary *melachah* of טוחן, *grinding wheat.* However, these *melachos* are not at all similar in purpose. One's intention in grinding wheat is to prepare it for eating — this is obviously not one's intention in grinding down iron. Since its purpose differs from that of the *av melachah,* it is a *toladah* (*Kilkeles Shabbos* ibid.).

4 **When is it permitted to perform melachah in an unusual manner?**

Melachah performed in an unusual manner is generally forbidden by Rabbinic decree (see note 11). However, in three situations, the Rabbis waived their decree:

A. *Where the act prevents monetary loss:* This rule is taught in *Shabbos* 153b, regarding a person who is carrying a bundle in the public domain when Shabbos arrives, and wishes to throw it into his house for safekeeping. Ordinarily, transferring an object from a public to a private domain is forbidden on Shabbos; however, since this person stands to suffer a monetary loss, he is permitted to throw his bundle into the house, so long as the act is performed in an unusual manner — e.g. by facing away from the door and throwing the bundle in backwards (*Shabbos* ibid. with *Rashi* ד"ה כלאחר יד; see *Mishnah Berurah* 266:32). See *Kesubos* 60a for another example of this rule.

B. *Where the act alleviates physical suffering:* For instance, if a person is ill (even with a non-life-threatening illness) and his cure requires him to suckle milk directly from an animal's udder, we permit him to do so on Shabbos. Now, milking an animal is usually prohibited on Shabbos (under the *toladah* of מפרק, *separating*). However, because this is not the way animals are usually milked, and because it will alleviate the person's suffering, it is permitted (*Kesubos* ibid.; see *Mishnah Berurah* 328:107). See further *Tosafos, Kesubos* ibid. ד"ה גונח.

C. *Where the act is done for the sake of a mitzvah:* The Sages teach that if, when *Erev Pesach* falls on Shabbos, a person forgets his slaughtering knife at home and is therefore unable to slaughter his *pesach* offering, he may stick the knife into the wool or between the horns of his offering, and allow the animal to transport the knife to the Holy Temple. Ordinarily, one may not perform a Shabbos *melachah* in conjunction with his animal (on account of the prohibition of מחמר — see below, *Iyunim* §6). Here, however, the *melachah* is performed in an unusual manner, for it is not common for sheep or goats (the animals used for the *pesach*) to carry loads. Furthermore, it is performed for the sake of a mitzvah (the *pesach* offering). Therefore, it is permitted (*Pesachim* 66b, with *Rashi* ד"ה כלאחר יד; see, however, *Tosafos* there, ד"ה הנח).

[These principles may not be applied in practice without consulting an expert in halachah. As with many halachic principles, their practical application is subject to various contingencies, whose enumeration is beyond the scope of this work.]

5 Is melachah performed in concert with an external force considered "indirect causation"?

In note 6, we discussed the *melachah* of זורה, *winnowing,* in which a person throws a mixture of grain and chaff into the air, and the wind carries off the chaff. Although the act is performed in conjunction with an external force (the wind), it renders one liable.

This law seems to contradict the rule that states that indirect causation (גרמא) of Shabbos *melachah* is permitted. For example, one may surround a fire with barrels full of water so that the fire will destroy the barrels and be extinguished. Because the actual *melachah* (extinguishing) is performed through the medium of an external force (the fire), it is permitted (see note 12). Yet, the *melachah* of winnowing, which also involves an external force, is forbidden!

A possible answer: Throwing grain into the wind is the usual method of performing the act of winnowing, and is the way it was performed in the *Mishkan*. Therefore, although the *melachah* is performed through an external force, it is forbidden on Shabbos. The *melachah* of extinguishing, by contrast, does not usually involve an external force. Therefore, when it *is* performed in this manner, it is permitted (*Imrei Binah,* דיני שבת §27 and *Avnei Nezer, Orach Chaim* §388, in explanation of *Rosh, Bava Kamma* 6:11; however, cf. *Pilpula Charifta* ad loc.).

Alternatively, one is *always* liable for a *melachah* performed in concert with an external force, whether or not it is the usual practice. As for the contradiction detailed above, it is resolved as follows: In the case of winnowing, the forbidden act is directly performed by the person, albeit in concert with the wind; it is not an act of indirect causation.

In the case of the fire, however, the person does *not* directly perform the *melachah* in concert with the fire. Rather, the person merely creates a situation in which an external force (the fire) is later empowered to perform a *melachah* on its own. Thus, the forbidden consequence — the extinguishing of the fire — is not a direct result of the person's act. Hence, his act is one of indirect causation, and is therefore permitted (see *Zera Emes,* vol. 1, §44).

6 One's Shabbos obligation with respect to his children, slaves and animals.

It has been mentioned (note 2) that our verse represents a prohibition against (a) allowing children to violate the Shabbos, (b) allowing slaves to violate the Shabbos, and (c) directing an animal in performance of *melachah* on Shabbos. Let us examine each of these categories:

A. *Children:* According to some authorities, the verse לא תעשה כל מלאכה אתה ובנך ובתך, *You shall not do any work, you and your son and your daughter,* is a prohibition enjoining adults from allowing their children to perform *melachah* on Shabbos (*Ramban, Shemos* 20:9; *Sefer HaChinuch* here; see *Teshuvos Chasam Sofer, Orach Chaim,* end of §83). However, this view appears to be at odds with the Gemara in *Shabbos* (121a), which equates the requirement to prevent a minor from violating the Shabbos with the general requirement to prevent minors from violating all Torah prohibitions. This implies that there is no specific Shabbos obligation. A similar inference may be drawn from *Shulchan Aruch* (*Orach Chaim* §343), which discusses one's Shabbos obligation vis-à-vis his children in the context of the general requirement, but makes no mention of a special Shabbos obligation. See also *Maggid Mishneh* to *Rambam, Hil. Shabbos* 20:7; see *Minchas Chinuch* end of §32.

B. *Slaves:* The words עבדך ואמתך, *your slave and your maidservant,* represent a command to prevent one's Canaanite slaves from violating Shabbos (*Rambam, Hil. Shabbos* 20:14; *Ramban,*

Shemos ibid.; *Sefer HaChinuch* ibid.). Although a slave is *personally* obligated to observe Shabbos, the Torah places a separate obligation upon the master to see to it that the slave complies (*Rambam* and *Ramban* ibid.). Other Rishonim maintain that there is no such obligation upon the master. Rather, the verse *your slave and your maidservant* refers to a גר תושב, a *resident alien* of Eretz Yisrael. This is a non-Jew who is pledged to abide by the seven Noahide Laws, but is not obligated to keep Shabbos. According to this view, the verse prohibits a Jew to employ a "resident alien" to perform *melachah* for him on Shabbos (*Hasagos HaRaavad* to *Rambam* ibid.).

B. *Animals:* The term ובהמתך, *and your animal,* prohibits a person to direct an animal (or bird) in performing a *melachah* on Shabbos, e.g. by leading it as it transports a load through a public domain. This *melachah* is commonly known as מחמר, *leading a laden animal* (see *Shabbos* 153b-154a, with *Ritva; Rambam, Hil. Shabbos* 20:1;

Sefer HaChinuch here); however, it applies not only to the *melachah* of carrying in the public domain, but to all Shabbos *melachos* (*Tiferes Yisrael, Kilkeles Shabbos* שביתת בהמתו ומחמר §2; *Toldos Shmuel, mitzvah* §32, 100:1; cf. *Pnei Yehoshua, Shabbos* 51b). According to some Rishonim, this prohibition encompasses not only the thirty-nine *melachos,* but also includes any case in which an animal is directed to perform work for a person on Shabbos, even if it is work that would not otherwise violate the Shabbos — e.g. carrying a load within a private domain (see *Rashba, Avodah Zarah* 15a).

The authorities disagree on whether the prohibition of מחמר is stated only regarding one's *own* animal, as implied by the word בהמתך, *"your"* animal, or whether it applies also to *melachah* performed with the animal of another. For discussion, see *Rashba* and *Chidushei HaRan* to *Shabbos* 153b; *Ran, Avodah Zarah* ibid.; *Yereim HaShalem* §332, as explained by *Eglei Tal,* חורש 13:2.

SITUATIONS IN HALACHAH

Question:
Can a Jew have *melachah* performed on his behalf on Shabbos, by a Jew for whom Shabbos has already ended?

Answer:
There are several possible scenarios where such a situation could arise. One involves a person who lives in one time zone, and owns a factory in a second time zone. Work is performed by Jews in his factory on his behalf after Shabbos, while it is still Shabbos where he lives. Now, obviously the Jews working in the factory are not violating any laws themselves, for Shabbos has ended where they live. However, we know that the principle of agency (*shlichus*) dictates that an act performed by a person's agent is deemed as if it was performed by the person himself. If we were to apply the principle of *shlichus* in this case, the owner of the factory would be viewed as if he were performing the work being done by the employees himself, thus desecrating the Shabbos!

At first glance, this would not appear to pose a difficulty, for this case is one where a transgression is involved, and the rule is that "there is no agency for an act of transgression" (אין שליח לדבר עבירה). Thus, the factory owner cannot be held liable for his employee's actions. However, this answer does not suffice. For the Gemara (*Bava Metzia* 10b) explains that this exception only holds where the agent is himself forbidden to perform the act (so that the fault is his for heeding the sender rather than Hashem — see *Tosafos* to *Kiddushin* 42b ד"ה אמאי). But in this case, the agent is doing nothing wrong, as Shabbos has ended for him. Accordingly, the rule of *shlichus* should apply, and the factory owner should be liable!

To answer this question, we must turn to a related discussion among the commentators with respect to the Rabbinic edict that forbids a Jew to ask a non-Jew to perform *melachah* for him on Shabbos (*amirah l'nochri*). The authorities wonder why such a decree was necessary. Seemingly, this would be forbidden in any case, for the non-Jew would be performing the *melachah* as an agent of the Jew, and the principle of *shlichus* should render the Jew liable!

To this question, *Beis Meir* (*Even HaEzer*, 5:14; see also *Teshuvos Chasam Sofer* §84) answers that the principle of agency does not apply to the performance of *melachah* on Shabbos. He explains that the Shabbos prohibitions are unique in that the essential violation of Shabbos is not the fact that one performed an act of *melachah* per se, but that in doing so, one has stopped "resting," (*menuchah*), which is the essential mitzvah of Shabbos. In other words, the 39 categories of *melachah* simply define exactly how to fulfill the mitzvah of "resting" by delineating which activities one must refrain from performing.

Consequently, the principle of agency does not apply to the performance of *melachah* on Shabbos, because that principle serves only to attribute *legal* responsibility for the agent's actions to the one who commissioned him. Attributing legal responsibility is only relevant where the essential prohibition is the performance of the act itself, for then we can view the one who commissioned the agent as having performed the forbidden act, thus he is liable to face the consequences. However, regarding the laws of Shabbos where the essential prohibition is not the actual performance of the *melachah*, but rather the fact that through its performance one's body stopped "resting," we cannot apply the principle of agency. [Similarly, one cannot fulfill one's obligation to put on *tefillin* by having one's agent put *tefillin* on himself, for the obligation is to place *tefillin* on one's *own* body. So too regarding Shabbos, the prohibition requires that one's *own* body should refrain from performing *melachah*.]

In the scenario discussed above, then, the same

reasoning would apply. Although *melachah* is being performed on behalf of the factory owner, since he himself is "at rest," he is not in violation of the Shabbos.

Other authorities, however, take a different approach, and maintain that when a non-Jew performs *melachah* for a Jew, the Jew *is* liable due to the principle of agency (see *Rashi* to *Shabbos* 153a ד"ה מ"ט, *Hagahos Rambam, Hil. Shabbos* 6:2, and *Kehillos Yaakov, Tractate Shabbos* §12). They explain that the Rabbinic decree against *amirah l'nochri* was needed to prohibit a Jew from telling a non-Jew on Shabbos to perform *melachah* for him after Shabbos [which obviously cannot be forbidden because of *shlichus*] (see further, *Avnei Nezer, Orach Chaim* 43:6, *Kehillos Yaakov, Shabbos* §55). According to these authorities, it would seem that the factory owner in the scenario discussed above *would* be liable. However, *Kehillos Yaakov* (§55) states that in truth, all views concur that there can be no true agency regarding the performance of *melachah* on Shabbos; and those authorities who do mention *shlichus* mean only that the Sages prohibited *amirah l'nochri* because it *appears* that the non-Jew is the Jew's agent. In our case, however, there would be no liability.

Another scenario where this question arises is when a Jew who accepted Shabbos upon himself early (before nightfall — see *mitzvah #31*, note 4) asks another Jew, who has not yet accepted Shabbos, to perform *melachah* for him. The halachah is that this is permissible, although the one asking has already accepted Shabbos upon himself (see *Shulchan Aruch, Orach Chaim* §263 [end] and *Mishnah Berurah* there §64). And, as explained above, the principle of *shlichus* does not apply (see *Teshuvos Yeshuos Yaakov, Even HaEzer* 5:5-6).

ILLUMINATIONS OF THE MITZVAH
Suggested Reasons & Insights

I. COMMEMORATING THE WORLD'S CREATION

❧ Creation and faith

It is an essential article of our faith that the world was willed into being by God at a definite point in time. The process of Creation lasted six days; on the seventh day God rested, having completed His work. Perpetuating the awareness of this elementary fact is the purpose of the law calling for the suspension of work on the Shabbos day (*Moreh Nevuchim* 3:43). The motivation for this law can be understood by way of a parable: The founding father of a country who designates a day to be celebrated as the anniversary of the state's inception; his hope is that the citizens, through this reminder of the past, will bring to mind the fact that they are subject to a higher authority — the man who founded the country (*Ikkarim* 3:26). All this is summed up by the Torah (*Shemos* 20:10-11): *The seventh day is Shabbos [dedicated] to Hashem, your God; do not do any work … for in six days God made the Heavens and the earth, the sea and all that is in them, and He rested on the seventh day.*

In addition to deepening our consciousness of the truth that the world had a beginning and did not always exist, the Shabbos prompts us to give thought to the process of Creation — how different things were created on each of six separate days, and then on the seventh, nothing at all, indicating a free-willed Creator. People who observe our inactivity on the Shabbos will inquire after the reason, and in this way many will be strengthened in their adherence to the true faith (*Chinuch* §32).

Recalling the Creation also provokes one to contemplate the majesty of the Creator, Who, by the

mere spoken word and without any exertion, called everything into existence out of nothing at all (*Radvaz, Ta'amei HaMitzvos* §91).

On the other hand, to desecrate Shabbos and engage in forbidden work is as serious as worshipping idols and denying God's existence. A Shabbos-breaker is considered a full-fledged apostate, "because he denies God's deeds, and bears false witness that God never rested from His creative activity on the seventh day" (*Rashi, Chullin* 5a).

There is a question, however, that must be addressed. Why should the *active* work of creation be commemorated by a day of *inactive* rest? (*Abarbanel, Shemos* 20:8) True, the fact that God rested on the seventh day implies the work that preceded that rest, but why not, in a more direct way, mark God's six days of creation by engaging in work throughout the six days? (*Maharal, Tiferes Yisrael* §40).

One answer offered is that the goal of Shabbos is to emphasize the fact that the world was created from nothing (*ex nihilo*), as opposed to all subsequent development, which involved only the production of new forms out of already existing matter. Once we accept that God ceased His creative work on the seventh day, when, in fact, He had every intention of developing it further — as the Torah itself states (*Bereishis* 2:3): *…that God created* **to make** — we are forced to conclude that His original work was different in nature from anything after it, *in that it was, uniquely, the creation of existence where there had been none before.* To commemorate this fact is the object of our Shabbos of rest (*Abarbanel,* ibid.).

That there has not been any true creation, *ex nihilo,* since the onset of the original Shabbos is a critical point, for if there had been, people would be tempted to view the appearance of new existence out of nothing as a natural phenomenon, and not the work of a willful Creator (*Malbim, Shemos* 20:11). We therefore mark the Creation specifically with the cessation of work on the seventh day, to symbolize the culmination of God's truly creative activity on the first Shabbos, and to highlight the difference between the events of the first six days from anything that was to occur thereafter.

It is also suggested that conveying the message of Creation by stopping all creative activity indicates the perfection achieved during the six days of creation. In general, the cessation of activity is a sign of completion; the fact that God rested on the seventh day served to show that His work of six days had fully attained its objective, and nothing more was left to be done (*Maharal, Tiferes Yisrael,* §40).

---— ✳ —---

✑ *Deference to the Creator*

Once one absorbs the lesson of Shabbos, that God is the world's Creator, he will inevitably be moved to humble himself and submit to His rule. If a person will visualize how, before the Creation, there was neither Heaven nor earth, and it was God who called it all into being, it is a small step to realize that He is the Master, and that, if He had the capacity to create all, He can also know all, sustain all, and oversee all (*Chochmah U'Mussar* II, p. 316).

It is not only by renewed faith that the Shabbos observer is brought to humility. The very effort to observe Shabbos by restricting one's activities amounts to an unspoken declaration that one's weekday accomplishments were realized only by the grant of God; none of it was the product of his own doing. This idea is alluded to in the seemingly superfluous verse dealing with Shabbos (*Shemos* 20:9): *Six days shall you labor, and accomplish all your work.* It is only by observing Shabbos that one's weeklong activity is sanctioned, for only through Shabbos does he acknowledge that although he labors, he cannot achieve, for achievement is in the hands of God (*Resisei Lailah* §27).

Truly, if not for Shabbos, "what safeguard [would ensure] that man in his position of honor would not forget God; that he would not look upon the world, which had been entrusted to him to govern according to God's will, as his own property; that in his controlling power over the things around him he would not regard himself as master; and that he would not live in God's world solely according to his human will?" (*R' Samson R. Hirsch, Chorev* §21).

That safeguard is Shabbos, which guarantees that men will "not forget the truth that every ounce of strength and every grain of power, and all that they might come to think was their own production, comes from God...; it is He Who has given them the strength and power they now enjoy and call their own, and Who expects them to acknowledge this fact with the twenty-four hour Shabbos sacrifice, by which they cease to exercise their 'creative' power in the control and regulation of the things around them" (*Commentary of R' Samson R. Hirsch, Devarim* 5:12-15).

II. COMMEMORATING THE EXODUS

✑ *The freedom to rest*

nly someone unconstrained by external control has the ability to abstain from work at his own convenience. When we were slaves in Egypt, such a prerogative was completely out of reach. After rescuing us from Egyptian bondage, God gave us the mitzvah to cease all work on the Shabbos day, thereby demonstrating our freedom to rest, and bringing to mind the miracles of the Exodus by which our benevolent God gave us this freedom (*Chinuch* §32). In addition, He granted us the privilege of becoming His servants (*Ramban, Devarim* 5:14, quoting the *Rambam's Moreh Nevuchim*). All this is summed up in the following passage (*Devarim* 5:15): *You shall remember that you were a slave in the land of Egypt, and Hashem, your God, removed you from there with a strong hand and an outstretched arm; therefore Hashem, your God, commanded you to make the Shabbos day.*

This explanation for the commandment to rest on Shabbos has been challenged, though, for the performance of this mitzvah does not evince a direct reference to the Exodus, and an observer is not likely to make the connection (*Ramban,* ibid.). In reply, it has been suggested that some mitzvos, although intended for perpetuity, were nevertheless rooted in the mindset of the generation that received the Torah. For them, freshly released from

Egyptian imprisonment, the statement made by the Shabbos rest could in no way be missed. That generation could be then counted on to pass on the message to their descendants, and the memory of the Exodus would thus be conveyed from one generation to the next, in the manner promoted in the exhortation of the prophet (*Yoel* 1:3), *Tell your children about it, and your children to their children, and their children to another generation* (*Ritva, Sefer HaZikaron* §12).

——— ❧ ———

❧ *Shabbos in Egypt*

The stoppage of work occasioned by Shabbos also serves as a reminder of the Exodus by virtue of the fact that in Egypt, when the Jewish slaves were finally granted a weekly day of rest in response to a petition by Moshe, it was the seventh day that they were given. This was the day that Moshe had asked for, and he later had great cause to rejoice when that day was designated as the holy day of Shabbos (*Seder HaYom, Seder Kiddush shel Shabbos*).

——— ❧ ———

❧ *A lesson in Divine Providence*

Reflecting on the kindness God displayed toward us through the miracles of the Exodus, and the plagues with which He humbled our enemies, reinforces one's belief that the Creator, after creating the world, did not leave it to be governed by chance. He retained control of the world and monitors all of its creatures; He sustains their existence, and gives each man according to the merits of his deeds. Inasmuch as resting on Shabbos calls to mind the events of the Exodus, the Shabbos observer will absorb the lessons those events have to teach about the Divine Providence over every creature. As the Torah enjoins (*Devarim* 5:15): *You shall remember that you were a slave in the land of Egypt, and Hashem, your God, removed you from there with a strong hand and an outstretched arm; therefore Hashem, your God, commanded you to make the*

Shabbos day. So that this conviction may become so ingrained in our psyche that it may endure for all time, we are obliged to manifest the idea with a positive act, for action presupposes fullness in thought; this is the function of the Shabbos rest. In general, with any important principle, a person has to believe it in thought, express it in speech, and confirm it in deed (*Ramban, Derashas Toras Hashem Temimah*).

[This faith in God's continuing control of the world, made evident to all by the events of the Exodus, is among the cardinal principles of the Torah. A Jew is expected to respond to the call "to rely on God with all your heart, and to believe in His Providence. So that the true concept of Unity may reside in your heart, you must believe that God's eyes penetrate every part of the world, and take notice of all of man's actions and thoughts. One who does not accept the full import of the words, ... *Who took you out of the land of Egypt* [indicating Divine Providence] does not truly believe that *I am Hashem, your God.* This idea forms the foundation for the entire Torah" (*Orchos Chaim L'HaRosh,* 1:26).]

——— ❧ ———

❧ *Shabbos: Every Jew's personal redemption*

Our liberation from Egypt was not meant to be a one-time event; on each and every Shabbos, a Jew is released from his own personal "Egypt" — the constraints imposed by the weekday world of mundane activity — and is given the opportunity to throw himself into the study of Torah, the quintessential service of God. Being that "there is no true freedom outside the study of Torah" (*Avos* 6:2), the liberation of Shabbos is complete.

This idea uncovers another layer of meaning in the Scriptural statement, made in the *Devarim* text of the Ten Commandments, that Shabbos serves as a memorial to the Exodus from Egypt (*Pri Tzaddik, Bo* §10). And just as the liberation of the Exodus was two-fold, physical as well as spiritual, so too, Shabbos affords freedom from the burden of bodily work as well as from spiritual benightedness. During the week, a person can have no peace, torn as he is between body and soul; the spirit strains Heavenward while the physical weighs him down. Only on Shabbos does the body, suffused with the holiness of the day, abandon the struggle and make peace with the soul (*Shem MiShmuel, Va'eira* 5678).

[The "Exodus-like" redemption of Shabbos and the inner peace it brings a person allow a person the leisure to reflect on God's Majesty, inspiring him to offer thanksgiving and to extol God's praises. Thus the Psalmist is moved to exclaim in the "Song for the day of the Shabbos" (92:6): *How great are Your deeds, O God!* Before the Exodus, the wonders of the Creator were masked by nature. As the Ten Plagues unfolded in defiance of all natural law, the process began by which the majestic glory of God was to be uncovered, a goal which became the national mission of the Jewish people. Jews therefore possess an instinctive desire to sing of God's praises and of their feelings of gratitude. For six days each week, this urge is suppressed, until the arrival of the Shabbos allows it free reign, giving rise to the Song that aptly begins, *It is good to give thanks to God, and to sing to Your Name, O Exalted One (Sefas Emes, Beshalach* 5661; *Shabbos HaGadol* 5647).]

This personal redemption of the spirit that is effected by Shabbos is accessible to any Jew, regardless of his spiritual level, again as is established by the precedent of the original Exodus. The Jews of Egypt had sunk to the forty-ninth degree of spiritual defilement and — uncircumcised — were almost indistinguishable from their Egyptian neighbors, but were all the same reclaimed by God and rescued from Egypt. [This, incidentally, is why there is a mitzvah to recall the Exodus on a daily basis. If a person should find himself in the grip of a sinful desire, and cannot find a way to extricate himself, he should remind himself of the Exodus, and he will be given new hope. Surely, he can reason, he has not sunk lower than those Jews of yore, and he, like them, can still look to God to pull him out of his bind.] So too, on Shabbos, God provides the Shabbos observer, without any initiative on his part, with an uplifting infusion of holiness (*Pri Tzaddik, Pesach*

§24; see also *Va'eschanan* §5; *Shem MiShmuel, Pekudei* 5675).

III. SHABBOS: THE GIFT OF REST

erhaps the most obvious of the reasons for Shabbos is that God, out of His loving concern for the welfare of His people, wished us to have a day of rest from the grind of the week. The weekly recess is simply good for the health, and it allows one to recharge his strength, along with that of his workers and animals, for the coming week (*Sefer HaBatim, Migdal David, Beur Aseres HaDibros;* cf. *Kuzari* III, 3). Shabbos ensures that at least one-seventh of one's lifetime will be spent in leisure, regardless of one's station in life; the benefit therefrom needs no elaboration (*Moreh Nevuchim* III, 43; cf. *Kad HaKemach, Shabbos*).

Not only the relaxation of Shabbos itself, but even the knowledge that at the end of the week awaits a day of rest, can invigorate a person in the midst of his work, lighten his burden, and improve his performance. In addition, when Shabbos is over he will return to his job with alacrity, while a worker who is never given a break will approach his job grudgingly and his work will be sluggish (*Derashos Rabbeinu Yonah, Vayakhel*).

IV. A DAY FOR THE SPIRIT

he *Talmud Yerushalmi (Shabbos* 15:3) states: "Shabbos and Festivals were given to Israel exclusively that they would spend them in the study of Torah." The pursuit of a livelihood generally occupies the bulk of a person's time during the week. God therefore designated one day a week on which we are required to refrain from mundane activities, allowing us for once to attend to the needs of the soul through the study of Torah, whether it be Scripture, Mishnah, or Talmud; each individual on his own level (*Akeidas Yitzchak* §55. cf. *Derashos Rabbeinu Yonah,* pp. 117, 146; *Meshech Chochmah, Devarim* 5:12). Without the opportunity afforded by Shabbos to give expression to one's spiritual side, the faculties of the soul would slowly wither and die. Shabbos, in this sense, is a balm for the soul, healing prior infirmities and preventing the onset of new ones (*Kuzari* 3:5). If not for the radiance of Shabbos, the darkness of materiality would envelop a person and drag him down, and he could not attain the spiritual growth and refinement necessary to cleave to his Creator. Abstaining from work on Shabbos pulls us away from the secular and earthly and raises us above the workday world. Of course, to completely cut off one's ties to his physical existence is impossible; one is, after all, part of this mundane world. But God, in His infinite wisdom, calculated the necessary measure of involvement in one's physical needs, and where detachment is indicated, directed us accordingly. This is the idea behind the various forms of work that were forbidden on Shabbos (*Derech Hashem* 4:7).

[In light of the foregoing, Shabbos is more than a passive desisting from forbidden work; it is a time waiting to be filled with spiritual content and active involvement in the service of God, in accordance with the Torah's description of the day as a *Shabbos [dedicated] to Hashem your God* (*Shemos* 20:10). This obligation is indicated by the words of the verse (*Shemos* 31:13), *The children of Israel shall keep Shabbos to* **make** *the Shabbos…*; that is, to transform Shabbos into the transcendent experience it was meant to be. It emerges that Shabbos calls for two different kinds of "rest," one preparing the ground for the other: the respite enjoyed by the body from the burden of weekday activity provides the soul with the leisure it needs to become fully involved in matters of the spirit. In this regard, the Torah instructs (ibid.): *My* **Shabbosos** *you shall keep,* referring to the two aspects of Shabbos, embracing both body and soul. Inasmuch as the primary objective of Shabbos is to achieve "rest" for the soul, the mere fulfillment of the negative commandment, *"You shall not do any work,"* is no guarantee that the positive commandment implied by *"a Shabbos [dedicated] to God"* has been fulfilled. This may be the intent of the Sages' assertion that the observance of *two* Shabbosos by the Jewish people would earn them immediate salvation — "two Shabbosos" be-

ing a reference to the two aspects of the Shabbos experience (*HaKesav VehaKabbalah, Shemos* 20:10 and 31:13).]

The Shabbos not only provides the time to develop the spirit; it actually sublimates the heart and mind, making them more receptive to spiritual stimulus. This is because the avoidance of engaging in physical work on the Shabbos nurtures the awareness that man is a foreigner in the physical world (*Reishis Chochmah, Shaar HaKedushah* §2), and it is only the acquisition of spiritual perfection that secures a person true life in his permanent home, the World of Souls (*HaKesav VehaKabbalah, Shemos* 31:16).

V. A PRIVATE AUDIENCE WITH GOD

he Shabbos marks a time of special closeness between God and Israel; the prohibition against work provides us with the liberty to sustain this bond and bask in our nearness to God. "It is commonplace for a king and queen to sit and converse with one another; the Shabbos facilitates just this kind of relationship between Israel and God, as it says (*Shemos* 31:17), *…between Me and the children of Israel*" (*Devarim Rabbah* 1:21; see there further). The intimacy with the Divine that the Jewish Nation attains on the Shabbos day is greater than that enjoyed by the ministering angels in Heaven, for concerning the Shabbos it is said (*Devarim* 26:17): *You have distinguished Hashem* **on the day** (היום) *to be a God for you,* meaning the special day, the Shabbos. By the same token (ibid. v. 18), *God has distinguished you* **on the day** (היום) *to be for Him a treasured people*; on the Shabbos He prefers you over the ministering angels (*Or Zarua, Shabbos* §42).

In a similar vein, the joy of Shabbos has been compared to a wedding celebration, with the groom being God and the bride, Shabbos itself. With this in mind, the Sages formulated the Shabbos prayers. The evening prayer opens with the phrase, *You have consecrated* (קדשת) *the seventh day…,* employing the same term used by the groom in betrothing the bride. The morning prayer is introduced with the words *"Let Moshe rejoice…"*, recalling the joy that marks every wedding. Following that is the *Mussaf* (Additional) Prayer, which reflects the extra concessions that the groom includes in his bride's *kesubah*. Alternatively, this prayer — and particularly the sacrificial offerings it represents — are intended to evoke a wedding feast. Finally, the *Minchah* prayer begins, *You are One, Your Name is One, and who is like Your people Israel, a unique nation on the earth?* alluding to the ritual seclusion (*yichud*) of the bride and groom (*Avudraham, Maariv L'Shabbos*).

The Shabbos moratorium on mundane work, aside from the advantages that accrue therefrom, constitutes a badge of distinction for the one nation to whom it was given. The fact that the Jews inherited, as their day of rest, the day on which God Himself had chosen to rest, indicates their status as God's treasured nation (*Chizkuni, Shemos* 31:13). Thus, on the verse *It is a sign between Me and you* (*Shemos* 31:13), *Rashi* comments: "It is a great sign between us that I have chosen you, this that I have bequeathed to you My day of rest for [your own] rest." This explains the Torah's frequent use of the possessive form in reference to the Shabbos (*Shemos* ibid.; *Vayikra* 19:3; et al.): **My** *Shabbosos you shall keep…,* and, in confirming the significance behind the endowment of this day for the benefit of Israel, the verse concludes, *…for it is a sign between Me and you, to know that I am God, Who consecrated you* as God's treasured people (*HaKesav VehaKabbalah, Devarim* 5:15).

VI. A RETURN TO THE HUMAN CONDITION PRIOR TO SIN

he act of refraining from work on the Shabbos represents a reinstatement of the idyllic state of existence that prevailed in the world just after Creation (*Maharsha, Shabbos* 10b). As long as Adam resided in the Garden of Eden, he had effortless access to all his needs. The trees of the garden were prepared for his sake, and, as the Sages relate, the ministering angels stood at his side, broiling meat and filtering wine. Only after he partook sinfully from the Tree of Knowledge was

it decreed that henceforth *with the sweat of your brow shall you eat bread* (*Bereishis* 3:19), imposing upon man the necessity of working for his food. On the Shabbos, however, the curse is suspended; all work is unnecessary and therefore forbidden, freeing one to toil instead in the study of Torah (*Pri Tzaddik, Bo* §10). We are thus reminded, in turn, that it is through the Torah that the world will eventually be cleansed from the effects of Adam's sin and finally restored to its former condition (*Derech Pikudechah, Lo Saaseh* §32).

As Shabbos lifts the Jewish people to the lofty plane the world was on before the advent of sin, it diffuses an enlightening radiance, a semblance of the resplendence that is hidden away for the righteous in the coming World, in accord with the Talmudic statement (*Berachos* 57b) that Shabbos is a sixtieth part of the World to Come. The cessation of work is suggestive of this, because in the future as well there will be no burden or toil; the Jews will sit serenely with their crowns on their heads in the proximity of the Divine Presence (cf. *She'iltos, Bereishis; Kad HaKemach, Shabbos; Reishis Chochmah, Sha'ar HaKedushah* §2).

[God wished to give us a small taste of the reward awaiting the righteous in the World to Come, for His overriding purpose in creating the world was to bestow goodness upon His creatures, and He can offer no greater bounty than to welcome a soul into His Presence. This will come to pass, in its fullest measure, in the seventh millenium, when the time will have come for rewards to be paid. That period is referred to as "the grand Shabbos." But even on an ordinary Shabbos, albeit on a far smaller scale, God benevolently lets through a bit of the light radiating from His countenance, and a person who has succeeded in refining his body, heart, and thoughts to receive the holiness of Shabbos is able to sense this Divine light. When he does, his heart will blaze with a Godly fire as his soul pines to cleave to God, and his heart will swell with a love that cannot be extinguished… (*Be'er Mayim Chaim, Bereishis* §2).

The flavor of the World to Come that Shabbos retains is evident not only in the prohibition against

engaging in work, but also in the way service of
God differs on Shabbos from that of the week, as
many of the Torah's mitzvos do not apply on Shabbos. This is because the six workdays are designated as the time for activity and the observance of
mitzvos, whereas Shabbos is primarily a time to
reap the rewards and to delight in one's closeness
to God. In this respect, Shabbos reflects the Eternal
World, which is entirely Shabbos; it is truly "the
grand Shabbos." The six workdays represent times
of movement and change; they symbolize the human lifetime of activity and effort toward the
achievement of one's purpose. Shabbos, on the
other hand, betokens the tranquility that comes
with the completion of one's work upon the attain-
ment of his goal, which, for life on this world, is to
merit a portion in the World to Come (*Akeidas
Yitzchak* §55). This is why many of the Torah's
mitzvos do not apply on Shabbos, when even mitzvah activity, relatively speaking, comes to a stand-
still (*Pri Tzaddik, Shevisas Shabbos* §1). For instance,
tefillin are meant to foster, through a positive act,
an awareness of the Name of God associated with a
Jew; the head-*tefillin* serve as a signal to others —

*All the peoples of the earth will see that the Name of
God has been proclaimed upon you* (*Devarim* 28:10;
see *Megillah* 16b) — and the arm-*tefillin* speak to
oneself, so that he may submit his heart to the service of God. But this mitzvah is performed on the
weekdays only. On Shabbos, the clear perception of
the Divine reality should be realized in one's mind
without the confirmation of a physical act, just like
in the coming World that will be entirely Shabbos,
being devoid of activity and the fulfillment of
mitzvos, where the spiritual enlightenment is bright
and apparent (*Dover Tzedek,* Introduction to *Kunteres Ner HaMitzvos*).]

VII. THE SOURCE OF ALL BLESSING

All the days of the week are anchored in
Shabbos, for any blessing they receive is
channelled through it (See *Zohar* II, 63b;
III, 144b). Shabbos is therefore not a time for work;
people must be free to properly prepare Shabbos
to serve as a receptacle for the outpouring of blessing from the Heavenly depositories (see *Toras
HaMinchah, Shemos, Derashah* §24).

THROUGH THE EYES OF THE SAGES
Stories, Parables & Reflections

I. THE CENTRALITY OF THE SHABBOS

∾ *Treasured by God*

The Holy One, Blessed is He, said to Bnei Yisrael: My children, do not make light of the Shabbos I have given you. Why? Because it is more dear to Me than all the other mitzvos, for I was the first to observe it, as it is written (*Bereishis* 2:3), *And God blessed the seventh day and sanctified it, for on [that day] He rested from all His work* (*Devarim Rabbah, Eikev* §1).

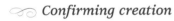

∾ *Confirming creation*

In what arrangement were the Ten Commandments given? Five were on one tablet, and five on the other … The fourth commandment inscribed on the first tablet was, *Remember the Shabbos day to sanctify it.* Directly opposite, on the second tablet, appeared the words, *You shall not bear false witness.* The Torah thus teaches that one who desecrates Shabbos in effect testifies in God's presence that He did not create the world in six days and then rest on the seventh. Conversely, one who observes Shabbos bears witness before God that He created the world in six days and rested on the seventh. As we were told by the prophet (*Yeshayah* 43:12): *You are My witnesses; so declared God* (*Mechilta, Yisro* §8; *Pesikta Zutrasa, Shemos* 20:13).

∾ *On a par with the rest of the Torah*

R' Yehoshua bar Nechemiah taught: God said to Israel: Safeguard Shabbos; it is equal to the whole of the Torah. For regarding Shabbos it is written (*Devarim* 5:12), *Safeguard* (שמור) *the Shabbos.*

And the same term is used in reference to the Torah in general (ibid. 11:22): *For if you carefully safeguard* (שמור תשמרון) *this entire mandate that I command you today …* (*Tanchuma, Ki Sisa* §33; see there for a second Scriptural source).

Rabbi Elazar bar Avina taught: That Shabbos is equivalent to the rest of the Torah can be inferred from the Torah, the Neviim (Prophets), and the Kesuvim (Writings). In the Torah, we find that when Moshe neglected to instruct the people to collect a double portion of manna each Friday, God rebuked Israel, (*Shemos* 16:28), *How long will you refuse to keep My commandments and My teachings?* The plural usage implies that they had disobeyed *all* of the mitzvos. But what immediately follows (ibid. v. 29)? *Realize that God has given you the Shabbos…"*

Where is this concept to be found in the Neviim? Yechezkel (20:13) quotes God's censure of the Jews thus: *But the House of Israel rebelled against Me in the Wilderness; they did not follow My decrees and they spurned My laws… What does it go on to say? And My Shabbosos they desecrated.*

Finally, in the Kesuvim, Israel recalled before God (*Nechemiah* 9:13), *Onto Mount Sinai You descended and spoke to them from Heaven; You gave them upright laws and teachings of truth, decrees and good commandments.* And then they continued (ibid. v. 14), *And you informed them of your holy Shabbos…*

The Holy One, Blessed is He, said to Israel: If you merit to observe the Shabbos, I will view you as having upheld all the mitzvos of the Torah. But if you desecrate it, I will view you as having transgressed all of the mitzvos. So says the prophet (*Yeshayah* 56:2), *He who guards Shabbos against desecrating it [thereby] guards his hand from committing every evil* (*Shemos Rabbah* 25:12; *Yerushalmi, Nedarim* 3:9; cf. *Devarim Rabbah* 4:4).

∾ *The essence of the Torah*

Shabbos is the embodiment of the Torah, and all the secrets of the Torah are tied to it. The preservation of Shabbos is, in effect, the preservation of

the entire Torah. One who observes Shabbos is regarded as if he observed all the laws of the Torah
(*Zohar* II, 92a; 47a; cf. 151a; et al.).

———— ঙ্গ ————

✎ *The severity of the prohibition*

One who desecrates Shabbos... is as if he violated every mitzvah in the Torah. So it is said
(*Yeshayah* 56:2), *He who guards Shabbos against desecrating it and [thereby] guards his hand from committing every evil,* implying that the failure to keep
Shabbos is akin to committing every evil. Shabbos
desecration is particularly severe; the prophet focused his admonishment of the Jews on desecration
of Shabbos alone (*Yirmiah* 17:27), *If you fail to listen
to Me to sanctify Shabbos day, and to refrain from carrying your burdens in through the gates of Jerusalem, I
will ignite a fire in its gates, and it will consume the
palaces of Jerusalem; it will not be extinguished*
(*Medrash Tannaim, Devarim* 5:15).

———— ঙ্গ ————

✎ *Akin to idolatry*

Speak to the Children of Israel and say to them: When
a person from among you shall offer a sacrifice to
God... (*Vayikra* 1:2). From among you, but not from
all of you. From here the Sages inferred that we accept sacrifices from the [impenitent] sinners of Israel
... with these exceptions: one who habitually pours
wine-libations to the idols, and one who is given to
desecrating Shabbos in public. From this it is apparent that worship of idols and Shabbos desecration are
of equal severity (*Eruvin* 69b; *Chullin* 5a; *Vayikra Rabbah* 2:9; *Tanna D'vei Eliyahu Rabbah* 6:12).

II. RETRIBUTION TO
THE WRONGDOER

✎ *Vulnerability*

ne who violates Shabbos will not be
guarded by God (Preface to *Tikunei Zohar,*
12a).

———— ঙ্গ ————

✎ *Impoverishment*

On account of three improprieties men of
wealth are divested of their holdings. [One of
these is] the practice of surveying one's properties
on Shabbos [to determine what improvements are
needed] (*Gittin* 38b).

———— ঙ্গ ————

✎ *Untimely death*

The Sages taught: For three transgressions (neg-
ligence in regard to *niddah, challah,* and Shabbos candles; cf. *Mishnah, Shabbos* 2:7) women die
as they give birth. R' Elazar said: For these three
sins, women die young (and not necessarily during
childbirth). R' Acha countered: The women die
young (not for these sins, but) for laundering their
children's soiled clothes on Shabbos (*Shabbos* 32a).

———— ঙ্গ ————

✎ *Disinherited in the future*

R' Elazar HaModa'i taught: One who desecrates
Shabbos ... although he may be in possession
of Torah and good deeds, he does not have a share
in the World to Come (*Avos D'Rabbi Nassan* 26:4,
according to the standard reading, confirmed by
the *Gra*; cf. *Binyan Yehoshua,* ad loc.).

———— ঙ্গ ————

✎ *Disgrace and Gehinnom*

R' Yaakov taught: The wicked people who corrupted their ways ... and profaned Shabbos in
public... — they descend to *Gehinnom* below and are
punished there, never again to emerge. However,
they will arise on the Day of Judgment, and they will
arise for the Resurrection of the Dead. Regarding
them it is said (*Yeshayah* 66:24), *And they will be the
object of disgrace* (דראון) *before all flesh.* What is
meant by the term 'דראון'? It is a contraction of
דֵּי רָאוֹן, "enough seen." All will say: It is enough that
they have been seen in their disgrace (*Medrash
HaNe'elam; Zohar* I, 107a).

———— ঙ্গ ————

The fires of Gehinnom

There is a section in *Gehinnom* designated for those who violated Shabbos. Since a person consigned to that area was guilty (in his lifetime) of kindling his lights before Shabbos came to an end, the functionary whose job is to re-ignite the fires of *Gehinnom* after the weekly respite of Shabbos would begin with his section, announcing: This is the place designated for So-and-so. And all the wicked people in *Gehinnom* would join him in setting fire to that place (*Zohar* III, 246b; see there further).

III. PUNISHMENTS TO THE PUBLIC

Depopulation

As a result of Shabbos desecration, beasts of prey proliferate, domestic animals perish, the human population dwindles, and the roads become desolate (*Shabbos* 33a).

————— ✥ —————

Fire

Fires occur only in places where Shabbos is desecrated, as it is said (*Yirmiyah* 17:27), *If you fail to listen to Me to sanctify the Shabbos day, and to refrain from carrying your burdens in through the gates of Jerusalem, I will ignite a fire in its gates, and it will consume the palaces of Jerusalem; it will not be extinguished.* What is meant by *it will not be extinguished?* Rav Nachman bar Yitzchak taught: The fire will break out at a time when people are not available to put it out [that is, on Shabbos] (*Shabbos* 119b).

————— ✥ —————

Foreign domination

Rav Yehudah taught in the name of Rav: If Israel had kept the very first Shabbos, no other nation could have gained control over them, as it is written (*Shemos* 16:27), *It happened on the seventh day that some of the people went out to collect [the manna], and they did not find.* And after that, what occurred (ibid. 17:8)? *Amalek came and waged war with Israel …* (*Shabbos* 118b; *Zohar Chadash* II, 37b).

————— ✥ —————

The fall of Jerusalem

Abaye taught: Jerusalem was destroyed only because Shabbos was desecrated [in public — *Halachos Gedolos, Hilchos Shabbos* 16] within its confines, as it is said (*Yechezkel* 22:26), *They averted their eyes from My Shabbosos, and I became profaned in their midst* (*Shabbos* 119b, cf. *Medrash Tannaim, Devarim* 5:15).

————— ✥ —————

Exile

They wandered [into exile] from before the sword … *from before the drawn bow* (קשת דרוכה) (*Yeshayah* 21:15). This was a consequence of their failure to keep Shabbos, of which it is written (*Nechemiah* 13:15), *In those days I observed in Yehudah people pressing* (דרכים) *grapes on Shabbos* (*Eichah Rabbah* 2:4; *Yerushalmi, Taanis* 4:5).

————— ✥ —————

A great city's downfall

The city of Tur Shimon would gather three hundred measures of bread to be distributed to the poor every Shabbos eve. So why was it destroyed? Some say because of immorality, and others say because they played games of sport on Shabbos (*Yerushalmi, Eichah Rabbah* ibid.).

his listing of the Shabbos *melachos* follows the order of the Mishnah in Tractate *Shabbos* (73a). There is one deviation; it is noted below. The list is focused primarily on the *avos melachos.* Although *tolados* (derivative *melachos*) are occasionally mentioned, the overwhelming majority of *tolados* are omitted. We have also omitted mention of Rabbinic decrees; hence, the listing is suitable for educational purposes only, and should not be used to decide questions of practical halachah.

1. זורע / sowing

This *melachah* consists of sowing seeds in the ground so they will grow (see *Rambam, Hil. Shabbos* 7:3). Included in the *melachah* are all acts of planting, such as setting seedlings into the ground, or grafting branches onto existing trees (*Shabbos* 73b; *Rambam, Hil. Shabbos* 7:3; see note 5 and *Iyunim* §3).

This *melachah* and the ten that follow include all the activities necessary for baking bread (see *Shabbos* 74a). All these *melachos* are derived from the cultivation and preparation of the herbs used in the *Mishkan* to produce dyes (see *Shabbos* 49b, with *Rashi* ד"ה הם זרעו) or the wheat used there to produce flour offerings (see following *melachah*).

2. חורש / plowing

This *melachah* is performed by softening the ground to prepare it for planting. It is not limited to actual plowing, but includes any act of digging intended to soften the ground prior to sowing (*Shabbos* 73b with *Rashi* ד"ה מלאכה אחת הן; *Rambam, Hil. Shabbos* 7:2).

During construction of the *Mishkan,* the builders cultivated herbs, from which they manufactured

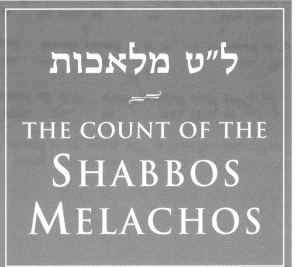

dyes, which were used to impart color to various tapestries and coverings. They would plow the ground to prepare it for planting the herbs (see *Shabbos* 103a; *Yerushalmi, Shabbos* 7:2). Some say that Shabbos *melachos* are based *both* on the activities performed while building the *Mishkan, and* on those performed while offering sacrifices there (see note 4). According to this view, the source of this *melachah* could also be the plowing that was done before they sowed wheat for flour offerings (*Rav Hai Gaon,* cited in *Chidushim MeiGeonim Kadmonim* to *Rambam, Hil. Shabbos* ch. 7).

[The Gemara (*Shabbos* 73b) notes that plowing is usually performed *before* sowing, and explains why the Mishnah reverses the order.]

3. קוצר / reaping

One who detaches produce from the place it is growing violates the *av melachah* of reaping. This applies both to produce that grows directly from the ground, such as grain or beans, and to that which grows from trees, such as grapes, dates or figs (*Rambam, Hil. Shabbos* 7:4). However, it does not apply to produce growing in a non-perforated pot (ibid. 8:3).

The *av melachah* of reaping is performed with a utensil; e.g. a sickle or knife. One who pulls up stalks of wheat or picks fruit or vegetables by hand has violated only a *toladah* of reaping (*Rambam* ibid., as explained by *Lechem Mishneh*).

4. מעמר / gathering

This refers to gathering grain or other produce into a single bundle or pile (*Tosafos Rid, Shabbos* 73b; see *Eglei Tal* מעמר 1:1). According to some, one violates the *av melachah* only if he ties the produce together, or causes its individual elements to adhere together, so that they form a single mass [as with pressed figs] (see *Rambam, Hil. Shabbos* 21:11, 8:6; *Minchas Chinuch* מוסך השבת 4:2).

The *melachah* of gathering is limited to items gathered in the place where they grew, e.g. sheaves in a field (*Tosafos, Beitzah* 31a; *Rashba* and *Ran* there, 33b; *Ritva, Shabbos* 73b; see, however, *Rambam, Hil. Shabbos* 21:11). With regard to whether it applies to non-agricultural items, see *Eglei Tal* מעמר §2.

5. דש / threshing

The *melachah* of threshing consists of separating inedible matter from food to which it is attached; the prime example is the removal of the husk from a kernel of wheat (see *Rabbeinu Chananel, Shabbos* 74a; *Aruch* ע' דש). The *av melachah* is performed by pounding the grain with a rod or utensil, or by having an animal trample it (see *Shulchan Aruch HaRav, Kunteres Acharon* to 510:1). Removing the husk by hand is a *toladah* of this *melachah*, namely: מפרק, *separating* (*Rashi, Shabbos* 73b ד"ה מפרק; *Rambam, Hil. Shabbos* 8:7; see *Shulchan Aruch HaRav* ibid.).

6. זורה / winnowing

Winnowing is performed by throwing grain into the wind with a pitchfork, so that the wind will blow away the chaff and leave the grain behind (*Rashi, Shabbos* 73a ד"ה הזורה). Throwing the grain into the wind by hand is a *toladah* of winnowing (*Eglei Tal* זורה §5; cf. *Minchas Chinuch* מוסך השבת מל' זורה). Similarly, blowing away the chaff with one's mouth is a *toladah* of winnowing (see *Rabbeinu Chananel, Shabbos* 74a; *Eglei Tal* ibid.).

7. בורר / selecting

The *av melachah* of selecting is defined as sorting out a mixture of inedible matter and food by picking out the inedible parts by hand, as, for example, when removing pebbles that are mixed

with kernels of wheat (*Rashi, Shabbos* 73a ד"ה הבורר; see *Rabbeinu Chananel, Shabbos* 74a).

8. טוחן / grinding

One who grinds wheat to make flour violates the *av melachah* of grinding. The *tolados* of grinding include cutting vegetables into tiny pieces, crushing spices in a mortar, or sawing wood in order to produce sawdust (*Shabbos* 74a; *Rambam, Hil. Shabbos* 7:5, 8:15, 21:18).

9. מרקד / sifting

This is the separation of inedible matter and food by means of a sieve (or any other utensil designed for this purpose); e.g. sifting flour to remove its impurities (*Rashi, Shabbos* 73a ד"ה המרקד).

[Winnowing, selecting and sifting share a single defining characteristic; namely, that all are intended to separate desired and undesired items. For discussion of the differences between these *avos melachos,* see *Shabbos* 73b-74a; *Rabbeinu Chananel* ibid. 74a; *Eglei Tal* זורה §3; *Shevisas HaShabbos,* foreword to מלאכת זורה בורר ומרקד.]

10. לש / kneading

This *melachah* is defined as mixing together a liquid and a solid, e.g. flour and water, and kneading it into dough (see *Shabbos* 18a; *Mishnah Berurah* 321:50).

11. אופה / baking

Although this *melachah* is called "baking," it is based on the cooking of herbs in the Mishkan to manufacture dyes. The *melachah* encompasses both cooking and baking (see *Rashi, Shabbos* 73a ד"ה אופה; see *Shabbos* 74b for why it is called "baking").

12. גוזז / shearing

This refers to cutting the wool or hair off any animal, whether alive or dead. It refers also to cutting wool or hair from an animal hide (*Rambam, Hil. Shabbos* 9:7). The *Mishkan* contained numerous items made of wool (e.g. the coverings); the wool was obtained by shearing sheep (see *Rashi, Shabbos* 73a ד"ה הגוזז). Cutting a person's hair (or nails) is forbidden as a *toladah* of shearing (see *Shabbos* 94b; *Rambam* ibid. 9:8; see *Beur Halachah* 340:1 ד"ה וחייב).

This *melachah* and the twelve that follow encompass all activities necessary to manufacture woolen articles. All these *melachos* are based on those performed during the production of woolen articles in the *Mishkan* (see *Rashi, Shabbos* 73a ד"ה הפוצע).

13. מלבן / whitening

This *melachah* is performed by washing raw wool or flax to remove impurities (*Rashi, Shabbos* 73a ד"ה המלבנו; *Rambam, Hil. Shabbos* 9:10). Some hold that washing clothing is a *toladah* of whitening (*Rambam* ibid. 9:11; see *Avnei Nezer, Orach Chaim* 165:1,3); others maintain that washing clothing is itself included in the *av melachah* (*Smag, Lo Saaseh* §65 ד"ה המלבן and *Yereim* 274:102, cited in *Avnei Nezer* ibid. §2).

14. מנפץ / disentangling

Before spinning raw wool into thread, one must disentangle the matted clump of wool by separating the individual fibers. Picking apart the fibers by hand constitutes the *av melachah* of disentangling (*Rashi,* to *Shabbos* 73a ד"ה המנפצו and 81b ד"ה ומפספס, to *Nazir* 42a ד"ה מפספס, and to *Bava Kamma* 93b ד"ה נפציה). Alternatively, the *melachah* of מנפץ consists of beating raw wool with sticks to remove sand and dirt (*Rambam, Commentary to the Mishnah* to *Shabbos* 73a).

15. צובע / dyeing

During construction of the *Mishkan,* it was necessary to dye wool to produce the colored tapestries that were used in the coverings and curtains. Dye was used also to color the reddened hides that formed one of the Tabernacle covers (*Rashi, Shabbos* 49b ד"ה הם זרעו).

16. טווה / spinning

Thread is manufactured by twisting together individual fibers of raw wool. One who performs this act violates the *av melachah* of spinning (see *Teshuvos Maharalbach* §23). The performance of this *melachah* during construction of the *Mishkan* is actually mentioned explicitly in Scripture (*Shemos* 35:25-26).

17. מיסך / warping

This refers to arranging warp threads on a loom in preparation for weaving. To explain: A weaving loom is a frame upon which are mounted a number of parallel threads. These constitute the warp; through them one passes the weft thread, over and under the alternating strands, until cloth is formed. After the warp threads are placed upon the loom, they are held taut and beaten with a stick, so that any crossing threads will fall into place. Placing the warp threads upon the loom constitutes the *av melachah* of warping (see *Rashi, Shabbos* 73a ד"ה המיסך, with *Targum HaLaaz* §47; *Rambam, Hil. Shabbos* 9:17,18). Beating the threads to straighten them (שובט) is a *toladah* of warping (see *Shabbos* 75b, with *Rashi* ד"ה שובט וד"ה שובט הרי הוא בכלל; *Rambam* ibid. 9:18).

18. עושה שתי בתי נירין / setting two heddles

The smooth passage of weft thread over and under the alternating threads of the warp is facilitated by simultaneously raising or lowering all the odd-numbered threads on the warp to one height, and all the even-numbered threads to another. This is accomplished by means of two harnesses, one of which controls all odd-numbered threads, the other which controls all even-numbered threads. The harnesses consist of frames, across which are stretched a number of cords equal to the number of odd- or even-numbered threads. Each cord has a loop, or ring, at its center; the warp threads pass through these loops. The looped cords are known as "heddles."

The *melachah* of setting two heddles refers to passing two of the warp threads through the loops of two heddles (*Rashi, Shabbos* 73a ד"ה בתי נירין; *Rav MiBartenura, Shabbos* 7:2; see *Tos. Yom Tov* ad loc.). Alternatively, it refers to placing two of the heddles upon the harness frame (*Tosafos Rid, Shabbos* 73b; see *Lechem Mishneh, Hil. Shabbos* 9:16).

19. אורג שני חוטין / weaving two threads

This is accomplished by passing the weft thread over and under the mounted warp threads. One who passes the weft between the warp threads twice has violated the *melachah* of weaving (Mishnah, *Shabbos* 73a; *Rambam, Hil. Shabbos* 9:17).

After the weft thread is passed through the warp, it is beaten down to produce a tight, dense fabric. This act of beating (מדקדק) is forbidden as a *toladah* of weaving (see *Shabbos* 75b, with *Rabbeinu Chananel,* printed on 76a; cf. *Rashi* 75b ד"ה מדקדק).

20. פוצע שני חוטין / severing two threads

This is accomplished by removing two threads from the warp or weft for a constructive purpose, such as to reweave a torn garment (*Rambam, Hil. Shabbos* 9:20). Alternatively, this *melachah* is performed by cutting away a newly-woven piece of cloth from the warp threads. One who severs even two of the threads has performed this *melachah* (*Hasagos HaRaavad* to *Rambam* ibid.; *Shenos Eliyahu, Shabbos* 7:2). For other interpretations of פוצע, see *Tosafos Rid, Shabbos* 73b; *Chidushei Ha-Ran, Shabbos* 73a.

21. קושר / knotting

The *av melachah* of knotting is performed by tying a knot that is intended to remain tied indefinitely, and is of a type tied by professionals, such as the knot used by cameleers in fashioning a permanent nose ring for their camels, or that used by sailors in fashioning a permanent docking ring for

their boats (*Rif* to *Shabbos* 112a, fol. 41b; *Rambam, Hil. Shabbos* 10:1). Alternatively, it must be a knot that is intended to remain tied indefinitely, but need *not* be of the type employed by professionals (*Rashi, Shabbos* ibid. ד"ה בדאושכפי; *Rosh* there §1; *Tur, Orach Chaim* §317).

This *melachah* was performed in the *Mishkan* by weavers, who would knot together warp threads that had snapped. Alternatively, it was performed by fishermen, who knotted ropes to form nets to catch the *chilazon,* an aquatic creature whose blood provided the *techeiles* dye that colored many *Mishkan* fabrics (see *Shabbos* 74b).

22. מתיר / untying

This *melachah* consists of untying the sort of knot that one would be liable for tying on Shabbos (*Rambam, Hil. Shabbos* 10:7). As we explained, this is a knot that is meant to remain tied indefinitely, and, according to some, is one used by professionals. In the *Mishkan,* the *melachah* of untying was performed by fishermen, who would sometimes obtain rope for their nets by unknotting old nets and reusing the rope (*Shabbos* 74b, with *Rashi* ד"ה קושרין ומתירין).

23. תופר שתי תפירות / sewing two stitches

The *av melachah* of sewing is performed by stitching together two pieces of cloth. As soon as one sews a second stitch, he has violated this *melachah.* The goat-hair covering of the *Mishkan* was made by stitching together cloth panels (*Rashi, Shabbos* 73a ד"ה ותופר וקורע). A *toladah* of this *melachah* extends the prohibition beyond sewing, to include any means by which two separate items are attached to one another (see *Rambam, Hil. Shabbos* 10:11; *Beur Halachah,* 340:14 ד"ה הרי זה תולדת תופר).

24. קורע / tearing

The *av melachah* of tearing applies where a person tears a cloth in order to re-sew it. For example, if a worm eats a round hole in a piece of cloth, it cannot be properly re-sewn without first tearing the cloth and then fitting together the edges so that they form a neat seam. This *melachah* was performed in the *Mishkan* when such holes were found in the panels of the goat-hair covering (see *Rashi, Shabbos* 73a, ד"ה ותופר וד"ה על מנת לתפור, from *Shabbos* 74b-75a).

25. צד / trapping

The *melachah* of trapping is performed by capturing an untamed creature; for example, by grasping it with one's hands, or penning it up in an area small enough to allow a person to recapture it at will. It must be the sort of creature whose capture is difficult to accomplish, as opposed to a slow-moving or sickly creature, which is captured with ease (see *Shabbos* 106a-b). The *melachah* of trapping was practiced in the *Mishkan* with the capture of the *tachash* beast, whose hide was used for one of the coverings of the *Mishkan,* and of the *chilazon,* whose blood was used to manufacture *techeiles* (see *Rashi, Shabbos* 73a ד"ה הצד; *Tosafos* ibid. 94a ד"ה רבי; *Pnei Yehoshua* ibid. 75a ד"ה פיסקא).

26. שוחט / slaughtering

The *av melachah* of slaughtering is defined as killing any living creature by cutting its throat, stabbing it, or striking it a blow (*Rambam, Hil. Shabbos* 11:1). Strangling is forbidden as a *toladah* of slaughtering (*Rambam* ibid.); see *Mirkeves HaMishneh* (ad loc.) for why strangling is not an *av*. It is forbidden under this *melachah* to take the life of any living creature on Shabbos, whether beast, fish, fowl or insect (see *Rambam* ibid.; *Shabbos* 107b).

This *melachah* was performed in the *Mishkan* with the slaughter of *tachash* beasts (*Rashi, Shabbos* 73a ד"ה הצד).

27. מפשיט / skinning

This refers to removing the hide of a dead animal [in order to make use of the hide]. In the *Mishkan,* they would skin *tachash* animals, whose hides were used for one of the coverings of the *Mishkan* (see *Rashi* ibid.).

28. מעבד / tanning (מולח / salting)

This is performed by tanning or salting animal hides to prepare them for use (see *Shabbos* 75b). In the *Mishkan,* they would perform this *melachah* when preparing the *tachash* hides (see *Rashi, Shabbos* 73a ד"ה הצד).

[In the Mishnah (*Shabbos* 73a), salting and tanning appear as two separate *melachos.* The Gemara (75b) protests that salting is actually a part of the tanning process. It therefore replaces one of these *melachos* with the *melachah* of משרטט, *tracing lines* (see below, *melachah* §33). *Rambam's* count of the Shabbos *melachos* (*Shabbos* 7:1) lists *tanning* and *tracing lines,* but not *salting.*]

29. ממחק / scraping

This *melachah* consists of smoothing animal hides by scraping off their hair (*Rambam, Hil. Shabbos* 11:5). In the *Mishkan,* they would perform this *melachah* by scraping the *tachash* hides used in the *Mishkan* covering (see *Rashi, Shabbos* 73a).

30. מחתך / cutting

One who cuts animal hide to a specific size or shape has performed the *av melachah* of cutting (see *Rambam* ibid. 11:7; *Mishnah Berurah* 322:18). This *melachah* was performed in the *Mishkan* upon *tachash* hides (see *Rashi* ibid.).

31. כותב / writing

This *av melachah* is performed by writing any two letters on Shabbos, whether one writes the same letter twice [e.g. אא] or two different letters [e.g. אב] (see Mishnah, *Shabbos* 103a, with *Rashi;* see *Avnei Nezer, Orach Chaim* 199:5-6; *Mishnah Berurah* 340:22-25, with *Shaar HaTziyun* §38). *Rambam* maintains that one is liable for writing the same letter twice only if the two letters form a meaningful word [e.g. תת, which means "give"] (*Rambam, Hil. Shabbos* 11:10, as explained by *Maggid Mishneh*).

The act of writing was performed in the *Mishkan* by inscribing letters upon the beams that formed the *Mishkan* walls. This was done to ensure that when the *Mishkan* would be reassembled after a journey, the beams would be placed in the correct sequence, with each beam occupying the precise spot (relative to the other beams) that it occupied before being dismantled (*Rashi, Shabbos* 73a ד"ה רושם, 75b ד"ה כתב, and 103a ד"ה כותב; see *Rambam, Commentary to the Mishnah, Shabbos* 12:3; *Avnei Nezer* ibid.).

32. מוחק / erasing

This refers to erasing writing or markings in order to create a blank space to write two letters (see *Rambam, Hil. Shabbos* 11:9). This act was performed in the *Mishkan* when the letters on the beams were inscribed incorrectly, and it was necessary to erase and rewrite them.

33. משרטט / tracing lines

Before cutting leather, it was customary to trace lines on it, to mark the pattern on which the cuts were to be made. In the *Mishkan*, this was done before cutting the ram and *tachash* hides used in the coverings (*Rashi, Shabbos* 75b ד"ה ועייל שירטוט). Alternatively, this *melachah* is performed by scoring parchment with lines, to aid the scribe in producing straight, even rows of letters (*Rambam, Hil. Shabbos* 11:17). See *Mishnah Berurah* 340:22, with *Shaar HaTziyun* §54.

34. בונה / building

"Building" is defined as joining together different components to form a unified whole, as is done when building a structure (see *Rambam, Hil. Shabbos* 7:6). *Tolados* of this *melachah* include: inserting one piece of wood into another to form a utensil (*Rambam* ibid. 10:13), and pressing together curds to form cheese (*Rambam* ibid. and

7:6; but cf. *Smak, mitzvah* §282; *Ritva, Shabbos* 102b). The act of building was performed in the *Mishkan* when its walls were assembled (*Yerushalmi, Shabbos* 52b, with *Pnei Moshe* ד"ה שהיו נותנין).

35. סותר / demolishing

The *av melachah* of demolishing applies where a person demolishes a structure in order to build a new structure in the same place (see *Shabbos* 31b; *Rambam, Hil. Shabbos* 1:18; see *Beur Halachah* 340:4 ד"ה סד"ה במשקין; *Avnei Nezer, Orach Chaim* 104:5; cf. *Rosh Yosef, Shabbos* ibid. ד"ה פסקא). Where, however, one's purpose in demolishing a structure is *not* to enable another to be built, the act is without constructive purpose; therefore, it does not violate the *melachah* (see *Rashi, Shabbos* ibid. ד"ה לעולם כר' יהודה; see above, note 8). During the wilderness era, this *melachah* was performed each time the *Mishkan* was dismantled in preparation for a journey (see *Shabbos* ibid.). [Although the *Mishkan* was reassembled in a different location each time, the *melachah* of demolishing requires rebuilding in the same place. See *Shabbos* ibid. for discussion of this issue.]

36. מכבה / extinguishing a fire

This *av melachah* is performed by extinguishing a flame or a glowing coal (see *Rambam, Hil. Shabbos* 12:2). According to some authorities, the *melachah* is limited to cases in which the purpose of extinguishing the fire is to create charcoal; extinguishing for other reasons (such as to prevent an object from being burned) is regarded as a *melachah* performed not for its inherent purpose, and does not violate the Shabbos [see note 10] (*Tosafos, Shabbos* 94a ד"ה ש"ר; for discussion, see *Mishnah Berurah* 278:3). In the *Mishkan*, this *melachah* was performed by extinguishing (or reducing) the fire beneath the cauldron in which they boiled the dyes (*Rashi, Shabbos* 73a ד"ה מכבה ומבעיר). Alternatively, it was performed by setting wood on fire, and then extinguishing the fire to produce charcoal, with which they would smelt metals for *Mishkan* use (*Tosafos* ibid.).

37. מבעיר / kindling a fire

This *av melachah* consists of kindling a fire for its heat or light (see *Rambam* ibid. 12:1). In the *Mishkan,* they would light fires beneath the cauldrons in which they would boil herbs to make dyes (*Rashi, Shabbos* 73a ד״ה מכבה ומבעיר).

38. מכה בפטיש / finishing

The *melachah* of מכה בפטיש, which translates as *striking a blow with a hammer,* is performed by perfecting, or finishing, an object; for example, by tapping lightly on a metal vessel with a hammer to smooth it out, or tapping on a brick to bring it in line with the others in its row (*Rabbeinu Chananel,* cited in *Ramban, Shabbos* 73a; *Tosafos, Shabbos* 102b ד״ה מכה; see also *Rashi, Shabbos* ibid. ד״ה המכה בפטיש, and 102b ד״ה מכה בפטיש). In the *Mishkan,* this *melachah* was performed whenever the builders would complete the manufacture of a service vessel [*kli shareis*] (*Tosafos* ibid.).

39. מוציא מרשות לרשות / transferring from one domain to another

In this *av melachah,* one picks up an object located in a "private domain" (רשות היחיד), transports it to a "public domain" (רשות הרבים), and places it

there. One is likewise forbidden to transfer an object from a public domain into a private domain; however, there is some question as to whether this is included in the *av melachah* or is a *toladah.* For discussion, see *Shabbos* 2a and 96b, with *Ramban* and *Rashba* to 2a; *Rambam, Hil. Shabbos* 12:8, with *Lechem Mishneh; Tosafos, Shabbos* 2a ד״ה פשט, and 2b ד״ה מי; *Rosh Yosef, Shabbos* 2a; *Chasam Sofer, Shabbos* 49b.

In the *Mishkan,* this *melachah* was performed after a journey, when the *Mishkan* beams were unloaded from wagons and lowered to the ground. The wagons were a private domain, the ground a public domain; hence, this was an act of transferring from a private to a public domain. Conversely, the *melachah* of transferring from a public to a private domain was performed *before* a journey, when the beams were loaded *onto* the wagons (see *Shabbos* 49b and 96b).

Carrying an object for a distance of four *amos* in the public domain is forbidden as a *toladah* of transferring (see *Tosafos, Shabbos* 2a ד״ה פשט; *Ramban* and *Ran* there 73a). However, some maintain that this too is included in the *av melachah* (*Rambam* ibid., as explained by *Minchas Chinuch,* מוסך השבת §39).

[A private domain is an enclosed area; a public domain is loosely defined as an open, unroofed public area that is at least sixteen *amos* in width. According to some, it must be used by at least 600,000 people daily.]

A. *The count according to Bahag*

 ahag lists the prohibition against performing work on Shabbos two times in his enumeration of the 613 commandments; once under the category of prohibitions for which the penalty is execution by stoning (§12), and again in the section in which he lists the negative commandments (§16). This presents an obvious difficulty: Why does *Bahag* list the same mitzvah twice? This question is easy resolved according to *Rambam's* understanding of *Bahag*. *Rambam* (*Sefer HaMitzvos, shoresh* §14) maintains that the mitzvos *Bahag* classifies by order of punishment do not refer to the actual prohibitions, but rather to the mitzvah incumbent upon *Beis Din* to administer the punishment the Torah specifies for each prohibition. Thus, according to *Rambam*, *Bahag* actually lists the prohibition against performing work on Shabbos only one time. However, *Ramban* (see *Hasagos* to *Sefer HaMitzvos* ibid. ד"ה וכתב עוד) contends that the mitzvos *Bahag* lists in sections categorized by punishment *do* refer to the actual prohibitions themselves. According to *Ramban*, then, the question remains.

Following are two approaches that have been suggested to resolve this difficulty:

1. *Bahag refers to a prohibition which does not carry the death penalty.*

Besides the prohibition against personally performing one of the thirty-nine categories of

forbidden labor on Shabbos, it is also forbidden to cause one's *animal* to perform one of these categories of labor. This prohibition, known as *mechamer* [מחמר], is derived from the same verse that forbids a person to perform labor on Shabbos (*Shemos* 20:10): *You shall not do any work, you, your son, your daughter … your animal* (*Shabbos* 153b; but see *Rambam, Hil. Shabbos* 20:1, who cites a different source for this prohibition). It does not, however, carry the death penalty (ibid. 154a). *Bahag* considers the prohibition against performing forbidden labor oneself, which carries the death penalty, and the prohibition against causing one's animal to perform forbidden labor, which does not carry the death penalty, to be two separate commandments. He lists the former prohibition under the category of prohibitions punishable by stoning; he lists the latter prohibition in his section of negative commandments (*Ramban, Hasagos* to *Rambam's Sefer HaMitzvos, shoresh* §14 ד"ה וכתב עוד).

2. *Bahag lists the commandment again as part of a subsection listing other prohibitions that relate to forbidden labor.*

Some answer that although *Bahag* lists the prohibition against performing forbidden labor on Shabbos in two places, he does not *count* this prohibition as two commandments of the 613. He includes it in his list of negative commandments simply because he wishes to set down in one place all the prohibitions forbidding

מפתח למוני המצוות

THE COUNT OF THE MITZVAH

Baal Halachos Gedolos / Lavin 16
בה"ג / לאוין טז

R' Saadiah Gaon / Lavin 156
רס"ג / לאוין קנו

R' Eliyahu HaZakein / Amud 35
ר' אליהו הזקן / עמ' 35

Rashbag / Lo Saaseh Os 59
רשב"ג / לא תעשה אות נט

R' Yitzchak El-Bargeloni / Lavin 16
ר"י אלברג'לוני / לאוין טז

Maamar HaSechel / Dibbur Revi'i 2
מאמר השכל / דיבור רביעי ב

Sefer Yere'im / 274
יראים / רעד

Rambam, Sefer HaMitzvos / Lo Saaseh 320
רמב"ם / לא תעשה שכ

Sefer Mitzvos Gadol (Smag) / Lo Saaseh 65
סמ"ג / לא תעשה סה

Sefer Mitzvos Katan (Smak) / 282
סמ"ק / רפב

Zohar HaRakia / Lavin 155
זוהר הרקיע / לאוין קנה

work on specific days. Thus, although he already listed the prohibition earlier, he lists it again in the category of negative commandments together with the prohibitions against working on Pesach, Shavuos, Rosh Hashanah, Yom Kippur, Succos and Shemini Atzeres. [These are prohibitions that do not carry the death penalty, and so are listed in *Bahag's* section of negative commandments.] It is clear that not all the prohibition in *Bahag's* list of negative commandments count toward the 613, since this list contains 282 prohibitions, and *Bahag* himself gives the total as 277! The difference represents five prohibitions that he counted elsewhere as part of the 613 (*R' A. S. Traub's introduction to Bahag*, 31-32).

B. *The count according to R' Saadiah Gaon*

In his count of negative commandments, *R' Saadiah Gaon* lists the prohibition *You shall not do any work* (§146). In his count of the positive commandments, he lists a requirement to *refrain* from performing labor on Shabbos (§34) [derived from *Shemos* 23:12: *Six days shall you accomplish your activities, and on the seventh day you shall rest*]. This presents a difficulty, for according to *R' Saadiah Gaon*, a commandment which is given as a prohibition and then repeated as a positive commandment is counted as only one commandment (see *R' Yeruchem Fischel Perla's introduction to Sefer HaMitzvos of R' Saadiah Gaon, §7, Shoresh §6*). Why, then, does he count the negative and positive commandments pertaining to forbidden labor on Shabbos as two separate commandments? (ibid., *Aseh* §34).

Two approaches have been suggested to resolve this difficulty:

1. *The positive commandment to refrain from work on Shabbos refers to strenuous activity in general.*

Some authorities maintain that the Torah commandment to refrain from working refers

not only to the thirty-nine categories of forbidden labor but to anything that requires exertion. The Torah commands that one rest on Shabbos, and not occupy himself in strenuous activity, even activities that do not fall under the thirty-nine categories of forbidden labor (see *Rambam, Hil. Shabbos* 21:1 with *Maggid Mishneh; Ramban, Vayikra* 23:24). Such activity is not included in the negative commandment that prohibits the thirty-nine categories of forbidden labor on Shabbos. Possibly, *R' Saadiah Gaon* subscribes to this view. Thus, he counts the prohibition against performing one of the thirty-nine categories of forbidden labor as one commandment, in his list of negative commandments, and the requirement to refrain from engaging in strenuous activity as a separate commandment, in his list of positive commandments (*R' Yeruchem Fischel Perla* ibid.).

2. *The negative commandment forbidding work on Shabbos refers to causing one's animal to do one of the forbidden labors.*

As noted above, *Bahag* maintains that the prohibition against causing one's *animal* to perform forbidden labor is a separate commandment. Perhaps *R' Saadiah Gaon* is of the same opinion. He thus lists two commandments pertaining to work on Shabbos. The positive commandment accounts for both the commandment to refrain from work on Shabbos and the *prohibition* against performing labor oneself (according to *R' Saadiah Gaon's* view that a commandment phrased in both negative and positive form counts as a single commandment). The negative commandment accounts for the prohibition against causing one's animal to perform a forbidden labor on Shabbos [which is not included in the positive commandment to refrain from work, as the verse states, *on the seventh day **you** shall rest*] (*R' Yeruchem Fischel Perla* ibid.).

Mitzvah 33

מִצְוַת כְּבוּד אָב וָאֵם

פרשת יתרו

To Honor
One's Father
& Mother

THE MITZVAH:

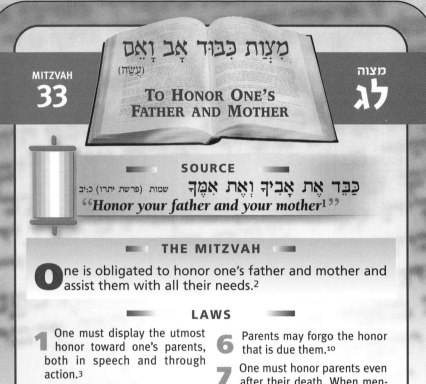

מִצְוַת כִּבּוּד אָב וָאֵם
(עֲשֵׂה)

MITZVAH 33

TO HONOR ONE'S FATHER AND MOTHER

מצוה לג

SOURCE

שמות (פרשת יתרו) כ:יב   כַּבֵּד אֶת אָבִיךָ וְאֶת אִמֶּךָ

"Honor your father and your mother[1]"

THE MITZVAH

One is obligated to honor one's father and mother and assist them with all their needs.[2]

LAWS

1 One must display the utmost honor toward one's parents, both in speech and through action.[3]

2 One must serve and assist parents with their needs, such as food and drink, clothing and escort[4] — all with a pleasant disposition.[5]

3 If parents can provide for themselves, a child need not spend his own money on their behalf. However, if they are financially incapable of doing so, the child must provide for them from his own funds.[6]

4 One must rise fully when a parent appears in view.[7]

5 A child may not heed a parent's request if it involves transgression of a Torah[8] or Rabbinic law.[9]

6 Parents may forgo the honor that is due them.[10]

7 One must honor parents even after their death. When mentioning them during the first year after death, one adds: הריני כפרת משכבו/ה.[11] After twelve months, one adds: זכרונו/ה לברכה.[12]

8 The mitzvah of honoring parents includes a requirement to honor certain other relatives as well.[13]

9 This mitzvah applies to both men and women,[14] in all places and at all times. However, a married woman's obligations to her husband supersede her obligations to her parents.[15]

10 The reward for this mitzvah is longevity.[16]

NOTE: For the laws of fearing one's parents (יראת אב ואם) see *mitzvah* #212.[17]

A REASON

A person must show his parents respect and gratitude, for they brought him into the world, and with tireless effort provided all his needs. Reinforcing this recognition will naturally cause a person to extend his gratitude to the Creator, Who created and sustains all life.

לע"נ אסתר בת אברהם יהושע ע"ה הרש
לע"נ אברהם בן אהרן הלוי ע"ה

1. The Gemara (*Kiddushin* 30b-31a) explains that the natural tendency of a child is to honor his mother more than his father, because she cajoles him with pleasant words. Hence, when speaking of honoring, the Torah places "father" before "mother," to indicate that a father must be equally honored. In the commandment to fear one's parents, however, the mother is mentioned first. Since a child naturally feels greater awe and reverence for his father, who teaches him Torah, the Torah places "mother" before "father." Thus, the Torah instructs us to treat both parents equally in regard to each of these commandments (*Rambam, Hil. Mamrim* 6:2; see below, note 8).

2. *Kiddushin* 30b; *Rambam, Hil. Mamrim* 6:1; *Tur* and *Shulchan Aruch, Yoreh Deah* 240:1.

Some say (based on a comment of *Zohar*) that included in this mitzvah is a requirement to love one's parents intensely (*Chareidim* 9:35-38; see, however, *Teshuvos HaRambam* [Blau ed.] §448). Additionally, there is a mitzvah to regard them as distinguished (*Chareidim* 9:35-38), regardless of other people's opinion of them (*Chayei Adam* 67:3).

Our verse states: *Honor your father and your mother.* Another verse states (*Mishlei* 3:9): *Honor Hashem with your wealth.* The shared wording of these verses teaches an analogy between them. *Mechilta* (*Shemos* 20:12; see also *Kiddushin* 30b) explains that the Almighty so values the mitzvah of honoring parents that He equated honoring them with honoring Him. See *Ramban* and *Rabbeinu Bachya* to our verse.

3. See *Mechilta, Shemos* 20:12; *Ralbag* there; *Igeres HaTeshuvah L'Rabbeinu*

AN EXPANDED TREATMENT

Yonah, final section; *Meiri, Kiddushin* 31a; *Chareidim* 12:1-2.

One must always speak to his parents with deference and respect, in a manner that exhibits his high regard for them. This is the simple understanding of the command, *Honor your father and your mother* (*Chareidim* ibid.). *Rabbeinu Yonah* (ibid.) writes that the fundamental requirement of the mitzvah of honoring parents is to give them satisfaction and pleasure, both through one's speech and through one's actions.

One must endeavor, through his words and actions, to increase the honor of one's parents. For example, if someone needs the cooperation of the members of a city in a project, and he knows that they will accede to his request either out of respect for him or for his father, he should ask them to do it on behalf of his father. In this manner, he assigns the honor being granted to his father (*Rambam, Hil. Mamrim* 6:4; *Shulchan Aruch, Yoreh Deah* 240:6). [However, if he intended to submit his request without mentioning any name, he need not mention his father's name (*Nachlas Tzvi* ibid., *Aruch HaShulchan* ibid. §23). For more details concerning this halachah, see *Tur* §240; *Perishah* 240:12; *Taz* ibid. §8; *Shach* ibid. §9, *Aruch HaShulchan* ibid.]

Even actions that have no direct connection to one's parents are governed by this commandment. Thus, one who truly wishes to honor his parents should engage in the study of Torah and performance of mitzvos. This is the greatest honor to parents, for it will cause observers to remark, "Fortunate are the parents who raised such a son!" Conversely, if one does not conduct himself in the proper way, his parents will suffer humiliation on his account. Such a child

shames them in the worst possible way (*Kitzur Shulchan Aruch* 143:21).

If a child hears a person speak falsely regarding his parents, he is obligated to protest (*Sefer HaYirah L'Rabbeinu Yonah* §197 ד"ה והתרחק מן הכבוד; *Sefer Chasidim* §72). However, if he knows that his protest will simply lead to further denigration, he should remain silent, so as not to increase their dishonor (*Sefer HaYirah* ibid.).

4. *Kiddushin* 31b; *Rambam, Hil. Mamrim* 6:3; *Tur* and *Shulchan Aruch, Yoreh Deah* 240:4.

These things are listed merely by way of example; the mitzvah actually obligates a person to see to all his parents' needs and to fulfill all their desires (see *Rambam, Commentary to the Mishnah, Kiddushin* 29a; *Ramban, Shemos* 20:12).

If necessary, one must physically attend to the needs of one's parents himself (see *Tos. Ri HaZakein, Kiddushin* 31b ד"ה מאכיל; *Rambam, Hil. Mamrim* 6:3; *Tur* and *Shulchan Aruch* ibid.§5, with *Bach* there ד"ה ומ"ש). Attending to parents' physical needs is not merely an act of kindness, but a basic component of the commandment to honor them. As *Rambam* (ibid.) writes: … And [a child] should serve [his parent] in [all] the ways that attendants serve their master…

Many Rishonim hold that where fulfillment of a parent's request would not benefit the parent personally, one is not obligated by this mitzvah to heed the request (see *Tosafos, Yevamos* 6a ד"ה שכן; *Ramban, Rashba* and *Ritva* there; *Beur HaGra, Yoreh Deah* ibid. §36; see *Maharik,* cited in *Darkei Moshe* there §10). Some maintain that since failing to obey would cause the parent anguish, while obeying would please the parent, one

should heed a request of this sort (see *Chazon Ish, Yoreh Deah* 149:8; see also *Rashi,* cited in *Ritva, Yevamos* ibid.; *Teshuvos HaRosh* 15:5; *Meiri, Yevamos* ibid.; *Chareidim* 16:1-2; see further, *Chazon Ish, Yoreh Deah* 149:8). See further, *Iyunim* §3.

5. Avimi the son of R' Abahu taught: One can feed his father [a delicacy, such as] *pisyon* birds (quail), yet this can drive him out of the world, if he shows that he does so begrudgingly. Conversely, one can make his father grind a millstone (a difficult labor), and this can merit him life in the World to Come [if he gently explains to him the necessity of doing this labor in a soothing, encouraging manner] (see *Kiddushin* 31a-b).

Rashi (ibid.) cites the following incidents related by *Yerushalmi* (*Peah* 1:1, *Kiddushin* 1:7), which served as the background for Avimi's comment: There was a man who customarily fed his father *pisyon* birds. Once, the father asked him how he could afford to do so. The son answered: Old man, what do you care? Grind [i.e. chew] and eat! With this disdainful remark, the son demonstrated that caring for his father was burdensome to him. There was another man, who worked at a mill, and who had an elderly father. When the king conscripted the father for work, the son said to him, "Father, you work in the mill and I will go in your place to perform the king's service, which can go on indefinitely."

6. When honoring one's parents entails spending money on their behalf, there is no obligation on the child to bear the expense. Rather, the father or mother must spend their own money to pay for their needs, e.g. food, clothing, and the like. This is true only when the parents have the

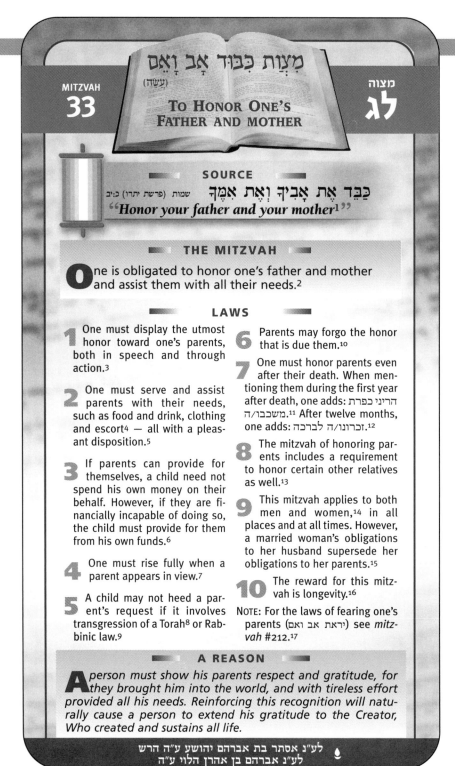

MITZVAH 33

מִצְוַת כִּבּוּד אָב וָאֵם
(עֲשֵׂה)

TO HONOR ONE'S FATHER AND MOTHER

מצוה לג

■ SOURCE ■

כַּבֵּד אֶת אָבִיךָ וְאֶת אִמֶּךָ שמות (פרשת יתרו) כ:יב

"Honor your father and your mother[1]"

■ THE MITZVAH ■

One is obligated to honor one's father and mother and assist them with all their needs.[2]

■ LAWS ■

1 One must display the utmost honor toward one's parents, both in speech and through action.[3]

2 One must serve and assist parents with their needs, such as food and drink, clothing and escort[4] — all with a pleasant disposition.[5]

3 If parents can provide for themselves, a child need not spend his own money on their behalf. However, if they are financially incapable of doing so, the child must provide for them from his own funds.[6]

4 One must rise fully when a parent appears in view.[7]

5 A child may not heed a parent's request if it involves transgression of a Torah[8] or Rabbinic law.[9]

6 Parents may forgo the honor that is due them.[10]

7 One must honor parents even after their death. When mentioning them during the first year after death, one adds: הֲרֵינִי כַּפָּרַת מִשְׁכָּבוֹ/ה.[11] After twelve months, one adds: זִכְרוֹנוֹ/ה לִבְרָכָה.[12]

8 The mitzvah of honoring parents includes a requirement to honor certain other relatives as well.[13]

9 This mitzvah applies to both men and women,[14] in all places and at all times. However, a married woman's obligations to her husband supersede her obligations to her parents.[15]

10 The reward for this mitzvah is longevity.[16]

NOTE: For the laws of fearing one's parents (יראת אב ואם) see *mitzvah* #212.[17]

■ A REASON ■

A person must show his parents respect and gratitude, for they brought him into the world, and with tireless effort provided all his needs. Reinforcing this recognition will naturally cause a person to extend his gratitude to the Creator, Who created and sustains all life.

לע״נ אסתר בת אברהם יהושע ע״ה הרש
לע״נ אברהם בן אהרן הלוי ע״ה

financial ability to pay for their needs. If they are impoverished, however, the children have an obligation to pay the necessary expenses of their parents out of their own pockets (*Rambam, Hil. Mamrim* 6:3; *Shulchan Aruch, Yoreh Deah* 240:5).

According to most Rishonim (*Rosh,*

Kiddushin 1:50; *Rif, Kiddushin* fol. 13b, *Ri* and *Rach* cited by *Tosafos, Kiddushin* 32a ד"ה אורו; *Tur* §240 et al.), this obligation derives not from the mitzvah to honor one's parents, but from the mitzvah to give charity. This view is adopted by the Poskim. Some therefore say that the obligation to

support one's parents is limited to the amount one is generally obligated to give to charity. Others maintain that the parental obligation extends even beyond that amount (see *Tur* §240; *Shulchan Aruch* and *Rama, Yoreh Deah* 240:5; and commentaries there). All agree, though, that support for one's parents comes ahead of support for other poor people, as stated in the laws of charity (see *Shulchan Aruch, Yoreh Deah* 251:3).

Rama (ibid. 240:5) concludes: Nevertheless, a curse should come upon a person of means who supports his parents from the money he has allocated for charity. The definition of "means" in this context is up to the Rabbinic judges to decide, according to the standards of each time and place.

According to the accepted view that the obligation to support one's needy parents derives from the obligation to give charity, a child who cannot afford this level of support has no obligation to solicit funds on behalf of his needy parent (*Shulchan Aruch* 240:5). Nevertheless, as a matter of propriety (*derech eretz*), it is proper for a child to do this for his parent, where possible (see *Ben Ish Chai, Shanah II, Mishpatim* §8). *Aruch HaShulchan* (240:22) adds that under no circumstances should one allow his mother to solicit funds for herself, since the shame experienced by a woman who must go begging is greater than a man's, due to her innate modesty. [Note: There are Rishonim who maintain that the obligation to support needy parents derives from the mitzvah of *honor your father and your mother,* and not from the law of charity (*Sefer HaChinuch; Ritva, Kiddushin* 32a; *Mordechai, Kiddushin* ch. 1 §498; *Smak, mitzvah* #50). According to this view, a person must support his parents even if he will have to beg for his own support as a result. Some maintain that he is even obligated to go begging for the money needed by his parents, or to take a job to earn enough money to support them.]

Even those who exempt a child from soliciting funds to *support* his parents agree that the child's obligation to attend to his parents' physical needs applies *even* if the child will be compelled to neglect his work, and the resulting loss of income will force him to solicit funds for his *own* livelihood. However, this applies only if the child has sufficient funds for that day's sustenance. If he does not, he is not obligated to neglect his work to attend to his father's needs (*Shulchan Aruch* ibid.).

7. The laws of rising for a parent are the same as those for rising for a teacher (*Rambam, Hil. Mamrim* 6:3). Hence, one must rise to his full height (*Aruch HaShulchan* 240:24), and one must rise from when he is able to see him in the distance until he disappears from view or sits down (*Chayei Adam* 67:7, as in *Shulchan Aruch* ibid. 242:16; but see *Aruch HaShulchan* ibid.). Likewise, "…one need only rise [twice daily, once] in the morning and [once] in the evening, unless he in the presence of others who are unaware that he previously arose for them. However, some maintain that one is obligated to rise even one hundred times each day" (*Chayei Adam* loc. cit.; see also *Shulchan Aruch* and *Rama Yoreh Deah* 242:16; *Shach* ibid. §37; *Beur HaGra* ibid. §53; *Birkei Yosef, Yoreh Deah* 242:21; *Aruch HaShulchan* ibid.)

As mentioned in Law 6, a parent may forgo the honor due him. This would be a practical suggestion for those who follow the more stringent opinion which mandates rising multiple times each day. Even when parents forgo the honor, however, it is a mitzvah for the child to show them "token honor" [*hiddur*] by rising

slightly from his seat, as if he intended to stand up fully (see *Kitzur Piskei HaRosh, Kiddushin* ch. 1 §53; *Shulchan Aruch Yoreh Deah* 242:32, 244:14).

8. The Torah instructs us (*Vayikra* 19:3): *Every man, your mother and your father you shall fear, and My Shabbosos you shall observe; I am Hashem, your God.* By juxtaposing these two commandments, and concluding with the words, *I am Hashem, your God*, the verse teaches that even when honoring one's parents, one must remember that "both you and your parents must honor Me [Hashem]." The verse thus teaches that one's parents should not be obeyed in instances where the parents' request contravenes the laws of Shabbos. This exclusion applies to all other mitzvos as well (*Rashi*, from *Yevamos* 5b-6a; see also *Bava Metzia* 32a; *Toras Kohanim, Vayikra* ibid.). Even if the parents do not directly instruct the child to transgress, but fulfilling their request will involve a transgression, one may not obey them (see *Chofetz Chaim, Hilchos Loshon Hora* 1:5 and *Be'er Mayim Chaim* there §8 and §9).

Where a person is faced by a choice between performing the mitzvah of honoring his parents and performing another mitzvah, this is the rule:

If the other mitzvah is one that cannot be put off until later (e.g. burying a corpse), and there is no one else to perform it now, he must set aside the mitzvah of honoring his parents and perform the other mitzvah instead (see *Kiddushin* 32a; *Rambam, Hil. Mamrim* 6:13; *Tur* and *Shulchan Aruch, Yoreh Deah* 240:12). This is because his parents too are obligated in the other mitzvah; therefore, it takes precedence (*Kiddushin* ibid.). [See *Teshuvos Machaneh Chaim* (I:85) regarding a case in which the parents are not obligated in the other mitzvah.]

However, if the other mitzvah is one that can be put off until later, or that can be performed by someone else, one should not set aside the mitzvah of honoring parents for its sake (*Rambam* ibid.; *Tur* and *Shulchan Aruch* ibid.).

9. See *Rambam, Hil. Mamrim* 6:12; *Shulchan Aruch, Yoreh Deah* 240:15. According to *Rambam* (*Sefer HaMitzvos, shoresh* §1) the obligation to obey Rabbinic legislation is based on the Torah commandment (*mitzvah* #496) *not to deviate from their word* [לא תסור] (*Devarim* 17:11). Therefore, violations of Rabbinic law are also included in the verse that exempts one from honoring parents where their honor would entail a violation of Torah law. *Ramban*, on the other hand, maintains that there is no Biblical obligation to obey Rabbinical legislation (*Ramban*, to *Rambam* ibid.). However, the authorities agree that even in *Ramban's* view, if a parent commands his child to violate Rabbinic law, the child may not obey. For the verse teaches that, "both you and your parents are obligated to honor Me (Hashem)." Since observing the Rabbinic laws is surely a form of honoring Hashem, requests that involve violating these laws are also excluded from the obligation of honoring one's parents (*Beis Yosef* 240:15). See also *Yam Shel Shlomo, Kiddushin* §63; *Kovetz He'aros, Yevamos* §18.

There is a dispute among the authorities concerning whether one is obligated to honor parents who are sinners. *Rambam* (*Hil. Mamrim* 6:11) rules that even if a father is a sinner, his son is obligated to honor him. This view is disputed by *Tur* (*Yoreh Deah* §240), who maintains that a son need not honor a father who is wicked unless he repents. *Shulchan Aruch* (240:18) follows the ruling of *Rambam*, while *Rama* (there) adopts *Tur's* position. However, even according to *Rama*, it is forbidden to cause

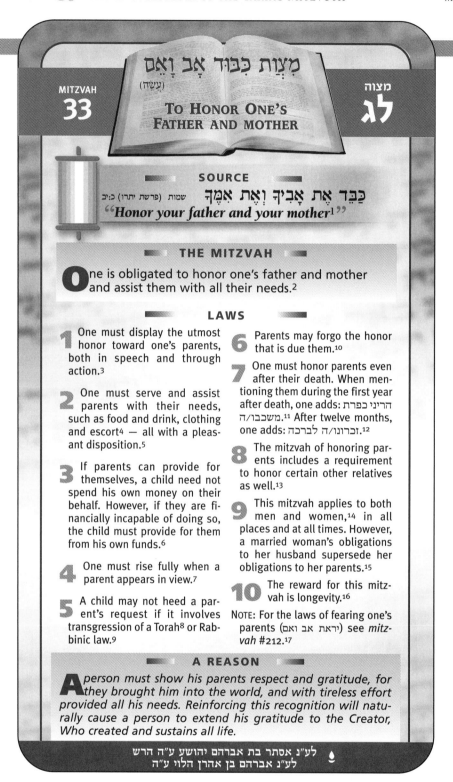

MITZVAH 33

מִצְוַת כִּבּוּד אָב וָאֵם
(עשה)
TO HONOR ONE'S FATHER AND MOTHER

מצוה לג

SOURCE

שמות (פרשת יתרו) כ:יב **כַּבֵּד אֶת אָבִיךָ וְאֶת אִמֶּךָ**
"Honor your father and your mother¹"

THE MITZVAH

One is obligated to honor one's father and mother and assist them with all their needs.²

LAWS

1 One must display the utmost honor toward one's parents, both in speech and through action.³

2 One must serve and assist parents with their needs, such as food and drink, clothing and escort⁴ — all with a pleasant disposition.⁵

3 If parents can provide for themselves, a child need not spend his own money on their behalf. However, if they are financially incapable of doing so, the child must provide for them from his own funds.⁶

4 One must rise fully when a parent appears in view.⁷

5 A child may not heed a parent's request if it involves transgression of a Torah⁸ or Rabbinic law.⁹

6 Parents may forgo the honor that is due them.¹⁰

7 One must honor parents even after their death. When mentioning them during the first year after death, one adds: הריני כפרת משכבו/ה.¹¹ After twelve months, one adds: זכרונו/ה לברכה.¹²

8 The mitzvah of honoring parents includes a requirement to honor certain other relatives as well.¹³

9 This mitzvah applies to both men and women,¹⁴ in all places and at all times. However, a married woman's obligations to her husband supersede her obligations to her parents.¹⁵

10 The reward for this mitzvah is longevity.¹⁶

NOTE: For the laws of fearing one's parents (יראת אב ואם) see *mitzvah* #212.¹⁷

A REASON

A person must show his parents respect and gratitude, for they brought him into the world, and with tireless effort provided all his needs. Reinforcing this recognition will naturally cause a person to extend his gratitude to the Creator, Who created and sustains all life.

לע"נ אסתר בת אברהם יהושע ע"ה הרש
לע"נ אברהם בן אהרן הלוי ע"ה

the parent anguish (*Shach* 240:20), or to hit or curse the parent (*Shulchan Aruch* 241:4).

[Even a *mamzer* born of a forbidden union must honor his parents (*Rambam* ibid.; *Shulchan Aruch* 240:18), provided the parents have repented their sin (*Rama* ibid.). The

mitzvah surely applies, then, where the *mamzer* was born of a *permitted* marriage; for example, the child of a convert who married a *mamzer*.]

10. By forgoing their honor, the parents release the child from liability for not honoring them. However, if the child

does honor them, he has fulfilled a mitzvah (*Tos. HaRosh, Bava Metzia* 32a ד"ה סד"א; *Radvaz*, cited by *R' Akiva Eiger* 240:19 and *Pischei Teshuvah* 240:16).

Parents can only forgo the honor due them, but they cannot allow their child to actively pain or disgrace them (*Teshuvos Rivash* §220, cited in *Kesef Mishneh, Hil. Talmud Torah* 7:13, *Minchas Chinuch* 212:6). Nor can parents permit a child to violate the prohibitions against hitting (#48) or cursing (#260) them (*She'iltos D'Rav Achai*, end of §60; *Haamek She'eilah* there; *Sefer Chasidim* §570; cf. *Minchas Chinuch* 48:3). See further, *Sdei Chemed*, מערכת כ' §31.

"It is forbidden for one to [overly] burden his children and demand meticulous honor [from them], lest he cause them to transgress [this mitzvah]. Rather, a parent should forgo [his honor] and look away" (*Rambam, Hil. Mamrim* 6:8, *Shulchan Aruch* ibid. §19; see *Sefer Chasidim* §152). A parent should emulate the example of Hashem, Who set aside His own honor and led the Jewish nation in the desert, as it says (*Shemos* 13:21), *Hashem went before them by day in a pillar of cloud to lead them on the way*, etc. (*Levush* 240:19).

If a parent wishes to serve and honor his child, the child is permitted to accept the parent's service (*Shulchan Aruch* ibid. §25), for his acquiescence to the parent's wishes is itself a form of honor (see *Yerushalmi, Kiddushin* 1:7; *Tos. Ri HaZakein, Kiddushin* 31b ד"ה מאימך קביל; *Tosafos* there ד"ה ר' טרפון). However, it is fitting that he not accept the service as his rightful due, but as something to which he is not entitled (see similarly, *Meiri, Kiddushin* 32a ד"ה האב).

11. *Kiddushin* 31b; *Rambam, Mamrim* 6:5; *Tur* and *Shulchan Aruch, Yoreh Deah* 240:9.

The phrase translates as: "I accept upon myself any evil that would befall his soul [for his misdeed]" (*Rashi, Kiddushin* 31b ד"ה הריני). One's punishment after death generally does not last more than a year; therefore, this formula is recited for that length of time only (*Rashi* ibid. ד"ה מכאן).

This law applies whenever one mentions the deceased parent, whether orally or in writing (*Shulchan Aruch* and *Rama* 240:9). Some earlier commentaries maintain that this only applies when quoting a Torah statement heard from his parent (see *Tos. Ri HaZakein, Kiddushin* 31b; *Teshuvos Maharil* §24). Others extend the rule to include any quotation from his parent, even regarding mundane matters (*Rabbeinu Yerucham, Nesiv* 1:4). The latter-day Poskim rule that one should add the prescribed formula even when just mentioning a parent's name conversationally (see *Kitzur Shulchan Aruch* 143:8; *Ben Ish Chai, Shanah* II, *Shoftim* §14).

Some maintain that the הריני כפרת משכבו formula (recited in the first year) is mentioned only when a deceased parent is quoted orally, not when he is quoted in writing (*Shiltei HaGiborim, Kiddushin,* fol. 13a in *dafei HaRif*).

12. The Gemara (*Kiddushin* 31b) quotes the appropriate formula as זכרונו לברכה לחיי העולם הבא, *May his memory be blessed for life in the World to Come.* However, *Rambam* (*Hil. Mamrim* 6:5) omits לברכה, *blessed,* and *Shulchan Aruch* (240:9) only writes the words זכרונו לברכה, *may his memory be blessed,* omitting the latter half of the formula. Many Poskim (*Shach* 240:13, *Chayei Adam* 67:6; *Aruch HaShulchan* 240:30; *Ben Ish Chai*) cite *Shulchan Aruch's* abbreviated version; however, others advocate reciting (and writing) the Gemara's complete version (*Taz* 240:13, *Kitzur Shulchan Aruch* 143:8).

It is customary to recite *kaddish* and lead the congregation in prayer during the first eleven months after the death of one's parents, and on their *yahrzeit* (see *Rama* to *Yoreh Deah* 376:4). Similarly, it is customary to study Torah (particularly Mishnah) and give charity in their memory, to name children after them (the sephardic custom is to honor one's parents by naming children after them even during their lifetime), and to title one's Torah publications with a reference to their name. In these ways and others, one fulfills the mitzvah of honoring one's parents after their passing (see *Teshuvos Maharik* §30; *Yam Shel Shlomo, Kiddushin* ch. 1 §63; *Chayei Adam* 67:6).

13. The list of relatives that one must honor include: (a) stepparents; (b) one's eldest brother, or, in some opinions, all older brothers (*Kesubos* 103a; *Rambam, Mamrim* 6:15; *Shulchan Aruch* 240:21-22); (c) grandparents (*Shulchan Aruch* 240:24; *Teshuvos Rama* §118); (d) a father-in-law or mother-in-law (*Medrash Tehillim* §7:4; *Shulchan Aruch* ibid.); (e) siblings of one's father or mother (*Sefer HaYirah L'Rabbeinu Yonah* §203; *Chareidim* 12:3-10, 16:3-12). Many of these obligations are of Biblical origin; others are mandated by Rabbinic law only. The nature and degree of these obligations vary depending on the relative. For greater elaboration, see *Shulchan Aruch, Yoreh Deah* 240:21-24 and commentaries there; see also *Iyunim* §4 at length.

14. *Kiddushin* 29a, 30b; *Rambam, Hil. Mamrim* 6:6; *Shulchan Aruch, Yoreh Deah* 240:17.

Women are obligated to honor their parents because it is a positive commandment whose obligation is not contingent upon time, and women are, as a rule, obligated in mitzvos of this kind (Mishnah, *Kiddushin* 29a). Furthermore, the obligation of women to honor parents is taught explicitly in a Scriptural verse, stated regarding the mitzvah of fearing parents, and this is applicable to honoring them as well. That verse states (*Vayikra* 19:3): איש אמו ואביו תיראו, *every man, his mother and father he must fear.* The plural form (תיראו) implies that the obligation applies to women as well as men (*Kiddushin* 30b). See *Kiddushin* 35a, where the necessity for this teaching is explained.

15. This is derived (*Kiddushin* 30b) in the following manner: Although both men and women are included in the obligation to honor parents, the verse specifies men (*every **man,** his mother and father he must fear* — *Vayikra* ibid.). This teaches that in some instances a woman need not honor her parents; namely, where she is married, and doing so would conflict with her marital duties (see *Kiddushin* 30b; *Shulchan Aruch, Yoreh Deah* 240:17).

If a husband chooses to forgo his rights, and allows his wife to see to her parents' needs before his own, she is fully obligated in all aspects of parental honor (*Sefer HaChinuch* here; *Shach* 240:19; *Chayei Adam* 67:17). *Sefer Chasidim* (§335) writes that a husband of refined character will allow his wife to give precedence to her parents' needs. Even if a husband does not permit this, the wife is still obligated to do for her parents whatever is possible without conflicting with her obligations to her husband (*Rambam, Commentary to Mishnah, Kiddushin* 29a; see *Ralbag, Shemos* 20:12).

[Some Rishonim maintain that a married woman is exempt from this mitzvah *not* because it conflicts with her marital duties, but for a practical reason — namely, that she does not live with her parents, and so cannot see to their needs (see *Tosafos, Kiddushin* ibid ד"ה שיש; *Tos. HaRosh* there). According to this view, if a

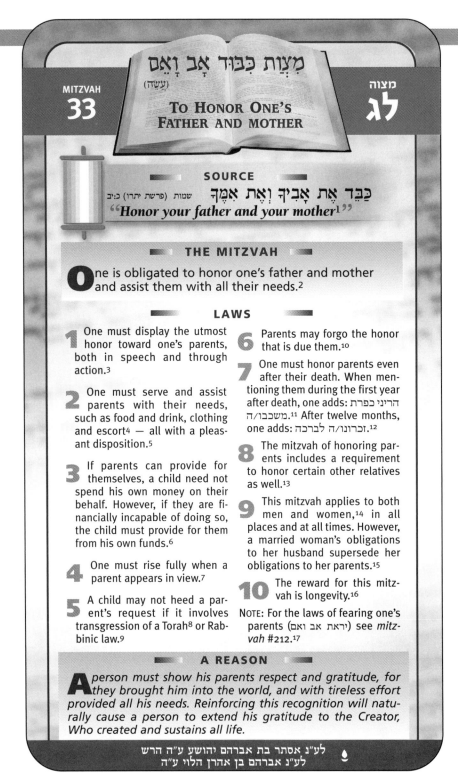

מִצְוַת כִּבּוּד אָב וָאֵם
(עֲשֵׂה)

MITZVAH
33

**TO HONOR ONE'S
FATHER AND MOTHER**

**מצוה
לג**

SOURCE

כַּבֵּד אֶת אָבִיךָ וְאֶת אִמֶּךָ שְׁמוֹת (פָּרָשַׁת יִתְרוֹ) כ:יב
"Honor your father and your mother[1]"

THE MITZVAH

One is obligated to honor one's father and mother and assist them with all their needs.[2]

LAWS

1 One must display the utmost honor toward one's parents, both in speech and through action.[3]

2 One must serve and assist parents with their needs, such as food and drink, clothing and escort[4] — all with a pleasant disposition.[5]

3 If parents can provide for themselves, a child need not spend his own money on their behalf. However, if they are financially incapable of doing so, the child must provide for them from his own funds.[6]

4 One must rise fully when a parent appears in view.[7]

5 A child may not heed a parent's request if it involves transgression of a Torah[8] or Rabbinic law.[9]

6 Parents may forgo the honor that is due them.[10]

7 One must honor parents even after their death. When mentioning them during the first year after death, one adds: הֲרֵינִי כַּפָּרַת מִשְׁכָּבוֹ/הּ.[11] After twelve months, one adds: זִכְרוֹנוֹ/הּ לִבְרָכָה.[12]

8 The mitzvah of honoring parents includes a requirement to honor certain other relatives as well.[13]

9 This mitzvah applies to both men and women,[14] in all places and at all times. However, a married woman's obligations to her husband supersede her obligations to her parents.[15]

10 The reward for this mitzvah is longevity.[16]

NOTE: For the laws of fearing one's parents (יִרְאַת אָב וָאֵם) see *mitzvah #212*.[17]

A REASON

A person must show his parents respect and gratitude, for they brought him into the world, and with tireless effort provided all his needs. Reinforcing this recognition will naturally cause a person to extend his gratitude to the Creator, Who created and sustains all life.

span of years (see *Mechilta* to *Shemos* ibid.).

[The Gemara in *Kiddushin* (39b) cites a Tannaic view (that of R' Yaakov) that interprets the reward of longevity mentioned in the verse as referring to reward in the World to Come. However, most Tannaim maintain that the verse promises reward in both this world and the next (see *Peah* 1:1 with *Tos. Yom Tov* and *Tos. Anshei Shem;* see also *Kiddushin* 40a with *Rashi* there). See also *Rashi* to *Shemos* 20:12 and *Rabbeinu Bachya* there. For further discussion of R' Yaakov's view, see *Rambam, Hil. Teshuvah* 9:1, and *Maharsha* to *Kiddushin* 39b.]

17. This refers to the separate mitzvah of fearing one's parents, which obligates one to hold them in awe and forbids any diminishment of their honor and esteem (see *Aruch HaShulchan, Yoreh Deah* 240:8). Some examples cited in the Gemara (*Kiddushin* 31b) are not to sit in one's father's place [e.g. at the head of the table], and not to contradict his words. See further, *Shulchan Aruch* 240:2-3.

The difference between honoring parents and fearing them is as follows: Honor is an active obligation; a child honors a parent by performing actions toward that end. Fear is a passive obligation; a child fulfills this obligation by refraining from actions that diminish the honor of his parents (see *To'afos R'eim* §4, to *Yereim* §222; see also *Malbim, Vayikra* 19:4). See *Aruch HaShulchan* 240:8.

married woman happens to live with her parents, she is fully obligated in the mitzvah of honor (*Teshuvos Rema MiPano*, §89).]

16. *Shemos* 20:12.
This is one of only two positive

commandments for which the Torah stipulates the reward of longevity. The other is the requirement of "sending off the mother bird" [שִׁלּוּחַ הַקֵּן] (*mitzvah #545*).

The punishment for failing to observe this mitzvah is a shortened

עיונים

A BROADER LOOK AT THE LAWS

1   Magnitude of honor:

"How far does the obligation to honor one's parents extend? Even if parents should take a purse full of gold coins belonging to their child and throw it into the ocean in front of him, the child should not embarrass them or display his anguish or anger [over this] in their presence. Rather, he should accept the Torah's decree [to honor his parents] and remain silent." [Note: Regarding a child's right to prevent his parents from causing him such damage, as well as his right to take legal action to recover his losses, see *Rama, Yoreh Deah* 240:8 and commentaries ibid. The practical details of this are numerous and complex, and are discussed at length in various halachic responsa.]

2   Seeking parents' blessings:

One should always endeavor to obtain the blessing of his father and mother. In addition to the obvious benefits of being blessed by a loving parent, whose heartfelt blessing is more likely to be fulfilled, one also thereby fulfills the mitzvah of honoring his parents. The Medrash teaches that all the success and dominion attained by the descendants of Eisav [i.e. Rome] comes from Eisav having esteemed the blessing of his father to the extent that he cried out loudly and bitterly [when he realized he had lost the blessing], *Bless me too, my father* (Bereishis 27:38).

The custom of receiving a blessing from parents on Friday nights and Erev Yom Kippur is especially widespread (see *Pele Yo'eitz* under 'berachos'; *Siddur Amudai Shomayim* by R' Yaakov Emden — customs of Friday night; see also *Chayei Adam* vol. II, 144:19).

It is a Sephardic custom to kiss the hands of one's father and mother upon receiving their blessing on Friday night (see *Chida* מורה באצבע §4:142;

Ben Ish Chai Shanah II, *Bereishis* §29; *Sdei Chemed*, מערכת קוף §7; *Kaf HaChayim, Orach Chaim* 262:17).

3   Honoring parents vs. Torah study and marriage:

A son may go to study in a yeshiva even though this will make him unavailable to serve his parents (*Shulchan Aruch, Yoreh Deah* 240:13). However, studying in a yeshiva frees him of the obligation to attend his parents only if the yeshiva is in a different city. If it is in the same city as his parents, the son must go to attend to his parents needs and then return to his studies (*Pri Chadash* cited in *Pischei Teshuvah, Yoreh Deah* ibid. §8; *Aruch HaShulchan* 240:36).

A son may choose to attend a yeshiva in a different city even over a parent's objection, if he thinks this will bring him greater success in his learning (*Shulchan Aruch* 240:25), even if such success is not assured (*Pischei Teshuvah* ibid.; *Aruch HaShulchan*). [Obviously, one should first consult with a Torah authority before making such a decision. Also, one must at all times take heed to present his position in a respectful manner, and avoid speaking in a way that affronts their honor.]

It is likewise permissible to select a spouse over a parent's objection (*Rama* ibid. §25). [Here, too, one should consult with a Torah authority before making such a decision.]

4   Honoring family members and elders:

As we have explained (see Law 8; and note 13), the mitzvah to honor parents includes a requirement to honor several other relatives as well. Let us examine these obligations more closely:

A. *Stepparents:* This is a Biblical obligation (*Kesubos* 103a; *Rambam, Hil. Mamrim* 6:15; see *Rambam, Sefer HaMitzvos,* beginning of *shoresh* §2; *Ramban* there; *Smak* §50; *Chareidim* 12:3). It is derived from the word את in the verse כבד את אביך ואת אמך, *Honor your father and your mother.* The verse could have stated simply: כבד אביך ואמך. Instead it states: את אביך and את אמך. The superfluous mentions of את are expounded to include the wife of one's father and the husband of one's mother in the mitzvah of honor (*Kesubos* ibid.). One must honor a stepfather or stepmother in all the ways that honors a parent (see *Chareidim* 16:3-12,18:1-2; *Minchas Chinuch* 33:1; *Chofetz Chaim, Pesichah, Asin* §10).

The obligation to honor the spouse of a parent is an extension of the obligation to honor the parent himself. Therefore, once the parent dies, the obligation disappears (*Kesubos* ibid.; *Rambam* ibid.; *Shulchan Aruch* 240:21; see *Teshuvos R' Akiva Eiger,* I:68). However, it is proper to continue to show them honor even after the parent's death (*Shulchan Aruch* ibid.). *Smak* maintains that even after the death of the parent, one remains obligated, by *Rabbinic* law, to honor the stepparent.

B. *Older brothers:* According to some, this refers to any brother older than oneself (see *Sefer Chasidim* §345; *Birkei Yosef, Yoreh Deah* 240:17; see *Teshuvos Chasam Sofer* VI:29). *Birkei Yosef* writes that older sisters too are included. Others maintain that the obligation applies only to the *bechor* of a family, i.e. a male firstborn (*Teshuvos Halachos Ketanos* §123; *Shevus Yaakov* I:76; *Beis Lechem Yehudah, Yoreh Deah* 240:12). In various ways, the obligation to honor an older brother is less comprehensive than the obligation to honor parents (see *Shiyurei Berachah, Yoreh Deah* ibid.; *Minchas Chinuch* 33:1).

According to some, this is a Biblical obligation, for it is derived from the superfluous letter Hebrew *vav* (which signifies the word *and*), of the Scriptural phrase ואת אמך (see *Kesubos* ibid.; *Rambam* ibid., as explained by *Kessef Mishneh* there and *Minchas Chinuch* ibid.; *Rambam, Sefer HaMitzvos* ibid.; *Chofetz Chaim, Aseh* §10). Others maintain that it is a Rabbinic obligation only (*Meiri, Kesubos* ibid.; *Chareidim* 47:32-36; see *Rambam* as understood by *Ramban, Sefer HaMitzvos* ibid.).

The *Poskim* disagree as to whether this obligation persists after the death of one's parents. For discussion, see *Rambam, Sefer HaMitzvos* ibid., with *Megillas Esther; Ramban* there; *Darchei Moshe, Yoreh Deah* 240:7; *Birkei Yosef* ibid.; *Teshuvos R' Akiva Eiger* ibid.

C. *Grandparents:* The obligation to honor grandparents is of Biblical origin (*Chareidim* 12:3-10), and applies to both sets of grandparents, both paternal and maternal (*Teshuvos Rama* §118; *Menoras HaMaor,* cited in *Chareidim* ibid.; cf. *Beur HaGra, Yoreh Deah* 240:34). One must honor a grandparent in all the ways one honors a parent (*Chareidim* 16:3-12; see *Chidushei R' Akiva Eiger* to *Yoreh Deah* 240:24); however, the honor of one's parent supersedes the honor of one's grandparent (*Teshuvos Rama* ibid.; see *Teshuvos R' Akiva Eiger,* I:68).

This obligation to honor a grandparent continues even after the death of one's parent (*Teshuvos Rama* ibid.; see also *Sefer Chasidim* §345).

D. *Parents-in-law:* The obligation to honor one's parents-in-law derives from the fact that a husband and wife are, from a legal standpoint, regarded as a single person (see *Kesubos* 66a; *Bechoros* 35b). It follows that the parents of one's spouse are like one's own parents; thus, they are included in the Biblical obligation to honor one's parents (*Chareidim* 12:3-10; see *Chayei Adam* 67:17).

There is some disagreement as to the degree of honor one must show parents-in-law. According to many, they are entitled to nothing more than the honor one must show a distinguished elder, as described in *mitzvah* #257. According to others, they are entitled to the same degree of honor one must show a parent. See *Medrash Tehillim* §7:4; *Chareidim* 16:3-12; *Bach, Yoreh Deah* 240 ד"ה וחייב לכבד; *Shach, Yoreh Deah* 240:22; *Chayei Adam* ibid.:24).

E. *Siblings of one's parents:* According to some authorities, the obligation to honor the siblings of one's parents is of Biblical origin, and one must honor them in all the ways one honors one's parents (*Sefer HaYirah L'Rabbeinu Yonah* §203; *Chareidim* 12:3-10, 16:3-12).

5 Honoring parents: Between man and God or between man and his fellow?

According to some authorities, the mitzvah of honoring parents falls into the category of mitzvos known as בין אדם לחבירו, *between man and his fellow,* which includes such mitzvos as the prohibition against stealing or the commandment to love one's fellow (*Rambam, Commentary* to *Peah* 1:1; see *Chareidim* 9:37-38). The rule regarding all such mitzvos is that if one transgresses, his sole means of atonement is to obtain forgiveness from the one he wronged. Without forgiveness, even Yom Kippur will not atone for his sin (see *Yoma* 85b). It follows that if a person fails to honor his parents, he must obtain their forgiveness. However, others maintain that the obligation to honor parents is classified as בין אדם למקום, *between man and God* (see *Ramban, Shemos* 20:13; *Malbim* ad loc.). Presumably, according to their view, a transgressor can obtain atonement without his parents' forgiveness. See further, *Minchas Chinuch* 33:3. [Even so, it is proper for the child to show contrition, and beg forgiveness of his parents. If the child is sincere, the parents should never withhold their pardon.]

שיח הלכה SITUATIONS IN HALACHAH

Q *Question:*
Is a person obligated to stand up to honor a blind parent, who cannot see him standing?

A *Answer:*
This question is identical to the issue dealt with by the Poskim in regard to the requirement of standing up to honor a blind *talmid chochom*. The root of the question is whether the honor shown to a *talmid chochom* is directed toward him, to make him feel respected, or whether it is meant to demonstrate honor for the essence of a *talmid chochom*, whether the *talmid chochom* in question is aware of it or not.

One proof cited in favor of requiring a person to stand up for a blind *talmid chochom* is the account given by the Gemara (*Kiddushin* 33a) of how Abaye would rise for his teacher Rav Yosef as soon as he saw the ear of his donkey appear in the distance. Although Rav Yosef was blind, as is well-known from the Gemara, and could not see his student standing up for him, Abaye nonetheless stood up.

Accordingly, the same should be true for standing up for one's parents. This is indeed evident from the words of *Rambam* (Hil. Mamrim 6:4): "A person must stand up for his [father] the same as he does for his teacher." This implies that they are identical in all respects. Thus, just as a student must stand up for his teacher who is blind, so too, one must stand up for his parent who is blind.

Some take issue with the proof from the Gemara, arguing that Rav Yosef may not yet have been blind when Abaye did this. Moreover, Abaye was clearly acting beyond the requirement of the

law, since he stood up even before his teacher was visible, and only the top of his donkey's head could be seen. Thus, we cannot prove from Abaye's actions that there is an obligation to stand for a blind teacher or parent, since he may have been acting beyond the requirement of the law in regard to this matter as well.

A number of other proofs and their deflections are discussed at length in the halachic literature on this subject. Nevertheless, the consensus of halachic authorities is that there is an obligation to stand up for a blind *talmid chochom* [and hence for a blind parent as well]. Support for this consensus may be found in the story related by the Gemara in *Chagigah* (5b): When Rebbi and R' Chiya arrived in one town, they made an effort to go pay their respects to a certain blind *talmid chochom* who lived there. When they took their leave of him, he gave them the following blessing: "You paid your respects to one who is seen but cannot see. May you merit to pay respects to the One Who sees but cannot be seen" [i.e. the Almighty, Whom we are commanded to "visit" and pay our respects to three times a year in the *Beis HaMikdash*]. Some support this ruling in regard to parents from the Biblical passage (*Bereishis* 48:10) which says: *And the eyes of Yisrael [Yaakov] had become dim with age, he could not see* ... Nevertheless, the passage continues (ibid. v.12), *And Yosef...prostrated himself [before his father Yaakov] with his face toward the ground.*

For further discussion, see *Teshuvos Ginas Veradim*, *Yoreh Deah*, *Klal* 2:4; *Teshuvos Perech Shoshan*, *Yoreh Deah*, *Klal* 4:1; *Teshuvos Shaar Ephraim* §78; *Birkei Yosef*, *Yoreh Deah*, 244:2. This is also the ruling of R' Akiva Eiger, *Yoreh Deah*, 240:7; *Ben Ish Chai*, Year II, *Parshas Ki Seitzei*; *Aruch HaShulchan*, *Yoreh Deah*, 244:7; *Teshuvos Shevet HaLevi*, VI:146.

| ברכת | |

THE BLESSING FOR THE MITZVAH

he Sages did not institute any blessing for the mitzvah of honoring one's parents. This is just one of a number of positive commandments for which the Sages did not institute a blessing. Various rules have been suggested to account for the absence of a blessing for these mitzvos, some of which explain why no blessing was instituted for the act of honoring one's parents. Two reasons unique to this mitzvah have also been suggested.

——— ❦ ———

A. *It is a mitzvah between man and his fellow man*

With any positive commandment [that deals with an obligation] between man and God ... one recites a blessing over it prior to its performance (*Rambam, Hil. Berachos* 11:2). "[*Rambam*] is careful to write "between man and God," to teach that with mitzvos between man and his fellow, such as acts of charity and the like, one does not recite a blessing for their performance" (*Kessef Mishneh* ibid.). Thus, in the view of those who maintain that honoring one's parents is a mitzvah performed by one person toward another (see above, *Iyunim* §5), there is no blessing for it.

——— ❦ ———

B. *It is a mitzvah whose fulfillment depends on others*

Many Rishonim have suggested that a blessing is not recited for any mitzvah whose fulfillment is not entirely in the hands of the person performing it, but requires the participation of another person. Since that other person may decline to participate, thereby negating the obligation to fulfill the mitzvah, the person attempting to perform the mitzvah does not recite a blessing. For this reason, one does not recite a blessing when performing the mitzvos of

visiting the sick and giving charity to the poor [because the sick person may decline to receive visitors and the poor person may refuse to accept the charity]. By the same token, since a parent who wishes to forgo his honor may refuse to accept it, in which case there is no mitzvah for the child to perform, a child does not recite a blessing when performing this mitzvah. [Some attribute this rule to *Ri ben Pelet*. It is also mentioned by *Rashba* in his *Teshuvos* 1:18, 1:254, 3:283, and in *Teshuvos HaMeyuchasos LaRamban* [attributed to *Ramban,* but actually authored by *Rashba*] §189. Other Rishonim who cite this rule include: *Raavad* in his *Teshuvos Tamim De'im* §179; *Sefer HaIttur,* Vol. II, *Tzitzis, Shaar* §3; *Abudraham, Shaar* §3; *Orchos Chaim* of *R' Aharon* of *Luneil, Hil. Berachos* 11:2; and *Rabbeinu Manoach* in his commentary on *Rambam, Hil. Berachos* 11:2. *Chasam Sofer, Orach Chaim* §54 writes that this is also the intent of *Rambam* [cited above], who says that a blessing is not recited for mitzvos between man and his fellow man.]

——— ❦ ———

C. *It is a mitzvah which applies at all times*

Blessings are recited only for mitzvos whose obligation is restricted to a specific time. Examples of these are *tzitzis, tefillin, succah* and the like. A blessing is not called for in the case of mitzvos whose obligation is always in effect, and from which one is never exempt; for example, the mitzvos of believing in Hashem and fearing Him, the mitzvah of honoring one's parents, etc. This is because a blessing expresses the love one feels for the mitzvah, and one does not feel the same fondness for mitzvos he is always obligated to perform as he does for mitzvos which he is only able to perform at intervals. Thus, no blessing is recited for them (*Or Zarua* vol. I:40).

——— ❦ ———

D. *It is a "rational mitzvah"*

Blessings are not said for the performance of "rational mitzvos" [מצוות שכליות]; i.e. mitzvos which reason alone would require us to perform, even if Hashem had not explicitly commanded us to do them. This is because the blessings for mitzvos express our gratitude to Hashem for the sanctification attained by fulfilling His will (as represented by His commandments) [as the blessing itself says: "Who has *sanctified* us with His commandments"]. This sanctification is evident primarily through our fulfillment of the "received mitzvos" [מצוות המקובלות] — i.e. those mitzvos that a person would not realize through his own intellect — for it is clear that we do not observe these mitzvos because of our intellect, but only because Hashem commanded us to perform them. It is our performance of the "received mitzvos" which sets us apart from the nations of the world and for which we are called a Holy People [see *Shemos* 19:6 — *And you shall be to Me a kingdom of priests and a holy nation*], a nation dedicated to the fulfillment of Hashem's will. This sanctification is not as evident in our performance of the "rational mitzvos," many of which even non-Jews fulfill simply because of the dictates of reason. Therefore, the Sages did not institute a blessing for "rational mitzvos." Honoring one's parents is a "rational mitzvah," and is practiced by almost all the nations of the world. Thus, no blessing is recited for it (*Rabbeinu Bachya*, in his commentary to *Bamidbar* 15:38 and in *Kad HaKemach, Tzitzis*; *Teshuvos Binyamin Zev* §169; see further *Aruch HaShulchan, Yoreh Deah* 240:4 and *Choshen Mishpat* 427:10).

—— ✿ ——

E. *It is almost impossible to fulfill the mitzvah to the extent the Torah requires*

There are two additional reasons for not reciting a blessing that are unique to the mitzvah of honoring one's parents. The first is that if one were to recite a blessing for any specific act of honoring his parents, he might feel that he has fulfilled his obligation for the moment. In reality, however, he has not performed even half the Biblically mandated measure of this mitzvah, whose obligation is so far-reaching. As the Gemara says regarding R' Tarfon and his elderly mother: Although [R' Tarfon] would

place his hands beneath [his mother's] feet to walk on as she went back to bed, the Sages, when told of this incident, responded that he had not yet done even half of what the Torah requires for honoring a parent (*Kiddushin* 31b; see also *Yerushalmi, Kiddushin* 1:7). For this reason R' Yochanan used to say, "Fortunate is the one who never saw them [his parents]", for not everyone can fulfill the stringent requirements of this mitzvah properly. Were a person to recite a blessing before performing an inadequate act of honoring his parent, he would not be blessing [Hashem] but insulting Him. The Sages understood that few people merit to perform this mitzvah properly, so they did not institute a blessing for it (*Maharit Algazy*, cited in *Sdei Chemed, Asifas Zekeinim, Maareches Berachos* 1:16).

—— ✿ ——

F. *In certain circumstances, the mitzvah results from a transgression*

The second reason why the Sages specifically did not institute a blessing for the mitzvah of honoring one's parents is that a blessing would have to be recited even by a *mamzer*, who is obligated to honor his parents even though they committed a grievous sin by conceiving him. Honoring them, though, is akin to a "mitzvah which comes through a transgression," and it is not appropriate to recite a blessing for such a mitzvah. [*Rashba* (*Teshuvos HaRashba* 1:18) cites this as the reason why the Sages did not institute a blessing for the mitzvah of returning what one stole, or returning the interest he (illegally) collected on a loan. Since there would be no requirement to fulfill the mitzvah of returning the stolen object or the interest had one not committed the sin of stealing or taking interest in the first place, the Sages did not institute a blessing for these mitzvos]. So as not to make exceptions in the requirement, the Sages did not institute a blessing even for an ordinary child (*Maaseh Avraham*, cited by *S'dei Chemed* ibid.; see also *S'dei Chemed's* further discussion of this matter).

ILLUMINATIONS OF THE MITZVAH
Suggested Reasons & Insights

I. DISCHARGING A DEBT

ur Sages have characterized the mitzvah of honoring parents as a repaying of a debt. Rav Avun said: ...The mitzvah [of honoring one's parents], is [in essence] the repayment of a debt, and ... the Torah states: *[Do so] in order that it go well for you, and in order that your days will be lengthened...* (*Yerushalmi, Peah* 1:1, see also *Tanchuma, Eikev* §2, et al.). Whatever one does to honor his parents is no more than repaying them for all the goodness they did to him by bringing him into the world, raising him and educating him (*Pnei Moshe* to *Yerushalmi*). For this reason, the *Chayei Adam* (63:1) states: One who does not honor his parents is labeled a *rasha* (wicked person), as the verse in *Tehillim* (37:21) says: *The wicked one borrows but does not repay.*

This rationale for the mitzvah does not exempt a person from honoring parents who were not involved in his upbringing. As *Meshech Chochmah* explains (*Devarim* 5:16): It is for this reason that the Torah states: *Honor your father and your mother as Hashem your God has commanded you,* that is, even in circumstances where your father and mother did not raise you, you must also honor them — as Hashem your God commanded you in the Wilderness. In the Wilderness, minimum effort was needed for fathers to raise their children, since manna would fall from heaven each day to feed them, water was readily available from the well of Miriam, meat was provided in the form of the quail, and the clouds of glory that surrounded the camp would launder their clothes. Despite all this, Hashem commanded you to honor your father and mother even then. So too shall you do, down to the last generation (see also *Ksav Sofer* to *Parashas Va'eschanan*).

II. AN EXPRESSION OF GRATITUDE

n a similar vein, numerous commentators explain the mitzvah of honoring one's parents to be based on the obligation to express gratitude to those who brought him into the world, and worked hard to raise him (*Sefer HaChinuch* §33; see further, *Beis Elokim, Shaar HaTeshuvah* ch.10). The performance of this mitzvah sensitizes a person to the general obligation to recognize the favors others have done for him and to repay them with kindness. In this manner a person learns not to be an ingrate, and not to act as a stranger to those who have done him a good turn, a trait utterly despised by God and man (*Sefer HaChinuch* ibid.). In this manner too, a person learns to recognize the beneficence and kindness bestowed upon him by his Father in Heaven (*Sefer HaChinuch* ibid.; *Ralbag, Shemos* 20:12; *Hadar Zekeinim, Shemos*; *Sefer HaBatim, mitzvah* §213). [See further *Derech Pikudecha* §33, who explains how this understanding of the mitzvah relates to the Torah's promise of length of days as a reward for performing the mitzvah; see also *Ralbag* to *Shemos* 20:12.]

There is an added element of gratitude that one must feel for his parents — that they brought him into the world as a Jew! The deepest gratitude a Jew must feel toward his parents is for their bringing him into the world with a body sanctified with the holiness of a Jew, which serves as a vehicle for performing the mitzvos of the Torah and enables him to gain the blessings of eternity (see *Pri Tzaddik, Kedoshim* §3).

———

A person should not be led astray by those who claim that children have no moral obligation to feel indebted to their parents. They argue that the parents merely had their own pleasure in mind; only incidentally were their children conceived, and once they were born, the parental instincts implanted in every father and mother impelled them to care for their children and raise them. It is no different, say they, than animals or birds, who nurture their offspring and prepare them for life, but do not receive in return any expression of gratitude … [Their logic is flawed, however,] for the same argument could be applied in regard to our obligations toward God Himself. We are, after all, the work of His hands; it is only natural that He show us compassion and bestow goodness upon us. Without a doubt, such people are, in their hearts, in denial of God (*Chayei Adam*, 67:2).

There are others whose lives are burdened with suffering, and they wonder why they must honor their parents for bringing them into the world. The truth is, however, that for the opportunity of receiving the reward in the World to Come of even the least worthy among us, it is worthwhile to endure whatever troubles one has in this world, and it is for this ultimate purpose, for the sake of which we live, that we have our parents to thank (*Likutei Halachos, Shevuos* §2; see *Toras Moshe, Shemos* 20:12, who observes that this explains why the mitzvah to honor one's parents was placed in the Torah beside the mitzvah of Shabbos, for the latter is likened to the World to Come).

Although it is true that, despite all the benefit that may be achieved in one's lifetime, the Sages concluded (*Eruvin* 13b) that man would have been better off not being created at all, one is still obliged to honor his parents for bearing and raising him. This is because, in the final analysis, God willed the creation of man, and it is incumbent upon us to defer to God's judgment and adopt His will as our own. Thus, one must honor his parents for bringing him into the world in accordance with the design of the Creator (*Maharal, Chidushei Aggados* IV, *Avodah Zarah* p. 30).

III. SHOWING HONOR TO HASHEM'S "PARTNERS"

ur Sages have taught (*Kiddushin* 30b; see *Niddah* 31a): There are three partners in [the formation of] a person: The Holy One, Blessed is He, the person's father, and his mother. Therefore, just as Hashem commands us to honor Him, so too He commands us to honor those who, so to speak, joined him in creating us

(*Ramban* and *Rabbeinu Bachya* to *Shemos* 20:12, *Kad HaKemach*). While it is true that the parents' share in the composition of their children is primarily limited to their material aspect, even that component of a human being is in reality the work of God, and we must honor those who served as a channel for the Divine plan (*Toras Moshe — Alshich, Shemos* 20:12).

[The mitzvah of honoring one's parents appears among the first five commandments, on the Tablet which deals with laws between man and God, rather than on the second Tablet, which deals with the laws between man and his fellow man. This is because the commandment to honor one's parents is directly related to the previous four commandments that deal with honoring God (see *Ramban* and *Rabbeinu Bachya* there for an elaboration; *Kad HaKemach* §20). For this reason, too, the Gemara states in *Kiddushin* 30b: When a person honors his father and mother, the Holy One, blessed is He, says: I count it for them as if I lived among them and they honored Me (*Maharal, Tiferes Yisroel* ch. 36; *Kli Yakar, Shemos* 20:12; *Derech Pikudechah* §33).

Indeed, in at least one respect the Torah is more demanding regarding the honor due one's parents than with the honor due God Himself. The *Yerushalmi* (*Peah* 1:1 and *Kiddushin* 1:7) observes: Regarding God it is written, *Honor God from your wealth*; that is, if you possess such wealth. But concerning one's parents it says simply, *Honor your father and your mother*, whether you are a person of means or not. The reason for this is that God's share in the formation of a person focuses on his spiritual qualities, so one who doesn't have money to spend on His honor need not exert himself physically. But the parents' share is manifest in the body of their child, and the Torah therefore demands of us, even if we cannot benefit our parents monetarily, to at least accord them honor by using our body to attend to their needs (*Beis Elokim, Sha'ar HaTeshuvah* §10).

IV. STRENGTHENING FAITH

y honoring one's parents, a person proclaims his belief in of the Creation of the world, and his rejection of the idea that the universe always existed. By acknowledging that his parents created him, he implicitly acknowledges that they too were created by their parents, and so forth back through the generations, until the very first "Progenitor," the Creator, Blessed is He. The Creator [by commanding the children to honor their parents] in turn bestows of His honor on those who follow in His path by bringing children into the world (*Maharal, Tiferes Yisrael* ch. 45; *Kli Yakar* to *Devarim* 22:7). It is for this reason that the *Bnei Yisrael* were commanded with regard to the Shabbos and honoring parents in Marah, even before they came to *Har Sinai* to receive the rest of the Torah (see *Sanhedrin* 56b). For these mitzvos logically precede other mitzvos [in that they epitomize the beliefs that form the foundation for all the mitzvos]. It is for this reason as well that these two commandments are associated with each other throughout the Torah (*Maharal* ibid.).

V. SAFEGUARDING THE CHAIN OF TRADITION

he mitzvah of honoring one's father and mother is a strong element in the preservation of the Torah and its mitzvos among the Jewish people. When a child submits to the authority of his parents, he will readily accept from them the traditions of Judaism (*mesorah*) that have been passed down from generation to generation, to which his parents now link him (*Ralbag, Abarbanel* to *Shemos* 20:12; see also *Meshech Chochmah* to *Vayikra* 13:3 and *Devarim* 5:16).

The *Sefer HaIkkarim* illustrates this point as follows: It is well-known that a ruler who founds a kingdom does not appear daily before his subjects. Thus, although the people who witnessed the original arrival of a king and pledged their allegiance to him may remember how he built up his kingdom and freed them from bondage to which they had previously been subject, the generation that comes after them, who did not personally experience his great deeds, may come in the end to think of the kingdom as having always been theirs, and rebel against the king. The only way to protect against such foolishness is to teach the younger generation subservience to the older one, and acceptance of their teaching and guidance. They in turn pass on to their children the knowledge of how oppressed they were until this king came and freed them, rebuilt their country and settled them peacefully in it.

Rabbi Samson Raphael Hirsch captures the essence of this reason in his inimitable fashion:

"The Exodus from Egypt and the Revelation of the Torah are the two foundations in fact on which the nation of Israel is built. It is they that serve as the basis for our submission to Hashem as the Ruler and Master of our destinies and lives. These two events are historical facts, and we know them and recognize them to be historical truths. However, the only guarantor of their truth is Tradition, and the basis for Tradition is a faithful transmission to children by their fathers, and a willing acceptance of it by the children from their fathers. The foundations of the great edifice established by God in Israel have survived the many long years only through the intellectual and practical obedience of children to their fathers and mothers. It emerges from this that respect for one's father and mother is the basic precondition for the eternity of the Jewish people. Through the father and mother, God imparts to the child not only his basic existence, but the link to his Jewish past that enables him to be a Jew. From the parents a child receives the tradition of the Jewish mission in knowledge, way of life and education. They transmit to him the lessons of Jewish history and the teachings of Torah, so that he too will bequeath them to his children when the time comes. Just as the child looks to his parents, so too his children will someday look to him. Without the bond between parents and children, the chain of the generations is broken, the hopes of the Jewish future are lost, and the faith of the Jews would cease to exist. Indeed, the role of parents in Jewish life is pivotal, and for this reason the Torah assigned them a place of prominence, by declaring in the Ten Commandments, *Honor your father and your mother*" (*Commentary to Shemos* 20:12).

However, again, even if one's parents failed to transmit to him Jewish tradition and values, the Torah requires (as noted above) that he nonetheless respect and honor them, just *as Hashem, your God, has commanded you.*

THROUGH THE EYES OF THE SAGES
Stories, Parables & Reflections

I. THE MAGNITUDE OF THE MITZVAH

Paramount precept

o honor one's father and mother is a formidable mitzvah among formidable mitzvos (*Yerushalmi, Kiddushin* 1:7; *Devarim Rabbah* 6:2, and elsewhere).

——— ❧ ———

Parallel to the honor of God

The Sages taught: Regarding one's parents, it says (*Shemos* 20:12): *Honor your father and mother*, and (in similar language) we find (*Mishlei* 3:9): *Honor God from your fortune*. The Scripture thus places the honor due one's parents on the same level as the honor due God (*Kiddushin* 30b; *Bava Metziah* 32a; *Mechilta* and *Mechilta D'Rashbi, Yisro; Sifra, Kedoshim* §1; et al.).

———

The Sages offered the following parable: A king had a servant who had fled from his service. The king pursued him in every country until the servant was finally returned to his custody. He brought him into his palace and showed him the abundance of gold and silver, precious stones, pearls and other such treasures that were in his possession. Then he led him outdoors to allow him a view of his gardens, orchards, and bountiful fields. The king also showed him his children and servants, young and old, and then he said, "Do you see, then, that I do not need you at all? [It is for your benefit only that I ask you to] come join the work of my children and servants, to show me respect, and to stand in awe of me." In the same way, the entire world belongs to God, and all He asks of a person is to honor and fear

his father and mother, and in so doing he will be considered as if he honors and fears God Himself. For God has equated honoring Him with honoring one's parents, as it says (*Malachi* 1:6), *A son honors [his] father, and a servant his master. If I am a Father, where is My honor…?* (*Tanna D'vei Eliyahu Rabbah,* 27:6).

———

The Sages taught: There are three partners in [the creation of every] person: The Holy One, Blessed is He, the father and the mother (see *Rashi* for elaboration).

———

When a person honors his father and mother, the Holy One, Blessed is He, says: I consider it as if I had lived among them and they had honored Me (*Kiddushin* 30b).

———

A person is obliged to honor his father and mother in the same way he honors God Himself, for his parents are partners with God. Similarly, one must stand in awe of his father and mother just as he is required to be in awe of God, and he must dignify his parents with all types of honor (*Zohar, Shemos* 93a, *Vayikra* 83a).

——— ❧ ———

Surpassing the honor of God

R' Shimon bar Yochai taught: Great is the mitzvah of honoring one's parents, for the Holy One, Blessed is He, prized it more highly than His own honor. For it says (*Mishlei* 3:9), *Honor God from your fortune*. With what must you honor Him? With what He has granted you. [Thus, if one is fortunate to have reaped a crop of grain,] he must leave behind in the field the gifts for the poor (*leket, shich'chah,* and *pe'ah*). From the harvested grain, he sets aside the Kohen's share (*terumah*), along with the various tithes (*maaser rishon, maaser sheni, maaser ani*), and, when it is later transformed into dough, he separates *challah*, to be given to the Kohen. He uses his earnings to prepare a *succah*, a *lulav*, a *shofar*, *tefillin*, and *tzitzis,* as well as to feed the poor and the hungry. All this is mandatory — if one possesses the means. But one who does not is completely absolved. By contrast, when it comes to honoring one's father and mother, the verse simply says, *Honor your father and mother.* Honor your parents, whether you are wealthy or not, even if it will reduce you to begging from door to door (*Yerushalmi, Peah* 1:1, *Kiddushin* 1:7; *Pesikta Rabbasi* §23).

——— ༄ ———

༄ Tantamount to transgressing the Ten Commandments

One who fails to fulfill the mitzvah of honoring his parents is considered as if he violated all of the Ten Commandments (*Batei Medrashos,* I — end of *Pirkei D'Rabbi Eliezer*).

———

A person who has food in his home, but does not give honor, food and sustenance to his father and mother, is viewed by God as someone who engaged in murder all his life ... as someone who engaged in adultery all his life ... as someone who engaged in kidnapping all his life ... as someone who engaged in bearing false witness all his life... as someone who coveted others' possessions all his life. This is true even when his parents are young, and all the more so when they are aged (*Tanna D'vei Eliyahu Rabbah* 26:26).

——— ༄ ———

༄ Retreat of God's Presence

When a person brings distress to his father and mother, the Holy One, Blessed is He, says: I did well not to live among them, for had I lived among them, they would have caused Me distress (*Kiddushin* 31a; cf. *Tanna D'vei Eliyahu Rabbah* 26:25)

II. REWARD FOR FULFILLING THE MITZVAH

༄ In this world and the next

hese are the precepts whose fruits a person enjoys in this world while the principal remains intact for him in the World to Come: ... Honoring one's father and mother, etc. (*Peah* 1:1). [See *Kiddushin* 39a, where one Tannaic view maintains that the "length of days" promised by the Torah in reward for this mitzvah (*Devarim* 5:16) refers to longevity in the World to Come.]

———

Whoever seeks for himself [productive] days and years, prosperity, honor and long life – in this world and the next, should perform the will of his Father in Heaven, and the will of his father and mother. It is therefore said (*Shemos* 20:8): *Remember the Shabbos day to keep it holy*, followed by (v. 12): *Honor your father and your mother, so that your days will be lengthened*, etc. (*Tanna D'vei Eliyahu Rabbah* 26:25)

———

When a person honors, feeds and supports his father and mother in their younger years and in their older years, to what is this comparable? To a king who was visited by the son of a close friend. The king said to him, "My child, where are you coming from?" The son replied, "From the house of my father and mother." The king asked him, "How are they doing?" He answered, "They have passed on in peace to their eternal rest." The king [who knew that this son had cared for his parents conscientiously] told him, "My child, you are blessed, and you will have contentment in this world for having given serenity to your father and mother until they passed on in peace to their eternal place. Come with me now to my palace and I will show you what your father and mother left with me for you." In the same vein, whoever honors, feeds and supports his father and mother until they pass on in peace to their eternal place, and who also walks in the ways of Heaven and thereby provides contentment to his father and mother — to such a person the Holy One, Blessed is He, says, "My child, come [with Me] and behold the Heavenly treasures that I have stored away for you, because you honored and sustained your father and mother, and you provided Me, as well as your father and mother, with contentment through your good deeds." As it is said (*Devarim* 28:2): *All these blessings will come upon you and reach you, if you listen to the voice of Hashem, your God.* When will all these blessings come upon you? If you listen to the voice of Hashem your God and go in His ways, the ways of Heaven (*Tanna D'vei Eliyahu Rabbah* 26:27).

———— ❧ ————

❧ The Blessing of children

Said God: *Who anticipated Me, that I can reward him? For whatever is under all the heavens is Mine* (*Iyov* 41:3). Is there anyone who took the initiative to honor his parents, and I did not grant him children? (*Tanchuma, Kedoshim* §15).

———— ❧ ————

❧ Protection from sin

The commandment to *Remember the day of the Shabbos to keep it holy* is followed by the mitzvah to honor one's parents. How are these two *mitzvos* connected? This is intended to teach us that as long as a person honors his father and mother, he may rest assured that the sin of Shabbos desecration will not come about through him, nor, for that matter, any other sin (*Tanna D'vei Eliyahu Rabbah* 26:24).

———— ❧ ————

❧ Reward for the wicked

Come and observe how cherished the mitzvah of honoring one's father and mother is before the Holy One, Blessed is He. For God does not deprive anyone of the reward for this mitzvah, whether the one fulfilling it is righteous or wicked. From where do we know this? From the wicked Eisav, who, because he honored his father, was granted all this honor by God. [The reference seems to be to the glories of the Roman Empire that was ruled by Eisav's descendants.]

R' Elazar says: The wicked Eisav shed three tears, one from his right eye, one from his left, and a third which formed in his eye but did not trickle out. When did this happen? When Yitzchak blessed Yaakov, as it says (*Bereishis* 27:38): *And Eisav raised his voice and cried.* Come and observe how much serenity the Holy One, Blessed is He, indulged him with because of these tears, as it says (*Tehillim* 80:6): *You fed them bread [on account] of a tear, and gave them to drink on account of three-fold tears.* It is not written 'three,' but 'three-fold,' because they were not three whole [tears, for one remained in his eye]. Now, if for having honored his father, God repaid this wicked man to such an extent, then how much more so will He reward a person who honors his parents and performs other mitzvos as well! (*Tanchuma, Kedoshim* §15).

III. THE FULFILLMENT OF THIS MITZVAH BY PERSONALITIES OF THE SCRIPTURE AND TALMUD

❧ Shem and Yefes

The verse states (*Bereishis* 9:23): *Shem took — and Yefes [too] — a garment, and laid it upon both their shoulders; they walked backward and covered their father's nakedness.* It does not say "they took" but rather "he (Shem) took." This teaches us that it was Shem who took the initiative to do this mitzvah, [and Yefes then joined him]. *They walked backward and covered their father's nakedness, and their faces were turned backward* ... This indicates that even after they had arrived [at their father's bedside], their faces remained turned away [i.e. at no point did they turn toward their father and see his nakedness]. How did the Holy One, Blessed is He, repay them? He paid Shem his reward with the *mitzvos* of *techeiles* (the blue *tzitzis* strings) and *tefillin*, with which to cover himself. And to Yefes He granted the merit of burial in *Eretz Yisrael* ... when Gog and Magog will, in the future, set upon Yisrael and God will defeat them, as was prophesied (*Yechezkel* 39:11), *It shall come to pass on that day that I will grant a burial site for Gog there in Yisrael* ... (*Tanchuma, Noach* §15; *Bereishis Rabbah* 36:6).

———— ✿ ————

✐ *Yitzchak*

The commandment, *Honor your father and your mother*, was truly fulfilled by Yitzchak, who allowed himself to be cast before his father like a sheep for slaughter (*Tanna D'vei Eliyahu Rabbah* 26:13; see *Vayikra Rabbah* 2:10).

R' Shimon began his discourse as follows: Scripture states (*Malachi* 1:6), *A son honors [his] father, and a servant his master.* 'A son honors his father' — this refers to Yitzchak, who honored his father Avraham. When did he honor him? At the time that Avraham bound him on the altar and was prepared to offer him as a sacrifice, Yitzchak was thirty-seven years old, while his father was aged. Had Yitzchak kicked him even with one leg, Avraham could not have withstood him. Still, Yitzchak honored his father and allowed himself to be bound like a sheep, in order to comply with the will of his father (*Zohar, Bereishis* 103a).

————————

As Yitzchak was walking with his father on the way to the *Akeidah*, the Satan took the appearance of a young man and stood on Yitzchak's right side. The Satan said to Yitzchak, "Where are you going?" Yitzchak replied, "To study Torah." The Satan asked, "In your lifetime or in death?" Yitzchak said, "Is there any person who can study Torah after his death?!" The Satan said to him, "You pitiful son of a pitiful woman, don't you know how many fasts your mother observed until you were born? And now this old man has lost his mind and is preparing to slaughter you [and you are cooperating]!" Yitzchak said, "Even so [I will continue on this path;] I will transgress neither the will of my Creator

nor the command of my father...[Later, when Yitzchak was bound on the Altar and Avraham was about to slaughter him, Yitzchak] said, "Father, [if you tell] my mother [that I died], do not tell her when she is standing near a pit or on the roof, lest she come to fall and die" (*Tanchuma, Vayeira* §22,23).

———— ✿ ————

✐ *Reuven*

The verse states (*Bereishis* 30:14): *Reuven went out in the wheat harvest season. He found mandrakes in the field and brought them to Leah his mother.* 'And he brought them to Leah, his mother' — [this phrase is meant] to tell you how much the honor of his mother was [felt] by Reuven, for he did not [even] taste them until he brought them to his mother (*Bereishis Rabbah* 72:2; *Pesikta Zutrasa, Bereishis* 30:14).

———— ✿ ————

✐ *Naftali*

At the inauguration, of the Tabernacle, the prince of each tribe brought a set of inaugural offerings. The verse states (*Bamidbar* 7:79) that the prince of Naftali brought such an offering as well: *His offering was one silver plate,* etc.

R' Yudan said: The prince of Naftali brought his offering corresponding to the *Avos* and the *Imahos*. Why so? Because Naftali honored his father to an extreme. His father was wont to send him on all kinds of missions, and Naftali was zealous in carrying them out. Yaakov derived satisfaction from him, and, in addition, Naftali's comments were pleasing to him. For this reason his father blessed him by [comparing him to] *a deer sent* [as a messenger] (*Bereishis* 49:21), for he ran to accomplish his missions like a deer. [See also *Sotah* 13a, where it is told that Naftali raced from Chevron to Mitzrayim to retrieve the contract of the transaction by which Yaakov had acquired Eisav's right to be buried in the Cave of Machpelah.] And for this reason he blessed him with [the phrase] *beautiful sayings,* for [Naftali's] sayings were beautiful.

Therefore, Naftali merited that the Holy One, Blessed is He, exacted revenge from [the Canaanite general] Sisera through Barak, who was from Kedesh Naftali (see *Shoftim* ch. 4). And since Naftali was careful in the honor of his forefathers, the prince of Naftali learned from his ancestor, followed in his ways and brought his offering such that it corresponded to the *Avos* and *Imahos* of the tribe of Naftali (*Bamidbar Rabbah* 14:11; see there at length).

———— ৵৶ ————

❧ *Yosef*

Honor your father and your mother — Yosef fulfilled this commandment, for it says (*Bereishis* 37:13): *And Yisrael said to Yosef: Are your brothers not grazing [the flocks] in Shechem? Go, for I am sending you to them.* [And Yosef complied, although he was aware of his brothers' sentiments toward him.] (*Tanna D'vei Eliyahu Rabbah* 26:13; *Pesikta Zutrasa, Shemos* 13:19).

————————

And Yisrael said to Yosef, "Are your brothers not grazing [the flocks] in Shechem? Go; I am sending you to them." And Yosef responded, "I am ready" (*Bereishis* 37:13). R' Chama bar Chanina taught: Yaakov would later reflect on these words [of Yosef], and his innards would churn. He would think: Yosef knew well that his brothers hated him and still he declared, "I am ready" (*Bereishis Rabbah* 84:13). According to *Medrash Aggadah* (*Bereishis* 37:13), Yosef replied, "Father, I know that they hate me. Kill me they might, but I shall not allow your request to go unfulfilled."

————————

Yosef applied himself to protect the honor of his mother … When Yaakov was returning to his father's home, and he was about to meet up with his brother Eisav, what did he do? He had his sons and their mothers come forward to bow down before Eisav, as it is said (*Bereishis* 33:6-7), *And the handmaids approached, they and their children, and*

they bowed down. Leah, too, approached with her children and they bowed down. But now take note of what is written of Rachel (ibid.): *Afterward, Yosef and Rachel came forward and bowed down.* Not 'Rachel and Yosef,' but 'Yosef and Rachel.' What is behind this? Yosef reasoned: There is no woman of beauty who can compare with my mother, and this evil man cannot be trusted. So he placed himself in front of his mother and obscured Eisav's view of her. This is why his father commended him (ibid. 49:22), *A handsome son is Yosef, a handsome son on the eye.* What is meant by 'on the eye?' It is a reference to his endeavor to cover the eye of the wicked Eisav, and prevent him from gazing upon his mother (*Pesikta Rabbasi* §12; cf. *Tanchuma, Ki Seitzei* §10).

————————

Yosef joyfully harnessed his chariot, as it is said (*Bereishis* 46:29), *And Yosef [himself] harnessed his chariot.* Did Yosef lack servants? Rather, he did it for the sake of his father's honor. Pharaoh also gleefully harnessed his chariot, as it is written (*Shemos* 14:6), *And [Pharaoh] harnessed his chariot.* Let the harnessing of Yosef, who acted for the purpose of going to greet his father, prevail over the harnessing of the wicked Pharaoh, who was on his way to pursue the Jews (*Mechilta, Beshalach* 1:7; cf. *Bereishis Rabbah* 55:8).

———— ৵৶ ————

❧ *The Twelve Tribes*

Yaakov heard … and his sons were with his livestock in the field (*Bereishis* 34:5). This comes to teach us that once his sons came of age they treated their father with esteem. They tended the sheep, allowing Yaakov to remain immersed in the study of Torah (*Medrash Sechel Tov, Bereishis* 34:5).

———— ৵৶ ————

❧ *Gidon*

An angel of God came and sat under the terebinth tree in Ophrah — the one that belonged to Yoash the Avi-Ezrite. Gidon, his son, was threshing wheat in a *winepress, so as to hide it from Midian. The angel of God appeared to him, and said, 'God is with you, mighty one!' Gidon responded, 'Please [answer this], my master, if God is truly with us, why has all this [tragedy] occurred to us? Where are all His wonders of which our forebears have told us, saying, 'Behold, God brought us up from Mitzrayim'? For God has now forsaken us and delivered us into the hands of Midian.' [The angel of] God turned to him and said, 'Go with this strength of yours, and you will save Yisrael from the hand of Midian; behold, I have sent you'* (Shoftim 6:11-14).

———— ❧ ————

The Medrash comments: The angel tarried [under the tree] until he found some merit for Gidon, and only then did he appear to him. The Sages elaborated: Gidon's father Yoash had been threshing the wheat. Gidon said to him, "Father, you are old. Go into the house, and I will do the threshing, for if the Midianites arrive, you will not have the strength to flee." The angel exclaimed, "You have fulfilled the mitzvah of honoring [your father]. You are thus worthy of having My children rescued through you." Immediately, 'the angel of God appeared to [Gidon]' (Radak ad loc.; see also Rashi there).

———— ❧ ————

❧ Yosam ben Uziyahu

Chizkiyah said in the name of R' Yirmiah, who said in the name of R' Shimon bar Yochai: [With my merits] I am able to exempt the entire world from [Heavenly] judgment, from the day I was created up until now. And if my son, Elazar, would join me — from the day the world was created up until now. And if Yosam ben Uziyahu would join us [we could exempt the world from judgment] from the day the world was created until its end (Succah 45b).

———————————

Rashi explains there: Yosam was a righteous man, and he was more humble than any other king. He was [particularly] meritorious in honoring his father, and it is regarding [Yosam] that the verse says (Malachi 1:6): *A son honors [his] father.* His father [Uziah] was afflicted with *tzaraas*, and it was

Yosam who ruled the people of the country [in his stead], as it is written (Melachim II 15:5): *And Yosam [oversaw] the palace and he ruled* … Yet, as long as his father was alive, Yosam did not wear the royal crown on his head, and any decree he issued, he issued in the name of his father.

———— ❧ ————

❧ The descendants of Yehonadav ben Reichav

The word came to Yirmiah from God during the days of Yehoyakim son of Yoshiah, king of Yehudah, saying: Go to the house of the Reichavites (the descendants of Yehonadav, son of Reichav, a scion of Yisro) and speak to them. Bring them to the Temple of God, to one of its chambers, and give them wine to drink.

So I took Ya'azaniah, son of Yirmiah, son of Chavatziniah, and his brothers and all his sons, and the entire house of the Reichavites. I brought them to the Temple of God … and I placed before the members of the house of the Reichavites bowls full of wine and cups, and I instructed them, 'Drink wine.'

They replied, 'We do not drink wine, for our ancestor Yehonadav son of Reichav commanded us (close to three hundred years before, for all his descendants — Radak) *, saying, 'You shall not drink wine, you or your descendants, forever. Houses you shall not build, seed you shall not sow, and vineyards you shall not plant, nor shall you possess any of these. Rather, you shall dwell in tents all your days, so that you may live for many years upon the land in which you sojourn.*

'And we heeded the call of our ancestor Yehonadav son of Reichav regarding all that he commanded us, not to drink wine all our days — we, our wives, our sons, and our daughters; not to build houses as our dwellings; and not to have vineyards, fields, or seed. Instead, we dwell in tents; we thus listened and acted according to all that Yehonadav our ancestor commanded us …'

… And to the house of the Reichavites, Yirmiah said, 'So said God, Master of Legions, God of Yisrael: Because you have heeded the instruction of your ancestor Yehonadav … Therefore, so said God, Master of Legions, God of Yisrael: There shall not cease to be a

man from the descendants of Yehonadav, son of Re-ichav, who will stand before Me (see below), *all the days* (*Yirmiah* ch. 35).

———

R' Nassan taught: The covenant that was made with [the family] of Yehonadav son of Reichav was greater than the covenant made with David. For the covenant made with David had a condition attached, as it is said (*Tehillim* 132:12), *If your sons keep My covenant and this testament of Mine that I shall teach them, then their sons, too, forever and ever, shall sit upon your throne.* But the covenant made with [the family] of Yehonadav son of Reichav was not subject to any condition, as it is written, *Therefore, so said God, Master of Legions, God of Yisrael: There shall not cease to be a man from the descendants of Yehonadav son of Reichav who will stand before Me, all the days* (*Mechilta, Yisro*).

———

R' Yehoshua taught: Can proselytes (as were these descendants of Yisro) truly enter the Hall of the Temple [to stand in God's service]? No one in Yisrael may enter the Hall (except for Kohanim, the descendants of Aharon). Rather, the intent is that they sat as members of the Sanhedrin, and their instruction was sought regarding matters of Torah. Some say: Some of their daughters married Kohanim, and among their descendants were those who brought sacrifices upon the Altar (*Sifrei, Beha'aloscha* §78).

——— ❧ ———

❧ *R' Tarfon*

R' Tarfon had an elderly mother whom he honored greatly. Whenever she wanted to climb into bed, he would bend down beside it and she would step upon him; whenever she needed to come down from the bed, he would bend over and she would step down upon him to get to the floor. R' Tarfon came and spoke proudly of his conduct to his colleagues in the Beis HaMedrash. They told him, "You have not yet reached even half the honor

that you owe your mother. Has it ever happened that she threw a bag of your money into the sea in your presence, and you refrained from shaming her?"(*Kiddushin* 31b).

———

R' Tarfon's mother once descended for a stroll in her courtyard on Shabbos. The strap of her shoe tore, and she could no longer wear it. [Since it was Shabbos, it was prohibited to knot it back onto the shoe — *Korban HaEidah*.] R' Tarfon went and placed his two hands beneath her feet and she walked upon them until she reached her bed. Once he became ill and the Sages came to visit him. His mother said to them, "Pray for my son Tarfon, because he honors me exceedingly." They said to her, "What does he do for you?" She related to them the [above] incident. They said to her, "Even if he had accumulated such deeds in the thousands, he would still not have reached even half the honor the Torah requires!" (*Yerushalmi, Kiddushin* 1:7; *Yerushalmi, Peah* 1:1. See also *Pesikta Rabbasi* §23, and *Tosafos, Kiddushin* 31b, ד"ה ר' טרפון).

——— ❧ ———

❧ *R' Yishmael*

R' Yishmael's mother once came before the Rabbis and complained about him. She said, "Rebuke my son Yishmael, for he does not show me respect!" At that moment, the Sages' faces turned red. They said [to themselves]: Is it possible that R' Yishmael does not behave with respect toward his parents? They asked her, "What has he done to you?" She said, "When he returns from the Beis HaMedrash, I wish to wash his feet and drink the water [out of my great affection for him—*P'nei Moshe*], but he does not let me." Upon which the Sages then told R' Yishmael, "Since this is her wish, this is her honor [and you should allow her to do so]" (*Yerushalmi, Peah* and *Kiddushin* ibid.; *Pesikta Rabbasi* §23)

———

R' Ze'ira used to say in distress, "Would that my father and mother still lived, so I could honor them and thereby inherit Gan Eden!" But once he heard these two lessons [regarding R' Tarfon and R' Yishmael], he exclaimed, "Blessed be the Merciful One that I no longer have a father and mother, for I would not have been able to conduct myself as did R' Tarfon, and I could not have complied with the ruling that R' Yishmael was given" (ibid.).

——— ✻ ———

∽ Rav Yosef

Whenever Rav Yosef heard the sound of his mother's steps approaching, he would say, "Let me stand up before the Divine Presence that approaches" (*Kiddushin* 31b).

——— ✻ ———

∽ Avimi, son of R' Avahu

R' Avahu taught: My son Avimi is an example of one who has truly fulfilled the mitzvah to honor one's parents. Avimi had five grown sons in his father's lifetime, yet when R' Avahu would come and call from the door, Avimi would run to open it himself, calling out as he ran, "Yes! Yes!" [to reassure his father that he was on his way]. One day R' Avahu said to him, "Bring me some water to drink." Avimi went off to carry out his request, but in the interim his father dozed off. Avimi stood over him, waiting, until he awakened, and in the meantime he succeeded in elucidating the Psalm entitled *Mizmor L'Assaf* (*Tehillim* ch. 79), something he had hitherto been unable to do (*Kiddushin* 31b).

——— ✻ ———

∽ Eisav

A son honors [his] father … (*Malachi* 1:6). This refers to Eisav, who honored his father outstandingly. Each day he would venture out to the fields and hunt game. He would bring back his catch, prepare the meat, and serve a meal to his father (*Shemos Rabbah* 46:4).

Rabban Shimon ben Gamliel said: All my life I served my father [to an unequaled degree — see *Devarim Rabbah* 1:15], but I did not do for him even one percent of what Eisav did for his father. When I attended to my father, I did so in my soiled clothes, and when I was out in the street, I wore my clean clothes. But Eisav, when he ministered to his father, did so only in royal garments [and not in the clothing he wore outdoors — see *Tanchuma* cited below]. Eisav said [to himself], "My father's honor warrants royal garments exclusively!" (*Bereishis Rabbah* 65:16; see also *Devarim Rabbah* 1:15 and *Tanchuma HaKadum V'HaYashan, Devarim,* Eshkol ed.).

———————

R' Yudan taught: When the Jewish people prepared to wage war [with Eisav's descendants], the Holy One, Blessed is He, showed Moshe the mountain where the Patriarchs are buried. He said to him, "Moshe, tell the Jewish people, 'You will not succeed in battle against him, for he is still owed reward for the esteem he showed those interred in this mountain.'" Where is this alluded to? In the passage [by which the Torah warns the Jewish people not to infringe upon the land of Eisav's descendants, but rather to pass around it and move on] (*Devarim* 2:3): *Enough of your circling this mountain.* (*Devarim Rabbah* 1:15; see also 1:17).

———————

A son honors [his] father, and a servant his master (*Malachi* 1:6). 'A son' refers to Eisav, for there never existed any human who honored his father as Eisav honored his. It was the respect he showed for his father that propelled him to dominance over the entire world (*Zohar, Bereishis* 146b. See *Pesikta Rabbasi* §23, where this merit of Eisav is blamed for delaying Yisrael's ascendancy).

——— ✻ ———

∽ Merodach-Baladan

At that time Merodach-Baladan, son of Baladan, the king of Bavel, sent letters and a gift to Chizkiah, for he heard that he had been ill, and then had recovered

(*Yeshayah* 39:1). Why is he called Merodach-Baladan? (His name was Merodach; his *father* was Baladan.) The Sages explained: Baladan had been king, but his face became disfigured and it came to resemble a dog's. His son took his father's place on the throne, and in all his correspondence, he would sign his name and that of his father, King Baladan, to enhance his father's prestige. He was therefore called [in the verse] by the name of his father, reflecting his signature (*Sanhedrin* 96a).

———— ✡ ————

ᔛ *Dama ben Nesinah*

R av Ulla's disciples once asked him: How far does the mitzvah of honoring one's parents extend? He replied: Go and observe the behavior of a certain idolater in Ashkelon; Dama ben Nesinah was his name. It once occurred that the Sages sought to purchase some merchandise from him that would have brought him a profit of six hundred thousand gold *dinars*. The key that was needed to access the merchandise was lying under the pillow on which his father was sleeping, and Dama declined to disturb him.

[A similar account:] Rav Yehudah related in the name of Shmuel: The disciples once asked R' Eliezer: How far does the mitzvah of honoring one's parents extend? He replied, "Go and observe the behavior of a certain idolater in Ashkelon; Dama ben Nesinah was his name. The Sages sought to acquire from him [precious] stones for the *ephod* (one of the vestments worn by the High Priest), that stood to bring him a profit of six hundred thousand gold *dinars* (Rav Kahana taught variantly: eight hundred thousand gold *dinars*). But the key needed to access the gems was lying under the pillow on which his father was sleeping, and Dama refused to disturb him. [The Sages went elsewhere and he lost the opportunity.] The next year, the Holy One, Blessed is He, gave him his reward and a *parah adumah* (an extremely rare "red cow" whose ashes are used for ritual purification) was born in his herd. The Sages of Yisrael came to him. He said to them, "I know that if I ask you for all the money in the world [in exchange for the cow], you will give it to me. However, I ask you only for the amount of money I lost on account of my father's honor."

R' Chanina commented [on this incident]: If one who performs a mitzvah without having been commanded to do so receives such a rich reward, then how much more will a person receive upon performing a mitzvah he has been commanded to do! For R' Chanina has taught: Greater is one who performs a mitzvah for which he has received a command than one who performs a mitzvah for which he has not received a command (*Kiddushin* 31a. For varying versions of this incident, and for more details, see *Yerushalmi, Peah* 1:1, *Kiddushin* 1:7; *Devarim Rabbah* 1:15; *Pesikta Rabbasi* §23).

————

W hen Rav Dimi came from the Land of Yisrael, he related the following: Dama ben Nesinah was once seated among the aristocrats of Rome, dressed in a gold-embroidered silk cloak. His mother stepped up to him and ripped off his cloak, hit him on the head and spat in his face; but he did nothing to shame her (*Kiddushin* ibid.).

————

D ama ben Nesinah was the ranking [Roman] official [in his region]. Once his mother slapped him in the presence of all his fellow dignitaries. [She was mentally ill — *Devarim Rabbah*.] As she did this, her glove fell from her hand, and he handed it back so she should not be distressed. R' Chizkiah recounted: Dama ben Nesinah was an idolater from Ashkelon, and he was the ranking [Roman] official [in the region]. Yet he was careful never to sit on the stone his father customarily sat upon. When his father died, he turned that stone into his object of worship (*Yerushalmi, Peah* and *Kiddushin* ibid.; *Pesikta Rabbasi* ibid.).

THE OBLIGATION TO HONOR ONE'S PARENTS IS COUNTED AS ONE MITZVAH

lthough the Torah's command to, *Honor your father and your mother* consists of two distinct requirements — an obligation to honor one's father and a separate obligation to honor one's mother — *Rambam* counts these obligations as one mitzvah (*Sefer HaMitzvos, Aseh* §210). This is consistent with *Rambam's* view that a single command which refers to multiple objects is considered one mitzvah in the count of the 613. Thus, for example, *Rambam* writes that the prohibition against eating the *Korban Pesach* when it is only partially cooked or when it is roasted (see *Shemos* 12:9) is counted as a single prohibition, although it refers to two different objects (see *Sefer HaMitzvos, shoresh* §9; see *Chinuch* §7, who also counts this prohibition as a single mitzvah). Although *Rambam* states this rule with regard to the Torah's negative commandments, it presumably applies to the positive commandments as well. Accordingly, he counts the obligation to honor one's father and one's mother as a single mitzvah, since the verse contains only a single command to honor (*Sefer Derech Mitzvosecha* from the author of *Mishneh LaMelech*, end of part one; see also *Ramban's* comments to *Sefer HaMitzvos, shoresh* §2, end of הב' (ד"ה העיקר הב').

Many Rishonim disagree with *Rambam's* principle, among them *Ramban* in his comments to

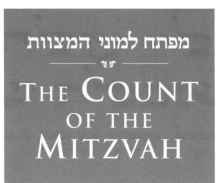

מפתח למוני המצוות
THE COUNT OF THE MITZVAH

Baal Halachos Gedolos / Asin 44
בה"ג / עשין מד

R' Saadiah Gaon / Asin 9
רס"ג / עשין ט

R' Eliyahu HaZakein / Amud 4
ר' אליהו הזקן / עמ' 4

Rashbag / Asin Os 24
רשב"ג / עשין אות כד

R' Yitzchak El-Bargeloni / Asin 20
ר"י אלברג׳לוני / עשין כ

Maamar HaSechel / Dibbur Chamishi 1
מאמר השכל / דיבור חמישי א

Sefer Yere'im / 222
יראים / רכב

Rambam, Sefer HaMitzvos / Aseh 210
רמב"ם / עשה רי

Sefer Mitzvos Gadol (Smag) / Aseh 112-113
סמ"ג / עשה קיב-קיג

Sefer Mitzvos Katan (Smak) / 50
סמ"ק / נ

Zohar HaRakia / Asin 26
זוהר הרקיע / עשין כו

Rambam's Sefer HaMitzvos (ibid. ד"ה והראוי; see also *Ramban's* list of the negative commandments ד"ה וכן אם תתן לבך, where he counts as separate mitzvos every case of multiple prohibitions that *Rambam* counts as a single mitzvah on the basis of this rule). According to this view, the separate obligations of honoring one's father and mother should seemingly be counted as two mitzvos. Yet, nowhere does *Ramban* indicate that this is the case (see *Derech Mitzvosecha* ibid.). Even more puzzling is the fact that *Ramban* does count as separate mitzvos other multiple positive obligations that are included in a single command. For example, he counts the obligation to recite the *Shema* morning and evening as two separate mitzvos, as well as the obligation to offer incense in the *Beis HaMikdash* in the morning and afternoon and the obligation to offer the *Tamid* sacrifice in the morning and afternoon (see his list of negative commandments ד"ה (ואתה אם תבין).

Some authorities explain that even according to *Ramban*, such obligations are counted as one mitzvah unless there is a specific reason to view them as separate mitzvos. In the case of the *Shema*, for instance, *Ramban* (ibid.) writes that the morning and evening *Shema* obligations are considered separate mitzvos because they apply at two different times. There is no similar reason to view the obligation to honor one's parents as two separate mitzvos, however, so *Ramban* agrees that they are counted as one mitzvah, since they are included in a single command (*Maayan HaChochmah, Aseh* §14; see *Chinuch* §7, who explains *Ramban's* view similarly).

[Note: Some authorities cite the Gemara in *Sanhedrin* (56b) as proof that the requirement to honor one's parents is considered one mitzvah. That Gemara states that the Jews were given ten mitzvos at *Marah*, even before receiving the Torah at Sinai (see *Shemos* 15:25): the seven mitzvos that are obligatory on non-Jews, as well as the obligation to establish a system of civil law, to honor one's parents, and to observe *Shabbos*. Clearly, the Gemara does not consider the obligation to honor one's parents as two separate mitzvos, or else it would have said that the Jews were given *eleven* mitzvos in *Marah*! (*Maharatz Chayes* to that Gemara; *Maayan HaChochmah* ibid.; *Kunteres K'sav Yad* of R' *Yosef Damesek* of Cracow). However, *Ramban* in his comments to *Rambam's Sefer HaMitzvos* (end of *shoresh* §14) writes that the commandments given to the Jews at *Marah* were given only in a general form. They were transmitted in all their detail when the Jews were given the rest of the commandments at Sinai. Many of these details are reckoned as mitzvos in their own right (for example, the forbidden relationships the Torah details in *Vayikra* ch. 18) However, until the details of each mitzvah were delineated at Sinai, it counted only as one mitzvah. If so, perhaps the command to honor one's parents was considered one mitzvah only in its general form given at *Marah*. Once these ten commandments were given with all their details at Sinai, however, the obligation of honoring one's parents may be considered two separate mitzvos.

THE OBLIGATION TO HONOR OTHER RELATIVES IS NOT COUNTED AS A SEPARATE MITZVAH

s we have seen, in addition to honoring one's parents, there is also a mitzvah to honor several of the parents' relatives. One is obligated to honor a father's wife and mother's husband, and his own eldest brother. Accordig to some (see *Iyunim* §4), This is derived through Biblical exegesis from the same verse that teaches the obligation to honor one's parents (see *Kesubos* 103a). According to *Rambam*, obligations that are derived by the Rabbis through Biblical exegesis are not included in the count of the 613 mitzvos (see *Sefer HaMitzvos, shoresh* §2). Thus, *Rambam* (ibid.) states that the requirement to honor these relatives is not considered one of the 613 mitzvos. He questions, however, *Bahag's* failure to include this requirement in his list of the 613 mitzvos, for *Bahag* maintains that obligations derived through Biblical exegesis *are* included. *Ramban* (to *Sefer HaMitzvos* ibid.) suggests two answers to *Rambam's* question:

A. As the Gemara in *Kesubos* (ibid.) states, one is obligated to honor these relatives only during his parents' lifetime (see also *Rambam, Hil. Mamrim* 6:15; *Shulchan Aruch, Yoreh Deah* 240:21). It is evident, then, that this requirement is simply a *means* of honoring one's parents. As such, it is not a mitzvah in and of itself, but part of the mitzvah of honoring one's parents. [Note: There is some question as to whether one is obligated to honor his own eldest brother even after his parents' death. If the requirement does apply after one's parents die, this reason of *Ramban* does not explain why *Bahag* does not count the obligation to honor one's eldest brother as a separate mitzvah (see *Ramban* ibid. and *Megillas Esther* there; see also *Pischei Teshuvah, Yoreh Deah* 240:18).]

B. As noted above, *Rambam* counts the obligation to honor one's father and one's mother as one mitzvah because it is a single command referring to multiple objects. For this reason, the requirements to honor one's father's wife, one's mother's husband and one's eldest brother cannot be reckoned as separate mitzvos, since the command which obligates one to honor these relatives is the same command which obligates him to honor his parents.

Mitzvah 34

אִסּוּר רְצִיחָה

פרשת יתרו

Not to
Murder

THE MITZVAH:

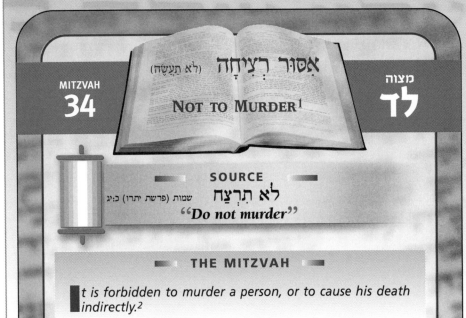

MITZVAH
34

אִסּוּר רְצִיחָה (לֹא תַעֲשֶׂה)

NOT TO MURDER[1]

מצוה
לד

SOURCE

לֹא תִרְצַח

שמות (פרשת יתרו) כ:יג

"Do not murder"

THE MITZVAH

It is forbidden to murder a person, or to cause his death indirectly.[2]

LAWS

1 It is forbidden to murder any person; man or woman, adult or child.[3]

2 It is also forbidden to hasten the death of a terminally ill or dying person; this too is murder.[4]

3 The penalty for deliberately murdering someone is execution by beheading.[5] One is not liable to this punishment unless he intended to kill,[6] and only if the victim was his intended target.[7]

4 One is not liable to execution for killing a *tereifah*.[8]

5 One who kills unintentionally violates this prohibi-tion, but is not liable to exe-cution. Rather, he is exiled to one of the "Cities of Refuge,"[9] and must remain there until the death of the *Kohen Gadol* [see *mitzvos #408, 410, and 520*].

6 This prohibition applies to both men and women, in all places and at all times.[10] Non-Jews are also forbidden to murder, as the prohibition against murder is one of the Seven Noahide Laws.[11]

7 If one is threatened with death if he refuses to mur-der someone, he must allow himself to be killed rather than commit murder.[12]

A REASON

That murder deprives the victim of his physical life is just one aspect of this terrible crime. The victim's spiritual growth is also curtailed; he can no longer fulfill the Torah and mitzvos to achieve the perfection that is the purpose of life.

לע"נ ר' יוסף בן יהושע בנימין ז"ל
לע"נ לאה בת אברהם חיים ע"ה

1. The prohibition forbids only the killing of someone who does not de-serve to be put to death. There are people, however, whom it is permit-ted, and in some cases even a mitz-vah, to kill. See *Iyunim* §1 for a list of such people.

2. For example, by tying him up in front of a lion so that he will be de-voured (*Rambam, Hil. Rotzei'ach* 2:2). The Gemara in *Sanhedrin* (77a) dis-cusses whether one is liable to execu-tion for such an act (see below, note 9); there is no question, how-ever, that he is guilty of murder.

The Scriptural source for this law is *Bereishis* 9:5, which states: *However, your blood which belongs to your souls I will seek [to avenge], from every beast I will seek [to avenge] it*. *Bereishis Rab-bah* (loc. cit.) expounds: "*From every beast* — this refers to one who placed another person in front of a wild ani-mal to be killed." Although he did not directly kill the victim, the Torah holds him responsible for the victim's death. Thus we derive that one who causes a person to be killed is guilty of murder.

Hiring someone to kill a person is also deemed a violation of the prohi-bition to kill (see *Kiddushin* 43a; *Rambam, Hil. Rotzei'ach* 2:2). Scrip-ture alludes to this indirect act of murder in *Bereishis* (9:5) as well: *However, your blood which belongs to your souls I will seek [to avenge] … as for man, from the hand of his fellow man, I will seek [to avenge] the life of man*. The words "from the hands of his *fellow man*" are expounded as referring to one who causes the death of another through his "fellow man"; i.e., by hiring someone to kill him (*Bereishis Rabbah,* loc. cit.; *Ram-bam, Hil. Rotzei'ach* 2:3). [As a rule, one is not held liable for a transgres-sion he instructs another to commit

AN EXPANDED TREATMENT

(אין שליח לדבר עבירה). One who hires someone to commit a murder, however, although he is not executed by *Beis Din* for his crime, *is* guilty of murder (see *Kiddushin* ibid.; see also Law 3 and below, note 9)].

Based on the language of the *Gemara* in *Kiddushin* (ibid.) and *Bereishis Rabbah* (ibid.), some contend that one does not transgress this prohibition if he merely *instructs* someone to commit a murder, but only if he *hires* him to do so [i.e., he pays the murderer to perform the murder] (*Mishneh LaMelech, Hil. Rotzei'ach* 2:2, citing *Ritva*, and explaining *Rambam, Hil. Rotzei'ach* 2:2). [See *Tosafos, Bava Kamma* 56a ד"ה אלא, who explain the rationale for this distinction as follows: While one who simply *instructs* another to commit a crime cannot be held responsible for the crime because he can argue that he did not expect the agent to heed his instructions in contravention of the law, one who *pays* someone to commit a crime cannot argue that he did not expect the agent to comply. See also *Rashba* to *Bava Kamma* ibid. ד"ה מהו, and *Rama, Choshen Mishpat* 32:2 and *Shach* there §3.] Others, however, maintain that there is no difference between paying someone to commit a crime and instructing him to commit a crime; in their view, one who instructs another to commit murder will also violate the prohibition (*Kiryas Sefer, Hil. Rotzei'ach* ibid.; *Ketzos HaChoshen* 32:1; *Teshuvos Chacham Tzvi* §138).

One who sends an agent to kill another is not liable to execution, but *is* liable to Divine retribution (*Rambam, Hil. Rotzei'ach* 3:10).

3. See *Sanhedrin* 84b; *Mechilta* to *Shemos* 21:12; *Toras Kohanim* to *Vayikra* 24:17; *Rambam, Hil. Rotzei'ach* 2:6.

It is also forbidden to kill an unborn fetus (see *Tosafos, Sanhedrin* 59a ד"ה ליכא מידעם; see also *Teshuvos Igros Moshe, Choshen Mishpat* vol. II §69 at length). However, one is not liable to punishment by *beis din* for doing so (see Mishnah, *Niddah* 44a).

One who kills a *nefel* [i.e. an immature nonviable baby who clearly will not survive] is also not subject to punishment at the hands of *Beis Din* (*Sanhedrin* ibid.; *Mechilta* to *Shemos* 21:12 and *Toras Kohanim* to *Vayikra* 24:17; *Rambam, Hil. Rotzei'ach* 2:6).

4. See *Sanhedrin* 78a; *Rambam, Hil. Rotzei'ach* 2:7. The fact that the murder victim would not have lived long in any case is irrelevant. The Torah does not measure the value of life in terms of life expectancy; it treats the killing of a very old person the same as it does the killing of a young child (*Minchas Chinuch* 34:4). [See Law 4 and below, note 8 regarding the murder of a *tereifah* or a person who is dying as a result of injuries inflicted by human agency.]

5. The only way to ascertain whether or not someone transgresses deliberately is to warn him beforehand not to perform the forbidden act. If he transgresses in spite of the warning, he undoubtedly did so deliberately (see *Sanhedrin* 8b; *Rambam, Hil. Sanhedrin* 12:2 with *Kessef Mishneh* and *Lechem Mishneh*). This warning is administered by the witnesses to the murder (*Beis Din* may not impose any capital or corporal punishment without hearing the testimony of two valid witnesses who saw the act in question [see *mitzvah* #82]). As part of this warning, the potential killer must also be informed of the severe consequences of the crime; i.e., that he will render himself liable to death if he commits

the criminal act (see *Sanhedrin* 40b; *Rambam* ibid.).

Numerous verses in the Torah prescribe death as the punishment for murder (see *Shemos* 21:12, 21:14, *Vayikra* 24:17, *Bamidbar* 35:16-21, ibid. 35:30). These verses do not state explicitly, however, the specific *method* of execution. Normally, the Torah's unqualified references to execution are understood as referring to the most lenient form of execution, strangulation. However, in the case of murder, the Sages derive exegetically that one is punished with a more severe form of execution — beheading — as follows: In describing the punishment for killing one's Canaanite slave, Scripture states that the slave shall be "avenged" (*Shemos* 21:20). Elsewhere in Scripture, we find the term "avenge" used in connection with the sword — *I will bring upon you a* **sword**, **avenging** *the vengeance of the covenant* (*Vayikra* 26:25). This teaches that the "vengeance" meted out to the murderer of a Canaanite slave is performed with a sword; i.e. beheading. And since it would be implausible to say that the penalty for killing a Canaanite slave is more severe than that for killing a full-fledged Jew, we must say that the punishment for killing a Jew is also beheading, and not strangulation (*Sanhedrin* 52b; see also *Rambam, Hil. Rotzei'ach* 1:1).

[The preceding exposition assumes that beheading is a more severe form of death than strangulation. However, there are Tannaim who maintain that beheading is a *less* severe manner of execution than strangulation (see Mishnah, *Sanhedrin* 49b with *Rashi*). According to this view, we cannot derive from the punishment given to the murderer of a Canaanite slave that one who kills a Jew is similarly beheaded, for perhaps the murderer of a Jew is

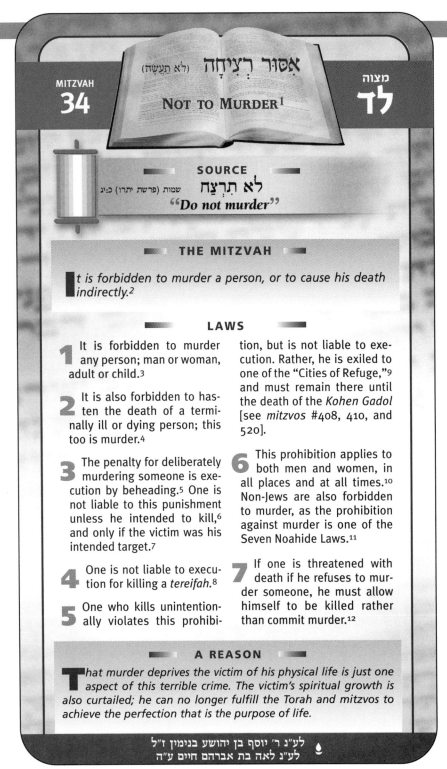

MITZVAH
34

אִסּוּר רְצִיחָה (לֹא תַעֲשֶׂה)

NOT TO MURDER[1]

מצוה
לד

SOURCE

לֹא תִרְצָח   שמות (פרשת יתרו) כ:יג

"Do not murder"

THE MITZVAH

It is forbidden to murder a person, or to cause his death indirectly.[2]

LAWS

1 It is forbidden to murder any person; man or woman, adult or child.[3]

2 It is also forbidden to hasten the death of a terminally ill or dying person; this too is murder.[4]

3 The penalty for deliberately murdering someone is execution by beheading.[5] One is not liable to this punishment unless he intended to kill,[6] and only if the victim was his intended target.[7]

4 One is not liable to execution for killing a *tereifah*.[8]

5 One who kills unintentionally violates this prohibi-

tion, but is not liable to execution. Rather, he is exiled to one of the "Cities of Refuge,"[9] and must remain there until the death of the *Kohen Gadol* [see *mitzvos* #408, 410, and 520].

6 This prohibition applies to both men and women, in all places and at all times.[10] Non-Jews are also forbidden to murder, as the prohibition against murder is one of the Seven Noahide Laws.[11]

7 If one is threatened with death if he refuses to murder someone, he must allow himself to be killed rather than commit murder.[12]

A REASON

That murder deprives the victim of his physical life is just one aspect of this terrible crime. The victim's spiritual growth is also curtailed; he can no longer fulfill the Torah and mitzvos to achieve the perfection that is the purpose of life.

arufah is expounded to teach that a murderer is put to death in the same manner as the *eglah arufah*, by decapitation (*Sanhedrin* 52b; see also *Mechilta* to *Shemos* 21:12).]

Normally, the execution of one who committed a capital offense is carried out by the witnesses who testified that he committed the crime. A murderer, however, is executed by one of the victim's close relatives, known as "the avenger of the blood" [גּוֹאֵל הַדָּם]. As the verse (*Bamidbar* 35:19) states: *The avenger of the blood, he shall put the killer to death* (see *Sanhedrin* 45b; *Rambam, Hil. Rotzei'ach* 1:2). [Anyone who inherits the victim qualifies as his "blood avenger" (*Rambam* ibid.).] If the "blood avenger" is unwilling or unable to execute the murderer, or if the victim has no relative who qualifies as a "blood avenger", *Beis Din* appoints someone else to carry out the execution (*Sanhedrin* ibid.; *Rambam* ibid.). From *Rambam* (*Hil. Sanhedrin* 13:1), though, it appears that, initially, the witnesses should carry out the execution [in the absence of a "blood avenger"]; only if the witnesses cannot execute the murder does *Beis Din* appoint someone else to execute him (see *Aruch HaShulchan, Choshen Mishpat* 425:2; *Chazon Ish, Sanhedrin* 19:2).

It is forbidden to accept ransom in exchange for the life of a murderer. See *mitzvah* #412 regarding this law.

6. If, however, he had never intended to kill his victim but only to injure him — for example, he intended to strike the victim with a blow to the thigh with insufficient force to kill him, but the blow landed on a more vital area of his victim's body (e.g., his chest), where it was sufficient to kill him — the murderer is not liable to death (see Mishnah, *Sanhedrin* 78b; *Rambam, Hil. Rotzei'ach* 4:2).

The reason the murderer is exempt from the death penalty in such

subject to strangulation, the more severe method of execution. These Tannaim derive the law that the murderer of even a Jew is killed by beheading from the verse regarding the *eglah arufah* [עֶגְלָה עֲרוּפָה], the calf that is decapitated to atone for the death of the victim of an unknown murderer (see

mitzvah #530). The verse (*Devarim* 21:9) states: *And you shall purge the innocent blood from your midst*; this teaches that even after the *eglah arufah* is decapitated, if the murderer is subsequently found, he must be executed. The reference to a murderer's punishment in the passage of the *eglah*

a case is that one is never liable to death for a capital crime unless he was forewarned that the act would render him liable to execution (see above, note 5). In this case, however, where his intention had not been to kill but to injure, albeit in a manner that *might* cause death, he cannot be warned with certainty that the act will *definitely* make the potential murderer liable to execution, but only that it *might* render him liable, for it is not certain that he will, in fact, kill the victim. Such an uncertain warning does not qualify as a valid warning [התראת ספק לא שמיה התראה], so the murderer is exempt from execution, just as someone who was not warned before committing a capital offense (see *Rashi* to *Sanhedrin* 79a ד"ה והיה בה; see further, *Iyunim* §3). Alternatively, the murderer is not liable to death in this case because his killing of the victim is considered accidental (*Yad Ramah, Sanhedrin* ibid. ד"ה נתכוון).

Moreover, a murderer is subject to the death penalty only if *Beis Din* determines that the blow he inflicted was capable, in and of itself, of causing the death of the victim. Among the factors *Beis Din* takes into consideration are: whether the type of instrument used to commit the murder can possibly be wielded with lethal force; the force of the blow (was it sufficient to cause death); and the health of the victim before he was killed. If, in *Beis Din's* estimation, the blow was insufficient to cause the victim's death, the murderer is not liable to execution for his death [because the victim's death may have been caused by other factors] (see *Rambam, Hil. Rotzei'ach* 3:1-7).

7. The Mishnah in *Sanhedrin* (79a) cites a dispute between the Tanna Kamma and R' Shimon as to whether one is liable when he kills someone other than his intended victim (see Gemara there). [All agree that if one intended to kill someone for whom he would not be liable to execution (e.g. a *nefel*; see above, note 3) and instead killed someone for whom there is liability to the death penalty, he is not liable. These Tannaim argue only when the intended victim was also someone for whose murder one would be liable to the death penalty (Mishnah ibid. 78b).] *Rambam* (*Hil. Rotzei'ach* 4:1) rules in accordance with R' Shimon that the murderer is exempt from execution in such a case. [Cf. *Raavad* there, who rules in accordance with the Tanna Kamma that the murderer *is* liable to execution; see also *Kessef Mishneh* there.]

A murderer is exempt from the death penalty not only if he had intended to kill a specific person and killed someone else instead, but even if he had no specific victim in mind. Thus, if one threw a rock [with lethal force] into a group of people, and it struck one of the group and killed him, the murderer is not liable to the death penalty, because he had not specifically intended to kill that particular person [even though he knew that he would likely kill *someone* in the group] (*Rambam* ibid.).

8. *Sanhedrin* 78a; *Rambam, Hil. Rotzei'ach* 2:8. A *tereifah* is someone who possesses one of a well-defined set of physical defects which will certainly cause his death (See *Rashi, Sanhedrin* ibid. ד"ה הכל for examples of physical defects that define one as a *tereifah*). Because of the physical defect he possesses, which will certainly cause his death, a *tereifah* is viewed, in many respects, as though he were already dead. Thus, one is not liable to punishment for killing a *tereifah*, for it is as if he had killed a "dead" person (see *Rashi, Sanhedrin* ibid. ד"ה שהוא פטור and *Chullin* 11b ד"ה טרפה הוה; see also *Ri MiGash*, cited by *Shitah Mekubetzes* to *Bava Kamma* 26b; *Rivam*, cited by *Tos. Rid* to *Shabbos* 136a). Although one who kills a *tereifah* is not liable to the death penalty, he *does* transgress the prohibition against murder (*Tashbatz*, cited by *Margaliyos HaYam, Sanhedrin* ibid.; see also *Rambam* ibid., who writes that one who kills a *tereifah* is not liable to punishment by *Beis Din*, implying that he *is* subject to *Divine* retribution; see also *Shulchan Aruch, Yoreh Deah* 339:1, for discussion of the extreme care one must take when attending to a dying person, so as not to hasten his death in any way). [However, *Minchas Chinuch* (51:18 ד"ה ונראה פשוט) posits that one who kills a *tereifah* does not transgress the prohibition against murder, since he killed a person who is already legally "dead."]

[It is noteworthy that according to Torah law, the prohibition against murder applies equally to a person who cannot contribute to society, such as one who is insane [שוטה] (*Teshuvos Maharil* §196; *R' Moshe Chaviv* in *Sefer Kol Gadol* §76; *Minchas Chinuch* 34:3; cf. *R' Yaakov Chagiz*, in *Sefer Halachos Ketanos* §37).]

The Gemara in *Sanhedrin* (78a) cites a Baraisa that teaches a dispute concerning one who kills a victim who is already dying as a result of injuries inflicted by others. The Rabbis compare him to a *tereifah*, and exempt his killer from execution; R' Yehudah ben Beseirah, however, holds him liable (see Gemara there for the Scriptural derivation of each view). *Rambam* (*Hil. Rotzei'ach* 2:7) holds that the halachah accords with the Rabbis. [Even according to the Rabbis, though, it is still forbidden to kill such a person.]

9. *Shemos* 21:13; *Bamidbar* 35:22-25; see Mishnah, *Makkos* 7a; *Rambam, Hil. Rotzei'ach* 5:1.

The accidental murderer must live in the city of refuge until the death of the *Kohen Gadol* (*Bamidbar* 35:25, 28; see Mishnah, *Makkos* 11a, and *Rambam, Hil. Rotzei'ach* 5:1). It

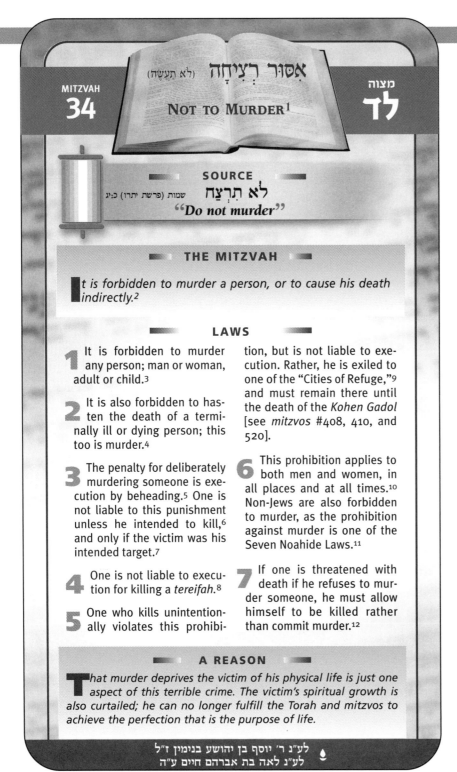

MITZVAH
34

אִסּוּר רְצִיחָה (לֹא תַעֲשֶׂה)

NOT TO MURDER[1]

מצוה
לד

SOURCE

לֹא תִרְצָח שמות (פרשת יתרו) כ:יג

"Do not murder"

THE MITZVAH

It is forbidden to murder a person, or to cause his death indirectly.[2]

LAWS

1 It is forbidden to murder any person; man or woman, adult or child.[3]

2 It is also forbidden to hasten the death of a terminally ill or dying person; this too is murder.[4]

3 The penalty for deliberately murdering someone is execution by beheading.[5] One is not liable to this punishment unless he intended to kill,[6] and only if the victim was his intended target.[7]

4 One is not liable to execution for killing a *tereifah*.[8]

5 One who kills unintentionally violates this prohibi-

tion, but is not liable to execution. Rather, he is exiled to one of the "Cities of Refuge,"[9] and must remain there until the death of the *Kohen Gadol* [see *mitzvos* #408, 410, and 520].

6 This prohibition applies to both men and women, in all places and at all times.[10] Non-Jews are also forbidden to murder, as the prohibition against murder is one of the Seven Noahide Laws.[11]

7 If one is threatened with death if he refuses to murder someone, he must allow himself to be killed rather than commit murder.[12]

A REASON

That murder deprives the victim of his physical life is just one aspect of this terrible crime. The victim's spiritual growth is also curtailed; he can no longer fulfill the Torah and mitzvos to achieve the perfection that is the purpose of life.

לע"נ ר' יוסף בן יהושע בנימין ז"ל
לע"נ לאה בת אברהם חיים ע"ה

the accidental murderer leaves the city of refuge before that time, the victim's "blood avenger" (see above, note 5) may kill him (*Bamidbar* ibid. 26,27; *Rambam, Hil. Rotzei'ach* 5:9,10). [See *mitzvah* #410 for details regarding this law.]

10. Although there are certain positive mitzvos from which women are exempt, they are, with few exceptions, subject to all the *negative* commandments of the Torah (see Mishnah, *Kiddushin* 29a).

Rambam, in his *Sefer HaMitzvos* (Lo

Saaseh §289), writes that the commandment, *You shall not kill* is directed to the judges of *Beis Din*, who are commanded not to impose the death penalty unlawfully. This would seem to imply that the prohibition does *not* apply to others. This interpretation, however, contradicts *Rambam's* own statement in *Hil. Rotzei'ach* (1:1) that *all* Jews are included in this prohibition. Moreover, elsewhere in *Sefer HaMitzvos* (Lo Saaseh §290), *Rambam* cites a *different* verse as the source for the prohibition against judges executing someone unlawfully: (*Shemos* 23:7) *Do not execute the innocent or the righteous* (see *mitzvah* #82). To resolve this contradiction, some commentators posit that *Rambam* holds that the prohibition of murder applies to everyone, as he writes in *Hil. Rotzei'ach,* and they attribute *Rambam's* words in *Sefer HaMitzvos* to a scribal error (*Dina D'chayei, Laavin* §160). This assertion is supported by manuscript versions of *Rambam's Sefer HaMitzvos* (see Frankel, Kappach, and Heller editions of *Sefer HaMitzvos*). Others defend the printed version, and maintain that *Rambam* subsequently retracted this view, and agreed that the prohibition applies to everyone, as he rules in *Hil. Rotzei'ach* (R' Yeruchem Fischel Perla, Commentary to Sefer HaMitzvos L'RaSag, Onshin §70).

11. The Gemara in *Sanhedrin* (56a) lists seven mitzvos that were given to non-Jews (the reference to Noahide Laws reflects the fact that all of mankind descended from Noah, whose family were the sole survivors of the Flood). They are: (1) the requirement to establish a system of civil laws (see *Rambam, Hil. Melachim* 9:14); (2) a prohibition against blasphemy (euphemistically referred to as "blessing" the Name of Hashem); (3) a prohibition against idolatry; (4) a prohibition against illicit relations (*arayos*); (5) a prohibition against murder; (6) a prohibition against theft; and (7) a prohibition against eating a limb torn from a live animal (אבר מן החי). The *Gemara* (ibid. 56b) derives these mitzvos from a verse in *Bereishis* (2:16), which speaks of Hashem's commands to *Adam HaRishon*.

12. This is true both of one who is forced by others to kill [i.e., he is offered a choice between killing someone or being killed himself] (see *Sanhedrin* 74a; *Rambam, Hil. Yesodei HaTorah* 5:2; *Tur* and *Shulchan Aruch, Yoreh Deah* 157:1) and one whose life is in danger (e.g., because of sickness) who can save himself only by taking the life of another (*Rambam* ibid. 5:6). [However, there is a difference between one who kills because others force him to on pain of death, and one who kills to save himself without being forced to. In the former case, the murderer is not liable to punishment for his deed (*Rambam, Hil. Yesodei HaTorah* 5:4). In the latter case, the murderer *is* guilty of murder, and is subject to the same punishment as a deliberate murderer (*Rambam* ibid. 5:6).]

The Gemara (*Sanhedrin* ibid.) derives this law through logic. The Gemara states that we say to the would-be murderer: "Why do you assume that your blood is redder than that of your victim?" *Rashi* there (ד״ה מאי חזית) explains: With regard to other commandments, one is permitted to transgress to save his life, because life is more precious to Hashem than mitzvah observance. But if one is faced with a choice of killing someone or dying himself, one person will die in any event. Now, there is no basis for assuming that one life is more precious in the eyes of Hashem than another. Thus, there is no valid reason for someone to save his own life at the cost of someone else's life.

The commentators discuss whether, in a case where one is being forced by others to kill, he may kill someone for whose murder there is no liability to execution [e.g. a *tereifah*; see Law 4] to save his own life; for the blood of such a person is *not* as precious as that of a regular person, as evidenced by the fact that there is no death penalty for his murder (*Minchas Chinuch* 296:24 [see also 296:7]; see also *Teshuvos Igros Moshe, Choshen Mishpat* vol. II 69:4)

It is forbidden not only to kill someone directly, but even to *cause* someone's death in order to save one's own life, for causing another's death is also murder [see above, note 2] (*Minchas Chinuch* 296:25). Indeed, the authorities rule that if an entire group of Jews is threatened by non-Jews with death unless they hand over a member of the group to be killed, the entire group must sacrifice their lives rather than deliver even a single Jew to be killed (*Rambam, Hil. Yesodei HaTorah* 5:5; *Rama, Yoreh Deah* 157:1).

עיונים

A BROADER LOOK AT THE LAWS

1 Circumstances under which killing a person is not forbidden

As mentioned above (see note 1), there are certain types of people that one is permitted (and sometimes even obligated) to kill. These include the following:

A. A *rodeif* — One who attempts to kill another person, or to violate a woman who is forbidden to him as an *ervah* (ערוה, a woman forbidden to him on pain of execution or *kares*; see *Vayikra* 20:10-21) is known as a *rodeif* [רודף, lit. *pursuer*]. It is permitted — indeed, one is *obligated* — to kill a *rodeif* in order to protect his intended victim (Mishnah, *Sanhedrin* 73a; *Rambam, Hil. Rotzei'ach* 1:6-8, 10-11; *Tur* and *Shulchan Aruch, Choshen Mishpat* 425:1-3). [This is true only when the victim cannot be saved in any other way, such as by incapacitating the *rodeif* without killing him (*Sanhedrin* 74a; *Rambam* ibid. 1:7; *Tur* and *Shulchan Aruch* ibid. 425:1).] See *Sanhedrin* 73a and *Rambam* ibid. for the Scriptural source for this law; see further, mitzvos #237, 600, 601.

A burglar is also considered a *rodeif* when it can be presumed that he is prepared to kill the homeowner if he tries to protect his property. Therefore, in such a case it would be permitted to kill a burglar during his attempt to break into one's home (see Mishnah, *Sanhedrin* 72a with *Gemara*, based on *Shemos* 22:1; *Rambam, Hil. Geneivah* 9:7-9; *Tur, Choshen Mishpat* §425 and *Rama* there 425:1).

B. During the Temple Era, when the Sanhedrin judged capital cases, they would condemn to death those found guilty of capital crimes. If a sinner was condemned to death by *Beis Din*, it is a mitzvah for *Beis Din* to kill him (see *mitzvos* #47,50,261,555). In addition, *Beis Din* has the authority to execute even a sinner who is not liable to the death penalty if the times require it;

e.g. if laxity in Torah observance has become so widespread that they feel that drastic measures are needed to rectify the situation (*Sanhedrin* 46a; *Rambam, Hil. Sanhedrin* 24:4; *Tur* and *Shulchan Aruch, Choshen Mishpat* 2:1).

C. A *rebel against the king* (מורד במלכות) — if someone rebels against the authority of a Jewish king in Eretz Yisrael, the king is permitted to put him to death. One who fails to heed even the most trivial command of the king, or who desecrates the king's honor or curses him, is considered a rebel (see *Sanhedrin* 48b-49a; *Rambam, Hil. Melachim* 3:8). This law does not apply nowadays.

D. An *unintentional murderer who leaves a "city of refuge"* — if an unintentional murderer, who is exiled to one of the cities of refuge [*arei miklat*] (see above, Law 5), leaves the city of refuge, his victim's "blood avenger" (see above, note 5) is permitted to kill him (Mishnah, *Makkos* 11b; *Rambam, Hil. Rotzei'ach* 5:10). Others are forbidden to kill the murderer, but are not liable to punishment if they do kill him (*Rambam* ibid., based on one textual version of that Mishnah; according to the version found in our texts, however, others *are* liable to execution for killing an unintentional murderer outside a city of refuge). [According to the Tanna R' Yose HaGlili, it is a *mitzvah* for the "blood avenger" to kill the murderer outside a city of refuge, and it is also permitted (though not a mitzvah) for others to do so.] This is only if the murderer *knowingly* leaves his city of refuge. If he leaves the city unwittingly, however, even the "blood avenger" is forbidden to kill him (*Makkos* 12a; *Rambam* ibid. 5:10-11). See further, mitzvah #410.

2 One who kills a Canaanite slave — The twenty-four-hour rule

One who kills a Canaanite slave [עבד כנעני; a non-Jewish slave owned by a Jew], is liable to execution just as if he had killed a Jew (*Mechilta* to *Shemos* 21:20; *Yalkut Shimoni* §334; *Rambam, Hil. Rotzei'ach* 2:10). In the context of this prohibition, a Canaanite slave is treated no differently than a full-fledged Jew (a Canaanite slave is obligated in mitzvos like a Jew, with the exception of those mitzvos from which women are exempt) and is considered a member of the Jewish nation (*Rambam, Hil. Rotzei'ach* 2:11). There is, however, a difference between one who kills his own Canaanite slave and one who kills the Canaanite slave of another. If one inflicts a mortal injury upon his own slave, he is not liable to punishment unless the slave dies within twenty-four hours of receiving the injury. This leniency does not apply to one who kills someone else's slave (see *Shemos* 21:21; *Rambam, Hil. Rotzei'ach* 2:12,13). [*Rambam* maintains, however, that one is exempt for mortally injuring his slave (if the slave does not succumb to his wounds until after twenty-four hours have elapsed) only if he inflicts the injury with an instrument normally used to administer discipline, such as a staff or a whip. In such a case, we assume that the owner had not intended to kill the slave, but to discipline him, and a murderer is not liable to punishment unless he assaults his victim with the specific intent of killing him (see Law 3). If he attacks him in a clearly non-disciplinary manner and kills him, he is liable even if the slave dies after twenty-four hours have passed.]

3 *Hasra'as Safek — Uncertain warning*

It was mentioned earlier (note 6) that according to *Rashi* (*Sanhedrin* 79a ד"ה והיה בה), one who strikes his fellow with intent to injure him, but kills him instead, is not liable to execution because the warning he received was an "uncertain warning" [*hasra'as safek*],

which is not legally valid. This requires further explanation, for in truth the question of whether a *hasra'as safek* is legally valid is debated by the Amoraim, R' Yochanan and Reish Lakish (see *Shavuos* 21a and *Makkos* 15b), and the halachah accords with R' Yochanan's view that such warnings are valid! (see *Rambam, Hil. Sanhedrin* 16:4).

To resolve this difficulty (and many others), see *Tiferes Yisrael* (*Sanhedrin* 9:2, *Boaz* §1) for a lengthy discussion of the many different categories of *hasra'as safek*. With respect to a case such as the one discussed here, he explains that R' Yochanan would concur in such an instance that the warning is invalid, because the intent of the attacker was to strike and injure, and therefore any warning about a possible, unintended outcome is not considered sufficient. [An example of an instance in which R' Yochanan and Reish Lakish *do* argue would be in a case where a person made an oath that he would not eat a certain loaf of bread (loaf A) *if* he eats another loaf (loaf B) as well. He then ate loaf A, followed by loaf B. Reish Lakish is of the opinion that he cannot receive *malkos* for violating his oath, since the warning he received before eating loaf A was a *hasra'as safek* (for if he never eats loaf B, loaf A is permitted to him). R' Yochanan, however, maintains that since eating loaf A is definitely the act that will become forbidden should he eat loaf B, warning him that eating loaf A will result in *malkos* if he eats loaf B is not a *hasra'as safek*. In this case, the intent of the eater to eat loaf A is clear, so R' Yochanan holds he can be warned not to do so. In our case, however, it is not at all clear that the act will even be an act of murder. See *Tiferes Yisrael* there at length for other examples and distinctions.]

SITUATIONS IN HALACHAH

Question:
Is suicide equivalent to an act of murder?

Answer:
The Gemara (*Bava Kamma* 91b) expounds the verse (*Bereishis* 9:5): *However, your blood, of your souls, I shall seek [to avenge]*. R' Elazar interprets this to mean: "From the hand of your souls [yourselves], I will seek your blood." The clear implication is that he who spills his own blood is viewed as a murderer.

Opinions diverge, however, on exactly how to classify the prohibition against suicide.

Beis Meir (*Yoreh Deah* 215:5) contends that once the Torah has branded a person who kills himself as a murderer, he is regarded as a murderer in every way, and he has violated the prohibition of *Lo Sirtzach* (see also *R' Y. F. Perla* on *R' Saadyah Gaon, Lo Saaseh* §59). In support of this approach, some authorities cite a Medrash (*Pesikta Rabbasi* §24) which teaches that the words לא תרצח, *You shall not kill,* should also be expounded as if they read לא תתרצח, "You shall not cause yourself to be killed," implying that to kill oneself is included in the commandment. *Chovos HaLevavos* (*Sha'ar HaBitachon* §4; see also *Chasam Sofer* to *Parashas Vayeitzei*) goes further, saying that killing oneself is *worse* than killing another person, because the act of suicide entails a treacherous abuse of the charge [one's life] entrusted to a person by God, and one who commits suicide has thereby forfeited his share in the World to Come (see also *Medrash Tehillim* §124).

Minchas Chinuch §34, however, maintains that while suicide is certainly an egregious sin, it cannot be seen as a violation of *Lo Sirtzach,* because that commandment applies only when the murderous act involves a crime against *another* person, whereas killing oneself is a sin against God. Suicide

is therefore a violation not of *Lo Sirtzach,* but of the separate prohibition derived, as mentioned above, from the verse, *However, your blood ... I shall seek.* [This prohibition is similar in nature to the law forbidding one to injure himself (see *mitzvah* #595).]

Rambam (*Hil. Rotzeach* 2:2) writes with respect to suicide: "One who kills himself has committed murder and is subject to Divine retribution, but he is not executed by *Beis Din.*" *Klei Chemdah* (*Bereishis* 9:5) wonders how it is appropriate to state about a person who has committed suicide (and hence is already dead) that "he is not executed by *Beis Din.*" *Minchas Chinuch* (ibid.) explains that *Rambam,* by adding these words, means to allude to a case where the culprit damaged someone's property at the very moment that he was killing himself. Now, there is a law that when someone damages another's property at the same time that he incurred the penalty of execution by *Beis Din,* he is not required to pay the money (קם ליה בדרבה מיניה). Accordingly, *Rambam* means to highlight the fact that the death penalty for someone guilty of suicide is administered by Heaven, not *Beis Din,* so the above rule does not apply, and his heirs must compensate the owner of the damaged goods. In any case, *Rambam's* words definitely indicate that one who commits suicide is not quite the same as a murderer. [For further discussion of *Rambam's* comments, see *Minchas Chinuch* (ibid.), *Klei Chemdah* (ibid.), and *Avi Ezri, Hil. Dei'os* §3.]

Additional proof that there is a distinction between suicide and murder is found in the words of the *Me'iri* (to *Bava Kamma* 91b) who writes that the prohibition against causing injury to oneself is also derived from the verse, *However your blood ... I shall seek.* This implies that suicide and self-injury are in the same category, both deriving from the same concept — that a person's body is not his property, and he may not handle it however he wishes. In *Meiri's* view, just as one who maims himself is surely not guilty of murder, neither, apparently, is one who commits suicide.

In another matter discussed by the *poskim,* there

are those (see *Teshuvos Shevus Yaakov* III:10 and *Radak* to *Shmuel* I 31:4) who suggest the novel idea that it is perhaps permitted to commit suicide to avoid being subjected to intense suffering. They cite as evidence the example of Shaul HaMelech, who was fighting a losing battle against the Plishtim. Shaul had good reason to suspect that, if captured, he would be abused by the victors, so he threw himself on his sword, fatally wounding himself (*Shmuel* ibid.). However, the commentators point out that this ruling can be true only if one follows the view that suicide is not classified as murder. If suicide has the status of an ordinary prohibition, it is possible that an allowance is made in order to escape great suffering, just as it is permitted to wound oneself for medical reasons (see, for example, *Minchas Chinuch* 48:5). But according to those who maintain that suicide is no different from murder, there can be no concession at all, for murder is one of the three sins which are not waived even to save one's life. [See *Teshuvos Chasam Sofer, Even HaEzer* §69 and *Yoreh Deah* §326, who concludes that *all* opinions agree that one should not take his own life in such a case, because the avoidance of suffering is, in fact, not sufficient reason to allow one to transgress the prohibition involved. And no proof can be brought from Shaul, who was worried that he would be coerced into sin (see *Gittin* 57b for a similar incident).]

[An intriguing inquiry related to our subject: Is someone who is about to kill himself classified as a *rodef* [a person in pursuit of another's life], who may be killed by any bystander? See *Nodah BiYehudah* (*Mahadura Tinyana, Choshen Mishpat* §60), who raises the question whether the permit to kill a *rodef* is merely a means to save the victim's life, or it is actually a variation of the death penalty prescribed for a murderer. In our case, killing the culprit would obviously do nothing to save his life, but as a penalty it may be appropriate, provided that committing suicide carries the same punishment as murder itself.]

ILLUMINATIONS OF THE MITZVAH
Suggested Reasons & Insights

I. MURDER: THE ULTIMATE CRIME AGAINST ONE'S FELLOW MAN

he Ten Commandments are arranged on the *luchos* (Tablets) in two groups: The first *luach* contained the five commandments focusing on man's relationship with God, and the second tablet contains the remaining five, governing man's relationship with his fellow man. At the head of the first group is the fundamental commandment, *I am Hashem, your God, Who took you out of the land of Mitzrayim...* And directly across, atop the second *luach,* appears the admonition, *You shall not kill.* Just as denying His existence is the ultimate sin against God, murder is correspondingly the ultimate offense against one's fellow man (*Akeidas Yitzchak* §45).

No sin is as grievous as murder (*Moreh Nevuchim III:*41), for it deprives the victim of the most precious commodity he has in this world ... his life (*RM"D Vali, Shemos* §20, לא תרצח). A person guilty of this crime is labeled a *rasha* (wicked person), and no amount of *mitzvos* accumulated in a lifetime can offset this sin and shield him from justice (*Rambam, Hil. Rotzei'ach* 4:9).

II. MURDER: DEATH OF THE PHYSICAL; DEVASTATION OF THE SOUL

he gravity of the crime a killer commits against his victim lies not merely in the fact that he has taken his physical life, but also in that he has cut short his spiritual development. A soul is placed in a body, after all, for no other reason than to achieve its ultimate purpose through the fulfillment of Torah and *mitzvos*, and by refraining from forbidden activities. In the process, one sanctifies his physical existence, and the body — as well as the soul

— becomes purified. The killer, by severing the soul from the body, aborts this process, and thereby robs the victim of his life's purpose (see *R' Saadiah Gaon, Emunos V'Dei'os* 3:2).

The tragic result is that the soul remains unperfected (*Ibn Ezra, Bereishis* 9:6, alternative approach). It is thus prevented, in the World of Souls, from retiring in peace to its rightful place in the צרור החיים, the "bond of life" (*Derech Pikudechah, Lo Saaseh* §34, *Cheilek HaMachshavah* §2). Since through the act of murder the soul is wounded, as well as the body, the killer is described as a שופך דמים, a "spiller of *bloods*," for there are *two* casualties: the body and the soul (ibid.).

There is more. When the killer abruptly brings a person's life to an end, the damage is not limited to the victim's own existence. The murderer is equally accountable for all the potential descendants who would have issued from the deceased had he survived (see *Rashi, Bereishis* 4,10). With his one evil act, he snuffs out the incalculable achievements that could have resulted from the efforts of all those people, and the world itself is left deprived of the perfection those activities might have accomplished.

"He who kills a man destroys all that he could have contributed to the physical world in the service of God. Hence, our Sages say (*Sanhedrin* 37a): Man was created singly, in order to teach that he who kills a man destroys a whole world" (*R' Samson R. Hirsch, Chorev* ch. 45).

III. MURDER: A THREAT TO CIVILIZATION

side from the enormous harm caused to the victim and his progeny, the act of murder is destructive to society (*Rambam, Hil. Rotzei'ach* 4:9). Man, by his nature, has little choice but to share his world with other people, for their mutual cooperation is the key to survival. But a community can only be viable under the rule of law, where the respect for others' lives and rights is observed and enforced. The act of murder breaches the boundaries of moral conduct, undermines the social order, and places the very underpinnings of human society into disarray (*Sefer HaIkkarim* 1:5. See also *Sefer HaBris II*, 13:13).

Moreover, God's intention in creating the world was that it be populated and settled. Upon creating man, He commanded him to reproduce and multiply, in order to fill the earth and civilize it. Those engaging in murder actively negate the Divine purpose by reducing the number of people inhabiting the world (*Chinuch* §34; *Rabbeinu Bachya*, *Shemos* 20:14; *Eileh HaMitzvos* §34, *Lo Saaseh* §20).

IV. MURDER: A STRIKE AGAINST A SERVANT OF GOD

n addition to bringing devastation to the world at large, the murderer, if he kills a Jew, also minimizes the glory of the Creator. The Jewish nation was conceived to serve God and to spread His glory, as it says (*Yeshayah* 43:21), *This people I formed for My sake; they will relate My praise*. By commanding *You shall not kill*, in effect, God was saying, "Take care not to destroy My handiwork by spilling human blood; I have created him for My honor and to offer thanksgiving to Me" (*Ramban*, *Shemos* 20:13). The murderer removes a servant from the effort to fulfill the will of the King, prevents him from producing future generations for the same purpose, and has thus diminished the honor of the Creator (*Derech Pikudecha, Lo Saaseh* §34, *Cheilek HaMachshavah* §2).

[Although God surely has an abundance of other servants attending His will, the absence of even a single person is noticed all the same, for each individual has a specially defined role in the service of God, which cannot be filled by any other person. *In an abundance of people lies the honor of the King* (*Mishlei* 14:28), for a great number of individual Jews is needed to make God's Divinity known throughout all the worlds. By removing the element of Divine revelation that was to have been brought about by that particular person, a murderer diminishes the Divine image [see the following segment] (*Likutei Halachos, Pesach* 9:28; see there further).]

V. MURDER: AN ASSAULT, AS IT WERE, AGAINST GOD HIMSELF

n addition to harming a servant of God and the world He created, the act of murder is a direct affront to the honor of God. Man was fashioned, as it were, in the image of his Creator (see *Rashi, Devarim* 21:23). To attack a human being, then, is to assail a likeness of God Himself.

The Medrash draws an analogy to a human king who had statues and portraits of himself displayed throughout his kingdom, and minted coins bearing his image. With the passage of time, the paintings were defaced, the statues broken, and the currency cancelled, thus diminishing the exposure of the king. In the same way, one who spills a person's blood is viewed by the Torah as having diminished the image [revelation] of the King of kings (*Mechilta, Shemos* §8. See also *Shemos Rabbah* 30:16; *Kli Yakar, Shemos* 20:13).

[To be sure, it is a fundamental tenet of Judaism that God has no body nor physical image; still, the human body deemed a reflection of the Divine image, for the parts of the body and their characteristics reflect different aspects of God's ways in dealing with the world (*Ramchal, K'lach Pischei Chochmah, Pesach 32*). This touches upon "a profound [kabbalistic] secret of the human form, a likeness of which is etched into God's Throne of Glory" (*Toras HaMinchah, Shemos* 20:13).

This concept is discussed by the *Zohar* (II 75:2): "God arranged in the human being representations of the Heavenly worlds and their secrets, along with representations associated with the lower world. All these are engraved in the human being, who stands in the image of God." (For further explanation, see *Sefer Pischei She'arim, Nesiv Igulim V'Yosher, Pesach* §1. See also *Tomer Devorah* §1, who notes that the fact that all the ways of God are represented in the human body — as an expression of the verse, *From my flesh I behold God* (*Iyov* 19:26) — is designed to teach us that just as God acts with the Thirteen Attributes of Mercy, so too "should these thirteen attributes be found in human behavior.") It is for this reason that one who causes a person's face to turn pale (by shaming him) in public is considered as if he committed murder (*Bava Metzia* 58b), for by causing the blood to drain from a face which bears the reflection of God, the offender has blemished that Divine image (*Alshich, Bereishis* 9:7. See also *Nesivos Olam, Nesiv Ahavas Ha'reia* §1).]

Murder is so grievous an offense against Heaven, that one who kills is considered to have repudiated God's existence and blasphemed Him (*Toras HaMinchah, Shemos* 20:14). This, then, can be another reason (see the beginning of this section) why the commandment, *You shall not kill,* the first of those on the second *luach,* was placed directly opposite the first commandment on the first *luach, I am Hashem your God,* — by which we are enjoined to acknowledge God's existence — because to violate the one is to contradict the other (*Toras HaMinchah* ibid.; cf. *Likutei Halachos, Pesach* 9:28. See also *Kli Yakar* (20:13), who uses this concept to explain why the forgiveness of the victim cannot absolve the killer, and why suicide is also deemed an act of murder: "It is unforgivable, for the victim represented an aspect of God's essence, and who has the authority to forgive Heaven's share?").

THROUGH THE EYES OF THE SAGES
Stories, Parables & Reflections

I. MURDER: THE SEVERITY OF THE SIN

～∞ *One blow; four victims*

man (אדם) *guilty of bloodshed will flee until the grave* (*Mishlei* 28:17). The letter *daled* in the word אדם ("man") is written here reduced in size, for the numerical value of the *daled* is four, and there are four parties who are, in effect, killed by an act of murder: the victim, his wife, his sons, and his daughters (*Alfa Beisa D'Rabbi Akiva* §4).

——— ৭৫ ———

～∞ *Future generations*

Capital offenses are unlike monetary crimes. In monetary crimes, the transgressor can make restitution and gain atonement. But when a murder is committed, the perpetrator bears responsibility for the blood of the victim and that of all his descendants until the end of time. This concept is found in connection with Kayin, who killed his brother Hevel. There it is said (*Bereishis* 4:10), *The voice of the* **bloods** *of your brother are crying out.* The plural form is used to include the blood of his seed (*Mishnah, Sanhedrin* 37a; *Avos D'Rabbi Nassan* 31:2; cf. *Bereishis Rabbah* 22:9; *Medrash Aggadah, Bereishis* 4:9).

——— ৭৫ ———

～∞ *One complete world*

Man was created singly for this reason: To teach that he who takes the life of one soul destroys a whole world, and he who saves the life of one soul preserves a whole world (Mishnah, *Sanhedrin* ibid.; *Avos D'Rabbi Nassan* ibid.; *Medrash Mishlei* 1:10).

——— ৭৫ ———

～∞ *Six and Seven*

The *following six God abhors, and seven are the abomination of His soul.* The six that God abhors are: ...Hands that have spilled innocent blood ... The following seven are the abomination of His soul: ... The act of murder... (*Medrash Mishlei* 6:16).

——— ৭৫ ———

～∞ *Elusive atonement*

Adam was commanded regarding six things: Idol worship, blasphemy, the preservation of justice, murder, illicit relations, and theft. For all of these prohibitions forgiveness can be attained (through repentance alone, without the atonement afforded by death), with the lone exception of murder, as has been established by the verse (*Bereishis* 9:6), *He who spills the blood of a man shall have his own blood spilled by man* (*Devarim Rabbah* 2:25).

——— ৭৫ ———

～∞ *Provoking the Satan*

When a human being dies, the soul generally departs by the hand of the Angel of Death. One may be inclined to believe that the soul of a murder victim is also removed by the Angel of Death. But that is not the case! The killer contrives to release the soul before the Angel of Death receives authority over the victim, thus cheating the angel out of what is rightfully his. As if it is not enough that the Angel of Death, who is also the Satan, is ever ready to denounce the world's people, this provocation will now cause his attacks to intensify. This yields an understanding of the verse (*Bamidbar* 35:33), *The land will not have atonement for the blood that was spilled in it, except through the blood of the one who spilled it.* This means that "the land," that is, the world at large, which is bound to suffer from the Satan's heightened hostility, cannot have relief except through the blood of the murderer who provoked his ire (*Zohar, Bereishis* 114a).

II. PERSONAL PUNISHMENTS

✑ This world and the next

or the following sins, one suffers the consequences in this world, while the principle punishment is reserved for the World to Come: ... Murder ... (*Yerushalmi, Pe'ah* 1:1, see there for Scriptural sources; *Tosefta,* ibid. 1:2; *Avos D'Rabbi Nassan* 40:1; cf. *Medrash Mishlei* 1:10).

———— ✑ ————

✑ Bubbling blood

It once happened that a man killed his brother. What did their mother do? She filled a cup with the blood of the victim, and placed it in a cabinet. Each day she would enter and find the blood seething. One time she checked and found it at rest, and she knew that her [surviving] son had been killed, in fulfillment of the verse (ibid.): *He who spills the blood of a man, shall have his own blood spilled by man* (*Devarim Rabbah* 2:25; cf. *Pesikta Rabbasi* §24).

———— ✑ ————

✑ Tzaraas

The afflictions of *tzaraas* come on account of the following seven sins: ...Murder, as it is written (*Shmuel* II, 3:29), *May there never cease from the house of Yoav* (who assassinated Avner) *contaminated men, lepers* ... (*Arachin* 16a; see also *Bamidbar Rabbah* (7:5), where the precedent given is that of Kayin, who upon killing his brother, was stricken with *tzaraas*).

———— ✑ ————

✑ Kill and be killed

Why are the two passages of *Shema* recited daily? R' Levi explains: Because they contain allusions to the Ten Commandments ... As for the commandment *You shall not kill*, it is implied by the phrase (*Devarim* 11:17), *And you will rapidly vanish,* for one who kills is bound to be killed himself (*Yerushalmi, Berachos* 1:5; *Medrash Aggadah, Devarim* 5:11. Other sources indicate that a murderer

does not necessarily meet with this fate; it is possible that the punishment will be deferred for the World to Come. See *Bereishis Rabbah* 34:14 and *Devarim Rabbah* 2:25).

———— ✑ ————

✑ Measure for measure

Hillel saw a skull floating in the water. [He recognized it as belonging to a known killer, who had been decapitated by other bandits like him.] He said to it, "Because you drowned others, they drowned you; and those who drowned you will be drowned themselves in the end (*Avos* 2:6; *Succah* 53a with *Rashi* there).

———— ✑ ————

✑ Vengeful vermin

In reference to the decapitated calf (עגלה ערפה) — the procedure observed upon the discovery of a corpse in the field that was the victim of an unwitnessed murder — the verse states (*Devarim* 21:8): *The blood shall thus be atoned for.* How so? The dead calf would become infested with worms. The worms would then find their way to the house of the person who had committed the crime, where they would attack and kill him (*Medrash Aggadah, Devarim* 21:8).

———— ✑ ————

✑ Redress at an inn

R' Shimon ben Lakish prefaced his discourse on the topic of murder with the following verse (*Shemos* 21:13), *One who did not lay in ambush, but God arranged for [the murder] to come to his hand...* Why would God do this? The verse refers to a scenario where two different people had each committed an unwitnessed homicide. One acted with forethought (a capital offense) and the second did not (but incurred the penalty of exile); neither one was brought to justice. So God draws the two to one inn, where the murderer sits at the foot of a ladder. The man guilty of unintentional killing climbs down from the top of the ladder and loses his footing. As witnesses look on, he falls off the ladder, fatally crushing the fellow below, who thus belatedly receives the execution he deserved. The witnesses bring the accidental killer to court, and he is sent off to the exile he had long been deserved. King David had this scenario in mind when he stated (*Shmuel* I, 24:13): *As the ancient proverb* (the Torah) *says, From the wicked flows wickedness* (*Makkos* 10b; *Pesikta Zutrasa, Shemos* 21:13).

———— ❧ ————

❧ *Avenged by a snake*

R' Shimon ben Shetach related: May I be deprived of witnessing the consolation of Yerushalayim if I did not truly once see a person pursuing his fellow into an abandoned building. I quickly followed him in and found a sword in his hand; it was dripping with blood as the victim writhed [in the throes of death]. I said to the perpetrator, "Wicked one! Who killed this man? It could only have been me or you! But there is nothing I can do, for the Torah prescribes (*Devarim* 17:6), *Only through the testimony of two or three witnesses shall the accused be put to death.* Rather, God Himself will settle with you." The Sages said: They had not yet left the premises when a snake appeared and bit the murderer; the bite proved fatal (*Shevuos* 34a; *Sanhedrin* 37b; *Tosefta, Sanhedrin* 8b; *Yerushalmi, Sanhedrin* 4:9; *Mechilta, Mishpatim* §20; *Medrash Tannaim, Devarim* 17:6).

III. COMMUNAL CONSEQUENCES

❧ *Famine*

s a result of four sins the rains are withheld: [One of them is] the sin of murder (*Yerushalmi, Ta'anis* 3:3; *Yerushalmi, Kiddushin* 4:1; *Sanhedrin* 6:7. Cf. *Medrash Shmuel* 28:5).

———— ❧ ————

❧ *The sword*

On account of murder, the world is visited upon by the [ravaging] sword (*Medrash Aseres HaDibros, Dibbur Shishi*).

————

You shall not kill (*Shemos* 20:13) If you would have upheld this commandment, you would have also beheld the fulfillment of this verse: *The sword will not pass through your land* (*Vayikra* 26:6). But since you have transgressed this commandment, a different verse will come to fruition (ibid. v. 33): *I will unsheathe the sword after you* (*Tanna D'vei Eliyahu Rabbah* 26:8).

———— ❧ ————

❧ *Worldwide destruction*

Because of eight misdeeds the world is subject to destruction: [One of them is] the spilling of blood ... The earlier generations (i.e. the Generation of Dispersion (דור הפלגה, the residents of Sodom, the generations of Pharaoh, Sancheiriv, and Nevuchadnezzar) were uprooted from the world for these eight very sins (ibid. 15:6).

———— ❧ ————

❧ *The Divine Presence*

The act of murder contaminates the land and the Divine Presence withdraws from Israel (*Yoma* 85a; *Mechilta, Ki Sisa; Bamidbar Rabbah* 7:10; cf. *Yalkut Shimoni, Devarim* §933 ד"ה כי תצא).

———— ❧ ————

❧ *The Temple's destruction*

Murder caused the Temple to be destroyed, and the Divine Presence to withdraw from Israel, for it is said (*Bamidbar* 35:34), *You shall not contaminate the land in which you live, and in the midst of which I dwell.* The message implied is that if you *do* contaminate the land in which you live, you will not live in it for long, nor will I dwell there (*Shabbos* 33a; *Toseftsa, Yoma* 1:10; *Tosefta, Shevuos* 1:3; *Bamidbar Rabbah* 7:10).

————

The First Temple was destroyed on account of three sins that were prevalent then: Idolatry, immorality, and murder ... They were guilty of murder, as is evident from this verse (*Melachim* II,

21:16): *Menasheh also shed much innocent blood, until he filled Yerushalayim from end to end [with blood]* [The preceding verses warn of the impending destruction of Yerushalayim.] (*Yoma* 9b; *Tosefta, Menachos* 13:4; *Yerushalmi, Yoma* 1:1, *Medrash Seichel Tov, Bereishis* §44; *Bamidbar Rabbah* 7:10).

───── ॐ ─────

ॐ *Exile*

Exile comes to the world because of ... murder... (*Avos* 5:9; cf. *Avos D'Rabbi Nassan* 38:4 according to the emendations of the *Gra; Bamidbar Rabbah* 7:10; *Yalkut Shimoni, Yeshaya* §443).

IV. ACTS OF MURDER IN THE ANNALS OF TANACH

A. *Kayin and Hevel*

nd Adam knew his wife Chavah, and she conceived and gave birth to Kayin, saying, 'I have acquired a man with God.' And she gave birth again, to his brother Hevel. Hevel became a shepherd, while Kayin became a worker of the soil. At the end of a period of time, Kayin brought, as an offering to God, some of the produce of the ground. Hevel as well brought some of the firstlings of his flock and from the choicest among them. God paid heed to Hevel and his offering, but to Kayin and his offering He paid no heed. Kayin was angered and his countenance fell ... Kayin conversed with his brother Hevel, and at a time that they happened to be in the field, Kayin rose up against Hevel his brother and killed him.* (*Bereishis* 4:1-8).

───── ॐ ─────

ॐ *How Kayin killed Hevel*

God said [to Kayin], *The voice of the **bloods** of your brother cries out to Me from the ground.* Rav Yehudah, son of R' Chiya, taught: The plural form teaches that Kayin inflicted a great many wounds on Hevel his brother. He did not know which wound would prove fatal, until he reached Hevel's neck (*Sanhedrin* 37b; *Tanchuma, Bereishis* §9; *Pesikta Zutrasa, Bereishis* 4:10; *Medrash Aggadah, Bereishis* 4:9).

───── ॐ ─────

ॐ *A club*

Rabban Shimon ben Gamliel taught: He killed him with a stick. For Lemech (who unintentionally killed Kayin) said to his wives (*Bereishis* 4:23), *Have I killed a man with a wound, a child with a **bruise** [with malicious intent, something Kayin once did to his brother Hevel]?* This indicates that Kayin used a stick, which tends to cause bruising (*Bereishis Rabbah* 22:8).

───── ॐ ─────

ॐ *A stone*

The Sages maintained that it was with a stone that he killed him, for Lemech had said, *Have I killed a man by my wound?* The weapon used was thus something that is apt to inflict open wounds (ibid.).

───── ॐ ─────

ॐ *Slaughter*

R' Yitzchak taught: Kayin took note of the way his father slaughtered the ox he sacrificed as an offering to God (cf. *Tehillim* 69:32 and *Shabbos* 28b; *Avodah Zarah* 8a; *Chullin* 60a). In like manner, he went and killed Hevel, cutting the two pipes in his neck (ibid.).

───── ॐ ─────

ॐ *A stone to the forehead*

Kayin took a stone and plunged it into Hevel's forehead (*Pirkei D'Rabbi Eliezer* §21; (see there, and *Biur HaRadal*, for the Scriptural source); *Targum Yonasan, Bereishis* 4:8).

───── ॐ ─────

ॐ *An iron rod*

And *Kayin rose up to* (אל) *Hevel.* The word אל is cognate to אלה (an iron staff with a rounded end — *Aruch, Erech Allah*). This, then, is the weapon that Kayin used against Hevel (*Pesikta Zutrasa, Bereishis* 4:8).

———— ৶৵ ————

 Bare teeth

R' Yitzchak taught: When Kayin set out to kill Hevel, he did not know how to cause his soul to depart. So he bit him with his teeth like a snake, over and over, until he finally killed him (*Zohar* I, 54b; II, 231a).

———— ৶৵ ————

B. *The Generation of the Flood*

God said to Noach, *The end of all flesh has come before Me, for the earth has been filled with crime* (חמס) *through them. Behold, I shall destroy them along with the earth* (*Bereishis* 6:13).

———— ৶৵ ————

The Crime of murder

R' Levi taught: The word חמס means murder, as it is said (*Yoel* 4:19), *Because of the* חמס *of the children of Yehudah, for they shed innocent blood in their land.*

C. *The men of Sodom and Amorah*

Guilty of murder

The people of Sodom *were wicked and sinful toward God, to a great degree* (מאד). The word מאד is a reference to the crime of murder, as we find elsewhere (*Melachim II,* 21:15), *Menasheh also shed much* (מאד) *innocent blood* (*Sanhedrin* 109a; *Tosefta,* ibid. 13:9; *et al*).

———— ৶৵ ————

Wayward walls

Until when will you plot treacherously against man? You all slay [others], like a leaning wall, a toppled fence (*Tehillim* 62:4). Rava expounded this verse: The people of Sodom would set their eyes on

men of wealth, and would entice them to sit beside a tottering wall. They would then topple the wall and crush him to death; they would then loot the victim's property (*Sanhedrin* 109a; *Yalkut Shimoni, Tehillim* 782).

———— ৶৵ ————

Criminal compassion

There was a young maiden in Sodom who would conceal bread in her water jug to give to a pauper on her way to the well. Eventually, her ruse was discovered. The enraged Sodomites coated her body with honey and placed her atop the city wall. The bees swarmed all over her and she was soon stung to death. God therefore said, in His indictment of Sodom (*Bereishis* 18:20), *The outcry [against] Sodom and Amorah has become great* (רבה), for the word רבה is cognate to ריבה which means a young maiden (*Sanhedrin* 109b; *Pirkei D'Rabbi Eliezer* §25; *Medrash Sechel Tov* §19; cf. *Yalkut Shimoni, Bereishis* §83).

———— ৶৵ ————

Sodomite Justice

I will descend and see. If they have truly done as evident from her outcry, which has come to Me — *then destruction it will be!* R' Levi explained: God was saying, "Even if I would prefer to remain silent, the injustice committed against the maiden would never allow it." For it happened that two girls went out to draw water. One said to the other, "Why do you appear so very sickly today?" Her companion replied, "Our food has run out, and I am starving to death." What, then, did her friend do? She filled her jug with flour and then the two exchanged jugs. When their fellow Sodomites learned of the matter, they seized the benefactor and burned her to death. For this reason, the verse refers not to "*their* outcry" but to "*her* outcry," as an allusion to this incident (*Bereishis Rabbah* 49:6; *Medrash Seichel Tov* §19. According to *Pirkei D'Rabbi Eliezer* §25, *Yalkut Shimoni, Bereishis* §83, and *Rashi* to this verse, however, the reference in this verse is to the maiden described in the previous story).

———— ৸৶ ————

D. *The slaying of Zechariah the Prophet*

*A*fter Yehoyada [the High Priest] died, the leaders of Yehudah came and prostrated themselves before the king; the king then began to be swayed by them. They abandoned the Temple of Hashem, the God of their ancestors, worshipping instead the asherah-trees and the idols. A Divine fury was aroused against Yehudah and Yerushalayim on account of this sin. God sent prophets among them to draw them back to Him; they admonished the people, who did not take heed.

Then the spirit of God came over Zechariah, son of Yehoyada the Kohen. He stood above the people and said to them, 'Thus said God: Why are you transgressing the commandments of God? You will not succeed! You have forsaken God, so He has now forsaken you.' But the people conspired against him and, by the command of the king, stoned him with rocks in the very courtyard of the Temple of God. The king Yoash did not bring to mind the kindness that the prophet's father Yehoyada had done for him; instead, he killed his son. As he was dying, Zechariah said, God will take notice and demand redress! (Divrei HaYamim II, 24:17-23).

———— ৸৶ ————

৩ *The Medrashic account*

*Z*echariah was killed, not in the women's or Israelite sections, but in the Kohanim's section of the Temple Courtyard. What's more, the people did not treat his blood as they would the blood of a deer or gazelle, for which the Torah provides (Vayikra 17:13), [The slaughterer] shall spill its blood and cover it with earth. Rather, they shed his blood onto the stones of the Temple floor, and there it remained, seething, for two hundred and fifty two years, from the days of Yoash until the reign of Tzidkiah (the last king before the fall of Yehudah). Why was it [arranged by God that it be neglected] so? In order to arouse His wrath and to exact proper

vengeance, as the prophet stated (Yechezkel 24:7-8), [Yerushalayim's] blood was within her, on a smooth rock she placed it. She did not pour it on the ground to cover it with earth. In order to stir up My wrath, to take vengeance, I have placed her blood upon the smooth rock, that it not be covered.

[Seven crimes were committed by Israel on that day: They killed an innocent man who was (1) a Kohen; (2) a prophet; (3) a judge; (4) they contaminated the Temple Courtyard; (5) they desecrated the Name of God; (6) it was Shabbos and (7) it was Yom Kippur as well — Eichah Rabbah.]

When Nebuzaradan (the general of the Babylonian army) came to destroy Yerushalayim, God signaled to the blood to start bubbling. The Jews heaped earth over it and tried every strategy — to no avail; the blood continued to seethe and boil. God said to the blood, "The time has come for you to collect your debt." When Nebuzaradan arrived, he noticed the blood, and he inquired about it. The Jews told him, "It is the blood from the many sacrifices that were slaughtered and offered here." The general called for bulls, rams, and sheep to be slaughtered before him, but the blood did not rest. He immediately seized the men who had given this answer, and had them hung from a tree branch. He demanded, "Tell me the truth about the nature of this blood; if you do not, I will rake your flesh with iron combs." They responded, "Since it is obvious that God seeks to avenge this blood, we will tell you the truth. There was a Kohen who was also a prophet and a judge; he was relaying a prophesy about the very devastation that you are presently bringing upon us. We did not believe him, and we assailed and killed him for daring to give us rebuke."

Nebuzaradan then [endeavored to appease the blood, and] had eighty thousand youthful Kohanim brought and slaughtered over the blood, but, instead of subsiding, it rose up and spread, to the point that it reached Zechariah's grave. Nebuzaradan went on and brought the members of the Great Sanhedrin and the secondary courts to be slain over the blood, but it still did not rest. He continued his attempt with the mass slaughter of youths and maidens, even school-aged children, but to no avail. The wicked general then cried out to the blood, "What is your merit? How is your blood so much more worthy than all the rest of this blood? Do you want your entire people to be wiped out over you?" At that point, God became filled with compassion. He said, "If even this cruel, wicked man, who has come to demolish My Temple, has been moved to feel compassion for them, how much more so should I, of Whom it is written (*Shemos* 34:6), *Hashem, Hashem, a Merciful, Gracious God*, and (*Tehillim* 145:9): *God is good to all, and his compassion is for all his works.*

With that, He signaled to the blood, and it immediately seeped into the floor (*Koheles Rabbah* 3:16; *Eichah Rabbah, Pesichta* §23; *Gittin* 57b; *Yalkut Shimoni, Yechezkel* §364).

he enumeration of this mitzvah as a separate prohibition presents a difficulty: There already exists a mitzvah of לא יוסיף, *Lest he continue to hit him,* warning not to add arbitrarily to the number of *malkos* [lashes] given by *Beis Din* (*mitzvah #595*), and this is seen to include a general prohibition against causing injury, in any form, to one's fellow Jew. Why, then, should the commandment not to kill be counted separately? After all, killing is certainly a way of inflicting injury, albeit in its most serious form. And many authorities who list the 613 *mitzvos* (following the lead of *R' Saadiah Gaon*) have presented a rule that when a particular mitzvah is simply a specific aspect of another, more general mitzvah, only the more inclusive one is counted.

[This question can actually be asked on a more fundamental level. Why did the Torah find it necessary at all to specifically proscribe murder, when causing less serious injury is already forbidden?]

Various approaches have been presented in answer to this question:

A. *Some forms of murder cannot be accounted for by the prohibition against causing injury.*

The commentaries advance various scenarios that involve an act of murder covered under *Lo Sirtzach,* but would not be in violation of the mitzvah forbidding injurious assault against another person.

1. One possible example is suicide. Some Rishonim maintain that self-injury does not infringe on *Lest he continue to hit him,* because that verse applies only to striking another person (*Tur, Choshen Mishpat* §420, quoting *Ramah*). Consequently, one who commits suicide transgresses only the prohibition of *Lo Sirtzach.* The *Rambam* (*Hil. Chovel U'-Mazik* 5:1), however, is of the opinion that injuring oneself *is* included in the prohibition against injuring a fellow Jew. Accordingly, suicide would not necessitate an extra mitzvah of *You shall not kill.* [See *Bava Kamma* 91 a-b, where there is an Amoraic dispute concerning whether a person is permitted to maim himself. See also Commentary of *R' Y. F. Perla* to *Sefer HaMitzvos L'Rasag, Lo Saaseh* §47-48.)

2. Another solution cited by the commentaries involves the killing of a Canaanite slave. The master of such a slave does not violate a prohibition when striking him, but is forbidden to kill him.

B. *A separate prohibition covering murder is needed so that the mitzvah of Lest he continue to hit him does not become an admonition that involves the death penalty.*

There is a rule throughout the Torah that a prohibition that carries a possible punishment of execution by *Beis Din* cannot be a cause for corporal punishment (*Rambam, Hil. Sanhedrin* 18:2). Even if the prohibition comprises two different acts, one that carries the liability to the death penalty, and another that does not, the second transgression does not incur *malkos*. That being the case, had there not been a separate mitzvah forbidding murder (which renders one liable to execution), and it was by default included in the prohibition of לא יוסיף, then that prohibition would be one capable of resulting in a penalty of death. As a consequence, the act of striking a fellow Jew would no longer be liable to *malkos*, and that was not the will of the Torah. It was therefore necessary to devote a new mitzvah to the crime of murder (*R' Y. F. Perla, Commentary* to *Sefer HaMitzvos L'Rasag, Onshin §70*).

Mitzvah 35

אָסוּר אֵשֶׁת אִישׁ

פרשת יתרו

Not to Have Illicit Relations With a Married Woman

THE MITZVAH:

אִסוּר אֵשֶׁת אִישׁ
(לֹא תַעֲשֶׂה)

NOT TO HAVE ILLICIT RELATIONS WITH A MARRIED WOMAN

מצוה **לה**

■ SOURCE ■

לֹא תִנְאָף[1]
שמות (פרשת יתרו) כ:יג

"You shall not commit adultery[2]"

■ THE MITZVAH ■

It is forbidden for a man and a married woman to engage in an adulterous relationship.[3]

■ LAWS ■

1 Once a woman has undergone the first stage of marriage, *erusin*,[4] it is considered adultery if she engages in intimate relations with someone other than her husband.[5]

2 The penalty for deliberately transgressing this prohibition is execution.[6] Depending on various factors, the form of execution for the transgression is either strangulation,[7] stoning,[8] or burning.[9]

The transgressors are executed only if they were warned beforehand that the act they intended to commit is forbidden and carries the death penalty.[10] One who transgresses unintentionally is not punished, but is obligated to

bring a *chatas* to atone for his transgression.[11]

3 A woman who commits adultery is permanently forbidden both to her husband and to the adulterer.[12]

4 This prohibition applies to both men and women, in all places and at all times.[13]

5 Adultery is forbidden to non-Jews as well, as it is one of the seven Noahide laws.[14]

6 One must allow himself to be killed rather than transgress this prohibition.[15]

7 It is forbidden to seclude oneself with someone else's wife (an act that can lead to adultery).[16]

■ A REASON ■

The bond of marriage between a husband and wife brings the Shechinah (Divine Presence) into the Jewish home. Adultery destroys this bond, causing the Shechinah to depart.

1. According to its literal meaning, the term ניאוף refers to any illicit act of intimate relations (see *Ibn Ezra* to *Shemos* 20:13). However, the Torah always uses this term in connection with illicit relations with a married woman (i.e., adultery), as in *Vayikra* 20:10 and *Yechezkel* 16:32, which use this term to describe an act of adultery. Thus, it is evident that the prohibition of לא תנאף refers specifically to an illicit relationship between a man and a married woman (*Rashi, Shemos* ibid.).

2. Like all of the Ten Commandments, the prohibition against adultery is repeated in *Devarim* ch. 5 (see verse 17 there). *Vayikra* 18:20 also forbids adultery; that verse, though, specifically refers to a *man* who engages in adultery with a married woman, and so teaches only that a *man* is forbidden to commit adultery; it does not teach, however, that the *woman* with whom he commits adultery is also guilty of a Biblical violation. That women are also forbidden to commit adultery is derived from the verses in *Shemos* and *Devarim* [which state simply that adultery is forbidden, without referring to either the man or the woman] (see *Rambam, Sefer HaMitzvos, Lo Saaseh* §347; *Smag, Lo Saaseh* §97). [As a rule, men and women are equally obligated in the Torah's negative commandments (see Mishnah, *Kiddushin* 29a). The adultery prohibition, though, is different, because the act that this prohibition forbids to a man does not apply to a woman. Thus, a separate verse is needed to teach that women are also forbidden to commit adultery (*Biurei HaMaharshal* to *Smag* ibid.).]

Some say that in addition to transgressing the negative commandments mentioned in *Shemos* and *Vayikra*, one who commits adultery

AN EXPANDED TREATMENT

also transgresses a positive commandment, derived from *Bereishis* 2:24, which states: *Therefore, a man shall take leave of his father and his mother and cling to his wife*. It can be inferred from this verse that one may "cling" only to *his* wife, but not to the wife of another (*Tosafos, Kiddushin* 13b ד"ה לכולי עלמא; as shall be seen below [note 14], this verse is the source for prohibiting a non-Jew from committing adultery). In addition, by committing adultery, a generally secretive act which strikes a blow at the bond between husband and wife, one renders himself liable to the curse stated in *Devarim* 27:24: *Accursed is one who strikes his fellow in secret* (*Pesikta Zutrasa* to that verse).

3. This prohibition forbids cohabitation between a married woman and any man other than her husband. The Gemara derives from Scripture that all acts of cohabitation are forbidden (see further, Mishnah, *Yevamos* 53b and Gemara there; see also *Rambam, Hil. Issurei Biah* 1:10). Even an incomplete act of cohabitation (known as העראה) is sufficient to violate the prohibition; for further details of this law, see *Yevamos* 55b-56a and *Rambam* ibid. 1:10-11; see also *Shevuos* 18a.

4. The bond of marriage is established in two stages: the initial stage, *erusin* [also known as *kiddushin*] (see *Rambam, Hil. Ishus* 1:1-2); and the second stage, *nisuin* (see *Rambam* ibid. 10:1). [A woman who has undergone *erusin* is known as an *arusah*; one who has also undergone *nisuin* is known as a *nesuah*.] Most of the laws that apply between a husband and wife take effect upon *erusin*. Certain laws, however, do not take effect until *nisuin* is performed (ibid.). With regard to adultery, *erusin* alone causes the prohibition to take effect.

5. See *Rambam, Hil. Ishus* 1:3. In several places, the Torah discusses the penalty for an *arusah* who has relations with someone other than her husband (see *Devarim* 22:13-21, 23-25). [Indeed, in certain cases the penalty for committing adultery with an *arusah* is more severe than the punishment for committing adultery with a *nesuah* (see below, note 8).] Clearly, with respect to the prohibition against adultery, an *arusah* is considered a married woman.

If one attempts to betroth a married woman with *kiddushin*, his act is meaningless; *kiddushin* cannot take effect upon a married woman.

6. As the verse (*Vayikra* 20:10) states: *A man who will commit adultery with [another] man's wife, who will commit adultery with his fellow's wife; the adulterer and the adulteress shall be put to death*. In addition, *Devarim* 22:22 states: *If a man will be found lying with a woman who is married to a husband, then both of them shall die, the man who lay with the woman and the woman, and you shall remove the evil from Israel*.

One case in which the death penalty does *not* apply for adultery is that of a married *shifchah charufah* [שפחה חרופה], a partially freed Canaanite maidservant (i.e. she was owned by two partners, one of whom freed her) who underwent *erusin*. Since *kiddushin* cannot take effect upon a Canaanite maidservant, this *erusin* is only legally effective upon the half of her that was freed. It does suffice, though, to forbid her to have relations with anyone besides her husband (see *Teshuvos Tzafnas Pane'ach*, I:2). Nevertheless, if one commits adultery with her, neither he nor she is liable to death (see *Vayikra* 19:20). Instead, the adulterer must bring an *asham*, a special sacrificial

offering, (ibid. v. 21). The adulteress incurs *malkos*, lashes (see *Kereisos* 11a; see further, *mitzvah* #129).

There is also no death penalty for committing adultery with the wife of a minor. This is derived from *Vayikra* 20:10, which states: *A man who will commit adultery with [another] man's wife … the adulterer and the adulteress shall be put to death*. The term *man* implies an adult male. Thus, the verse indicates that one is only liable for committing adultery with the wife of an adult, but not with a *minor's* wife (*Kiddushin* 19a).

[Under normal circumstances, it is not possible for a minor to have a wife, for a minor does not have the legal maturity needed to effect *erusin* or any other legal transaction. A minor *can* acquire a wife, however, through the mechanism of *yibum*. The Torah provides that if a husband dies childless, his brother should marry his widow. This marriage, which can be effected only with an act of cohabitation, is called *yibum* (see *mitzvah* #598). Even the *yibum* of a minor as young as nine years old is effective (see Mishnah, *Niddah* 45a). It is to this circumstance that the verse refers when it teaches that the death penalty does not apply to adultery committed with the wife of a minor (*Kiddushin* ibid.). Although the minor's *yibum* is fully effective, and he thus acquired his sister-in-law as a wife thereby, if she then commits adultery, neither the adulterer nor the adulteress is liable to death (see *Rashi* there ד"ה דמדאורייתא; *Raavad*, cited by *Rashba* there ד"ה מהו דתימא; *Ramban, Yevamos* 96b).

[Many Rishonim disagree with this view, and maintain that a minor cannot acquire a wife on the Biblical level even through *yibum*. In their opinion, a minor's *yibum* is effective only on the Rabbinic level, but not on

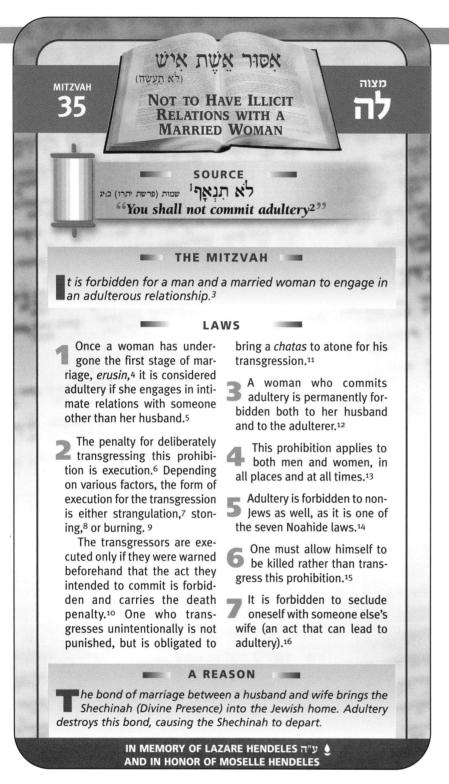

the Biblical level necessary for the Biblical punishments for adultery to apply. Indeed, these Rishonim cite *Vayikra* 20:10 as the source for the law that a minor's *yibum* is ineffective. They interpret the verse as teaching that one is not liable for committing adultery with the wife of

a minor who performed *yibum,* because she is not considered legally married to him (*Tosafos, Kiddushin* ibid. ד"ה ומדאורייתא; *Rashba* ibid.).]

7. This form of execution is performed by wrapping a scarf around the neck of the condemned. One person pulls

one end of the scarf and another person pulls the other end until the condemned is strangled to death. See Mishnah, *Sanhedrin* 52b for further details.

With the exception of those cases of adultery for which the Torah specifically prescribes a different form of capital punishment (see below, notes 8 and 9), strangulation is the standard form of execution the Torah mandates for adultery. This is derived from *Vayikra* 20:10, which states: *A man who will commit adultery with [another] man's wife … the adulterer and the adulteress shall be put to death.* The verse mandates the death penalty for adultery without specifying a particular form of execution. Therefore, we must interpret the verse as referring to the most lenient form of execution. Of the four types of capital punishment (stoning, burning, beheading, and strangulation), strangulation is considered the most lenient method (*Sanhedrin* 52b). [Some Tannaim maintain, however, that *beheading* is the most lenient form of execution (see Mishnah, *Sanhedrin* 49b with *Rashi* ד"ה סקילה). According to these Tannaim, we derive from Scripture that whenever the Torah mandates execution without indicating which method should be used, the intended method is strangulation (see further, *Sanhedrin* ibid.; see also *Rambam, Hil. Sanhedrin* 14:1).]

8. This form of capital punishment consists of pushing the condemned off an elevation twice the height of the average-sized man (six *amos* [cubits], approximately ten feet). If the fall itself does not kill the condemned, he is pelted with stones until he dies. For a detailed description of the procedure for stoning, see Mishnah and Gemara, *Sanhedrin* 45a-b.

If one commits adultery with a *naarah* (a woman who attained adulthood within the past six months) who has undergone *erusin* but not *nisuin* [such a woman is known as a *naarah hameorasah*, נערה המאורסה], both adulterer and adulteress are subject to execution by stoning. Although the punishment for adultery is normally strangulation (see previous note), the Torah makes an exception in the case of a *naarah hameorasah*, and mandates this more severe form of execution. As *Devarim* 22:21, which refers to an adulterous *naarah hame'orasah*, states: *And they shall take the naarah to the entrance of her father's house, and the people of her city shall pelt her with stones and she shall die.* Similarly, vs. 23-24 state: *If there will be a virgin naarah who has undergone erusin with a man, and a [different] man finds her in the city and lies with her; then you shall take them both out to the gate of that city and pelt them with stones and they shall die.* This exceptional form of execution applies only to the specific case of adultery with a *naarah* who is an *arusah*. If one commits adultery with a *naarah* who is a *nesuah*, or with an *arusah* who is a *bogeres* (a woman who attained adulthood more than six months previously), the regular punishment of strangulation applies. See further, *Iyunim* §1, for circumstances in which even adultery with a *naarah hameorasah* is punished with strangulation.

According to the view of the Sages in *Sanhedrin* 66b, one who commits adultery with an *arusah* who is a minor is liable to stoning, just like one who committed adultery with an *arusah* who is a *naarah*. The Tanna R' Meir disagrees, arguing that adultery with a minor is treated no differently than adultery with a *bogeres*, for which the penalty is strangulation even if she is only an *arusah*. The halachah is in accordance with the Sages, who state that the adulterer is executed by stoning (see *Rambam, Hil. Issurei Biah* 3:5).

[The *adulteress*, however, is not punished at all, for minors are not held responsible for their transgressions (see Mishnah, *Kereisos* 11a).]

9. This method of execution is performed by pouring molten lead down the throat of the condemned (see Mishnah and Gemara, *Sanhedrin* 52a for details).

The penalty of burning applies specifically to a Kohen's daughter who commits adultery, as the verse (*Vayikra* 21:9) states: *If the daughter of a Kohen will be desecrated through illicit relations … she shall be consumed by the fire.* Through Biblical exegesis, the Gemara (*Sanhedrin* 50b) derives that the act of "illicit relations" to which the verse refers is adultery.

Only the adulteress is executed by burning. The adulterer is subject to the same form of capital punishment to which he would be subject if the adulteress was not the daughter of a Kohen (*Sanhedrin* 51a); either stoning (if the adulteress is a *naarah hameorasah* — see previous note) or strangulation (in all other cases; see above, note 7). See further, *Iyunim* §2, for circumstances in which the adulterous daughter of a Kohen is not executed by burning.

10. See Baraisa cited in *Sanhedrin* 80b. According to the Tanna R' Yehudah cited there, the transgressor must be warned of the specific method of execution to which he will be subject for committing the sin. The halachah, however, is in accordance with the Sages, who maintain that it suffices if he is warned that the transgression carries the death penalty (see *Rambam, Hil. Sanhedrin* 12:2).

Some maintain that the warning must make mention of the Scriptural verse which forbids the action the transgressor is about to commit (see *Rashi, Shevuos* 20b ד"ה ואזהרתיה; see further, *Minchas Chinuch* 32:2 ד"ה והנה). In the case of adultery, a reference to

either of the two verses that forbid adultery (*Shemos* 20:13, *Vayikra* 18:20; see above, note 2) suffices to meet this requirement (*Minchas Chinuch* 35:1). [Note: This is true only of the warning issued to the man. The warning issued to the woman, however, must refer to the verse in *Shemos*, because the verse in *Vayikra* does not apply to women (see above, note 2).]

If the transgression was not committed before witnesses (note that the witnesses need only testify that they saw the couple together "in the manner of adulterers" — see *Makkos* 7a and *Rambam, Hil. Issurei Biah* 1:19), or there was no proper warning, the violators are liable to *kares* — Divinely imposed premature death. See Mishnah, *Kereisos* 2a; *Rambam, Hil. Issurei Biah* 1:1. [According to the Gemara in *Moed Katan* (28a), this refers to death between the ages of fifty and sixty. *Kares* can also take the form of sudden death (at any age); even someone over sixty can be subject to this type of *kares*. According to *Yerushalmi* (*Bikkurim* 2:1), one who is liable to *kares* dies *before* the age of fifty. Some say that while some forms of *kares* involve the premature death of the transgressor, the *kares* of those who engage in the types of illicit relations listed in *Vayikra* ch. 18 refers to a *spiritual* punishment, not a physical one. The transgressor is not subject to premature death as a result of his transgression, but after death his *soul* is "cut off" from Heavenly life (*Ramban, Vayikra* 18:29).] Some Rishonim maintain that included in the punishment of *kares* is childlessness, or, if the transgressor has children, that they die prematurely (see *Rashi, Kereisos* 7a ד"ה כרת; *Rabbeinu Tam*, cited by *Tosafos, Shabbos* 25a ד"ה כרת). Others, however, contend that this is true only where the Torah specifically states that the transgressors will die without children (*Riva*, cited by

MITZVAH 35

אִסוּר אֵשֶׁת אִישׁ
(לֹא תַעֲשֶׂה)

NOT TO HAVE ILLICIT RELATIONS WITH A MARRIED WOMAN

מצוה לה

SOURCE

לֹא תִנְאָף¹ שמות (פרשת יתרו) כ:יג

"You shall not commit adultery²"

THE MITZVAH

It is forbidden for a man and a married woman to engage in an adulterous relationship.³

LAWS

1 Once a woman has undergone the first stage of marriage, *erusin*,⁴ it is considered adultery if she engages in intimate relations with someone other than her husband.⁵

2 The penalty for deliberately transgressing this prohibition is execution.⁶ Depending on various factors, the form of execution for the transgression is either strangulation,⁷ stoning,⁸ or burning. ⁹
The transgressors are executed only if they were warned beforehand that the act they intended to commit is forbidden and carries the death penalty.¹⁰ One who transgresses unintentionally is not punished, but is obligated to bring a *chatas* to atone for his transgression.¹¹

3 A woman who commits adultery is permanently forbidden both to her husband and to the adulterer.¹²

4 This prohibition applies to both men and women, in all places and at all times.¹³

5 Adultery is forbidden to non-Jews as well, as it is one of the seven Noahide laws.¹⁴

6 One must allow himself to be killed rather than transgress this prohibition.¹⁵

7 It is forbidden to seclude oneself with someone else's wife (an act that can lead to adultery).¹⁶

A REASON

The bond of marriage between a husband and wife brings the Shechinah (Divine Presence) into the Jewish home. Adultery destroys this bond, causing the Shechinah to depart.

Tosafos ibid.; see also *Ramban, Vayikra* 18:29).

At the end of the passage which lists all the forbidden relationships (*Vayikra* ch. 18), among them illicit relations with a married woman (ibid. v. 20), the Torah (v. 29) states: *For if anyone commits any of these abominations, the people doing so will be cut off from among their people.* The term "cut off" refers to the punishment of *kares*.

Some say that the verse in this passage which forbids adultery (v. 20)

refers specifically to adultery with a *nesuah*. According to this view, there is no *kares* for adultery with an *arusah* (*Maharam MiRothenburg*, cited by *Tos. HaRosh, Yevamos* 34a; see also *Teshuvos R' Chaim Or Zarua* §164). However, it is evident from *Toras Kohanim* (to *Vayikra* 4:1) that adultery with an *arusah* is indeed punishable by *kares* (see next note).

11. One who inadvertently violates any of the *kares*-bearing prohibitions must bring a *chatas* to atone for his transgression, provided the transgression involves positive action on the part of the violator. Adultery is committed with an act, so its unintentional violation requires a *chatas* (Mishnah, *Kereisos* 2a; *Rambam, Hil. Shegagos* 1:1:1-2). [See previous note for the view that there is no penalty of *kares* for adultery with an *arusah*. According to this view, there is also no requirement to bring a *chatas* if such adultery was committed unintentionally. However, *Toras Kohanim* (cited in that note) states explicitly that one who inadvertently commits adultery with an *arusah* must bring a *chatas* (from which it follows that in the view of *Toras Kohanim*, one who intentionally commits adultery with an *arusah* is subject to *kares*).]

12. Mishnah, *Sotah* 27b; see *Rambam, Hil. Sotah* 2:12. Even if the husband subsequently dies or divorces her, she may not marry the adulterer (*Yevamos* 11b, 24b). Any child that is the result of an adulterous union is a *mamzer*, and may not marry an ordinary Jew (see Mishnah, *Kiddushin* 66b and *Rambam, Hil. Issurei Biah* 15:1).

The Rishonim discuss whether a husband is *required* to divorce an adulterous wife, or whether he may choose to remain married to her [and abstain permanently from marital relations]; see *Tosafos, Zevachim* 2b ד"ה סתם אשה; *Rambam, Hil. Ishus* 24:18;

Rama, Even HaEzer 117:1 with *Beis Shmuel* §8; see also *Even HaEzer* 115:6-7 with *Chelkas Mechokeik* §23 and *Pischei Teshuvah* §37.

In Biblical times (up until the latter part of the Second Temple era — see *Sotah* 47a), a woman under legal suspicion of adultery would, in certain specific circumstances, be subjected to a special test, the drinking of the מי המרים, *bitter waters*. This test, which is described in *Bamidbar* 5:11-31 (see also *Rambam, Hil. Sotah* ch. 3), would miraculously reveal if the woman was guilty or innocent (see further, *mitzvah* #365). When the spiritual level of the Jewish nation fell from its lofty standards, however, the test ceased to be effective (see *Ramban, Bamidbar* 5:20).

13. See above, note 2, end of first paragraph.

14. The Gemara in *Sanhedrin* (56a) lists seven mitzvos that were given to non-Jews (the reference to Noahide Laws reflects the fact that all of mankind descended from Noah, whose family were the sole survivors of the Flood). They are (1) the requirement to establish a system of civil laws (see *Rambam, Hil. Melachim* 9:14); (2) a prohibition against blasphemy (euphemistically referred to as "blessing" the Name of Hashem); (3) a prohibition against idolatry; (4) a prohibition against illicit relationships (see *Sanhedrin* 57a); (5) a prohibition against murder; (6) a prohibition against theft; and (7) a prohibition against eating a limb torn from a live animal (אבר מן החי). The source of this prohibition is *Bereishis* 2:24, which states: *Therefore a man shall take leave of his father and his mother and cling to his wife*, which implies that one may not "cling" to *someone else's* wife [see above, note 2] (*Sanhedrin* 58a). This verse was stated to Adam, hence it applies to all his descendants (see *Rashi, Sanhedrin* ibid. ד"ה על כן).

15. That is, if one is threatened with death if he does not commit adultery, he must choose death. This is true not only of adultery, but of *all* illicit relations (*Sanhedrin* 74a; *Rambam, Hil. Yesodei HaTorah* 5:2; see further, *mitzvah* #295). With regard to this law, however, there is a difference between a man and a woman. As long as she remains completely passive throughout the act of cohabitation, a woman is not required to sacrifice her life to avoid illicit relations (see *Sanhedrin* 74b; see *Tosafos* there ד"ה והא אסתר). A man, however, cannot remain passive, so he must always choose death rather than commit adultery.

16. It is forbidden for a man to seclude himself with any woman that is forbidden to him (*Kiddushin* 80b) [with the exception of his mother or daughter (Mishnah, *Kiddushin* ibid.), his wife while she is a *niddah* (*Rambam, Hil. Issurei Biah* 22:1; *Shulchan Aruch, Even HaEzer* 22:1), and to a lesser extent, his sister (according to some authorities; see *Chelkas Mechokeik* 22:1 and *Beis Shmuel* 22:1)]. *Tur, Even HaEzer* §22, writes that this prohibition is Biblical; however, see *Beis Yosef, Bach* and *Derishah* there, who cite *Rambam* (*Hil. Issurei Biah* 22:2) as maintaining that the prohibition is only Rabbinic in nature. In addition, the Sages prohibited seclusion with a non-married Jewess, and even a non-Jewess (see *Avodah Zarah* 36b).

One who secludes himself with a non-married woman receives *makkos mardus*, Rabbinically imposed lashes (see *Kiddushin* 81a with *Rashi* ibid.). However, the Rabbis waived this punishment in the case of one who secludes himself with a married woman, for fear that if she would be flogged, people might take this as an indication that she had actually committed adultery, and will suspect her children of being illegitimate (see *Kiddushin* ibid.).

A BROADER LOOK AT THE LAWS

1 The Laws of a Naarah Ha'meorasah Who Committed Adultery

∽ Method of execution

As noted above (note 8), the penalty for adultery with a *naarah ha'meorasah* is stoning. Twice, in two separate verses, the Torah mandates this punishment: In *Devarim* 22:21, which states: *And they shall take the naarah to the entrance of her father's house and the people of her city shall pelt her with stones, and she shall die, for she committed an outrage in Israel, to commit adultery in her father's house*; and ibid. vs. 23-24, which state: *If there will be a virgin naarah who has undergone erusin with a man, and a [different] man finds her in the city and lies with her; then you shall take them both out to the gate of that city and pelt them with stones and they shall die*. From these verses it is derived that the penalty of stoning applies only in the following circumstances:

A. The woman was still a *naarah* at the time of the adulterous act (Mishnah, *Sanhedrin* 66b), as verse 23 states: *If there will be a ... **naarah** etc*. If she was a *bogeres*, she and the adulterer are not subject to stoning but to strangulation, the standard punishment for adultery (*Sanhedrin* 66b; *Rambam, Hil. Issurei Biah* 3:4). [As noted above (note 8), the Sages and R' Meir argue whether this verse also excludes a minor.] If she sinned as a *naarah* but was not convicted until she became a *bogeres*, the penalty of stoning still applies (*Kesubos* 45b; see below regarding the execution site for this *bogeres*).

B. She was still a virgin at that time (Mishnah ibid.), as the verse (ibid.) states: *If there will be a **virgin** naarah etc*. If she was not a virgin, she and the adulterer are subject to death by strangulation (*Sanhedrin* ibid.; *Rambam* ibid.).

C. She was still an *arusah* (Mishnah ibid.), as the verse (ibid.) states: *If there will be a virgin naarah **who has undergone erusin,** etc*. If she had already undergone *nisuin* at the time she committed adultery, the standard punishment of strangulation applies (*Sanhedrin* ibid.; *Rambam* ibid. 3:4).

D. At the time of her adultery, she had not yet left her father's house to enter the house of her husband. [An *arusah* continues to live in her parents' house as she did before undergoing *erusin*. Leaving her parent's house for her husband's is one of the means of effecting *nisuin*.] If, however, her father had given her over to agents of her husband to bring her to her husband's house, she and the adulterer are liable to death by strangulation, and not by stoning (Mishnah ibid.; *Rambam* ibid.). This is derived from v. 21, which condemns an adulterous *naarah ha'meorasah* to stoning for the outrage of committing adultery **in her father's house.** The verse thus teaches that if she had already left her father's house when she committed the adulterous act, she is not liable to stoning, even if she had not yet entered her husband's house and completed the act of *nisuin* (*Sanhedrin* ibid.).

E. She was born a Jew. If she is a convert, however, the standard penalty of strangulation applies (Mishnah, *Kesubos* 44a; *Rambam* ibid. 3:7). This is derived from the wording of the verse (ibid.), *for she committed an outrage in **Israel,*** which implies that the penalty the verse describes applies only to a born Jewess (see *Kesubos* 44b; see also *Rashi* to the Mishnah ibid. ד"ה הרי זו בחנק). Someone whose mother converted after his conception but before his birth is, in many respects, considered a convert himself. With regard to the law of *naarah ha'meorasah,* however, even a woman whose mother converted after conceiving her is considered to be "in Israel" (Mishnah ibid.; see also *Rambam* ibid. 3:11; see Gemara there 44b for the Scriptural source for this law).

Site of execution

Usually, a sinner who was sentenced to stoning is executed at "the stoning place" [בית הסקילה], a site specifically designated for carrying out this execution (see Mishnah and Gemara, *Sanhedrin* 42b). In the case of an adulterous *naarah ha'meorasah,* however, Scripture mentions other places as the site of execution. The two verses that mandate death by stoning for this adultery (*Devarim* 22:21 and ibid. v. 24) each refer to a different site for the execution. One verse (v. 21) states: *And they shall take the naarah to* **the entrance of her father's house,** *and the people of her city shall pelt her with stones and she shall die.* The other verse (v. 24) states: *And you shall take them both to* **the gate of that city** *and pelt them with stones and they shall die.* [This refers to the gate of the city in which the adultery was committed — see *Tosafos, Kesubos* 45b ד"ה סוקלין אותה.] A Baraisa (cited by the Gemara in *Kesubos* 44b-45a) explains that the two verses refer to two different circumstances. The first verse refers to a case in which the witnesses who saw her sin did not testify until after she had undergone *nisuin* and moved to her husband's house [as is evident from the earlier verses in that passage (see *Rashi* ibid. 45a ד"ה סוקלין אותה).] In that case, the Torah stipulates that she be stoned at the entrance of her father's house, to publicize the fact that although she was not convicted until after she was a *nesuah* living in her husband's house, she had sinned while yet an *arusah* living in her parents' house [and therefore is liable to stoning, not to strangulation] (see *Rashi* ibid. ד"ה ראו גידולים). The second verse, which states that she is stoned at the gate of the city, refers to a case in which the witnesses testified when she was still an *arusah*. Since it is known that she was still an *arusah* when she sinned, the Torah does not mandate stoning her in front of her parents' house.

Rambam (*Hil. Issurei Biah* 3:9), based on a different version of the aforementioned Baraisa (see *Maggid Mishneh* there), cites other factors as determining where an adulterous *naarah ha'meorasah* is stoned. According to *Rambam,* if she committed adultery while living, as most *arusos* do, in her father's house,

she is stoned at the entrance of his house (regardless of where she was living at the time that the witnesses testified). However, if at the time she sinned she happened to be living in her *father-in-law's* house, she is stoned by the gate of the city.

There are circumstances in which an adulterous *naarah ha'meorasah* is not stoned at the entrance of her father's house even if the witnesses did not testify until after she underwent *nisuin* (or, according to *Rambam,* even if she sinned while still living with her parents). These are:

A. Where it is not *possible* to stone her at the entrance of her father's house; for example, she has no father, or her father has no house (*Kesubos* 45b; see also Mishnah there, 44a). According to a Baraisa cited by the Gemara (ibid.), in this case she is stoned at the gate of the city. [*Rambam* (ibid. 3:11), however, rules that she is stoned in "the stoning place".]

B. Where her mother had converted after conceiving her, but before giving birth to her (Mishnah, *Kesubos* 44a; *Rambam* ibid.). Such a girl has the same status as an adulterous *naarah ha'meorasah* who has no father (*Shitah Mekubetzes* to Mishnah ibid. ד"ה אין לה). In this case, she is stoned at the gate of the city (*Rambam* ibid.).

C. The witnesses who saw her sin did not testify until after she became a *bogeres* (*Kesubos* 45b). In this case, her stoning takes place at the "stoning place" (*Rambam* ibid. 3:10; for the source of this law, see *Shitah Mekubetzes, Kesubos* ibid. ד"ה האמר ליה).

D. According to some, if the witnesses did not testify until after she underwent *nisuin* and had intimate relations with her husband, she has the same status as a *naarah ha'meorasah* whose witnesses did not testify until after she became a *bogeres* (*Rambam* ibid.). Others, however, disagree (*Hasagos HaRavad* there).

An adulterous *naarah ha'meorasah* is executed at the gate of the city only if most of the city's inhabitants are Jews. If the majority of inhabitants are not

Jews, however, her execution takes place near the entrance of the *Beis Din* that sentenced her (*Kesubos* 45b).

2 The Daughter of a Kohen Who Committed Adultery

∞ *Form of execution*

As noted above (note 9), the Torah prescribes burning as the method of execution for a *bas kohen* (*kohen's* daughter) who committed adultery. There are three views concerning when the adulteress is subject to burning, and the manner of her execution when the penalty of burning does not apply:

A. The view of the Rabbis (*Sanhedrin* 50b) is that an adulterous *bas kohen* is subject to burning only if she is not a *naarah ha'meorasah*. A *bas kohen* who is a *naarah ha'meorasah,* however, is subject to the same penalty as any other *naarah ha'meorasah* — stoning. This distinction is not based on any explicit indication in Scripture. Rather, it is predicated on the Rabbis' view that stoning is a more severe form of execution than burning. Now, the Torah does not intend to subject a *bas kohen* to a *less* severe form of execution than applies to the daughter of a non-*kohen*. Thus, the verse which prescribes burning for the adulterous *bas kohen* must not be referring to a case in which she would be subject to stoning had she not been the daughter of a *kohen* (i.e. when she is a *naarah ha'meorasah*), but to where she would otherwise have been subject to the standard penalty for adultery — strangulation — which is less severe than both stoning and burning (*Sanhedrin* 50b; see also *Rashi* there 50a ד"ה ומדאפקיה).

B. R' Shimon disagrees with the Rabbis (see *Sanhedrin* ibid.) and maintains that an adulterous *bas kohen* is *always* subject to burning, even if she is a *naarah ha'meorasah*. R' Shimon contends that since the verse that mandates burning for an adulterous *bas kohen* does not distinguish between a *bas kohen* who is a

naarah ha'meorasah and one who is not, this penalty applies regardless of the *bas kohen's* status. R' Shimon's view is consistent with his opinion that burning is a more severe form of execution than stoning. Thus, by mandating burning as the punishment for an adulterous *bas kohen* who is a *naarah ha'meorasah,* the Torah is imposing a more severe penalty than the punishment of stoning to which a non-*bas kohen* is subject, not a less severe one (*Sanhedrin* ibid.). [Indeed, the law of a *bas kohen* is the source from which R' Shimon derives that burning is more severe than stoning. Since the Torah clearly did not intend the penalty for an adulterous *bas kohen* to be less severe than that for a non-*bas kohen,* the fact that the Torah mandates burning for a *bas kohen* who is a *naarah ha'meorasah* indicates that the Torah considers burning more severe than stoning (see *Sanhedrin* ibid.) with *Rashi* ד"ה אימא).]

R' Akiva also subscribes to this view, although on the basis of a different source than R' Shimon (ibid. 51b).

C. R' Yishmael is of the opinion that an adulterous *bas kohen* is subject to burning only if she is a *naarah ha'meorasah*. If she is not a *naarah ha'meorasah,* she is subject to strangulation, just like a non-*bas kohen*. He derives exegetically that the verse refers specifically to an adulteress who would have been subject to a more severe form of execution than the standard strangulation even if she was not a *bas kohen;* i.e. a *naarah hameorasah,* who, if she is a non-*bas kohen,* is subject to stoning instead of strangulation (*Sanhedrin* 51b). [It follows from this that R' Yishmael agrees with R' Shimon that burning is a more severe form of execution than stoning, for otherwise the Torah would not replace the penalty of stoning, to which a regular *naarah hameorasah* is subject, with a less severe punishment in the case of a *bas kohen* (see ibid. 51a with *Rashi* ד"ה ואי רבי ישמעאל).]

The halachah is in accordance with the Rabbis, who state that an adulterous *bas kohen* is subject to stoning if she is a *naarah hameorasah,* and to burning in all other cases (*Rambam, Hil. Issurei Biah* 1:5; see also *Chinuch* §35).

 Exceptions

A *bas kohen* who is a *chalalah* [חללה] (i.e. the offspring of a *kohen* and a woman forbidden to him), is not subject to the penalty of burning for committing adultery (*Meiri, Sanhedrin* 51a, from *Yerushalmi, Terumos* 7:2).

[It should be noted that many commentators to *Yerushalmi* ibid. understand this point to be the subject of a dispute there.]

According to the Tanna R' Meir (*Terumos* 7:2), the penalty of burning does not apply to an adulterous *bas kohen* who was married to someone forbidden to her. The Sages there, however, disagree. The halachah is in accordance with the Sages (*Rambam, Hil. Issurei Biah* 3:3).

SITUATIONS IN HALACHAH

Question:

Are wives of those men who ascended alive to Heaven permitted to remarry?

Answer:

We learn in *Tanach* that Eliyahu HaNavi (the prophet Elijah) never died. Rather, he ascended alive to Heaven (see *Melachim* II 2:11; see also *Targum Yonasan* to *Bereishis* 5:24 and *Tosafos* to *Yevamos* 16b ד"ה פסוק in regard to Chanoch). *Terumas HaDeshen* (2:102; see *Beis Shmuel, Even HaEzer* 17:11) cites an inquiry as to whether Eliyahu's wife would have been permitted to remarry after her husband ascended to Heaven. On the one hand, she no longer had a husband on Earth; yet on the other hand, her husband had not died. He concludes that she would indeed have been permitted to remarry, as the prohibition of adultery only forbids relations with *Eishes Rei'eihu, the wife of his fellow* (*Vayikra* 20:10), implying that it is permissible to engage in relations with the wife of an angel — and one who has ascended to Heaven has the status of an angel.

R' Elchanan Wasserman (*Kovetz Shiurim* 2:27-28) elaborates the inquiry: In the case of a husband's death is it the absence of the husband which permits the wife to remarry? Or does the husband's death terminate the marriage, and it is for this reason that the wife may remarry? If it is the absence of the husband that allows the wife to remarry, then since Eliyahu is absent from Earth, his wife would be permitted to remarry. However, if it is the death of the husband that terminates the marriage, then since Eliyahu did not die, his marriage was not terminated, and hence his wife would not be permitted to remarry.

The Gemara (*Kiddushin* 13b) derives the right of a woman to remarry after her husband's death from the link the Torah makes between the death

of a husband and a divorce (see *Devarim* 24:3). It would thus seem that death severs the marriage bond in the same way that a divorce severs that bond. If so, it would seem that in cases like that of Eliyahu, in which no death occurred, the wife should remain forbidden to remarry. As we have seen, however, *Terumas HaDeshen* rules otherwise. His ruling is based on the logic that once a person has become an angel, he is no longer eligible to be considered a husband. Hence the marriage is automatically terminated (see *Minchas Chinuch* to §203 and *Teshuvos R' Meshullam Igra, Even HaEzer* §28).

Question:

Are wives of men who died, but were then miraculously resurrected, permitted to marry other men?

Answer:

There are examples in *Tanach* and in the Gemara of people who died but were then miraculously resurrected (see *Melachim* I 17:17-24; *Melachim* II 4:8-38, and *Megillah* 7b). The authorities differ as to whether the wife of such a man — who, it would seem, became permitted to remarry after her husband's "death" — reverts, upon her husband's resurrection, to being *his* wife and, therefore forbidden to other men. *Teshuvos Avnei Nezer* (*Even HaEzer,* end of §56) writes that she remains permitted to remarry, while *Birchei Yosef* (*Even HaEzer* 17:1) and *Teshuvos Nefesh Chayah* (*Even HaEzer* §63) writes that she reverts to her former status, and is therefore forbidden to remarry. Here too, the question is whether it is the death or the absence of a husband that allows the wife to remarry: If it is his death, then once a man dies, his marriage is terminated. However, if it is the absence of a husband, then if the man returns to life — i.e. is no longer absent — the marriage ensues again. [See *Knesses HaGedolah* to *Tur, Even HaEzer* 17:2 for a discussion of a case in which a wife died but was then restored to life (see *Kesubos* 62b for such a case).]

ILLUMINATIONS
OF THE MITZVAH
Suggested Reasons & Insights

I. A CRIME AGAINST ONE'S FELLOW MAN

he prohibition of adultery is counted among the interpersonal *mitzvos* (cf. *Ibn Ezra, Shemos* 20:13), for it involves the theft of a person's most personal treasure (*Akeidas Yitzchak* §65); it is an injustice rejected by common sense (*Chinuch* §35).

However, this is not the only rationale for the mitzvah, for if it were, the prohibition, and the death penalty it incurs, would apply only when the perpetrator defrauds the husband, in the manner of the classic adulterer described in the Scripture (*Iyov* 24:15), *The adulterer's eye awaits the night, saying, "No eye will see me!" and he applies himself [to sin] in concealment.* The Torah therefore elaborates in another place (*Vayikra* 20:10), *A man who will commit adultery with a man's wife, who will commit adultery with his fellow's wife; the adulterer and the adulteress shall be put to death,* to indicate that even if the husband approves the union, it is still a capital sin (*Ha'amek Davar, Vayikra* ad loc.). Moreover, an extramarital relationship is considered adultery even when it actually serves the husband's interest. For instance, a man incapable of having children, who is eager for a son to carry on the family name, may be tempted to find someone he can trust with a secret to impregnate his wife, in the hope that she will bear a son. He will then claim the boy for himself, and his "son" will go on to perpetuate his name. To make clear that even this is forbidden, the Torah states in a third passage (*Vayikra* 18:20): *With your fellow's* (עמיתך) *wife you shall not lie to [produce] seed.* Even with the wife of a man who is "with you" — in collaboration with you — you shall not lie, although your altruistic intention is *to produce seed* for the childless husband. In this way, the Torah pursues the evil inclination in every avenue it may take to justify a forbidden act (*Meshech Chochmah, Vayikra* ibid.).

II. A THREAT TO THE FAMILY AND COMMUNITY

he cornerstone of a healthy society is the family unit, complete with parents and children. The family system could never withstand the prevalence of adultery; children would not be able to identify their fathers and siblings, nor fathers their children. The resulting quarrels and enmity would sever relationships and divide families, and in the process undermine civilization itself, which is founded on the harmonious cooperation of large numbers of people (*Toras HaMinchah* §24).

III. AN OBSTACLE TO MITZVAH OBSERVANCE

afeguarding the sanctity of marriage and the integrity of the family unit is key to the proper fulfillment of many of the Torah's commandments. If adultery would prevail, sowing confusion regarding paternity, the children of compromised marriages would be deprived of the mitzvah to honor their fathers, and would be vulnerable to unwittingly entering into incestuous marriages with sisters and other relatives whom they never knew (*Chinuch* §35). This concern is alluded to in the language of the prohibition (*Vayikra* 18:20), *You shall not lie with the wife of your fellow, to [produce] seed,* the last words being an allusion to one of the reasons for the law: children will be born, and they will not know the identity of their fathers and family (*Ramban, Vayikra* ad loc.). Adultery also breeds violence; it is natural for the offended husband to avenge his humiliation, and even murder could conceivably result (*Chinuch* §35; cf. *Ralbag, Vayikra* 16-18).

Adultery would discourage fathers from properly raising their children. Being uncertain that the children are his own, a father would not be driven to exert himself to discipline them and correct their behavior. The children's development would then inevitably be deficient, for (*Bereishis* 8:21) *the inclination of man's heart is evil from his youth* (*Ralbag,* ibid., and in his commentary on the Ten Commandments).

The tainted offspring of an adulterous relationship are inherently more likely to be led astray by vice and evil, progressing eventually to the worship of idols. The formation of a fetus at the time of conception is influenced by the intention of the union that brought it about; if the union is sinful, the conception is sinful, and this can impact negatively upon the offspring (*Toras HaMinchah* §24).

IV. Subduing one's passions

 t is the Divine will that a person strive to sanctify himself by asserting the reign of the intellect over bodily lust. Various commandments were designed toward this aim, including the laws limiting the union of man and woman to the framework of marriage, and regulating whom one may marry. The prohibition of adultery accords with this purpose, and, beyond its obvious application to a forbidden relationship with another man's wife, also intimates the imperative to avoid, in general, shameful overindulgence in sensual pleasure (*Abarbanel, Devarim* §5; see also *Moreh Nevuchim* II:

36). One should not allow marital relations to become an animalistic act meant solely to achieve the gratification of the senses (*Binah L'Ittim* 1:3), for otherwise, even legitimate relations would be devoid of the spirit of holiness residing therein (*Be'er Mayim Chaim, Bereishis* §2).

V. Producing "fruit according to its own kind"

 mong the ideas underlying this mitzvah is that God desires that the world be settled in accordance with His will. And God determined for the world a definite natural order: All living things reproduce in their kind, and the various species should not be mixed. In the same way, God ordained that the offspring of humans not be confused, and each individual should know from whence he came (*Chinuch* §35). And not only in the production of offspring does adultery interfere with the natural order, but even the act itself is akin to a cross-breeding of separate species. This is because every man, unique in his qualities, has been designated an appropriate mate; by reaching out to take the wife of another, the adulterer mingles these diverse qualities, and will pay with his life to the King of the world (*Alshich, Shemos* 20:13).

THROUGH THE EYES
OF THE SAGES
Stories, Parables & Reflections

I. THE SEVERITY OF THE SIN

Adultery is hateful in Hashem's eyes

he God of these people [the Jewish nation] abhors promiscuity (*Sanhedrin* 93a and 106a; *Yerushalmi Sanhedrin* 10:2; see *Eichah Rabbah* 5:11).

———— ৸৶ ————

The adulterer denies Hashem's scrutiny

The adulterer's eye awaits the night, saying, *No eye will see me* (*Iyov* 24:15). The adulterer thinks, No one knows about me, because all his adulterous deeds are carried out in darkness. And so it says (*Mishlei* 7:8-9): *Passing through the marketplace, next to her corner, he strode toward her house in the twilight shadows of the day, in the blackness of the night and utter darkness.* An adulterer thinks that because he carries out his deeds in darkness (where no can see him) the Holy One, Blessed is He, is not aware of him either. And similarly it says (*Yeshayah* 29:15): *Woe to those who attempt to hide in the depths, to conceal [their] plans from Hashem, whose deeds are [performed] in darkness: They say, "Who sees us and who is aware of us?"* This is the way of all transgressors; they think that the Holy One, Blessed is He, will take no notice of their actions ... And so it says: *The adulterer's eye awaits the night, saying, "No eye will see me."* He does not say, "No person will see me," but rather, "No eye will see me"; that is, neither a human eye below nor the heavenly Eye above (*Bamidbar Rabbah* 9:1; see also there §9 and *Tanchuma, Naso* §4).

———— ৸৶ ————

An adulterer is like an idol worshipper

The last five commandments correspond to the first five commandments ... *Do not commit adultery* corresponds to *Do not recognize other gods.* [The Ten Commandments were written on two tablets containing five commandments each; *do not commit adultery,* which is the second commandment of the second tablet, corresponds to the commandment of *Do not recognize other gods,* the second commandment of the first tablet.] The Holy One, Blessed is He, said: If you commit adultery, I consider it as if you worshipped idols (*Pesikta Rabbasi* §21: see *Zohar, Shemos* 90a).

———— ৸৶ ————

The adulteress repudiates the Holy One, Blessed is He

Any man [ish, ish] whose wife shall stray and commit treachery against him (*Bamidbar* 5:12). Now, this verse need only have said: *A man [ish] whose wife shall stray;* what does the Torah intend to teach us by using the double expression, *"ish, ish?"* That this wayward woman rejects *two* [different individuals]. One *ish:* When she acts promiscuously, she rejects her husband, who trusted her to be faithful to him. And the other *ish:* She repudiates the Holy One, Blessed is He, who commanded her, *"Do not commit adultery."* ... And where do we see that the Holy One, Blessed is He, is referred to as *ish?* For it says (*Shemos* 15:3): *Hashem is a man [ish] of war,* etc. Similarly, it says (*Mishlei* 2:17): *[She] who forsakes the husband of her youth and forgets the covenant of her God.* Thus, we see that a woman who is unfaithful to her husband rejects Hashem's authority as well (*Bamidbar Rabbah* 9:2; *Tanchuma, Naso* §5; see below).

———— ৸৶ ————

Adultery leads to the transgression of all the Ten Commandments

The disciples of Rav Huna the father of Rav Acha asked him: You have taught us that an adulterer and an adulteress transgress the Ten

Commandments. We understand how they come to transgress nine of the ten, but we do not understand how they come to transgress the commandment to keep the Shabbos. They transgress the other nine commandments as follows:

———————

I am Hashem, your God — because every adulterer denies the Holy One, Blessed is He, as it says (*Yirmiah* 5:7-10,12): *They acted adulterously … each man signaling to the wife of his acquaintance. Shall I not punish for these things — the word of Hashem. And from a nation such as this, shall My spirit not exact vengeance? … for they are not loyal to Hashem. They denied Hashem, and they said: It is not so…*

———————

You shall not recognize other gods – for it is written in this commandment: *You shall not bow down to them and you shall not serve them, for I am Hashem, your God, a jealous God.* And it says twice in regard to the wayward wife (*Bamidbar* 5:14): *And a spirit of jealousy passed over him,* etc. Why is this phrase stated two times? Because she causes jealousy both to the Holy One, Blessed is He, and to her husband. Similarly, it says regarding the *minchah* brought by the wayward wife: *For it is a minchah of jealousies,* that is, two jealousies (as implied by the verse's use of the plural, *jealousies*).

———————

Do not take the Name of Hashem in vain — for he commits adultery, and may then swear that he did not commit this sin.

———————

Honor your father — because if one commits adultery with a faithless wife and she conceives a child from him, she will likely tell her husband that the child is his. The child will grow up and show honor to her husband, thinking that he is his father, when in fact he is not; and when passing through the marketplace, he will perhaps curse the adulterer, thinking that he is not his father, when in fact he is.

———————

Do not murder — because the adulterer enters the house of the adulteress prepared to kill or be killed if he is caught by her husband.

———————

Do not commit adultery — this is obvious, for he is committing adultery.

———————

Do not kidnap — because the adulterer steals the 'well' of his fellow (i.e. he is stealing his fellow's wife in a certain sense). And similarly it says (*Mishlei* 9:17): *Stolen waters are sweeter, and bread [stolen and eaten] in hideaways is more pleasing.* [It is evident from the context of this verse that it refers to promiscuity; thus we see that the Scripture speaks of adultery in terms of theft].

———————

Do not testify falsely — because the adulterous wife testifies falsely [to her husband], saying, "I am with child from you."

———————

Do not covet — because one who commits adultery with another's wife covets everything that person has. How so? Because when the husband is about to die, he thinks that the son born from the adulterous union is his. Accordingly, he writes a will leaving everything he has to that son, not knowing that he is not his son. Thus, besides coveting his fellow's wife, an adulterer covets *everything* his fellow has.

———————

The disciples said to Rav Huna: We have explained nine [of the Ten Commandments]; tell us how he transgresses *Remember the Shabbos day to keep it holy?* Rav Huna said to them: I will tell you: Sometimes a *Kohen* has a wife, and an Israelite adulterer has relations with her, and she gives birth to a son, and people think he is the son of the *Kohen* [when in fact he is not]. That son will proceed to serve in the Temple, offering *olah* sacrifices on the Shabbos. He thereby desecrates the Shabbos [because as a non-*Kohen*, he is not permitted to perform the Divine service, and his invalid service does not override the Shabbos Laws].

Thus, the adulterer and adulteress can come to transgress all of the Ten Commandments. And regarding an adulterous woman Shlomo HaMelech said (*Koheles* 7:26): *I have found more bitter than death the woman who is snares, whose heart is nets, whose arms are chains. He who is [judged] good before God will escape her, but the sinner will be caught by her.* Woe to the transgression through which one transgresses the Ten Commandments! (*Bamidbar Rabbah* 9:12; *Tanchuma, Naso* §2; see *Pesikta Rabbasi* §21; see *Bamidbar Rabbah* 9:11 and *Sifrei Zuta* to *Bamidbar* 15:39 regarding other transgressions that are linked to adultery; see also *Sotah* 37b, which teaches that all the curses uttered on Mt. Gerizim and Mt. Eival (*Devarim* 27:11-26) are directed toward the adulterer and adulteress).

II. PENALTIES FOR THE INDIVIDUAL

✆ *Punishment in this world and in the next*

here are four things for which punishment is exacted from a person in this world, yet the principal [punishment] awaits him in the World to Come, and they are as follows: ... and illicit relations (*Yerushalmi Peah* 1:1).

— ✆ —

✆ *Punishment is administered immediately*

R' Azaryah and R' Yehudah bar R' Simon said in the name of R' Yehoshua ben Levi: In regard to all [sins], the Holy One, Blessed is He, defers His wrath, with the exception of promiscuity. What is the source for this? For the verse states (*Bereishis* 6:2): *The sons of the powerful saw ... and they took themselves wives from whomever they chose.* This refers even to married women (see *Rashi* ibid.). What is written later (ibid. v. 7)? *And Hashem said, "I will erase Man"* (*Bereishis Rabbah* 26:5; see *Vayikra Rabbah* 23:9, and *Tanchuma, Vayeira* §9).

— ✆ —

✆ *Afflictions of tzaraas*

R' Shmuel bar Nachmani said in the name of R' Yochanan: *Tzaraas* afflictions come upon a person on account of any one of seven things: ... on account of illicit relations, as it is written (*Bereishis* 12:17): *And Hashem afflicted Pharaoh with severe afflictions, on account of the matter of Sarai, the wife of Avram* (*Arachin* 16a; *Zohar, Bamidbar* 206a-b; see *Vayikra Rabbah* 18:3, *Bamidbar Rabbah* 7:5; *Tanchuma Tazria* §11 and *Metzora* §4).

———

R' Shimon ben Lakish said: How brazen are those who engage in immorality! If a person cohabits with a married woman, *tzaraas* appears upon his flesh, as it says (*Mishlei* 6:32): *He who commits adultery with a woman lacks an [understanding] heart.* What is written afterward, in the next verse? *Affliction [nega] and shame will he discover* (*Midrash Pisron Torah, Parashas Bamidbar*).

— ✆ —

✆ *Suffering and Gehinnom*

Regarding an adulteress, it is stated: *I have found more bitter than death the woman...* (*Koheles* 7:26). How is she more bitter than death? Because she causes him suffering in this world. Why? Because he strays after her. And ultimately, she lowers him into *Gehinnom,* as it says (*Mishlei* 2:16,18): *To save you from the foreign woman ... for her house declines toward death.* And it says further (ibid 5:3-5): *For the lips of a foreign woman drip with honey ... but ... her feet descend to death, her footsteps carry to she'ol* [*Gehinnom*] (*Bamidbar Rabbah* 9:12).

———

All those who descend to Gehinnom eventually ascend from there, except for three who descend and do not ascend, and they are as follows: He who commits sins with a married woman ... (*Bava Metzia* 58b; see *Tosafos* there).

— ✆ —

❧ The loss of the adulterer's wisdom

He who commits adultery with a woman lacks an understanding heart (*Mishlei* 6:32). R' Zavda said: What does the verse mean when it says: *He lacks an understanding heart?* That the Omnipresent removes wisdom from his heart. And wisdom refers to Torah, as it says (*Tehillim* 19:8): *The Torah of Hashem is perfect … making the simple one wise.* Not only that, but the appearance of his face becomes altered to reflect a lack of wisdom. And from where do we know that a person's facial appearance reflects his wisdom? As it says (*Koheles* 8:1): *A man's wisdom lights up his face; and the boldness of his face is altered* (*Medrash Mishlei* 6:32).

— ❧ —

❧ No forgiveness for the adulterer (without repentance and punishment)

R' Shimon ben Menasyah says: If a person steals, he can return the article he stole and by so doing correct his misdeed. If a person robs, he can return the article he robbed and thus correct his misdeed. But if one sins with a married woman and thereby renders her forbidden to her husband, he is banished from the world and must go away (i.e. he will descend to *Gehinnom* and not be released quickly) Repentance is not entirely effective for him, because his transgression causes irreparable harm (*Chagigah* 9b, with *Rashi* and *Maharsha* there; *Tosefta Chagigah* 1:10; *Bamidbar Rabbah* 9:6; *Koheles Rabbah* 1:15)

———

R' Yehoshua ben Levi said in the name of Bar Kappara: The Holy One, Blessed is He, provides atonement for everything (i.e. every kind of sin), except for illicit relations, as it says (*Mishlei* 6:29): *So is one who has relations with his fellow's wife; anyone who touches her will not be exonerated* (*Tanchuma Yashan, Vayeira* §14; see *Tanchuma, Vayeira* §9).

———

R' Zavda said in connection with the verse (*Mishlei* 6:32): *He who commits adultery with a woman lacks an understanding heart:* the ill repute he (the adulterer) bears can never be erased, as it says (ibid. v. 33): *Affliction and shame will he discover, and his disgrace will not be erased.* Furthermore, when he comes to the Day of Judgment, the Holy One, Blessed is He, will not forgive him; rather, the Holy One, Blessed is He, will become full of anger on account of him (*Medrash Mishlei* 6:32).

———

What is the meaning of the verse (ibid. v. 26): *A married woman can trap a precious soul?* … Rava said: it means that anyone who sins with a married woman, even if he has learned Torah — of which it is written (ibid. 3:15): *It is more precious than pearls (peninim),* that is more precious than the *Kohen Gadol* who enters the innermost sanctum *(lifnai vilifnim)* — she will trap him into the judgment of *Gehinnom* (*Sotah* 4b; see there and 5a).

———

Whoever sins with another's wife, it is as if he betrays the Holy One, Blessed is He, and the Jewish nation. And for that the Holy One, Blessed is He, will not provide atonement through mere repentance. Rather, the effect of his repentance is suspended until he dies. That is the meaning of what is written that (*Yeshayah* 22:14): *this sin will not be atoned for you until you die.* And when *will* it be atoned? When he enters the World to Come amid repentance. And yet he must receive a punishment … He is not accepted with his repentance until the judgment of *Gehinnom* is imposed upon him (*Zohar, Vayikra* 44b).

III. PENALTIES FOR THE PUBLIC

❧ The stricken sun [as an evil portent]

he Rabbis taught a Baraisa: On account of any one of four sinful things the sun is stricken (a sign of coming tribulation): …

And because of a betrothed maiden, who was violated and cried out for help in the city, yet no one saved her (*Succah* 29a; *Derech Eretz Rabbah* §2).

———— ✒ ————

❧ The degradation of produce

R' Shimon ben Gamliel says: R' Yehoshua testified that from the day the Temple was destroyed, there is no day without a curse, and dew does not descend as a blessing, and the true flavor of fruit was taken away. R' Yose says: The richness of fruit was also taken away. R' Shimon ben Elazar says: The abandonment of purity removed the flavor and aroma of fruits; the abandonment of tithing removed the richness of grain. But the Sages say: Promiscuity and sorcery destroyed everything (Mishnah, *Sotah* 48a).

———— ✒ ————

❧ Famine

On account of five sins the rains do not fall: On account of the sin of ... those who engage in illicit relations ... From where do we know that the rains do not fall on account of those who engage in illicit relations? As it says (*Yirmiah* 3:2): *You have brought guilt upon the land with your adulteries ...* And it says in the next verse: *The raindrops have been withheld and there was no late rain ...* (*Bamidbar Rabbah* 8:4; see *Yevamos* 78b; *Medrash Shmuel* 28:5).

———— ✒ ————

❧ Inflation and poverty

There was once an incident in the town of Kfar Sachanya in which the going price for forty *seah* of grain (a huge quantity) had been only a *dinar,* but then the buying power of one *dinar* went down by a single *seah,* so that it could now buy only thirty-nine. The citizens investigated the cause of this inflation, and found that a father and son had sinned with a betrothed maiden on Yom Kippur. They brought them to *Beis Din* and stoned them, and the rate returned to what it had been originally (*Gittin* 57a).

———— ✒ ————

❧ Plague of death

R' Simlai said: Wherever you find promiscuity, catastrophe befalls the world and kills the good together with the bad (*Bereishis Rabbah* 26:5; *Vayikra Rabbah* 23:9; *Tanchuma, Bereishis* §12; *Yerushalmi Sotah* 1:5).

———— ✒ ————

❧ The destruction of the world

The world is subject to destruction on account of any one of eight things: On account of ... engaging in illicit relations. The earlier generations were uprooted from the world only because they sinned in these eight matters (*Tanna D'vei Eliyahu Rabbah* 15:6).

———— ✒ ————

❧ The destruction of the Sanctuary and Temple

Why was [the Sanctuary at] Shiloh destroyed? Because of two iniquitous things that existed there: Engaging in illicit relations ... (*Yoma* 9a).

————————

Why was the First Temple destroyed? Because of three iniquitous things that existed there: ... and engaging in illicit relations (*Yoma* 9b; see also *Bamidbar Rabbah* 7:10).

———— ✒ ————

❧ Exile

Exile comes upon the world on account of ... engaging in illicit relations (*Pirkei Avos* 5:9; *Bamidbar Rabbah* 7:10).

————————

Because of the sin of engaging in illicit relations ... exile comes upon the world; invaders exile the inhabitants and others come and dwell in their place, as it says in the passage dealing with illicit relations (*Vayikra* 18:27): *For the inhabitants of the land who were there before you committed all these abominations,* and it is written (ibid. v. 25): *And the land became contaminated, and I visited its iniquity* upon it [and the land vomited out its inhabitants]. And it is written (ibid. v. 28): *Let not the land vomit you out for having contaminated it* (*Shabbos* 33a).

———— ✿ ————

✿ Departure of the Divine Presence

R' Yishmael bar R' Yose said: Whenever promiscuity is rampant among the Jewish people, the Divine Presence departs from them, as it says (*Devarim* 23:15): *So that He will not see an immodest thing from among you and turn away from behind you* (*Bamidbar Rabbah* 7:10; *Avos D'Rabbi Nassan* 38:4; *Sifri* to *Devarim* 23:15; see also *Sotah* 3b).

IV. YOSEF HATZADDIK — HIS TEST AND HIS TRIUMPH

✿ The test

nd it was after these matters, that the wife of Yosef's master cast her eyes upon Yosef and said to him, "Lie with me." But he refused. He said to his master's wife, "Behold, my master knows not what transpires with me in the house, and whatever he has, he has placed in my trust. There is no one greater in this house than I, and he has withheld from me nothing but you, since you are his wife. How then can I commit this enormous evil, and I will have sinned against God!" And she spoke to Yosef coaxing him day after day; but he would not listen to her to lie beside her, or to be with her. And it was on that day that he entered the house to perform his work — and not one of the men of the house was present in the house — that she caught hold of him by his garment saying, "Lie with me!" But he left his garment in her hand, fled and went outside (*Bereishis* 39:7-12).

———— ✿ ————

✿ The intensity of the test and its details

And it was after these matters, etc. This refers to thoughts of certain matters. Who pondered these matters? Yosef pondered them ... He said to himself, "Father was tested; my grandfather was tested. But as for me — am I not to be tested?" The

Holy One, Blessed is He, said to him, "By your life, I will test you more than them" (*Bereishis Rabbah* 87:4).

————

But he refused. Why did he refuse? R' Yehudah bar Shalom said: Because he saw the image of his father, and his father said to him, "Yosef, Yosef! The names of your brothers are destined to be written on the *ephod* stones (worn by the *Kohen Gadol* in the Temple). Do you want your name to be missing from among them, and [instead] to be known as a companion of harlots?" For this reason he refused... *He said to his master's wife ... and I will have sinned against God!* Yosef said, "I take an oath to God that I will not commit this enormous evil!" *And she spoke to Yosef, coaxing him day after day (yom yom)*; R' Yehudah bar Shalom said: The words *day after day* indicate a year, as it says (*Esther* 3:7): *From day to day and from month to month, the twelfth [month]*. When she would come by to chat with him, he would lower his head to face downward in order not to look at her. What did she do? Rav Huna bar Idi said: She had an iron spike placed underneath his beard so that if he faced downward the [point of the] spike would strike him, as it says (*Tehillim* 105:18): *They afflicted Yosef's leg with fetters; his soul came into iron*. Nevertheless, he did not listen to her. She said to him, "Why do you not listen to me? Am I not a married woman (so even if I conceive, no one will realize that I sinned with you)?" He said to her, "Now, the single women among you are forbidden to us (as non-Jews), all the more so the married women among you!" For it says regarding even single non-Jewish women (*Devarim* 7:3): *And you shall not intermarry with them*. Despite all her urging, he did not listen to her. R' Yehudah bar Nachman said this last exchange is analogous to an idolater who said to a Jew, "I have a superb dish to feed you." The Jew asks him, "What is it?" He replies, "Pork." The Jew says to him, "Fool! Even meat from a kosher animal that you slaughtered is forbidden to us! All the more so pork!" And that is what Yosef told her, "Even your single women are forbidden to us; certainly a married woman!" (*Tanchuma, Vayeshev* §8; see also *Sotah* 36b and *Bereishis Rabbah* 87:10).

———————

They say to the wicked person when he is brought for judgment before the Heavenly Court, "Why did you not engage in Torah study?" If he responds, "I was good-looking and caught up with my evil inclination," they will say to him, "Were you better looking than Yosef?" They said in regard to Yosef HaTzaddik: Each and every day, Potiphar's wife would attempt to seduce him with words. The clothes she wore for him in the morning she would not wear for him in the evening; the clothes she wore for him in the evening she would not wear for him on the following morning. She said to him, "Give yourself up to me." He said to her, "No!" She said to him, "I will confine you in prison!" He said to her, *Hashem releases the imprisoned* (*Tehillim* 146:7). She said, "I shall bend over your stature!" He replied, *Hashem straightens the bent* (ibid. v. 8). She said, "I will blind your eyes!" He said, *Hashem gives sight to the blind* (ibid.). She gave him one thousand talents of silver to persuade him to listen to her, *to lie beside her, to be with her* (see *Bereishis* 39:10), but he did not want to listen to her, *to lie beside her* in this world, *to be with her* in the World to Come. Thus, we

find that "... Yosef obligates the wicked who do not study Torah, for if Yosef was able to withstand the test engendered by his good looks, certainly the Heavenly Court has a valid claim against them (*Yoma* 35b; see *Bereishis Rabbah* 87:10; *Tanchuma, Vayeshev* §5; *Avos D'Rabbi Nassan* 16:2).

——— ৬ ———

∾ Yosef's merit, the sanctity of the Jewish people and their redemption from Mitzrayim

R' Pinchas said in the name of R' Chiya bar Abba: Because the Jewish people while in Egypt restrained themselves in matters relating to immorality, they were redeemed from Mitzrayim … Rav Huna said in the name of R' Chiya bar Abba: Our Matriarch Sarah descended to Mitzrayim and restrained herself in a matter relating to immorality (see *Bereishis* 12:10-20); as a consequence, in her merit all the women (her descendants) practiced restraint. Yosef descended to Mitzrayim and restrained himself in matters related to immorality; in his merit, the Jewish people to practiced restraint. R' Chiya bar Abba said: This restraint in regard to immorality was sufficient a merit in itself that the Jewish people could have been redeemed through it alone (*Vayikra Rabbah* 32:5; see there at greater length).

——— ৬ ———

Having seen some of our Sages' comments on the severity of the ban against adultery — a severity that derives in a substantial measure from the destructive effect adultery has on the sacred institution of marriage — it would seem appropriate to follow with a brief selection of the Sages' statements on marriage. The passages cited will touch on the sanctity of marriage, the reward in store for those who conduct their marriage in a way befitting that sanctity, and the importance of cultivating domestic harmony.

∾ The Divine Presence

R' Akiva expounded: If a husband and wife are meritorious in regard to the sanctity of their marriage (i.e. they do not engage in adulterous relations — *Rashi*), then the Divine Presence rests in their midst. (Indeed, God divided His [two-letter] name and caused it to lodge between a husband

and wife, for איש, man, contains the *yud*, while אשה, woman, was given the *heh* — *Rashi*). However, if they are not meritorious in regard to their marriage, they will be consumed by אש, a fire (that is, God removes the letters of His name from between them, at which point איש and אשה, now stripped of their *yud* and *heh*, are reduced to אש and אש — fire and fire — *Rashi*) (*Sotah* 17a).

✆ *Virtuous children*

When a woman lives with her husband in holiness (i.e. she entertains no thought of another man), God brings forth from her righteous offspring. This we find in connection with Chanah, who lived with her husband in holiness, and God did not withhold her reward: He gave her a son (Shmuel) who was as righteous as Moshe, as it is said (*Yirmiah* 15:1), *If Moshe and Shmuel were to stand before Me...* And it is said (*Tehillim* 99:6), *Moshe and Aharon were among His priests, and Shmuel among those who invoke His name* (cf. *Bamidbar Rabbah* 18:5). Chanah confirmed that, *This is the child that I prayed for* (*Shmuel* I 1:27). Why [was this child so virtuous]? Because he was conceived in holiness.

God declared [to Israel]: In this world I spurned all the other nations ... and I chose you because you are of faithful seed, as it is said (*Yirmiah* 2:21), *I planted you from a choice vine, entirely of faithful seed.* And it says (*Devarim* 14:2), *God has chosen you for Himself to be a treasured people.* In the future as well I shall choose no one but you, for you are the product of holy seed, blessed by God, as it is written, (*Yeshayah* 65:23), *They will not toil in vain, nor produce for futility , for they are the offspring of those blessed by God* (*Medrash Tanchuma* §7).

✆ *A wellspring of blessing*

R' Tanchum taught in the name of R Chanilai: A person that is without a wife abides without joy, blessing, or goodness. Without joy: For it is written (*Devarim* 14:26), *And you shall rejoice — you and your household* (a reference to one's wife — *Rashi*). Without blessing: As it is said (*Yechezkel* 44:30), *To bring blessing to rest upon your household.* And without goodness: As it is said (*Bereishis* 2:18), *It is not good that man be alone.*

In the west (i.e. in the Land of Israel, to the west of Bavel) it is taught: A person who is without a wife abides without Torah and without protection. Without Torah: As it is written (*Iyov* 6:13), *If my helpmate is not with me, wise counsel is thrust away from me* (for he is distracted by the cares of his home, and in time his learning will be forgotten — *Rashi*). Without protection: For it is said (*Yirmiah* 31:21), *The woman encircles the man.* Rava bar Ulla adds: Without harmony, for it is said (*Iyov* 5:24), *You will know that your tent* (representing one's wife—*Rashi*) *is at peace...* (*Yevamos* 62b).

✆ *Respect for one's wife*

R' Chelbo taught: A person should be very careful of his wife's honor, for the blessing that is found in a person's home is granted only on account of his wife, as it is said (*Bereishis* 12:16), *And he treated Avram well for her sake.* This was the rationale behind Rava's advice to the residents of Mechoza: "Honor your wives so that you may become wealthy" (*Bava Metzia* 59a).

✆ *R' Akiva's marriage to Rachel*

R' Akiva was originally a shepherd for [the enormously wealthy] Kalba Savua. Kalba's daughter, Rachel, observed that this shepherd possessed a modest and refined character. She said to him, "If I agree to become betrothed to you, will you go and study at an academy of Torah? [Although R' Akiva was a complete boor at this time, she recognized his potential for Torah greatness — see *Maharsha*.] He answered affirmatively. So she quietly married him, and sent him off to study Torah. Her father learned of what she had done, and [in his anger over her marriage to an ignoramus] he drove her out of his house, and made a vow forbidding her to derive benefit from his property. R' Akiva stayed in the yeshiva for twelve years. When he finally made his way back, he brought along with him twelve thousand disciples. As he drew near his home, he overheard a certain neighbor asking his wife, "How much longer will you remain like a widow in your husband's lifetime?" She replied, "If he would only listen to me, then he would spend another twelve years in the academy!" When R' Akiva heard that, he said, "Then I have her permission!" He turned around and went back to his studies for another twelve years. When he left once again to come home, he brought with him twenty-four thousand disciples. His wife, informed of his imminent arrival, set out to greet him. Her neighbors advised her, "Borrow some finery to wear in his honor." She said to them (*Mishlei* 12:10), *The righteous man knows his animal's soul* (i.e. a *tzaddik* appreciates even his livestock; certainly my husband is well aware of my impoverished state, and does not expect me to appear in fancy attire). When she reached her husband, she fell to her face and kissed his feet. The sage's attendants began to push her away, but R' Akiva said to them, "Let her be. All [the Torah] that is mine and yours is in reality hers."

Kalba Savua heard that a great man had come to town. He said to himself, "Let me call on him; perhaps he will find a way to annul my vow [by which I disowned my daughter]." He came before R' Akiva [and related his problem]. The sage questioned,

"Did you intend for your vow to take effect even in the event that your son-in-law would become a great man?" Kalba answered, "Had I known he would learn as much as one chapter, or one halachah, I would never have taken the vow." R' Akiva said to him, "Well, it is I." Kalba Savua fell to his face and kissed him on his feet; he then signed over to him half of his wealth.

R' Akiva's daughter did for her husband, Ben Azzai, what her mother had done for her father (sending him off to study for many years). [In another place (*Yevamos* 63b) it is related that Ben Azzai, in his passion for Torah study, separated from his wife. *Maharsha*, in light of the passage cited above, concludes that his lofty spiritual level was due to his wife's own insistence that he remain in yeshiva.] This gave rise to the saying, "The ewe (רחל) follows the lead of the ewe (רחל). The deeds of the mother are reflected in the deeds of the daughter" (*Kesubos* 62b-63a).

The count according to Bahag

*B*ahag lists the prohibition against adultery a total of four times in his count of the 613 commandments: 1) adultery with a *naarah hame'orasah* in the section in which he enumerates the prohibitions for which the penalty is execution by stoning (§14); 2) adultery with a *nesuah* in the section of prohibitions for which the penalty is death by strangulation (§36); 3) adultery with the daughter of a *Kohen* in the section in which he lists prohibitions for which the penalty is burning (§28); and 4) as a general prohibition against adultery in his section of negative commandments (§29). This is one of several instances in which *Bahag* lists a prohibition according to the punishment for transgressing it, and lists it again in the section of negative commandments. According to *Rambam* (*Sefer HaMitzvos, shoresh* §14), those mitzvos that *Bahag* classifies by order of punishment do not refer to the actual prohibitions, but rather to the mitzvah incumbent upon *Beis Din* to administer the punishment the Torah specifies for each prohibition. Thus, according to *Rambam's* understanding of *Bahag*, while commandments related to adultery account for four of the 613 commandments on *Bahag's* lists, only one of these commandments — the one *Bahag* lists in the section of negative commandments — refers to the prohibition itself. *Ramban*

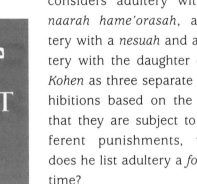

מפתח למוני המצוות

THE COUNT OF THE MITZVAH

Baal Halachos Gedolos / Lavin 29
בה"ג / לאוין כט

R' Saadiah Gaon / Lavin 92
רס"ג / לאוין צב

R' Eliyahu HaZakein / Amud 57
ר' אליהו הזקן / עמ' 57

Rashbag / Lo Saaseh Os 11
רשב"ג / לא תעשה אות יא

R' Yitzchak El-Bargeloni / Lavin 30
ר"י אלברג'לוני / לאוין ל

Maamar HaSechel / Dibbur Shevi'i 1
מאמר השכל / דיבור שביעי א

Sefer Yereim / 18
יראים / יח

Rambam, Sefer HaMitzvos / Lo Saaseh 347
רמב"ם / לא תעשה שמז

Sefer Mitzvos Gadol (Smag) / Lo Saaseh 97
סמ"ג / לא תעשה צז

Sefer Mitzvos Katan (Smak) / 292
סמ"ק / רצב

Zohar HaRakia / Lavin 10
זוהר הרקיע / לאוין י

(see *hasagos* to *Sefer HaMitzvos* ibid. ד"ה וכתב עוד), however, contends that the mitzvos *Bahag* lists in sections categorized by the form of punishment *do* refer to the actual prohibitions. This presents an obvious difficulty: Even if *Bahag* considers adultery with a *naarah hame'orasah*, adultery with a *nesuah* and adultery with the daughter of a *Kohen* as three separate prohibitions based on the fact that they are subject to different punishments, why does he list adultery a *fourth* time?

Some possible answers to this question:

A. *The prohibition, You shall not commit adultery, includes other activities besides actual adultery.*

Besides the prohibition against having illicit relations with a married woman, several other prohibitions are derived from the Torah's commandment of *You shall not commit adultery*:

1. That it is forbidden to act as an agent for an adulterer; i.e. to assist someone in finding women with whom to commit adultery (*Shevuos* 47b; see also *Smag, Laavin* §103).

2. That it is forbidden to cause a seminal emission in vain (*Niddah* 13b; see also *Smak* 292; see, however, *Rambam, Peirush HaMishnayos, Sanhedrin* 7:4 ד"ה אשה המביאה, who derives this prohibition from a different source).

3. That it is forbidden for one to smell the perfume of a woman forbidden to him, since this can arouse one's desires (*Pesikta Rabbasi* §24; see also *Rambam, Peirush HaMishnayos* ibid.).

These prohibitions are not accounted for by the prohibitions against adultery with a *naarah hame'orasah*, a *nesuah* and the daughter of a *Kohen*, for they do not carry the death penalty as actual adultery does; indeed, they do not relate specifically to a married woman. Thus, they must be counted as a *separate* commandment of the 613. Possibly, the commandment of *You shall not commit adultery* which *Bahag* includes in his section of negative commandments refers to these prohibitions.

[Interestingly, in his *Azharos*, *R' Eliyahu HaZakein* (whose count of the 613 commandments is based on *Bahag* — see *R' M. Slutzki's* introduction to *Azharos* of *R' Eliyahu HaZakein*) lists having illicit relations with a married woman and the prohibition of *You shall not commit adultery* as two separate prohibitions. He defines the latter prohibition, as forbidding "following in the footsteps of an adulterer," a phrase the *Gemara* (*Shevuos* ibid.) uses to refer to one who assists another in committing adultery, the first additional prohibition noted above.]

B. *Bahag lists the commandment again because it is one of the Ten Commandments*

Some answer that although *Bahag* repeats the prohibition against adultery in his list of negative commandments, he does not *count* it as a separate mitzvah distinct from the three prohibitions against adultery he listed elsewhere. He includes it in this list simply because it is one of the Ten Commandments, and he wishes to present in one place all the prohibitions contained in the

Ten Commandments. Thus, although he already listed the prohibition earlier, he lists it again in the category of negative commandments together with those prohibitions of the Ten Commandments that are not listed elsewhere. It is clear that not all the prohibitions in *Bahag's* list of negative commandments count toward the 613, since this list contains 282 prohibitions, and *Bahag* himself gives the tally of prohibitions in this list as 277! The difference represents five prohibitions that he already counted elsewhere as part of the 613 (*R' A. S. Traub's* introduction to *Bahag*, 31-32).

The count according to R' Saadiah Gaon

In his count of the 613 commandments, *R' Saadiah Gaon* lists the prohibition of *You shall not commit adultery* (*Laavin* §92), and another prohibition against having illicit relations with a married woman (ibid. §97). Why does *R' Saadiah Gaon* count the prohibition against adultery as two commandments? [*R' Saadiah Gaon* also lists the prohibition a third time, in connection with the punishment that is meted out to an adulterer or adulteress. However, this does not refer to the actual prohibition against adultery, but rather to the mitzvah incumbent upon *Beis Din* to administer the punishment the Torah mandates for adultery (see *R' Yeruchem Fischel Perla's Introduction to vol. III of Sefer HaMitzvos of R' Saadiah Gaon*, §2).]

Possibly, the prohibition of *You shall not commit adultery* which *R' Saadiah Gaon* lists does not refer to actual adultery, but to the other prohibitions that are derived from this verse, as noted above. These are not included in the prohibition against having illicit relations with a married woman, so they are counted as a separate negative commandment, as explained above.

Mitzvah 36

אִסּוּר גְּנֵבַת נֶפֶשׁ

פרשת יתרו

Not to Kidnap

THE MITZVAH:

MITZVAH 36

אִסּוּר גְּנֵבַת נֶפֶשׁ
(לֹא תַעֲשֶׂה)
NOT TO KIDNAP

מצוה לו

■ SOURCE ■
לֹא תִגְנֹב
שמות (פרשת יתרו) כ:יג
"Do not steal"

■ THE MITZVAH ■

It is forbidden to seize a person and take possession of him against his will.[1] [This mitzvah relates specifically to kidnapping. Burglary or robbery of another's property are forbidden by other prohibitions; see mitzvos #224 and #229.[2]]

■ LAWS ■

1 This prohibition is transgressed only when the kidnapper takes the victim into his own domain,[3] or when a halachic act of acquisition is used to acquire the victim.[4]

2 This prohibition applies equally to the kidnapping of a man, a woman or a minor.[5]

3 One who transgresses this prohibition is liable to execution by strangulation[6] [see mitzvah #47].

However, to be liable to execution, the kidnapper must make use of his victim physically;[7] subsequently, he must sell his victim in the manner of a Canaanite slave,[8] to a buyer who is not one of the victim's relatives.[9] [When the kidnapper sells his victim, he also transgresses the prohibition of selling a Jewish slave on the auction block. See mitzvah #345.][10]

4 This prohibition applies to both men and women,[11] in all places and at all times.

5 Non-Jews are prohibited to kidnap as well, as this is included in the prohibition against theft, one of the Seven Noahide Laws.[12]

6 One who abducts any person who is easily accessible to him, such as his son, is not liable to execution.[13]

■ A REASON ■

Man, who was formed in the Divine Image, was created so that he could freely exercise his will and guide his own life. Such a being ought to be servile to God alone. A kidnapper denies him this ability, and defies the Divine element inherent in man.

1. See Mishnah, *Sanhedrin* 85b, and Gemara there; see also *Rambam, Hil. Geneivah* 9:1.

The verses dealing with this prohibition use the term *"geneivah,"* which generally connotes theft. The commentators discuss whether the Torah's use of this term was meant to restrict the prohibition to clandestine kidnapping, or if *"gezeilah,"* kidnapping a person openly, would also be included. See *Iyunim* §1 for further discussion of this question.

2. The Torah prohibits "stealing" in two separate verses; *"Lo Signov,"* "You shall not steal" (*Shemos* 20:13), and *"Lo Signovu,"* "You (plural) shall not steal" (*Vayikra* 19:11). The first verse, one of the Ten Commandments, is understood as a prohibition against kidnapping, while the second verse in *Parashas Kedoshim* is understood to prohibit theft of property. *Chazal* (*Mechilta, Shemos* 20:14; see also ibid. 21:16) explain that this is derived through the use of one of the thirteen principles of Biblical exegesis: דבר הלמד מעניינו, *a matter elucidated by its context*, as follows:

Since *Lo Signovu* is situated between two verses dealing with monetary prohibitions, we learn that it, too, is a monetary prohibition, forbidding the theft of property. And since *Lo Signov* is situated next to two mitzvos which incur capital punishment (*You shall not murder* and *You shall not commit adultery*), we learn that it, too, is a prohibition incurring capital punishment, viz. kidnapping (see *Sanhedrin* 86a and *Aruch LaNer* there).

Despite the distinction derived by the Medrash cited above, we do find various occurrences of *Lo signov* being referred to as prohibitions against monetary theft (see *Mechilta, Shemos* 21:6, *Otzar HaMedrashim* [Eisenstein] p. 488, et al.). Moreover, many Torah

AN EXPANDED TREATMENT

commentators explain *Lo Signov* as a general prohibition which includes all forms of theft (*Ibn Ezra, S'forno,* and *Malbim* et al. to *Shemos* 20:13).

3. The verse states concerning a kidnapper (*Shemos* 21:16): *One who kidnaps a man and sells him and he was found to have been in his hand* (בידו), *he shall surely be put to death.* The Mishnah (*Sanhedrin* 85b) derives from the word בידו, *in his hand,* that the kidnapper must take the victim into his domain (*Rashi* to *Sanhedrin* ibid., from *Mechilta, Shemos* 21:16; see *Rambam, Hil. Geneivah* 9:2).

4. The requirement of בידו can also be satisfied, according to many commentators, if the kidnapper performs a *kinyan* upon the victim, even without bringing him into the kidnapper's own domain (see *Tosafos* to *Sanhedrin* 85b ד״ה עד, and *Minchas Chinuch* 36:3). Not every type of *kinyan* is effective, however. One example of a halachic form of acquisition that can be used in the case of kidnapping is *meshichah,* pulling. This would be accomplished by physically transferring the victim out of his own domain. [Regarding whether he must be transferred to a domain under the kidnapper's control in order to effect acquisition, or whether the *kinyan* is in effect once the victim is taken to a public domain, see *Kesubos* 31b, *Rambam, Hil. Geneivah* 3:2, and *Shulchan Aruch, Choshen Mishpat* 351:1, with *Sma* there §3.]

If a kidnapper performs *hagbahah,* lifting with intent to acquire, upon his victim without removing the victim from his own domain, the Rishonim are in doubt as to whether he is liable for kidnapping. On the one hand, it is possible that he is exempt, for the verse states: *When a man is found kidnapping one of his brothers*

(מאחיו) ... *he shall be put to death* (*Devarim* 24:7). The term "מאחיו" — literally, from his brothers — implies that the victim must be removed from his family, i.e. taken out of his own domain. Thus, it may be that any method of acquisition that does not remove the victim from his domain would not incur liability (*Tosafos* to *Sanhedrin* 85b, ד״ה עד). On the other hand, perhaps he is liable, for the word בידו used in *Shemos* 21:16 implies that the kidnapper is liable for any situation in which the victim is legally deemed to be in his hand, even if the victim never left his domain. Thus, *hagbahah* performed in the victim's domain *would* make the kidnapper liable (*Tosafos* ibid.; see also *Ramban* to *Shemos* 21:16).

5. The verse in *Devarim* (24:7) uses the word נפש, *soul,* to describe the kidnap victim; this term includes men, women, and minors (see *Mechilta, Shemos* 21:16 in *Sanhedrin* 85b; see also *Rambam, Hil. Geneivah* 9:6).

6. See *Rambam, Hil. Geneivah* 9:1. The kidnapper's death penalty is stated explicitly in two verses: *One who kidnaps a man ... shall be put to death* (*Shemos* 21:16), and *When a man is found kidnapping ... he shall be put to death ...* (*Devarim* 24:7). The Torah does not specify which method of execution is to be used, but there is an Oral Tradition received by Moshe Rabbeinu at Sinai that whenever the method of death penalty is unspecified in the Torah, the intended method is *chenek,* strangulation (*Rambam, Hil. Sanhedrin* 14:1. See also *Mechilta Shemos* 21:16, *Sanhedrin* 52b, and *Yad Ramah* there).

It must be noted, however, that *Beis Din* may not impose any capital or corporal penalty, without hearing the testimony of two valid witnesses who saw the act in question [see

mitzvah #47]. Regarding kidnapping, *Chazal* derive from the Torah that both the abduction and the selling of the victim must have been witnessed for the transgressor to incur the death penalty (*Mechilta Shemos* 21:16). Nor can *Beis Din* impose capital punishment unless the perpetrator of the crime was warned by two valid witnesses that he would incur the death penalty for his action. Regarding kidnapping, the witnesses must give warning both before the abduction and before the selling of the victim, because both are integral aspects of the transgression (see *Tosafos* to *Sanhedrin* 86b, ד״ה גניבה; *Minchas Chinuch* 36:16. For further discussion, see also *Iyunim* §2).

[If the witnesses gave warning for both the abduction and the selling at the onset of the transgression, and there was no undue interruption (*hefsek*) between the two acts, it is possible that such warning is sufficient (*Chazon Ish, Bava Kamma* 19:1).]

7. This requirement is derived (see Mishnah, *Sanhedrin* 85b) from the verse (*Devarim* 24:7): *If a man is found kidnapping one of his brothers ... and he makes use of him and sells him, he shall surely be put to death.*

Any degree of physical benefit the kidnapper derives from his victim, even if it is of negligible monetary value, such as leaning on him, is enough to fulfill this condition (*Sanhedrin* ibid.; *Rambam Hil. Geneivah* 9:2). Even if the victim was asleep and he was used as a cushion, it is also considered "usage" (*Rambam* ibid.; see *Maggid Mishneh* there).

If the kidnapper does not fulfill this condition (or the condition of sale — see below), he is exempt from punishment, but has still transgressed the prohibition of "*Lo Signov*" (*Minchas Chinuch* 36:1).

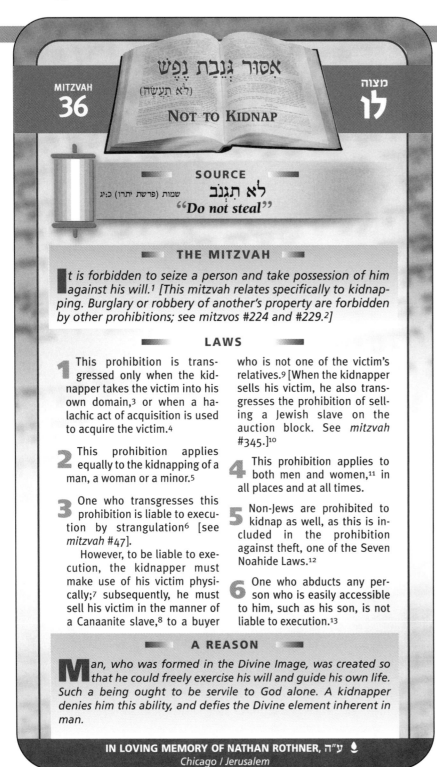

אִסּוּר גְּנֵבַת נֶפֶשׁ
(לֹא תַעֲשֶׂה)

NOT TO KIDNAP

מצוה
לו

■ SOURCE ■

לֹא תִגְנֹב
שמות (פרשת יתרו) כ:יג

"Do not steal"

■ THE MITZVAH ■

It is forbidden to seize a person and take possession of him against his will.[1] [This mitzvah relates specifically to kidnapping. Burglary or robbery of another's property are forbidden by other prohibitions; see mitzvos #224 and #229.[2]]

■ LAWS ■

1 This prohibition is transgressed only when the kidnapper takes the victim into his own domain,[3] or when a halachic act of acquisition is used to acquire the victim.[4]

2 This prohibition applies equally to the kidnapping of a man, a woman or a minor.[5]

3 One who transgresses this prohibition is liable to execution by strangulation[6] [see mitzvah #47].

However, to be liable to execution, the kidnapper must make use of his victim physically;[7] subsequently, he must sell his victim in the manner of a Canaanite slave,[8] to a buyer who is not one of the victim's relatives.[9] [When the kidnapper sells his victim, he also transgresses the prohibition of selling a Jewish slave on the auction block. See *mitzvah #345*.][10]

4 This prohibition applies to both men and women,[11] in all places and at all times.

5 Non-Jews are prohibited to kidnap as well, as this is included in the prohibition against theft, one of the Seven Noahide Laws.[12]

6 One who abducts any person who is easily accessible to him, such as his son, is not liable to execution.[13]

■ A REASON ■

Man, who was formed in the Divine Image, was created so that he could freely exercise his will and guide his own life. Such a being ought to be servile to God alone. A kidnapper denies him this ability, and defies the Divine element inherent in man.

8. This requirement, too, is derived from the verse in *Devarim* cited in the previous note (see Mishnah *Sanhedrin* ibid., and *Rambam, Hil. Geneivah* ibid.). The sale of the victim does not take effect, even when a valid method of acquisition is used — thus, the victim does not belong to the buyer (see *Bava Kamma* 68b, and *Rashi* there ד"ה גניבה בנפש). Regarding the reason for this, and for a discussion of why the kidnapper is liable only if he uses the normally effective methods of acquisition, see *Iyunim* §3.

Because the sale of the victim is ineffective, it follows that the kidnapper is liable for the *attempted* sale — that is, the transaction of a *kinyan* intended to transfer ownership of the victim. The commentators discuss what type of *kinyan* must have been attempted to render the kidnapper liable. *Minchas Chinuch* (36:6) cites three possibilities: (1) any *kinyan* that would transfer a Canaanite slave (money, a document of sale, or a proprietary act [*chazakah*]); for the prohibition against selling a kidnap victim is derived from the verse in *Vayikra* (25:42), which speaks of selling a Jew as a Canaanite slave; (2) any *kinyan* that would transfer a Jewish slave (money or a document, but *not* a proprietary act); for the kidnap victim is, in fact, a Jew; (3) any *kinyan* that would transfer movable items (such as *hagbahah* [lifting] or *meshichah* [pulling]). Since, in fact, the victim is not a slave at all, it is possible that *kinyanim* effective for transferring slaves are not relevant to him.

If the kidnapper gives away his victim as a gift, or if he consecrates him to the Temple treasury, he is exempt from punishment, for the verse states: *One who kidnaps a man and sells him … shall be put to death* (Shemos 21:16). Since the verse specifies selling, giving away or consecrating are excluded (*Rashba* to *Bava Kamma* 78b ד"ה גנב ונתן; see *Minchas Chinuch* 36:7).

Regarding a case in which the buyer takes possession of the victim in the kidnapper's domain, but does not remove him to his own domain, there is a dispute among the Rishonim as to whether the kidnapper is liable. Their dispute revolves around how one understands the verse: *One who kidnaps a man and sells him, and he was found to have been in his hand, he shall surely be put to death* (Shemos 21:16). Some understand that the verse requires that the victim must be found in the *buyer's* hand, i.e. the buyer's domain, in order for the kidnapper to incur a penalty. Therefore, if the victim is never removed from the kidnapper's domain, the kidnapper is exempt (*Ramban* to *Shemos* ibid.). Others explain this phrase as referring to the act of kidnapping, not the sale, and it requires that the kidnapper remove the victim from his own domain in order to be liable (see above, note 4). If so, no such requirement is stated regarding the act of selling, and therefore the kidnapper is liable whether the victim stays in the kidnapper's domain or not (see *Ramban* loc. cit., regarding the opinion of *Rashi* in *Sanhedrin* 85b ד"ה ועדיין; see *Rambam, Hil. Geneivah* 9:3 and *Maggid Mishneh* there).

9. This exclusion is derived from the phrasing of the verse (*Devarim* 24:7): *When a man is found kidnapping one of his brothers* (מאחיו) ... The term "מאחיו" — literally, "from his brothers" — implies that the victim must be removed from his brothers, i.e. his family. Therefore, a kidnapper who sells his victim to the victim's own relatives is exempt from punishment, as this condition has not been fulfilled (*Sanhedrin* 85b; *Rambam, Hil. Geneivah* 9:3).

The commentators discuss what degree of kinship is encompassed by this exemption: Does it exclude only selling to those relatives who are unfit to give testimony against the victim as a result of their relation, or would even more distant relatives be included? (see *Minchas Chinuch* 36:9).

Even if the victim is sold to his own relatives, and the kidnapper is exempt from punishment, he nevertheless has transgressed the prohibition against selling a Jewish slave on

the public auction block (see *Minchas Chinuch* 36:1 and *mitzvah* #345).

10. See *Sanhedrin* 86a; *Rambam, Hil. Geneivah* 9:1.

This mitzvah prohibits selling a Jew in the same manner that one would sell a Canaanite slave. It encompasses the case in which a kidnapper sells his victim in the manner of a Canaanite slave, even though that case is prohibited by *Lo Signov* as well (*Rambam* ibid.).

11. In general, all prohibitions in the Torah apply equally to men and women (see Mishnah, *Kiddushin* 29a, and Gemara there 35a). With regard to kidnapping, however, the verse in *Devarim* (24:7) mentions a *man* who kidnaps, which could lead one to assume that this prohibition applies only to men. To dispel this notion, the verse in *Shemos* (21:16) refers simply to *one* who kidnaps, indicating that the prohibition applies to both men and women kidnappers (see *Mechilta, Shemos* 21:16, and *Sanhedrin* 85b; see also *Rambam, Hil. Geneivah* 9:6).

12. The Gemara in *Sanhedrin* (56a) lists seven mitzvos that were given to non-Jews (the reference to Noahide Laws reflects the fact that all of mankind descended from Noah, whose family were the sole survivors of the Flood). They are: (1) the requirement to establish a system of civil laws (see *Rambam, Hil. Melachim* 9:14); (2) a prohibition against blasphemy (euphemistically called "blessing" the Name of Hashem); (3) a prohibition against idolatry; (4) a prohibition against illicit unions (see *Sanhedrin* 57a); (5) a prohibition against murder; (6) a prohibition against theft; and (7) a prohibition against eating a limb torn from a live animal (אבר מן החי).

The Gemara (ibid. 56b) derives these mitzvos from a verse in *Bereishis* (2:16), which speaks of Hashem's commands to Adam HaRishon. With respect to theft, the Gemara states that Adam was told he could eat *of every tree in the garden* — which implies that fruit stolen from *other* trees would be forbidden. Kidnapping is also included, as it too is a form of theft.

[It should be noted that in the view of some commentators, Shechem was liable to be killed because he violated this law when he kidnapped Dinah, the daughter of Yaakov (see *Ramban* to *Bereishis* 34:13).]

13. This is derived from the verse in *Shemos* (21:16), which states: *One who kidnaps a man and sells him, and he was found to have been in his hand, he shall surely be put to death.* The verse implies that the victim was found to be in the kidnapper's hands *as a result of the kidnapping*, from which it is derived that if the victim had been in the kidnapper's hand (i.e. readily accessible to him) *before* the kidnapping, the death penalty does not apply (*Sanhedrin* 86a; see *Mechilta* of *Rashbi* to *Shemos* ibid.).

The same exemption will apply to a teacher who kidnaps his student (*Sanhedrin* ibid.; see *Rambam, Hil. Geneivah* 9:5, and *Minchas Chinuch* 36:11). There are other victims whose kidnap does not render the kidnapper liable to the death penalty. Examples include: (1) a Canaanite slave or half-slave/half-freeman [where one of two people who owned him in partnership set his half of the slave free] (*Minchas Chinuch* ibid.); (2) a nonviable child (*nefel*), or any child who might be a *nefel* (see *Mechilta* of *Rashbi* to *Shemos* ibid.); or (3) a *tereifah* [a person who possesses one of a defined set of fatal physical defects] (see *Medrash Cheifetz* to *Shemos* ibid.).

A BROADER LOOK AT THE LAWS

1 The act of kidnapping: exclusively "geneivah," or can it be "gezeilah"?

There are two terms the Torah uses to refer to monetary theft; *geneivah*, theft, that is performed surreptitiously, without the owner's knowledge, and *gezeilah*, robbery, that is performed openly.

The three verses dealing with kidnapping all use the term *geneivah*: "*Lo Signov*" (*Shemos* 20:13), "*Goneiv ish u'mechoro …*" (ibid. 21:16), and "*Ki yimotzei ish goneiv nefesh …*" (*Devarim* 24:7). Some infer from this that the prohibition of kidnapping is restricted to kidnapping which falls within the parameters of *geneivah*. Thus, if one kidnaps his victim openly, with the knowledge of his family, he is not liable. This is implied in the verse (*Devarim* 24:7) which states: *When a man is found kidnapping another from his brothers,* which can be understood to mean that the victim was stolen secretly from his relatives (who are deemed to be his "owner" for the purposes of this prohibition). [A possible explanation of this limitation is that when one kidnaps another openly, with his relatives' knowledge, they would surely do everything in their power to free him. When one kidnaps covertly, however, the victim has a much smaller chance of being rescued. Accordingly, the Torah views this act much more severely (see Responsa of *R' Betzalel Ashkenazi* §39; *Minchas Chinuch* 36:14).]

Others disagree with this inference, and make no distinction between *geneivah* and *gezeilah* with respect to the act of kidnapping. They reason that a person is his own "owner," and therefore any victim of kidnap is perforce a victim of *gezeilah*, since he is aware that he is being kidnapped. They further explain that the Torah's usage of the term *geneivah* is simply due to the reality that most victims of kidnapping are children (see *Ibn Ezra* to *Shemos* 21:16), whose awareness is not considered halachically valid, thereby making their kidnapping an act

of *geneivah* (Commentary of *R' Y. F. Perla* to *Sefer HaMitzvos* of *R' Saadiah Gaon* [*RaSag*], *Lo Saaseh* §91 [p. 127b]; see there at length).

2 Does one incur the death penalty for selling alone, or only for kidnapping and selling?

The verse states: *One who kidnaps a man and sells him, and he was found in his hand, he shall surely be put to death* (*Shemos* 21:16). There is an Amoraic dispute in the Gemara (*Sanhedrin* 86b) as to which element of the prohibition incurs the death penalty. Chizkiah maintains that capital punishment is given solely for the act of selling the victim. Accordingly, since the act of kidnapping alone is not a capital offense, one who kidnaps — but does not sell — his victim would incur the punishment of *malkos* (lashes), as per the law for transgressions of prohibitions that do not carry the death penalty. [However, if he does sell his victim in a manner which makes him liable to the death penalty, he is exempt from *malkos*, since one who incurs a minor penalty and a more severe penalty simultaneously is exempted from the lesser one [קם ליה בדרבה מיניה] (*Rashi* to *Sanhedrin* ibid. ד"ה לחודה).]

R' Yochanan disagrees, and argues that the capital punishment is given for the combined act of kidnapping and selling. Therefore, one who kidnaps but does not sell does not receive *malkos*, as is the rule for any transgression which can potentially carry the death penalty (see *Rambam*, *Hil. Sanhedrin* 18:2).

The dispute between these two Amoraim has another ramification: If the witnesses who testified to the kidnapping were subsequently contradicted by a second set of witnesses in a manner which fulfills the conditions of "*hazamah*" [see *mitzvah* #524], they are rendered *zomemim* witnesses (see *Makkos* 5a), and are liable to receive the punishment of "*ka'asher zamam*" — that is, they receive the punishment they attempted to cause their victim to receive. According to Chizkiah, the *zomemim* would receive *malkos*, for in his view, this is the punishment they attempted to impose upon the supposed kidnapper. According to R' Yochanan, however, they would be exempt from *malkos*, since their testimony alone would not have resulted in any punishment (see *Sanhedrin* ibid. and *Rashi* there).

The halachah follows the opinion of R' Yochanan. Therefore, one who kidnaps, but does not sell his victim, does not receive *malkos* (*Rambam, Hil. Geneivah* 9:1). However, the kidnapper transgresses the prohibition against kidnapping even in this case (*Minchas Chinuch* 36:1).

Witnesses to the kidnapping who were rendered *zomemim* would not incur *malkos*; only witnesses who testified to both the kidnapping and the selling and were rendered *zomemim* with respect to both testimonies could be punished by the laws of *ka'asher zamam*. And in that case, they would receive the punishment of strangulation, for this is the punishment they would have imposed on their victim, the supposed "kidnapper" (*Rambam, Hil. Eidus* 21:9).

3　The sale is invalid, but must be attempted in a halachically valid manner

As mentioned above, the sale of the victim is completely invalid, even when carried out with halachically valid methods of transaction (see *Bava Kamma* 68b, and *Rashi* there ד"ה גניבה בנפש). The commentators explain that since the victim is not, in fact, a slave, the kidnapper has no rights to sell him (*Minchas Chinuch* 36:6). Nevertheless, the kidnapper is exempt from punishment unless he attempts to sell his victim using a halachically valid

method of transaction, as if he were his master (see above, note 8).

There are, however, two cases in which even an attempted sale that was performed correctly may not result in liability to capital punishment: (1) where the buyer is a non-Jew. The commentators disagree as to whether a sale to a non-Jew fulfills the condition of "selling" to obligate the kidnapper. Some maintain that there is no difference who the buyer is (*Lechem Mishneh, Hil. Eidus* 21:9; see also *Kessef Mishneh* ibid.; *Minchas Chinuch* 36:6). Others maintain that one who sells to a non-Jew would be exempt from punishment. *Zera Avraham* (*Responsa* 14:6, explaining *Rambam, Hil. Eidus* 21:9) explains that the nature of this sale must be such that if it were performed under normal conditions, it would be valid. Since one can never sell one's Jewish slave to a non-Jew (see *Rambam, Hil. Avodim* 1:3), such a sale cannot fulfill this condition [For another possible explanation, see *Tzafnas Pane'ach, Terumos* 1:23]; (2) where the kidnapper retracted his sale. If the kidnapper retracted his attempted sale in a manner which would normally annul a sale's validity, i.e. if he retracted *toch k'dei dibbur* (literally: within the time it takes to make an utterance; this is defined by the Gemara [*Makkos* 6a, *Bava Kamma* 73b] as the few seconds it takes to greet one's teacher), he is exempt from the death penalty. Here too, since the sale would have been invalidated had it been an actual sale, it cannot fulfill the condition of "selling" the victim (*Minchas Chinuch* 36:12).

SITUATIONS IN HALACHAH

Question:
Did Yosef's capture and sale render his brothers liable to the penalty of death?

Answer:
The Medrash (*Medrash Eileh Ezkarah*; see *Beis Medrash II, VI; Baal HaTurim, Devarim* 24:7) relates that a Roman governor came upon the verse, *One who kidnaps a man and sells him, and [the victim] is found in his hand, he shall be put to death* (*Shemos* 21:16). Recalling at once the story of Yosef and his brothers, the tyrant ordered ten Jewish Sages to appear before him, and sentenced them to death as punishment for the sale of Yosef. He argued that they, as the successors of the ancient tribes and great leaders of Israel, bore responsibility for their sin. These *Asarah Harugei Malchus,* the Medrash tells us, were, in fact, the ones whom Heaven had chosen to effect atonement, once and for all, for the sale of Yosef (*Medrash Heichalos Rabbasi* 5:5; *Medrash Mishlei,* 1:13; see also *Zohar Chadash*, end of *Eichah* [117a]; see further in *Through the Eyes of the Sages* section). The clear implication is that Yosef's abduction involved a capital crime, a violation of the prohibition of *Lo Signov*.

However, although there was undoubtedly some degree of fault to be found in the brothers' behavior, many commentators cite various arguments that somewhat mitigate the brothers' crime against Yosef:

❧ *The abduction of Yosef did not meet all the conditions for the Torah's classic case of kidnapping.*

Chasam Sofer (*Toras Moshe, Vayeishev* [p. 161]) asks: What did Yehudah expect to gain when he broached the idea of rescuing Yosef from the pit, and to sell him instead as a slave? The act of kidnapping Yosef and selling him into slavery would

carry the penalty of death, while leaving Yosef to die in the pit was an indirect act of killing, one that would not incur capital punishment. So, at least from the standpoint of the severity of the respective penalties, it would seem that he should have opted to leave Yosef where he was.

Some suggest that the answer is alluded to in the language of the verse (*Bereishis* 37:28): *They **pulled** and hoisted Yosef out of the pit.* What would be missing had the verse simply stated, "They hoisted Yosef out of the pit?" The superfluous term "pulled," these commentators say, was added to inform us that the brothers took special care to raise him from the pit with a pulling action only — by dragging him up along the walls of the pit — as opposed to *lifting* him up in the air. This is because the brothers were anxious to avoid performing an act of acquisition on their victim, a requisite ingredient in the type of kidnapping prohibited by the Torah (see above, Law 1). Now, the halachah provides that while the acquisitional method of הגבהה, *lifting*, is effective even in a public domain, the method of משיכה, *pulling,* is not (see *Bava Basra* 76B and *Tosafos* to *Kesubos* 31b). By refraining from lifting Yosef, the tribes, who were in a public domain, effectively avoided transgressing *"Lo Signov"* (see *Bris Shalom* by R' Pinchas MiVoldavi).

Chasam Sofer (ibid.; see also *Minchas Yitzchak, Vayeishev*) himself suggests that the brothers reasoned that even a valid act of acquisition would not render them liable, because the halachah is that if the kidnap victim was never removed from his own domain into the property of the kidnapper, there is no penalty, even though an abduction took place (see *Rambam, Hil. Geneivah* 9:3; see above, note 4). That being the case, the abduction of Yosef could not have met this condition, because the entire episode took place in Eretz Yisrael, which belonged to his father, Yaakov. Even today, our claim to Eretz Yisrael derives from that of our forefathers, which indicates that the land was already the legal possession of our forefather Yaakov, a member of whose household Yosef was. He was thus never removed from his own domain. In the same vein,

Binyan David (by *R' David Meisels* of *Uhel*) points out that the sale of Yosef took place in the area of Shechem, which was his *own* territory (see *Bereishis Rabbah* 97:6). Certainly, then, he remained in his own domain throughout the actual kidnapping.

 Other conditions for liability that were absent in the sale of Yosef

Other commentators (*Binyan David, VaYitzbor Yosef*) find the solution to our problem in the *Rambam's* law that when the kidnapper's victim is readily available to him, he is not liable to the death penalty (see above, Law 6). Yosef, one of the youngest of Yaakov's sons, lived with his brothers in the same household, as it says (*Bereishis* 37:2), *Yosef, at seventeen years old, would shepherd the flock with his brothers …* It can be said, then, of Yosef, that he had previously been under the "hand" of his brothers, exempting them from liability to the death penalty. *Chasam Sofer* (ibid.) suggests yet another approach: A condition for liability to the death penalty is that the abductor "make use" of his victim before selling him (see Law 3), something the brothers took care to avoid. An allusion to this can be seen in the verse, *Let us not lay our hands on him …* (*Bereishis* 37:27).

VaYitzbor Yosef cites the Medrash (*Bereishis Rabbah, Vayeishev* 84:17), which states: "The brothers said, *'Let us go and sell him …'* What is meant by the wording, 'Let us go?' The brothers said to one another, 'Let us go, and adopt the ways of the world. Was not Canaan the son of Cham, who sinned, cursed to be a slave in punishment for his sin? This one [Yosef], is no different; let us go and sell him!'" We see from this Medrash that the tribes were of the opinion that Yosef, as a result of his sins, was *de facto* a slave. And we have learned (see above, note 13) that one who kidnaps a slave is not liable to punishment.

It is interesting to note that according to some Rishonim (see *Rashbam* and *Rabbeinu Bachya*), Yosef was not actually sold by his brothers at all; it was the passing *Midianites* who seized him and sold him to the Arab merchants. This view is, in fact, borne out by the simple reading of the verse (*Bereishis* 37:28), *Some Midianite men, merchants, passed by; they pulled and hoisted Yosef from the pit, and sold Yosef to the Ishmaelites for twenty silver [pieces].* According to this view, the brothers were sitting at a distance from the pit, eating their meal while waiting for the Ishmaelite caravan from Gilaad to arrive. They were preempted by the Midianites, who removed Yosef from the pit and sold him for a profit. Although the brothers did not have a direct hand in the sale, they were still held accountable for their passive role in Yosef's abduction.

ILLUMINATIONS OF THE MITZVAH
Suggested Reasons & Insights

I. KIDNAPPING: AN ASSAULT ON THE PERSON; A STRIKE AT THE SOUL

he Torah's prohibition against kidnapping is founded on the elementary principle that a person is born to be free. To kidnap a person is to strip him of a most basic right that is much treasured by mankind (see *R' Samson R. Hirsch* to *Shemos* 20:13 & 21:16).

Kidnapping tears the victim away from his family and native environment, which in itself takes a heavy toll on his quality of life. Moreover, it is by no means impossible for an abduction to eventually lead to the death of its victim, as he may be abused in captivity. If he winds up being sold as a slave to an overbearing master, who drives his slaves to work to the hilt, he is liable to be beaten, perhaps even to death, when he fails to perform to the expected degree (see *Bava Basra* 8b).

The damage of kidnapping does not end with the havoc it wreaks on the victim's earthly life. The transformation of a proud, free man into a captive slave cannot but harm him spiritually too. If he is sold to an idolater, who will have little sympathy for his religious observance, the danger is plain. But even if he is bought by a Jew, presumably his new owner assumes that he is an idolater, for otherwise he would not enslave him. The master will thus allow for his observance of only those mitzvos which a Canaanite slave is obliged to perform — those that are not time related. The rest of his mitzvos will remain unfulfilled. Furthermore, the master is bound to arrange for his new "slave" a union with a Canaanite maidservant, something forbidden to a Jewish man unlawfully possessed; his children will thus be born into slavery. In sum, the kidnapper brings his victim to sin, which, our Sages have established, is worse than killing him, for it deprives

him not only of true life in this world, but also eternal bliss in the next (see *Sifrei, Devarim* §252, and *Meshech Chochmah, Devarim* 24:7; see also *Eileh HaMitzvos, Lo Saaseh* §35).

One mitzvah which a kidnap victim may be prevented from performing is singled out by the commentators — that of honoring one's parents. The prohibition against kidnapping appears in the Torah (*Shemos* 21:16) between two verses dealing with a child's relationship to his parents — one prescribing the punishment for hitting one's parents, and the other for cursing them. This placement is seen as alluding to the concern that kidnap victims, who are often children who will grow up ignorant of their parents' identities, will come one day to unwittingly strike, or curse, the very people who brought them into the world (*Ramban* and *Ibn Ezra, Shemos* 21:15, citing *R' Saadiah Gaon*; see also *Bamidbar Rabbah* 9:7). And even if such a thing never occurs, such children are deprived of the opportunity to honor their parents, and, as a result, will always suffer from a spiritual handicap (see *Ramban, Shemos* 20:13). The chain of Jewish tradition and faith is made of links formed by the bonds connecting parents and children; by demonstrating respect to his parents, a child reinforces the message that he is on the receiving end of this life-giving legacy and dependent upon it.

II. KIDNAPPING: A MENACE TO THE SOCIAL ORDER

he act of abduction is more than just an offense against one individual; it attacks the social framework that allows people to live peacefully with one another. Human society cannot endure if people are given free reign to kidnap their neighbors. The Torah thus considers this a capital crime, for at stake is the viability of human civilization itself. If only the offender would have paused to consider, perhaps he would have realized that, by causing the breakdown of society's norms for justice and fair play, he ultimately harms himself. In an environment where the tethers of brotherly relations are undone, no individual is safe (*Sefer HaBris* II, 13:13).

III. KIDNAPPING: ROBBING A MAN OF HIS MISSION

he victim and society are not the only casualties of the kidnapper's actions. A kidnapper negates the very purpose of human existence. The fundamental human entitlement to freedom derives from the fact that man — as reflected by the Divine image that he bears — has been created so that he may freely exercise his will and guide his own life. Such a being ought to be servile to God alone. The kidnapper, by mocking this liberty, defies the Divine element inherent in man (*Recanti, Taamei HaMitzvos, Lo Saaseh* §21).

This holds true in regard to the kidnapping of any human being. Beyond that, however, a kidnapper who preys on a *Jewish* victim repudiates God's efforts in taking the Jews out of Egypt. The aim of the Exodus from Egypt was to liberate the Jewish people, not only from Egyptian servitude, but from all external forces, empowering us to dedicate our lives to God's service alone. Imagine if a human king had singled out one of his subjects, exempting him from all his civil duties so that he may become fully devoted to the royal service. If one had the audacity to seize this man and make him his personal slave, is there any doubt that the king would call for his head? (*Derech Pikudechah, Lo Saaseh* §36, *Cheilek HaMachshavah* §9, citing *R' Menachem HaBavli*).

A Jew conscious of his noble calling would never, and indeed must not, submit himself to the servitude of another man. He is already a member in the company of servants devoted to God, as He Himself has declared, *They, whom I have taken out of the land of Mitzrayim, have become My servants; they must not be sold in the manner of a slave* (*Vayikra* 25:42). The Gemara (*Kiddushin* 22b) explains Hashem's intent: "They are *My* servants, and are not to be servants to other servants."

This is not a matter to be taken lightly, as it involves nothing less than an element of idol worship, one of the worst of all sins. To subject oneself to the control of another man is not so far removed from the deplorable inclination to place oneself under the domination of a force other than God, which is the essence of idol worship (*Be'er Mayim Chayim, Yisro* 20:2; see there for elaboration). If this has been said of one who becomes a slave of his *own* accord, how much more grave is the sin of one who uses force to enslave another man against his will!

There is yet more. One need not go so far as to kidnap a person in order to violate the sublimity of a Jewish soul. If a person in a position of authority, in an unjustified way, lords over others and instills in them fear, he also has infringed on this precept. It is not appropriate for a servant of God to be cowed by the fear of a mortal being. Upon its inception, God exhorted the Jewish nation: *And you shall be to Me a kingdom of nobles and a holy nation* (*Shemos* 19:6). All Jews are nobility; they must live as men with no other lord than God alone (*Shaarei Teshuvah*, 3:167).

THROUGH THE EYES OF THE SAGES
Stories, Parables, & Reflections

I. THE KIDNAPPING AND SELLING OF YOSEF

ne of the fundamental narratives in the genesis of the Jewish nation is the incident of Yosef's kidnapping; how his brothers took him and sold him into slavery. The story is very difficult to understand, for it is a story in which both merit and shame are intertwined. On the one hand, the brothers' sale of Yosef was predestined, and resulted in a positive development — the descent of Yaakov and his offspring to Mitzrayim, where the Jewish people and its spiritual mission would incubate, and from which they would be liberated and chosen as the eternal nation of Hashem (see *Tanchuma, Vayeishev* §4). On the other hand, *Chazal* present the sale of Yosef in a negative light as well: They speak of it as a grave sin whose executors were held to account while still alive, and which caused much misery for the Jewish people in later generations. Nevertheless, amid the depiction of the brothers' deeds and guilt, the Sages take care to highlight their righteousness, as is seen in the following Medrash: "Even though the hands of the brothers were indeed involved in the sale of Yosef, do you think that this incident took place for the simple reason that they were wicked in general? [I.e. that Heaven presented them with the opportunity to sin in this matter because they were wicked people, in accordance with the rule that God chooses the wicked as His agents to effect predestined harmful events?] *No!* Rather, they were thoroughly righteous men, and they committed no sin other than that one, as it is written (*Bereishis* 42:21): [*The brothers*] *said to one another* [many years later, after being falsely accused and imprisoned for treachery in Mitzrayim], *'Indeed, we are guilty concerning our brother ... that is why this anguish has*

come upon us.' That is, they were engaging in introspection, trying to understand why they had been arrested by the Egyptians, and could find nothing but this sin alone. Thus, from the description of their shame, Scripture intimates their virtue; that they were guilty of only this sin. And because the sale of Yosef was [ultimately] a benefit for him — since it brought him to rule [Mitzrayim] — and a benefit for all of his brothers and his father's household — since it led to their sustenance in the years of famine — for these very reasons, Yosef was sold through them, for Heaven causes acts of merit to occur through the meritorious" (*Bamidbar Rabbah* 13:18).

Within this section, we will present several statements of *Chazal* regarding the crime of Yosef's sale and its negative repercussions. They are presented here in order to emphasize the severity of kidnapping and selling a person. However, it is necessary to emphasize that although the brothers' conduct toward Yosef seems severe, it was not unreasoned. Aside from the fact that they did not transgress the prohibition of kidnapping in its strict halachic sense (see *Responsa, Maharitatz* I:165 at length; see also *Siach Halachah* section), they had solid reasons for what they did, even taking into account the conceptual sense of this prohibition. Indeed, the Holy One, Blessed is He, Himself joined them, as it were, in instituting a ban against anyone who would disclose Yosef's sale to Yaakov (see *Tanchuma, Vayeishev* §2). Therefore, it is incumbent upon the reader to relate to what follows with a sense of reverence for these spiritual luminaries. They were our spiritual progenitors, and the continued existence of the Jewish people, both materially and spiritually, is based upon their righteousness and merit.

——— ❦ ———

❧ *The Episode of the pit*

And so it happened, when Yosef came to his brothers, they stripped Yosef of his tunic, the tunic of fine wool upon him (*Bereishis* 37:23). R' Elazar said: [Yosef] came to them full of praises and joy. How did they react? *They stripped Yosef* — this refers to his frock; *his tunic* — this refers to his long shirt; *the tunic of fine wool* — this refers to his decorated cloak; *upon him* — this refers to his trousers. The verse states further: *And they cast him into the pit; the pit was empty; there was no water in it* (*Bereishis* 37:24). From the plain meaning of that which it says *the pit was empty*, do I not know that it had no water? Rather, what does the Torah mean to teach us by saying, *there was no water in it*? (see *Shabbos* 22a). *There was no water in it*, but there were snakes and scorpions in it. [According to some, there were two pits: One was full of stones and one was full of venomous snakes and scorpions. Once they put him inside the (second) pit, Shimon gave the command and they commenced to throw stones at him from the first pit in order to kill him (*Tanchuma Yashan; Yalkut Shimoni*).] R' Acha said: The words *the pit was empty* are meant to teach us that *Yaakov's* pit became empty; that is, Yaakov's sons became empty of words of Torah, in that they did not realize the punishment for the matter. The words *there was no water in it* teaches us that in each of the brothers there were no words of Torah, which are symbolized by water, as it says (*Yeshaya* 55:1): *Ho, every thirsty person, go to the water*. In what respect were they ignorant of Torah? It is written (*Devarim* 24:7): *If a man is found kidnapping a person of his brethren … that kidnapper shall die*. Yet, of them it could be said, "You are selling your brother!" (*Bereishis Rabbah* 84:16; *Tanchuma Yashan, Vayeishev*).

——— ❦ ———

❧ *The sale*

Let us go and sell him to the Yishmaelites (*Bereishis* 37:27). The brothers said, "Let us go and follow the way of the world: Canaan sinned; was he not cursed to be a slave? (see ibid. 9:25). This one too [Yosef] (whom they held had sinned by bringing a bad report about them to their father), let us go and sell him to the Yishmaelites" (*Bereishis Rabbah* 84:17; *Pesikta Zutresa, Vayeishev*).

———

How many bills of sale were written for Yosef (i.e. how many times was he sold)? R' Yudan said: Four: (1) from his brothers to the Yishmaelites (see *Bereishis* 37:28); (2) from the Yishmaelites to the "merchants" (see ibid.); (3) from the merchants to the Midianites (see ibid. v. 36); and (4) the Midianites sold him to Mitzrayim (see ibid.). Rav Huna said: Five, [for] the Midianites sold him to the provincial administrator of Mitzrayim and Potiphar came and bought him from the provincial administrator (*Bereishis Rabbah* 84:22).

——— ❦ ———

❧ *The price*

They sold Yosef to the Ishmaelites for twenty silver coins (*Bereishis* 37:28). They proceeded to sell him for twenty silver coins, two silver coins for each [of the ten brothers] to buy shoes for their feet [as it is written (*Amos* 2:6): *For their selling a righteous man for silver and an indigent man for shoes* (*Medrash HaGadol* and *Yalkut Shimoni* to *Bereishis* ibid.).] Now do you really think that a young man as handsome as Yosef would have been sold for only twenty silver coins? Rather, after Yosef was cast into the pit, the shine of his countenance dimmed, the blood fled from his features and his face appeared greenish. Therefore, they sold him for only twenty silver coins for shoes (*Tanchuma, Vayeishev* §2; *Medrash HaGadol, Bereishis* ibid.).

———

Once Yosef saw himself among those wild creatures (the snakes and scorpions mentioned above), he became despondent and said, "Woe is to me, that I shall not be saved from these wild creatures!" Out of his intense fear and trepidation, he lost his [handsome] form and beauty. However, the Holy One, Blessed is He, closed the mouths of the wild creatures and they did not harm him. And when the brothers saw a caravan of Ishmaelites, they hauled him out of the pit unclothed and sold him that way. The Holy One, Blessed is He, said, "Should a righteous man such as this stand unclothed in front of people?" The Sages said: There was one thing he was still wearing, an amulet hung around his neck. The Holy One, Blessed is He, sent the angel Gavriel and he extracted from that amulet a garment and clothed him. Once the brothers of Yosef saw that he was miraculously clothed, they said to the Ishmaelites, "Give us back this garment, for we sold him to you unclothed only." The Ishmaelites replied, "We will not return the garment to you." They argued until the Ishmaelites agreed to add another four pairs of shoes to the price they had already paid them. In that garment, they brought Yosef to Mitzrayim (*Medrash Asarah Harugei Malchus*).

———— ❧ ————

❧ "Returning the stolen property"

Yosef's bones, which the children of Israel had brought up from Mitzrayim, they buried in Shechem (*Yehoshua* 24:32). Why Shechem? R' Chama bar R' Chanina said: It was from Shechem that they kidnapped him (see *Bereishis* 37:14), so it is to Shechem that his lost object [his body] should be returned (*Sotah* 13b).

II. Mitzvos and offerings intended to atone for the sale of Yosef

❧ The redemption of the firstborn

he Holy One, Blessed is He, said: You sold Rachel's son for twenty silver *maos,* which equal five *selaim;* therefore each and every one will have to dedicate the valuation of his firstborn son — five *selaim* in Tyrian currency (*Bereishis Rabbah* 84:18; see *Rashi* to *Bamidbar* 3:46).

———— ❧ ————

❧ The half-shekel

R' Yehudah ben Shimon said: The Holy One, Blessed is He, said to the brothers: You sold Rachel's son for twenty silver coins [which is two silver coins, or a half-*shekel,* for each of the ten brothers,] therefore each and every one of you is required to give a half-*shekel* every year (*Bereishis Rabbah* ibid.; *Yerushalmi, Shekalim* 2:3).

———— ❧ ————

❧ The eighth-day inaugural offering

What motivated the Jewish people to bring more [offerings] than Aharon? [On the eighth day of the inauguration of the *Mishkan,* Aharon was commanded to bring only a young bull and a ram (see *Vayikra* 9:2), whereas the Jewish people were commanded to bring a calf, a he-goat, a sheep, a bull, and a ram (ibid. vs. 3-4).] Moshe said to the Jewish people, "You are responsible for an initial sin and a concluding sin: You have the initial sin of [the sale of] Yosef, which involved a he-goat, as it says (*Bereishis* 37:31): *And they slaughtered a he-goat and dipped the tunic in the blood.* And you have a concluding sin, as it says (*Shemos* 32:8): *They made for themselves a molten calf.* Let the he-goat come and atone for the goat incident, and let the calf come and atone for the calf incident" (*Toras Kohanim, Shemini, Miluim* §3).

———— ❧ ————

❧ The offerings of the princes

In connection with the offering of Nachshon ben Aminadav, prince of the Tribe of Yehudah, the verse (*Bamidbar* 7:16) states: *One he-goat for a chatas.* This corresponds to an event in the life of Yehudah, for he brought to his father the fine woolen tunic of Yosef that he had dipped in the he-goat's blood, as it says (*Bereishis* 37:31): *And they slaughtered a he-goat, etc.* Yehudah brought it to his father and said (ibid. v. 32): *Identify, if you please: Is this your son's tunic or not?* (*Bamidbar Rabbah* 13:14; *Medrash Aggadah Bamidbar* 7:16). Indeed, *Medrash Aggadah* (*Bamidbar* 28:26) states that wherever the Jews were commanded to offer a he-goat, it was to atone for the sin of Yosef's sale.

III. THE IMMEDIATE PUNISHMENT

av Mana says: As a result of the sale of Yosef, the brothers were stricken, and their iniquity was not atoned for until they died. Regarding them the verse states (*Yeshayah* 22:14): *That this sin will never be atoned for you until you die.* It is for this reason that a famine visited the Land of Canaan for seven years, and the ten brothers of Yosef went down to buy provisions from Mitzrayim (*Tanchuma, Vayeishev* §2; *Pirkei D'Rabbi Eliezer* §38).

————

Neither are riches to the discerning (*Koheles* 9:11). This refers to the sons of Yaakov who were men of discernment, and wealthy, as it says (*Bereishis* 31:16): *But all the wealth that God has taken away from our father [Lavan] belongs to us and to our children.* However, they lost their assets because they sold Yosef (*Medrash Sechel Tov, Vayeishev*).

IV. THE PUNISHMENT FOR LATER GENERATIONS

 ### Exile in Mitzrayim

he Holy One, Blessed is He, said to the brothers: You sold Yosef into slavery; by your lives, you [i.e. your descendants] will recite every year (*Haggadah shel Pesach*): "We were slaves to Pharaoh in Mitzrayim!" (*Yalkut Shimoni, Tehillim* §648).

———— 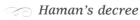 ————

Haman's decree

The Holy One, Blessed is He, said to the brothers: You sold your brother amid food and drink, as it says (*Bereishis* 37:25): *They sat to eat bread* (after casting Yosef in the pit and before selling him) — I will do the same to you: Your descendants will be sold in Shushan, the capital city amid food and drink. That is the meaning of what is written (*Esther* 3:15): *The king and Haman sat to drink,* after issuing the decree of annihilation against the Jews (*Esther*

Rabbah 7:25; *Medrash Tehillim* §10; *Yalkut Shimoni* ibid.).

———— ————

The Asarah Harugei Malchus (literally: the ten murdered by the regime) and those murdered in every generation

R' Yehoshua ben Levi said: The *Asarah Harugei Malchus* were given over to the wicked regime by Heaven solely because of the sin of Yosef's sale. R' Avin said: I would say that ten people are punished in each and every generation; yet, that sin endures still (*Medrash Mishlei* 1:13).

The verdict issued against the Asarah Harugei Malchus

Once Lulianus Caesar was sitting, engaging in the study of the Torah, and he found written (*Shemos* 21:16): *One who kidnaps a man and sells him, and [the victim] was found to be in his possession, shall certainly die.* So he went and plastered shoes all over the room, sticking them to the walls. He sent for Rabban Shimon ben Gamliel and his colleagues and said to them, "A person who kidnaps a Jewish person and proceeds to sell him — what is his sentence?" They told him, "He is liable to the death penalty." He said to them, "If so, then you are liable to the death penalty. Accept upon yourselves the judgment of Heaven!" They said to him, "Why are we liable to the death penalty?" He said to them, "Because of Yosef's brothers who sold Yosef, as it is written (*Bereishis* 37:28): *And they sold Yosef;* and it is written (*Amos* 2:6): *For their selling a righteous man for silver and an indigent man for shoes.*" It was for this reason that Caesar plastered the room with shoes, so they should take note of the item for which Yosef was sold. The Sages said to him, "If Yosef's brothers sold their brother, what crime have we committed? Why should you kill us?" He replied, "If Yosef's brothers were still alive today, I would arrest them and administer justice to them. Now that they are not alive, I shall administer justice to you, for you are the equals of the brothers of Yosef, who participated in his sale."

They said to him, "Give us some time — three days — until we determine if this decree comes from Heaven. If it does, then we will accept upon ourselves the judgment of Heaven." He gave them three days' time. These future martyrs of the regime gathered together, and these were their names: Rabban Shimon ben Gamliel, R' Yishmael ben Elisha the *Kohen Gadol,* R' Akiva ben Yosef, R' Yehudah ben Bava, R' Chanina ben Teradyon, R' Yeshevav the Scribe, R' Elazar ben Dema, R' Chanina ben Chachinai, R' Chutzpis the Meturgeman (translator), and R' Elazar ben Shamua. These were the ten martyrs of the regime murdered because the brothers sold Yosef, and the smallest of all of them was the great Sage, R' Yishmael the *Kohen Gadol.* R' Yishmael said to the others, "If you are willing to share responsibility with me in the offense entailed in my mention of the Name of God, then I will ascend to Heaven and we will know: If this decree issued from Heaven, we will accept it upon ourselves; but if it is not from Heaven, then I can nullify it with the Name." They told him, "Your offense is split among us."

When R' Yishmael would want to ascend to Heaven, he would mention the Name and a wind would lift him up, and he would fly in the air and ascend to Heaven. The angel Gavriel would greet him and tell him whatever he wanted to know. This time when he mentioned the Name, he was received by a storm wind, which brought him up to Heaven. Once he ascended, the angel Metatron encountered him. Metatron said to him, "Who are you?" He answered, "I am Yishmael ben Elisha, the *Kohen Gadol.*" He asked him, "Are you the Yishmael in whom your Creator takes pride every day, and He says [to me], 'I have a servant on Earth who is like you: His shine is like your shine and his appearance is like your appearance?'" R' Yishmael ben Elisha, the *Kohen Gadol,* humbly replied, "I am Yishmael." Metatron said to him, "What are you doing in this place?" He replied, "The government issued a decree against us to murder ten of the Sages of Israel,

so I ascended to find out if this decree is from Heaven, in which case we will accept it upon ourselves. But if not — if it is not from Heaven — then we are able to nullify it." Metatron said to him, "In what way could you nullify it?" [R' Yishmael] replied, "With the Name." Metatron *Sar HaPanim* said to him, "Fortunate are you, O Israel, to whom the Holy One, Blessed is He, has revealed the secret of the Name, a secret that He has not revealed to the ministering angels. For you can nullify decrees with the Ineffable Name. However, woe is to you, Yishmael, my son! This is what I overheard from beyond the Curtain: The echo of a Heavenly voice wailed, saying, 'Ten of the Sages of Israel have been given over to the government!'" R' Yishmael said to him, "Why?" He replied, "Because there was an argument that took place before the Holy One, Blessed is He, between Samael (the angel of Edom/Eisav — see *Rashi, Sotah* 10b. Samael is also identified with the Satan — see *Shemos Rabbah* 18:5 and *Devarim Rabbah* 11:10) and Michael (the angel who advocates for the Jewish people — see *Daniel* 10:21 with *Metzudas David*). Samael said before Him, 'Master of the Universe! Have You ever written one letter in Your entire Torah for no purpose? Is it not written (*Devarim* 32:47): *For it is not an empty thing for you,* etc. (i.e. there is nothing in the Torah written in vain — see *Rashi* ad loc.). Yet it is written (*Shemos* 21:16): *One who kidnaps a man and sells him,* etc., and You have not collected their due from the sons of Yaakov who sold Yosef!' Immediately, the Holy One, Blessed is He, decreed execution on ten of the Sages of Israel." R' Yishmael said by way of response, "But could the Holy One, Blessed is He, not find ten from whom to exact the judgment regarding Yosef other than us?" Metatron said to him, "Woe, Yishmael! By your life, the Holy One, Blessed is He, did not find ten who were the equals of the sons of Yaakov other than you." Once R' Yishmael was finished listening to Metatron's statements, he descended to the earth and found his colleagues immersed in prayer and fasting. They said to him, "What news do you have?" He told them, "Go, wash yourselves, purify yourselves and don your burial shrouds, for it is a decree from before the Holy One, Blessed is He."

R' Yishmael said: When I came and testified this testimony [i.e. I related the conversation that I had with Metatron before the Throne of Glory], all my colleagues rejoiced. They sat before R' Nechuniah ben Hakaneh, held a feast and engaged in rejoicing. R' Yishmael and Rabban Shimon ben Gamliel, his partner, sat together. They were rejoicing and mourning: mourning with the left hand (i.e. to a lesser degree), because a sentence of death by unusual means had been meted out to them; but rejoicing and dancing with the right hand (i.e. to a greater extent), because the Holy One, Blessed is He, had told them they were the equals of the sons of Yaakov. Not only that, but amid their rejoicing, the Nasi, Rabban Shimon ben Gamliel said, "May the God of Israel accept our

souls as an offering, using them to [take] revenge against wicked Rome. Let us be merry and rejoice, and make music with the harp and flute."

The Sages were sitting and engaging in the study of the laws of Pesach. They were reciting the Mishnah in *Pesachim* (3:1) that speaks of *chametz* mixtures that one may not possess on Pesach. They did not manage to finish the Mishnah before a royal official arrived with an unsheathed sword in his hand. He said to them, "Are your minds still untroubled with your fates that you are instead delving into the Torah? But you know your end, that a death sentence has been pronounced upon you!" (*Medrash Asarah Harugei Malchus*; *Pirkei Heichalos* §5. For additional versions of this story, and its details, see *Otzar HaMedrashim,* p. 439; the *piyut* "*Eileh Ezkerah*" in the *Yom Kippur Mussaf;* the *kinah* "*Arzei HaLevanon*" in the *Kinnos* for *Tishah B'Av*).

ahag lists the prohibition against kidnapping two times in his count of the 613 commandments; once in the section in which he enumerates the prohibitions for which the penalty is execution by strangulation (§32), and again in the section in which he lists the negative commandments in general (§30). This is but one of several instances in which *Bahag* lists a prohibition in one of the sections categorized by the punishment to which one is subject for transgressing the prohibition, and then again in the section of negative commandments. This presents an obvious difficulty: Why does *Bahag* list the same mitzvah twice? This question is not difficult to answer according to *Rambam's* understanding of *Bahag*. *Rambam* (*Sefer HaMitzvos, shoresh* §14) maintains that the mitzvos which *Bahag* classifies by order of punishment do not refer to the actual prohibitions, but rather to the mitzvah incumbent upon *Beis Din* to administer the punishment the Torah specifies for each prohibition. Thus, according to *Rambam*, *Bahag* does not actually list the prohibition against kidnapping twice. However, *Ramban* (see *Hasagos* to *Sefer HaMitzvos* ibid. ד"ה וכתב עוד) contends that the *mitzvos Bahag* lists in sections categorized by the form of punishment *do* refer to the actual prohibitions themselves.

According to *Ramban*, then, the question remains. Some answer that although *Bahag* lists the prohibition against kidnapping in two places, he does not *count* this prohibition as two commandments of the 613. He includes it in his list of negative commandments simply because it is one of the Ten Commandments, and he wishes to set down in one place all the prohibitions contained in the Ten Commandments. Thus, although he already listed the prohibition earlier, he lists it again in the category of negative commandments together with those prohibitions of the Ten Commandments that are not listed elsewhere. That not all the prohibitions in *Bahag's* list of negative commandments count toward the 613 is evident from the fact that although this list contains 282 prohibitions, *Bahag* himself gives the tally of prohibitions in this list as 277! The difference between *Bahag's* tally and the actual number of prohibitions he lists in this section represents the five prohibitions that are also listed elsewhere. He does not include these prohibitions in the total, because they were already counted as part of the 613 (*R' A. S. Traub's* Introduction to *Bahag*, pp. 31-32).

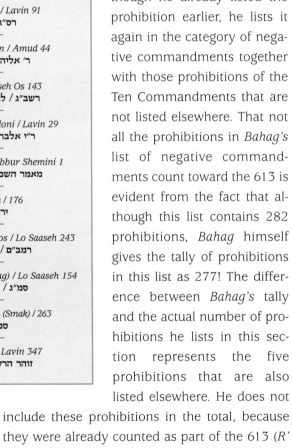

מפתח למוני המצוות

THE COUNT OF THE MITZVAH

Baal Halachos Gedolos / Lavin 30
בה"ג / לאוין ל

R' Saadiah Gaon / Lavin 91
רס"ג / לאוין צא

R' Eliyahu HaZakein / Amud 44
ר' אליהו הזקן / עמ' 44

Rashbag / Lo Saaseh Os 143
רשב"ג / לא תעשה אות קמג

R' Yitzchak El-Bargeloni / Lavin 29
ר"י אלברג'לוני / לאוין כט

Maamar HaSechel / Dibbur Shemini 1
מאמר השכל / דיבור שמיני א

Sefer Yere'im / 176
יראים / קעו

Rambam, Sefer HaMitzvos / Lo Saaseh 243
רמב"ם / לא תעשה רמג

Sefer Mitzvos Gadol (Smag) / Lo Saaseh 154
סמ"ג / לא תעשה קנד

Sefer Mitzvos Katan (Smak) / 263
סמ"ק / רסג

Zohar HaRakia / Lavin 347
זוהר הרקיע / לאוין שמז

Mitzvah 37

אִסוּר עֵדוּת שֶׁקֶר
פרשת יתרו

NOT TO
TESTIFY FALSELY

THE MITZVAH:

MITZVAH 37

אִסּוּר עֵדוּת שֶׁקֶר
(לֹא תַעֲשֶׂה)
NOT TO TESTIFY FALSELY

מצוה לז

SOURCE

לֹא תַעֲנֶה בְרֵעֲךָ עֵד שָׁקֶר שמות (פרשת יתרו) כ:יג
"Do not bear false witness against your fellow[1]*"*

THE MITZVAH

It is forbidden to give false testimony,[2] or to testify regarding an incident one did not personally witness, even if he heard about the incident from reliable sources.[3]

LAWS

1 It is forbidden to give false testimony, whether the testimony is offered orally or in writing,[4] or by signing as a witness on a document.[5]

2 It is forbidden to testify falsely even if the purpose of the false testimony is to substantiate a claim one knows to be true.[6]

3 The prohibition applies only to effective testimony,[7] given by qualified witnesses.[8]

4 The prohibition applies only to testimony offered by the witness in court.[9]

5 The prohibition applies in all places and at all times,

to men but not to women.[10]

6 The punishment for transgressing this prohibition[11] is *malkos*, lashes.[12]

7 If the witnesses are proven false through the testimony of a second set of witnesses, who testify that the first witnesses were with them elsewhere at the time of the alleged incident, and could not have witnessed it, they are known as *zomemim* witnesses, and are subject to special punishment.[13]

NOTE: It is a mitzvah for witnesses to offer *true* testimony in *Beis Din* — see *mitzvah* #122.

A REASON

A healthy society depends on the preservation of justice; and judges depend on accurate testimony to determine the truth about disputed events, and to arrive at decisions that are just and fair. Bearing false witness sabotages this system.

לע"נ ר' יוסף בן יהושע בנימין ז"ל
לע"נ לאה בת אברהם חיים ע"ה

---

1. This prohibition is repeated in *Devarim* 5:17. That verse, though, states, *You shall not bear vain witness against your fellow.* *Ramban* (in his Torah commentary to that verse; see also *Chizkuni* there) explains that the term "vain witness" includes even false testimony that will have no practical consequences (the term "vain" connotes something which is pointless — see *Rashi, Shevuos* 3b ד"ה וכדרבא); for example, testimony that one declared that he would give a sum of money to a second party. This testimony would not result in a loss, since the courts would not enforce such a non-binding commitment in any case (see *Bava Metzia* 48a). Nevertheless, it is forbidden to offer such testimony. Others, however, maintain that one does not transgress the prohibition for offering legally inconsequential testimony (see *Minchas Chinuch* 37:3 ד"ה וראיתי; see also *Yereim HaShalem* §178 and *Semag, Laavin* §216). Interestingly, *Ramban* himself seems to subscribe to this latter view in *Sefer Milchamos Hashem* (*Sanhedrin* 19a ff.).

Based on the wording of the verse, some say that only false testimony to the detriment of ("against") another person ("your fellow") is included in this prohibition; for example, testimony that a person committed a punishable offense, or that he owes money to someone else. False testimony *in support* of someone (for example, falsely testifying that a certain person did *not* commit a crime), or testimony that is not directed against a person (such as testifying that one saw the new moon on the thirtieth day of the month, and that that day should be declared *Rosh Chodesh* [see *mitzvah* #4]), is not forbidden under this prohibition [although there are other prohibitions

AN EXPANDED TREATMENT

which forbid such testimony; see below, note 3] (*Teshuvos R' Akiva Eiger, Mahadura Kamma* §176 ד"ה הדברים רחוקים; see also ibid. *Mahadura Basra* §47). Others maintain that the prohibition applies to any testimony that affects another person, even if it is not directed *against* that person. According to this view, this prohibition *does* prohibit giving false testimony regarding the proper day to establish *Rosh Chodesh*, since this affects all Jews (see *Koveitz Shiurim, Bava Basra* §328; see also *Minchas Chinuch* 4:13).

2. According to some authorities, one who gives false testimony also transgresses the positive commandment of, "*Distance yourself from a false word*" (*Shemos* 23:7; see *mitzvah* #74), which forbids lying (*Minchas Chinuch* 37:11; see *Shevuos* 31a). This would also seem to be the view of *Smag* (*Aseh* §107) and *Smak* (§226). However, *Rambam* and *Chinuch* do not interpret this verse as a positive commandment forbidding lying. In their view, this verse applies only to judges, and enjoins them to accept only qualified witnesses (for an extensive discussion of both views, see *Commentary of R' Y. F. Perla to Sefer HaMitzvos L'RaSag, Aseh* §22 [p.156 ff]).

Based on the Gemara in *Makkos* (23a), *Rambam* (*Sefer HaMitzvos, Lo Saaseh* §281 and *Hil. Sanhedrin* 21:7) and *Chinuch* (§74) maintain that one who testifies falsely also transgresses the prohibition of, "*Do not accept a false report*" (*Shemos* 23:1), which is understood as not only forbidding accepting a false report, but also causing a false report to be accepted by offering false testimony in court (see also *Rashbam, Pesachim* 118a ד"ה וקרי ביה). Other authorities, though, disagree with this interpretation of the

Gemara in *Makkos,* and contend that the Gemara means that one who testifies falsely transgresses the prohibition stated at the end of that verse (*Shemos* 23:1) "*Do not place your hand together with the wicked to become a corrupt witness*" [*mitzvah* #75] (*Rivan, Makkos* ibid. ד"ה אל תשת ידך). [*Rambam* (*Sefer HaMitzvos, Lo Saaseh* §286) and *Chinuch* (§75), however, understand the prohibition against "*placing your hand together with the wicked,*" too, not as referring to testifying falsely, but rather as an exhortation to the judges, not to accept the testimony of a witness who is unqualified to testify due to his sins.]

3. See *Shevuos* 31a; *Rambam, Hil. Eidus* 17:1,5; *Tur, Choshen Mishpat* §28; *Rama* there 28:1.

This is forbidden only if the witness testifies that he witnessed the incident himself. If, however, he tells the court that he did not personally witness the incident and is simply repeating what he heard from a trustworthy source, he does not transgress the prohibition (see *Aruch HaShulchan, Choshen Mishpat* 28:6; cf. *Teshuvos Binyamin Ze'ev* 412).

4. The question of whether one can violate this prohibition through written testimony is dependent upon a more basic question: whether testimony submitted in written form (e.g. an affidavit) is admissible in court in the first place. The validity of written testimony is a subject of dispute among the Rishonim. Seemingly, the Torah requires that testimony be given in court orally, as the verse (*Devarim* 19:15) states: *Through the mouths of two witnesses or three witnesses he shall be put to death*; the expression, "through the *mouths* of two witnesses," which implies oral testimony,

teaches that written testimony is invalid (see *Yevamos* 31b). However, *Rabbeinu Tam* (cited by *Tosafos, Yevamos* ibid. ד"ה דחזו; see also *Sma, Choshen Mishpat* 28:42) maintains that written testimony is invalid only if the witness is *unable* to testify orally; e.g. he is mute, or he is unable to come before the *Beis Din* to testify in person (see *Sema* ibid. §43). Someone who is capable of giving oral testimony, however, can also testify in writing. Thus, according to *Rabbeinu Tam*, in certain circumstances it is possible to transgress the prohibition against testifying falsely through written testimony. Most Rishonim, though, maintain that written testimony is invalid under *any* circumstances (see *Rambam, Hil. Eidus* 3:4; *Rashi, Devarim* ibid. ד"ה על פי שני עדים; regarding a document signed by witnesses, see next note). According to this view, one cannot transgress the prohibition by testifying falsely in writing, since such testimony is inadmissible in court in any event.

5. [For example, by signing a forged loan document or *get* (divorce document).] A document signed by witnesses is an exception to the rule (cited in the previous note) that invalidates written testimony. Most Rishonim maintain that a signed document is considered valid testimony on the Biblical level; in their opinion, the verse in *Devarim* from which it is derived that written testimony is invalid refers to testimony delivered in written form, not to signatures on a document (see *Ramban, Hasagos to Rambam's Sefer HaMitzvos,* end of *shoresh* §2; *Rashi, Gittin* 71a ד"ה ולא מפי כתבם). *Rambam* (*Hil. Eidus* 3:4), however, disagrees. He maintains that Biblical law does not differentiate between a signed document

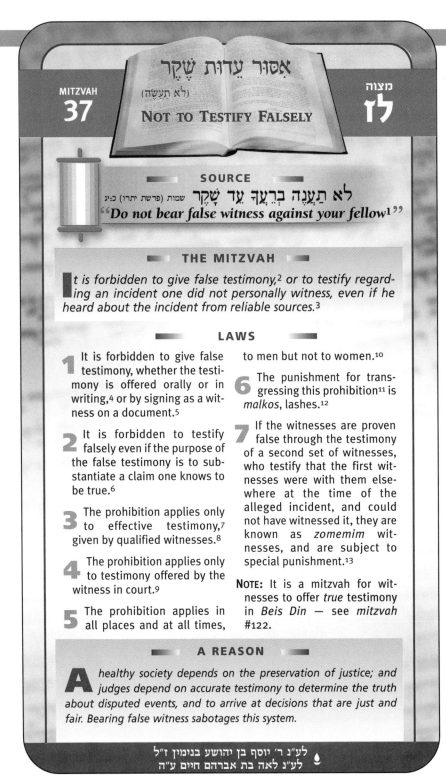

MITZVAH 37 / מצוה לז

אִסּוּר עֵדוּת שֶׁקֶר
(לֹא תַעֲשֶׂה)
NOT TO TESTIFY FALSELY

■ SOURCE ■

לֹא תַעֲנֶה בְרֵעֲךָ עֵד שָׁקֶר שמות (פרשת יתרו) כ:יג

"Do not bear false witness against your fellow[1]"

■ THE MITZVAH ■

It is forbidden to give false testimony,[2] or to testify regarding an incident one did not personally witness, even if he heard about the incident from reliable sources.[3]

■ LAWS ■

1 It is forbidden to give false testimony, whether the testimony is offered orally or in writing,[4] or by signing as a witness on a document.[5]

2 It is forbidden to testify falsely even if the purpose of the false testimony is to substantiate a claim one knows to be true.[6]

3 The prohibition applies only to effective testimony,[7] given by qualified witnesses.[8]

4 The prohibition applies only to testimony offered by the witness in court.[9]

5 The prohibition applies in all places and at all times, to men but not to women.[10]

6 The punishment for transgressing this prohibition[11] is *malkos*, lashes.[12]

7 If the witnesses are proven false through the testimony of a second set of witnesses, who testify that the first witnesses were with them elsewhere at the time of the alleged incident, and could not have witnessed it, they are known as *zomemim* witnesses, and are subject to special punishment.[13]

NOTE: It is a mitzvah for witnesses to offer *true* testimony in *Beis Din* — see *mitzvah #122.*

■ A REASON ■

A healthy society depends on the preservation of justice; and judges depend on accurate testimony to determine the truth about disputed events, and to arrive at decisions that are just and fair. Bearing false witness sabotages this system.

לע"נ ר' יוסף בן יהושע בנימין ז"ל
לע"נ לאה בת אברהם חיים ע"ה

and other types of written testimony; both are Biblically invalid forms of testimony. According to *Rambam*, the validity of a signed document as testimony is a special Rabbinical leniency, instituted by the Rabbis so that people would not refrain from lending others money for fear that they would be unable to collect the debt because of the witnesses' deaths or their inability to come to court to testify (or, in the case of a *get*, so that the woman would be able to remarry even if her witnesses died or could not testify in person). Nevertheless, although according to *Rambam,* the written testimony of witnesses' signatures on a document is only Rabbinically valid, if the testimony is false, the witnesses transgress the *Biblical* prohibition against giving false testimony (*Maharam Schick* 37:3; see also *Iyunim* §1).

6. *Ritva* (*Gittin* 63b [Mossad HaRav Kook ed.], cited in *Teshuvos HaRadvaz* vol. IV:85,276) discusses a case in which two messengers delivered a *get* from a husband to his wife. The woman then lost the *get*, which, besides being the instrument of a woman's divorce, is also the written proof that she is free to remarry. *Ritva* states that these messengers may not prepare and sign another *get* for this woman to use as proof that she was divorced, because they are thus testifying that she was divorced through this second *get*, when in fact she was divorced through the first *get*. Although this woman's claim that she is divorced is true, they may not testify falsely to support it.

Ritva writes that such false testimony is either a violation of this prohibition, or a violation of the commandment to distance one's self from falsehood (*mitzvah #74;* see above, note 2). Similarly, he writes that witnesses that saw a woman divorced may not testify that she is widowed, or vice versa (even where she had children, so *yibum* is not a concern, and she is free to remarry in either case), because the testimony itself is false.

7. One does not transgress this prohibition if his testimony was never given credence by the court in the first place. This rule excludes testimony by a single witness in cases that require two witnesses, such as cases of criminal and monetary law [see *Devarim* 19:15; *Rambam, Hil. Eidus* 5:1], and matters related to forbidden marital relationships [דבר שבערוה — see *Gittin* 2b; *Rambam, Hil. Geirushin* 1:13] (see *Minchas Chinuch* 37:1). [If one witness testifies falsely *together* with a truthful witness, though, he does transgress the prohibition, for his testimony is effective in conjunction with the testimony of that other witness. This is evident from the Gemara in *Shevuos* (31a), which discusses a case in which one has only a single witness to testify that he is owed money by someone else. Because *two* witnesses are required to prove a monetary claim, the lender asks a second person to join that witness to testify in support of his claim. The Gemara states that if the second person does testify that he witnessed the loan being made, he is guilty of transgressing the prohibition against bearing false witness.]

There are matters for which the testimony of even a single witness suffices. For example, the testimony of a lone witness suffices to establish a man's death, thus allowing his wife to remarry (see Mishnah, *Yevamos* 117b; *Rambam, Hil. Geirushin* 13:29). Similarly, if a single witness identifies a murderer, the town nearest to where the body of the victim was discovered is exempt from having to perform the *eglah arufah* ritual [the rite the Torah prescribes for the town nearest to where the victim of an unidentified murderer was found — see *mitzvah* #530] (*Sotah* 47b; *Rambam, Hil. Eidus* 5:2). And if a lone witness testifies that a suspected *sotah* (a woman who ignored her husband's warning against secluding herself with a man with whom he suspects her of committing adultery) indeed had illicit relations with the man she was warned against, she loses her *kesubah* and does not drink the "bitter waters" otherwise used to determine her guilt or innocence [see *mitzvah*

#365] (Mishnah, *Sotah* 31a; *Rambam* ibid.). In all these cases, if a lone witness testifies falsely, he *does* transgress the prohibition, since his testimony is effective (*Minchas Chinuch* 37:1; see also *Yereim* §178).

If both litigants in a monetary dispute agree to accept the testimony of a lone witness, his testimony is effective. Nevertheless, if such a witness testifies falsely he does not transgress the prohibition, because the testimony of a single witness is halachically insignificant in cases of monetary law; it is effective in this case simply because of an agreement made between the parties involved in the litigation (*Teshuvos R' Akiva Eiger, Mahadura Kamma* §179 ד"ה אח"כ נזכרתי and *Minchas Chinuch* 37:3 ד"ה ולכאורה נראה, based on *Ran, Shevuos* fol. 15b (ד"ה והם).

The testimony of a single witness also suffices in cases of prohibitory law [i.e. testimony relating to the permissible or forbidden status of an item] (see *Gittin* 2b). However, for reasons that will be discussed below (note 10), many authorities maintain that a witness who testifies falsely in matters of prohibitory law does not transgress the prohibition.

8. The Torah forbids bearing "false *witness*," a term which denotes the testimony of a *qualified* witness. Excluded, therefore, is anyone who is an unqualified witness, even in cases where his testimony is admissible (see below). Certainly, in cases in which his testimony is *inadmissible* in the courts, an ineligible witness does not transgress the prohibition if he testifies falsely.

The category of unqualified witnesses includes someone who committed a crime punishable by death or *malkos*, a thief [though his crime is not subject to *malkos*, and certainly not the death penalty] (see *Sanhedrin*

27a), someone who is closely related to the person affected by his testimony [e.g. he is related to one of the litigants in a monetary dispute] (Mishnah, *Sanhedrin* 27b), a woman (see *Shevuos* 30a), a Canaanite slave (see *Bava Kamma* 88a), and a minor (see *Bava Basra* 155b). [See *Rambam, Hil. Eidus* ch. 10 for a complete list of those who are not qualified to be witnesses.]

Now, wherever the testimony of a single witness is effective (see above, note 8), the testimony of an unqualified witness is also effective (see *Rambam, Hil. Eidus* 5:3). Nevertheless, if an unqualified witness testifies falsely in these matters, he does not transgress the prohibition, because an ineligible witness does not have the legal classification of a "witness," even in those cases in which his testimony is effective. Similarly, while the testimony of ineligible witnesses is effective in monetary disputes if both litigants agree to accept it (see *Rambam, Hil. Sanhedrin* 7:2; *Shulchan Aruch, Choshen Mishpat* 22:1), the witnesses do not transgress the prohibition if they testify falsely, since they cannot be categorized as "witnesses" (*Minchas Chinuch* 37:3 ד"ה ולכאורה; *Teshuvos R' Akiva Eiger, Mahadura Kamma* 179 ד"ה ולפי"ז; cf. *Yere'im* §178). [Some posit, though, that this is true only of *inherently* unqualified witnesses, (e.g. slaves), who are ineligible to testify in any matter that requires "witnesses." However, a relative, who is inherently an eligible witness, and is disqualified from testifying only when he is related to one of the affected parties, *is* considered a "witness" in cases in which his relationship does not disqualify him from testifying. Thus, if he gives false testimony in such cases, he does transgress the prohibition (*Minchas Chinuch* 37:4 ד"ה ונראה לי).]

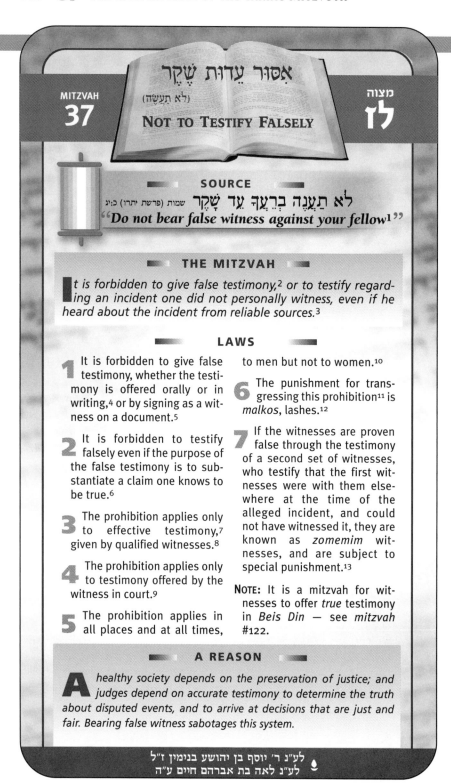

MITZVAH 37 / מצוה לז

אִסּוּר עֵדוּת שֶׁקֶר
(לֹא תַעֲשֶׂה)
NOT TO TESTIFY FALSELY

■ SOURCE ■

לֹא תַעֲנֶה בְרֵעֲךָ עֵד שָׁקֶר שמות (פרשת יתרו) כ:יג

"Do not bear false witness against your fellow[1]"

■ THE MITZVAH ■

It is forbidden to give false testimony,[2] or to testify regarding an incident one did not personally witness, even if he heard about the incident from reliable sources.[3]

■ LAWS ■

1 It is forbidden to give false testimony, whether the testimony is offered orally or in writing,[4] or by signing as a witness on a document.[5]

2 It is forbidden to testify falsely even if the purpose of the false testimony is to substantiate a claim one knows to be true.[6]

3 The prohibition applies only to effective testimony,[7] given by qualified witnesses.[8]

4 The prohibition applies only to testimony offered by the witness in court.[9]

5 The prohibition applies in all places and at all times, to men but not to women.[10]

6 The punishment for transgressing this prohibition[11] is *malkos*, lashes.[12]

7 If the witnesses are proven false through the testimony of a second set of witnesses, who testify that the first witnesses were with them elsewhere at the time of the alleged incident, and could not have witnessed it, they are known as *zomemim* witnesses, and are subject to special punishment.[13]

NOTE: It is a mitzvah for witnesses to offer *true* testimony in *Beis Din* — see *mitzvah #122.*

■ A REASON ■

A healthy society depends on the preservation of justice; and judges depend on accurate testimony to determine the truth about disputed events, and to arrive at decisions that are just and fair. Bearing false witness sabotages this system.

לע"נ ר' יוסף בן יהושע בנימין ז"ל
לע"נ לאה בת אברהם חיים ע"ה

---

in cases in which it is effective, may be retracted. Only irrevocable testimony is included in the prohibition, so one who gives false testimony outside of court does not transgress this prohibition (see *Yereim* §178; *Semag, Lavin* §216). See *Iyunim* §2 regarding the law when such testimony is presented *in* court.

Others disagree with this criterion, and maintain that even testimony given outside of court is included in the prohibition, as long as it would be effective. Thus, according to this view, one who testifies falsely outside of court in a matter pertaining to prohibitory law *does* transgress the prohibition. One who gives false testimony outside of court in a matter pertaining to criminal or monetary law, however, or in a matter pertaining to forbidden marital relations, does not transgress, since such testimony is invalid in any case (*Minchas Chinuch* 37:1). See further, *Iyunim* §2.

10. Although, in general, men and women are equally subject to the Torah's negative commandments (see Mishnah, *Kiddushin* 29a), this prohibition does not apply to women, because women never testify in monetary or criminal proceedings (see *Shevuous* 30a and *Rambam, Hil. Eidus* 9:2).

11. Of course, one cannot be subject to punishment for giving false testimony unless it can be proven that he testified falsely. Normally, one is proven guilty of a crime through the testimony of witnesses. With regard to the crime of giving false testimony, however, witnesses do not always suffice to prove the transgression. If a second set of witnesses contradicts the first set — for example, they testify that the incident described by the first set never occurred — this does not prove that the first set lied, for it may be that the second set is lying and the

---

9. Some authorities maintain that this rule excludes not only out-of-court testimony pertaining to monetary law, criminal law and forbidden marital relations (which is effective *only* when presented in court) but even testimony pertaining to prohibitory

law (i.e. testimony relating to the permissible or forbidden status of an item), which is effective outside of court as well. The significance of testimony given in court is that once given in court, it cannot be retracted. Testimony given outside court, even

first set testified truthfully. Clearly, one pair of witnesses is lying, and there is no reason to believe the second pair more than the first! (see *Bava Kamma* 74b; *Rambam, Hil. Eidus* 18:2; see also Mishnah, *Makkos* 5a). Witnesses can be proven false in one of two ways: (a) through irrefutable evidence that they lied; for example, they testified that a certain person was dead, and that person was subsequently discovered to be alive (see *Bava Kamma* ibid.). (b) through a process known as *hazamah* (הזמה), whereby other witnesses testify that these witnesses could not possibly have witnessed the incident they described because they were together with these second witnesses in a different location at the time the incident is alleged to have occurred. Although logically in this situation, too, the second pair of witnesses should not be given more credence than the first pair, the Torah decrees that in such a situation, the second pair is believed, and the first witnesses are considered proven false. Witnesses discredited through this process are known as *zomemim* witnesses [עדים זוממים] (Mishnah, *Makkos* ibid.), and they receive a special punishment (see note 13).

12. *Rambam, Sefer HaMitzvos, Lo Saaseh* §285; *Chinuch* §37.

The prohibition against testifying falsely is an exception to the rule that one does not receive punishment for transgressing a prohibition which involves no action [לאו שאין בו מעשה]. Although the presentation of false testimony is not considered an action, the Torah specifically imposes the punishment of *malkos* for this transgression. The Gemara (*Makkos* 2b) derives this from *Devarim* 25:1-2, which states: *If there will be a dispute between men, and they come to the court and they judge them, and they exonerate the innocent one and convict the*

guilty one. Then it will be that if the guilty one is liable to lashes, and the judge bends him over and lashes him, etc. The Gemara interprets the passage as referring to witnesses who discredited other witnesses through *hazamah*, thus "exonerating" the intended victim of the false witnesses' testimony, and "convicting" the first set of witnesses (the "guilty ones") of the crime of bearing false witness. As the verse states, the punishment for these false witnesses is *malkos*.

This prohibition is also an exception to the rule that one is not subject to corporal punishment (i.e. *malkos* or the death penalty) for committing a crime unless he was first warned that his transgression would result in that penalty. False witnesses receive *malkos* even if they were not warned prior to giving testimony that they would be liable to *malkos* for testifying falsely (*Kesubos* 33a; *Rambam, Hil. Eidus* 18:4; see also *Makkos* 4b).

13. The *malkos* penalty applies to witnesses whose testimony was discredited through irrefutable evidence [see note 11] (see *Bava Kamma* 74b; see, however, end of this note). Witnesses who were proven false through *hazamah*, however, do not always receive *malkos* as their punishment. The Torah prescribes a unique punishment for *zomemim* witnesses, known as *ka'asher zamam*, the "reciprocal punishment"; i.e. they are punished with the very penalty that would have resulted from their testimony had it not been discredited (see *Devarim* 19:19). [For example, if the witnesses had testified that a person is guilty of a crime which carries the death penalty, and then they are found to be *zomemim*, they are put to death. If they testified that one person owes another a sum of money, and they were found to be *zomemim*, they must pay the defendant that sum (the law of *ka'asher zamam* applies only when certain

conditions are fulfilled; see *Iyunim* §3 and see further, *mitzvah* #524). In the Mishnah in *Makkos* (4a), the Tannaim argue as to whether the penalty of *ka'asher zamam* is in *addition* to the *malkos* false witnesses normally receive, or if it is *instead* of *malkos*. R' Meir maintains that *zomemim* witnesses receive two punishments; *malkos* for bearing false witness, and, because they were discredited through *hazamah*, whatever punishment they had intended to cause the victim of their false testimony to receive. The Sages, however, contend that *zomemim* witnesses do not receive two punishments for the single crime of testifying falsely. Since the Torah mandates that they are punished with the consequences they intended for their victim, they do not receive *malkos* (see *Makkos* 4b; see also *Kesubos* 32b). The halachah is in accordance with the Sages (see *Rambam, Hil. Eidus* 18:1; *Tur, Choshen Mishpat* 38). [There are situations in which the fate the *zomemim* witnesses sought to impose upon the victim cannot be reciprocated (see *Makkos* 2a-b). In such cases, all agree that the witnesses receive *malkos*. The passage in *Devarim* ch. 25, which mandates *malkos* as the punishment in a case of *zomemim* witnesses, refers to such a case (see Mishnah and Gemara, *Makkos* 2a-b).]

As mentioned above, witnesses that are proven false through means other than *hazamah* receive *malkos* (see *Bava Kamma* 74b), since the Torah does not mandate "reciprocal punishment" in cases other than *hazamah*. This is the view of most Rishonim. Others, however, contend that the punishment of *malkos* applies only to *zomemim* witnesses, for the passage that mentions the punishment of *malkos* (*Devarim* ch. 25) refers to a case of *hazamah*. Witnesses that are proven false in another manner,

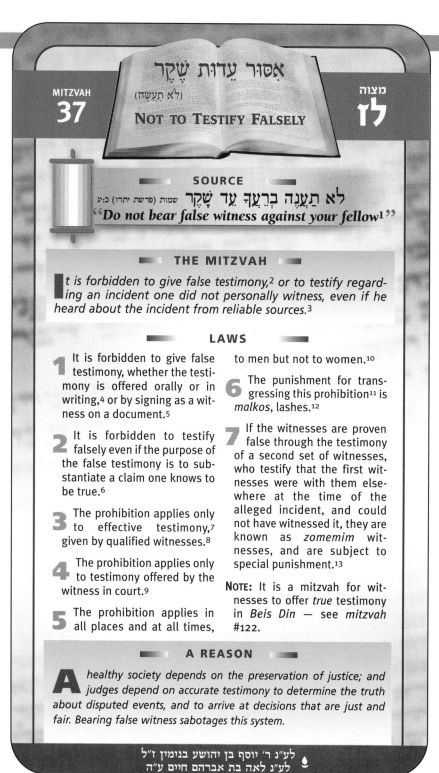

אִסּוּר עֵדוּת שֶׁקֶר

(לֹא תַעֲשֶׂה)

NOT TO TESTIFY FALSELY

MITZVAH 37

מצוה לז

SOURCE

לֹא תַעֲנֶה בְרֵעֲךָ עֵד שָׁקֶר שמות (פרשת יתרו) כ:יג

"Do not bear false witness against your fellow¹"

THE MITZVAH

It is forbidden to give false testimony,² or to testify regarding an incident one did not personally witness, even if he heard about the incident from reliable sources.³

LAWS

1 It is forbidden to give false testimony, whether the testimony is offered orally or in writing,⁴ or by signing as a witness on a document.⁵

2 It is forbidden to testify falsely even if the purpose of the false testimony is to substantiate a claim one knows to be true.⁶

3 The prohibition applies only to effective testimony,⁷ given by qualified witnesses.⁸

4 The prohibition applies only to testimony offered by the witness in court.⁹

5 The prohibition applies in all places and at all times,

to men but not to women.¹⁰

6 The punishment for transgressing this prohibition¹¹ is *malkos*, lashes.¹²

7 If the witnesses are proven false through the testimony of a second set of witnesses, who testify that the first witnesses were with them elsewhere at the time of the alleged incident, and could not have witnessed it, they are known as *zomemim* witnesses, and are subject to special punishment.¹³

NOTE: It is a mitzvah for witnesses to offer *true* testimony in *Beis Din* — see *mitzvah* #122.

A REASON

A healthy society depends on the preservation of justice; and judges depend on accurate testimony to determine the truth about disputed events, and to arrive at decisions that are just and fair. Bearing false witness sabotages this system.

P'nei Yehoshua, Makkos 2b ד"ה ותיפוק ליה). However, most authorities maintain that although the passage in *Devarim* indeed refers to a case of *hazamah,* the penalty of *malkos* it refers to is not a unique function of the law of *hazamah,* but is the ordinary consequence of having violated the prohibition against false testimony. The verse simply teaches that this prohibition is an exception to the rule that one does not receive *malkos* for a violation that involves no action. Thus, the punishment applies regardless of the manner in which the witnesses were discredited (see *Tosafos, Makkos* 4b ד"ה ורבנן; *Ramban, Makkos* 2b ד"ה ותיפוק ליה; *Ritva, Makkos* 2b ד"ה ותיפוק ליה; *Raavad,* cited by *Shitah Mekubetzes, Bava Kamma* 74b ד"ה לוקין משום לא תענה; see also *Baal HaMaor, Sanhedrin* fol. 19a ד"ה איתמר; *Rashi, Bava Kamma* 74b ד"ה לוקין; *Ketzos HaChoshen* 38:1; see further *Iyunim* §3). See *Iyunim* §4 for other cases in which false witnesses do not receive *malkos*.

---

however, receive no punishment. According to this view, this *malkos* penalty is not the result of having violated the prohibition against testifying falsely (which is a transgression that involves no action, and is thus not a punishable offense), but is a unique

hazamah-related penalty the Torah imposes when "reciprocal punishment" is not applicable. Thus, just as witnesses that were proven false through other means do not receive "reciprocal punishment," they do not receive *malkos* either (see *Meiri, Makkos* 2a;

A BROADER LOOK AT THE LAWS

1   Testifying falsely regarding a matter of Rabbinical law.

There are those who maintain that the Biblical prohibition against testifying falsely applies only to testimony pertaining to matters of Biblical law. However, if witnesses testify falsely regarding a matter of Rabbinic law — for example, they testify that someone is Rabbinically disqualified from serving as a Kohen — they do not transgress the Biblical prohibition against testifying falsely, for such testimony is insignificant on the Biblical level (although they are certainly guilty on the *Rabbinic* level). As such, they do not receive *malkos* for their false testimony, since this punishment applies only to Biblical transgressions (*Ramban, Makkos* 2a ד״ה והא דתנן; *Ritva, Makkos* ibid. ד״ה מעידנו). Others, however, seem to rule that witnesses who give false testimony regarding matters of Rabbinic law *do* transgress the Biblical prohibition and are punished with *malkos* (see *Rambam, Hil. Eidus* 20:8). In their opinion, the Biblical prohibition forbids any false testimony that has a *practical effect*. Testimony relating to Rabbinic law certainly has a practical effect, even if not on the Biblical level. Thus, it is included in the Biblical prohibition against bearing false witness (see *Aruch LaNer, Makkos* 2a; *Teshuvos R' Akiva Eiger, Mahadura Kamma* §179 ד״ה ובהההיא ענינא).

2   Testifying falsely in court regarding a matter of prohibitory law.

As noted above (see note 9), many authorities maintain that the prohibition against testifying falsely does not apply to testimony concerning prohibitory law because such testimony is valid even when stated outside of court, and the prohibition against testifying falsely applies only to testimony given in front of a court. Some authorities take this a step further, and contend that even if the witness should happen to present his false testimony *in court*, he does not transgress. They maintain that there is no significance to the fact that the testimony was given in front of a court, since testimony regarding prohibitory law does not *require* a court (see *Nesivos HaMishpat, biurim* 38:2). Others, however, argue that although testimony relating to prohibitory law does not require a court, if a witness does present false testimony in court, he transgresses the prohibition, since such testimony is irrevocable (see *Meshovev Nesivos* 38:2)

3   Malkos: a function of hazamah or of the violation of the prohibition?

We have seen (see note 13) that the authorities argue as to whether the penalty of *malkos* mandated by the Torah for testifying falsely is a *hazamah*-related penalty, or if it is a penalty for violating the prohibition against testifying falsely. One ramification of this dispute, noted above (ibid.), concerns witnesses discredited through means other than *hazamah*. This dispute can also manifest itself in cases of *zomemim* witnesses. If the *malkos* is a *hazamah*-related penalty, then its application is subject to any limitations that apply to the "reciprocal punishment" *zomemim* witnesses usually receive; if, however, it is a penalty for transgressing the prohibition on testifying falsely, it is not subject to these limitations. Now, the law is that *zomemim* witnesses who testified falsely in a capital case receive the death sentence they intended for their victim only if they were proven false *before* the court had a chance to carry out the sentence on their victim. If, however, they were discredited after the victim was [wrongly] executed, they do not receive "reciprocal punishment" (see *Makkos* 5b). Some authorities maintain that in such a case, the witnesses do not even receive *malkos*. In their opinion, *malkos* is a *hazamah*-related penalty, and just as "reciprocal punishment" does not apply to witnesses discredited after the sentence was carried out, so, too, the penalty of *malkos* does not apply (*Gevuros Ari, Makkos* 5b ד״ה חייבי מלקיות; *Chiddushei HaRim, Choshen Mishpat* 1:36). Many others, however, contend that the witnesses *do* receive *malkos*. These authorities maintain that the *malkos* is not related to *hazamah*, but is rather imposed for the witnesses' violation of the prohibition against testifying falsely. As such, its application is not limited by the laws of *hazamah*. Thus, although the novel penalty normally imposed on *zomemim* witnesses does not apply, the *malkos* penalty still applies (*Teshuvos R' Akiva Eiger, Mahadura Kamma* §176; *Nesivos HaMishpat, biurim* 1:3; *Tzlach, Makkos* 2b; *Mirkeves HaMishnah, Hil. Eidus* 20:2).

4 Cases in which witnesses do not receive malkos for testifying falsely.

A. False witnesses receive *malkos* only if they are proven false after the court issued a verdict on the basis of their testimony (see *Makkos* 5b with *Rashi* ד"ה חייבי גליות). This is understandable if we say that *malkos* is a *hazamah*-related penalty (see above), for the Mishnah in *Makkos* (5b) derives from Scripture that the penalty for *hazamah* does not apply if the witnesses were found to be *zomemim* before the court handed down a verdict. But if *malkos* is a result of transgressing the prohibition against testifying falsely, as many maintain, why are false witnesses not liable to *malkos* as soon as the court accepts their testimony, at which point they violate the prohibition? (see note 9). The commentators explain that the witnesses cannot be punished for this transgression as long as the court did not issue a verdict, because they performed no action, and one is not punished for transgressions that involve no action. Although the passage in *Devarim* 25:1-2 teaches that the prohibition against bearing false witness is an exception to this rule (see note 12), that passage refers to a case in which the court issued a verdict on the basis of the witnesses' testimony. In such a case, their testimony at least *resulted* in an action (the issuance of the verdict). Although this would not normally be considered "action" with regard to the aforementioned rule, the verse teaches that in the case of false witnesses even this "action" suffices to punish the witnesses with *malkos*. If the court never issued a verdict, however, the transgression involved no action whatsoever, so the witnesses are not punished (*Or Same'ach, Hil. Eidus* 18:6; see also *Chazon Ish, Bava Kamma* 18:12).

B. Another case in which false witnesses do not receive *malkos* would be in a case where witnesses testified that a certain person is a murderer, and the witnesses were proven false when the alleged victim was discovered alive. Although the witnesses are guilty of giving false testimony, they do not receive *malkos* for their transgression. This is because giving false testimony in this case rendered them potentially liable to the death penalty, for if they would have been discredited through *hazamah*, they would have been liable to execution under the *ka'asher zamam* penalty (just as they intended the person they accused of murder to be executed). And the law is that one is not punished with *malkos* for a transgression which potentially carries the death penalty (see *Bava Kamma* 74b).

SITUATIONS IN HALACHAH

Question:

Does the prohibition of *Lo Saaneh* apply to testimony that a Jew testifies concerning a non-Jew?

Answer:

In stating the prohibition of *Lo Saaneh*, the Torah writes (*Shemos* 20:13): *Do not bear false witness against your fellow*. Since elsewhere the term "your fellow" is expounded to exclude non-Jews (see, for example, *Bava Metzia* 87b and 111b), it would seem that the prohibition of testifying falsely should only apply to testimony offered concerning fellow Jews, and that there is no prohibition that would prevent a Jew from testifying falsely concerning a non-Jew. *Chasam Sofer* (*Kovetz Teshuvos* §90 ד"ה ואני נבוך and *Miluim* ad loc.) therefore asks: How can a *Beis Din* ever accept the testimony of a Jew in a case involving a non-Jew?

Chasam Sofer resolves the question, ruling that a Jew's testimony against a non-Jew is in fact subject to the prohibition of *Lo Saaneh*. He explains that here the term *your friend* does not exclude testimony against non-Jews from the prohibition of *Lo Saaneh*. Here, *your fellow* refers not to one's fellow man, but to Hashem Himself! As the source of this interpretation, he cites *Ramban* (*Emunah U'Bitachon*, ch. 19): "The verse states: *Do not bear false witness against your fellow*. Now, may one testify falsely against one who is not his fellow? Surely not! Rather, *your fellow* here refers to Hashem [see *Mishlei* 27:10 and *Rashi* ad loc.; see *Shemos Rabbah* 27:1 and *Vayikra Rabbah* 6:1; see also *Ramban* to *Bereishis* 48:25], for anyone who violates His mitzvos is as if he testifies falsely against [Hashem] Himself... that is why [the verse] says, *against your fellow*, and not *against your brother*" [which would have excluded testimony against non-Jews from the prohibition — see *Bava Metzia* 111b; see also *Tosafos* to *Gittin* 9b ד"ה העולים].

Thus, concludes *Chasam Sofer*, this prohibition also applies to testimony concerning a non-Jew, and therefore a witness's testimony concerning an non-Jew can be accepted in *Beis Din*.

Question:

Is the testimony of a witness acceptable only if he is subject to the prohibition of Lo Saaneh?

Answer:

Chasam Sofer's question as to how a *Beis Din* can accept the testimony of a Jew in a case involving a non-Jew if such testimony is not subject to *Lo Saaneh* (see above) is based on an assumption: that the testimony of a witness is only acceptable if it is subject to the prohibition of *Lo Saaneh*. However, this is not universally accepted. *R' Akiva Eiger* (*Teshuvos R' Akiva Eiger* §176) writes that witnesses who testify that they saw the new moon are not subject to the prohibition of *Lo Saaneh*, as they are not testifying against a person. It thus seems that according to *R' Akiva Eiger*, witnesses need not be subject to this prohibition in order for their testimony to be accepted. Rather, we may assume that a witness will tell the truth regardless of whether his testimony is subject to *Lo Saaneh* or not. [On the other hand, *Kovetz Shiurim* (to *Bava Basra*, §329, 562, 566 and 583), asks how testimony regarding the new moon, if it is not subject to the prohibition, can be valid? Clearly, *Kovetz Shiurim* is of the opinion that only testimony that is subject to the prohibition of *Lo Saaneh* can be accepted in *Beis Din*.] However, it may be that even *R' Akiva Eiger* would agree that testimony that concerns another person must be subject to *Lo Saaneh*, and the case of witnesses of the new moon is unique.

Question:
Can the testimony of a witness who is suspect to violate *Lo Saaneh* be accepted?

Answer:
R' Moshe Feinstein (*Igros Moshe* in several places — see, for example, *Even HaEzer* IV:32) writes that people who reject the Torah automatically reject the existence of the prohibition of *Lo Saaneh*, and are hence suspect of violating the prohibition. He therefore rules that such people cannot serve as witnesses. [Clearly, he too is of the opinion that only testimony subject to the prohibition of *Lo Saaneh* may be accepted in *Beis Din*.] Moreover, even if the person who rejects the Torah is a *tinok shenishba* (literally: a captured infant; a person who, through no fault of his own, was raised without knowledge of the Torah and mitzvos), who is unaware of the prohibition to testify falsely and its parameters, he is nevertheless not fit to serve as a witness. As a result, R' Moshe rules that if such a non-observant person served as one of the witnesses of a marriage ceremony, the ceremony is considered to lack proper testimony, and is invalid.

ILLUMINATIONS OF THE MITZVAH

Suggested Reasons & Insights

I. FALSEHOOD: AN ABOMINATION IN THE EYES OF GOD

he wrongdoing inherent in uttering lies does not need much elaboration, for falsehood arouses nothing but disgust in intelligent people (*Chinuch* §37; see *Shaarei Teshuvah* 3:179). God in particular, Who has adopted Truth as His seal (*Yerushalmi Sanhedrin* 1,1), abhors people who pervert the truth, as it says (*Tehillim* 101:7): *In the midst of My house shall not dwell a practitioner of deceit; one who tells lies shall not be established before My eyes.* This disdain for falsehood per se, regardless of whether it causes any harm, is expressed in numerous Scriptural verses: *I have hated falsehood, and abhorred it* (*Tehillim* 119:163). *False lips are an abomination to God* (*Mishlei* 12:22). *God hates these six … haughty eyes, a false tongue…* (*Mishlei* 6:16-17). *A duplicitous mouth I have hated* (*Mishlei* 8:13). False speech is thus a considerable crime; adherence to truth is among the mainstays of the soul (*Shaarei Teshuvah* ibid. §184).

One who bears false witness has attached himself to the circle of deceivers and liars, of whom the Sages have said (*Sotah* 42a), "Four groups shall not greet the presence of God: Scoffers, flatterers, liars, and slanderers (*Shaarei Teshuvah* ibid. §178).

The commandment prohibiting false testimony applies even when no damage results; this is the lesson of the wording used for the commandment in *Parshas Va'eschanan, You shall not bear **vain** witness against your fellow.* "Bearing vain witness" implies testimony which holds no consequence for the defendant. For example, to testify (falsely) that he entered into a verbal agreement to make a gift to his fellow, something which — even if true — does not legally bind him if it was not implemented by a valid act of acquisition (*Ramb[...]* Furthermore, this commandme[...] when no person is indicted by[...] the witness is only testifying t[...] person suspected of a sin which[...] such as desecrating the Shabbos. This is so because the wording *You shall not bear **vain** witness* indicates that the commandment is intended to condemn false testimony of any kind, regardless of the consequences, or lack thereof (*HaKesav VehaKabbalah,* ad loc.).

Implicit in this prohibition against bearing false witness is the exhortation to adhere to the truth in all aspects of life (Commentary of *R' Avraham ben HaRambam* to *Shemos* 20:13).

II. FALSE TESTIMONY: SUBVERSION OF SOCIAL JUSTICE

he system of justice which supports any society is to a large degree dependent on the accurate testimony of witnesses to determine the truth about disputed events, enabling the judges to arrive at decisions that are just and fair. To corrupt this crucial element in the legal process is to undermine that justice, without which civilization cannot be sustained (see *Derech Pikudecha, Lo Saaseh* §37, *Cheilek HaMachshavah* §14).

On the other hand, witnesses faithful to the truth who come forward to provide the court with the information it needs are, for the same reason, performing a mitzvah (*Akeidas Yitzchak* §45) and are seen as upholding the world (*Chinuch* §37; *Beis Elokim, Shaar HaYesodos* §31).

The inclusion of this mitzvah in the Ten Commandments is indicative of this matter's importance for the preservation of social order. Thus the Torah here emphasizes the use of falsehood in testimony "against your fellow," although, in fact, all forms of untruthfulness are forbidden, as stated elsewhere (*Shemos* 23:7): *Distance yourself from a false word* (*Ha'amek Davar, Shemos* 20:13).

II. FALSE TESTIMONY: AN AFFRONT TO GOD HIMSELF

cripture teaches the concept that God bestows His presence upon a court of Torah law, and even involves Himself in the legal process (*Tehillim* 82:1): *God stands in the Divine assembly; in the midst of judges shall He judge.* Thus one who is prepared to come before a *Beis Din* and perjure himself thereby betrays his disregard for not only the cause of justice, but the God before Whose presence he stands (*R' Menachem HaBavli*). "Said Rabbi Levi: So declares God — 'If you testify falsely against your fellow, I shall consider you to have proclaimed that I am not the Creator of Heaven and earth'" (*Yerushalmi, Berachos* 1:5).

Moreover, by demonstrating a belief in his ability to benefit one person at the expense of another by perverting the truth, a false witness repudiates the teaching that every person's financial affairs for the entire year are predetermined on Rosh Hashanah. His actions also disavow the fact that God is the ultimate arbiter of justice, as attested to by the verse, *...For the judgment is God's* (*Devarim* 1:17), and *...For it is not for man's sake that you judge, but for God's* (*Divrei HaYamim* II, 19:6). It cannot be that he truly accepts the concept of Divine Providence, for how otherwise could he entertain the thought that he is capable, by artificial means, of altering the distribution of property as established by Heavenly decree? Indeed, his efforts will not bear lasting fruit, as the prophet (*Yirmiyah* 17:11) warns: *Like a [bird] calling to itself chicks it did not bear, so is one who garners wealth unjustly; in the middle of his days it will leave him, and at the end he will be branded a scoundrel.* Nevertheless, he will be censured for "inconveniencing" God to undo what he wrought, as the Sages taught (*Sanhedrin* 8a): "God has remarked, 'It is not enough that the wicked unlawfully take money from one person for the sake of another, but they cause Me the trouble of arranging restoration of the money to its rightful owner!'"

In fact, the commandment was worded to reflect this aspect of the perjurer's crime: *You shall not bear false witness against your fellow.* God has been referred to as man's fellow, as it is written (*Mishlei* 27:10), *Your Fellow and the Fellow of your father you shall not forsake.* One who testifies falsely does so against his fellow man, as well as his Fellow in Heaven (*Recanti, Taamei HaMitzvos, Lo Saaseh* §23).

The act of bearing false witness also offends God Himself from another perspective. A human being reflects the image of the Divine [*tzelem Elokim*], and testifying against him is thus like testifying against God (*Zohar* III, 12a).

THROUGH THE EYES
OF THE SAGES
Stories, Parables & Reflections

I. THE SEVERITY OF THE PROHIBITION

Confrontation with God

he witnesses must bear in mind Whom they may affect by their testimony (there is a risk of "inconveniencing" God, Who has committed to redress any miscarriage of justice — *Rashi*), before Whom they are testifying (for God's Presence is manifest in a court of Torah law), and Who will exact from them retribution (if they dare testify falsely). Thus it is said (*Devarim* 19:17), *And the two men* (i.e. the witnesses) ... *shall stand before God* (*Sanhedrin* 6b).

——— ৭৫ ———

Denial of God

R' Levi taught: God declared, "If you dare testify falsely concerning your fellow, I will view it as a testimony that I did not create heaven and earth" (*Yerushalmi, Berachos* 1:5. Cf. *Pesikta Rabbasi* §21; *Zohar, Shemos* 90a).

——— ৭৫ ———

Reflection of the Divine

You shall not bear false witness against your fellow. And in the Torah's account of Creation (*Bereishis* 1:26) we find: *God said, Let Us make man in Our image.* A witness who testifies falsely against his fellow, who bears the image of God, is considered as one who testified against God Himself, as it were (*Zohar, Vayikra* 12a).

——— ৭৫ ———

An ignominious end

One who gives false testimony against his fellow is deserving of being thrown to the dogs (he is considered unworthy of receiving a proper burial after his death; for his corpse is fit to be thrown to the dogs — *She'iltos D'Rav Achai* §45). From where is this derived? In the Torah it is said (*Shemos* 22:30), *To the dog you shall throw it.* And the verse then continues (ibid. 23:1) *You shall not accept* (תשא) *a false report,* a phrase that can also be read, *You shall not convey* (תשיא) *a false report.* From the juxtaposition of these two verses, it is evident that one guilty of conveying a false report is fit to have himself cast to the dogs (*Pesachim* 118a; *Makkos* 23a).

II. THE PUNISHMENTS FOR TRANSGRESSION

Tzaraas

The following six God abhors, and the seventh is an abomination to His soul: haughty eyes, a false tongue, and hands that spill innocent blood. A heart that formulates iniquitous thoughts, and feet that hurry to run to evil. A false witness spouting lies, and one who stirs strife among brothers (*Mishlei* 6:16-19). R' Yochanan taught: All of these make one subject to the affliction of *tzaraas*... As for the "false witness spouting lies," how is it derived that he becomes exposed to *tzaraas*? It is deduced from the experience of those who worshipped the Golden Calf. By proclaiming (*Shemos* 32:4), *These are your gods, O Israel,* they were guilty of giving false testimony, and we find that they were stricken with *tzaraas*, for it is said (ibid. v. 25), *And Moses saw that the people were* "פרוע" What does this word denote? R' Yochanan answered: This teaches that they developed *tzaraas*, regarding which it is said (*Vayikra* 13:45), *And his head shall be* "פרוע" (literally: unshorn) (*Vayikra Rabbah* 16:1; *Medrash Pisron Torah, Metzorah.* Cf. *Tanchuma, Metzora* §4, and *Zohar, Bamidbar* 206a-b).

——— ৭৫ ———

Death

A maul, a sword, and a sharp arrow (the trade-tools used by the Angel of Death — *Maharsha* to *Sanhedrin* 37a), *[are brought forth by] a man who bears false witness against his fellow* (*Mishlei* 25:17. See below, "Preparing the Witnesses for Testimony").

———— ❧ ————

✑ *Drought and famine*

As a result of the sins committed by false witnesses, the clouds form but the rain does not fall, and famine comes upon the world (*Targum Yonasan ben Uziel, Shemos* 20:13, *Devarim* 5:17. See below, "Preparing the Witnesses for Testimony").

————————

As a result of four things, the luminaries become stricken [a sign of an impending calamity]: ... On account of those who bear false witness (*Succah* 29a; *Tosefta* ibid. 2:6; *Maseches Derech Eretz Rabbah* §2).

———— ❧ ————

✑ *Destruction of Jerusalem*

You shall not bear false witness. If you would have upheld this commandment, you would have been the fulfillment of the verse (*Yeshaya* 43:12), *You are My witnesses, said God.* But now that you have transgressed the commandment, you will instead become the subject of another verse (*Eichah* 2:13), *With what shall I bear witness for you? To what can I compare you, O daughter of Jerusalem? To what can I liken you that I may comfort you, O maiden daughter of Zion?* (*Tanna D'vei Eliyahu Rabbah* 26:11).

III. PREPARING THE WITNESSES FOR TESTIMONY

✑ *Words of warning*

ow does the *Beis Din* examine the witnesses? They would bring them into a room and strike fear into them ... What would they tell them? Rav Yehudah said: This they would tell them: *Clouds and wind without any rain is [caused by] a man who applauds himself for a false gift* (*Mishlei* 25:14). [Bringing gain to one's fellow by bearing false witness on his behalf is not a genuine

gift, for it comes at no cost to the giver — *Maharsha*. A result of this sin is that the rains are held back, and, though the skies may cloud up with a blustery wind, no rain will materialize — *Rashi*.] The witnesses will thus fear to bring a drought to the world.

Rava objected: If so, the witnesses could take comfort in the adage that 'a famine can persist for seven years, but through the door of a tradesman it will not pass." [That is, since it would not personally affect them, they will not heed the warning.] Rather, Rava taught, this they would tell them: *A maul, a sword, and a sharp arrow [are brought forth by] a man who bears false witness against his fellow* (*Mishlei* 25:17). [This teaches that pestilence will result from the sin of false testimony — *Rashi*.]

Rav Ashi took exception: If so, the witnesses can take comfort in the adage that "a plague may last for seven years, but no man dies before his time." Rather, Rav Ashi taught in the name of Nassan bar Mar Zutra: This is what we say to them: Know that false witnesses are despised even by those who recruit them, as we find in the counsel of King Achav's advisors [on how best to dispose of Navos of Yizre'el, whose vineyard Achav coveted]: *Then seat two men, unscrupulous people, opposite him, and they will testify [falsely] against him, saying, 'You blasphemed God and the king!* [*Melachim* I, 21:10] (*Sanhedrin* 29a).

————————

How do the judges intimidate the witnesses [so that they fear to perjure themselves]? For capital cases, the judges bring them into a room and proceed to strike fear into their hearts, saying, "Is it possible that you plan to testify based on conjecture, or hearsay, or perhaps on information you learned from some reliable source, or from an eyewitness? You must surely be aware that we will, in due course, examine you rigorously. Please be advised that capital cases are quite different in nature from monetary judgments. In the case of monetary matters, a witness who lies, and then seeks to repent, can readily make restitution and gain his atonement. But when the defendant's life is in question, the witnesses are accountable not only for the blood of the accused, but for every one of his potential descendants, down until the end of time.

This we find in connection with Kayin, who murdered his brother. There it is written (*Bereishis* 4:10), *The voice of the **bloods** of your brother cry out to Me.* The plural form was deliberately used, so as to include the blood of his seed … For this reason, too, the first man was created alone, to teach us that one who causes the death of one person has destroyed a whole world, and, conversely, one who saves the life of one person has saved a whole world. If this is so, you may wonder, why become involved in such a serious matter? For the Torah has stated (*Vayikra* 5:1): *[If] he is a witness, and he saw or he knew, if he does not testify, he shall bear his iniquity.* Perhaps you will say: Why make ourselves liable for this criminal's death? You have nothing to fear; there is no guilt or blame, as it said (*Mishlei* 11:10), *When the wicked perish, there is [cause for] glad song* (see *Sanhedrin* 37a).

IV. FALSE WITNESSES BEFORE SHLOMO HAMELECH'S THRONE

nd the king fashioned a great throne of ivory, and overlaid it with sparkling gold. The throne had six steps, and a rounded top from behind… (Melachim I, 10:18-19). Shlomo HaMelech overlaid his great throne with sparkling gold, studded with an assortment of gems — sardonyxes, garnets, jacinth, emeralds, and all sorts of fine pearls. The throne had no equal in the annals of royalty, and there was no kingdom that could duplicate it. These were its features: Twelve golden lions stood on each of its steps; opposite each lion was an eagle of gold. The number of lions totaled seventy-two, and the eagles likewise numbered seventy-two.

The throne had a rounded top above the seat of the king, and was fronted by six golden steps, as mentioned in Scripture. On the first step crouched a golden ox on one side; directly opposite was a golden lion. On the second step crouched a golden wolf, facing it was a golden sheep; on the third step crouched a golden leopard, and facing it a golden camel; on the fourth step crouched a golden eagle,

and opposite it a golden peacock; on the fifth step crouched a golden cat, and facing it a golden rooster; on the sixth step crouched a golden hawk, and opposite it a golden pigeon. Atop the throne stood a golden pigeon with a hawk of gold in its grip.

Above the throne loomed a golden menorah with all its accessories: lamps, tongs, scoops, and decorative knobs, goblets, and flowers. From one side of the stem extended seven golden branches, on which were engraved the seven patriarchs of the world: Adam, Noach, Shem, Avraham, Yitzchak, Yaakov, with Iyov amongst them. On the second side extended another seven branches, bearing the images of seven of the world's saintly personalities: Levi, Kehas, Amram, Moshe, Aharon, Eldad, Medad. Attached to the top of the menorah was a golden jug filled with pure olive oil, which was used to kindle the lamps of the Temple. Fixed underneath it was a golden basin, bearing the likeness of Eli the High Priest; it was filled with pure olive oil which was earmarked for the menorah's lamps. Two golden branches, engraved with the images of the two sons of Eli, Chophni and Pinchas, extended from the great basin, and from among these extended two golden tubes, on which were depicted Nadav and Avihu, sons of Aharon. There were two golden seats flanking the throne, one for the High Priest and the other for his deputy. Above the top of the throne, seventy golden chairs were installed, to be used by the seventy members of the Great Sanhedrin, who would sit in judgment in Shlomo HaMelech's presence … Twenty-four grapevines of gold were affixed above the top of the throne; they provided shade for the king. The throne was equipped with a silver serpent that resembled a revolving wheel, and whenever Shlomo HaMelech wished to go somewhere, the throne would move along underneath him, propelled by a mechanism that was developed for it.

When he would set his foot on the first step, the golden ox would lift him up to the second step. From the second step he would be placed on the third, and from the third to the fourth, and from the fourth to the fifth, and from the fifth to the sixth. When he reached the sixth step, the eagles would descend and sweep Shlomo HaMelech up in their wings, seating him at the head of the throne.

When word of Shlomo HaMelech's throne reached the kings of the world, they came as a group and bowed down before him, exclaiming, "In all the kingdoms, a throne like this has never been made, and no other people exist that could produce anything like it." And when the kings fully appreciated the design of the throne, they began extolling the praises of the One Who willed the world into being.

When Shlomo HaMelech would ascend the throne, the great eagle would take the royal crown and place it on his head, the lions would sprinkle fragrances of many varieties. and the great serpent would revolve by way of an inventive design. Then the lions and eagles would begin revolving as well, and they would rise up above Shlomo HaMelech's head, providing more shade. The golden pigeon would descend from its pillar and open the Ark to remove the Torah Scroll, which it would place in the arm of the king, in fulfillment of the verse from the Torah of Moshe (*Devarim* 17:19-20), *It shall remain with him, and he shall read from it all the days of his life … in order that his reign shall endure, for him and his descendants, in the midst of Israel.*

When the *Kohen Gadol* and the elders would arrive, they would greet the king, and seat themselves around the throne, to its right and its left, and begin judging the people. In the event that false witnesses would appear before Shlomo HaMelech, the revolving devices would begin moving, and the oxen would start lowing, the lions roaring, the wolves howling, the sheep bleating, the leopards growling, the camels bawling, the cats wailing, the peacocks moaning, the roosters crowing, the hawks shrieking, and the birds chirping clamorously. All this to spark fear in the hearts of the witnesses and to dissuade them from falsifying their testimony. The witnesses would then say to themselves: We must tell the truth, for if we don't, we will be uprooted from the world, and the world itself will be destroyed on our account (*Targum Sheni* to *Megillas Esther* 1:2, based on the Hebrew translations of *Pas'sheggen HaKsav* and *R' Tzvi Cohen, Targum Sheni,* Bnei Brak, 1996).

מפתח למוני המצוות
THE COUNT OF THE MITZVAH

Baal Halachos Gedolos / Lavin 31
בה"ג / לאוין לא

R' Saadiah Gaon / Lavin 34
רס"ג / לאוין לד

R' Eliyahu HaZakein / Amud 56
ר' אליהו הזקן / עמוד 56

Rashbag / Lo Saaseh Os 13
רשב"ג / לא תעשה אות יג

R' Yitzchak El-Bargeloni / Lavin 31
ר"י אלברג'לוני / לאוין לא

Maamar HaSechel / Dibbur Tish'i 1
מאמר השכל / דיבור תשעי א

Sefer Yere'im / 178
יראים / קעח

Rambam, Sefer HaMitzvos / Lo Saaseh 285
רמב"ם / לא תעשה רפה

Sefer Mitzvos Gadol (Smag) / Lo Saaseh 215
סמ"ג / לא תעשה רטו

Sefer Mitzvos Katan (Smak) / 236
סמ"ק / רלו

Zohar HaRakia / Lavin 17
זוהר הרקיע / לאוין יז

Mitzvah 38

אָסוּר חֲמוּד

פרשת יתרו

NOT TO COVET THAT WHICH BELONGS TO ANOTHER

THE MITZVAH:

MITZVAH 38

אִסוּר חִמּוּד
(לֹא תַעֲשֶׂה)

NOT TO COVET THAT WHICH BELONGS TO ANOTHER

מצוה **לח**

SOURCE

לֹא תַחְמֹד   שמות (פרשת יתרו) כ:יד

"Do not covet"

THE MITZVAH

One is forbidden to exert any sort of pressure upon his fellow to convince him to surrender his property.

LAWS

1 All types of pressure or efforts to convince a person to relinquish his property are forbidden; this includes enticing him with large sums of money.[1] Merely admiring another's property is not included in the prohibition.[2]

2 The prohibition applies only to property that, when transferred, is no longer possessed by its original owner.[3] Therefore, one who pressures his fellow to teach him a skill or a trade does not violate this prohibition.[4]

3 The prohibition also applies to coveting another man's wife. Accordingly, one who attempts to separate a wife from her husband in order to marry her himself violates this prohibition.[5]

4 One has violated this prohibition only if he succeeds in acquiring the coveted object.[6]

5 The prohibition applies only to efforts aimed at acquiring a property or object that one covets from its owner. Efforts aimed at acquiring an identical object from another source are permitted.[7]

6 This prohibition applies to both men and women, in all places and at all times.[8]

7 One who violates this prohibition does not incur lashes.[9]

NOTE: Another prohibition (*mitzvah #416, Lo Sis'aveh*) is closely related to this one. However, the conditions for transgressing each of the two prohibitions differ somewhat.[10]

A REASON

One who covets the property of another lacks faith in God. A person of faith trusts that God will provide him with all his needs. One who trusts in God's benevolence will feel no desire for the property of others.

לע"נ הרב אברהם יעקב בן הרב שלמה יהודה ע"ה
לע"נ הרב נתן צבי בן הרב אביגדור ע"ה

1. See *Mechilta* to *Shemos* 20:14; *Rambam, Hil. Gezeilah Va'Aveidah* 1:9; *Tur, Choshen Mishpat* §359, and *Shulchan Aruch* 359:10.

The prohibition of לא תחמוד is limited to *repeated* requests or demands that are difficult for the owner to withstand (these may come from the person himself, or people he sends to persuade the owner to give up the property). Therefore, making a simple request of a person to relinquish his property, without applying pressure upon him, would not violate this prohibition. However, if the request is made by a prominent person, whose first request would also be difficult to refuse, even a simple request is forbidden (*Shaarei Teshuvah* 3:43; *Orchos Chaim* [R' Aharon HaCohen MiLuneil] III:43; *Hagahos HaSmak* §19).

Of course, one is always permitted to inquire whether a particular item is for sale, or to make efforts to acquire an item known to be for sale.

2. According to *Rambam* (*Hil. Gezeilah Va'Aveidah* 1:9), one violates the prohibition of *Lo Sachmod* only if he actually sets a plan in motion with the aim of acquiring the coveted property (see, however, note 6). It seems that in the opinion of *Rambam* (ibid. 1:10), simply desiring to obtain another's property, while certainly improper behavior (as it will often lead to transgression), not only is not prohibited by *Lo Sachmod*, but is not even forbidden by *Lo Sis'aveh* (another prohibition, *mitzvah* #416, closely related to ours), unless he devises a scheme to obtain the coveted property. This opinion is cited in *Shulchan Aruch, Choshen Mishpat* 359:10. However, other Rishonim write that even

An Expanded Treatment

though one does not transgress *Lo Sachmod* by desiring to obtain another's property, he does transgress *Lo Sis'aveh* (*Rambam, Sefer HaMitzvos, Lo Saaseh* §266; *Sefer HaChinuch* §416). A third opinion found in the Rishonim maintains that though *Lo Sachmod* is not violated unless he is successful in acquiring the coveted property, the desire to do so is itself an element of this prohibition (*Smak* §19; *Orchos Chaim*: ibid.). Still others are of the opinion that the prohibition of *Lo Sachmod* applies even to the mere desire in one's heart to obtain the property of another (*Rabbeinu Bachya* to *Shemos* 20:14; *Ibn Ezra, Peirush HeAruch* ibid.). See further, note 10 and *Iyunim* §1.

3. For example: real estate, slaves, or livestock, all of which are mentioned in the Biblical verses that teach this prohibition (*Shemos* 20:14; *Devarim* 5:18). Although the Torah specifies these items, it does not mean to exclude other items from the prohibition. Rather, it lists them to establish a general category; that is, anything that transfers from one person to another, and is lost to the original owner once transferred [see next note] (see *Mechilta* to *Shemos* ibid.; *Rambam* ibid.; *Tur* ibid.; *Aruch Ha-Shulchan, Choshen Mishpat* 359:9, 10).

Another criterion of this category (expounded in *Mechilta* ibid.) is that all of the items mentioned are things that can be acquired *only* with the owner's consent. *Mechilta* explains that this rule is intended to permit a person to attempt to convince a father to allow his daughter to marry a particular man, or his son to marry a particular woman. One might imagine

that since children can be said to "belong" to their parents in a certain sense, it would be forbidden to exert pressure on a parent to consent to a specific match for his child. To dispel this notion, we derive from the Torah's choice of examples that the prohibition applies only where the owner's consent is necessary. In the case of marriage, the parents' consent is *not* needed, for children *may* marry without the permission of their parents. Since the parents' agreement is not required, pressure exerted upon them does not fall under the prohibition of לא תחמוד (see *Aruch HaShulchan* to *Choshen Mishpat* ibid. §11).

4. Knowledge is not something that transfers from one person to another, as the knowledge, even after it is imparted to the student, still remains with the teacher. Thus, the student has not pressured the teacher to relinquish anything. Therefore, pressuring one to share knowledge is not included in this prohibition (see *Mechilta* ibid.; *Aruch HaShulchan* ibid. §9, 10).

One is also permitted to covet another person's level of accomplishment in Torah and mitzvos. Since these, too, are things retained by their owner even after they are acquired by another, they do not fall under the prohibition of לא תחמוד. In fact, it is actually meritorious to covet such worthy accomplishments [as the Gemara states (*Bava Basra* 22a): Jealousy among scholars increases wisdom]. One who does so will surely be rewarded (*Rabbeinu Bachya, Shemos* 20:14).

Zohar (vol. 2, 93b) derives the permissibility of coveting another's Torah accomplishments in this

manner: The items specified in the verse — houses, fields, slaves — are all mundane things of the physical world. The Torah thereby implies that the prohibition applies only to items such as these, but not to Torah, which is of the spiritual realm. See also *Mirkeves HaMishneh* and *Shevus Yehudah* (p. 80) to *Mechilta* ibid.

5. The Torah specifically prohibits coveting *the wife of your fellow* (*Shemos* ibid.; *Devarim* ibid.). Therefore, one who attempts to cause the divorce of a married woman from her husband in order to marry her himself violates the prohibition of *You shall not covet* (see *Sma, Choshen Mishpat* 359:19; cf. *Bach* ibid.).

By specifying "the *wife* of your fellow," the verse implies that one is permitted to covet an unmarried woman, and to endeavor to win her hand in marriage (*Aruch HaShulchan* ibid. §11).

6. *Mechilta* (*Shemos* 20:14) derives this requirement from an unrelated verse that is written with regard to the prohibition against deriving benefit from idols. The Torah states (*Devarim* 7:25): *The carved images of their gods you shall burn in fire; you shall not covet (Lo Sachmod) the silver and gold that is on them, and take it for yourself; lest you be ensnared by it.* This verse connects the prohibition of coveting the idols with the taking of the valuables they contain; we derive that regarding the prohibition of *Lo Sachmod*, too, only coveting that ends in the acquisition of the desired item is forbidden (see, however, the various opinions cited above, note 2). See also *Rambam, Hil. Gezeilah Va'Aveidah* 1:9.

The question of whether the object must be obtained against the

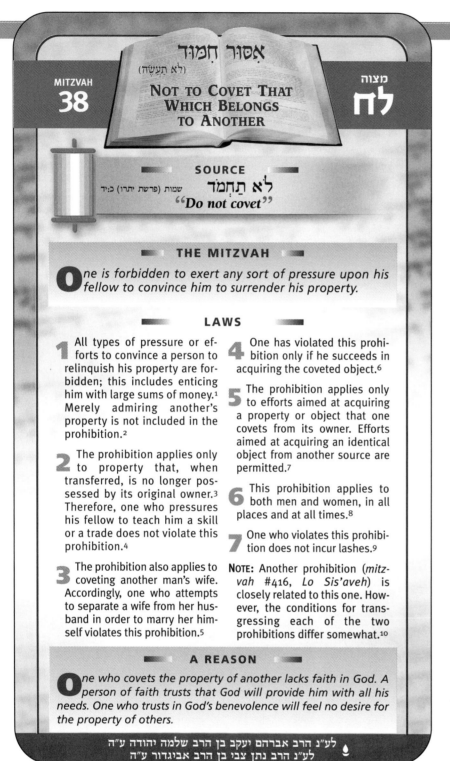

אִסּוּר חֲמוּד
(לֹא תַעֲשֶׂה)

MITZVAH 38

NOT TO COVET THAT WHICH BELONGS TO ANOTHER

מצוה לח

■ SOURCE ■

לֹא תַחְמֹד
שמות (פרשת יתרו) כ:יד
"Do not covet"

■ THE MITZVAH ■

One is forbidden to exert any sort of pressure upon his fellow to convince him to surrender his property.

■ LAWS ■

1 All types of pressure or efforts to convince a person to relinquish his property are forbidden; this includes enticing him with large sums of money.[1] Merely admiring another's property is not included in the prohibition.[2]

2 The prohibition applies only to property that, when transferred, is no longer possessed by its original owner.[3] Therefore, one who pressures his fellow to teach him a skill or a trade does not violate this prohibition.[4]

3 The prohibition also applies to coveting another man's wife. Accordingly, one who attempts to separate a wife from her husband in order to marry her himself violates this prohibition.[5]

4 One has violated this prohibition only if he succeeds in acquiring the coveted object.[6]

5 The prohibition applies only to efforts aimed at acquiring a property or object that one covets from its owner. Efforts aimed at acquiring an identical object from another source are permitted.[7]

6 This prohibition applies to both men and women, in all places and at all times.[8]

7 One who violates this prohibition does not incur lashes.[9]

NOTE: Another prohibition (*mitzvah #416, Lo Sis'aveh*) is closely related to this one. However, the conditions for transgressing each of the two prohibitions differ somewhat.[10]

■ A REASON ■

One who covets the property of another lacks faith in God. A person of faith trusts that God will provide him with all his needs. One who trusts in God's benevolence will feel no desire for the property of others.

owner's will for *Lo Sachmod* to be violated is discussed extensively by the Rishonim, and several different opinions exist. *Rambam* maintains that even if the owner parts with the item willingly, *Lo Sachmod* has been violated. Others go to the other extreme

and maintain that in order to violate *Lo Sachmod*, the person must take the object against the owner's will *and not pay for it at all* (see *Tosafos* to *Bava Metzia* 5b ד"ה בלא, with *Maharsha* and *Maharam Schif*, see also *Tosafos* to *Sanhedrin* 25b ד"ה מעיקרא,

first explanation, and *Smag, Lo Saaseh* §158). A third group of Rishonim, *Raavad* among them, take a middle position: They maintain that while the item must be taken against the owner's will to violate *Lo Sachmod*, it need not be stolen outright; even if the owner was given money, the prohibition is violated as long as the seller does not consent to the sale (see *Tosafos* to *Bava Kamma* 62a ד"ה חמסן and to *Sanhedrin* ibid., second explanation; see also *Sefer Yereim* §115). [According to the latter two views, one cannot violate *Lo Sachmod* without violating the prohibition against robbery as well; for discussion of why a separate prohibition of *Lo Sachmod* is needed, see *Rabbeinu Bachya* to *Shemos* 20:14. See also *Derishah* §9 to *Choshen Mishpat* §371, for what appears to be a fourth view.]

7. Since by attempting to acquire an identical item one does not cause the owner of the original item to relinquish anything, he has not violated the prohibition [see above, notes 2 and 4] (see *Rabbeinu Avraham ben HaRambam* to *Shemos* 20:14).

8. This is in conformance with the general rule that men and women are equated by the Torah with regard to prohibitions (see Mishnah, *Kiddushin* 29a, and Gemara there, 35a).

9. *Rambam* writes (*Hil. Gezeilah Va'Aveidah* 1:9) that one who violates *Lo Sachmod* does not receive *malkos* because it is a לאו שאין בו מעשה, *a prohibition that does not involve an action.* This is somewhat difficult to understand, given that *Rambam* himself rules that *Lo Sachmod* is not violated unless the person ultimately acquires the item — which certainly *is* an action! (see *Hasagos HaRaavad* ibid.). For further discussion, as well as an alternate explanation, see *Iyunim* §2.

10. According to *Rambam* (ibid. 1:9-10), the distinction between the prohibition against desiring acquisition of another's property (*mitzvah* #416 — *Lo Sis'aveh*, which appears in the *Devarim* text of the Ten Commandments) and the prohibition of *Lo Sachmod* is as follows: As soon as one concludes in his mind that he wishes to acquire another's property, and he begins to scheme and plan ways to accomplish this, he has violated *Lo Sis'aveh* — even if he has not yet set any plans into motion. Once he begins to actually carry out his plans, he has violated *Lo Sachmod* as well (as noted above, however, to transgress *Lo Sachmod,* he must be sucessful in ultimately acquiring the object). [According to *Rambam*, merely desiring the property of another without a mental resolution to obtain it violates neither prohibition, although it is improper behavior; see above, note 2.]

Others disagree with *Rambam's* explanation; for further discussion, see *Iyunim* §1.

A BROADER LOOK AT THE LAWS

1 Lo Sachmod and Lo Sis'aveh — one prohibition, or two?

As mentioned above (notes 2 and 10), *Rambam* maintains that *Lo Sachmod* and *Lo Sis'aveh* are two distinct prohibitions, with *Lo Sis'aveh* prohibiting scheming to acquire a coveted property, and *Lo Sachmod* prohibiting the setting of such schemes in motion. Others, however, disagree. *Smag* (*Lo Saaseh* §158) notes that in the *Devarim* text of the Ten Commandments (5:18), the Torah states both *Lo Sachmod* and *Lo Sis'aveh* — *Lo Sachmod* with regard to another man's wife, and *Lo Sis'aveh* regarding another man's house. Can it be, asks the *Smag*, that the Torah was stricter with regard to coveting another's house (forbidding even scheming) than concerning coveting another's wife (forbidding only the carrying out of those schemes)? Certainly not! Therefore, *Smag* concludes that *Lo Sachmod* and *Lo Sis'aveh* are one and the same — both forbid the scheming to obtain another's possession. [For a defense of *Rambam*, see *Bach* to *Choshen Mishpat* §359 (end).]

[Note that according to *Rambam*, one can violate *Lo Sis'aveh* even if he does not ultimately obtain the coveted item (as the exposition requiring this applies only to *Lo Sachmod*; indeed, *Rambam* only mentions this condition with respect to *Lo Sachmod*). According to *Smag*, however, one does not violate even *Lo Sis'aveh* unless he ultimately obtains the item (see *Bach* ibid.).]

It must also be noted that there are commentators (*Shaarei Teshuvah* 3:43) are of the opinion that even merely desiring to compel another to relinquish his property is forbidden by *Lo Sachmod*. Others are of the opinion that even the *desiring* of another's property itself, without an accompanying desire to compel him to relinquish it, is also forbidden by *Lo Sachmod* (*Rabbeinu Bachya* to *Shemos* 20:14; *Ibn Ezra* ibid.). Indeed, it is concerning this aspect of *Lo Sachmod* that *Ibn Ezra* (*Shemos* 20:14) asks his famous question: How can the Torah expect a person not to covet a beautiful item that he sees? Granted that he knows that he may not steal it; but how can he be expected to not even feel a desire to obtain it? *Ibn Ezra* replies with a parable: A simple villager, if he is of sound mind, will not observe the princess of his kingdom and desire her for his mate. He understands that she is above his station, and desiring her for a wife is just as silly as desiring wings with which to fly. Nor does one desire to marry his mother, as he has known all his life that she is forbidden to him. Similarly, says *Ibn Ezra*, every Jew must realize that desirable property belonging to another was awarded to that person by Hashem. As such, it should be as unattainable in his eyes as the princess to the villager, and as forbidden as one's own mother. Should Hashem wish to grant him such items, he will receive them; he must realize that scheming to obtain them is unnecessary.

2 Why is there no liability of malkos for transgressing Lo Sachmod?

As mentioned above (note 9), *Rambam* states that one does not receive *malkos* for violating *Lo Sachmod*, because it is a לאו שאין בו מעשה — *a prohibition that does not involve an action*. This is challenged by *Raavad*, who argues that the taking of the coveted item should certainly qualify as an action! He therefore advances a different reason — that since the coveted item must be returned to its original owner, one who violates the prohibition of *Lo Sachmod* is similar to a robber. And just as one who robs does not receive *malkos* — for the prohibition against robbery is a לאו הניתק לעשה, *a prohibition that can be remedied through the performance of a positive commandment* — so, too, one who violates *Lo Sachmod* does not receive *malkos*.

Maggid Mishneh (to *Rambam* ibid. 1:9) explains that *Rambam* and *Raavad* differ in a fundamental question: Is the acquisition of the coveted item *part* of the transgression of *Lo Sachmod*? Or is it perhaps only a condition that must be fulfilled for the person to have violated *Lo Sachmod*: that is, if the coveted object is not ultimately obtained, this shows us that the level of maneuvering done by the person did not reach the level necessary to violate *Lo Sachmod*. But the obtaining itself is not part and parcel of the prohibition. He states that *Rambam* is of the opinion that the obtaining of the object is not part of the prohibition — indeed, *Rambam* holds that even if the original owner parts with the object willingly as a result of the coveter's persuasion, the prohibition has still been violated (although there is no liability to return the item in such a case). Accordingly, *Rambam* considers *Lo Sachmod* a prohibition that does not involve an action. *Raavad*, on the other hand (see also *Sefer HaChinuch* §38), considers the obtaining of the item against the will of the owner to be part of the prohibition (for this reason, *Raavad* rules that if the owner ultimately parts with the item willingly, *Lo Sachmod* has *not* been violated). In his view, therefore, *Lo Sachmod* does involve an action, and does not receive *malkos* only because the prohibition must be remedied through the return of the item.

One final point remains to be addressed, however: Granted that according to *Rambam*, the obtaining of the object is not an active part of the transgression, but what of the plans the coveter sets in motion to obtain the item? Surely they often involve action! *Maggid Mishneh* (ibid.) addresses this point, and explains cryptically that השתדלות לא היה מעשה, *in the attempt, there is no action.*

The commentators differ as to the meaning of this answer. Some maintain that in cases where the plans *do* involve action (such as where the owner is physically compelled to give up the object), the prohibition *does* involve action, and *malkos* is not received only because the item must be returned (see *Minchas Chinuch* here §3, and 229:7; see also *Even HaAzel, Hil. Gezeilah Va'Aveidah* 1:9). Others state that since in most cases no action is involved, the prohibition is classified in all cases as a prohibition that does not involve action (see *Achiezer*

vol. I, 22:6). [It is also possible that *Maggid Mishneh* simply means that there is no act that can be singled out as an act that will violate this prohibition, since it is never known with certainty whether the owner will bow to the pressure, or which plan will succeed. Therefore, all plans and schemes are not acts of violation — rather, it is the mindset that causes one to put such plans in motion that is forbidden.]

3 Does one receive malkos for coveting a married woman?

A practical ramification of the dispute as to why the violator of *Lo Sachmod* does not receive *malkos* (see above, §2) can be found in the case of a man who pressures his fellow to divorce his wife, so that he can marry her himself. If one is exempt from *malkos* because the prohibition does not involve action, this person too is exempt, since "attempting" is not legally regarded as an action. But if the reason is that the transgression can be rectified, the exemption should not apply to one who pressures his fellow to divorce his wife and then marries her himself; for once he marries the woman, she is not permitted to return to her first husband (see *mitzvah* #580). Since the act cannot be rectified, he would be liable to lashes (see *Megillas Sefer, Lo Saaseh* §158, p. 83).

4 Demands made upon prospective in-laws

A *choson* (bridegroom) may not demand gifts from his future parents-in-law beyond those stipulated at the engagement (e.g. in the *tenaim* document). One who does so violates the prohibition of *Lo Sachmod* (*Sefer HaMitzvos HaKotzeir, Lavin* §40). The same applies to the parents of the *choson* and *kallah*. Once the financial arrangements of the match have been finalized, the two sets of parents are forbidden to pressure each other to provide gifts beyond those stipulated in their agreement. However, as long as the agreement has not been finalized, they may make whatever demands they wish (*Shemiras HaLashon*, second afterword to vol. 2 [end of §12]).

5 Distancing oneself from coveting another man's wife

A single Hebrew word, depending on how it is pronounced, can assume many different meanings. The different pronunciations of the phrase לא תחמד (which in Scripture is spelled without the letter *vav*) yield several meanings that are complementary to the verse's primary thrust. If the verse is vowelized as לֹא תֶחְמַד, it translates as: *do not make yourself desirable.* This is a command to a man to refrain from beautifying himself in order to find favor in the eyes of another man's wife [whom he covets]. Alternatively, the verse can be pronounced as לֹא תְחַמֵד, which translates as: *do not make [a woman] desirable.* According to this understanding, one is enjoined against praising the beauty of a married woman to a man other than her husband, lest he cause the second man to sin by coveting her (*Sefer Chasidim* §99; see also *Sefer HaYirah L'Rabbeinu Yonah* ד"ה אל תשבח, and *Orchos Chaim L'HaRosh* §98).

SITUATIONS IN HALACHAH

Question:

Are there situations in which coveting another's possessions or pressuring someone to part with his property is not a violation of *Lo Sachmod*?

Answer:

The Poskim discuss several situations where it is possible that the prohibition of *Lo Sachmod* does not apply. Some examples are:

A. Pressuring someone to sell (or give) a nonspecific item

The prohibition of *Lo Sachmod* only applies to the coveting of a specific item. Thus, pressuring someone to give a gift (e.g. pressuring one's parents for a birthday present without requesting a specific item) is not a violation of *Lo Sachmod* (see *Rav Berachos* [by the *Ben Ish Chai*] p.93ff; see also *Commentary* of *R' Y. F. Perla* to *Sefer HaMitzvos L'Rasag, Lo Saaseh* §271).

B. Pressuring someone to give his property to a third party

Ben Yehoyada (to *Kiddushin* 59a) writes that one only violates *Lo Sachmod* if he desires another's property for himself. In his view, suggesting that a person should give his property to another does not violate the prohibition. [It should be noted, however, that from *Ben Yehoyada's* proof it is clear that he subscribes to the view that merely *desiring* another's possessions is sufficient to violate the prohibition, and it is in relation to this that he limits the prohibition to a selfish desire. It is possible that even *Ben Yehoyada* would concur that *pressuring* one to give property to a third party is also forbidden.]

C. Pressuring someone to sell an easily obtainable object

If a person is hungry, and can easily obtain food, but pressures his fellow to sell him food instead of

going to buy it himself, he has not violated *Lo Sachmod* according to some Poskim (*Teshuvos Eretz Tzvi* I:4, citing *Imrei Emes* and others). The rationale for this would seem to be that in such a case the person really does not covet the food; he is simply lazy, and his pressuring the person to sell him the food stems from a desire to prevent exertion, not from a desire for the object itself.

D. Pressuring someone to sell a mitzvah object

In the opinion of some Poskim (see *Toldos Shmuel* 38:1:6; *Rav Berachos* p. 92), *Lo Sachmod* does not apply to mitzvah objects. Thus, if Reuven owns a particularly beautiful *esrog*, Shimon may pressure Reuven to sell it to him. [Of course, Reuven must ultimately consent to sell the *esrog* for it to be fit for Shimon's use, as a stolen *esrog* is invalid for the mitzvah.] Others, however, maintain that with respect to *Lo Sachmod* there is no distinction between mitzvah objects and any other objects, and they rule that Shimon would indeed violate *Lo Sachmod* in such a case (see *Teshuvos Machaneh Chaim, Orach Chaim* II:32).

E. Pressuring someone to sell his share of a partnership

When two people own an object in partnership, each partner has the right to dissolve the partnership at any time. If the object cannot be divided between them (for example, an automobile), either one can tell his partner, "Either buy my share of the item, or allow me to buy your share" (see *Bava Basra* 13a; *Rambam, Hil. Shecheinim* 1:2; *Tur* and *Shulchan Aruch, Choshen Mishpat* 171:6). One is legally entitled to exercise this option even if he knows that his partner does not have sufficient funds to purchase his share of the object, and will thus be forced to sell (*Shach* to *Shulchan Aruch* ibid. 6). The authorities debate the question of whether one violates *Lo Sachmod* by exercising this buy/sell option, since he is, in effect, forcing the other partner to sell his share against his will (see *Teshuvos Mishpatim Yesharim* I:69).

טוב טעם

ILLUMINATIONS OF THE MITZVAH
Suggested Reasons & Insights

I. COVETOUSNESS: A PERIL TO BODY AND SOUL

ovetousness stems from the deplorable feeling of envy (*Reishis Chochmah, Sha'ar HaAnavah* §7; *Orchos Tzaddikim* 14; *Mesillas Yesharim* §11), an emotion which should be kept far from one's heart.

An envious person, who desires what others possess and cannot be satisfied with what he himself has, is an unfortunate person indeed. He will never know the serene feeling of contentment; instead, he is destined to squander his life pursuing empty illusions, only to end up unsatisfied, as our Sages observed (*Koheles Rabbah* 1:13): No person dies having attained even half of his desires. The *Mesillas Yesharim* (ibid.) writes, "Envy imprisons a person for life; it places on his arms the burden of laborious work, as it is written, *He who loves money will never be sated with money* (*Koheles* 5:9). It distracts him from the service of God; how many prayers are lost, and how many mitzvos neglected, as the price of excessive involvement in business activity, to say nothing of the study of Torah?"

Observance of the Torah's prohibition against covetousness, then, is of great benefit to a person in terms of his physical health, spiritual development, and even his economic well-being. A covetous person is wont to wear down his strength and spirit, and to squander his money in the endless struggle to attain his desires. It is this that the Sages pithily taught (*Avos* 4:1), Who is the wealthy person? He who is content with his lot, as it is said (*Tehillim* 128:2), *When you consume the work of your hands, you are praiseworthy and the good will be yours* (*Migdal David, Sefer Mitzvah, Azharah* §266).

II. COVETOUSNESS: A DEFICIENCY IN FAITH AND RELIANCE ON GOD

esiring another's possessions is a symptom of weakness in one's belief that the Creator of the universe is He Who apportions to every one of His creatures all that it needs for its ultimate good (*Ibn Ezra, Shemos* 20:14; *Shaarei Kedushah* 2:4; *Derech Pikudecha, Lo Saaseh* §38, *Cheilek HaMachshavah* §3). A true believer rests assured that whatever he lacks, God does not wish to give, and what God will not give, there is no way to get (*Ibn Ezra, Shemos* ibid.). In the words of the Mishnaic Sage Ben Azai: "They shall call you by name, they shall sit you in your place, they shall give you what is yours. No person can touch what is assigned to his fellow, even as much as a hair" (*Yoma* 38a-b). One who relies on God's judgment and is content with his lot acquires for himself a sense of serenity and fulfillment, the antithesis of envy; this kind of absolute faith, which frees one from worrying about what will be on the morrow, is the foundation underlying the whole of the Torah (*Gra, Even Sheleimah* §3).

It is for this reason that this commandment was left for last among the Ten Commandments, so that it may be linked to the first, "*I am Hashem, your God*" (calling for faith in God). The Torah thereby teaches that one presupposes the other. Warding off envy demonstrates faith, and both commandments come to fulfillment. Conversely, to fall victim to envy negates the message of "*I am Hashem*," for if one truly believed, he would have no cause to covet (*Kad HaKemach, Chemdah*; cf. *Takanas HaShavin* §6). Indeed, one must purge from his heart the inclination to covet as earnestly as one eradicates any trace of idolatry (*Akeidas Yitzchak* §45; see there for elaboration).

III. AN OBSTACLE TO THE LOVE OF GOD

n envious person, instead of asserting the rule of his intellect, allows himself to be drawn after worldly enticements, thinking that they hold the key to human success (*Derashos Rabbeinu Yonah, Shemos*). As a result, he becomes more and more distanced from that which is truly good (*Mesillas Yesharim* §1).

The preoccupation with material goals prevents one from developing more refined aspirations. "The desire itself is a sin against God, and a sin against yourself as well, for your heart should be kept free for only pure and proper ambitions" (*R' Samson R. Hirsch, Shemos* 20:14).

One basic goal pushed out of one's heart by feelings of envy is the cultivation of a heartfelt love for God, as mandated by the Torah. This mitzvah was communicated to us with the words, *You shall love Hashem, your God, with **all** your heart...*, which amounts to a call for this sentiment to fill one's whole heart, until no room is left for the love of anything else. Indeed, one who truly longs to draw close to God and bask in His presence will scoff at the transient pleasures this world has to offer; those thrills lose all attraction to one who has experienced the bliss and delight found in a close connection to God (*Sefer HaBris* II, 14:14; *HaKesav VeHaKabbalah, Yisro*; cf. *Sefas Emes, Yisro* 5636).

[If a person has previously been immersed in the pursuit of wealth and pleasure, and was thus far removed from the mitzvah to love God, he can be assured that if he will take the initiative and do what he can to attune his heart to such spiritual sentiments, he will receive Heavenly assistance in attaining his goal. A promise in this regard is explicit in the following verse (*Devarim* 30:6): *Hashem, your God, will circumcise your heart and the heart of your offspring, to love Hashem, your God, with all your heart and with all your soul. Ramban* explains that covetousness and earthly desires comprise the foreskin of the heart, and to banish such feelings is the heart's circumcision (ad loc.).]

IV. A SPRINGBOARD FOR TRANSGRESSION

side from compromising one's spiritual values, feelings of envy can bring one to sin in a very practical sense. Once a person, with his desires aroused, has set his heart on something in his fellow's possession, he will not be deterred until he gets what he wants. If the owner will not sell it, he will take it by force (*Sefer HaChinuch* §38), and if his fellow resists, he may even kill him (ibid.; *Rabbeinu Bachya, Shemos* 20:17; cf. *Ralbag* ad loc.). Only those who do not covet are not prone to harm their fellow (*Ramban, Shemos* 20:14), and therefore the observance of this mitzvah is deemed crucial to the world's very survival (*Beis Elokim, Sha'ar HaYesodos* §31).

A person who is envious of what others have surely covets what is already his own, and is not likely to part with his property for charitable causes (*Kad HaKemach, Chemdah*). While it is true that the Torah only forbids one to covet "all that belongs to your fellow," and this commandment is seen primarily as an interpersonal mitzvah, one may also interpret "your fellow" as a reference to God (see *Mishlei* 27:10). The portion of one's possessions that ought to be used for the service of God can be described as belonging to God, and even its nominal owner may not covet it for himself (*Derech Pikudecha, Lo Saaseh* §38, *Cheilek HaMachshavah* §2).

[This concept need not be confined to tangible money or property. Deeper reflection on the underlying intent of the Torah brings one to realize that even to begrudge the effort and energy that should be invested in the proper service of God is, in effect, a violation of this prohibition. For both life and limb are not really one's own; they are the property of man's "Fellow" in Heaven. A person who seeks to appropriate them for himself, to the exclusion of his duties toward God, infringes on the prohibition of *You shall not covet ... what belongs to your Fellow* (*Derech Pikudecha* ibid.).]

A covetous person is made vulnerable to a broad range of transgressions. In the relentless pursuit of personal gain, he can easily be induced to bear false witness, steal, or take a false oath. His envy of others can lead to assault, adultery or murder. He will be loathe to spend money on mitzvah observance, such as to honor his parents, or to sacrifice profit by observing Shabbos. He may even progress to idol worship if he becomes convinced the pagan gods can deliver the pleasures he craves. In sum, avarice and desire can bring a person to all forms of evil, up until and including the denial of God (*Toras HaMinchah, Shemos* §24; see also *Reishis Chochmah, Sha'ar HaAnavah* §7). Even if a person is usually inhibited by fear of God and His retribution, his lust can blind his judgment as he gropes for rationalizations to justify forbidden indulgences (*Be'er Mayim Chayim, Devarim* 7:25). In the final analysis, all sin and transgression can be traced to covetousness (*Gra, Even Sheleimah* §3).

[Because this sin is the source of so many others, the Torah placed the commandment that proscribes it at the end of the Ten Commandments, indicating that it is equivalent to all those that precede it. For if one will not beware of this sin, he will wind up transgressing the others as well. Once a person covets, he will eventually steal (*You shall not steal*), and then, being brought to trial, will swear in denial (*You shall not take a false oath*). He will, on occasion, steal on Shabbos (*You shall not do any work*), and when the law catches up with him, he will convert for protection (*You shall not recognize other gods*), etc. (*Kad HaKemach, Chemdah*; see *Akeidas Yitzchak* §45).]

THROUGH THE EYES
OF THE SAGES
Stories, Parables & Reflections

I. THE MAGNITUDE OF THE SIN

He who covets is considered as if he transgresses the entire Torah

eb Yakum says: A person who transgresses *Lo Sachmod* is considered as if he transgresses the [entire] Ten Commandments (*Pesikta Rabbasi* §21; see further there; *Zohar Chadash, Ki Sisa* 74b).

The last commandment of the Ten Commandments is: *You shall not covet another man's wife.* [It is the concluding commandment] because it encompasses everything: A person who covets another's wife is as if he transgresses the entire Torah (*Zohar, Vayikra* 78b).

Elisha said to his assistant Geichazi [after Geichazi manipulated Naaman into giving him the gift that Elisha had refused (see *Melachim* II ch. 5):] "And you — wicked man! — you have tainted me. You have sworn falsely and coveted Naaman's gift, and have thus transgressed the entire Torah!" (*Zohar, Vayikra* 51a).

Coveting leads to theft

From where do we know that if a person allows himself to desire something, he will eventually covet it? For it says (*Devarim* 5:18): *Do not desire, ... Do not covet.* From where do we know that if a person covets something, he will eventually steal it? For it says (*Michah* 2:2): *And they coveted fields and stole them* (*Mechilta DeRabbi Shimon Bar Yochai* 20:14).

Coveting can cancel the honor due one's parents

How were the Ten Commandments given? Five on this tablet and five on the other ... It is written on the first tablet, *Honor your father and your mother*, and opposite it, it is written, *You shall not covet*' [The commandment, *Honor your father and your mother*, is the last of the five commandments on the first tablet, and *Lo Sachmod* is the last of the five commandments on the second tablet.] This tells us that whoever covets his fellow's wife will eventually father a child who will curse his father and mother and honor someone who is not his father (*Mechilta, Yisro* §8; *Zohar, Shemos* 90a; *Pesikta Zutresa, Shemos* 20:13).

Coveting leads to the world's destruction

The world is destroyed through eight things ... And some say: also through coveting. The earlier generations were uprooted from the world only because they sinned in these eight matters (*Tanna D'vei Eliyahu Rabbah* 15:6).

Coveting leads to exile

R' Huna said: We find that the Jewish people were not exiled from their land until they transgressed the sin of coveting, as the verse states (*Michah* 2:2): *They coveted fields and stole [them], houses and took them; they oppressed a man and his household, a person and his inherited portion* (*Pesikta Rabbasi* §24).

The decree of the Temple's destruction was sealed on account of coveting

Rav Yehudah said in the name of Rav: Regarding which incident is it written (*Michah* ibid.): *They coveted fields and stole (them) ... they oppressed a man and his household, a person and his inherited portion*? There was once an incident in which a man coveted the wife of his master; that is, his master in carpentry (i.e. he was an apprentice to this carpenter). One time, the master needed to borrow money, and the apprentice said to him, "Send your wife to me and I will give her the money." The master sent his wife over to his apprentice, who spent three days with her. The master arose early on the fourth day and went to the apprentice. The master asked him, "Where is my wife, whom I sent over to you?" The apprentice replied, "I sent her off immediately, but I heard that some [immoral] youths misbehaved with her on the way." Distraught, the master asked him, "What should I do?" The apprentice answered, "If you want to take my advice, divorce her!" The master said to him, "I cannot afford to divorce her, for the amount of money I would have to pay for her *kesubah* settlement is enormous." The apprentice replied to him, "I will lend you money so that you will be able to give her the money for her *kesubah*." The master went and divorced her. The apprentice then married her. When the time came for the master to repay the loan and he did not have the wherewithal to pay him, the apprentice said to him, "Come and work for me to pay off your debt." They (the apprentice and his wife) would sit, eat and drink while he, the former master, stood over them serving them beverages, and tears would fall from his eyes into their cups. At that moment, the decree of the Temple's destruction was sealed in Heaven (*Gittin* 58a; see *Maharsha* there).

II. THE PUNISHMENT FOR THE SIN

 The coveter loses even what is rightfully his

he Rabbis taught: The *sotah* (adulteress) set her eyes upon someone who was not fit for her; what she sought was not given to her (i.e. she is forbidden to marry the man with whom she committed adultery) and what she had, they took from her. For if she drinks the "bitter waters" used to test a *sotah*, she will die; if she chooses instead to admit her guilt, she becomes forbidden to her husband. This is a general principle: Anyone who sets his eyes upon something that is not his,

what he seeks is not given to him, and what he has, is taken from him.

And so we find in regard to the primordial snake, which set its eyes upon something that was not fit for it (for it coveted Chavah, the wife of Adam HaRishon): What it sought, it was not given; and what it had in hand was taken from it. The Holy One, Blessed is He, stated, "I had declared the snake king of all the animals and beasts, but now it is cursed beyond all the animals and beyond all the beasts of the field (see *Bereishis* 3:14). I had said that the snake would walk upright; now it shall go upon its belly (see *Bereishis* ibid.). I had said that the snake's food would be the same as human food; but now, it shall eat dust (ibid.). The snake had said to itself, 'I will kill Adam and marry Chavah'; but now (ibid. v.15), *I will place enmity between you and the woman, between your offspring and her offspring.*"

And so we find that this principle applied regarding Kayin. Kayin was born with one sister, his brother Hevel with two. Kayin desired the extra sister born with Hevel. To obtain her, he killed Hevel, for which he was sentenced by God to exile, and eventually killed by his own descendant Lemech. It also applied to Korach, who coveted the *Kehunah*, and ultimately was swallowed up by the earth; Bilam, who demanded great sums of money from Balak for cursing the Jewish people, was killed in Midyan when he went to receive payment for the 24,000 Jews who died as a result of his advice (see *Sanhedrin* 106a); Doeg, one of the greatest Torah scholars in the times of Shaul, who became jealous of David and attempted to belittle him in Shaul's eyes, was punished with an early death (see *Sanhedrin* 93b, 101b); Achitofel, who desired the kingship in the times of David, was punished with an early death (see *Sanhedrin* 101b); Geichazi, who coveted the property of the Aramean general, Naaman, was punished with *tzaraas* for taking it (see *Melachim* II Ch. 5); Avshalom, who wanted to usurp the kingdom of his father, king David, met an untimely death in the rebellion he instigated (see *Shmuel* II Ch. 5-18); Adoniyahu, David's son, who coveted David's attendant, Avishag of Shunem, was subsequently killed (see *Melachim* II ch. 2); Uziyahu, one of the kings of Yehudah, who coveted the status of Kohen, was stricken with *tzaraas* (see *Divrei HaYamim* II 26:16-21); and Haman, who desired honor, and decreed that everyone must bow down to him — this led to his downfall and subsequent execution. All these men set their eyes upon something not fit for them. What they sought was not given to them, and what they had in hand was taken from them (*Sotah* 9a-b with *Rashi*; *Tosefta Sotah* 4:5; see also *Zohar, Bamidbar* 176a).

Chamor and his son Shechem said to their citizens regarding Yaakov's family (*Bereishis* 34:23): *Their livestock, their property and all their animals — will they not be ours? Let us but accede to them and circumcise ourselves, and they will dwell with us.* From here we see that they did not undergo circumcision for the sake of Heaven; rather, they set their eyes on Yaakov's wealth. But they did not receive any wealth; and the wealth that was in their hands, the children of Yaakov took from them [see ibid. vs. 28-29] (*Medrash Seichel Tov Bereishis* 34:23).

A person who hopes his wife will die so he may inherit her, or so that he may marry her sister, or anyone who hopes that his brother will die without children so that he may marry his wife through the institution of *yibum* (where the brother has no children, for otherwise the wife of one's deceased brother is forbidden to him); in the end, they will bury him in their lifetime. [Similarly, if a wife hopes that her husband will die so that she may marry another, in the end he buries her (*Tosefta*).] Regarding such a person, the verse states (*Koheles* 10:8): *He who digs a pit will fall into it, and he who breaches a fence will be bitten by a snake* (*Avos D'Rabbi Nosson* 3:3; *Tosefta Sotah* 5:5).

With regard to Bilam, who came to claim payment for the 24,000 Jews whose death he brought about through his advice, and not only failed to receive payment, but was also killed at that time, people have a saying: The camel went to demand horns, but instead his ears were shorn from him (*Sanhedrin* 106a).

Do not set your eyes on money that is not yours, for it will darken you (i.e. make you evil) as black as the black of night and darkness (*Derech Eretz Zuta* §4).

Do not set your eyes on money that is not yours, for those assets will sink into the earth (i.e. they vanish from the world — *Tuvei Chaim*), even if they originally amounted to so much that they reached the gates of the Heavens (*Derech Eretz Zuta* 4; *Tanna D'vei Eliyahu Zuta* 16:1).

--- ৵৵ ---

The story of Achav and Navos

A prime example of forbidden coveting, which resulted in grave consequences and punishment, can be found in the story of Achav and Navos. This narrative is related at length in *Melachim* I, Chapters 21 and 22. Achav, the king of Shomron, coveted the vineyard of Navos. In Achav's attempts to acquire it, he became implicated in the sins of theft, false testimony and even murder. [See *Rambam's Sefer HaMitzvos, Lavin* §266 and *Hil. Gezeilah* 1:9.] Indeed, the Sages have established Achav for all generations as the archetype of a sinful coveter. *You shall not covet — Achav repudiated this* (*Pesikta Rabbasi* 21; *Tanna D'vei Eliyahu Rabbah* 26:2). Achav suffered a bitter end on account of this sin. Although he was in any case a wicked king about whom the verse testifies, *Achav did more to anger Hashem, God of Israel, than all the kings of Israel who had preceded him* (*Melachim* I 16:33) and, *There had never been anyone like Achav who did what was evil in the eyes of Hashem with abandon* (ibid. 21:25), his bitter fate was sealed only because of his criminal behavior toward Navos. This story serves as a moral lesson of the severity of the prohibition of *Lo Sachmod* and the severe consequences it entails.

III. SELECTIONS FROM MELACHIM I, CHAPTERS 21-22

t happened after these matters: There was a vineyard [belonging] to Navos, the Yizre'elite, in Yizre'el that was next to the palace of Achav, king of Shomron. Achav spoke to Navos, saying, "Give me your vineyard, so that I may use it as an herb garden, for it is close to my house; in its place, I will give you a superior vineyard, or, if you prefer, I will pay you its price in money." But Navos said to Achav, "God forbid that I should give my ancestors' heritage to you!"

Achav came home, sullen and upset over the matter that Navos the Yizre'elite had spoken to him, for he said, "I will not give you my ancestors' heritage." [Achav] lay on his bed, turned his face [to the wall] and would eat no bread.

Izevel, his wife, came to him and said, "Why is it that your mood is so sullen and you eat no bread?" He said to her, "Because I spoke to Navos the Yizre'elite and said to him, 'Give me your vineyard for money, or, if you prefer, I will give you a vineyard in its place.' But he said, 'I will not give you my vineyard.'" His wife, Izevel, said to him, "Are you now wielding your sovereignty over Israel? [It is fitting for a king to find a clever way to have his will fulfilled, not to be sullen and upset (*Metzudas David*).] Arise. Eat your bread and let your heart be merry. I shall present you with the vineyard of Navos the Yizre'elite!"

She then wrote scrolls in Achav's name and sealed them with his signet. And she sent [the] scrolls to the elders and the officials who were in his city, who dwelt with Navos. She wrote in the scrolls, saying, "Declare a fast [on a fast day, the people were accustomed to examine the sins of which they were guilty — *Rashi*], and seat Navos at the head of the people. Then seat two unscrupulous individuals opposite him, so that these may [later] testify against him, saying, 'You blasphemed God and the king!' Then take him out and stone him, so he will die."

The men of his city — the elders and the officials who dwelt in his city — acted according to the instructions Izevel sent them, according to what was written in the scrolls that she had sent them. They declared a fast and seated Navos at the head of the people. Two unscrupulous men came and sat opposite him, and these men testified against Navos in the presence of the people, saying, "Navos has blasphemed God and the king." Then they took him outside of the city, and stoned him with rocks and he died. They then sent word to Izebel, saying, "Navos has been stoned and has died."

When Izevel heard that Navos had been stoned and had died, Izevel said to Achav, "Arise and inherit the vineyard of Navos the Yizre'elite, which he refused to give you for money; Navos is not alive, for he is dead." When Achav heard that Navos had died, Achav arose to go down to the vineyard of Navos the Yizre'elite to inherit it. [Some say that Achav was entitled to inherit Navos because the property of those executed by the government belongs to the king; others say that Navos was Achav's cousin, and that Achav also killed Navos's sons, so that he was the sole remaining heir (*Rashi*).]

The word of Hashem then came to Eliyahu HaTishbi saying, "Arise and go down to meet Achav, king of Israel, who dwells in Shomron. Behold he is in the vineyard of Navos, which he has gone down to inherit. Speak to him, saying, 'Thus said Hashem: Will you murder and also inherit?' Then speak to him again, saying, 'Thus said Hashem: In the place where the dogs licked up the blood of Navos, the dogs will lick up your blood as well.'"

Achav said to Eliyahu, "Have you found me guilty, my foe?"

Eliyahu replied, "I have found you guilty because you have done what is evil in the eyes of Hashem with abandon. Behold, [says Hashem] I am bringing evil upon you and I shall eliminate all extensions of you; I shall cut off from Achav every wall-wetter [this is an idiomatic expression; not even a dog, which relieves itself against a wall, will remain of Achav's family and possessions (*Radak*)], every item of hidden property, and every item of public property in Israel. And I shall make your house like the House of Yeravam ben Nevat and like the House of Basha ben Achiyah, because of the provocation with which you have provoked Me, and because you caused the Jewish *people to sin. Hashem has spoken concerning Izevel as well, saying: 'The dogs shall consume Izevel in the Valley of Yizre'el.' Anyone belonging to the House of Achav who dies in the city shall be eaten by the dogs; and anyone belonging to that house who dies in the field, shall be eaten by the birds of the Heavens (Melachim I 21:1-24).*

In the next chapter, Scripture recounts how Achav joined Yehoshaphat, king of Yehudah, in considering battle against the king of Aram. A large group of false prophets prophesized that Achav would be victorious in battle. However, there was one true prophet, Michayahu ben Yimlah, who informed him that he would fall in battle, as indeed happened in fulfillment of Eliyahu's curse. In his prophecy, he describes the following vision:

"I saw Hashem sitting upon His throne, with all the hosts of Heaven standing next to Him, to His right and to His left [on one side of God stood those who were defending Achav; on the other side were those who were prosecuting him (*Rashi*)]. *And Hashem said, 'Who will entice Achav to enter [battle] so that he may fall in Ramot Gilead?' Then the spirit* (see *below*) *came forth and stood before Hashem and said, 'I shall entice him.' And Hashem said, 'How?' The spirit replied, 'I will go out and become a spirit of falsehood in the mouths of all his prophets.' And Hashem said, 'You will entice him and you will succeed! Go forth and do so.' And now — behold! — Hashem has put a spirit of falsehood in the mouths of all these prophets of yours, for Hashem has decreed evil upon you (Melachim I 22:19-23).* R' Yochanan said: The spirit mentioned in the verse was the spirit of Navos the Yizre'elite, who sought to cause Achav's death (*Shabbos* 149b; *Sanhedrin* 89a and 102b; see *Zohar, Bereishis* 192b).

Thus, we see that Achav's punishment came as a result of his sin of coveting Navos's field, and the sins that followed from it: Just as Navos was falsely accused and executed, Achav too was seduced by false prophets into fighting the war in which he lost his life.

I. WHY LO SACHMOD IS COUNTED AS A SEPARATE COMMANDMENT

s noted above (Law 4), one does not violate the prohibition of *Lo Sachmod* unless he succeeds in acquiring the object he covets. Moreover, according to many authorities, one transgresses only if he obtains the item against its owner's will (see note 6). Now, taking an item from someone without his consent, even with payment, constitutes robbery. If so, the Rishonim ask, why did the Torah find it necessary to specifically forbid "coveting," given that the act which the prohibition proscribes is forbidden in any case under the prohibition against robbery? (*mitzvah* #229). [*Tosafos* do not mean to ask why the prohibition of *Lo Sachmod* is necessary at all, for there are certain items for which one does not transgress the prohibition against robbery even if he takes them without their owner's consent — e.g. real estate and Canaanite slaves (see *mitzvah* #229). The prohibition of *Lo Sachmod*, however, does apply even to these items, as the verse explicitly states. Thus, the commandment is necessary to forbid acquiring even real estate and Canaanite slaves against their owner's will. The verse, however, also explicitly includes in the *Lo Sachmod* prohibition objects to which the prohibition against robbery *does* apply — livestock. The point of *Tosafos'* question is, why

did the Torah find it necessary to forbid the coveting of *these* objects? (*Ma'ayanei HaChochmah, Bava Metzia* ibid.).] They answer that while it is true that the act which constitutes "coveting" is forbidden as robbery, the Torah wished to add a *second* prohibition forbidding this act (*Tosafos, Bava Metzia* 5b ד"ה בלא דמי).

This answer, though, does not explain why *Lo Sachmod* is counted as a separate commandment of the 613. For some authorities maintain that a prohibition against an act that is forbidden in any event by a different prohibition, is not counted as a separate commandment of the 613 (see *R' Y. F. Perla* to *Sefer HaMitzvos L'Rasag,* introduction to *shoresh* §9, who ascribes this view to *R' Saadiah Gaon*). Since *Lo Sachmod* forbids the same act as the prohibition against robbery, why, according to this view, is it counted as a separate commandment of the 613?

To resolve this difficulty, we must say that those who subscribe to this view maintain either: (a) that even one who obtains a coveted item legally, with its owner's consent, violates *Lo Sachmod* (as stated above, note 6, this is the opinion of *Rambam*); or (b) that one violates the prohibition merely by virtue of his *desire* for the coveted object, even if he does not succeed in obtaining it (see note 2 for a list of those who are of this opinion). According to either of these two views, it is possible to transgress *Lo Sachmod*

מפתח למוני המצוות
THE COUNT OF THE MITZVAH

Baal Halachos Gedolos / Lavin 32
בה"ג / לאוין לב

R' Saadiah Gaon / Lavin 90
רס"ג / לאוין צ

R' Eliyahu HaZakein / Amud 45
ר' אליהו הזקן / עמ' 45

Rashbag / Lo Saaseh Os 11
רשב"ג / לא תעשה אות יא

R' Yitzchak El-Bargeloni / Lavin 32
ר"י אלברג'לוני / לאוין לב

Maamar HaSechel / Dibbur Asiri 1
מאמר השכל / דיבור עשירי א

Sefer Yereim / 115
יראים / קטו

Rambam, Sefer HaMitzvos / Lo Saaseh 265
רמב"ם / לא תעשה רסה

Sefer Mitzvos Gadol (Smag) / Lo Saaseh 158
סמ"ג / לא תעשה קנח

Sefer Mitzvos Katan (Smak) / 19
סמ"ק / יט

Zohar HaRakia / Lavin 12
זוהר הרקיע / לאוין יב

without violating the prohibition against robbery. Thus, *Lo Sachmod* is counted as a separate commandment.

II. WHY LO SACHMOD IS NOT COUNTED AS MORE THAN ONE COMMANDMENT

The enumeration of *Lo Sachmod* as a single commandment of the 613 presents a difficulty: The verse of *Lo Sachmod* actually states *two* prohibitions against coveting; one in connection with the house of another, and a second in connection with various other possessions of another [(a) *You shall not covet your fellow's house; (b) You shall not covet your fellow's wife, his manservant, his maidservant, his ox, his donkey, nor anything which belongs to your fellow*]. While it is true that both prohibitions refer to a single act, that of coveting, and they merely enumerate different objects one may not covet, they seemingly should be counted as separate commandments, in accordance with *Rambam's* (*Sefer HaMitzvos, shoresh* §9) rule that multiple prohibitory phrases (e.g. *You shall not, You may not*) used in a verse count as separate prohibitions even when they refer to the same act (*Minchas Chinuch* 38:1 ד"ה ולכאורה צריך עיון וד"ה ולכאורה צריך ביאור).

Some answer that *Lo Sachmod* is not counted as two commandments because there is a specific reason why the verse repeats the prohibitory phrase. As mentioned above (*Iyunim* §1), most authorities maintain that *Lo Sachmod* (in *Shemos* 20:14) and *Lo Sis'aveh* (in *Devarim* 5:18; *mitzvah* #416), although they apply to the same objects, are two separate negative commandments. But the verse of *Lo Sis'aveh*, while it lists most of the same objects that are included in *Lo Sachmod*, does not include another's wife in its list! From where is it known that *Lo Sis'aveh* applies to another's wife as well? This is derived from the fact that the verse of *Lo Sachmod* uses an additional prohibitory phrase which includes another's wife in the list of objects which are forbidden to covet.

This seemingly superfluous phrase teaches that just as those other objects are subject to *Lo Sis'aveh* in addition to *Lo Sachmod*, so, too, another's wife is subject to *Lo Sis'aveh*. Thus, the purpose of repeating the prohibitory phrase is not to add an additional prohibition, but to show that *Lo Sis'aveh* applies to the desire for another's wife as well (see *Maayan HaChochmah, Lo Saaseh* 24:17).

The question remains though, according to *Ramban*. *Ramban* (*Hasagos* to *Sefer HaMitzvos* of *Rambam, shoresh* §9 ד"ה וכן הגזירה) maintains that wherever a verse uses one prohibitory phrase in reference to several objects, each reference is counted as a separate commandment, as if the verse had stated a prohibition with regard to each object individually. Thus, for example, the prohibition against eating the *Korban Pesach* when it is only partially roasted, or when it is cooked — as the verse states: *You shall not eat it partially roasted or cooked in water, only roasted over fire* (*Shemos* 12:9) — is counted as two separate negative commandments, as though the verse were written, You shall not eat it partially roasted and You shall not eat it cooked (see also *Ramban's* list of the negative commandments at the end of *Rambam's Sefer HaMitzvos*, ד"ה וכן אם תתן לבך; see also *Minchas Chinuch* 38:1 ד"ה וגם, who ascribes this view to *Smag* as well). Now, the verse mentions several objects in connection with *Lo Sachmod* [(a) *your fellow's house* (b) *your fellow's wife,* (c) *his manservant,* (d) *his maidservant* (e) *his ox,* (f) *his donkey,* (g) *nor anything which belongs to your fellow*]. According to *Ramban*, then, the prohibition against coveting should be counted as *several* negative commandments, one for each object to which the prohibitory phrase refers!

Some answer that *Ramban's* rule applies only to acts that are inherently two separate prohibitions, but for which the verse uses one prohibitory phrase. In the case of a *korban pesach*, for example, eating a partially roasted *korban* and eating one which is cooked are two different prohibitions. Thus, although the verse uses one prohibitory phrase to prohibit both acts, they are considered two separate negative commandments. If, however, the prohibited act is essentially the same for all the objects specified in the verse, *Ramban* agrees that the separate references do not constitute separate commandments, for the verse intends merely to *elaborate* on the prohibition, to teach which

objects it applies to (see *Chinuch*, end of *mitzvah* §7). Clearly, the forbidden act of coveting is the same regardless of the particular object being coveted. Therefore, the references to the various objects one may not covet are not understood as constituting separate commandments, but merely as a list of items that are included in the single negative commandment of *Lo Sachmod* (*Minchas Chinuch* 38:1 ד"ה וגם הרבה דברים).

Appendix

1. צ"ע מדוע לא מנה הרמב"ן בספר המצוות מצות עשה זו כמו שמנה את הלאו. ואינו קשה כל כך, כי את פירושו על התורה כתב הרמב"ן בזקנותו אחר שכבר כתב את השגותיו על ספר המצוות.

2. וכן שהאריך בזה רבינו נסים בדרשותיו (הדרוש החמישי נוסח ב') וז"ל: "כבר ביארו שאלו השני המאמרים השיגו אותן כל ישראל בבירור בלא חידה [ומשל], וזו באמת מדרגה גדולה בנביאים שתהא נבואתם מבוארת, כאשר העיד על ה' יתברך על אדון כל הנביאים (במדבר, י"ב ח') 'במראה ולא בחידות', ועם היותם שלא היו כל ישראל שלמי החכמה והמידות, השיגו עתה כל ישראל זאת ההשגה לקיום התורה, שאלו לא השיגו הם בנבואה, אלא כאשר יגיד משה להם מה שֶצֻּוָּה מאתו יתברך, לא היתה האמונה במשה שלמה, כי לא יאמת דבריו אלא כפי מה שראינו אותותיו". עכ"ל.

ובהמשך דבריו משיב הר"ן על הטענה, כיצד עלו כל ישראל למדרגת השגה עליונה במעמד הר סיני מבלי שהשלימו בעצמם את המעלות והשלמויות הנצרכות לנבואה, למרות שאמר רבי יוחנן [נדרים ל"ח ע"א]: "אין הקב"ה משרה שכינתו אלא על גיבור ועשיר וחכם ועני". ונראה מדבריו של הר"ן בהמשך שם שחסרון תנאי הנבואה של רבי יונתן הוא טעם הרמב"ם במורה נבוכים הסובר שלא שמעו ישראל את הדיברות ממש, אלא רק קול דברים בעלמא בשתי הדיברות הראשונות, ומשה פירשן להם בפיסוק תיבות. והיינו, דכיוון שלא השלימו עצמם את התנאים הנחוצים לנבואה לא היו יכולים לשמוע את הדברים כהוויתם ממש.

ובעצם השאלה הזו, איך עלו ישראל למדרגה עליונה בלי ההכנות הראויות לנבואה, ובפרט לשמוע את קול ה' פנים בפנים, שהיא דרגת נבואה עליונה שבעליונות, מבואר הדבר בשו"ת הרשב"א (חלק ד' סימן רל"ד): "זה הכתב שלח הרשב"א ז"ל אל החכם ר' שמואל הסלמי ז"ל, המכונה סאסקליעה, אל שאלה ששאלוהו בעניין מעמד הר סיני וכו'. עוד אמרת, שהוגד לך בשמי, מה שמאמין אני במעמד הנכבד, מעמד הר סיני, שהיה כולו נבואי, וישר בעיניך. אלא שהוקשה לך, איך הגיע כל העם, שאינם חכמים כחכמים, למדרגת הנבואה. שכבר נודע שהוא מן הנמנע, שיגיע למדרגת הנבואה, רק מי שהשיג הקדמות הראויות לה". עיי"ש שהאריך מאד הרשב"א לענות על שאלה זו, ופלפל הרבה בדברי הרמב"ם בזה, ודחה את דבריו, ובסוף כתב הרשב"א: "זה אינו בנמנע, שיחכים השי"ת כרגע לכל העם, שעמדו במעמד הנכבד ההוא. והוא שהיה בו השפע הגדול במראות אלקים. וכאשר אמר בבצלאל: 'ואמלא אותו רוח אלקים, בחכמה ובתבונה ובדעת, ובכל מלאכה' [שמות ל"א, ג']. והוא קטן בשנים מאד וכו'". וכן כתב בשו"ת הרדב"ז ח"ב בסימן תתי"ז, עיי"ש.

3. וכדרשת רבי עזריה ורבי יהודה ב"ר סימן [במדרש חזית, שהוא שה"ש רבה הנ"ל] על הפסוק (דברים ל"ג, ד') "תורה צוה לנו משה", דרש גם רבי שמלאי בגמרא מסכת מכות [כ"ג ב'], אלא ששם הסיום הוא ' 'אנכי' ו'לא יהיה לך' מפי הגבורה שמענום". וזה לשון הגמרא שם: "דרש רבי שמלאי, שש מאות ושלש עשרה מצות נאמרו לו למשה שלש מאות וששים וחמש לאוין כמניין ימות החמה ומאתים וארבעים ושמונה עשה כנגד איבריו של אדם אמר רב המנונא מאי קרא? "תורה צוה לנו משה מורשה" תורה בגימטריא שית מאה וחד סרי, הוי 'אנכי' ו'לא יהיה לך' מפי הגבורה שמענום". ע"כ. ועיין עוד במדרש תנחומא וילך [ב]: "ולא נקראת תורה עד שנתנה בסיני ועל מניין המצות נקראת תורה כי המצות של תורה הן תרי"ג, תורה עולה בגימטריא תרי"א והשניים שנפחתו מן תרי"ג אלו שנים שניתנו מפי הגבורה. וזהו שאמר הכתוב (תהילים ס"ב, י"ב) 'אחת דיבר אלקים שתים זו שמעתי', וזהו 'תורה צוה לנו משה' כמניין "תורה" צוה לנו משה, והשניים צוה הקב"ה, כמו שפירשתי בפרשת וישמע יתרו. וב"פרקי דרבי אליעזר" (פרק מ"א) "כל המצות שבתורה תרי"ג מצות ושתים שדיבר הקב"ה. לפיכך נקראת תורה ומניין תורה תרי"א ושתים דיבר הקב"ה, שנאמר: 'אחת דיבר אלקים שתים זו שמעתי'", הרי תרי"ג.

4. יש להקשות: מה התועלת באמירת כל הדיברות בדיבור אחד אם אינן מובנות לשומעיהן וצריך לחזור ולפרטן?

ועיין להגר"י הוטנר בספר "פחד יצחק", (שבועות מאמר ל"ב), שכתב יסוד, שכל התרי"ג מצות נערכים כאברים של קומה אחת. ובאופן, שכשיחסר קיום איזו מצוה תוכל חברתה להשלימה, כמו בגוף, שאבר אחד מקבל על עצמו תפקידו של חבר. ולכן ישנה מציאות של "בא דוד והעמידם על אחת עשרה, בא ישעיה והעמידם על שש וכו' עד שבא חבקוק והעמידם על אחת" [מכות כ"ד ע"א]. וכתב, ששורש דבר זה היא אמירת כל עשרת הדיברות ע"י הקב"ה בדיבור אחד, ואח"כ חזר ופירש כל דיבור ודיבור, וכדברים המכילתא. וכשם שמצאנו את שורש הדברים בנתינת התורה במעמד הר סיני, כך הוא הדין בכלליות התרי"ג מצות

ועיין לשון הריטב"א (יבמות מ"ט ב'): "איספקלריא המאירה ושאינה מאירה. סודם עמוק ונשגב וידועים לבעלי האמת ששניהם היו במעמד הר סיני כדכתיב (דברים ד', ל"ו) 'מן השמים השמיעך את קולו לְיַסְּרֶךָ' ועל הארץ הראך את אשו הגדולה', וסודם ליודעים חן". משמע שהיו שתי דרגות בשמיעה במעמד הר סיני, דרגא דאיספקלריא מאירה ודרגא דאיספקלריא שאינה מאירה. ויתכן שזהו החילוק לדעת הריטב"א בין השמיעה של שתי הדיברות הראשונות שמפי הגבורה שמענום, לבין הדיברות האחרונות. ונמצא, להריטב"א שבשתי הדיברות הראשונות התעלו ישראל לדרגת משה רבינו שנתנבא באיספקלריא מאירה. ועיין ב"ערבי נחל" פרשת ואתחנן שהאריך בעניין זה שישראל התעלו במעמד הר סיני למדרגת משה רבינו עצמו, ונתנבאו באיספקלריא המאירה, עיי"ש שפירש את הפסוקים לפי זה.

והאברבנאל [דברים פרק ל"ד עמ' שנ"ט] האריך ליישב קושיית המפרשים איך אמר הכתוב שרק משה ידע את ה' פנים בפנים, והרי בתורה כתוב בפירוש שישראל שיזכו למדרגה זו [פנים בפנים דיבר ה' עימכם, דברים ה', ד'], ע"ש שהביא את דברי הרמב"ן שכלל ישראל שמעו קולו מתוך האש בלבד ולא ראו פנים. אמנם הוא עצמו כתב שם, שהיה זה חסד עליון ממדרגתם לשם נצחיות התורה כדי שתתחקק בלבם בלי שום ערעור ופקפוק, עיי"ש דבריו באורך. וכדבריו כתב גם הר"י אלבו בספר העיקרים מאמר שלישי סוף פ"ח, עיי"ש.

שניתנו באחידות כתרי"ג אברים של קומה אחת. עכת"ד. ויש
להוסיף, דלפי הרס"ג שכל התרי"ג מצוות כלולים בעשרת
הדיברות, וכמבואר להלן (עיין הערה 26), הרי הדברים כפשוטן
ממש, שכל התרי"ג מצוות ניתנו בדיבור אחד ממש, להורות שכולן
קומה אחת שלימה ומאוחדת, כדברי ה"פחד יצחק" הנ"ל.

ועיין בספר "עבודת הקודש" (ח"ד פרק ל"ג), שביאר הטעם למה
אמרו הדיברות בדיבור אחד ע"פ סוד: "הנה בָּאֲמָרָם שֶׁאֲמָרָם
כולם בדיבור אחד יורו שאין ביניהם שום הבדל והכלל הוא הפרט
והפרט הוא הכלל, ואין בכלל אלא מה שבפרט, ואין בפרט אלא מה
שבכלל, כולם בהשוואה אחת ובהשגה שוה, אין ביניהם שום
הבדל, ולזה הְשָׁוָה כולם בדיבור אחד, ויורה לנו זה נפלאות בייחוד,
כי עשרת הדיברות כנגד עשרה מאמרות, סוד עשר ספירות, סוד
האצילות שהוא בדיבור אחד ובייחוד אחד", עיי"ש באורך.

5. כך למד הרא"ם [ונדפס בתמצית בגליון רש"י שמות כ', א'],
והסכים איתו רבי דוד פארדו במשכיל לדוד, שכתב "אין לנו אלא
דברי הרא"ם ז"ל", וכן פירש תלמיד רבי דוד פארדו בפירושו "באר
בשדה", ורבי מרדכי יפה בעל הלבושים בפירושו "לבוש אורה".
וכבר קדמם החזקוני על אתר, עיי"ש.

וכן הוא גם משמעות ה"תיקוני זוהר", (תיקון כ"ב) "ואיהו דיבור
חד דכליל עשר אמירן. ורזא דמלה (תהילים ס"ב, י"ב) 'אחת דיבר
אלקים שתים זו שמעתי', לאחזאה בה דעשר דברן בדיבור אחד
אתאמרו. שתים זו, אלין "אנכי" ו"לא יהיה לך" [תרגום: "והוא
דיבור אחד הכולל את עשרת הדיברות. וסוד הדבר [תהילים ס"ב,
י"ב] 'אחת דיבר אלקים שתים זו שמעתי', להראות בו שעשר
הדיברות נאמרו בדיבור אחד. 'שתים זו' – אלה הם 'אנכי' ו'לא
יהיה לך' "], עיי"ש בביאור הגר"א שפירש שם ע"ד דברי החזקוני
והרא"ם הנ"ל. ולהדיא כתב הגר"א שכן היא שיטת רש"י. אלא שיש
חידוש בדברי הגר"א, והוא ששתי הדיברות 'אנכי' ו'לא יהיה לך'
נאמרו בהשמעה השנייה בדיבור אחד, מה שלא נזכר בדברי
הרא"ם ודעימיה. ועיין גם בשפתי חכמים (שמות כ', א') בביאור
המכילתא, שלמד כדברי הגר"א, שכן כתב על שאלת המכילתא אם
כן מה ת"ל אנכי ולא יהיה לך: "כלומר, הואיל וכולן בדיבור אחד
נאמרו, למה כתיב במקום אחר אחת דיבר אלקים שתים זו שמענו
[שמעתי], דמשמע, דווקא אנכי ולא יהיה לך בדיבור אחד נאמרו,
ומתרץ שחזר ופירש וכו'". הרי להדיא שהבין כהגר"א את שאלת
המכילתא.

והנה, עיין בדברי הרא"ם שעיקר סמיכתו ותמיכתו בפירוש דברי
המכילתא הוא על שינוי הלשון בין שתי הדיברות הראשונות ובין
שאר הדיברות. שהשתים הראשונות, שהן "אנכי" ו"לא יהיה לך",
מדברות בלשון נוכח והאחרות בלשון נסתר, שמשום כן הוקשה
(לדעתו) לבעל המכילתא אם הכל נאמר בדיבור אחד מה נשתנו
אלו מאלו, והרי הדיבור אינו מתחלק? ויישב שחזר ודיבר כל דיבור
בפ"ע. עיי"ש. ולכאורה קשה להוציא את המכילתא מפשוטה,
שהרי לא הזכירה דבר וחצי דבר מכל שינוי הלשון הזה. [עיין ב"גור
אריה" שהשיג כן, ועיי"ש שהשיג גם על סברת הרא"ם שדיבור
אחד אי אפשר לחלקו ללשון נוכח וללשון נסתר.]

ובעניין שכתב הרא"ם: "כי לא יתכן שה' ידבר דבריו קצתן בלשון

מדבר [מדבר, היינו גוף ראשון] וקצתן בלשון נסתר", הנה
האברבנאל בשמות (כ', א') הביא רשימה של פסוקים המכחישים
זאת, וכגון: "זה לך האות כי אנכי שלחתיך [מדבר] תעבדון את
האלקים על ההר הזה [נסתר]" (שמות ג, יב), וכן: "עד אנה מאנתם
לשמור מצוותי ותורותי [מדבר] ראו כי ה' נתן לכם השבת [נסתר]"
(שמות ט"ז, כ"ח), ועוד הרבה, ועיין עוד להלן (הערה 10) שהביאנו
דברי הראב"ע שהוכיח כן ממש"כ (שמות כ"ג, י"ח): "לא ילין חלב
חגי", ואחריו אמר (שם פסוק י"ט): "בית ה' אלקיך". וע"ע
ב"עבודת הקודש" (ח"ד פל"ד) שהאריך להראות דוגמאות רבות
נוספות על זה, וכתב שם, שעניין זה שפותח בלשון מדבר וגומר
בלשון נסתר יש בו סוד בעניין הייחוד הגמור, עיי"ש.

6. זוהי שיטת הרמב"ם ב"מורה נבוכים" (ח"ב פל"ג). אולם עיין
היטב בלשון הרמב"ם (פ"ח מהלכות יסודי התורה ה"ג) שכתב:
"אלא בעינינו ראינוה ובאזנינו שמענוה כמו ששמע הוא". וכן היא
לשונו ממש באיגרת תימן שכתב שישראל שמעו בסיני "כמו
ששמע הוא". ומשמע שישראל שמעו את הדיברות כמו ששמע
משה בלא הבדל, והיינו בפיסוק תיבות. ויש לעיין אם חזר בו
הרמב"ם ממש"כ ב"מורה נבוכים", או האם תיבת "כמו" אינה
מתפרשת על אופן השמיעה אלא על עצם השמיעה. ועיין בשו"ת
מהר"ם אלשקר (סימן קי"ז) שעמד על הלשון "כמו ששמע הוא",
הכתובה באיגרת תימן [ולא הזכיר שכן היא הלשון בספר "משנה
תורה"], וכתב להשוות לשון זו עם מה שכתב הרמב"ם ב"מורה
נבוכים". וכך כתב: "ועתה יתיישב בטוב מאמרם ז"ל שאמרו 'אנכי'
ו'לא יהיה לך' מפי הגבורה שמעום". הודיענו שלא שמעו ישראל
מפי הגבורה אלא הקול המורה על שתי הדיברות האלו, אבל כשאר
הדיברות לא שמען כי אם משה ע"ה לבדו. וזה הדרך האחרון הוא
אצל רבינו הרב ז"ל העיקר שכתב שנתייחדו בו הכתובים ודברי
חכמים. וכבר נתבארה כוונתו ז"ל בזה הפרק למבינים, ונתבאר
שאע"פ שלא שמעו הקול כל כך מפורש ולא כל כך צח כמו משה
רבנו ע"ה הנה שמעו מפי הגבורה הקול כשהיה מדבר עמו. משל
למה הדבר דומה, למלך שהיה מדבר עם שני אנשים והיה האחד
מהם קרוב למלך יותר מחברו, או שהיה לאחד מהם חוש השמע
יותר חזק משל חברו, האחר הקרוב או אותו שהחוש שלו יותר חזק
שמע חתיכת [חיתוך] הדברים יותר מהאחר, אבל מ"מ שניהם ראו
ושמעו את הקול יוצא מפי המלך. וכן נאמר בכאן, שמשה וישראל
שמעו עיקר הקול מפי הגבורה, אלא שמרע"ה השיג ממנו יותר
מהם, ומצד הקול ששמעו כשהיה מדבר למשה האמינו בו אמונה
שלמה בלי ראיה ומופת, כמו שכתב רבינו ז"ל באריכות באותו
לשון שכתבנו למעלה בשמו בתחילת פ"ב, שכתב באגרת תימן."

7. ביאור הדברים, שהרמב"ם סובר כנראה שלא יתכן שעלו
ישראל למדרגה גבוהה כמו משה רבינו עליו השלום בלי ההכנות
המצטרכות אל הנבואה, ורק בשתי הדיברות הראשונות שהן
הגיוניות, וניתנות להוכחה בשכל האנושי, היו ישראל מסוגלים
לשמוע את דבר ה' ממש [היינו, שהן "מושכלות" בשכל, ואינן
בחינת מפורסמות]. ועיין היטב בדברי הרשב"א בתשובה (ח"ד
סימן רל"ד) שהקשה שהדעת נוטה ההיפך. ש"לא תרצח" ו"לא

תנאף" וכו' שהן "המפורסמות" לא יצטרכו כל הקדמות ויוכלו להשיג ישראל כמו משה. ועיין עוד להלן בדברינו]. וכיוון שהשגתם השכלית בדיברות אלו לא היתה שלימה, הרי שבצירוף הנבואה ששמעו את קול ה', נכון יהיה לומר שלא תתייחס מסירתם למשה רבינו, אף שהוא אשר מסר להם בפועל את הדיברות האלו בפיסוק תיבות, אלא כמו אמרו חז"ל (מכות כ"ד, א') ש"אנכי ולא יהיה לך מפי הגבורה שמענום". ועוד יתברר לפנינו שהרמב"ם פירש את דברי חז"ל: "מפי הגבורה", שהכוונה ל:"גבורת המופת", ועיין בר"ן בדרשותיו דרוש חמישי נוסח שני, שהשיג על הרמב"ם קשות, ועיין גם בשו"ת הרשב"א הנ"ל שהקשה עוד קושיות רבות על שיטת הרמב"ם בזה. ועיין גם ב"ספר העיקרים" מאמר שלישי פי"ח, ועוד עיין בספר "עבודת הקודש" ח"ד פל"ג, ובספר "עקידת יצחק" שער מ"ה ושער פ"ט, שדחו את דברי הרמב"ם, כל אחד וסגנונו.

8. ועדיין קשה על שיטת הרמב"ם [ועל ריב"ל במדרש חזית] מהפסוקים המורים להדיא שהקב"ה אמר את כל עשרת הדיברות אל כל הקהל, וכמו שהבאנו לעיל מפרשת יתרו ופרשת ואתחנן ופרשת עקב. וצריכים אנו לומר או שהרמב"ם ידחק ויאמר, שפסוקים אלו מדברים על שתי הדיברות הראשונות בלבד, או שיפרש כפשוטן לדברים דמיירי בכל עשרת הדיברות, אלא שהכתוב אומר שהקב"ה דיבר את כל הדברים כנגד הקהל – אך ישראל לא שמעו אלא את השתים הראשונות בלבד, וגם אותן שמעו ללא הבנה, ואילו את שאר הדיברות לא שמעו כלל רק משה שמעם, או שיפרש שהקב"ה "אמר" את כל הדברים באופן שהיה מגביר את קולו של משה לדבר את הדיברות לכל ישראל, וכדאיתא במכילתא שהובאה לעיל, שהיה הקב"ה מסייעו לתת בו כח להיות קולו מגביר ונשמע. ולפ"ז מש"כ: "אל כל קהלכם" (דברים ה', י"ט), הכוונה היא שישמיע משה את הדברים לכל הקהל.

ויש להעיר עוד, דמה שהביא הרמב"ם סיוע לדבריו ממדרש חז"ל על הפסוק (תהילים ס"ב, י"ב): "אחת דיבר אלקים שתים זו שמעתי", דמתפרש שאמר הקב"ה את שתי הדיברות הראשונות בלבד בקול אחד ואנו שמענום בלא הבנה, ו"שתים זו שמעתי", ששמענו אותן בהבנה כשתי דיברות חלוקות ע"י משה. אמנם מה שציין הרמב"ם על מדרש חזית, הוא "שיר השירים", לא נמצא כן שם במדרש, ואולי גירסא אחרת היתה לו לרמב"ם במדרש. ועיין במדרש תנחומא (דברים פרשת ואלך אות ב'), וכן ב"פרקי דרבי אליעזר" (פרק מ"א) שאכן ובא שם הפסוק הנזכר בתהילים ביחס למתן תורה, אמנם שם מבואר ש"שתים זו שמעתי" פירושו ששמענו [בהבנה] את שתי הדיברות הראשונות מפי הקב"ה בעצמו, ולא מפי משה כדברי הרמב"ם (ומשמע כשיטת הרמב"ן). יתר על כן, בבמדבר רבה (פרשה י"א ז') מבואר להדיא ש"אחת דיבר אלקים" הכוונה היא שהקב"ה אמר את כל עשרת הדיברות בדיבור אחד, ודלא כמש"כ הרמב"ם שרק את שתי הדיברות הראשונות אמר הקב"ה בקול אחד. וכן מוכח להדיא מהמכילתא שהביא רש"י (שמות כ', א'), שתחילה אמר הקב"ה את כל הדיברות בדיבור אחד (ולא רק את השתים הראשונות כדכתב הרמב"ם).

אכן הלשון: "'אנכי' ו'לא יהיה לך' בדיבור אחד נאמרו" איתא בילקוט (ירמיה רמז רס"ו), וכן ישנה לשון דומה ב"תיקוני זוהר",

(תיקון ל"ב דף ע"ו ע"א) "אנכי ולא יהיה לך דאתאמרו בדיבורא חדא". וכן ב"זוהר חדש" (יתרו דף ס"ח ע"ב) "אנכי ולא יהיה לך בדיבורא חדא איתאמרו", ואולי יש במקורות אלה סמך לשיטת הרמב"ם. ועיין ברש"י (מכות כ"ד ע"ד ד"ה מפי הגבורה) שכתב: "דכתיב (תהילים ס"ב, י"ב) 'אחת דיבר אלקים שתים זו שמעתי', במכילתא". וצ"ע שלא נמצא במכילתא פסוק זה על שתי הדיברות הראשונות. ויתכן שרש"י גרס כן במכילתא דפרשת החודש שהביא רש"י (שמות כ', א') וכמו שפירש הגר"א הנ"ל את המכילתא, עיי"ש בדבריו.

ואין להקשות על הרמב"ם ממה שאמרו חז"ל (ראש השנה כ"ז ע"א): 'זכור ושמור' בדיבור אחד נאמרו", שלכאורה קשה להרמב"ם 'זכור ושמור' נאמרו ע"י משה, שהרי הם אינם מהדיברות הראשונות ששמענו מפי הגבורה, ומה שייך "בדיבור אחד" כשנאמרו על ידי משה (כן הקשה גם האלשיך הק' בספרו "תורת משה" פרשת ואתחנן פרק ה'). וזה אינו קשה כלל, שהרי הרמב"ם ודאי מודה שאת כל הדברים אמר הקב"ה בכבודו ובעצמו, ורק מבחינת השומעים כתב הרמב"ם שישראל שמעו את שתי הדיברות הראשונות בלבד, אולם משה רבינו שמע פשיטא ששמע מפי הגבורה עצמה את כל הדיברות, ובכלל זה את "זכור ושמור" שנאמרו בדיבור אחד. ועיין בספר "מעשי ה'" לרבי אליעזר אשכנזי שהרבה להקשות על מש"כ הרמב"ם שקול דברים ששמעו ישראל הוא קול הברה בלתי מובן, מהרבה מקראות שמוכח שקול דברים הוא דבר המובן, וכמו שאמר הכתוב (דברים ה', כ"ה) "וישמע ה' את קול דבריכם", ועוד הרבה. וכן הקשה מפסוק מפורש שישראל שמעו "דברים" ולא רק "קול", וכמו שכתוב (דברים ד', ל"ו) "מן השמים השמיעך קולו וגו' ודבריו שמעת וגו'", הרי ששמענו דברים ולא רק קול, עיי"ש במש"כ שם עוד להשיג על דברי הרמב"ם. וגם בספר "עבודת הקודש" (ח"ד פל"ג) ובפירוש אברבנאל (שמות כ', א') הרבו להקשות על הרמב"ם.

9. יל"ע, לשם מה נאמרו שמונה הדיברות האחרונות ע"י הקב"ה אם לא ניתן היה להבינם, דבשלמא לשיטת הרמב"ם ששתי הדיברות הראשונות נאמרו בלא הבנה, ופירשן משה, סוף סוף היתה תועלת ששמעו ישראל את קול ה' בעצמם וידעו כי ה' מדבר עליהם. אך להרמב"ן הרי כבר הושגה תועלת זו באמירת שתי הדיברות הראשונות שנשמעו להדיא מפי הגבורה, ומה צורך היה עוד בהשמעת הדיברות האחרונות בלא הבנה [ובשלמא מש"כ במכילתא שמתחילה נאמרו כל עשרת הדיברות בדיבור אחד, כבר נתבאר עניין זה בדברי המפרשים שהוא להורות על כל הדיברות, שרשי כל התורה כולה, שהן קומה אחת שלימה, אבל שמונה הדיברות שנאמרו לישראל בפעם השנייה כל דיברה בנפרד, ובאופן ששמעו אותן ישראל בלא הבנה, מה תכליתן?]. וכבר הקשה כן מהר"י גבאי בספר "עבודת הקודש" (חלק סתרי תורה פל"ג) על שיטת הרמב"ן וז"ל שם: "והקול ההוא ששמעו בשאר הדיברות בלא הבדל למה? [=לשם מה?] הלא מותר הוא ודבר בלתי צריך". ונראה לומר, דס"ל להרמב"ן שהיתה חשיבות סגולית ששמעו ישראל את כל הדיברות ע"י הקב"ה ממש אף שלא בהבינו, כדי שיושרשו העיקרים האלו של כל התורה כולה בנשמתם של

ישראל, וכעין שכתב ה"משך חכמה" (דברים ל"ג, ד'), שחקוקה
בצורת נפש הישראלי [=היהודי] כל ההתפעלות אשר נרגש ונפעל
הישראלי בעמדו על הר סיני. וצריך לומר, שההשמעה הראשונה
של הדיברות שהוזכרה במכילתא יתרו, שהייתה בדיבור אחד
ממש, לא השיגה אף את התכלית הזו.

10. שיטת הראב"ע והרלב"ג מבוארת בפירושיהם בפרשת יתרו.
וזה שנאמרו שתי הדיברות הראשונות בלשון מדבר, ואילו שמונה
האחרונות בלשון נסתר, אין בכך כלום, שכן דרך התורה בהרבה
מקומות להתחיל בלשון מדבר ולסיים בלשון נסתר. וכבר העיר כן
הראב"ע, וז"ל: "דע כי עשרת הדברים כאשר הם כתובים בפרשה
הזאת ה' אמרם כולם. כי כתב: 'וידבר אלקים את כל הדברים
האלה לאמר'. ותחילתם 'אנכי' וסופם 'וכל אשר לרעך'. וגם משה
אמר כאשר הזכיר עשרת הדברים בשנית [דברים ה', י"ט]: 'את
הדברים האלה דיבר ה' אל כל קהלכם' ואין הפסק ביניהם. ועוד,
כאשר נכתבו כולם באצבע אלקים, כן אמרם ה' כולם. והעדות
שהביאו, שהכתוב בדיבור השלישי והרביעי והחמישי אינו על דרך
המדבר, יש להשיב, אחרי שֶׁקִּבַּלְתָּ זה ה' להיות לך לאלקים על כן
אמר [שמות כ', ז']: 'לא תשא את שם ה' אלקיך לשוא', גם (שמות
כ', י"א): 'כי ששת ימים עשה ה''. ועוד כי משפט אנשי לשון הקודש
לדבר ככה. כתב (שמות כ"ג, י"ח): 'לא ילין חלב חגי' [=חג שלי-
מדבר], ואחריו כתוב (שמות כ"ג, י"ט) 'תביא בית ה' אלקיך'
[=לבית שלו- נסתר]. ורבים כאלה". עכ"ל הראב"ע. ועיי"ש
ב"עבודת הקודש" ובפירוש אברבנאל ובספר "עקידת יצחק" (שער
פ"ט), שהביאו דוגמאות רבות מפסוקי התורה הפותחים בלשון
מדבר ומסיימים בלשון נסתר.

11. דברי הרמב"ן קצת צ"ע, שהרי במדרש שיר השירים מבואר
שהיא מחלוקת רבנן ורי"ל, ואם כדבריו הרי אין מחלוקת, דגם
רי"ל, שהוא בשיטת רבי שמלאי, מודה שהקב"ה אמר את כל
הדברים לכל ישראל. וצ"ל שהרמב"ן למד שרבנן חולקים על רי"ל
וסוברים שאין חילוק כלל בין שתי הדיברות הראשונות
והאחרונות, וכמ"ש מהר"ם גבאי בעבודת הקודש ודעימיה,
שיובאו דבריהם להלן. והרמב"ן תפס כעיקר את שיטת רי"ל ורבי
שמלאי מפני חילוק הלשון שבין שתי הדיברות הראשונות
שנאמרו בלשון מדבר, ובין הדיברות האחרונות, שנאמרו בלשון
נסתר, וכמו שפתח הרמב"ן את דבריו.

12. מבואר כאן בדעת הרמב"ן היא דעיקר סמיכת חז"ל לומר
שרק "'אנכי' ו'לא יהיה לך' מפי הגבורה שמענום", היא בגלל
השינוי בין הלשונות של הדיברות, שהשתיים הראשונות נאמרו
בלשון מדבר, ואילו השאר נאמרו בלשון נסתר, ומכאן שיטתו
של הרמב"ן להלן שמשה פירש לישראל את שאר הדיברות. ועיין
בספר "עקידת יצחק" (שער פ"ט), שהקשה קושיה חזקה על
הרמב"ן.

13. וכן כתב החזקוני במפורש שרש"י הוא כדברי הרמב"ן. וגם
הגר"א בביאורו על התיקונים תכ"ב (דף ע"א ע"ב) כתב שרש"י

למד כך את המכילתא. [נראה שכוונת הגר"א לרש"י במסכת מכות
(כ"ד ע"א) בשם המכילתא, והביא שם את הפסוק (תהלים ס"ב,
י"ב): "אחת דיבר אלקים שתים זו שמעתי", והשתיים ששמענו הן
שתי הדיברות הראשונות אנכי ולא יהיה לך, שמפי הגבורה
שמענום, דנתכוון רש"י לומר ששתים אלו שמענו בהבנה כי
נאמרו בחיתוך הקול]. ועיין בדברי האריז"ל ב"ספר הליקוטים"
(תהלים ס"ב) וז"ל: "אחת דיבר אלקים שתים זו שמענו וכו'" –
פירוש, הקב"ה דיבר כל עשרת הדיברות בדיבור אחד, משא"כ כח
בבשר ודם. וזהו "וידבר אלקים את כל הדברים האלה
לאמר"(שמות כ', א'), כלומר כאחד, ובדיבור אחד. אבל ישראל לא
שמעו באזניהם, כי אם שתי דיברות לבד, שהם אנכי ולא יהיה לך,
וזהו: 'שתים זו שמעתי וכו'. וזה מה שאמרו רז"ל: "'אנכי' ו'לא
יהיה לך' מפי הגבורה שמענום". וזהו "ישקני מנשיקות פיהו"
(שה"ש א', ב'), מיעוט רבים שנים, והם הב' דיברות. ולפי שלא יכלו
לסבול, אמרו למשה רצוננו לראות מלכנו ולשמוע מפיו, ואחר
שראו שאין בהם כח כמשה רע"ה, אמרו (שמות כ', ט"ז) דַּבֶּר אתה
עימנו ונשמעה ואל ידבר עימנו אלקים וכו'". הרי שסובר שישראל
שמעו שתי דיברות בלבד, ומשמע מדבריו שדיברות אלו לא היה
צורך שיבארן, ודלא כהרמב"ם. והנה, מלשון האריז"ל משמע עוד,
לא היו שתי הַשָּׁמַעו ת של עשרת הדיברות, אלא הקב"ה אמר את
עשרת הדיברות בדיבור אחד, ובהשמעה זו גופא הבינו ישראל את
שתי הדיברות הראשונות, ואת האחרונות שמעו מפי משה, ואולי
כן היא גם שיטת הרמב"ן. וזה דלא כהחזקוני, הרא"ם והגר"א
שכתבו שהיו שתי השמעות.

והאור החיים הק' (שמות כ', א') כתב ששתי הדיברות הראשונות
הן שורש לכל מצוות עשה ומצוות לא תעשה. וז"ל שם: "וראיתי
לתת טוב טעם בהשמעת ה' לישראל שתי דיברות, 'אנכי' ו'לא
יהיה לך', כי הם שני שרשים לשתי כללות המצוות [=לשתי מצוות
כלליות]: מצוות עשה, ומצוות לא תעשה. 'אנכי' הוא עיקר ושורש כל
מצוות עשה, 'לא יהיה לך וגו' הוא עיקר ושורש כל מצות לא תעשה.
לזה נטע ה' בהם מפי אל עליון שרשי שני עיקרי המצוות, שבזה לא
תמוש תורה מזרעינו לעולם ועד". עכ"ל. אלא שיש להעיר, שאף
ששיטת האור החיים הק' קרובה לשיטת הרמב"ן, היא שונה ממנה.
לדעתו, השיגו ישראל שתי דיברות הראשונות מהקב"ה עצמו
[כהרמב"ן], אולם את שאר הדיברות שמעו ממלאכים שנוצרו
מהדיבורים של הקב"ה, ולא רק מפי משה, עיי"ש (ועיין עוד בדברי
האור החיים הק' דברים ד', י"ב, ושם בדבריו על פסוק י"ג).

14. עיין בחידושי הריטב"א למסכת יבמות (מ"ט ע"ב) שהבאנו
לעיל (סוף הערה 2). ומשמע מדברי הריטב"א שהיו שתי דרגות
בשמיעה במעמד הר סיני, דרגא דאיספקלריא מאירה ודרגא
דאיספקלריא שאינה מאירה. ויתכן שזהו החילוק לדעת הריטב"א
בין השמיעה של שתי הדיברות הראשונות שמפי הגבורה שמענום,
לבין שאר הדיברות, וכדברי בעל "עקידת יצחק". ועיין גם בפירוש
"כלי יקר" (שמות כ', ב') שכתב כעין דברי ה"עקידת יצחק" וז"ל:
"ולדעת האומרים שכל הדיברות שמעו מפי הגבורה הנה הב'
דיברות ראשונות דיבר איתם ה' פנים אל פנים בנוכח כדי שיכירו
מי הוא מלכם, ואחר זה הם חייבים לשמוע בקולו אף אם אינם רואין

השי"ת בעצמו לישראל פנים בפנים מבלי אמצעות משה אין כח
ביד שום נביא לומר דבר כנגדם ולא להחלישם בשום עניין, ואפי'
בהוראת שעה, וזהו אמרו מפי 'הגבורה' שמענום ולא אמר מפי
הקב"ה שמענום [א']: אבל במדרש שיר השירים כתוב מפי
הקב"ה שמענום, כאלו באר, שהנאמר על פי נביא יש בו כח לבטלו
אם בהוראת שעה ואם לפי מה שיהיה העניין נותן, כירמיה שביטל
מנין החדשים מניסן. אבל הנאמר לאדם ע"פ ה' בלי אמצעות נביא,
אין כח ביד נביא לבטלו ואפי' בהוראת שעה. וזהו שאמרו [ע'
סנהדרין צ' ע"א], הנביא האומר לעבוד ע"א אפי' לשעה אין
שומעין לו. אבל אם יאמר שנחלל שבת או שנעבור על אחת מן
המצוות בהוראת שעה, או בעניין שלא יהרוס שרשי הדת, ראוי
שנשמע לו, משום שנאמר אליו תשמעון (דברים י"ח, ט"ו). ואם
יאמר ה', צוונו שתתפללו לכוכב פלוני או למלאך פלוני להיות
אמצעי בינו וביניכם, לא נאבה לו ולא נשמע אליו, לפי שזה כנגד
אנכי ולא יהיה לך ששמענום מפי הגבורה, ואי אפשר לשום נביא
לשמוע אל נביא אחר לבטל מה ששמע הוא מפי ה', כמו שבארנו
בתחילת זה הפרק". [יש לחקור בשיטת בעל העיקרים: האם ס"ל
כשיטת הרמב"ן שרק את שתי הדיברות הראשונות שמעו בהבנה,
או דס"ל כשיטת המפרשים המובאים להלן שישראל שמעו את כל
עשרת הדיברות בהבנה. ומדכתב: "כי אנכי ולא יהיה לך שמעום
מפי ה' מבלי משה, ושאר הדיברות היו שומעים את הקול אומר
אותם למשה ומשה חוזר ומבאר אותם להם", משמע שסובר
העיקרים כשיטת הרמב"ן, שאת שתי הדיברות הראשונות שמעו
מה' עם הבנה, ואת שאר הדיברות שמעו רק קול ה' ולא דברים
חתוכים, והוצרך משה לבאר להם. וכן הוא פשוט בדעתו, שאם היו
שומעים את כל הדיברות בהבנה אזי לא היה יכול נביא לבטל גם
את שאר הדיברות אפילו בהוראת שעה. ומטעם זה מסתבר שגם
שהר"ן חולק על המפרשים דלהלן הסוברים שאת כל הדיברות
שמעו ישראל בהבנה. אלא שיש להסתפק בשיטתו של הר"ן, שאף
אמנם שחולק הוא על הרמב"ם ב"מורה נבוכים" בעניין שתי
הדיברות הראשונות, וכותב במפורש ששמעו ישראל אותם
בבהירות והבנה כמו משה רבינו, עדיין לא פירש לנו הר"ן כיצד
נשמעו שמונה הדיברות האחרות, האם לא שמעו כלל את קול ה',
וכשיטת הרמב"ם בעניין זה, או ששמעו את קול ה' בלא הבנה,
והוצרך משה לבאר להם כשיטת הרמב"ן. ואם לפי הצד הראשון,
יצא ששיטת הר"ן היא שיטה נוספת על השיטות שהבאנו בפנים].
ויתכן עוד שיש ליישב, [ע"פ את שיטת הרמב"ן, שלשתי הדיברות
הראשונות הייתה להם עדות שמיעה ממש בהבנה], ע"פ דבריו
הנפלאים של המבי"ט בספר "בית אלקים" (שער היסודות באמצע
פרק שנים עשר בד"ה ונראה וכו') שהאותיות של כל עשרת
הדיברות שנאמרו ע"י הקב"ה נחקקו כולם על הלוחות, והניסיות
של חקיקת האותיות הספיריים [=שבאבן הספיר] היא עדות
עצומה על אמיתות דבריו של משה רבינו ע"ה. ונמצא, שהייתה
להם עדות שמיעה שהייתה בה הבנה על שתי הדיברות הראשונות
[לדעת הרמב"ן] ועדות קריאה מן הלוחות על שאר הדיברות.
[אומנם לרמב"ם לא יעלו דבריו ארוכה, כי סוף סוף לא הייתה להם
עדות שמיעה עם הבנה על דברי ה', ואפילו לא על שתי הדיברות
הראשונות]. וז"ל המבי"ט: "ונראה שהיו כל האותיות של עשרת

תמונה זולתי קול, אף על פי שגם בראשונות לא ראו שום תמונה,
מ"מ הדיבור בנוכח מורה על הדיבור אל פנים כמ"ש (דברים
ה, ד): 'פנים בפנים דיבר ה' עימכם וגו', אבל שאר הדיברות דיבר
בלשון נסתר להודיע כי הוא אל מסתתר ואעפ"כ חייבים לשמוע
בקולו אחר קבלת עול מלכותו פנים בפנים". עכ"ל.

15. וכעין זה כתב הר"ן בדרשותיו דרוש חמישי [נוסח ב'] וז"ל:
"וכן מצינו במעמד הר סיני שזכו כל ישראל להשגה עצומה, עד
שבשתי הדיברות הראשונות לא הוצרכו שיגיד משה אליהם כי הם
השיגום כמו שהשיגם משה, שכן אמר במכות (כ"ג ע"ב): 'דרש רבי
שמלאי שש מאות ושלש עשרה מצות נאמרו למשה בסיני, אמר רב
הונא (שם בגמ' הגירסא רב המנונא) מאי קראה "תורה צוה לנו
משה" (דברים ל"ג, ד'), תורה בגימטריא הכי הוי, תורה שית מאה
וחד סר הויין, אנכי ולא יהיה לך מפי הגבורה שמענום', כבר ביארו
שאלו שני המאמרים השיגו אותן כל ישראל בברור בלא חידה
[ומשל], וזו באמת מדרגה גדולה בנביאים שתהא נבואתם
מבוארת, כאשר העיד השי"ת על אדון כל הנביאים [במדבר י"ב,
ח']: 'במראה ולא בחידות', ועם היות שלא היו כל ישראל שלמי
החכמה והמידות, השיגו עתה כל ישראל זאת ההשגה לקיום
התורה. שאלו לא השיגו הם בנבואה, אלא כאשר יגיד משה להם
מה שצווה מאתו יתברך, לא הייתה האמונה במשה שלמה, כי לא
יאמת דבריו אלא כפי מה שראינו באותיותיו, ואם יקום נביא אחד
וינגד דבריו [=יסתור דבריו] וייתן אות או מופת, היינו צריכין
להעריך [=להשוות] אותות משה עם אותותיו ותהיה התורה
בספק. אבל עכשיו שראינו בעניינו השגת משה, וכי השגנו אנחנו
עמו ונתבררה אצלנו השגתו והשגתו, אין אנו צריכים לנבואתו
אות או מופת, וכיון שנתבררה לנו נבואתו שהיא אמת, ושהוא
נתנבא שזאת התורה לא תשתנה לעולם, לא נביט לדברי המדבר
בהפך, שכבר נתברר לנו באור שהוא שלם משקר ומתנבא מה שלא
שמע. ולכן בהיות יסוד תורתנו השגה עצומה שהשיגוה אבותינו,
היה רצון השי"ת שיזכו כולם לאותה מדרגה במעמד ההוא, אע"פ
שהיו שם הרבה שלא היו ראויים אליה. ונתייחדו אלו המאמרים
בהיותם יסוד הדת, והם האמונה בה' יתברך והאזהרה בעבודה
זרה, ושתי פינות אלו קיימות לעולם, לא ידחו אפילו להוראת
שעה, כי האמונה בה' לא תשתנה לעולם. וכן המניעה בעבודה זרה
כבר אמרו בסנהדרין [צ' ע"א]: 'אמר ר' אבהו אמר ר' יוחנן בכל אם
יאמר לך נביא עבור על דברי תורה שמע לו, חוץ מעבודה זרה
שאפילו מעמיד לך חמה באמצע הרקיע אל תשמע לו'. ולפי שאלה
המצות קיימות לעולם, ולא תהיה להם ביטול אפילו לשעה,
נתייחדו אלו בפרט לשמעם מפי הגבורה, כדי שתתקיים אצלנו [כל
השלמים] פינות התורה כמו שביארנו, ואע"פ שלא היינו כולנו
ראויים לכך ולא השיגו כל השלמויות שהזכיר ר' יונתן". עכ"ל. וכן
כתב ב"ספר העיקרים" (מאמר שלישי פי"ח): "וזה יורה על ההבדל
שיש בין "אנכי" ו"לא יהיה לך" לזולת מן הדיברות, כי "אנכי" ו"לא
יהיה לך" שמעום מפי ה' מבלי משה, ושאר הדיברות היו שומעים
את הקול אומר אותם למשה ומשה חוזר ומבאר אותם להם, וע"כ
באו בלשון נסתר כמו שאמרנו. ולזה אמרו: 'אנכי ולא יהיה לך מפי
הגבורה שמענום', כלומר, כי שתי אלו הדיברות אחר שאמרם

אומנם יוחס אליו להיות המאמר אשר שמעו רבינו משה ע"ה, בֵּרְאוּ וחידשו כמו שברא כל מה שֶׁבֵּרְאוּ וחידשו". ע"כ. אכן, עיין בספר "עבודת הקודש" (ח"ד פל"א) ובספר "לקח טוב" [הנקרא פסיקתא זוטרתא], אשר תקפו את שיטת הרמב"ם, ודבריהם כעין דברי ספר השל"ה הק' מסכת שבועות תורה אור (דף ל"ט ע"א), שכתב וז"ל: "[כתב] הרב המורה ז"ל (ח"ב פל"ג), שהקול ההוא העצום אשר השיגו ישראל בו נתנה התורה היה נברא כו'. ואסור לשמוע הדברים, אלא הקול הוא קול יהו"ה, 'מן השמים השמיעך את קולו'" (דברים ד',ל"ו). ועיין בספר תורה שלימה (חלק ט"ז עמוד רי"ד), שהביא סימוכים לדברים אלה מאבות דרבי נתן פ"א: "משה קיבל תורה מסיני לא מפי מלאך ולא מפי שרף אלא מפי מלך מלכי המלכים הקב"ה". אלא שהעלה ביישוב שיטת הרמב"ם, די"ל שכוונתו שהקב"ה ברא קול ודיבור שהיו שומעים בו את המלה "אנכי", ואין רצונם לומר שברא הקב"ה בריה לדבר "אנכי", אלא אותו הדיבור שנברא הוא הוא הבריה, עיי"ש עוד בתורה שלימה, ואכמ"ל.

17. כתוצאה מן העובדה ש"זכור" ו"שמור", וכן "שקר" ו"שוא" בדיבור אחד נאמרו יש נפקותות הלכתיות, וכמבואר בגמרא ובראשונים. [עיין שבועות כ' ע"ב ש"זכור ושמור בדיבור אחד" בא ללמדנו חיוב נשים בקידוש, ו"שוא" ו"שקר" בא ללמדנו מלקות או קרבן בשבועת שוא. ועיין תוס' ב"ק (נ"ד ע"ד בה"המתך) שזכור ושמור בדיבור אחד מועיל להחשיב את הדיבורים של שבת סמוכים לעניין כלל ופרט וכלל. ועיין בתוס' שבועות (כ"א ע"א בה"ה קמ"ל) שדייקו מהגמרא שם שחזרה בה ממה שאמר ש"שוא" ו"שקר" בדיבור אחד, אולם הביאו שהמשך הגמרא שם ומהירושלמי (נדרים פ"ג ה"ב ושבועות פ"ג ה"ח) מוכח שנאמרו בדיבור אחד. וב"תורת משה" לאלשיך הק' (דברים פרק ה') כתב שמה שנאמר "בדיבור אחד נאמרו", אינו רק על "זכור ושמור" ו"שוא ושקר", אלא כל הדיברות שנאמרו בראשונה, וכל הדיברות שנאמרו באחרונה בדיבור אחד נאמרו, ולכן גם לא תחמוד ולא תתאוה בדיבור אחד נאמרו. [ע"ש שכתב שמה שהזכירו חז"ל "זכור ושמור" ו"שוא ושקר" הם רק דוגמא, ומהם נקיש על יתר הדברים. ועיין גם "מגילת ספר" (סמ"ג) לאוין קנ"ח, שכתב ע"פ דברי התוס' (ב"ק נ"ד ע"ב בד"ה בה"המתך) שאמרו ש"זכור ושמור" נקראים סמוכים כיון שבדיבור אחד נאמרו, שלפי"ז גם "לא תחמוד" ו"לא תתאוה" נקראים סמוכים כיון שנאמרו בדיבור אחד, ותירץ בזה את הרמב"ן (פ"א מגילה ה"ט) מהשגת הראב"ד, עיי"ש.] ברם המהר"ל ("תפארת ישראל" פמ"ד) חולק, וסובר שלא נאמר הדבר אלא ב"זכור ושמור", וב"שוא ושקר" – ומה שכתוב במכילתא יתרו שכל הדיברות נאמרו בדיבור אחד, והוא עניין אחר, שמדבר על עשרת הדיברות ראשונות שנאמרו כולם בבת אחת, ולא על עשרת הדיברות הראשונות שבפרשת יתרו שנאמרו בדיבור אחד עם עשרת הדיברות האחרונות שבפרשת ואתחנן. [עיין להמהר"ש אלגאזי בספרו "שמע שלמה", שהקשה ע"פ המכילתא, למה אמרו "זכור ושמור בדיבור אחד נאמרו", הרי כל עשרת הדיברות בדיבור אחד נאמרו. וקושייתו לכאורה צ"ע, שהרי, כאמור, מה שנאמר במכילתא שנאמרו כל עשרת הדיברות

הדיברות שהן תרי"ג מלבד [המילים] "אשר לרעך" כתובות זו אחר זו מבלי הפסק בין תיבה לתיבה ובין פסוק לפסוק, אלא כולן כמו תיבה אחת מחולקת לכמה שיטות שוות, כל כך אותיות בשיטה אחת כמו בשיטה אחרת עד סופן, שהרי אמרו חז"ל (מכילתא) "את כל הדברים האלה לאמר", ומה ת"ל "אנכי" ו"לא יהיה לך", אלא מלמד שאמר המקום עשרת הדיברות בדיבור אחד, מה שאי אפשר לבשר ודם לומר כן, וחזר ופרטן. ואמרו ג"כ על הפסוק (שמות כ',ט"ו): 'וכל העם רואים את הקולות', ראו דיבור של אש יוצא מפי הגבורה ונחצב על הלוחות, שנאמר (תהילים כ"ט, ז'): 'קול ה' חוצב להבות אש'. ובהצטרף ב' מאמרים אלו, נאמר שכל עשרת הדיברות שנאמרו בדיבור אחד נחצבו על הלוחות מיד בבת אחת האותיות זו אחר זו בלי הפסק תיבה ופסוק ופרשה, להורות על הנס הגדול שנעשה בעשרת הדיברות שנאמרו בדיבור אחד מה שאי אפשר לבשר ודם, ובהיותם תרי"ג אותיות רומזות לתרי"ג מצוות, הרי כל אות יש לה הוראה על המצוה המיוחדת או נרמזת בה ואינה נקשרת עם שלפניה ושל אחריה, ואחר שחזר ופרטן נקשרו ד' אותיות הראשונות ונקראו אנכי, וכן כל תיבה ותיבה ופסוק ופסוק ופרשה ופרשה, כמו שהן כתובות בס"ת שכתב אח"כ מרע"ה מפי הגבורה בהפסק בין אות לאות ובין שיטה ובין פרשה לפרשה, ולכך נקראו "לוחות העדות" שהן עדות שהמקום ב"ה נתן עשרת הדיברות בדיבור אחד מה שאי אפשר לבשר ודם, ושנחקקו מיד כשיצא הקול מפיו על הלוחות. ומפני שאין עדות בפחות משנים נחקקו בשני לוחות. וכן הן עדות למרע"ה שפירש להם עשרת הדיברות מפי הגבורה ולא מפי עצמו בהיות עשרת הדיברות נחצבות על הלוחות כמו שאמרן הוא מפי הגבורה, ואין מקום לאפיקורסים לומר שהוא חקקן, כי "הלוחות מעשה אלקים המה והמכתב מכתב אלקים הוא חרות על הלוחות" (שמות ל"ב, ט"ז), כי מן הלוחות עצמן ומגשם הספירי שלהן וריבוען ואלכסונן ועניינן היה נראה לכל באי עולם דבר גלוי ומפורסם שהיו מעשה אלקים נבראות כך כמו שהיו ולא היו נחצבות מאבן גדולה, וכן המכתב היה נראה שהיה מכתב אלקים בלי שום ספק שלא על יד אדם, כי בשמיר ג"כ לא היה אפשר לחקוק ולחרות האותיות כמו שהיו חקוקות וחרותות ומאירות על הלוחות, וא"כ היו עדות לישראל ולמשה שעשרת הדיברות נאמרו מפי הגבורה בשווה, וא"כ תר"ך אותיות שבעשרת הדיברות, שסימנם כת"ר, נחצבו על הלוחות בדיבור אחד בשיטות שלמות שהם כמו דיבור א', בהיות שכל אותיות שווה בכל השיטות ולא יישאר מקום פנוי בסוף שיטה אחרונה ולא יותר לשיטה אחרת, והרי הם כדיבור אחד."

16. במהות קול ה' אשר שמעו ישראל במעמד הר סיני כתב הרמב"ם ("מורה נבוכים" ח"ב פל"ג) וז"ל: "אמנם 'קול ה' רצוני לומר, הקול הנברא אשר ממנו הובן ה'דיבור' – לא שמעוהו אלא פעם אחת לבד – כמו שאמרה התורה וכמו שבארו החכמים במקום אשר העירותיך עליו, והוא ה'קול' אשר יצאה נשמתן בשמעו והשיגו בו שתי הדיברות הראשונות". עכ"ל. וע"ע במש"כ שם ב"מורה נבוכים" (ח"א פס"ה) וז"ל: "וכל שכן בהסכם כל אומתנו שהתורה ברואה, הכוונה בזה, דברו המיוחס לו נברא,

ופמ"ד, וב"גור אריה" (שמות כ', ח'; ודברים ה', י"ב), שמשה רבינו הוסיף ביאורים על הדברים, וכדרכו בספר משנה תורה, מלבד אותן לשונות שאי אפשר לומר שהוסיפם כיון שהן מחליפות לשונות אחרות הכתובות בדיברות הראשונות, ולכן אמרו בהם חז"ל שאותם דברים נאמרו בדיבור אחד. והיינו "זכור ושמור", ו"שוא ושקר". ועיין גם בספר "מעשי ה'" פרשת יתרו לרבי אליעזר אשכנזי שכתב כן. ועיין בגמרא בב"ק (נ"ד ע"ב) [שהובאה להלן בפנים]: "שאל רבי חנינא בן עגיל את רבי חייא בר אבא, מפני מה בדיברות הראשונות לא נאמר בהם "טוב", ובדיברות אחרונות נאמר בהם "טוב"? אמר לו: עד שאתה שואלני למה נאמר בהם טוב שאלני אם נאמר בהן טוב אם לאו, שאיני יודע אם נאמר בהן טוב אם לאו, כלך אצל ר' תנחום בר חנילאי שהיה רגיל אצל ר' יהושע בן לוי שהיה בקי באגדה. אזל לגביה, אמר לו: ממנו לא שמעתי, אלא כך אמר לי שמואל בר נחום אחי אמו של רב אחא ברבי חנינא, ואמרי לה אבי אמו של רב אחי ברבי חנינא, הואיל וסופן להשתבר. וכי סופן להשתבר מאי הוי, אמר רב אשי: חס ושלום פסקה טובה מישראל". ובספר פני יהושע שם (נ"ה ע"א) הביא מתחילה שיש כמה טעמים לשינויים בין הדיברות הראשונות לאחרונות. טעם ראשון הוא משום שנשתנו בערבות מואב מפי משה, ולפי זה לא נאמרו מפי הקב"ה אלא פעם אחת בלבד. אבל במדרשים איתא שבדיבור אחד נאמרו, אלא שזה שייך רק היכא שיש שינוי לשון כגון "זכור ושמור", ו"שוא ושקר". ועוד הסביר ה"פני יהושע" (ע"פ מכילתא, יתרו), שהקב"ה אמר בפעם הראשונה את הכל בדיבור אחד כמו שכתוב בפרשת יתרו, ושוב פירש להם ואמר כל אחד לחודיה, כמו הנוסח שבפרשת ואתחנן [ולפ"ז אמר הקב"ה את הדיברות פעמים]. וזהו ביאור המחלוקת בירושלמי אם הלוחות היו חמש דיברות מול חמש דיברות, או עשר דיברות מול עשר (עיין להלן הערה 19, שנרחיב שם את הדיבור בזה). דהיינו דפליגי [=שחלוקים] אם הקב"ה אמר את עשרת הדיברות פעם אחת, וכמו הדרכים הקודמות, או שתי פעמים כהדרך האחרונה, שאם אמר פעמים, אזי גם על הלוחות היו כתובות שתי הנוסחאות, עשר מול עשר. [ולפי כל זה לא מצאנו הכרח שהנוסח של פרשת ואתחנן היה כתוב על הלוחות השניות, אמנם כך יוצא מתשובת רבי שמואל בר נחום, וכמו שנביא להלן בפנים]. ושאלת רבי חנינא בן עגיל אם היתה, דכיון ש"למען ייטב לך" אינו שינוי אלא הוספה, מדוע אינו כתוב בפרשת לוחות הראשונות, דבשלמא השינויים, יש לומר שנכתבו קצתם בראשונות וקצתם באחרונות, אבל בהוספה צריך טעם למה הושמטה מהראשונות. ועל זה נסתפק באמת רבי חייא בר אבא, אם נאמר "למען ייטב" במתן תורה או שהיה זה הוספת רבינו בערבות מואב, וממילא לא היה כתוב לא על הלוחות הראשונות ולא על השניות.

19. יש עוד מדרש (שמות רבה פרשה מ"ו, א'), שבלוחות ראשונות היו רק עשרת הדיברות, ובשניות היה כלולים גם הלכות מדרשים ואגדות, וכמו שאמרו חז"ל שם: "התחיל מצטער על שבור הלוחות ואמר לו הקב"ה אל תצטער בלוחות הראשונות שלא היו אלא עשרת הדיברות לבד, ובלוחות השניים אני נותן לך שיהא בהם הלכות מדרש ואגדות, הה"ד (איוב י"א, ו') "ויגד לך תעלומות

כאחד, אמרו כן על עשרת הדיברות של הדיברות ראשונות מיניה וביה, או של הדיברות אחרונות מיניה וביה, או של שתיהן כל אחד מיניה וביה. ועיין ב"ילקוט שמעוני" ירמיהו רמז רס"ו שהעתיק דברי הגמרא בתענית (סוף דף ה' ע"א) בפירוש הפסוק (ירמיהו ב, יג): "שתים רעות עשה עמי", דמיירי בעוון ע"ז שהיא שקולה כשתים, ואיתא שם בילקוט: "דאמר מר אנכי ולא יהיה לך בדיבור אחד נאמרו מה שאין הפה יכול לדבר ואין האוזן יכולה לשמוע". וכן ישנה לשון דומה בתיקוני זוהר, (תיקון ל"ב דף ע"א) "'אנכי' ו'לא יהיה לך' דאתאמרו בדיבורא חדא". וכן ב"זוהר חדש" (יתרו דף ס"ח ע"ב) "'אנכי ולא יהיה לך' בדיבורא חדא איתאמרו". וע"פ, גם מאמר זה אינו דומה למאמרי חז"ל "זכור ושמור בדיבור אחד" ו"שוא ושקר בדיבור אחד", כי מדבר על דיברות ראשונות מיניה וביה. ועיין מש"כ לעיל בהערה 5 דברי הגר"א בפירוש דברי התיקוני זוהר].

18. פירושו של שו"ת מהר"ם אלשקר סימן ק"ב מובא בפירוש "יפה תואר" למהר"ש יפה על מדרש רבה רבה יתרו. ועיין בסנהדרין נ"ו ע"ב: "'כאשר צוך ה' אלקיך' (דברים ה', י"ב) – במרה", וכתב על זה רש"י שם: "כאשר צוך ה' אלקיך – כתיב בדיברות האחרונות, גבי שבת וכיבוד אב ואם. והיכן צוך? האי ליכא למימר דמשה הוה אמר להו [=זה אין לומר שמשה אמר להם] בערבות מואב, דמשה לאו מאליו היה שונה להם משנה תורה ומזהירם על מצוותיה אלא כמו שקיבלה הוא, והיה חוזר ומגיד להם, וכל מה שכתוב בדיברות האחרונות היה כתוב בלוחות וכן שמע בסיני". הרי דס"ל לרש"י שכל מה שנאמר בדיברות אחרונות שבפרשת ואתחנן נאמר במעמד הר סיני, ולכן מוכרח שפירוש "כאשר צוך" שנאמר בדיברות אחרונות הוא שצוך במרה, ואין הפירוש שצוך בסיני. ועיין בערוך לנר בסנהדרין שם מש"כ על דברי רש"י אלו. ועיין בדברי הנצי"ב מוולאז'ין בפירושו "העמק דבר" (דברים ה', י"ט) שהשינויים והתוספות שנכתבו בפרשת ואתחנן הם הדברים ששמעו ישראל במעמד הר סיני בקול הברה ולא הבינו. וכגון שאמרו (ר"ה כ"ז, א') "זכור ושמור בדיבור אחד נאמרו", "זכור" הבינו, ו"שמור" לא הבינו. "זכור" שהבינו נכתב בראשונות, ו"שמור" שלא הבינו נכתב באחרונות. ומשמע מדבריו שם שלא רק "זכור ושמור", אלא כל השינויים כגון "למען ייטב לך" הם בכלל זה, שנאמרו ע"י הקב"ה בסיני, ולא הבינום ישראל [וכדאיתא במכילתא יתרו, שכל עשרת הדיברות נאמרו בדיבור אחד, וממילא מבואר שלא הבינום ישראל], והוצרך משה רבינו לחזור עליהם. וב"תורת משה" לאלשיך הק' (דברים פרק ה') כתב להדיא [=בפירוש] שאת כל התוספות שנאמרו בדיברות אחרונות שמעו ישראל במעמד הר סיני, וכאשר דיבר אותם משה במשנה תורה זכרו ישראל ששמעו את הדברים בסיני.

אלא שבפירושו "יפה מראה" על הירושלמי (נדרים פ"ד ה"א) הקשה המהר"ש יפה על פי דברי הגאונים: "מי הזקיקם לכל זה [ללמוד שכל הכתוב בדיברות אחרונות נאמר למשה בסיני ממה שאמרו "זכור ושמור בדיבור אחד נאמרו"], אחר דהגמרא נתנה טעם לחייב נשים בקידוש, דכל דאיתנהו [=שכל שישנו] בשמירה איתנהו בזכירה. וכן כתב המהר"ל ב"תפארת ישראל" פמ"ג

חכמה כי כפלים לתושייה". ועיין בדברי הנצי"ב ב"העמק דבר" (שמות ל"ד, א') שהביא מדרש זה וביארו באופן זה: "והכוונה בכל זה, דבלוחות הראשונות לא ניתן כח החידוש, אלא מה שקיבל משה דיוקי המקראות והלכות היוצא מזה אבל לא לחדש דבר הלכה ע"י י"ג מידות וכדומה הויות התלמוד. ולא היתה תורה שבע"פ, אלא דברים המקובלים מפי משה, ומה שלא היה מקובל היו מדמים מילתא למילתא. אבל בלוחות השניות ניתן כח לכל תלמיד ותיק לחדש הלכה ע"פ המידות והתלמוד". עיין עוד ב"העמק דבר" (שם פסוקים כ"ח-כ"ט; ודברים ד',י"ד; ושם י',א') [עיין להלן בפרק "עשרת הדברות כוללים את כל התרי"ג מצוות" דברים חולקים מבעל "הכתב והקבלה" ובעל "בית הלוי"]. באשר לגמרא בב"ק, (נ"ד, ב'-נ"ה, א') עיין בפירוש הרי"ף על "עין יעקב" שם, ובספר "המקרא והמסורה" להגר"ר מרגליות סימן א'; ועיין ב"ספר המפתח" על בבא קמא מהדורת פרנקל רשימה של קרוב לשלושים אחרונים שיישבו גמרא תמוהה זו. עכ"פ, הרי יוצא מן הגמרא שבלוחות ראשונות לא היה כתוב "למען ייטב לך" ובלוחות אחרונות היה כתוב. מוכח דעת רבותינו, שבלוחות הראשונות היו כתובות הדיברות הראשונות, ובלוחות השניות היו כתובות הדיברות האחרונות. ה"פני יהושע" (ב"ק נ"ה ע"א, עיין בהערה הקודמת) כתב לבאר בשיטת רבנן בתלמוד ירושלמי (שקלים פ"ו ה"א), שהדיברות, הן לפי הנוסח שבפרשת יתרו והן לפי הנוסח שבפרשת ואתחנן נכתבו כולן בלוחות הראשונות, ושלפי"ז היו עשר דיברות בלוח אחד, ועשר דיברות בלוח שכנגדו. וכן נראה שיטת הרדב"ז ח"ב סימן תתי"ז, ושיטה זו חולקת על הבבלי הסובר ש"למען ייטב" לא נכתב בלוחות הראשונות, מפני שסופן להשתבר. ויש לעיין אם לשיטת רבנן בירושלמי נכתבו הדיברות בשני הנוסחים גם בלוחות אחרונות, כמו בלוחות ראשונות, ונראה שְׁכֵּן, מדלא חילק הירושלמי בין לוחות ראשונות ללוחות שניות. ושיטת הרי"ף בעין יעקב היא, שרבי חייא בר אבא בבבלי (גמ' ב"ק שם) צידד לומר, שגם על הלוחות הראשונות היה כתוב כהנוסח שבפרשת ואתחנן, ולא כהנוסח שבפרשת יתרו.

אולם הרמב"ן (שמות כ', ח') כתב: "ואני תמה, אם נאמר 'זכור' ושמור' מפי הגבורה, למה לא נכתב בלוחות הראשונות? ויתכן שיהיה בלוחות הראשונות ובשניות כתוב 'זכור', ומשה פירש לישראל כי 'שמור' נאמר עמו וזו כוונתם באמת". הרי שסובר הרמב"ן שבלוחות האחרונות היה כתוב "זכור" כמו בלוחות הראשונות, ולא "שמור' כמו שנאמר בפרשת ואתחנן, ומשה פירש לישראל בעל פה ש"שמור' נאמר יחד עם ה"זכור" בסיני. ועיין בשו"ת הרדב"ז (ח"ג סימן תקמ"ט), שכתב: "במה שכתב [הרמב"ן] כי בלוחות הראשונות והאחרונות היה כתוב בהם 'זכור', אין אני מודה לו. אלא 'זכור ושמור' היה כתוב בהן, שכל מצוות התורה ודקדוקים היו כתובים בלוחות, כמו שנבאר לקמן בעזה"ת". והנצי"ב ב"העמק דבר" (דברים ה', י"ט) כתב, שבלוחות הראשונות היה כתוב 'זכור' ובשניות היה כתוב 'שמור'. והוכיח כן מלשון הסידור בתפילת שחרית של שבת, שכתוב: "ושני לוחות אבנים הוריד בידו וכתוב בהם שמירת שבת", הרי "שמירת" הוא מלשון "שמור", ומוכח שהיה כתוב על הלוחות [האחרונות] לשון "שמור", ודלא כדברי הרמב"ן שהיה כתוב "זכור". ועיין עוד בדברי הנצי"ב שם

בדברים להלן (י', ד') שכתב דיוק נפלא: ""אשר דיבר ה' אליכם'. ולעיל (ט', י') כתיב: 'ככל הדברים אשר דיבר ה' עמכם'. והוא כמש"כ לעיל (ה', י"ט), דבלוחות הראשונות היה כתוב דיברות הראשונות ששמעו ישראל מפי הגבורה והיינו אשר דיבר ה' עמכם. אבל בלוחות שניות היה כתוב דיברות השניות שלא שמעו באוזניהם אלא משה שמע 'שמור וזכור בדיבור אחד'. וכן כל השניים מה שאין הפה יכול לדבר ואין האוזן יכולה לשמוע. אבל משה שמע ולימד לישראל. מש"ה כתיב: 'אשר דיבר ה' אליכם', דמשמעו כמו: 'וידבר ה' אל משה ואל אהרן', דמשמעו משה דיבר עם אהרן [עיין ויקרא י"א, א' ורש"י שם], ה"נ משה דיבר עם ישראל."

וצ"ע בדברי הרמב"ן, שהרי ממסקנת הגמרא בבבא קמא הנ"ל נראה, שמה שנאמר בדיברות אחרונות היה כתוב על הלוחות האחרונות, ואיך אומר הרמב"ן שבלוחות האחרונות היה כתוב "זכור" ולא "שמור". ויש ליישב דעת הרמב"ן, שאותן תוספות שיש בדיברות האחרונות, כגון "למען ייטב לך" וכיו"ב, הן שנכתבו על הלוחות האחרונות, ולכן לא נכתב "למען ייטב" בלוחות ראשונות מפני שסופן להשתבר. אך הדברים המחולפים, כגון "שמור" במקום "זכור", ו"שוא" במקום "שקר", לא נכתבו על הלוחות כלל, ורק נאמרו לישראל ע"י משה שכך שמע הוא את הדברים האלו שנאמרו בדיבור אחד, ואילו על הלוחות היה כתוב רק מה ששמעו ישראל, והיינו "זכור", ו"שקר". ועוד יש לומר, שהרמב"ן מפרש דברי רבי שמואל בר נחום בבבא קמא שלא נכתב "טוב" בלוחות הראשונות מפני שסופן להשתבר, שלאו דוקא בראשונות לא נכתב, אלא מאחר שלא נכתב בראשונות לא נכתב גם באחרונות, אע"פ שאין בהם הטעם הנזכר, כי לא נכתב באחרונות מה שלא נכתב בראשונות].

20. בספר "פרי צדיק" פרשת בא (אות י') כתב שאחר חטא העגל ירדו ישראל ממדרגתם למדרגת אדם הראשון אחר החטא ['אכן כ"אדם" תמותון' (תהילים פ"ב, ז'); עיין מסכת עבודה זרה ה' ע"א שאחרי מתן תורה לפני חטא העגל לא היה מלאך המות שולט בהם], ונעשו שייכים לעמל הפרנסה וצורך ההשתדלות, ולכן טעם השבת בדיברות האחרונות הוא היציאה מעבדות, והמנוחה מהעמל והטורח, "למען ינוח עבדך ואמתך כמוך", והעיקר הוא הימנעות והשמירה שלא לעשות מלאכה, בחינת "שמור". [ועיין ב"צדקת הצדיק" בסוף אות רל"ז שכתב באופן אחר: "ובדיברות ראשונות נאמר "זכור", שֶׁדֵּי בזכירה לבד שזוכר היום שבת ובזה מקבל הקדושה. ודיברות אחרונות שאחר החטא נאמר "שמור", שעל ידי השמירה מעשיית מלאכה וקיום הלא תעשה על ידי זה הוא קבלת הקדושה. ושניהם בדיבור אחד נאמרו, דבאמת צריך שניהם, רק ההבדל הוא מי שבולט יותר ושהוא עיקר קבלת שבת, אם על ידי "סור מרע" דיצר רע או על ידי "עשה טוב" וקבלת קדושה ה' יתברך"]. ועיין בספר "סנהדרי קטנה" לסנהדרין נ"ו ע"ב, דלפי מהלך זה מובן גם מדוע נאמר "כאשר צִוְךָ" רק בדיברות אחרונות, משום ש"כאשר צוך" מרמז שהצווי הוא קדמון, והוא אותו הצווי שהיה כבר במרה קודם מתן תורה, וכדברי חז"ל בגמרא בסנהדרין (שם), וה"כאשר צוך" מבאר, שבדיברות אחרונות

ישראל הם כמו במעמדם ומצבם במרה, ששם נצטוו על השבת בראשונה, שזה היה קודם שפסקה זוהמתן, שהרי עדיין לא עמדו למרגלות הר סיני, והם כמו אדם הראשון אחר החטא. אולם בדיברות ראשונות לא נאמר "כאשר צוך" [במרה], משום שהציווי של דיברות ראשונות היה במדרגה גבוהה יותר ממדרגתם במרה. והוסיף ה"סנהדרי קטנה", שבמרה, שהיו במדרגה נמוכה הוצרכו להבטחה של שכר בעולם הזה, שלא תהיינה להם המחלות שהיו במצרים, וכן הזכיר להם "כאשר צוך" במרה, בדיברות אחרונות אחר חטא העגל שירדו למדרגה נמוכה. אולם בדיברות ראשונות הספיקו להם הבטחות השייכות לעולם שכולו ארוך.

עיין בחזקוני דברים (ה', י"ב) שהלך במהלך אחר החולק על זה, וכתב שה"זכור" שבדיברות הראשונות בא להזכיר את השבת של מרה, ובדיברות אחרונות שנאמרו לדור הבנים בערבות מואב אי אפשר היה להתייחס לשבת וכיבוד אב ואם שנצטוו במרה בלשון "זכור", שהרי לא היו שם, וכדי להזכיר את השבת וכיבוד אב ואם שנצטוו במרה. נאמר במצוות אלו לשון "כאשר צוך",דהיינו במרה, וכדברי הגמרא בסנהדרין. עוד עיין בתורת משה להחת"ס (דברים שם), ודבריו שם מסבירים את עניין השמטת ה"כאשר צוך" בדיברות ראשונות במצוות שבת, אך אינם מסבירים את השמטתם במצות כיבוד אב ואם.

עכ"פ, דרשת חז"ל זו, ש"כאשר צוך" מרמז לציווי במרה קודם מתן תורה, מובנת ומוכרחת מאד אם נאמר שגם התוספות של הדיברות האחרונות נאמרו במעמד הר סיני. אך אם נאמר כדברי המהר"ל וסיעתו (עיין לעיל הערה 17), שאת התוספות הוסיף משה בערבות מואב, צ"ע, דלכאורה אין הכרח גמור לומר שצוך במרה, די"ל בפשיטות, שההכוונה שצוך בסיני בדיברות ראשונות, וכמו שביאר הרשב"ם (דברים ה', י"ב). [ומזה משמע שהרשב"ם לומד כשיטת המהר"ל, שמשה הוסיף את התוספות בערבות מואב]. ועיין בדברי התוספות (שבת פ"ז ע"ב ד"ה ואמר רב יהודה כאשר צוך במרה), שכתבו: "האי קרא במשנה תורה כתיב. וליכא למימר "כאשר צוך" במתן תורה, שהרי משה לא היה מספר אלא על הסדר וכולהו לא כתיב כאשר צוך". ולפי זה אתי שפיר גם לשיטת המהר"ל ודעימיה.

21. כבר הקשו האחרונים, מדוע לא חייש לכתוב "למען יאריכון ימיך" בלוחות ראשונים העתידים להשתבר. עיין "תורת חיים" לב"ק (נ"ה ע"א) בד"ה מפני, "פנים מאירות" ח"א בסוף ההקדמה, "חתם סופר" לב"ק (נ"ד ע"ב), "ערוך לנר" לדף האחרון במסכת נדה, ברכת ראש פתחו רבתי אות ט"ז, ועוד (מובאים ב"ספר המפתח" על ב"ק). ועיין עוד בחידושי אגדות להמהר"ל לב"ק שם שכתב, שעיקר הקפידא הוא על עניין ה"טוב", שכתוב ב"למען ייטב לך", כי מדרגה זו מורה על האדם במציאותו הרגילה בעולם הזה, שהוא כמו שעשאו האלקים, שאמר עליו "כי טוב", וכשעמדו ישראל למרגלות הר סיני עלו למדרגת מלאכים, וכמו אדם הראשון קודם החטא שהיה במדרגה של גן עדן שאינה במציאות העולם הזה, ומדרגה זו של מלאכים פשיטא שבטלה עם שבירת הלוחות, [ולכן אין לחשוש אם כתוב "למען יאריכון ימיך", שהוא מדרגה של עולם הבא, כנ"ל ביאור דבריו]. אך אם היה כתוב בלוחות

הראשונים "טוב" הייתה בטילה מישראל גם המדרגה הרגילה של "אדם", והיו נופלים לגמרי. ע"ש. ודבריו צ"ע, שפירש שמדרגת "טוב" מתאימה לישראל אחר חטא העגל, ולאדם הראשון אחר החטא, דקשה לומר שהתורה תקרא "טוב" על בריאת האדם לפי מצבו שלאחר החטא. ועיין בספר מכתב מאליהו ח"ה עמודים 453–454 שמבאר היפך המהר"ל, והוא, שמדרגת ה"טוב" היא המדרגה הגבוהה השייכת למצבו של אדם הראשון קודם החטא, והגמרא מלמדת שהיה זה לטובתם של ישראל שלא נכתב "למען ייטב" על הלוחות הראשונים, כי אם היה נכתב "טוב" בלוחות הראשונות, שהם בחינת המדרגה הגבוהה של אדם הראשון קודם החטא, כאשר עדיין לא נקבע הדבר בלבם כראוי ע"י מעשה, אלא נשאר בגדר השגה בעלמא, אזי כשהיו מאבדים מעלה זו בשבירת הלוחות, שוב לא היו יכולים לזכות במעלה זו לעולם, כי שבירת הלוחות היא הביטול הגמור. אך מחסד ה' היה שלא תקבע בלבם מעלה גבוהה שיאבדו אותה לבלי שוב, ולכן לא נכתב "טוב" בלוחות הראשונים. ועיין גם בפני יהושע ב"ק שם, שהבין כהמהר"ל, שמדרגת "למען ייטב" היא מדרגה נמוכה יותר מ"למען יאריכון ימיך", אולם לא מטעמיה, אלא שביאר ש"למען ייטב", הוא עולם שכולו טוב, ו"למען יאריכון", הוא עולם שכולו ארוך, כדאמרו חז"ל בקידושין (ל"ט ע"ב) ובחולין (קמ"ב ע"א), והם שני מושגים שונים. עולם שכולו טוב הוא עולם הנשמות או עולם התחייה, ושניהם שייכים לאחר המיתה דווקא. ואילו עולם שכולו ארוך הוא העולם שעתיד הקב"ה לחדש לעתיד לבוא, ואינו תלוי במיתת האדם, אלא אפילו לא ימותו יחדש הקב"ה את עולמו. ולכן בלוחות ראשונים שהגיעו בהם ישראל למצב של חירות ממלאך המות, ולא הייתה מיתה שולטת בהם, לא היו צריכים להבטחה של "למען ייטב", לעולם שכולו טוב, שזה שייך אחר המיתה בלבד, ורק בלוחות אחרונים, שהם אחר חטא העגל, הוצרכו להבטחת "למען ייטב", כי חזרו למצב של "אכן כאדם תמותון" (תהלים פ"ב, ז'). עכ"ד. ולכאורה דבריו צ"ע, דלפי טעם זה לא הייתה הגמרא צריכה לנמק מדוע לא נכתב למען ייטב בלוחות ראשונים בטעם שעתידים הלוחות להשתבר ושאז הייתה פסיקת הטובה מישראל, דלדברי ה"פני יהושע" מעיקרא לא שייך לכתוב "למען ייטב" בלוחות ראשונים, ויש ליישב.

22. כך כותב הכלי יקר: "בדיברות ראשונות לא הזכיר "ושורך וחמורך" כי הוא בכלל "בהמתך", אבל בדיברות אחרונות נאמר "שורך וחמורך" לדרוש מהם גזירה שוה שור לחסימה, חמור חמור לפריקה (בבא קמא נד ע"ב) כי כבר קבלו ישראל כל הדיברות ומצוות פריקה וחסימה שנאמרו אחר מתן תורה, אבל האומות קודם ששמעו עשרת הדיברות רצה הקדוש ברוך הוא לנסותם תחילה אם יקבלו עליהם דיברות אלו ואם היו מקבלים עליהם הדיברות היה מצוה להם אח"כ גם שאר המצות וחסימה ופריקה גם כן, ועל כן לא היה לו לכתוב כאן "ושורך וחמורך" לגזירה שוה, כי עדיין כל המצות בספק אם יקבלום, אבל ישראל אמרו 'כל אשר דבר ה' נעשה ונשמע' (שמות כ"ד, ז'), היינו מה שיצוה לנו עוד."

23. מהלך שלישי בביאור ההבדלים שבין הדיברות הראשונות

והדיברות האחרונות מציע המהר"ל ("תפארת ישראל" פמ"ג – פמ"ה; "גור אריה" לשמות כ', ח', ולדברים ה', י"ב): שהדיברות האחרונות ניתנו בתוספת ביאור מפי משה. מהלך זה מבוסס על הכלל האמור בגמרא (מגילה ל"א ע"א) בהבדל בין משנה תורה לבין שאר התורה, והוא, שהתורה נאמרה מפי הקב"ה ומשנה תורה נאמר מפי משה. [עיין שם בדברי המהר"ל שח"ו שמשה אמר את משנה תורה מפי עצמו, אלא ההבדל הוא, שבכל התורה דיבור שיצא מפיו של משה היה שמע מאת ה' (בחינת שכינה מדברת מתוך גרונו). ואילו ב"משנה תורה", משה שמע מפי ה' והיה אומר את הדברים בקולו שלו:] ["כמו השליח שמדבר כאשר צוה לו המשלח."]

והטעם הוא כי התורה היא בבחינת ברית, ובברית ישנם שני צדדים, צד הנותן וצד המקבל. ולכן, ארבעת חומשי התורה נאמרו מפי הקב"ה הנותן, ו"משנה תורה" נאמר מפי משה שליחם של המקבלים. ולכן ארבעה החומשים ניתנו כפי ערך הנותן, ו"משנה ורה" ניתן כפי ערך המקבל, שהוא בשר ודם, צריך בהכרח שיֵ מֵר בתוספת ביאור, וכמו שכתוב (דברים א', ה'); (ועיין ב"חידושי הגרי"ז" על התורה" שם, ויל"ע אם הדברים עולים בקנה אחד עם דברי המהר"ל, ואכמ"ל): "הואיל משה 'באר' את התורה הזאת."

ולפי עיקרון זה מבאר מהר"ל את כל התוספות שבדיברות אחרונות, שהן באות לצורך ביאור הדברים וחיזוקם, ולפי הכלל שהדברים נאמרו ב"משנה תורה" לפי ערך המקבלים. אמנם לגבי השינויים המחולפים שבין הדיברות הראשונות והאחרונות, כגון "זכור ושמור", וכן "שוא ושקר", שאין לתלות אותם בתוספת ביאור, שהרי אין כן תוספת אלא שינוי ממש בעצם המצוה. ואמרו חז"ל (ראש השנה כ"ז, ע"א, שבועות כ', ע"ב; ועיין עוד ב"ספר הכתב והקבלה" דברים ה, יז) על דיבורים אלו שנאמרו בדיבור אחד, כדי שלא יהיה חיסרון ומגרעת בעשרת הדיברות הראשונות והאחרונות. אלא השינוי מוסבר בהבדל המהותי שבין הדיברות הראשונות שניתנו כפי ערך הנותן, לעומת הדיברות האחרונות שניתנו לפי ערך המקבלים.

בשלושת הפרקים הנ"ל שבספרו "תפארת ישראל", מאריך המהר"ל לבאר על פי יסודות אלו את כל השינויים שבין הדיברות הראשונות והאחרונות, ללא יוצא מן הכלל, כולל חסרות ויתרות שבתיבות שבדיבור "לא יהיה לך", וכולל קשר הווי"ו שבארבע הדיברות "לא תנאף", "לא תגנוב" וכו' שבפרשת "ואתחנן", ועוד הרבה שינויים שלא נתבארו ע"י המפרשים. ומפני עומק של הדברים וריבויים לא הובאו כאן. [בעניין קשר הווי"ן ראוי לציין את דברי רבינו בחיי (דברים ה', ט"ז) שפירש, שהיות ומשה הוא שאמר את הדיברות האחרונות, לכן קשר את הדיברות הקצרות האחרונות בו"ין, כמו אדם המספר מה שידוע כבר, וקושר את הכל במחרוזת אחת. ומשמע מדברי רבינו בחיי שנוקט שהדיברות האחרונות הן מדברי משה בערבות מואב, וכשיטת המהר"ל ודעימיה, עיין לעיל.]

24. עיין במהרש"א בסוף מסכת מכות (כ"ג ע"ב) שביאר, שריבוי המצוות בכל התורה ובעשרת הדיברות הוא מצידנו, שאי אפשר לנו להבין דברים אלא בריבוי – אך מצד נותן התורה, הקב"ה, שהוא אינו חומר וכן שהוא מעל הזמן, כל המצוות כולן נכללות

בעשרת הדיברות, וכל עשרת הדיברות הכוללות את כל התורה בדיבור אחד נאמרו (מכילתא יתרו). ודיבור זה, ששמענוהו מפי הגבורה ("אנכי" ו"לא יהיה לך"), הוא מצות האמונה בה. וביחודו, אשר מצוה זו כוללת את כל המצוות, וכמו שאמרו (שם כ"ד ע"א): "בא חבקוק והעמידן על אחת: 'וצדיק באמונתו יחיה' (חבקוק ב', ד')". והמהר"ל ב"גור אריה" (שמות כ', ד'), ביאר, שהכוונה בהתכללות כל התורה בעשרת הדיברות, ושוב, בהתכללות כל עשרת הדיברות בדיבור אחד, וכמו שאמרו במכילתא, שעשרת הדיברות בדיבור אחד נאמרו, להורות על היותה של התורה קומה אחת שלימה ומאוחדת, ומתוך כך, כל הכופר בדבר אחד מן התורה ואומר שאינו מן השמים, כופר בכל התורה כולה, ועליו נאמר: "כי דְבַר ה' בָּזָה" (במדבר ט"ו, ל"א; עיין סנהדרין צ"ט ע"א). ועוד טעם, כדי להורות על נותן התורה שהוא האחד האמיתי. ועיין למעלה בהערה 4 שהבאנו מסֵפֶר "עבודת הקודש" (ח"ד פל"ג) שכתב על דרך טעמו השני של המהר"ל. וכן עיי"ש במה שהבאנו מסֵפֶר "פחד יצחק" (שבועות מאמר ל"ב), שכתב כעין הטעם הראשון שכתב המהר"ל. ועיין גם בשו"ת "בית הלוי" (ח"ב דרוש י"ח), שהאריך לבאר שכל התורה הייתה כתובה על הלוחות בדרך נס.

25. מן הטעמים האחרים: כנגד שבעה קולות במזמור "הבו לה'" (תהילים פ"ב), שבהם ניתנה תורה [שהם: קול ה' על המים, קול ה' בכח, קול ה' בהדר, קול ה' שובר ארזים, קול ה' חוצב להבות אש, קול ה' יחיל מדבר, קול ה' יחולל אילות] (שו"ת הרדב"ז ח"ג סימן תקמ"ט, מנורת המאור אלנקוה ח"ג עמ' 328.); כנגד שבעה ספרי תורה [המבוארים במסכת שבת קט"ז ע"א, והם: בראשית, שמות, ויקרא, ריש במדבר עד "ובנחה יאמר", פרשת "ובנחה יאמר", משם עד סוף במדבר, ספר דברים. שבעה ספרים אשר עליהם נאמר "חצבה עמודיה שבעה"] (כן הביא ב"תורה שלמה" כרך ט"ו עמ' ר"ה בשם ילקוט כת"י כורדיסטאן); כנגד שבע ספירות [שהן: חסד, גבורה, תפארת, נצח, הוד, יסוד, מלכות] (כ"כ בפירוש "מתנות כהונה" על המדרש שם בשם המקובלים). ועיין בפירוש רבינו בחיי על התורה פרשת יתרו (שמות כ', יד), שכתב שעשרת הדיברות הן כנגד עשר ספירות, כשכוללים את ספירות כתר חכמה ובינה. ושבע היתרות על תרי"ג משלימות למניין כת"ר [שש מאות ועשרים] מרומזות לשבע ספירות הבניין, שהן חסד גבורה תפארת נצח הוד יסוד מלכות, שהן כנגד שבעה קולות שנִתְּנָה בהם התורה (עיין בדבריו שם כנגד פסוק א). ועיין בספר עבודת הקודש (ח"ד פל"ד), שכתב שמטעם זה באו הדיברות חתומות בשם אהי"ה, שהוא שם ספירת הכתר, שתחילתן אל"ף וסופן ד', א"ך גימטריא אהי"ה. והנה ניתן לייחס את יתרת האותיות לתיבות האחרונות שבדיברות, דהיינו "אשר לרעך" (סה"כ ז' אותיות), וכתב השל"ה הק' (שם בשער האותיות, וכתב שהבין כן מספר ציונו [פרשת יתרו]) שהוא משום ש"אשר לרעך" הוא הבסיס לכל התורה כולה, וכמו שענה הלל לגר בפרק במה מדליקין (שבת ל"א ע"א), עיי"ש.

26. כתב החכם רבי עזריאל תלמיד רבי יצחק סגי נהור החסיד בן הראב"ד בעל "ההשגות", בפירושו הידוע על שיר השירים המיוחס להרמב"ן (ד', י"א): "דְּבַש וחלב תחת לשונך וריח שלמותיך כריח

המנהג רווח בתפוצות ישראל יש (אמנם בקהילות הספרדים יש
חילוקי מנהגים בזה, עיין בשו"ת "ישכיל עבדי" הנ"ל). אולם
בשו"ת "יביע אומר" (ח"ח סימן ט"ו) ובשו"ת "יחוה דעת" (ח"א
סימן כ"ט) האריך לאסור ע"פ תשובת הרמב"ם (הוצאת פריימן
סימן מ"ו) שכתב שיש למנוע את העמידה בעשרת הדיברות מפני
תרעומת המינים. וכתב שאלו ראו החיד"א ודעימיה את תשובת
הרמב"ם לא היו מתירים, ועיין בשו"ת "ציץ אליעזר" בתשובה
הנ"ל מה שהשיב על זה. ועיין עוד בשו"ת "ישכיל עבדי" (ח"ז סימן
א') שראה דברי הרמב"ם בתשובה והחזיק בדעתו. ע"ע בשו"ת
משנה הלכות (חלק י"א סימן קי"ח) שהביא דברי "שערי אפרים"
(ש"ז סקל"ז) שמנהג ישראל לעמוד בעשרת הדיברות. וכתב
ה"משנה הלכות" כמה סברות לומר שאין כאן תרעומת המינים,
דלא אמרו מפני תרעומת המינים אלא כשתיקנו לומר עשרת
הדיברות בדברים מה שליכא חיוב כזה כעת. אבל כשיש חיוב לקרות
עשרת הדיברות ממילא, כגון בשבועות שחיוב הקריאה בתורה
בעניינו של יום כולל את עשרת הדיברות והקהל עומדים בקריאה
זו, אין זה בכלל החשש. ועוד כתב, שכל שאנו עומדים גם לשאר
קריאות, וכמו שפשט המנהג שהרבה עומדים בכל קריאות
הפרשיות בציבור, וכן שעומדים בכמה מקומות בתפילה, וכגון
ב"אז ישיר" וכו', תו אין חשש לתרעומת המינים שיאמרו שקמים
רק לעשרת הדיברות, ע"ש באורך. וכ"כ סברא זו ב"אגרות משה"
בתשובה הנ"ל. סוף דבר, שחוץ מה"יביע אומר", כל הפוסקים
האשכנזים והספרדים מתירים עמידה בעשרת הדיברות.

29.   החיד"א (בספר "כסא רחמים") התקשה מדוע לא חששו כאן
חז"ל לתרעומת המינים שיאמרו שרק עשרת הדיברות קבלו
ישראל מסיני, שהרי רק הם נשתנו במעלתן שטעונים ברכה
לפניהם ולאחריהם. ותירץ, שהואיל וקוראים אותם בכלל הפרשה
שקוראים בכל שבת – ואין כאן קריאת עשרת הדיברות לחוד – אין
לחוש לתרעומת המינים, שהרי ידוע לכל שיש לעשות זכר למעמד
הר סיני, ועשרת הדיברות נכתבו בלוחות והם יסודי התורה
(וסברא דומה כתב החיד"א בספרו "טוב עין" (סימן י"א) כשהשליך
[=הֵגֵן] על המנהג לעמוד בעת עשרת הדיברות, עיין בהערה
הקודמת).

30.   יש בין הגאונים שיטה מחמירה מאד, שהנשבע בספר תורה
או בעשרת הדיברות אין לו הפרה עולמית, שכיוון שעשרת
הדיברות כוללות את כל התורה, כספר תורה הם. [ז"ל תשובות
הגאונים "שערי תשובה" (סימן קמ"א): "וששאלתם הנשבע
בעשרת הדיברות ובס"ת אין לו הפרה לעולם, שכיוון שיש בעשרת
הדיברות כל התורה ומקראות והזכרות כספר תורה הם ואין לו
הפרה."]. ואין כן שיטת הש"ס, דמשמע שיש התרה אפילו בנשבע
בספר תורה. וכן כתב הר"ן (נדרים כ"ב ע"ב): "ואע"ג דאמר גאון,
מאן דאשתבע בספר תורה או בעשרת הדיברות אין לו הפרה
עולמית, ליתא למילתא כלל". מ"מ, משום חומרת עשרת הדיברות
אכן היה נהוג, שיהודי הנשבע היה מניח ידו בעת השבועה על
עשרת הדיברות (שו"ת "שאילת יעבץ" ח"ב תשובה נ"א).

הלבנון" [כהמשך לביאורו על פסוק זה כתב רבנו עזריאל את
קונטרסו על המצוות, והמדפיסים סדרום כנספח אחר פירושו על
שיר השירים]: "בקול ההוא שנאמר עליו: 'קול גדול ולא יסף'
[דברים ה', י"ט], אין ספק כי בו נרמזו תרי"ג מצוות, ויש לנו לפרש
כפי דרכנו כל מצוה ומצוה מאיזו מידה היא". ואכן, סידר רבי
עזריאל קונטרס שלם הנקרא: "תרי"ג מצוות היוצאים מעשרת
הדיברות" להראות בפירוט עצום כל מצוה ומצוה שבתורה באיזה
דיבור מעשרת הדיברות היא תלויה. אמנם הדרך שבה חילק את
המצוות שונה מדרכו של רבי סעדיה גאון אשר קדמו במלאכה
זאת, אשר כתב באזהרות שלו את מספר מצוות הכלולות בכל
אחת ואחת מעשרת הדיברות. ולפי החלוקה שלו, המספרים הם:
אנכי – שמונים; לא יהיה – ששים; לא תשא – ארבעים ושמונה;
זכור – שבעים וחמש; כבד – שבעים ושבע; לא תרצח – חמישים;
לא תנאף – חמישים ושמונה; לא תגנוב – חמישים ותשע; לא
תענה – חמישים ושתים; לא תחמוד – חמישים וארבע. [והביא
הרס"ג חשבון זה גם בפירושו על ספר יצירה, והעתיקו הר"י
ברצלוני בפירושו על ספר יצירה (דף רע"ח). כמו כן הביאו את דברי
רס"ג גם הרקאנטי בפירושו עה"ת פרשת יתרו, והציוני בפרשת
יתרו. ושם בספר ציוני כתב שחלוקה זו היא מסורת וקבלה איש
מפי איש עד משה רבינו ע"ה. ובספר "תורה שלמה" (חלק ט"ז עמ'
ר"ח) העיר שבמאמר השכל הביא מנין זה בלי לציין על רס"ג,
וכנראה שמסורת זו היתה ידועה גם ממקור אחר, וכדברי ספר
ה"ציוני" שהיא מסורת מקובלת עד משה רבינו ע"ה].

27.   ה"מגן אברהם" (או"ח סימן א' סק"ט) אסר לכתוב את עשרת
הדיברות על קונטרס מיוחד לציבור, מפני תרעומת המינים. ועיין
בשו"ת "ציץ אליעזר" חי"ד סימן א' שאסר על פי דברי המג"א הללו
הפצת לוחות שמודפסים בהם עשרת הדיברות, דיש לחשוש
מהכופרים בתורה מן השמים, ובפרט בזמננו.

28.   אמנם בשו"ת "טוב עין" (סימן י"א) הצדיק החיד"א את
המנהג, ברם בספרו "לדוד אמת" (סימן ז' אות ה') החמיר, וכתב
שלדעת האריז"ל שאסור לאמרם אפילו ביחיד הוא הדין שאסור
לעמוד, אפילו היחיד. ודבריו סותרים למש"כ בטוב עין הנ"ל שאין
לדמות את נידון האמירה לנידון העמידה. וכבר יישב את דברי
החיד"א בשו"ת "ישכיל עבדי" ח"ב (או"ח סימן א'), שהחיד"א
נוקט להיתר, ולא אמר את דבריו ב"לדוד אמת", שם נקט לחומרא
אלא לדברי הרב מהר"י אלגזי שלא חילק בין הנידונים. ועיין
בשו"ת "אגרות משה" או"ח (ח"ד סימן כ"ב) דשדא נרגא בסברת
החיד"א לחלק בין הנידונים, כי הרי גם בבית המקדש היו קורין
קריאת שמע יחד עם אמירת עשרת הדיברות, ובכ"ז חששו
לתרעומת המינים, שיאמרו שרק עשרת הדיברות נאמרו למשה
בסיני. אלא שהתיר לעמוד מטעם אחר, והוא, דאין לך בו אלא
חידושו, דרק בעניין האמירה של עשרת הדיברות, שמצאנו
שקלקלו בו המינים, באו חכמים ובטלו את אמירתן, מה שאין כן
בעניין העמידה בעשרת הדיברות לא מצאנו שקלקלו בזה המינים,
ואין לנו לחדש גזירות חדשות. גם בשו"ת "ציץ אליעזר" (חי"ז
סימן כ"ו) האריך להתיר העמידה בעשרת הדיברות, וכתב שכן הוא